Introduction to Early Childhood Education

A MULTIDIMENSIONAL APPROACH TO CHILD-CENTERED CARE AND LEARNING

Francis Wardle

Red Rocks Community College, Colorado

Photos by the author

Boston ▪ New York ▪ San Francisco ▪ Mexico City
Montreal ▪ Toronto ▪ London ▪ Madrid ▪ Munich ▪ Paris
Hong Kong ▪ Singapore ▪ Tokyo ▪ Cape Town ▪ Sydney

Series Editor: Traci Mueller
Editorial Assistant: Erica Tromblay
Senior Marketing Manager: Elizabeth Fogarty
Editorial-Production Administrator: Beth Houston
Editorial-Production Service: Kathy Smith
Composition and Prepress Buyer: Linda Cox
Manufacturing Buyer: Megan Cochran
Cover Administrator: Linda Knowles
Design: rosa+wesley, inc.
Electronic Composition: Omegatype Typography, Inc.

Library of Congress Cataloging-in-Publication Data
Wardle, Francis, 1947–
    Introduction to early childhood education : a multidimensional approach to
child-centered care and learning / Francis Wardle.
        p. cm.
    Includes bibliographical references and index.
    ISBN 0-321-07707-5
    1. Early childhood education. 2. Child development. I. Title.

LB1139.23 .W37 2003
371.21–dc21

                                                            2002028384

Printed in the United States of America

10 9 8 7 6 5 4 3 2 1   07 06 05 04 03 02

CHAPTER 3

Important People and Movements: Past and Present   54

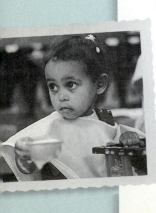

Contents

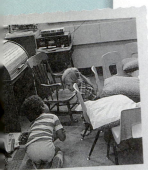

CHAPTER 7

Teachers as Professionals   192

Preface

My favorite TV show is *The Simpsons.* And my favorite character is Bart. The episodes of the program I find most interesting are those that involve Bart and his school. In particular, I remember the time Bart was taking a test that would enable him to move on to second grade—something very important to him. He completed the test, gave it to his teacher, and then waited anxiously for the results. His teacher corrected the test with a bright red pencil, then put a big, fat F at the top of the paper, circled. Bart burst into tears, and his teacher said something to the effect of, "Bart, I'm surprised you're crying; you should be used to getting Fs by now!"

Then Bart started telling his teacher about the French and Indian wars in western Pennsylvania, and George Washington's battle with the British against the French (I remember this well, because I once lived three miles from Fort Necessity, where Washington surrendered to the French). As a result of Bart's "oral report," his teacher let him move on to second grade, much to Bart's relief.

Bart's various struggles with his school, teacher, and principal usually illustrate what we should not do with young children. We really do know what young children need, however, and we generally know how to meet those needs—especially when we build strong partnerships among the program (child care or school), the home, and the community. This book discusses many of the ways to provide what children and families need. Because Chapter 1 serves as a general introduction to the rest of the book, there is no need to provide an introduction here. And the table of contents gives a clear outline of the structure and subject matter addressed.

Introduction to Early Childhood Education: A Multidimensional Approach to Child-Centered Care and Learning is a direct outgrowth of my experiences with all children who have taught me so much over the years. I cannot name them all, but there's Timotheo—my smiling, barefooted friend in the village of Panimasiguan, in the highlands of Guatemala—who always wore a shirt several sizes too large; Robert and Ricky, whom I taught during the day at Da Nahazli school and cared for in their one-room adobe home on the high Taos plateau, as well as Emmy, Andrea, Sarah, and Tammy, my Taos folk dancers. Then there are Trell and his sister, Tonya, who visited me in Greeley, Colorado, when their Kansas City schools were on strike; and redheaded Charlie, Bonnie, and sweet Colleen from PACERS school. Stanley, Pablo, and Jared kept me on my toes in our kindergarten class at New Meadow Run School; Evelyn taught me the difference between purple and house finches; and Erica showed me how mothers in her native Bolivia carry their infants on their backs. And finally, there are my friends from Minas Gerais, Brazil, Maria Teresa and Maria Luiza, who made me feel so much at home when I was far from my family.

But maybe I've learned most about children and families from my own children: Maia, serious,

dancer, gymnast, and carer; Eirlys, headstrong, affectionate, driven; Kealan, smiling, artist, soccer player, and computer wiz; and RaEsa, independent, artist, French expert, and lacrosse player.

Whenever I teach and write about early care and education, I naturally think of my own early years. I am so grateful for that time, and to all the teachers and caregivers who allowed me to explore the bracken-covered Titterstone Clee Hill; put my feet into the clear, cold mountain streams; and pick foxgloves, primroses, and sweet-smelling white violets on our farm in Wheathill, England. My early teachers nurtured in me a deep joy in dance, art, woodwork, music, and learning. They exposed me to the rich worlds of nature, human diversity, and compassion. And they patiently waited for my (very) late academic skills to blossom. I am the result of those full, exciting years of school at Cleeton Court, camping in the Wild Wood, watching sheep dipping and shearing on the farm, and picking purple heather on the moors.

Finally, I wish to acknowledge and thank Adam Beroud, my development editor, and reviewers Pamela Davis, Henderson State University; Smita Guha, Temple University; Leslie Minor-Evans, Central Oregon Community College; and Terrie F. Ozelis, West Chester University who reviewed the book manuscript and provided suggestions. I would especially like to thank Angela Baum, Ohio University; Dora Chen, University of Nebraska at Omaha; Martha Dever, Utah State University; and Janie Humphries, Louisiana Tech University, who reviewed the manuscript at several stages of writing. Because *Introduction to Early Childhood Education: A Multidimensional Approach to Child-Centered Care and Learning* is the first textbook I have written, their feedback, suggestions, and constructive criticism were invaluable.

Dedication

I dedicate this book to my wonderful parents, Derek and Madge Wardle, who were also two of my first teachers; and to Ruth Elaine—wife, mother, companion on life's journey, and soul mate.

About the Author

Francis Wardle started his work with young children when he volunteered in a kindergarten program during his senior year in high school. Since then he has cared for infants and toddlers in a children's program at a religious institution, taught children of preschool through elementary-school age in a variety of schools, and been a teacher in a before- and after-school program. His Head Start involvement began in 1973 when he volunteered in a friend's classroom in Ault, Colorado, and includes serving as a Policy Council volunteer, a member of the National Head Start Association board of directors, an education coordinator, and a Head Start director. Dr. Wardle has also been the national education director for Children's World Learning Centers, a consultant with Bright Horizons Family Solutions, and a playground designer. Currently Dr.  Wardle teaches at Red Rocks Community College and the University of Phoenix/ Colorado Campus, consults for the National Head Start Migrant Program, and writes for a variety of national publications.

CHAPTER

I

The Need *for* Child Care *and* Early Childhood Programs

*O*ver the past thirty years, the care of children by some-one other than a member of the extended family has become more and more acceptable in the United States. Further, the care of other people's children now also includes infants and toddlers as well as school-age children. Each day in this country, an estimated thirteen million children under the age of 6 spend part of their day being educated or cared for by someone other than their parents (Children's Defense Fund [CDF], 2001). Add school-age children under age 13, and the number rises to sixteen million.

Globally, child care and early education are acceptable ser-vices in most industrial countries, and they are also gaining importance in developing countries (Jaffe, 1999). As women's rights and economic involvement in developing countries expand, the demand for early care and education increases. And according to Decker and Decker (1997), next to the computer industry, early childhood education is the fastest-growing enter-prise in the world. The Bureau of Labor Statistics forecasts a rise in employment opportunities in early care and education in the United States, at least through 2006. Many public schools are increasing their early childhood services; programs like Head Start and state-supported programs continue to expand (recently Head Start introduced Early Start, a program for infants and preschool-age children), and federal block-grant funds for child care slowly increase each year. The welfare reform of 1996, requiring able-bodied parents to work, has also

Questions to Consider

1. When we think about caring for young children, do we really know what the children need?

2. Has recent brain research affected our view of caring for and edu-cating young children? How?

3. Why is there such a need for high-quality child care in the United States today?

4. Are the needs for child care and high-quality education global phenomena?

5. Can early childhood and school programs have a positive impact on children and families under stress?

6. What are future trends in early childhood care and education in this country and the world?

7. Why is there such a conflict between child care and early education?

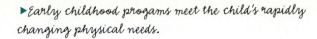

▶*Early childhood programs meet the child's rapidly changing physical needs.*

expanded federal and state involvement in child care, along with public acceptance of caring for young children outside the extended family. Adding to the trend, recent brain research has confirmed what many early childhood professionals have always believed—the crucial importance of the first five years in developing brain structures required for later school and life success. As early care and education programs have gained popularity and institutional acceptance, school reform efforts are placing emphasis on the early years of formal schooling, kindergarten through third grade (K–3). Many believe students must experience social and academic success during these early grades to lay the foundation for future school success.

In this chapter I discuss the rising need for child care, early childhood programs, and school-age care; describe the two distinct forms of care, child care and early education; and outline efforts and programs designed to improve the quality of K–3 grades for more children. This first chapter also serves as an overview of the whole book, introducing a variety of concepts that I will trace throughout: meeting the needs of all children; parent participation, involvement, and communication; issues of diversity and children with special needs; the vast range and variety of programs, including philosophical differences; the purpose of early childhood programs in various societies and communities; and globalization of child care and early education.

Throughout *Introduction to Early Childhood Education*, I use the terms *child care* and *early childhood education* to encompass the age range from birth through 8 years (third grade); and *teachers*, *caregivers*, and *child-care providers* to describe professionals who teach and care for other people's children—in their home, in centers and religious programs, and in schools. Words in boldface type are defined in the glossary at the end of the book. ■

Child Care for Families

Clearly, a fundamental purpose of child care is to provide for the care and safety of children while their parents work. Organized child care on a major scale occurred in this country during World War II, when men were away fighting and women were working in factories providing war materiel (Jaffe, 1999). Both business and government involvement in child care started at that time.

Child care for working parents can be broken into two forms—care for children from infancy to school entry (usually kindergarten)—and care for school-age children—before and after the school day, and during vacations. There is, of course, overlap, such as wraparound child care (see Chapter 2), and many organizations provide both kinds of services.

Child Care before School Enrollment

The increasing number of parents in the workforce, and a growing acceptance that high-quality care provides a solid foundation for young children's later school success, are the central reasons for the increased demand for early childhood programs in this country (CDF, 2001). Not only do children need safe and secure care while their parents work (or participate in training and college programs), but there is also a need to prepare children for later success in formal school programs.

Two Working Parents. In 1976, in 33 percent of two-parent families who had young children, both parents were employed, at least for a time; in 1998 this number had risen to 58 percent (Bachu, 2000). And in 1998, 58 percent of women with babies less than a year old were employed, up from 31 percent in 1976 (Bachu, 2000). More and more, both parents in two-parent homes choose to be employed, even when they have young children. Also, sometimes while one parent is employed, the other parent is completing needed schoolwork or training. Many parents believe they cannot sacrifice their careers to stay home and care for their young children, though this trend is beginning to change. Mothers and fathers who do leave work for a while to care for their children often find it difficult to reenter the workforce, and must enter at their previous level of seniority and pay, if they are lucky enough to do so.

Single-Parent Families. According to the Census Bureau, in 1999, 71 percent of single mothers were employed (Smith, 2000). The numbers of households headed by a single male and of single parents of adoptive and foster children have also steadily increased. Clearly, single parents who work—or are going to school—need child care for their children. There are also single grandparents and other extended-family members raising children, and they often need child care, temporarily or permanently.

Welfare Reform. The Welfare Reform Act of 1996 requires able-bodied welfare parents to work. Thus, a network of family and child-care programs in local communities is needed to care for children from welfare homes. Temporary Assistance for Needy Families (TANF) provides direct funding to states for this child care, along with bonuses for states that improve the accessibility, quality, and affordability of child care for these families.

Specialized Programs. The need for child-care programs for specialized populations increases the overall demand for child care. Specialized populations include children of college students (campus child care), children in crisis (for those removed from their families by social services, temporarily or for the long term), those needing therapeutic foster care, children of homeless families and in women's shelters, young children with special needs, children from homes with substance abuse, and children whose parents serve in the military (which has a large number of young families, of whom one parent is often on assignment). There is also a need for temporary drop-in programs (at hotels, airports, conferences, city services, and the like).

Before- and after-School Programs for Children

In 1997, 78 percent of mothers in homes with children between the ages of 6 and 13 were employed. There are thirty-nine million children between 6 and 14 in this country. Children whose parents work need safe, appropriate care. An article by Halpern (1999) documents that in Seattle, only 35 percent of school-age children are being served in appropriate school-age programs; in Boston, 14 percent; and in Chicago, only 9 percent. According to the U.S. General Accounting Office, the known supply of school-age programs and services can serve only one-third of the children with employed parents. Nearly one in ten children aged 5–11, and more than four in ten children aged 12–14, go home to empty homes after school (CDF, 2001). Although it is obvious that children home from school need to be cared for, specific statistics (CDF, 2001) highlight the problem:

- Juvenile violence is most frequent between 3:00 and 7:00 P.M.
- Almost forty-five million children younger than age 14 are injured at home every year.
- Most injury-related deaths of children occur when children are unsupervised.
- Children unsupervised after school are at a greater risk of truancy, early pregnancy, poor academic performance, mental depression, and substance abuse.
- Children need care not only before and after school, but also during teacher in-service training days and vacations. Clearly, parents whose work hours keep them from being able to care for their children before and after the traditional school hours also need care for their children during these times. Some of these children might attend school-sponsored activities during vacations, such as summer school and summer camp, but most need supervised care. An additional complication for many parents is the growing number of year-round schools—with a school calendar that alternates school time and off-school time throughout the year. Care for children during the off periods is crucial.

Even as full-day child care has become an acceptable mode for providing for the care and safety of our children, schools and most early childhood educational programs are on part-day, part-year schedules. The care of children beyond traditional school hours is considered a supplemental program, with additional costs that parents are often required to pay. Students from families that cannot afford school-age care are left alone at home or on the streets.

Who Cares for the Children?

More than sixteen million children in the United States under the age of 13 are currently cared for outside the extended family for at least part of the week (Neugebauer, 2000). One in every two children under the age of 6 is enrolled in an early childhood center or a family child-care home, or has a baby-sitter (one-on-one care). One in five school-age students (6–12) participates in care outside the home. And overall, early childhood centers are the most popular form of care by nonrelatives. Since 1965 there has been a dramatic shift from family care providers to child-care centers, resulting in the following distribution of care (Neugebauer, 2000):

- 30 percent of children aged 0–5 and 11 percent of school-age children are enrolled in centers;
- 14 percent of children aged 0–5 and 5 percent of school-age children are in family child-care homes;
- 4% of children aged 0–5 and 3 percent of school-age children are with nannies or in other forms of one-on-one care.

Six Trends in Center-Based Care. According to Allen (1998), there are six major trends that will greatly affect the demand for center-based child care and early education in the beginning of the twenty-first century.

1. Increased growth in women's labor-force participation will lead to modest growth in the overall need for child care.

2. The growth in the U.S. population of children under age 6 will be among children of color and children of Hispanic origin.

3. All parents—those who work and those who do not—are increasingly enrolling their children in early childhood programs, which emphasize education, as opposed to child-care programs, which emphasize care. This is especially true of middle-class families. In 1995, 53.3 percent of children of nonworking mothers and 63.3 percent of children of working mothers attended some form of early education program.

4. Parents who seek flexibility in their family and work lives are more likely to choose center-based care, enabling them to juggle careers and family responsibilities.

5. The ten fastest-growing jobs over the next ten years (from 1998) will be concentrated at the upper and lower ends of the income scale. Six of them are in traditionally female, low-income occupations; only two are what one would consider middle-income—truck driving and nursing, and the remaining two are upper-income professional occupations. Increasing jobs at the extremes of the pay range adds to the existing discrepancy between rich and poor, and child-care and early education programs serve primarily low-income and well-to-do families.

6. Projected increases in government subsidies of programs for young children will be in early education, not child care. Politicians believe that problems with K–12 school performance can be addressed by investment in early education, and apparently most parents agree.

Setting the Foundation for School Success

In 1965, Head Start was born to address the reality that low-income children lag behind their middle-class peers in preparation for entry into school, in the belief that a quality preschool program would enhance later school success of low-income children. Since 1965, this belief has produced an expansion of these programs, with many states initiating their own efforts, schools providing early childhood options, and private and religious programs joining the trend. As the nation has increased its critical examination of the perceived deficiencies of public schools—particularly in serving low-income and minority children—high-quality early childhood programs have been viewed as a solution to this dilemma.

Impact of Brain Research

Over the past fifteen years, advances in the field of neuroscience have revolutionized the way we think about the development of the human brain and have made us aware of the crucial importance of the first years of life. "Brain research suggests that we have from birth to the age of ten to help children develop the wiring of the brain . . . Strengthening a child's neural network then becomes the job of helping the child develop patterns and relationships and helping him or her make connections between those patterns and relationships and all new information" (Schiller, 1998, p. 50). Before birth, the brain builds neural pathways at a staggering rate, continuing after birth. Further, other kinds of development—motor skills, cognitive development, self-esteem, and use of all the senses—are influenced by brain development. We have learned that the early years are a window of opportunity—or a critical period—for optimal brain development, and that this development is totally dependent on the child's physical and social environment. "We know that engaging in rich language experiences with significant others influences vocabulary and quality for speech, and is correlated to later academic functioning. We have learned that participation in an environment filled with interesting sights, sounds, and people enriches a child's schemes of thought and action" (Lally, 1998, p. 46).

Clearly, neurological research has sparked a strong interest in the years of infancy and early childhood and has demonstrated the crucial importance of high-quality early childhood experiences—ones that support, stimulate, and nurture maximal brain development. The specifics of how the young child's brain is nurtured and stimulated are covered in later chapters; what's important here is that brain research clearly demonstrates that the early years (0–8) are an essential period for child development, and that only certain environments—physical and social—will assure maximal development.

Because most of today's parents work outside the home, educators and politicians have emphasized the need for high-quality early childhood and child-care programs to provide the needed brain-compatible environments. Unfortunately, however, the focus (both money and legislation) has been on educational programs rather than on child care.

Preparing for School

Goal One of Goals 2000, established by the federal government in 1989 (see Chapter 4), states that "by the year 2000, all children in America will start school ready to learn." The purpose of this

▶ *Early childhood programs must provide children with places where they can get away and be on their own.*

goal is to encourage parents to spend time reading to their children, to make sure that children are physically healthy when they enter school, and to provide access to high-quality early childhood programs for preschoolers (CDF, 2001). Because parents are busy working and holding the family together, high-quality child care and early child-hood experiences are the most obvious ways to meet this goal. A large number of stud-ies consistently show the relation between the quality of early childhood experiences and school success, entering college, and reduction of juvenile crime and misbehavior. The famous Perry Preschool Longitudinal Studies (Schweinhart and Weikart, 1997), the Abecedarian project (CDF, 2001), and other research continue to support this relation-ship. Because private preschool and center-based child care are expensive, in 1999, 70 percent of children from high- and middle-income families attended center-based preschool programs, while only 57 percent of children from low-income homes did so (CDF, 2001). The gradual expansion of Head Start, the introduction of a variety of state-funded early childhood programs, and early childhood programs at local schools are attempts to provide good preschool programs for low-income families. High-quality publicly funded early childhood programs are viewed by many as a way to prepare children for successful school entry and to lay the foundation for a successful school experience.

K–3 Programs

Based on their belief in the crucial importance of the early years, educational reform-ers are stressing the importance of the K–3 grades. It is regarded as vital that during these years children experience school success, learn how to learn, develop a disposition toward learning and knowledge, and learn the social skills needed to be successful in schools. Efforts to improve the quality of K–3 programs include:

- reducing class size (see the STAR project, described in Chapter 15);
- emphasis on literacy development;
- looping (see Chapter 4);
- earlier identification of gifted students, and better programs for gifted students;
- better identification and services for children with special needs;
- mixed-age grouping;
- development of national and state standards (see the math standards for pre-kindergarten through age 8 in Chapter 13);
- more effective bilingual programs;
- more effective approaches to parental involvement;
- charter schools with a single philosophical focus;
- using a variety of new models in public education, such as Montessori, Waldorf, Core Curriculum, school uniform requirements, and so on;
- use of technology in the early grades;
- developing effective transition programs and models between early childhood programs and public schools (including seamless processes for children with special needs);
- incorporating methods that have proved effective in early childhood programs into K–3 programs (better parental involvement, comprehensive services, integrated learning, use of volunteers, and the like).

To set a more effective foundation for future school success, some schools are creating an organizational unit covering preschool through third grade. Further, these schools hire K–3 teachers whose certification includes early childhood education. While it is clear that experiences at these ages are crucial to future school success, however, the move toward developmentally appropriate practice and parent-friendly programs is offset by the national trend for standards, texts, and pushing down the school curriculum. This tension will be discussed throughout the book.

Specific Early Childhood and School Programs

Research indicates that all high-quality child-care and early childhood programs enhance the likelihood that children will enter school with the needed skills and will succeed in school in the later grades. Here I briefly cover programs specifically designed to prepare children for school and to develop a solid foundation of success during the early grades.

Head Start. In 2000, 761,853 children were served in regular Head Start programs throughout the fifty states (Department of Health and Human Services, Administration for Children, Youth and Families, Head Start Bureau [Head Start], 2001). Additional children were served by the Migrant and the Indian programs. The Head Start Migrant programs are located in communities that use migrant workers; they serve migrant children, infants to school age, and their families. The programs are concentrated in Arizona, Texas, Florida, the east and west coasts, and Wisconsin. Programs move from the south to the north as families follow the crops. But more and more places grow crops year-round—such as the Imperial Valley of California—and therefore need farm workers to work throughout the year. Indian Head Start programs are located on Native American reservations, are run by local tribal councils, and emphasize each nation's culture, traditions, learning styles, and expectations. Both the Migrant and the Indian programs follow the same general performance standards used by all Head Start programs and have the same comprehensive approach to serving families. Most Head Start children are aged 3–5, though Head Start also serves children aged infants–3 in their Early Start Programs. Head Start's popular and political success has prompted the creation of a number of state-funded programs for at-risk children. Head Start is characterized by a comprehensive approach (including education, health, mental health, and nutrition), parental involvement and empowerment, and local control. In Chapter 2 I cover Head Start in more detail.

State-Supported Initiatives. Although child care and early education are vital for all working parents, and for ensuring that all children enter school ready to learn, many low- and moderate-income families are unable to afford them (Adams & Poersch, 1997). To help defray some of the costs, government subsidies are needed. Over the past few years, states have become more involved in this issue. Starting with federal block-grant funds, and then with the 1996 Welfare Reform Act, federal money for child care has been distributed to individual states, which have increased control over child-care and education policies. The recent trend has been to shift responsibility for the care and welfare of our most vulnerable citizens from the federal government to the states, which then often administer local programs through the counties.

As I also mentioned, many states have developed early childhood programs designed specifically to enhance children's likelihood of being ready to succeed in school. Some of these state-supported programs are based on the comprehensive Head Start model—addressing every aspect of the child's and family's needs. Most, however, are more narrowly focused on early learning and meeting the kindergarten entry requirements of local public schools. States have also found vastly different approaches to funding these programs, from their general education budget to lottery funds and other sources.

The administration and operation of state-supported preschool programs differ from state to state. In Colorado the funds are administered through the local school districts, which then select the program provider (mostly public schools); in Georgia the state gives the funds, through a competitive-bid process, to local private, nonreligious providers; in other states these programs are simply downward extensions of the local public school.

Local Public-School Early Childhood Programs.

Public schools have always been involved in the upper end of what is considered the early childhood years—ages 6, 7, and 8. Over the years more districts have introduced kindergarten programs, though many of these are still only half-day. But public schools that serve a high number of low-income and minority families have found a variety of ways to provide full-day kindergarten and preschool programs.

Most local schools provide preschool programs (ages 3–5) by combining a variety of funding, including but not limited to Title I funds, state preschool moneys, special education funds (for preschoolers with documented disabilities), and some district moneys. Of course, quite a number of schools across the country, including city school districts such as Detroit and Philadelphia, directly run the local Head Start program. Other districts are delegate agencies, contracting with the local Head Start grantee to provide a number of Head Start classrooms and other services. Even Start, a federal literacy program for families with young children, is run through the local schools.

Title I Programs.

Title I of the Elementary and Secondary Education Act (ESEA) is the largest source of federal aid to educational programs—more than $8 billion annually. This act targets schools in low-income areas, especially at the elementary level. The money is distributed based on the number of low-income children in the school, with schools with the largest percentage of children from low-income homes receiving the greatest amount of money. These funds are used to provide additional academic support and learning opportunities to help low-achieving children meet state standards in core academic areas—reading, math, science, computers, preschool programs, and after-school programs. All children at these schools can take advantage of these programs. The funds are distributed to local school districts through each state's department of education. Charter schools are also eligible.

Private and Religious Preschool Programs.

Almost all religious and private child-care centers provide a curriculum that includes basics and religious instruction. Many parents are convinced that the preschool years are when children should prepare for school entry. Obviously, many private and religious early childhood programs are part of private and religious schools, and simply take a seamless approach to preparing children to enter the next phase of their school experience. Some parents also choose religious options for the early grades, then transfer their children to public or private schools as they grow older. In later chapters I discuss the vast array of private models, including Waldorf, Montessori, international (bilingual) programs, university-based lab schools, and exclusive, upscale academies. Religious options include Catholic, Quaker, and Jewish schools; and other religions, including those of more recent immigrants, such as Muslims, have established a variety of programs.

Almost all religious and private preschools provide an extended-day option for working parents. Because these programs exist to serve parents—and depend for much of their funding on tuition—they are highly responsive to their clients, who often need full-day child care.

Improving Schools

While many policymakers—from the federal architects of Goals 2000 to the developers of state preschool initiatives—believe that money and effort should be used to prepare children to enter schools, many educators and child advocates believe the problem is better addressed by changing the schools children enter, so that schools are ready for our children. Although this text will reflect the tension between these two opposing positions, my underlying belief is that for educational programs to be effective, they must be flexible and responsive enough to meet the needs of each child. The notion of a specific entry-level plateau that must be reached before children can fully utilize the services of the school is not only not developmentally appropriate (see Chapter 3) but also ignores the tremendous diversity of public-school students. Traditional K–12 schools must find ways to take children as they are, affirm their identity, and then create a developmental and educational path that maximizes their education.

The Needs of Young Children

Clearly, young children need safe and healthy care while parents work, and they deserve to receive the appropriate preparation for school entry and subsequent school success. But beyond these general purposes, what do young children really need? In other words, beyond the adult need to work (and thus have their children cared for) and the educational community's need to prepare children for school, what are the basic needs of children themselves?

The Irreducible Needs of Children

In 2000, two leading experts published *The Irreducible Needs of Children: What Every Child Must Have to Grow, Learn, and Flourish*. In this book, T. Berry Brazelton and Stanley I. Greenspan outline what they believe children need. Their list of seven needs unflinchingly goes beyond health, safety, and preschool cognitive preparation (Greenberg, 2001).

Nurturing Relationships. All young children need good-quality human relationships in which parents or caregivers interact directly with the child, one-on-one, in a variety of ways—cuddling, holding on their lap and reading a book, playing cute interactive games, pretend play, and other activities in which the child receives the adult's exclusive attention (Greenberg, 2001). Two-thirds of a child's time should be spent with parents and other people who are important to the child, in direct involvement and supportive activities. Supportive activities are those that assist children in investigating the environment—use of toys, the outdoors, art materials, and more. Brazelton and Greenspan believe that good human relationships and emotional interactions are the most crucial foundation for a child's social and intellectual growth. Because of the essential nature of human interactions, these authors believe that the same caregiver—the primary caregiver—should stay with an infant for three to four years.

Physical Protection, Safety, and Regulation. This need corresponds to the first three levels of Maslow's **hierarchy of needs.** Children should feel secure and loved, and have a consistent environment—in the home, community, and child-care program. Children also require good nutrition, safety from other children and abusive adults, and a sense of order. They should be protected from inappropriate media exposure to acts of violence, disrespect, and intolerance. Thus, families that experience drug and alcohol abuse, domestic violence, and lack of consistency can be extremely detrimental to children's development. Further, the authors stress how important low teacher–child ratios are for caring for children: for infants up to one year old, three babies to one adult; for 1- to 2-year-olds, four infants to one adult; and for 3- to 4-year-olds, five to eight children per adult. A typical preschool classroom should have fifteen children and two adults (a teacher and an aide). Low adult–child ratios are particularly vital for children who do not get physical protection, safety, and regulation at home (Greenberg, 2001).

Experiences Tailored to Individual Differences. Another reason small adult–teacher ratios are so crucial is that each child is unique. "Nurture works with nature much as a key does in a lock: the right experiences can open up the lock of nature and help children realize their potential. Parenting and teaching customized to fit the individual can work wonders" (Greenberg, 2001, p. 11). According to scores on Brazelton's **Neonatal Behavioral Assessment Scale,** newborn babies have unique physical and personality characteristics. These should be shared with parents, and used to plan activities and interests for children. Different children need different patterns of parent and teacher responses, which will help them use their temperament constructively, or they will begin to have problems.

▶ *Early childhood programs are places where children can feel safe and enjoy their childhood.*

Developmentally Appropriate Experiences. We need to lay down five basic things during the first three years of a child's life (Greenberg, 2001, p. 8):

- self-esteem—"I matter, I can dare to care about myself";
- more than enough self-esteem, so the child has some to spare and can be altruistic;
- motivation for learning;
- sense of humor; and
- impulse control.

The developmentally appropriate experiences that develop these attributes come in two forms—both at home and in the child-care program. These are, first, activities in which the parent or caregiver facilitates interactions between the child and other children or the environment (primarily structuring, intervening, asking questions, and responding to the child); and, second, activities in which the adult interacts one-on-one with the child (holding, cuddling, playing peekaboo games, lap reading, experimenting with materials, and so on). These activities should consume at least two-thirds of the child's waking hours and should match the child's need for strong adult contacts and interaction with the real world—not watching TV or "playing away from adults."

Limit-Setting, Structures, and Expectations. "The ability to set limits has gone way down in this generation" (Greenberg, 2001, p. 9). Parents have a tough time setting limits; they come home tired after a day's work and don't feel like being disciplinarians. They need all the help we can give them to provide reasonable, consistent discipline of the child. Discipline comes from having enough time to nurture children: spending lots of time with children during which parents can lead, innovate, and direct activities. Children who receive plenty of nurturing—at home and in programs—are open to limits, structure, and expectations. And one-on-one attention in a program helps this nurturing, especially for children with disciplinary problems. Parents and teachers cannot simply discipline without providing lots of nurturing first.

Stable, Supportive Communities and Cultural Consistency. Providing for the basic needs of children requires three components all working together: the family (parents), early childhood programs and child care, and the community. What we do in the program should be consistent with what is done in the home and the community. To help early childhood programs work effectively with the home and the community, Brazelton has developed Touchpoints Guiding Principles (Brazelton & Greenspan, 2000, p. 14):

- Value and understand the relationship between you and the parent.
- Use the behavior of the child as your language.
- Recognize what you bring to the interaction.
- Be willing to discuss matters that go beyond your traditional role.
- Look for opportunities to support parent mastery.
- Focus on the parent–child relationship.
- Value passion wherever you find it.
- Value disorganization and vulnerability as opportunities.

Protecting the Future. Children need adults and institutions that profess to care about children and are committed to the needs of children throughout the world. Children in poor countries who don't have enough food to eat, adequate shelter, or medical care, and children around the world who are abused and neglected, need our sympathy and commitment. We also need to develop this sympathy and commitment in our children.

Health and Safety

Clearly, our first mandate when caring for young children is to care for their health and safety. Thus programs concentrate on limiting the spread of germs through handwashing, proper diaper changing procedures, toothbrushing, and sterilizing toys and utensils. Environments—inside and outdoor—are carefully set up to limit potential hazards of choking, falling, strangulation, and other accidents. And staff are trained to take care in monitoring health and safety in family care and center programs.

Additionally, early childhood care and education programs implement the nationwide health and safety agenda. As institutions that have direct contact with a vast number of parents and families, child-care programs can have a powerful impact on a variety of health- and safety-related interventions. Often the child-care program is the first institution through which struggling parents have contact with the larger world and issues relating to medical care, substance and physical abuse, nutrition, and safety can be addressed. The network of family child-care homes, child-care centers, schools, and early intervention programs provides a highly effective way for governments, public health programs, and educators to communicate with families and to implement health and safety programs.

Immunizations. A generation or two ago, most people were scared of contracting a contagious debilitating illness, such as polio or diphtheria. As a young boy growing up on an isolated farm in England, I contracted polio in 1953 and was hospitalized for a while with the illness. Luckily I was not left with any severe disabilities. Today, through the development and use of vaccines, medical science has all but eliminated these illnesses in developed countries. To keep these diseases at bay, however, all children in this country are required to take a series of shots on a specific schedule. For low-income families who have limited access to medical care, and for new immigrant families who may not know of the immunization requirements and schedules (which periodically change), early childhood programs serve as a place to get needed information and to obtain knowledge of free clinics and programs. Further, early childhood programs are not allowed to enroll children who are not current with their immunizations, providing an incentive for parents to get the shots for their children.

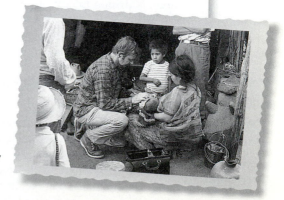

▶ *Early childhood programs provide a place to address critical health needs. In places where they don't exist, like the highlands of Guatemala, doctors must travel to each home.*

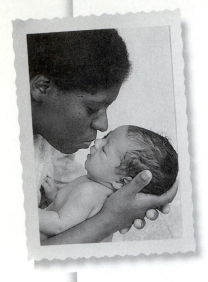

▶ *Good early childhood programs serve the whole family.*

One year when I was a Head Start director, we had a hepatitis epidemic in our community. It was very simple for the Head Start health coordinator to require all our families—and other low-income families from the neighborhood—to come to one of our locations and receive a hepatitis shot from the county health doctor.

Nutrition. More and more research demonstrates the central importance of nutrition for the maximal physical and mental development of all children, but particularly young children. Recent brain research is simply the latest example. According to the Children's Defense Fund (2001), approximately 13.6 million children from low-income families suffer from malnutrition in the United States. Further, 25–29 percent of U.S. children are overweight (Endres & Rockwell, 1994). The surgeon general of the United States believes that obesity in America may soon cause as much disease and death as cigarette smoking. To combat the problem, he contends that schools must provide daily physical education for each grade, offer healthier food options, and enforce federal rules restricting students' access to junk foods (Kim, 2001).

Because the goal of nutrition education is to help people develop the knowledge, skills, and motivation needed to make correct food choices, the early years are one of the best times to provide this education. The knowledge and habits gained will last a lifetime. Children served by family and early childhood programs receive nutritional services in a variety of ways: U.S. Department of Agriculture (USDA) meals, access to federal supplemental food programs such as Women, Infants and Children (WIC), and information about good nutrition for infants and children. All family and center child-care programs that serve low-income children are eligible to serve nutritionally balanced USDA meals, as are schools that serve the same population. The special supplemental food program for WIC is a federal initiative that provides food supplements—free milk, cereal, and other foods—to pregnant women and to women with infants and young children. Nutrition Education and Training Program (NET) provides nutrition education to early childhood programs and schools. The federal government, states, and university extension services also provide information about good nutrition for children, as do some commercial entities, such as the National Milk Council and Dole, which has a comprehensive school program to teach children about the five-fruits-and-vegetables-a-day approach to proper nutrition, and so on.

Substance Abuse. Drug and alcohol abuse by parents (or by grandparents who are the primary caregivers of their grandchildren) is a serious problem that has a negative impact on children. Early childhood professionals can help young children of addicts and alcoholics by developing caring relationships, maintaining consistent routines, and providing therapeutic play in the classroom. These professionals can become the caring, warm, special adult in the child's life that these children so desperately

Figure 1.1

Early childhood programs and schools must be at the forefront of addressing nationwide health and safety concerns. Poor food choices are leading to a national health crisis.

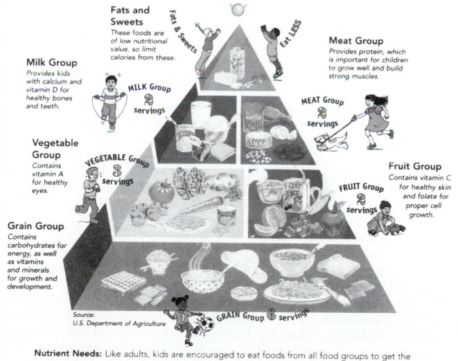

HEALTHFUL EATING
FOR HUNGRY KIDS

Are you concerned about what and how much to feed young children? There's good news! The United States Department of Agriculture's (USDA) new Food Guide Pyramid for Young Children offers nutrition guidelines for 2- to 6-year-olds, emphasizing a variety of kid-friendly food choices and physical activity.

The pyramid illustrates the importance of starting nutrition education at a young age when children are beginning to form lifelong eating habits. So, to give kids a healthy start in life, follow the pyramid!

Fats and Sweets
These foods are of low nutritional value, so limit calories from these.

Fats & Sweets

Eat LESS

Meat Group
Provides protein, which is important for children to grow well and build strong muscles.

Milk Group
Provides kids with calcium and vitamin D for healthy bones and teeth.

MILK Group **2** servings

MEAT Group **2** servings

Vegetable Group
Contains vitamin A for healthy eyes.

VEGETABLE Group **3** servings

Fruit Group
Contains vitamin C for healthy skin and folate for proper cell growth.

FRUIT Group **2** servings

Grain Group
Contains carbohydrates for energy, as well as vitamins and minerals for growth and development.

Source:
U.S. Department of Agriculture

GRAIN Group **6** servings

Nutrient Needs: Like adults, kids are encouraged to eat foods from all food groups to get the nutrients they need. According to the USDA, most young children are consuming fewer than the recommended number of servings from the Vegetable, Fruit, Grain and Meat groups.

need. Other ways programs can meet the needs of these families, include (Rice and Sanoff, 1998):

- posting announcements for community meetings of Alcoholics Anonymous and other recovery groups on the program's bulletin board;
- offering workshops for parents on family stressors (include family substance abuse in these series);
- creating a safe, confidential place for parents to talk with staff or with one another;
- knowing that children often communicate their worries through behaviors, not words, and carefully observing their play and art activities for such behaviors;
- using children's books in the program that discuss sensitive issues like substance abuse, to help children tell their own stories;
- including activities that help children talk about what's going on in their daily lives, especially sensitive, scary issues;
- helping children and parents develop long-term, trusting relationships with a primary caregiver.

As helping professionals we have a responsibility to assist children and parents in homes where addiction is present. We can also offer a variety of connections with community agencies designed to assist these families. "It is our responsibility to lend a hand and believe in the vision that a better future for everyone is possible in recovery" (Rice & Sanoff 1998, p. 33).

Child Abuse and Neglect. All states have laws that require professionals to report suspected abuse and neglect to the appropriate authorities. This requirement, of course, includes all people working with young children—in family child-care homes, child-care centers, and schools. According to the U.S. Department of Health and Human Services, in 1998 2.9 million children were reported to child protective services as suspected of being abused or neglected. The same year, 903,000 children were determined to be victims of mistreatment—half of neglect, half of physical or sexual abuse. Infants and toddlers had the highest rates of abuse and neglect; preschool children under age 5 made up 78 percent of the 1,100 children who died of abuse or neglect in 1998 (HHS, 2000).

Additionally, it appears that child abuse and neglect go hand in hand with domestic violence. Children who experience domestic violence often exhibit a range of emotional and behavioral problems, physical disorders, and academic challenges. These children are more likely to perpetuate the cycle of violence when they become parents themselves.

As Brazelton and Greenspan point out, for children from abusive families, a strong, warm, consistent relationship with a caring teacher or provider is crucial for the child's healthy development (Greenberg, 2001). Child-care programs also try to address child abuse and neglect by adopting curricula that allow for lots of dramatic play, art activities, and gross motor play, encouraging children to explore and come to terms with the violence and abuse at home and in their communities. Also, programs help address child abuse and neglect by working closely with mental health agencies, providing referrals to women's shelters, organizing parent support groups, and posting information about family counseling resources in the community.

Unfortunately, state laws that require teachers and child-care providers to report all cases of suspected child abuse and neglect can backfire. Although the reports are supposed to be confidential, parents can often figure out who made the report; and in my experience with Head Start and child care, the parents then remove the children from the program. Further, many professionals who work with young children have not been trained to discriminate between suspected abuse or neglect and normal childhood accidents. Of particular concern is suspected sexual abuse: even professionals cannot agree on what behaviors, language, or other indicators should be considered suspicious (Wardle & Moore-Kneas, 1995). While there are many ramifications to unsubstantiated reports, one common result is that parents take the child out of the child-care program—often the only secure, loving environment the child has.

Violence. Every year, children die from guns—victims of either the accidental use of guns by others or their own accidental use. In 1998, 3,761 persons under the age of 20 died from firearms (CDF, 2001). According to the U.S. Department of Health and Human Services, Centers for Disease Control and Prevention, more children under age 15 died in 1998 from guns than from cancer, pneumonia, influenza, asthma, and AIDS complications combined (CDC, 2000). Further, as the previous discussion of domestic violence indicates, violence in this society is very destructive for children. Gang membership, rape, and child abuse are indicators of the problem. Child-care centers and schools have taken on the task of trying to address the issue of violence in children's lives. They do so through specific antiviolence curricula, classroom and reading materials, staff training, and working with parents and communities. These professionals also try to reduce children's exposure to violence in the media (TV, videos, films, CDs, and video games), and to pressure the entertainment industry to reduce violent content in what children watch and listen to. Since the Columbine massacre, many schools have initiated various forms of anti-bullying programs.

Special Needs and Diversity

Early intervention is at the root of the mission of helping children who have or are at risk for a disability (Wolery & Wilbers, 1994). Children with special needs differ from children without disabilities: they have all the needs other children have, plus they have needs that children without disabilities do not. These children need environments designed to minimize the effects of the child's disability and to promote learning. They require professionals who can meet the general needs of all young children and also promote the learning of children with disabilities. Finally, these children need professionals who are good at working with other specialists and in partnership with the child's family. Because these children have unique educational needs, the earlier they are identified, the better.

Identification. There are various ways to identify children with special needs. "Perhaps the most relevant classification system deals with their eligibility for early intervention and special education services" (Wolery & Wilbers, 1994, p. 3). The Individuals with Disabilities Education Act (IDEA) defines thirteen categories of disability: deafness, dual-sensory impairments, hearing impairments, mental retardation, multiple handicaps, orthopedic impairments, other health impairments, serious emotional disturbances, specific learning disabilities, speech (language) impairments, visual impairments and blindness, dramatic brain injury, and autism. Many states use the broad term **developmental delay** to cover all these categories. Each state has specific criteria and measurement procedures to determine a child's eligibility for early intervention services. Most disabilities can be placed in one of these categories: for instance, cerebral palsy, spina bifida, and muscular dystrophy fall under orthopedic impairment. Children with ADHD (attention deficit hyperactivity disorder) fall under one of several categories (there is no single category for children with ADHD).

Role of Early Childhood Programs. Many young children with special needs are not identified when they first enter a family child-care or early education program. Early childhood caregivers and teachers are a key to identifying children who may have developmental delays. This identification can occur through informal observation, screening with developmental tools, or visual or hearing screening. As I discuss later, if a screening tool indicates a possible special need, a more intensive assessment must be conducted, resulting, if required, in a full staffing and the development of an Individual Education Plan or Individual Family Service Plan.

Early intervention programs exist to provide early and intensive stimulation to children who are born with a disabling condition—with the intent of enhancing learning while reducing or preventing school failure or further delays. Early childhood programs provide the primary setting in which children with disabilities receive specialized services. Current practice requires this service to be within the **least-restrictive environment** and in equal partnership with a parent or legal guardian. Early childhood programs—be they family child care, center-based programs, Head Start, or schools—play a vital role in meeting the needs of children with disabilities, both through early identification and by providing direct, integrated services.

Diversity. Although our society is becoming more and more diverse, most children come from quite homogeneous homes and communities, be they white, black, Hispanic, Asian American, or Native American. Poor kids tend to grow up in rural areas or low-income neighborhoods; middle-class children in suburbs and college towns. Generally, a child's entry into a center-based early childhood program is the first direct exposure to racial, ethnic, and possibly economic, national, and linguistic diversity. And for many children, enrollment in an early childhood program is their first real exposure to children with various disabilities. As children get older and move into the local school and a wider physical area of involvement, their exposure to diversity increases.

Since this country is becoming ever more diverse and the world is becoming smaller, all children should be exposed to all forms of diversity. As children move into schools and the workplace, they will need to be able to function effectively in a variety of diverse settings. Further, as the United States of America becomes more pluralistic, children must learn to accept and tolerate differences of religion, values, race, ethnicity, language, and abilities.

Developmentally Appropriate Practice

Parent Education

Historically, educating parents has been an important part of child-care programs; Head Start has made it the core of its philosophy, and the majority of nursery schools in the field's early years were parent cooperatives (Hewes, 2000). In today's early childhood programs—family child care, center-based programs, and schools—the need for family involvement continues to increase. One of the central functions of family involvement is parent education—dissemination of a vast range of information and knowledge to help parents with their roles as providers, nurturers, role models, advocates for children, and to help them be effective users of family-oriented services and agencies.

Immigrant Families

According to Allen (1998), the growth of the U.S. population under age 6 will come from children of color or Hispanic origin, while the percentage of the white, non-Hispanic population will drop (Hispanics or Latinos can be of any race). Obviously, these young children will move on into our schools. By 2027, minority (nonwhite and Hispanic) children will be the majority in the United States. Many of their families come from outside the country: Mexico, Central America, South America, Africa, and Asia. Currently, there is also a significant influx of families from Russia, eastern Europe, and the Balkans. These new families bring with them their own languages, cultural practices, religions, and values to our country and to early childhood programs. While (as I discuss in Chapter 6) these immigrants will maintain important aspects of their unique cultural heritage, they must also become somewhat Americanized: learn the language, customs, attitudes, and expectations necessary to succeed in this country. After all, new immigrants come here for a better life, and they are interested to learn how to achieve that life.

Language Issues. Many early childhood programs struggle with families whose main language is not English. As programs find ways to educate children who don't speak English while supporting their home language, they also expose parents to the English language and provide opportunities for parents to learn English. Some schools, Head Start programs, and other community agencies provide English as a Second Language (ESL) classes for new parents; others refer parents to classes provided by local community colleges, extension services, county and city agencies, or private providers.

Other ways non–English-speaking parents begin to learn English are when their children come home speaking English, when they need to talk to the teacher (who may not know their language), when they try to help their child with homework, and when they begin to make friends with English-speaking parents and teachers. Obviously, well-integrated early childhood and school programs are more effective at helping non–English-speaking parents learn English. Programs that encourage activities in which all parents—from diverse language and ethnic or national backgrounds—participate also encourage the learning of English. Early childhood programs can be very instrumental in encouraging new immigrants' efforts to learn English, while supporting their need to retain their own language, cultural heritage, and sense of belonging.

Acculturation. I have been lucky enough to spend time in several foreign countries, including Brazil. On my first visit there, I returned to my room in my host's house after a breakfast of presweetened black coffee, melons, and cheese rolls, to discover that my bed had been made and my dirty clothes were gone! On inquiry, I discovered that middle-class Brazilians use maids in their homes, who pick up after the family and do the cooking and laundry. Making my bed and washing my clothes are signs of Brazilian hospitality.

Every culture has its own way of doing things and expects that people in the culture will follow those ways. Each of us functions comfortably within our own culture, and we are usually unaware of our own behaviors and values until we travel or meet someone from another culture. New immigrants face the huge challenge of learning our cultural norms and expectations, and then learning how to follow them without rejecting their own family's cultural heritage—what some call a **bicultural practice.** Child-care centers and schools provide an excellent place for new immigrants to learn our values relating to education, the role of parents working closely with the school, and how Americans raise their children. Immigrant parents can also ask other parents when they are puzzled, need additional information, or simply want to know how it is done here. Because all parents of young children struggle with the same issues of balancing child rearing, employment, and family stresses, early childhood programs can be wonderful places for new immigrants to receive support, knowledge, and referrals.

Parent Advocacy

Anyone who has been—or is—a parent knows that parenting is an all-consuming, difficult task, especially when children are young. When my four children were young, I often felt I was in the middle of a struggle between my family and the rest of society: the media spreading morals and values I did not agree with, advertisers telling my children they deserved toys, clothes, and fat-filled food I didn't want for them, and social service agencies that seemed more interested in parents making mistakes than in helping families under stress. Child-care and school programs are settings in which parents should feel solidarity and empowerment, and in which their needs and those of their family are met.

Parenting Skills. We all can learn to be better parents. Raising children in today's society is extremely difficult and stressful. Early childhood programs understand this, and good programs provide a range of ways to help parents with their parenting skills. They work as partners with parents to serve the best interests of the children. Approaches programs use to work with parents include:

- parenting classes;
- newsletters;
- parent libraries, containing books, magazines, and video and audio tapes;
- parent groups, socials, and discussions;
- sponsoring parent activities in the community, such as brown-bag lunches, speakers, children's festivals, and others;
- visits by experts to the program;
- referrals to community agencies (child psychologists, mental health agencies, parenting experts, support groups, adoption experts, hospitals, and the like);
- direct advice;
- parent committees to address school-related issues and policies;
- membership on the school board, PTAs, advisory boards, or policy councils;
- opportunities to learn from other parents.

Working with Schools and Other Agencies. When I was a Head Start director, some of my parents were concerned about the way one of our local schools stereotyped their children as poor and minority, and therefore as children who could not succeed in their school. So we worked closely with the school to try to change their view, and to make sure our children and parents were welcome. Also, because our families were all low-income, we worked very closely with the local food bank and food distribution center, the county office of social services, and the area's federal job training center. We found better ways for our families to have access to the local libraries, and made sure there were good transition programs in place between our centers and the neighborhood public and Catholic schools.

All communities offer a vast array of services for children, from information regarding the safe use of infant car seats to making available free food and health insurance for low-income families. Counties provide mental health and public health services, local schools and community colleges offer parenting classes and ESL course for parents, libraries schedule family time and group reading activities, and university extensions teach many classes for families. A variety of not-for-profit agencies and local businesses also offer services for families. While programs like Head Start are required to work very closely with many of these community services and to provide referrals to their families, all child-care programs and schools are excellent places to disseminate information about family-friendly community programs and services.

Good early childhood programs usually go beyond simply informing parents of resources and work directly with community agencies to make sure the agencies know the needs of the program's families, and to reduce barriers that might keep families from benefiting from any agencies that don't encourage full family participation. To assure that local agencies are responsive to family needs, child-care programs should consider some of these activities:

- have someone from the child-care program or school sit on the agency's board;
- meet regularly with officials from various agencies;
- sit on community boards that include other agencies, such as the United Way, the local Community Development Block Grant (CDBG) board, and others;
- join social groups that include people from other agencies, such as Rotary or Lions clubs;
- join political advocacy groups;
- always invite members of the community to visit the child-care program or school, especially for special events and occasions;
- support events at the center or school that bring the community together;
- support child- and family-friendly community events by allowing teachers and other staff to participate, on company time;
- regularly invite representatives of agencies to come and give a presentation to staff and parents about the programs and services they offer.

Global Early Childhood Programs

Clearly, children around the world have the same basic needs of health and safety, nutrition, stimulation, and preparation for their future. As more women enter the workforce, the needs of the children increase. Children will have to be cared for by others, and the collaboration of government, industry, and local communities is required to provide for the welfare of the next generation. For decades most developed nations have recognized the need for programs that support working families and help protect their children, prepare them for school, and care for them before and after school hours. Now developing countries are also addressing these concerns. Finally, as the world becomes smaller and technology becomes a driving force, children in all countries need high-quality early educational opportunities to succeed.

The Foundation

In the 1920s, the socialist government in Brazil passed a law requiring factories in urban areas to provide child care as an employee benefit. Some of these business-based programs survived through the 1970s (Jaffe, 1999), and some programs exist today that are based on that legislation. I visited a school for low-income children in a town called Diamantina, in the state of Minas Gerais. The program was a cross between a Head Start program and a community-center before- and after-school program—playground, classrooms with sewing machines and desks, social activities for older children, and adult supervision. The school was funded by local industry and the municipality of Diamantina.

In the 1980s, the Ecuadorian Congress required all companies that employed fifty people or more to provide child care for the children of their workers. In 1985 the Ecuadorian government developed a series of workplace-based child-care centers to demonstrate its own compliance with the law. Since then the country has supported a series of programs called *guaderias*—child-care centers that combine care of children with medical services, and serve the child-care and medical needs of the entire community.

And, as I mentioned earlier, the advent of World War II led to the first large-scale child care in this country. Federal legislation established funding for child-care centers, which were subsidized by the government to give mothers access to them. Often these programs operated around the clock. Hundreds of centers were established across the country by 1942 and continued to function throughout the war. The centers run by Kaiser Industries are the best known of these wartime programs (Jaffe, 1999).

Global Child-Care Needs

Whether children are in China, Poland, Nigeria, or the United States, they are at similar stages of development during their preschool years, David Weikart pointed out in an interview (Child Care Information Exchange, 1999, p. 8): "We found children in all countries engaging in the same tasks—sliding, swinging, jumping, and playing tag." In studying children from fifteen different nations, Weikart discovered that while children appear very different—in physical features, dress, and cultural mannerisms—they behave in very similar ways: they run, jump, and manipulate materials in much the same manner.

Weikart and his colleagues also found that in most of those fifteen countries, teachers and parents had the same expectations for preschool-age children. Both parents and teachers in almost all of the countries studied believed that the most important skill was to learn to relate to peers; the least important was learning to relate to adults. Additionally, teachers and parents in most countries believed that it was essential to develop language skills and personal self-sufficiency skills during the early years.

The only area of major disagreement was regarding the acquisition of academic skills. In Finland, 3 percent of the teachers and 14 percent of parents viewed the development of academic skills in preschool children as important; in Nigeria, 75 percent of parents and 73 percent of teachers viewed the acquisition of academic skills as most important. Also, Nigerians did not view self-sufficiency as a skill for preschoolers to learn, because in their culture children learn at an early age how to care for their younger siblings and other self-sufficiency skills (Child Care Information Exchange, 1999).

The Netherlands. In Holland, local communities are required to plan for child care. Any new business must determine the number of child-care spaces it needs, based on the number of its employees. Then it is required to pay into a local child-care fund for the expansion of child-care spaces—either at its own facility or at a community child-care center—or else the company can contract with local private or public providers for the care of its children (Jaffe, 1999). This law has stimulated a rapid increase in corporate-sponsored child care, and one large child-care company has tripled its number of centers to more than 120—mostly serving children in collaboration with corporations and local governments. A wide variety of businesses, from local companies to international corporations, provide for the children of their employees.

China. In China, the majority of preschool children are still cared for in their homes, either by parent or by grandparents. In urban areas, 80 percent or more of preschool-age children attend preschools; in rural areas, approximately 20 percent of children attend such programs. The main sponsors of preschool programs are employers, education institutions, and the government—with employers being the main providers, and programs being located at or near the workplace (Child Care Information Exchange, 1999). The groups in these programs are very large—a ratio of one adult for every forty-five children in urban programs, and one adult for every sixty children in the rural ones. According to teachers in these programs, areas of greatest importance for this age are language and self-sufficiency skills; according to parents, areas of greatest importance are language and preacademic skills.

Nigeria. A very small percentage of children in Nigeria attends either home care programs or centers. Because there is almost no governmental support of programs for young children, only parents who can afford the full cost have access to them. The average adult–child ratio in a formal preschool-age program is one to twenty-one, with a maximum of one to sixty. Both teachers and parents in Nigeria named preacademic skills as the most important to teach preschool children, and self-sufficiency as the least important.

Finland. The Day Care Law of 1973 guarantees public child care for every child between the ages of 1 and 6. Services are provided through family child-care homes and centers, funded primarily by local and national government entities. Religious organizations also provide very popular play groups for a few hours every week. Because of Finland's other family-friendly policies, parents can often stay home with their infants and young children. Finland has a training system for all teachers and caregivers—both those who work in family homes and those in child-care centers. The average ratio in Finland's children's programs is one to six, with a range between one to three and one

▶ *As more women enter the workforce, child care and early education is becoming a worldwide phenomenon, such as this setting in Brazil.*

to nine. Teachers and parents believe that social skills with peers and self-sufficiency skills are the most important areas to develop at this time; preacademic skills are rated the least important.

Brazil. Brazil is essentially a developing country with two distinct classes, upper-middle class and poor. Historically the Brazilian upper-middle-class families have relied on maids to help care for their young children, along with doing tasks such as shopping, cooking, and cleaning the house. A visitor to a large city park, such as the Municipal Park in the center of Belo Horizonte, or Sarah Kubitscheck Park in Brasilia, will observe maids accompanying one or two young children. The maids are usually minority (black and mixed-race), the children white and Asian. There is beginning to be a shift away from the maid system, with a variety of child-care programs sprouting up in the wealthier sections of urban areas. These parents also have access to a variety of international preschool models, such as Montessori and Waldorf.

In Brazil many poor parents take their children to work with them—in the fields, and selling produce and wares along the side of the road. Another popular option is care by relatives. A variety of religious programs and service organizations have set up nurseries to care for children of the poor, including homeless and street children. And there are a few local-government (city) programs operating in poorer parts of towns.

Conclusion

The need for good-quality child care and early education is increasing in this country and around the world. The primary functions of these programs are to provide safe and consistent care for children while parents are at work, and to prepare children for successful school entry and completion. Many of these programs also look after school-age children before and after their regular school day and during vacations. The first years of formal education, kindergarten through third grade, are receiving renewed attention in the United States, other developed nations, and developing countries. Beyond care and education, high-quality early childhood programs also function in a variety of ways to support parents and families, promote national agendas of health and safety, address issues of various forms of diversity, and help immigrant families to develop a solid foundation in their new country. In this country, the federal and state governments are increasing their support for educational programs for young children; but they are more concerned with sponsoring education programs than supporting high-quality child-care programs.

Questions and Projects

1. Find an article (Internet, library) on global child care, and report back to the class.

2. Interview two or three parents of children under age 5. Do they have children in an early childhood program? How many hours a day? Is it child care, education, or both? Write a three- to five-page paper.

3. Find a specialized child-care program in your community. Receive permission from your instructor. Visit the program and write a short paper.

4. Identify a kindergarten program—public, private, or religious. Determine where children come from to enter the program (other programs, no program, feeder programs). Determine if the teacher feels they are "ready" for the kindergarten program. Are there any transition programs in place?

5. Identify an elementary school with a significant number of non–English-speaking students. How does the school meet the needs of these students? How does it work with their parents? Does it provide non-English services to all families, or just those who speak Spanish? Provide an oral report to the class.

CHAPTER 2

Types *of* Early Childhood Programs

*T*he purpose of this chapter is to describe the wide range of approaches to child care, early childhood education, and primary-school programs that exist in this country. The chapter describes different funding sources, philosophies, structures, and purposes of various programs. Types of programs covered include part-day parent co-ops, federally funded Head Start programs; religious programs; full-day, full year child care; Title I programs; and diverse private early childhood and elementary-school options. While approaches to caring for young children are often divided into child care—programs whose primary role is to care for children while their parents work or go to school—and early childhood programs—part-day educational programs designed to give children a preschool preparation for school entry—this chapter will not be divided in that manner, because the lines between the two extremes are blurring all the time, and the distinction is not particularly helpful in exploring the options for early care and education. ■

A Need for Child Care and Early Education

Like other struggling families, we had to find care for my first child, Maia, shortly after her birth. Initially, Maia's caregivers alternated among my wife's mother, me in the evenings, and my wife during the day while she studied. Sometimes Maia would

Questions to Consider

1. Who uses family day-care homes, and why?
2. Should all Head Start programs be part of the local public school?
3. What is the role of religious early childhood programs?
4. How do international early childhood approaches such as Waldorf, Montessori, and British Infant schools fit into the American options for early care and education?
5. What is the role of the federal and state government in early childhood programs and child care? Will this role expand?
6. What is the role of private child-care chains, private schools, and independent early childhood programs?

sleep in her carrier or play with toys on a blanket on the floor in my office at Big Brothers and Sisters. Because I was a manager, I could bring her with me to work without anyone objecting. But we soon had to find a more permanent solution. I remember meeting with a family day-care provider in her home. It was a dark room, there was fine crystal on shiny wooden tables and in cupboards, and three children were quietly watching the TV. When I asked the provider how she kept the crystal from being broken, she replied that she simply taught all the children to mind.

We finally found a variety of programs for Maia, including a mother who cared for Maia and another child along with her own child, a Catholic school that served primarily black families, and several preschool programs attached to small private schools. My second daughter, Eirlys, was cared for with several other children by a Sikh in an ashram. This was a wonderful nurturing, caring environment for her. To this day I believe Eirlys's strong, secure temperament reflects that early care.

When we moved from Kansas City to Denver, my wife decided to stay home for a while to care for our four children. By this time Maia was in first grade, but we decided to teach her with the other three children at home. It was cheaper for Ruth to stay home and care for them than to have Maia go to school and an after-school program, and the others attend a child-care program.

Many child care and early childhood programs have different eligibility criteria, and some are not full-day, full-year programs. Further, there is considerable overlap among programs. For example, some Head Start programs are run by public schools, while others simply rent space in public schools; Catholic Charities and other charities administer Head Start programs, and many others are community not-for-profit programs. There are even home-based Head Start programs.

Willer et al. (1991) provide terminology that help define the different ways young children are cared for and educated in this country. **Center care** refers to a situation in which children are cared for in a group in a nonresidential setting for all or part of the day. Center care is subdivided into nonprofit centers, both sponsored and independent; and for-profit centers, both independent and chains. Nonprofit, sponsored programs are further categorized by auspices, including centers sponsored by Head Start, public schools, religious organizations, and others, including employers or community agencies. **Family child care** is care providing for a small group of children in a caregiver's home. Often a family child-care provider is a mother with children of her own at home. Family child care may be regulated or unregulated. Unregulated care includes providers who are not licensed or registered, regardless of whether they should

Variety of Programs to Care for and Educate Young Children (0–8)

Head Start and Early Start

Military child care

Religious programs (various denominations)

Family child care

Public school early childhood programs, including Title I and Special Education programs

Care by relatives

Nanny service

Not-for-profit community centers

For-profit independent community centers

For-profit child-care chains

Public school K–3 programs

Private schools (Montessori, Waldorf, international/bilingual, British Infant Schools, early childhood, and K–3 programs)

Employer-sponsored care

Specialized care (homeless, special needs, therapeutic, gifted programs, and others)

Campus child care

School-age programs (before- and after-school care), private, public, contract

▶*Some programs stress early academics; others have a more whole-child approach.*

be. **In-home care** is care provided by a nonrelative who comes into the family home, such as a nanny. Sometimes the provider brings her own children with her. Care provided by a relative in the child's home or the relative's home is called **relative care.**

Public School Early Childhood Programs

Public schools have traditionally provided K–12 programs. Additionally, many public schools administer a variety of early childhood programs. For several reasons, these programs are increasing in popularity and number of children served.

Figure 2.1

Percentage of children under age 14 enrolled in nonrelative child care, part- or full-time.

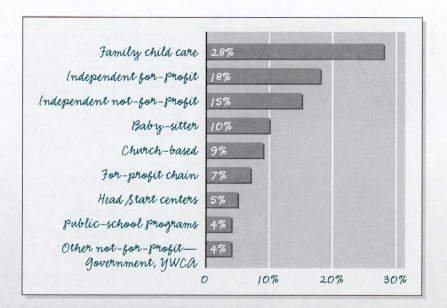

Category	Percentage
Family child care	28%
Independent for-profit	18%
Independent not-for-profit	15%
Baby-sitter	10%
Church-based	9%
For-profit chain	7%
Head Start centers	5%
Public-school programs	4%
Other not-for-profit— Government, YWCA	4%

Source: Neugebauer 1998.

Programs include some Head Starts, Title I programs, special education programs, state-funded preschools, tuition-based programs, and programs funded from the school's regular budget. Sometimes public school programs are an integral part of the local school; others are contracted by them or simply run out of their buildings. The increase in early childhood programs in public schools is a result of two main trends: the need for full-day care for children of working families; and the belief that young children, especially those from low-income backgrounds, need early childhood programs to prepare them for public school success.

Almost all public schools offer kindergarten; some are full-day, others only part-day sessions. In certain middle-class communities, schools offer half-day regular kindergarten and half-day tuition-based programs. Sometimes these half-day options are run by the school itself; more often they are contracted to an independent provider or a child-care chain.

While public schools that have early childhood programs try to create a full-day, seamless approach to child care by collaborating with Head Start, state-funded programs, and community child-care providers, this is often difficult to accomplish. There are many **turf issues,** conflicting regulations, incompatible funding streams, and opposing philosophies.

State-Funded Preschools

Many states are directly funding prekindergarten initiatives. A variety of funding streams is used to support these programs: Colorado uses state general-fund moneys; Georgia's early childhood program is funded with lottery money. In fiscal year 1991–1992, states spent a total of $700 million on prekindergarten programs; in 1998–1999, almost $1.7 billion (Children's Defense Fund [CDF], 1999), and the 2000–2001 outlay was estimated to be $2.54 billion. Forty-two states plus Washington, D.C., fund programs; twenty-four were increasing their funds for the 2000–2001 academic year (Dateline Child Care 2000). From 1991 to 2000, the number of children served by these programs grew from 290,000 to 725,000. States that are increasing their support for these programs the most are Texas, New York, North Carolina, California, Georgia, Illinois, Ohio, Florida, Massachusetts, and Michigan.

Philosophies, administrative support, and scope of preschool programs differ from state to state. Some are part-day, some full-day; some are focused academic programs, others are based on the comprehensive Head Start model. State-supported programs in some states are offered only through the local public schools, while in other states the programs are provided through a variety of community-based settings, including private, for-profit centers.

Georgia is the only state that funds its program at a high enough level to serve all children whose parents want the program and to assure high-quality programs (Schulman, Blank, & Ewen, 1999). Most programs limit eligibility to low-income families or families with other risk factors; but still only a small percentage of those eligible are actually served.

Most of the state-funded programs serve 4-year-olds. Eighteen states limit eligibility to one year; thirty-one states limit it to two years, to allow the maximum number of children to benefit from the programs, and to follow the original Head Start philosophy, which held that one year of a good-quality early childhood program could provide a significant "head start" for school success.

State programs in Massachusetts and Connecticut provide money for facilities costs—building, renovation, or buying. All other state programs fund only the program operation itself—teachers, administrators, and materials. The lack of financial support for buildings can cause major problems, especially for school districts whose increasing population makes it difficult to house their K–12 students. The Georgia program solved this dilemma by encouraging private child-care providers to administer the program in their own centers. It is much easier for these providers to provide full-day, full-year **wraparound child care** than it is for schools and part-day Head Start programs, because child care is their business.

Quality Standards. The quality of state-funded early childhood programs varies a great deal, because there are no overall state or federal standards for schools (most public-school standards are state- and district-specific) and because public-school standards do not apply well to young children (Wardle, 1989). For example, kindergarten classrooms often have twenty-five or more children, yet child-care licensing for the same age requires much smaller groups. Some schools simply rely on the local school standards or the state's child-care licensing codes. Others have created their own standards, based on existing guidelines such as the Head Start Performance Standards and the accreditation criteria of the National Association for the Education of Young Children (NAEYC, 1998).

Most states do, however, set qualifications for teachers and stipulate student–teacher ratios. Teacher qualifications reflect the educational establishment's belief in formal education, which is often used to separate school programs from child care; student–teacher ratio is a program-quality indicator that professional early childhood programs have insisted on (NAEYC, 1998). In fact, these are both considered quality indicators. Student–teacher ratio is one area in which early childhood programs (small ratios) and schools (large ratios) differ to an extreme.

Comprehensive versus Academic Models. Fourteen of the state preschool programs have no provisions beyond a prekindergarten readiness program, which reflects a public-school curriculum concept that tends to focus on the scope and sequence of academic skill acquisition (see Chapter 4), rather than the whole-child early childhood philosophy that characterizes Head Start and other comprehensive programs (Bredekamp & Copple, 1997). Unwittingly, Goal One of Goals 2000 (every child will enter school ready to learn) promoted some of these traditional preschool programs. Nevertheless, some state programs do include a variety of nonacademic components, including health screening and full-day services.

Parental Involvement. Although most of the state preschool programs call for parental involvement, parents are not full partners in many of them (Schulman, Blank, & Ewen, 1999). Parental involvement is another watershed difference between traditional school programs and early childhood programs, and it is also viewed by many as an indicator of program quality. While many public schools profess parental involvement, they often struggle to implement it fully, especially in low-income and minority schools. Georgia and Wisconsin provide grant funds specifically targeted for parent activities, involvement, and training.

Clearly, state-supported early childhood programs are here to stay. Still unclear are the particular curricular and programmatic forms they will take, and whether they will primarily exist in public schools or remain a mix of public and private providers.

Title I Programs

Title I programs constitute the largest single federal allocation to public schools, with a budget of more than $8 billion a year in 2000. As part of the Elementary and Secondary Education Act (ESEA) of 1965, Title I is short for "Part A of Title I of Improving America's School Act of 1994, Reauthorization of the Elementary and Secondary Education Act of 1965." The majority of Title I money is targeted at children from low-income families "who are failing, or most at risk of failing, to meet state academic standards" (Colorado Department of Education, 2000, p. 1). Schools whose enrollment includes at least 50 percent of students from poor families are eligible for Title I funds for schoolwide programs. These programs "provide additional academic support and learning opportunities to help low-income children master challenging curriculum and meet state standards in core academic subjects." (CDE 2001, p. 1). Examples are instruction in reading, math, science, and computers; preschool programs for targeted students; after-school programs; and summer programs. Title I serves children in preschool through twelfth grade.

Although the vast majority of these funds go to public schools, parochial, charter, and private schools that serve a significant low-income population are also eligible for them. The federal government allocates moneys to state departments of education based on the census poverty figures for each state. The state then reallocates funds to each district, which in turn provides moneys to schools with the most children from low-income homes, to support programs for the entire school, not just the poor children in the school.

While Title I funds do not go just to preschool children and their families, as do Head Start funds (except for the Early Head Start program), a significant portion does assist children from preschool through grade three. These funds supplement a community's Head Start moneys and a school's special education (IDEA) funds.

Some of the kinds of initiatives funded by Title I include

- smaller classes;
- additional teachers and assistants;
- extra training for school staff;
- extra time for instruction;
- a variety of teaching methods and materials;
- counseling and mentoring;
- bilingual paraprofessionals.

Special Education and Even Start Programs

There are various federally funded programs that serve children, from infancy through age 21, identified as having disabilities. Some of the disabilities are obvious physical, emotional, and behavioral challenges, but many are learning disabilities that inhibit a child's ability to learn effectively. Most of the children are served in public-school programs, including preschool programs; however, children in religious programs, private centers, and Head Start programs, as well as those cared for at home, are also eligible for special-education services. The specifics of the program differ for children aged 0–3 and for children over age 3. These programs are discussed in detail in Chapter 6.

▶*Charter schools select a specific philosophy, such as the arts or technology.*

Even Start is a literacy program also funded by the revised ESEA of 1994. It provides money to local school districts to offer services to the nation's low-income families by integrating early childhood education, adult basic literacy or adult education, and parenting education into a family literacy program. This program is separate from Title I, Head Start, and state-funded programs.

Charter Schools

Charter schools—popular in Colorado, Arizona, and other states—are self-contained public schools with a very specific focus, such as technology, arts and performance, core curriculum, gifted and talented, alternative, or expeditionary learning curricula. They are funded by the local school district but don't follow many of the district's policies and procedures. A charter school must demonstrate both parental support and a program approach that is not otherwise available in the district. Various charter school options include Waldorf; Montessori; Core knowledge schools; specialized curricula developed by private companies, such as the Edison Project and Mosaica; Roots and Wings (the Johns Hopkins University); various gifted models; the British Infant Schools model; and arts and technology approaches. I discuss some of these options in this chapter under Private-School–Based Early Childhood Programs, because they are typically viewed as private school choices.

A few states—Wisconsin, Ohio, Florida—are also experimenting with vouchers to fund elementary schools. This approach allows parents to select a school for their children, including private and religious schools.

Religious Early Childhood Programs

For one year I taught a kindergarten class at a school in a religious community, the Bruderhof, in rural Pennsylvania. A typical day started at 7:30 A.M. My students' fathers dropped the children off on their way to work at the woodworking shop, school, medical offices, or maintenance building. We started our morning in our two small classrooms. After reading a story together, we headed off across the fields to a small barn. We fed a flock of laying hens and collected their eggs, then put the eggs in a bucket near the door so we could pick them up on returning from our walk. Next we hiked up a pathway through hardwood trees to the pond. We spent time fishing, watching the colorful fall leaves floating on the water, tossing objects into the water to observe their concentric rings, and playing in the bushes (Wardle, 1995a).

On our return we took the eggs to the communal kitchen and went back to the classroom. After taking off our outdoor clothes, unloading all our new specimens on the science table, and eating a quick snack, we broke into our learning centers, where children engaged in woodworking, dramatic play, reading in the loft, playing with unit blocks, splashing in the water table, or listening to tapes. At 12:15 P.M. we walked over to the dining room for a communal lunch with the children's families and everyone else in the community.

Most of my days followed this familiar pattern. But we also went on field trips to the local firehouse with the father of one of the children in class, who was a volunteer firefighter; we visited a farm at milking time; and we participated in a maple-sap operation that included extracting the sap, processing it into sugar, and making sugar cookies.

This early childhood program is one of thousands of religious early childhood programs and schools in this country. The philosophy of the program revolves around high-quality care and supervision, exploration of the natural environment, learning the songs and stories of the community's culture, and helping in community life. There is also an emphasis on arts and crafts—woodworking, ceramics, painting, and crafts—with little attention to the academic subjects of reading, writing, and arithmetic until first grade.

Religious education programs in this country include Jewish, Mormon, Amish, Hutterite, Baptist, Catholic, Lutheran, Episcopalian, Muslim, Buddhist, and Quaker schools. Most people are familiar with the network of Catholic schools that exists in every major city. In addition to religious schools, there are also various preschool and child-care programs run out of churches. These programs are a service to members and the community and often provide a revenue source for the church.

According to *The Demand and Supply of Child Care in 1990* (Willer et al., 1991), 15 percent of preschool children who are in child-care centers nationwide are in religious programs. This compares to 6 percent in for-profit chains, 9 percent in Head Start, and 8 percent in a public-school program. And this percentage does not include children in religious schools (over 5 years old), or those in before- and after-school programs in religious school settings. Nearly 1.5 million children attend weekday early childhood programs housed in religious facilities, and most of these programs are operated directly by the religious order. Nearly one in six child-care centers in the United States is housed in a house of worship, with a total of 26,750 religious child-care centers in this country (Neugebauer, 2000b). The largest child-care providers in this country are the Catholic Church and the Southern Baptist Convention (Neugebauer, 2000b).

While providing nurturing care and love is the number one reason churches care for young children, the second major reason is providing spiritual education and development. Further, churches are greatly expanding their programs as they realize they have the space to do so (initially created for Sunday school programs). Interestingly, as we become aware of worldwide early childhood efforts (see Chapter 8), we recognize the significant role of religious programs in other countries, including Uruguay, Namibia, and Brazil.

Head Start Programs

In the fall I volunteer to help my friend, Keith, in his Head Start classroom, in the small town of Ault, Colorado. The Head Start program is located in the ground level of an old house, right on main street, which has been remodeled into classrooms and a kitchen. As we start to set up the classroom for the day's activities, children begin to arrive. These are children from local agricultural workers' families, Hispanic and white. Keith greets each parent and child warmly. A recent Peace Corps volunteer in Peru, he is fluent in Spanish, and speaks to the children in the language they are most comfortable with (and he even tries to teach me some Spanish!).

We quickly work into the routine of eating breakfast, brushing teeth, reading a book, and engaging in individual activities. We then go out behind the house, away from the main street, to play.

But there is nothing to do! Although the program has done a nice job remodeling the inside of the house, the back is an empty yard. As usual, money seemed to run out before the outdoor playground could be built. So we take the children down to the local city park. But the park is designed for older children, so this is not a good solution. Also, taking the children through town along the streets is not easy or safe.

As we clean up after the children leave and prepare for the next day, we discuss the lack of an adequate outdoor playground. We decide to find out whether parents would be interested in helping us design and build a playground in the back yard. Several fathers are recruited to help us. Because all the parents are involved in farming, they have access to a variety of materials and tools, and have the carpentry and masonry skills needed to build the playground.

We set to work on our playground. A dump truck delivers a huge tire from a road grader, which we fill with sand to make a sandbox; a group of fathers drops off several cable spools, and the rest of us diligently transform a fire escape to the upstairs apartment (which is empty) into a slide with a big curve at the bottom. The stairs of the fire escape become the steps for the slide. By the end of a day we have transformed the empty back yard into a fun playground for a group of Head Start children.

Head Start encourages parents to volunteer in their program, and communities are required to contribute directly to the operation of the local program. This requirement is a way to assure community support. Parent volunteers, businesses, scout troops, dentists, doctors, and mental health professionals are just some of those who contribute thousands of hours every year to local Head Start programs. Head Start programs also work out agreements to work collaboratively with other local community agencies.

History of Head Start

Head Start was developed as part of President Lyndon Johnson's **Great Society Program.** It was part of a collection of programs known as the **War on Poverty**—Job Corps, VISTA, CETA, LEAP, CAP agencies, and others. Head Start is one of the few remaining War on Poverty programs, and in 1999 it had an annual budget of $4.6 billion (Head Start, 1999).

Head Start, initiated in the summer of 1965, grew out of a national commission seeking ways to meet the needs of children with mental retardation. Fundamental to Head Start was the belief that many low-income children entering public school were already behind their middle-class counterparts. Further, its creators believed that for a variety of reasons, many schools did not serve low-income children and their families

▶ *Head Start is a federally funded program, primarily for children aged 3 to 5 years old.*

adequately. The first national Head Start program was funded at a level of $96,400,000 and served 561,000 during only the summertime (Head Start, 2000). By contrast, the 1998 program served 822,316 children for the school year. Since its inception, Head Start has served 17,713,000 children.

Comprehensive Approach

The Head Start philosophy views the years before school as a time to address a range of family and children's issues. Thus local Head Start programs cover many areas, including family partnerships, community partnerships, child health and development services, education and early childhood development, child health and safety, child nutrition, and child mental health.

Family Partnerships. Parents are recognized as the first educators of the child. Head Start also recognizes that improvements in a child's educational environment start with parental behavior and attitudes. Local programs are required to develop and implement approaches to involve parents: as volunteers in the classroom; through membership in classroom, center, and program policy committees; by holding paid positions in the program; and by direct participation in program activities and community affairs. Head Start staff are also required to visit homes regularly and to work with parents to help meet their children's needs.

Local Head Start programs have done a wonderful job of encouraging low-income parents to volunteer in the program, training them, and eventually hiring them as full-time staff. Many current Head Start employees were originally parents of Head Start children (30 percent of current staff were parents of Head Start children, according to the Head Start Bureau [Head Start, 1999]. In the program I directed, my manager for family partnerships was originally a parent, a migrant worker employed in the fields of southern Colorado.

Community Partnerships. Head Start works closely with community agencies to help meet the needs of its students' families. These agencies include food banks, the welfare office, public schools, emergency clothing banks, hotels for the homeless, organizations that provide supplemental heating funds, and mental health services. The intent is to coordinate all existing services, to break down barriers, and to empower parents to be advocates for their children.

Nutrition. Many low-income children have inadequate food and poorly balanced diets. All local Head Start programs receive USDA money for breakfast, lunch, and snacks. The program is charged with making sure these meals are balanced and nutritious, and with educating both parents and children about healthy food choices and habits. The program's nutritionist works closely with the teachers to integrate nutritional information into the curriculum.

Health and Safety. Low-income families do not have access to adequate health care, and children with health-care needs have more difficulty in school. The health component of Head Start works closely with local clinics, doctors, and agencies to address any chronic health issues before a child starts formal school. Further, the program assists families to get access to services, to change behaviors, and to advocate for their children, so that when their children enter school they are ready to learn. Dental health and good dental habits are addressed in the same way.

Mental Health. Because of the pressures of poverty, lack of health insurance, substance abuse in the family, and dysfunctional families, many Head Start children must deal with mental health issues. Like the program's approach to physical health, Head Start works closely with the family to find community resources, develop healthy behaviors, and include specific mental health issues in the classroom curriculum. Local Head Start programs work very closely with **Child Find** to identify children with disabilities, develop programs for them, and assure a smooth transition from Head Start into the school district's special education program. Thirteen percent of Head Start enrollment consists of children with disabilities (Head Start, 1999). The focus is on early detection and intervention, working with the child's family, **inclusion,** and transition to the public school.

Education and Early Childhood Development. In most Head Start programs, education is provided through a variety of classroom options; however, some children attend home-based programs. In 1998, 42,743 Head Start children received home-based services out of the total 822,316 children (Head Start, 1999). I once reviewed a home-based program deep in the Ozark Mountains of northern Arkansas. We drove miles and miles along narrow, twisting roads to visit families tucked away in the valleys. One family lived in an old frame house, with an outhouse, that had been in the family for generations; another was a hippie family living in a geodesic dome. The home-based option is for rural programs that simply cannot get the children to classrooms on a regular basis. In such situations, the children meet once a week in a community building for social activities.

Head Start's educational philosophy is centered on a concept known as social competence—the idea that children should develop the skills, attitudes, and abilities to be successful in a variety of settings (see Chapter 3). Social competence in children is developed through field trips, play, exposure to a variety of people, and interacting positively with peers and staff.

Local Control

Although Head Start is a federally funded program with national goals and performance standards, it has a strong focus on local control. Federal funds for Head Start go directly from Washington to the local agency that runs the program. This agency works with the federal government in writing grants, providing required reports, upgrading services, and responding to new initiatives. Diverse agencies run local programs. Examples of local Head Start agencies include city and county governments, community colleges, training institutions, public schools, single-purpose agencies, regional governments, and community agencies like the Cerebral Palsy Association, Catholic Charities, and community child-care organizations.

Every Head Start program must have a local **policy council.** This is a governing group made up of parents and community volunteers, which works with the local **grantee agency** to run the program. The policy council has specifically mandated responsibilities that must be met, such as approving the annual budget and approving all hiring and firing of Head Start staff.

Head Start expects each local program to tailor its activities, approaches, staffing patterns, and skills to meet local needs, and to allocate resources in the best way to meet those needs. To know how best to meet the local needs, every program must conduct an extensive community needs assessment every three years as part of its grant reapplication process.

Head Start Quality Standards

Since its inception, Head Start has recognized the need for standards. Standards are crucial because many Head Start services are unique and therefore need their own quality indicators, and because of the emphasis on local solutions to local problems. Another reason standards are important is that there are different opinions regarding what constitutes a high-quality early childhood program. For example, early critics of Head Start believed its purpose should be to increase children's IQ scores. It was only after results of the **Perry Preschool Project** (Schweinhart & Weikart, 1997) were published that people began to see Head Start as successful. The research studied social skills, indicators of success like staying in school and not getting into trouble with the law, and a **cost–benefit analysis** of children attending Head Start–type of programs. This analysis measured whether the cost of providing a high-quality preschool program would ultimately benefit a society by reducing future expenditures (jail time, special education, counseling, and so on). The Perry Preschool researchers indicated that for every dollar spent on the program, society would save six dollars in future reduced services.

Head Start Performance Standards. Head Start **performance standards** outline overall standards to be met in each area, while requiring local programs to develop local responses to these standards. For example, under the education and child development components, programs are expected to have a well-articulated curriculum that specifically meets the needs of their local children and families. For example, one community might have a significant number of Spanish-speaking families that require a strong bilingual or Spanish-language program; another program might need to work closely with the Hmong community to understand their culture and maximize the learning of the Hmong children in their program.

Current Status of Head Start

Head Start is by far the largest federally funded preschool program (Title I receives more federal funds, but it is not just for preschool children). For the 1999 financial year, Head Start's allocation from the government was $4.66 billion. Added to this amount is the 20 percent **local match** required of all grantees. This match is most often provided not in direct dollars but in community contributions, such as space, legal and financial services, medical support, and volunteer time in classrooms and on buses.

Some descriptive data for Head Start in 1998 give a thumbnail sketch of the program (Head Start, 1999).

Ages of children being served:
4-year-olds	59%
3-year-olds	31%
5-year-olds	6%
Under 3 years old	4%

Additionally, about 35,000 children are served in Early Head Start (0–3 years old).

Racial-ethnic composition of families served:

Native American	3.4%
Hispanic	26.4%
black	35.8%
white	31.5%
Asian American	2.9%

The average cost per child in 1998 was $5,147.

Future of Head Start

Architects of Head Start viewed the program as a way to enable poor families to climb out of poverty. They believed children who received Head Start services would subsequently be successful in their public school experience, and eventually move out of poverty. Framers of the program believed the comprehensive nature of Head Start—particularly its parent partnership—would assure this upward mobility. This has not happened: today there are Head Start families who have had children in the program since its inception.

Head Start is receiving considerable criticism. One reason is that it has not achieved some of its original goals. Another is that the program has been slow to adjust to the changing needs of poor families, especially the need for full-day, full-year programs. Most local Head Start programs are still part-day, and part-year. Head Start is attempting to address this problem by creating wraparound solutions—linking with other not-for-profit child-care providers, both state-funded and community-based, to provide full-day, full-year programs. The comprehensive nature of the program opens it to criticism from those who advocate narrowly academic preschool programs. Further, many state governments would like to have the federal funds to distribute how they see fit.

The future of Head Start is unclear. The trend in federal programs is to give the money to states in block grants (unrestricted federal funds). If this were to occur, the money would go to public schools serving children with the greatest need, much the way Title I programs are funded. And the trend is for public schools to push academics further and further downward.

Military Child-Care Programs

The U.S. Department of Defense runs the largest employer-sponsored child-care program in the nation, serving two hundred thousand children a day in three hundred locations (Date Line Child Care, 2000). In the 1970s and 1980s, the U.S. military developed a strong reputation for providing good-quality early childhood programs, both on domestic bases and on bases abroad. In many ways they have become the standard by which other programs are measured. These centers are essential support services for young military families, which are often under considerable stress as one parent goes on assignment for prolonged periods of time.

Military child care established state-of-the-art centers on bases throughout the world, often with the latest indoor and outdoor equipment. A network of family care providers is offered on the bases for parents who prefer this option, especially for infants.

Military child care set the standard by emphasizing its own quality standards: providing continual staff training, allocating sufficient resources at every level, and supporting accreditation (Date Line Child Care, 2000). The military developed a Child Development Associate (CDA) program (see Chapter 7) based on its own curriculum and training, a model that has been adopted by a variety of other large child-care providers and some Head Start programs. It also established the first standards for school-age programs.

As the military budget was drastically reduced during the 1990s, its approach to child care changed. Now many of the services are contracted out to private providers, which run the child-care centers with supervision and guidance from the military. It is not yet clear whether these changes will affect the overall quality of care provided by the military.

Private-School–Based Early Childhood Programs

The discussion of private-school–based early childhood programs describes several different options. The curricula associated with these programs are discussed in more detail in Chapter 4.

Waldorf Schools

The Waldorf philosophy is probably the most maturational of all educational philosophies, encouraging children to progress naturally through three general developmental stages, and expecting them to focus on academics in the middle-childhood developmental stage. The Waldorf program does not support pushing children academically, and it includes a strong arts and music component. What is also interesting about this philosophy is that, like Montessori, British Infant Schools, and Reggio Emilia (see Chapter 3), it is a popular educational philosophy worldwide.

Waldorf schools are based on the educational theories of an Austrian, Rudolf Steiner (1861–1925). Steiner was a philosopher before he was an educator (Montessori, Piaget, and Vygotsky, discussed in Chapter 3, were not trained educators either). He was asked to start a school for children of workers at the Waldorf Astoria Cigarette factory in Stuttgart, Germany, and opened his first school, called Die Freire Waldorfschule (The Free Waldorf

▶ *The Waldorf philosophy is probably the most maturational of all philosophies. It does not believe in pushing children academically.*

School), in 1919. His philosophical bent was anthroposophical (Steiner, 1926). Like Froebel, Steiner was interested in developing the whole child; unlike many modern U.S. approaches, he believed the early childhood years should be intrinsically valued, not simply regarded as a time of preparation for later school success. He believed the child's being is made up of spirit, soul, and body, and that all of these components develop through three distinct developmental stages: early childhood, middle childhood, and adolescence. Because of his belief about the child's spirit and soul, he was very concerned to protect children from the world's adult evils, including early academic expectations and other unhealthy influences.

Waldorf education nurtures and responds to each individual child's natural educational and emotional stages of development. Waldorf education carefully balances academic, creative, and practical activities to prepare a child's self-confidence and self-reliance, while fostering personal integrity and a sense of responsibility and community (Denver Waldorf School, n.d.). Worldwide, there are 740 Waldorf schools, 1,087 kindergartens, and 300 special-needs centers in forty-four countries. In the United States, Waldorf schools are a rapidly growing alternative for parents who do not wish their children to attend the back-to-basics, accelerated programs espoused by more and more U.S. private and public schools. There are more than 200 Waldorf schools in the United States (Denver Waldorf Schools, n.d.).

Waldorf early childhood curriculum and activities center on dramatic play, physical activities, art and creative expression, games, and practical tasks like preparing meals. As the child progresses, academic concepts and skills are integrated into activities meaningful to the child, and each class pursues a single project for two hours a day over several weeks. This project integrates all aspects of academic skill and concept development.

Montessori Programs

Montessori programs are a significant choice for parents of young children around the world; and more and more public Montessori early childhood and school options are available across the United States. There are Montessori schools in Russia, Taiwan, Japan, Korea, Australia, New Zealand, South Africa, Tanzania, Colombia, India, and Canada. Within the United States, there are close to five thousand private Montessori schools and about two thousand public ones. Two Montessori organizations, the Association Montessori Internationale and the North American Montessori Association, train and certify teachers, and accredit local programs. There is also a wide variety of schools using the Montessori name that do not adhere strictly to the guidelines of either of these associations (Kahn, 1995).

Although Maria Montessori developed her approach to work with poor children whom the Italian educational establishment had rejected as impossible to educate, her schools today tend to attract upper echelon families in most nations and communities. This is partly because private schools are, obviously, expensive in all societies, and also because the word *Montessori* has come to be associated with high-quality education. Many parents and politicians who have no concept of the history and philosophy of the Montessori method still believe it is a good educational approach.

Maria Montessori was born in Chiaravalle, Italy, in 1870. In 1896 she became the first female physician in Italy, and in 1907 she founded her first *casa dei bambini* (children's house), in the San Lorenzo district of Rome. The program was for sixty children of poor, working parents. There she developed her method of early education. She died in the Netherlands in 1952.

The Montessori approach is centered on nurturing children's initiative to explore, discover, and order the natural world on their own. Thus Montessori places great emphasis on providing an environment that encourages exploration and mastery at the child's developmental level. The role of the teachers is to structure and restructure the environment, and to support the child's natural developmental path: it is not to teach directly (Kahn, 1995). This environment is characterized by order, aesthetics, and child-size furniture and equipment. Children develop skills through the use of solid, attractive, carefully made materials based on Montessori's original designs. (The pink tower is the most familiar one among non-Montessori educators). These materials are designed to teach sequential skills in a single skill or concept area. They can be used in only one way; thus they are what Montessori educators call self-correcting.

Students in Montessori programs work in mixed-age groups—3-, 4-, and 5-year-olds in the same classroom. Each child usually stays with the same teacher for three years. This matches Montessori's concept of three-year cycles. The curriculum is divided into four areas: practical life skills, sensorial, mathematics, and language.

British Infant Schools

As the name implies, this approach comes from England. Infant schools there are programs for kindergarten and elementary grades. During the 1960s and 1970s—when U.S. public schools had open classrooms and experimented with multi-age groupings, and the free school, or alternative school, movement was strong—the British Infant Schools philosophy was very influential. Its emphasis on child-directed learning, developmental progression, and constructive knowledge lent itself well to the educational philosophy of that time. As our educational preferences have turned back to emphasis on the basics, early academics, and the standards approach of the 1990s and beyond, this model is far less popular today.

Characteristics of the British Infant Schools approach include grouping of children in mixed-age clusters, with teaching teams that follow the same child for several years (in today's parlance we call this mixed-age grouping and looping); use of play, learning centers, integrated learning, and the project approach; and an emphasis on learning how to learn, the process of learning, and building on a child's previous knowledge and current experiences.

British Infant Schools, along with Waldorf schools, are highly consistent with the U.S. philosophical approach called developmentally appropriate practice (Bredekamp & Copple, 1997), discussed further in Chapter 3.

▶ *A number of programs make extensive use of the outdoors.*

Core Knowledge Schools

Over the years, American educational approaches have come under a great deal of criticism from a variety of sources. One contemporary brand of criticism holds that schools have lost sight of the traditional values and curricular content that made them successful. The belief is that progressive education, multiculturalism, developmentally appropriate practice, multi-age grouping, and other current educational approaches have drastically reduced the quality of American education by having a negative impact on the curriculum and instructional approaches used in our schools and classrooms.

Two proponents of this view are William Bennett, secretary of education under Ronald Reagan, and E. D. Hirsch, a noneducator. Hirsch has developed the **core knowledge curriculum,** which is a back-to-basics approach structured around a specific list of content and skills that he believes every child should know. He has published books that outline the content to be taught, and at what ages it should be taught. Private schools and public charter schools that attract conservative, back-to-basics parents often use Hirsh's core curriculum and are called Core Knowledge Schools. William Bennett has written several books for parents that cover required cultural content.

Gifted Programs

Programs for children identified as gifted have become part of the educational landscape. Most of these programs, however, don't start until mid-elementary school, and many lack quality and comprehensiveness. This scarcity of good public-school programs for gifted and talented students has led to the establishment of private schools for the

Hope Center for Gifted Children

Six years ago, George Brantley developed a program for inner-city preschoolers. The program is housed in an old, abandoned warehouse, which was remodeled thirty-nine years ago to serve children with a variety of learning challenges. According to Brantley, one of the reasons he decided to establish the Hope Center for Gifted Children was to challenge the historical notion that inner-city schools and social-service programs just target children who struggle to learn. Further, he felt that gifted minority students must be identified early on, or "they can very easily move in an anti-social direction and be utilized against society" (Yettick, 2001, p. 22A).

Over the six-year history of the program, the Hope Center has screened between two hundred and three hundred children and served seventy-five with IQs of 120 and above. Parents pay for the program on a sliding scale. Unfortunately,

when children leave the center and move into the local schools, not only are there no gifted programs for them, but they return to programs that focus only on children—especially minority children—who struggle to achieve in school.

Brantley believes that there is an acceptance in minority communities, and in schools and social-services agencies that serve these communities, of the need to serve minority children who struggle academically, but there is little pressure to serve gifted minority children. He would like to see gifted children treated just like children with disabilities—that way, "all gifted kids could be identified and served, not just the ones who can afford a private school for the gifted, or who attend a school where testing for giftedness is as common as testing for reading disabilities" (Yettick, 2001, p. 23A).

gifted, which often include early childhood components. Many of these schools are free-standing private schools; others are college-campus–based programs such as the Richie Early Childhood Center at the University of Denver, in Colorado. Most are tuition-based, but there is an increasing interest in efforts to identify and serve gifted and talented low-income and minority students before they are misidentified, or lost in large city school systems (Wardle, 1999c).

Other Educational Approaches

There is a vast range of other private-school and independent early childhood approaches. Many of these independent schools have unique philosophies and provide preschool programs designed as feeder programs for their school. The Denver International School, which three of my children once attended, is an example. There is also a growing movement of national private schools (Neugebauer, 1999). The Edison Project has already established itself as a provider of charter schools, which contract with local school districts to run an individual elementary school, offering early childhood programs as part of their services. The Edison schools emphasize small classes, use of technology, intensive literacy training, and active parental involvement.

Private Early Childhood Programs

Independent Community Centers

One week a few years ago I attended meetings of two local Denver early childhood programs. I was the academic adviser for one program, providing input on policies, curriculum, staff training, and child development; for the other program, in which three of my own children were enrolled, I was an elected parent board representative. Both programs are single, not-for-profit corporations.

The board members of Montview Community Preschool and Kindergarten, a parent cooperative, meet monthly in a large community room in a Presbyterian church. We sip instant coffee and herbal teas, listen to a budget report, and discuss a proposal of the church's youth minister. The program uses the local church facilities for free. Parents pay tuition and are required to volunteer their time—either in the classroom or in various fund-raising activities. The board of the school is composed of representatives from the church, teachers, administration, and parents. Business is conducted according to the program's bylaws.

Montview Community Preschool and Kindergarten serves mostly white middle- and upper-middle class liberal families in an older, integrated neighborhood of Denver. Its primary purpose is to provide a high-quality early childhood experience in the city. A secondary purpose is to showcase a high-quality program that is built around a state-of-the-art philosophy, staff benefits, and staff training. The program is part-day, but full-day child-care service is provided for those families that need it.

At the board meeting of the second early childhood program, we discuss, over a bottle of good French red wine, the prospective visit of officials from France. This is the Denver International School, a bilingual French-American school that was started by local French educators. It serves children 4 to 11 years old in a renovated farm building in an area of single-family homes on the edge of Denver. The school is also funded through parent tuition and work bonds (required volunteer work). Additionally, the school receives support from the French government: the director is a French government employee, as are the teachers who teach the French curriculum. Colorado certified teachers teach the American curriculum.

In structure and unique educational philosophy, the Denver International School is typical of the thousands of small private schools scattered across this country. The board is made up primarily of community members and parents. The main purpose of the preschool component of the school is to provide a feeder to the school. In fact, because the school is truly bilingual, American students who don't enter at age 4 do not have the language ability in French to be successful at the school. The *maternelle* of the Denver International School is a full-day program (as is the *maternelle* in France), and before- and after-school care is also available for parents who need supervision of their children outside of regular school hours.

These two early childhood programs are radically different. Their curricula reflect these differences. Montview Community Preschool and Kindergarten focuses on developmentally appropriate practice (Bredekamp & Copple, 1997), multicultural and nonviolence education, working closely with families, and teacher training and support. The Denver International School, on the other hand, emphasizes bilingual education and provides a curriculum that meets both Colorado state requirements and the requirements of the French government.

The independent child-care and education options in a community are numerous and extremely diverse. Some are co-ops, some are run by an individual or couple, and some are stand-alone companies. The majority of child-care centers in this country that serve preschool children—54 percent—are independent community for-profit and not-for-profit centers (Willer et al., 1991).

Child-Care Chains

Private for-profit child-care chains account for about 6 percent of centers nationwide. They tend to be in suburban areas, and serve primarily children of middle- and upper-income families (Willer et al., 1991). From 1974 to 1989, the six largest chains expanded by more than 1,000 percent (Neugebauer, 1999). This growth leveled off until 1999, when growth took off again. In 1999, 582,472 children were served by national chains (Neugebauer, 2000a). Most of these centers also provide school-age programs, and all are dependent almost exclusively on parent tuition. Many also contract directly with employers to provide on-site child care. Employers are private companies, a variety of government agencies, and colleges and universities.

The philosophies of all for-profit chains are, understandably, market-driven, because their profits are based on tuition. Thus they must give parents what they want. Most of their parents are well educated, competitive people, so the programs

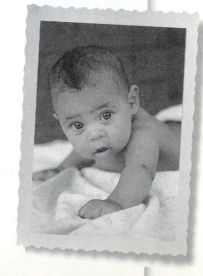

▶ *A variety of programs (religious, private, and not-for profit) serve infants.*

tend to have very attractive buildings, upscale playgrounds, and curricula that emphasize computers and the academic skills of reading and writing. Because parents are very concerned with quality, and with what they perceive as indicators of quality, many national chains are at the forefront of supporting accreditation of early childhood programs.

Employer Child Care. Bright Horizons Family Solutions is an employer child-care company—an organization that works almost exclusively to provide direct services to employees of specific companies and government agencies. The companies they serve subsidize the cost of providing the child-care service—by providing facilities, direct financial subsidies, and other forms of support. These employers then have some input into the program's philosophy and daily operations. One result of this arrangement is that Bright Horizons Family Solutions is able to provide somewhat better salaries and benefits to its employees than other child-care chains can.

There is continued growth of employer child care, as employers view it as a major employee benefit. Eighty-five percent of private employers with more than two thousand employees offered some form of child-care assistance to employees, up 64 percent since 1990 (Day Care, USA, 1996). Employers large and small provide a variety of options to assist their employees with child care. Eighteen percent of companies that provide assistance subsidize on-site or near-site centers, 5 percent give discounts with providers, 5 percent give vouchers to employees, and 6 percent provide reimbursement for employees using outside care. Ninety-six percent of large corporations allow employees to pay for child care as a pretax expense (Day Care, USA, 1996).

With corporate restructuring, downsizing, and international competition, many companies have fewer, more stressed-out employees, and are looking at child-care options as a way to support them (Neugebauer, 1996). Employer child-care programs have moved from the novelty and pilot stage to become a stable part of employers' benefit packages (Neugebauer, 1996). More and more companies are looking at this option as a way to retain employees and to support their families' lives. Further, because major companies are interested in quality, they insist that these centers are, or quickly become, accredited.

Not-for-Profit Programs

Not-for-profit programs (excluding religious programs) are government-supported child-care programs that are outside of a school setting and usually provide care for the entire day. According to Willer et al. (1991), these programs make up 25 percent of the centers serving children up to 5 years old. They are funded by a variety of funding streams, including parent tuition (often on a sliding scale), state subsidies for poor women who work or are receiving training, and **federal block grant money.** They also might be funded by specific training programs, welfare reform efforts, women's shelters, city child-care initiatives, and other programs designed to provide child-care services for low-income working parents. When I was a Head Start director, I started a wraparound child care program for Head Start children whose parents were involved in a federally funded training and job placement program. Later the program also served children whose mothers were in a local women's shelter. More and more not-for-profit programs are working closely with Head Start programs, state-funded preschool programs, and other early childhood educational programs to provide full-day wraparound care.

Campus Child-Care Programs

Campus child-care programs are a growing phenomenon in this country. They exist principally to provide care for the children of students—especially older, nontraditional students—and children of faculty members. While this service is clearly a community asset and provides needed quality care for children, a major rationale for its existence is

Programs for Homeless Children

There are various early childhood programs that serve specialized populations of young children, including children with HIV, children in women's shelters, and foster and adoptive children who require therapeutic care. One such program is the Community Children's Center, in Dorchester, Massachusetts, funded by the Bright Horizons Initiative, the not-for-profit foundation of Bright Horizons Family Solutions. The program serves seventy-one preschool children aged 2 months to 5 years. "By giving parents an opportunity to leave their children in a safe, nurturing environment, they are free to pursue employment, schooling, job training and find permanent housing" (Bright Horizons Family Solutions, 1997, p. 4). The program also provides parent training and sometimes hires parents as case providers.

Programs that serve homeless children have an unusual challenge because the lives of homeless children are so different from the lives of children who have permanent homes. These children have unique needs that stretch a program's abilities. In fact, there are increased numbers of children entering early childhood programs who come from environments that are not conducive to traditional and familiar approaches to education, which present a distinctive challenge. For homeless children, there is no certainty, no order, no predictability (Boxhill, 1993). When these children arrive at an early childhood program they are often tired, hungry, starved for individual attention, and needing a sense of order. Other characteristics of the homeless child, as outlined in an article by N. A. Boxhill (1993), include

- Homeless children lack any kind of consistency in any area. They have trouble making friends and creating attachments, because they instinctively know these won't last; but if they stay alone and aloof, they know they will miss out on all the fun.
- Homeless children need lots of food most of the time, and they need help in choosing and eating nutritious foods.
- Homeless children need lots of safe, open space where they can run, climb, shout, and be children without being constantly yelled at. They also need the opportunity to be alone. In homeless shelters, children are constantly being observed, supervised, and watched.
- These children need to be allowed to rest. There should always be a place away from noise and activities where children can sleep, when they need to, without interruptions.
- Because homeless children exist outside the normal world of care and adult attention, their behavior in a child-care center may appear to be disruptive, scattered, and lacking focus. They desperately seek meaningful, purposeful adult attention.
- Many homeless children like to spend lots of time playing in the housekeeping area. They seem to like the order and normalcy of home life in their play, since their real home life is so disordered and disorganized.
- Homeless children have little place to store anything, so be careful about what you send home. Ask parents how much stuff they can reasonably take home.
- Teachers in early childhood programs for homeless children can provide security by understanding these children and by providing them with secure, honest relationships.

to attract both students and faculty to the institution. More than 170,000 children are served by campus child-care programs; two-thirds of all colleges provide some form of child care for students and faculty (Neugebauer, 1998).

Two additional purposes of campus child care are to provide a base for ongoing research in child development, psychology, learning theory, and models of child care; and to supply a convenient site for student teaching, practicum, and student project activities. As I discuss later in the book, however, these two functions are being questioned by educators and researchers. Because campus child-care programs primarily serve children of students and faculty, the children in these programs are largely white, well educated, well fed, medically cared for, and from well-educated, middle-class families. This means the research **sample** is skewed, giving results that are useful only for one kind of child and family. Further, early childhood teachers who work at these centers often don't learn strategies and approaches to work effectively with more diverse populations.

Campus Support of Child Care

Because campus child-care programs are an asset to the college or university, most receive some kind of direct or indirect support from the institution. The support may be free or reduced cost for space, utilities, or maintenance; enhanced staff salaries; or tuition subsidies. Almost all campus child-care programs receive training support for their staff in child development, psychology, and child management. And because these programs are used for student teaching, they generally have a very low student–teacher ratio, and often more and better equipment than the average early childhood program.

As one can imagine, more and more campus child-care programs are moving to provide full-day service, with flexible schedules available for those students who need care for their children only while attending class, the library, or study sessions (Neugebauer, 1998). About 10 percent of the programs are open in the evenings and on weekends.

Campus child-care programs are administered in a variety of ways. Almost 50 percent are operated by a student association, 20 percent by a department of the university (for example, the child development department), 10 percent by the personnel office, and 20 percent independently. Of the independent programs, 5 percent are contracted to outside vendors, often a child-care chain.

Many campus child-care centers participate in state and federal subsidy programs, such as free and reduced-cost lunches (USDA), social-service reimbursement, and funding from the Higher Education Act. Half of campus child-care programs are also open to the entire community, not just people associated with the campus.

My son, Kealan, attended the early childhood program at the Aurora campus for a time. This child-care center serves the three colleges that make up the Aurora campus in Denver: Metropolitan State University, the University of Colorado at Denver, and the Community College of Denver. While neither my wife nor I was a student or faculty member at any of these institutions, we chose this program because of the low student–staff ratio, innovative approaches (especially in art activities, which Kealan loved), and diversity activities, including an African storyteller.

Professional Organization

The National Coalition for Campus Children's Centers (NCCCC) is the professional organization that focuses on the needs of campus child care. It has a membership of more than four thousand centers, provides a well-attended annual conference, and is headquartered in Alexandria, Virginia. Most national early childhood and school associations are located in or near Washington, D.C., to have access to the national government and national policymakers.

The growth of campus child care has occurred at the same time traditional college-based lab schools have declined. The decline of the **traditional lab school** has occurred largely because universities could not justify their cost. Many institutions felt the lab activities of the school—research, student teaching, field testing new ideas—could better occur in local public schools. These public schools more accurately represent a true sample of America's children and offer student teachers a more realistic and relevant experience. They also enable universities and colleges to provide direct services, support, and partnerships to the community.

Family Child Care

Family day care is "care provided for a small group of children in the caregiver's home. Often a family day care provider is a mother with children of her own at home. Family child care may be regulated or nonregulated. Nonregulated care includes providers who are not licensed or registered, whether or not they are subject to such regulation" (Willer et al., 1991, p. 3). "There is no question that family day care has been the most frequently used form of out-of-home child care . . . although recently the numbers are dropping off for mothers who work full-time or have children over three years of age" (Kontos, 1992, pp. 2–3). Experts estimate that there are more than five million children in family child care in this country, and that between 60 percent and 90 percent of family child care is unregulated (Kontos, 1992). There are about 225,000 regulated family day-care homes in the United States (Kontos, 1992); but estimates suggest that there are actually one to two million family child-care providers (Hofferth & Phillips, 1987). Family child care is very difficult to study because some states do not require regulations; and in those that do, many family child-care homes operate outside the regulations.

Family child care is used mostly by families with mothers who are employed part-time and families with children under age 3. Thirty-six percent of children served in family child care are under age 3; 20 percent of preschool children of employed mothers are in family child care, 28 percent in centers. The use of family child care is increasing at a rate slower than the use of center-based care (Hofferth & Phillips, 1987). As children move into preschool years, they are more likely to be in centers. This trend has developed over time. For families that use centers—full-time and part-time programs—use peaks when children are 3 and 4 years old. Forty-three percent of employed mothers and 30 percent of unemployed mothers use centers as their primary supplemental arrangement; 20 percent of employed mothers and 5 percent of unemployed mothers of infants and toddlers reported centers as their primary supplemental care (Willer et al., 1991).

Choice of Families

In the Willer et al. study (1991), parents reported different reasons for choosing center care and family child care. The main reasons for family care were warm, loving caregivers, a low adult–child ratio, and the provider being known to the family. Other research includes a preference for family child care because of flexible hours, perceived affordability, and a convenient location (Kontos, 1992). The main reasons stated for center-care preference were warm, loving care, training of staff, providers known to the family, child–staff ratio, and preparation of the child for school (the smallest percentage). Family child-care programs can be much more responsive to families' individual needs. Their hours are more flexible, and they are often responsive to concerns parents might have regarding their children. Some research also suggests that parents can select family child care that most closely approximates their own childrearing and discipline philosophies and practice. While many parents perceive family child care to be cheaper than center-based care, research suggests that the costs are about the same (Hofferth, 1989).

One of the advantages of family child care is that it covers the time parents are away from home, including travel to and from work or school. Some homes even care for children when parents are working or training in the evening. This means that home care providers work very long hours. Work weeks of forty-five to fifty hours are the norm for family care providers (Kontos, 1992). The majority of family care providers work nine hours a day or more, and, as reported in a study by Kontos (1989), 29 percent worked eleven or more hours a day.

Regulating Family Child Care

One of the confusions of early care in this country is the differing ways regulation of early childhood programs takes place. For example, most child-care centers are licensed by a state department of social services, yet early childhood programs in schools are often not subject to these same regulations. All fifty states and the District of Columbia have some form of regulation requirements for family child care; the military also regulates its family child-care programs (Kontos, 1992). Willer et al. (1991) report that only 10 percent to 18 percent of family child care providers are regulated. Of the states that regulate family child care, three different approaches are used: licensing (twenty-one states), registration (sixteen states), and certification (five states). Five states use a combination of registration and certification; three, other approaches.

- *Licensing.* States set minimum standards for providing care that must be kept, monitor compliance of the standards, and have the right to revoke the license.
- *Registration.* This is a voluntary system in which individual providers self-inspect and sign a statement acknowledging awareness of the state child-care standards; parents are given copies of the standards in the hope that they will help monitor the process by selecting care that follows them. Inspections occur only if complaints are received.
- *Certification.* Certification is like registration, except that it requires providers to be certified if they are to serve subsidized children (children whose care is paid for by the state). This obviously is a convenient way to monitor the child-care home.

What Is Regulated? States regulate six broad areas of family child care (Children's Foundation, 1990):

1. General criteria, which include the minimum number of children in a group (people who care for fewer than the minimum number are not regulated), maximum allowable group size, caregiver–infant ratios, space requirements, nature of state oversight, and, liability insurance (a fairly recent requirement).

2. Caregiver qualifications. Eighty-four percent of the states that have regulations require caregivers to be at least 18 years old; the remaining states have age requirements from 19 to 21. Two states have a maximum age level. Tuberculosis tests and criminal background checks are now required in many states.

3. Training and orientation. Eleven states require orientation training; twenty-nine states have some type of training requirements, from CPR and first aid to training in child development. These requirements are usually defined by a set number of hours in a specific subject-area training.

4. Zoning. Most states (thirty-six) require family child-care homes to comply with zoning ordinances for small businesses. This requirement means that many home-care providers operate outside the law because, naturally, they live in residential areas.

5. Discipline. Thirty-nine of the states prohibit corporal punishment; those that permit it do so under specific conditions.

6. Sick care. Twenty-two states address the conditions under which sick children should be isolated, or sent home, and other situations.

Many experts believe that increasing state requirements will actually lead to an increase in the number of providers who are not regulated, because some providers cannot afford the expense and many simply will avoid the hassle (Kontos, 1992).

Accreditation. The National Association of Family Child Care (NAFCC) accredits family child-care programs, and more and more programs are being accredited. Further, many states are supporting these accreditation efforts. Much of the accreditation effort involves provider training, which is often combined with training of center-based staff.

School-Age Care

"School-age care is the fastest growing segment of the early childhood arena . . . and possibly the least visible" (Neugebauer, 1998, p. 35). School-age care is an ill-defined, little-understood service, for variety of reasons. These include the multiplicity of providers, the fact that school-age care exists outside of the traditional school day, its short history in this country, and the continual conflict between educational programs and child-care services.

Europe has had school-age programs for years. I remember being part of these programs while growing up in England. Since I was raised in a community with strong German ties, these programs—after school, on holidays, and on some weekends—were called Hort. They were staffed by people who were not our teachers (often quite young); activities ranged from helping harvest the farm's produce (strawberries, potatoes, currants) to sports, outdoor games, hiking in the countryside, and arts and crafts activities. As I pointed out earlier, on my recent trip to Brazil I observed a before- and after-school program for children, of kindergarten age through grade 4, in a program funded by local businesses.

The fairly recent growth of school-age care in this country is a direct result of parent demand. More than 80 percent of parents say they want their children to participate in such programs (Neugebauer, 1998). Clearly, the need is based on the number of parents working and of single-parent homes, in which there is no one home to take care of the children. Parents are willing to leave their children in school-age programs; unfortunately, demand far exceeds supply, especially in low-income neighborhoods. Almost all school-age programs serve children of preschool and elementary-school age. There are beginning to be some programs for middle-school students, but these are few and far between.

Parents' number one reason for placing their children in after-school programs is safety (Neugebauer, 1998). After safety, parents' expectations for these programs run the gamut, including recreation, tutorials, homework help, and supervised social experiences. These parental expectations sometimes conflict with the goals of the schools, which tend to view these programs as a way to meet their specific needs, such as extending the school day, providing instruction in basic skills, offering mentoring programs, meeting state standards, or providing enrichment for gifted students.

Currently 30 percent of all school districts offer some school-age care. In some cases schools set up their own programs; in others they contract with outside for-profit or not-for-profit providers. Because private schools are beholden to parent needs, they have set the example in school-age care. The majority of private schools provide some kind of school-age program.

School-age care providers include child-care centers, public and private schools, youth recreation programs, and national child-care chains. Child-care centers are the primary providers of school-age care, especially for younger children ages 4, 5, and 6 years old). More than a third of school-age programs are operated by centers of all kinds: military, private, religious, and not-for-profit. Some of these programs pick up children at the school and transport them to their programs.

A wide variety of recreational and youth programs—such as the local YMCA, YWCA, boys' and girls' clubs, city recreation centers, and teen programs—provide school-age services. There is a growing attempt to coordinate these programs with local public schools, especially in low-income areas, where the supply is so limited. Several national for-profit organizations have developed specifically to provide school-age care. These include Voyager, Explorer, and Medallion (Aramark Educational Services).

Parents still provide the bulk of financing for school-age programs. These costs, however, are offset somewhat by programs in public schools—especially those run by the school districts themselves, because they don't pay for building rent, utilities, janitorial services, and other basic expenses. Additionally, private foundations and large companies are beginning to assist in offsetting some of the costs, and the federal government is also becoming more involved in providing grant funds to school-age programs.

School-Age Organizations

There are several national organizations that are involved in leading and standardizing school-age care in this country. The first organization, now called the National Institute on Out of School Time, was created in 1978 at Wesley College. *School-Age Notes* was started twenty years ago by Rick Scofield. With a subscription base of six thousand, *School-Age Notes* communicates information of importance to the field, and has also become a strong advocate for a variety of national school-age care issues, policies, and initiatives.

The National School-Age Care Alliance (NSACA) was founded in 1987 as a national professional organization. This organization boasts a membership of six thousand, advocates for all forms of after-school care that meet family needs, and sponsors an annual school-age conference. NSACA has also developed school-age care standards to help improve program quality.

Conclusion

Children from infancy to 8 years old are served by a wide variety of programs. These include family child care, private community-based programs, for-profit chains, religious options, Head Start programs, and traditional public-school programs. Further, private schools have increased their services to young children, and school-age programs are becoming popular. Traditionally, services for children under school age were paid for by parents; programs for older children were either free in public school, or tuition-based in private and religious schools. But because the majority of parents work all day, federal and state governments are becoming more involved in not only paying for preschool programs, but also supporting before- and after-school programs. Finally, the line between part-day, academically focused preschool programs and full-day child care is blurring, with full-day early childhood programs and a variety of wraparound options.

Questions and Projects

1. Design your own early childhood program. Choose elements from the various programs studied to create your program. Cover philosophy, curriculum, funding, teacher qualifications, and students served (ages, family income, ethnicity, location, number of students).

2. Select three early childhood programs you are familiar with. Compare them on funding, parent involvement and control, philosophy, length of day, eligibility (whom they serve), teacher qualifications, curriculum, and your own personal beliefs.

3. Is before- and after-school care the responsibility of society or of families? How should this important issue be addressed? What kinds of programs would work best? Who should pay for this service?

4. As a parent—or a potential, prospective parent—argue for one of the child-care options discussed in this chapter. What criteria did you use to make your decision? What age is the child for whom you selected this option? Why? Would you change options as the child grows older?

Resources

NSACA
1137 Washington St.
Boston, MA 02142
(617) 298-5012

School-Age Notes
P.O. Box 40205
Nashville, TN 37204
(800) 410-8780

National Institute on Out of School Time
Wellesley College Center for Women
Wellesley, MA 02181
(781) 283-2547

Association of Waldorf Schools of North America (AWSNA)
3911 Bannister Rd.
Fair Oaks, CA 95628
http://www.waldorfeducation.org
(916) 961-0927

North American Montessori Teacher's Association
11424 Bellflower Rd., NE
Cleveland, OH 44106
(216) 421-1905

CHAPTER

3

Important People *and* Movements: Past *and* Present

*E*arly childhood programs in this country are based on the historical movements of ideas, significant people, and government legislation, such as compulsory education and the belief that an educated populace is required as the foundation for democracy. This chapter traces the development of trends, ideas, policies, and influences from around the world and from different disciplines, to help the student understand the emergence of a strong focus on early education in the United States. ▨

Early Childhood Perspective

Women Raise Young Children

Historically, caring for young children has been the role of women—mothers, grandmothers, nannies, maids, and slaves. All cultures gave this important responsibility to women, while men were primarily involved in protection, politics, building, and earning a living. In some cultures, the nuclear and extended family were charged with raising children; in cultures with a more communal and social structure, child care, protection, and education of children were assigned to women in general. Traditions, customs, skills, and information needed to care for and raise children were passed from grandmothers to mothers to children and grandchildren. In some cultures, female leaders helped provide the transmission of information and skills needed for rearing and education—a practice still followed in a few contemporary cultures. As societies began to use some of their members to raise the children of others, they employed women. European royalty and aristocracy used nannies to care for their young; the wealthy in the Colonial United States, Brazil, and other New World countries used slaves, including wet nurses. Even today, nannies are a popular method for well-off U.S. and European families to care for children; maids are still the primary caregivers for middle- and upper-class families in South America.

With the development of more organized child care and early education options, it was still women who cared for the children: teachers, directors, and child-care providers. In fact, until very recently, most elementary school teachers and principals in this country were women.

As we begin the twenty-first century, caring for young children is still viewed by all societies as principally a woman's job. It is part of our cultural values; it has also resulted in the low pay and status of early childhood workers in many societies.

Research on families and the role of parents in families—parenting styles, discipline approaches, the impact of divorce—has almost exclusively looked at the role of the mother. Only recently have researchers really cared about the role of the father in the home. Some educators, psychologists, and social theorists have suggested that fathers are not really needed for the development of healthy children. The extremely high level of fatherless families in this country, Brazil, Europe, and elsewhere, with the resultant negative impact on social institutions such as the criminal justice system, education, and social service agencies, has led to a new interest in the role of fathers.

White Men Write about Raising Young Children

Piaget, Vygotsky, Erikson, Skinner, Brazelton, Froebel, Rousseau, Dewey, Gardner, Bruner, and Kohlberg are some of the people who have greatly influenced the early childhood field. This chapter details their important contributions and those of others. Ironically, even though caring for young children has been the role of women, all these people are white men, from Europe and the United States (King, 1999). There are notable exceptions—including Montessori, Smith and Sprague, and Sylvia Ashton-Warner—but the majority of the contributors to this field, until very recently, have been white men.

Education in any society reflects the important values of that society. And, of course, many of the values of the U.S. **dominant culture** are based on the ideas, philosophies, and politics of white men—Thomas Jefferson, the Greek philosophers, and the English legal scholars. Our political, legal, and educational systems are based on these ideas and knowledge. This is not necessarily bad; it simply means that much of what we do in early childhood programs and schools reflects a white, male, English-speaking, European and U.S. perspective. As we examine the foundations of our field, it is important to keep this in mind.

European Precursors

I start the discussion about European descendants with Rousseau and Pestalozzi because they represent a radical change in their approach to children and childhood. Before them, children were viewed as being born evil, and the role of educators was to rid them of this evil. In the religious sense, children were born bad. Further, children were "to be seen and not heard"—being only of value when they could assist with adult activities. Rousseau and Pestalozzi believed children were born good, with the potential to blossom in their own unique way. They also believed children had needs that required an approach that recognized they were far more than simply down-sized adults.

Jean-Jacques Rousseau and Johann Heinrich Pestalozzi

In 1762 Rousseau published the book *Émile* about raising a fictional child. In it he expressed his belief that children are naturally good, and that education should support and encourage a child's natural development. He felt that each child is unique and should be encouraged to develop in a unique way. Environments and methods should be responsive to individual needs, and to the child's penchant for learning and development. The child's natural development is to be nurtured, and the early years stressed. He also believed that children should be encouraged to learn using natural and concrete materials, not pushed into abstract, adult activities.

Early childhood beliefs that focus on the individual child, faith in children's ability to control and direct their own learning, concrete learning materials, and natural environments all have their roots in Rousseau's writings. Philosophies that stress uniqueness and autonomy also go back to Rousseau.

J. H. Pestalozzi (1746–1827) was a Swiss educator and children's advocate who was the first writer to stress the whole-child approach, involving the head, hands, and heart. The head meant intellectual learning, the heart the child's emotional responses, and the hand learning basic practical skills that could be directly taught. To some extent Pestalozzi was more interested in the children of commoners, by contrast to Rousseau's involvement with children of the elite. He suggested ways mothers could work to enhance the development of their children at home. Unlike Rousseau, he addressed issues of the school environment, and the value of children working together in groups. He wrote *How Gertrude Teaches Her Children* and the *Book for Mothers*.

Friedrich Froebel: Kindergarten

My kindergarten experience in England was in a Froebel program. I have vivid memories of my preschool and kindergarten years: almost all my time involved exploring the outdoors, painting, playing with blocks, and having fun in the sandbox. We also enjoyed German *Sing Spiel* (a combination of songs, dances, and group games). Our preschool and kindergarten classroom opened onto a hardtop area, which was surrounded by a large area of grass, trees, and sandboxes. Beyond were woods, fields, and streams that we explored with our group.

Froebel is, of course, the father of the kindergarten. He founded the first kindergarten, in Blankenburg, Germany, in 1837. *Kindergarten* is a German word that literally means "children's garden," a term he used to convey his belief that young children are like flowers, who need to be nurtured, cared for, and protected. But like flowers, he felt, children should naturally unfold and blossom, and not be forced to grow too quickly. He thought that the best medium for this natural unfolding was play; and he believed play could occur only if a child were provided a stimulating environment and allowed to pursue play in self-directed ways.

To assist in this unfolding, Froebel created "gifts" for children to use in their play. These gifts are an early example of educational toys. Froebel believed young children

▶ *Froebel believed children unfold like flowers; he also felt they needed to explore nature.*

learn best using concrete materials and through exploration of the natural world. He also thought it was important to teach parents how best to work with their young children. The ten gifts Froebel developed were yarn balls; a set of solid wooden cubes, cylinders, and spheres; one-inch wooden cubes; solid wooden rectangles; a collection of cubes, half-cubes, and quarter-cubes; a collection of rectangular and square blocks and six narrow columns; a box of colored parquetry tiles, which included squares, circles, half-circles, and rectangles; metal rings and sticks; wooden beads, with a grid to use to make patterns with these beads; and a collection of peas and sticks.

Froebel also developed ten different occupations (activities), which included painting, modeling with clay, cutting paper, drawing, sewing, and weaving with paper. These focused on the development of fine motor skills.

As a result of the immigration of many Germans to this country in the 1850s, the kindergarten movement was brought to America. Germans created private, independent kindergartens in many American cities. The first such program was established in Watertown, Wisconsin, in 1856 by Mrs. Carl Schurz, a pupil of Froebel's; the second was in Columbus, Ohio. The first English-speaking kindergarten was established by Elizabeth Peabody, a strong and influential advocate of kindergartens, in Boston in 1860. St. Louis had the first public kindergarten program; Milwaukee followed soon after, in 1882.

Now all American public schools include kindergarten programs; unfortunately, most have rejected much of Froebel's philosophy, especially his advocacy of play and his warning against pushing children's academics too soon. Nevertheless, many of his gifts and occupations can still be found in many preschool programs today: using blocks of different kinds, cutting, art activities, patterning with beans, and using differently shaped materials to form patterns and pictures. Some programs still continue the practice of having children explore nature through caring for gardens and going on field trips.

Maria Montessori

Maria Montessori (1870–1952) was the first female physician in Italy. In 1907 she opened a school for slum children in Rome, called Casa dei Bambini. The children in this school were children the Italian educational establishment had rejected as being uneducable. Montessori worked with children before they were 5 years old, and developed an approach that soon attracted worldwide attention.

Montessori schools are now common in America, with even some public schools among their number. I discuss the Montessori approach in detail both in Chapter 2 and in Chapter 4. Montessori schools are extremely popular around the world today, especially serving middle- and upper-middle-class families in private programs. Some basic Montessori concepts include:

▶ *Maria Montessori developed her method for low-income Italian children. Many of her ideas can be found in all good early childhood programs. (Getty Images)*

- *The absorbent mind.* Montessori believed that young children learn a great deal of information, which led her to concentrate on working with this age group rather than waiting until the formal school years.
- *Prepared environment.* Montessori strongly believed in the central importance of an ordered and aesthetic environment (maybe because the children she served came from neither). The environment needs to be orderly, the furniture child-sized, and the materials especially designed for children's learning. A central focus of all Montessori programs is the carefully designed and crafted (and thus expensive) learning materials that are used. Teachers are responsible for preparing and maintaining the environment.
- *Individual learning.* Children are to use the planned environment and self-correcting educational materials to develop their own knowledge individually. Teachers demonstrate and guide, but do not directly instruct. Teachers model the correct way to use the Montessori materials; children must then perfect this correct approach. Materials and activities are introduced in a carefully planned sequence.
- *Daily living.* Activities such as setting the table, sweeping the floor, and washing the table are central components of the Montessori curriculum. They teach specific skills and develop a sense of order and discipline.
- *Use of all the senses.* Montessori believed that children learn to organize the world using all their senses, and that concepts are easier to learn if more than one sense is used. She was particularly interested in the sense of touch. She developed concrete materials and materials that use a variety of senses as academic learning aids; examples are the sandpaper letters and a movable alphabet.
- *Artistic development.* Music and art activities are stressed in a Montessori curriculum.
- *Freedom of choice.* In the Montessori program, children are expected to choose their activities and materials; once the choice has been made, however, they must use the materials in the correct, prescribed manner.
- *Sensitive periods.* Montessori believed children go through a series of sensitive periods, during which they are more responsive to different and particular kinds of learning.

Montessori programs emphasize individual child development; development of skills such as concentration, observation, and perception; concept formation; problem solving; and reading and writing skills. Montessori programs are not concerned with specific content, narrow outcomes, or specific curricular objectives.

▶ *Jean Piaget has contributed a vast amount of information about how children construct knowledge, including the notion that a child's view of the world is very different from an adult's view. (Bill Anderson, Photo Researchers)*

Jean Piaget: Constructivist Theories

Jean Piaget (1896–1960) was trained as a biologist, and as a young teenager he published an article in a biology journal. His interest in the biological world laid the foundation for some of his basic assumptions about cognitive theory. Later he studied children's answers to common, easy questions and became fascinated by their incorrect answers. He began to focus on how children think—how they come up with the answers to specific questions. Piaget developed a method of research that allowed him to follow the way children's thought processes work. This method is called *méthode clinique.*

Piaget then studied his own children in depth. He gave them specific problems, and then recorded how they solved them. He asked them the reasons for their responses, and the process they went through: "Why is there more water in that container?" "How do you know where the sun goes at the end of the day?" Based on his research, Piaget developed his theory of **cognitive development.** I discuss this theory in more depth in Chapter 9; here I touch on a few characteristics. His theory focuses on how children think; he was not interested in their physical, psychological, or emotional development. He used the idea of the metamorphosis of a butterfly to propose a theory in which each stage of cognitive development is qualitatively different from the previous stage; and once a child has progressed to a stage, it is impossible to return (a butterfly cannot go back to being a chrysalis). This is called a **stage theory,** with each stage sequential, progressive, and **invariant.**

Piaget's cognitive theory is driven by children's continual attempt to match their view of the world (an internal construction) with the external reality. As children have new experiences, they are continually revising their internal constructs. Because children are continually constructing their reality through this process, this is known as a **constructivist theory.** The theory is based on both a child's genetically programmed script to progress through specific stages in a specific order, and the influence of a rich, stimulating, and responsive environment. To progress successfully through each stage, a child must be an active learner.

Piaget had a powerful influence on early childhood approaches. Early childhood practices that are greatly influenced by him include child-directed and child-centered learning, well-designed and de-

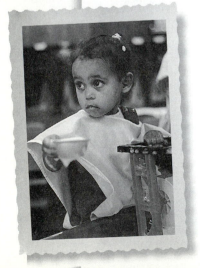

▶ *Piaget believed children must actively interact with the environment to create mental structures.*

Figure 3.1
Piaget's Stages of Cognitive Development

Formal Operations Period (11+)

Children can think abstractly, can hypothesize, can predict the results of conflicting variables, and can determine the results of actions and interactions not personally experienced. Can solve complex math and science problems.

Concrete Operations Period (7–11)

Uses logical thinking and rules to solve problems. Has learned conservation and reversibility. However, the child can only think logically about things personally experienced. Thus they believe, "It won't happen to me."

Preoperational Period (2–7)

The child can think abstractly/representationally, but not logically. When there is a conflict between concrete information and abstract knowledge, the concrete information dominates. The child has achieved object permanence. A very egocentric stage; and centrism predominates.

Sensorimotor Period (0–2)

The infant learns about the world through physical movement and all the senses. Much knowledge comes through mouthing objects. Lacks fully developed object permanence.

veloped educational environments, emphasis on the vital importance of play, multi-age groupings (so students can learn from others who are one stage ahead of them in development), and a curriculum based on concrete activities and experiences that match a child's development. Discovery learning, problem solving, and the project approach are also approaches consistent with Piaget's philosophy.

Lev Vygotsky: Sociocultural Theory

Lev Vygotsky was born the same year as Piaget, in 1896, in the small rural Russian village of Orsha. His father was a banker, his mother a teacher. As Russian Jews the family had many restrictions on where they could live and what they could do for a living. Like Piaget, Vygotsky did not initially study psychology or child development; he studied law. Because Jewish students were confined by Russian law to 3 percent of the university student enrollment, Vygotsky had difficulty entering the university. But he studied at Moscow University and graduated in 1917. He then went on to teach at Gomel's Teacher's College, then at the Psychological Institute of Moscow.

Vygotsky came to know all the great thinkers of his time, including Freud, Piaget, Jung, Luria, Leont'ev, Benet, and American psychologists. Vygotsky's knowledge of eight languages helped him understand the ideas of all these thinkers. Because he was not officially trained as a psychologist, he brought a fresh and somewhat new perspective to the work of these intellectuals.

In Moscow he collaborated closely with Luria and Leont'ev. They became known as the troika of the Vygotskian School. Luria and Leont'ev continued Vygotsky's work after his death from tuberculosis, in 1934, at the age of 38. Vygotsky's work was slow to come to the West because after his death his work was banned by Stalin for twenty years, all his work needed to be translated from Russian, and during that time intellectuals in the West were enamored of Piaget and American behaviorism.

Vygotsky's theory of how children grow and develop is called a sociocultural theory. "People are products of their social and cultural worlds and . . . to understand children, we must understand the social, cultural, and societal context in which they develop" (Berk & Winsler, 1995, p. 1). According to Berk and Winsler, sociocultural theory can be summarized by the following ideas:

- *The developmental method.* Human behavior can best be explained by examining its development—we need to know the developmental progression that leads to specific behaviors.
- *Two lines of development.* Children develop along two distinct paths: the natural development of biology in developmental stages, and cultural growth in learning the rules, skills, language, and expectations of a specific culture.
- *Cross-cultural variations.* Higher-order mental processes in people differ from culture to culture because of each culture's unique tools, words, expectation, and activities.
- *Lower versus higher mental functions.* The mental activity of humans is controlled by two forces, those shared with other mammals and those unique to human beings. The latter functions include language and other cultural tools that control the way we think and act.
- *General genetic law of cultural development.* All higher mental functions occur at two levels; first, at the social or interpersonal level; and, second, at the individual or psychological level. Language acquisition is a good example: children hear language first from outside, through social interactions; later, they internalize it and it becomes part of their psychological makeup.
- *Language is central.* Language is the essential tool used by humans to develop higher-order thought processes and to structure thought. Since language is culturally based, individual mental structures become culturally defined.

- *Education leads development.* Because formal education is the culture's way of socializing its citizens to the society's beliefs and values, formal education is very important. (This is one of the central differences between Piaget and Vygotsky: Piaget saw little value in formal education assisting cognitive development.)

While Vygotsky has contributed to our knowledge of learning and teaching in a variety of ways, his most important contributions include analyzing the relation between culture and knowledge, emphasizing the powerful impact of language on **mental functions,** and articulating the role of the teacher and other experts (volunteers, parents, peers) in learning. These ideas are discussed at length in Chapter 9.

Rudolf Steiner: Waldorf Education

Rudolf Steiner (1861–1925) was a German educator who developed a school for factory workers' children. His philosophy today is followed in schools worldwide. Steiner based his theory on his theosophical beliefs, and divided development into three distinct stages: Will (0–7 years), Heart (feelings; 7–14 years), and Head (spirit and body; 14 and above). Because of this stage approach, he believed the early childhood years are a discrete period in a person's development, not simply a time to set the foundation for later development and learning. The Waldorf philosophy is very much one of child-directed learning, yet the role of the teacher is to carefully select the environment, and to protect and support the child's development.

Contemporary Waldorf programs provide a fully integrated approach that stresses the arts and individual development, does not give tests, and resists TV watching. The approach is in direct conflict with many of the characteristics of public school early childhood and elementary education programs in this country.

Erik Erikson: Psychosocial Stages

The father of Erik Erikson (1902–1994) was Danish and his mother Jewish. But he never knew his father, as he was illegitimate. He was trained in art, and also took a course in Montessori education. He became an art teacher in Vienna and later studied psychoanalysis, graduating from the Vienna Psychoanalytic Society. He knew many of the great thinkers in Europe at the time: Freud, Anna Freud, Jung, and others. In 1931 he moved to Boston, where he set up a private practice as a child psychoanalyst.

Although he had no formal university degrees, Erickson taught at Harvard Medical School, Yale University, and the University of California at Berkeley. Through his private practice and extensive study of various Native American tribes, Erikson formed a psychosocial theory of development. This theory has eight distinct stages and spans a person's entire life; it is often called **life-span development.** Each stage contains a conflict that must be positively resolved for the person to move on to the next stage. A less-than-positive resolution to the conflict will cause problems for the person's psychosocial development in later life.

Erikson's theory addresses social, psychological, and emotional development—how people feel about themselves, and how they relate to others. He details the needs he sees for mature adult assistance in helping children progress through each childhood stage. Although the material environment is important for progress to be made through each stage (especially stages that involve trust, mastery and competence), Erikson stresses the role of the entire human environment in healthy development.

Erikson's theory has had an impact on early childhood education. Not only does he provide information about the psychosocial stages of young children, but his adult stages help us understand the life issues of new parents, grandparents (if they are raising grandchildren), and teen parents. Further, his theory enables us to consider children's noncognitive development when creating ways to meet their needs. This is particularly important as we serve younger and younger children, serve children for longer periods of time every day, and try to meet the emotional and psychological needs of homeless children, children from abusive homes, and those in foster care.

U.S. Pioneers

While the early childhood field in this country is greatly influenced by European precursors, we have developed a uniquely American early childhood field. Contributors to our view of early childhood education include our public school philosophy, American researchers and theorists, pioneer educators, and civil rights activists. In addition, specific federal laws that affect children have helped shape the early childhood field as we know it today.

Ye Old Deluder Satan Act: The First U.S. Public School

The first public school (a school funded by taxes so all citizens can attend free, regardless of income) was created in the Massachusetts Colony by laws passed in 1642 and 1647. These laws required an elementary school for every fifty families and a grammar school for every one hundred families. The laws that established these schools were called Ye Old Deluder Satan Act, because their purpose was to provide instruction in reading so students could read the Bible, thus "deluding" Satan's influence. It was only natural for the first schools to reflect the religious beliefs of the time. Later schools in the southern and middle colonies reflected the religious affiliations of their inhabitants.

The significance of these early publicly funded schools lies in the belief by the early settlers in the need for public education for all children. When the U.S. Constitution was adopted, however, there was no direct reference to public schools—only a guarantee regarding the "general welfare" of citizens. Specifics regarding the funding, organization, curriculum, and practices of local public schools was left up to the government of each state. This contrasts with other industrial societies—and most countries that provide any form of publicly funded education—which have a national system of funding, curriculum policies, and outcomes.

The universal, free, public educational system in this country is of tremendous significance to the early childhood field. All states now have free education, starting at kindergarten. More and more public schools are reaching downward to provide programs for children 3 and 4 years old, while some schools also provide care for infants of teen parents. These public-school programs are funded by a variety of options, including district funds, local Head Start programs, Even Start, and state-funded early childhood programs (see Chapter 2). As the need for high-quality early childhood programs becomes more accepted, a logical solution is to provide all of these programs through existing public schools and finance them through the same system that funds the local schools.

While preschool programs attached to public schools become natural feeders to the school, this model also results in school curricula, content, and methods (large class sizes, and so on) being pushed down to the preschool level, in direct conflict with the developmentally appropriate approach to early childhood education.

Maids and House Slaves

Rousseau's writings about raising and educating children was based on the typical European upper-middle-class model of the child and tutor, or child and nanny. Naturally, this way of raising children was brought by Europeans to this country—especially in the middle and southern colonies. As slavery became more institutionalized in the southern colonies, the role of caring for young children became more and more the responsibility of slaves; the duties of most female house slaves in the South included cooking, cleaning, and caring for the young children. Many of these children spent more time with their nannies—or slaves—than with their parents. Accounts of this period relate in detail the love and attachment between these children of the plantation owners and the slaves who cared for them.

Contemporary forms of this approach to early care and education include nannies and maids. Nannies are in general well-paid young women who live in a person's home, with the sole responsibility of caring for children (with some cleaning and car-driving responsibilities). Often students from Europe, these young people are employed only by upper-income parents. As the result of newfound technology wealth, nannies' popularity increased at the beginning of the twenty-first century in communities serving this industry.

Many middle-class families in developing countries, such as those in Latin America, use maids extensively to take care of their children. I observed this phenomenon on one of my visits to Brazil. I watched children playing in the city park of Belo Horizonte, accompanied by a maid; each home I visited during my stay had a maid who cooked and cared for the children. These maids often live in the child's home and are paid, though poorly. But the maid approach to caring for children is becoming less popular, as these countries develop, provide education for all their citizens, and offer increased opportunities for these women.

John Dewey: Progressive Education

John Dewey lived from 1858 to 1952. He was raised in Vermont and became a professor of philosophy at both Columbia University in New York and the University of Chicago. He became a giant in U.S. educational thought, writing a large variety of books and journal articles. Dewey and his colleagues developed what came to be known as **progressive education.** This is a problem-solving,

▶ *John Dewey is a giant in American education. He insisted that the school's curriculum be based on the child's experiences; further, he believed that education for young children must include the arts. (Bettmann Archive)*

▶ *John Dewey believed children learn through experience.*

inquiry-based approach that stresses the importance of individual student experiences in the educational process, and it dramatically opposed the traditional educational approach of his time. Describing traditional education in comparison to progressive education, Dewey wrote, "to imposition from above is opposed expression and cultivation of individuality; to external discipline is opposed free activity; to learning from texts and teachers, learning through experience; to acquisition of isolated skills and techniques by drill, is opposed acquisition of them as means of attaining ends which make direct vital appeal; to preparation for a more or less remote future is opposed making the most of opportunities of present life; to static aims and materials is opposed acquaintance with a changing world" (Dewey, 1938, p. 5).

Dewey believed children learn through experience. He thought the nature of that experience should structure the central components of education: discipline, content, scope and sequence, and goals and objectives. Students' experiences have built into them a desire to learn, to grow, and to acquire knowledge. "I assume that amid all uncertainties there is one permanent frame of reference: namely, the organic connection between education and personal experience; or, that the new philosophy of education is committed to some kind of empirical and experimental philosophy" (Dewey, 1938, p. 7). According to Dewey, there are two kinds of experiences in schools that are educational— those that interest, stimulate, and absorb the student; and experiences that "live fruitfully and creatively in subsequent experiences" (p. 7). In other words, educational experiences must both be interesting and individually captivating, and lead to future experience and learning.

Dewey's ideas can be seen in many aspects of early childhood education. His concept of the value of experience underlined the free-school movement of the 1960s and 1970s and is the rationale for many contemporary approaches, such as expeditionary learning (Outward Bound) and Reggio Emilia; his concept of personal meaning is threaded throughout the work of Gardner, memory theorists, and programs for gifted and talented students; and his view of experience leading to future learning opportunities is the basis of the notion of **dispositions.**

Arnold Gesell: Maturation Theory

Arnold Gesell (1880–1961) established the Clinic for Child Development at Yale University, where he collected data on children's physical growth, data that were later used as the basis for well-baby checkups given by physicians across the country.

Gesell was particularly interested in the concept of maturation—the preprogrammed pattern of physical growth that each child follows. He believed this predetermined pathway was outside the normal influence of the environment. Gesell's view of a child's natural development over time is called a **maturation theory.** The Gesell Institute in Chicago was established to further these ideas, and along with Frances Ilg and Louis Ames, Gesell developed and presented this concept, describing normal maturational growth from infancy to adolescence. Gesell and his colleagues believed pushing children to accelerate their development was a practice that should be avoided.

Today "ages and stages"—the concept of progressive development through specific stages at specific ages—is still used as a guide to development (the books describing each level of development are still available); and Gesell's ideas can be seen in such policies and attitudes as kindergarten readiness (social and emotional maturation for kindergarten).

Bank Street College

Bank Street College is a world renowned college of education known for its innovations in the field of early childhood education. Founded by Lucy Sprague Mitchell, today the college includes an early childhood lab school, a teachers college, a workshop for writers of children's literature, and a bulletin to disseminate information about how young children learn and should be taught (Greenberg, 1987).

Lucy Sprague Mitchell. Lucy Sprague Mitchell (1878–1967) was the founder of the Bank Street College of Education (part of Columbia University in New York). Later she became president of the same institution. She worked as a teacher of young children and a teacher of teachers, and she wrote many books on early childhood education, especially regarding children's literature. She helped establish a lab school at Bank Street College for young children. Mitchell and the colleagues she collected around her systematically observed young children and implemented their ideas regarding early childhood education, training, and mentoring for future teachers. She also worked closely with Caroline Pratt and directly supported Pratt's experimental schools.

Caroline Pratt. Born in Fayetteville, New York, in 1867, Caroline Pratt became a teacher in a one-room school at age 16. She later attended Teachers College in New York, where she rebelled against traditional teaching methods and became attracted to early childhood education. At the turn of the century she started teaching in a small school in New York City. There she could begin to apply methods she had developed as a result of her unhappiness with the traditional educational approach. To this end she became an ardent supporter of children's play, but she had no materials to support and extend the play. Using woodworking skills learned in her occupational training experience, she began to create wooden blocks and toys.

She then developed an early childhood program called a Play School in a settlement house, where she used her new wooden materials. She wanted play to go beyond simple entertainment; she believed she could structure an entire early childhood curriculum around her blocks. At the Play School she experimented with this concept. Out of this experience she developed unit blocks, along with a specific curricular approach to enable children to take their own unique experiences and structure play using the blocks. She viewed play as a learning experience guided by appropriate materials and expert adult assistance (Winsor, 1996). She believed children need good-quality materials and support to enhance the quality of their play—what we now call complex play.

Together with Harriet Johnson and Mitchell, Pratt worked at the City and County School in New York. There she observed children and teachers. The approach to early childhood education that she developed has three major parts:

- "The power to deal effectively with his environment accrues to a child through the free use of constructive materials;
- "Possibilities are offered by blocks and similar materials for expressing rhythm, pattern, and design;
- "By means of these materials, children may review, rehearse, and play out their past experience" (Johnson [1928], 1972, pp. 182–189).

Pratt also believed that blocks could stimulate creative, exploratory involvement of other materials—clay to mold miniature figures and animals, cloth to create awnings and tents, and furniture and wood to make vehicles for roads and cities created with the blocks. According to Pratt, children need to use their ingenuity and problem-solving skills to find ways to use these basic, undefined materials. (I discuss the value of unit blocks in Chapter 8).

Patty Smith Hill. Patty Smith Hill (1868–1946) was trained in the Froebel kindergarten approach, and she worked with G. Stanley Hall and Dewey. She became directly involved with the Bank Street lab school at Columbia University and was a founding member of the National Association of Nursery Education (NANE), which later became the National Association for the Education of Young Children (NAEYC).

Bank Street College at Columbia University has had a profound impact on early childhood education. The college was very influential in implementing Dewey's Progressive Education, kept alive the fundamental ideas of Froebel, and further developed approaches to educating each child through an insistence on play, respect for the individual child's worth and unique experiences, and the development of unit blocks. Equally important, it established what is now the largest and most influential early childhood association in this country, NAEYC. The document *Developmentally Appropriate Practice* (Bredekamp & Copple, 1997) has as its foundation much of the work of the Bank Street women (Wardle, 1999c).

Kaiser Child-Care Centers

In 1941 Congress passed the Lanham Act, which provided federal funds to communities affected by the war; these funds were used for a variety of programs, including building and operating nurseries. At one time, two-thousand nurseries were active in forty-one states (Hurwitz, 1998).

The child-care program built and operated by the Kaiser Shipyard in Portland, Oregon, is the most famous of these programs. Early on, Edgar Kaiser realized that issues relating to children caused high levels of absenteeism and tardiness among his five thousand female employees. As a consequence, he had two centers built, each with a capacity of a thousand children, and hired Meek Stotz and James Hymes to run the programs. Each center consisted of fifteen rooms that radiated around an outdoor play area; each classroom had a bathroom and a covered porch area.

The Kaiser child-care centers opened in November 1943. To run the programs, staff were recruited from across the country and were paid according to the Kaiser company's salary scale, as opposed to a separate, lower child-care scale. Open twenty-four hours a day and 364 days a year, the centers served children aged 18 months to 6 years for three eight-hour work shifts, and also provided school-age care before and after school and during vacations. Meals were provided, including meals that parents could take home when they picked up their children, along with sick care, immunizations, and a library for parents.

Parents paid a very small percentage of the cost of caring for their children; Kaiser Shipyard picked up the rest, which they then passed along to the federal government as part of the cost of building the ships. At the end of the war the child-care centers closed down, but their offspring can be seen in corporate centers run by companies such as Bright Horizons Family Solutions (see Chapter 2).

B. F. Skinner and Behaviorism

B. F. Skinner, along with other behaviorists such as John B. Watson, Edward L. Thorndike, and Albert Bandura, has had a tremendous influence on child development, childrearing, schools, child therapy, and early childhood programs. Behaviorism, the most American of all psychological theories, is based on an environmental approach consisting of reinforcers, punishment, and associations. The approach is discussed in detail in Chapter 9.

Skinner perfected the behavioral approach known as operant conditioning. He and his students conducted a variety of experiments using pigeons, mice, and rats to help develop the theory. **Behaviorism** claims that all behavior can be taught, changed, or modified based on external reinforcers and punishments; that the internal state of the child can be ignored. Behaviorism is a total-environmental—or nurture—approach that dismisses concepts such as motivation, stages, information processing, moral reasoning, private speech, and schemas.

Skinner was quick to expand his ideas to society in general, in articles and books such as *Walden Two* (about a behaviorist commune) and *Beyond Freedom and Dignity*. He believed a more just and humane society could be developed by rewarding socially acceptable behavior and punishing unacceptable behavior.

Skinner's work was not originally intended for use in schools. In fact, because operant conditioning requires immediate reinforcement and carefully planned schedules of reinforcement, Skinner felt it was impractical for use in the classroom. But scholars took Skinner's work and created the behavior modification approach for use in schools.

The work of Skinner and other behaviorists has had, and continues to have, a strong impact on early childhood programs. Behavior modification, time out, token economies, and various forms of punishment are direct results of this work (see Chapter 12). Specific techniques used to modify the behavior of difficult children and to work with special-education children with behavioral problems are other examples. The use of modeling to change behavior, and the use of popular role models by programs and schools to promote socially desired behavior, are based on the work of Bandura. Another major contribution of behaviorism is its ability to help early childhood educators understand the powerful impact of the community and overall society on children, their expectations, and what they see as important. When athletes are reinforced (money, clothes, cars) for being athletes, and rock stars are reinforced for outrageous clothes and inappropriate language, young children want to imitate these behaviors and see them as culturally appropriate. Bandura has shown how models on TV and in films can have a similar impact on our children. The often-heard advice for parents to "model reading to their children" is another example. And finally, schools that reward their athletes (with assemblies, plaques, attention) teach their students that athletics is more socially and culturally desirable than academics.

1950s through 1970s

Brown v. Board of Education of Topeka

In the landmark Supreme Court decision ***Brown v. Board of Education of Topeka,*** the highest court determined that segregation by race is unequal and therefore unconstitutional. Before the decision, many public schools for black and other minority children were physically separate from those for white children. Black children were educated in different buildings, with different budgets and different curricula. Not only did the Supreme Court decision finally place minority students on a legal footing equal to white

Time Line of People and Movements

Ye Old Deluder Satan Act: first U.S. public school, 1642 and 1647

Jean-Jacques Rousseau, 1712–1788; wrote *Émile* in 1762

J. H. Pestalozzi, 1746–1826; wrote *How Gertrude Teaches Her Children* in 1801

Friedrich Froebel, 1782–1852; in 1827 wrote *Education of Man*

Kindergartens established in Germany, 1827

First Kindergarten in the United States, Watertown, Wisconsin, 1856

Rudolf Steiner, 1861–1925; Waldorf Education

John Dewey, 1858–1952; progressive Education

Patty Smith, 1868–1946; a founder of NAEYC

Caroline Pratt, 1867–1954; Unit blocks

Maria Montessori, 1870–1952; Montessori Programs

Lucy Sprague Mitchell, 1878–1967; Bank Street College

Arnold Gesell, 1880–1961; Maturation Theory

Lev Vygotsky, 1896–1934; Sociocultural Theory

Jean Piaget, 1896–1980; Constructivist Theory

Erik Erikson, 1902–1994; Psychosocial Theory

B. F. Skinner, 1904–1988; Behaviorism

Albert Bandura, 1925–; Social Learning Theory, Modeling

Lanham Act and Kaiser Shipyard child-care centers, 1941–1945

Reggio Emilia, 1945–present

Brown v. Board of Education of Topeka, 1954

Free schools, 1960–1975

Head Start established, 1964–1965

Lawrence Kohlberg; moral reasoning, 1927–1987

Bilingual education, 1968 (Act), 1974 (*Lau v. Nichols*)

Pedagogy of the Oppressed, by Paulo Freire, 1970

Individuals with Disabilities Education Act (IDEA), 1975 and 1990

Multicultural education, 1980s and 1990s

Technology, 1980s and beyond

In a Different Voice, by Carol Gilligan, 1982

Black Children, by Janice Hale, 1982

Gardner; Multiple Intelligences, 1983

Character education, 1920s, 1960s, 1990s

New brain research, 1990s

Comer Process for reforming education, 1996

students, but it opened the gates for the equality of other students, such as those with disabilities and those who do not speak English. Today, schools cannot legally separate students by race, disability, gender, or economic status; however, most of our city public schools tend to be primarily minority schools, and rural and suburban schools serve primarily white students. Many early childhood programs also are segregated, with many Head Start and block-grant child care programs primarily serving minority children (Head Start is mandated to serve only poor children) and private options such as Montessori and child-care chains tending to serve middle-class, white children. Even campus child care often serves primarily white, educated parents' children.

Head Start

Two momentous events led to the creation of Project Head Start. The first was the Civil Rights movement of the early 1960s, which coincided with the passage of legislation by the U.S. Congress guaranteeing the rights and protection of minorities in this country—an important achievement that finally gave blacks the equality they were promised with Emancipation and that extended to members of other minority groups. (Later legislation expanded to include women, the disabled, and age bias.) The second event was President Lyndon Johnson's War on Poverty, which included a wide range of programs for the poor, including Head Start. The structure, philosophy, and current status of Head Start programs in this country are covered extensively in Chapter 2.

Project Head Start also benefited from a cadre of motivated civil rights workers and a willingness on the part of local communities to contribute resources (buildings, services, medical experts) to the cause (Greenberg, 1969). Head Start grew out of a national advisory panel of experts convened by President John F. Kennedy to address the needs of children with mental disabilities. Its scope later expanded to cover all low-income children, who enter public school with severe disadvantages. The belief was that a high-quality, comprehensive early childhood program could provide enough of a head start for low-income children that they could then be successful in the local school. To some extent this assumption was based on the theory of early childhood being a critical developmental period that, if completed successfully, would guarantee a child future school success. In the summer of 1965 the first program was launched. This program's philosophy included:

- A comprehensive approach: educational, dental, medical services; family involvement; parent training; and employment of low-income parents.
- A stress on **social competence**—the idea that a child can learn new and important information in a variety of settings.
- Local control: national guidelines and standards were written in such a way that local programs made important decisions, such as the choice of the educational curriculum.
- Parent involvement: the heart of each local program is the parent policy council. In addition, parents are to be used as volunteers and hired at all levels of the program.
- Community commitment: local communities must contribute resources to help run the local program (buildings, medical services, legal and financial support, and the like).

After the 1965 summer Head Start project, Westinghouse funded a research study of the program that was conducted by Ohio State University. Researchers used IQ tests given to Head Start students and a similar group who did not attend the program as the basis of their study. Results showed no difference between the two groups. The future of Head Start appeared dim until the Perry Preschool Project research appeared (1997). This study analyzed the success of a program similar in nature to Head Start that had been developed by the High/Scope Foundation in Ypsilanti, Michigan. The research carefully matched low-income students who attended the program with similar students who did not. Research showed that students who did not attend the Perry Preschool Program were more likely to need additional social, educational, and juvenile justice programs throughout their school years, including special education, juvenile services, early pregnancy services, and intervention (Schweinhart & Weikart, 1997).

Head Start has had a tremendous impact on early childhood programs in this country. It is largely responsible for an acceptance of publicly funded early childhood programs for low-income students; it established the idea of parental involvement for all parents, including low-income, uneducated ones; and it pioneered the concept of a comprehensive early childhood approach. Because of the success of Head Start, many public schools—especially in low-income areas—have created their own early childhood programs.

Free Schools and Alternative Schools

From 1970 to 1976 I taught in free schools in Taos, New Mexico; and Kansas City, Missouri. Afterward I wrote about my experience. "What is a free-school? . . . Most definitions involve the word 'free'—free in terms of spirit, not finances . . . free both for the children and teachers. How much freedom differs with each particular school . . . A. S. Neill's writings—including *Summerhill*, about the free school he ran in England—were influential in starting the free school movement in this country. Paul Goodman, John Holt, George Leonard, George Dennison, and Ivan Illich severely criticized the present public school system, and suggested alternative approaches to education. Other influential factors in the growth of the movement were young idealistic teachers, dissatisfied parents, and unhappy children" (Wardle, 1978).

The school where I taught in Taos served children from the various communes scattered in the mountains around the town, along with middle-class families seeking alternatives for themselves and their children. The school in suburban Kansas City, Missouri, served primarily suburban families wanting a more creative, innovative, and experiential education for their children.

The emergence of free schools in the United States was a natural part of the searching of the 1960s and 1970s for alternative approaches to all established U.S. institutions—family, religion, community, nation, and school. The basic concept of the free-school philosophy is placing the child at the center of the entire educational process, trusting the child to direct and control the learning process. An example of this philosophy can be seen from the Kansas City school: every morning the entire school (ages 4–12) met to go over school offerings and activities students wished to present during the day; at any time during the day, any student could call a meeting to address a problem; problems were resolved democratically, through a one-person, one-vote system (including teachers); students developed their own procedure for cleaning the school, with a rotating student supervisor; students worked together on multi-age projects; and students chose whether to participate in all learning activities (Wardle, 1978). Free schools were small, parent-run schools housed in a variety of homes and commercial buildings scattered across the country. Clearly this approach held that individual children could choose what was best for their educational needs. Critics, of course, said this would not work. Recently I have had contact with three former students of mine; one is teaching English in the Philippines, a second is a city manager in Oregon, and the third became a Rhodes scholar and is now a college professor.

Free schools pushed the envelope on many aspects of education. They influenced contemporary educational approaches, including multi-age learning, the project approach, the concept of a school and classroom as a community, conflict-resolution programs that use peer mediators, student rule making, team teaching, and the use of the community for experiential learning.

Moral Reasoning

The 1960s were a time of upheaval when many of our rules and moral values were challenged. When this happens, we tend to look at our schools for answers. (The first character education movement was during the "Roaring Twenties.") Thus, a new effort to address the moral education of students began to emerge, called Moral Reasoning.

Lawrence Kohlberg. One morning when teaching at the free school in Kansas City, I sat with children of different ages in a circle on the floor. I posed to them a moral problem, then facilitated their discussion and arguments about how best to solve the problem. We were engaged in a Magic Circle Activity—a curriculum adaptation of Lawrence Kohlberg's concept of **moral reasoning.**

Kohlberg was a Piaget scholar. He reasoned that if children develop cognitively through a series of stages, in which they think qualitatively differently at each stage, then it makes sense to assume that children think differently about moral behavior during each stage. Further, if they think differently about morality, then surely they will behave differently in moral situations. Kohlberg used the Piaget research method to pose moral dilemmas to children of different ages, observed how they resolved the problems, and, more important, asked participants to explain the moral reasoning behind their decisions. From the results of these experiments Kohlberg developed his theory of moral reasoning. The theory is structured into three levels of development; each level is further divided into two stages. A child moves progressively through these stages, from Stage 1, Level One, to Stage 6, Level Three. His stages and levels are as follows:

Stage 1: Punishment and obedience orientation ⎤ Level One:
Stage 2: Individualism and relevant orientation ⎦ Preconventional Morality

Stage 3: Mutual interpersonal expectations ⎤ Level Two:
Stage 4: Social system and conscience ⎦ Conventional Morality

Stage 5: Social contract ⎤ Level Three:
Stage 6: Universal ethical conduct ⎦ Postconventional Morality

Kohlberg's moral reasoning theory was used to develop school programs known as **values clarification.** The purpose of these programs was to help children think about moral problems and behaviors, and then engage in appropriate moral behaviors. While these programs have fallen out of favor, Kohlberg's work has influenced the way we view moral development and provided ideas for supporting that development in the schools. Most important, Kohlberg showed us that children's sense of moral reasoning—the way they think about right and wrong, good and bad—develops in stages throughout childhood.

Carol Gilligan. Carol Gilligan was a student of Kohlberg's. She noted that all the studies he performed to create his theory of moral reasoning were conducted on boys (white, lower- and middle-class boys, to be exact). She believed that as a result of this single-gender sample, Kohlberg's stages are only accurate for males, and not applicable to female moral reasoning. She believed Kohlberg's stages are an example of a theory based on the dominant culture's perspective.

Gilligan interviewed women who were experiencing, or had recently experienced, a personal crisis, and asked them to describe the reasoning they used to solve the crisis. She discovered that women were very concerned about who would be hurt by their actions and what would be the results for each step to the solution—not just the final outcome. The women were also very concerned with where they could get help to resolve the problem. Based on these studies, Gilligan believes that the underlying reasoning for behaving morally (why we are honest, follow the law, are loyal to friends, and so on), differs between men and women. Men, she believes, are linear thinkers who logically determine individual rights and responsibilities, while women are guided more by social needs, and by a sense of caring and protection. Women are concerned about how people feel, and about minimizing suffering. Gilligan believes men make moral decisions with little regard to who may be hurt along the way, or to a sense of caring for others.

Paulo Freire: Critical Pedagogy

Paulo Freire was born in Recife, Brazil, in 1921, into a middle-class family. But as Brazil experienced the impact of the Great Depression, his family joined the extreme poverty of many others, and Freire came to understand the misery of poverty in a developing country. In 1959 Freire received a doctorate of education from the University of Recife, and later became a professor of history and philosophy of education at the same university, where he developed an approach to teaching literacy to impoverished adults. This approach was implemented throughout northeastern Brazil.

In 1964 Freire, along with thousands of other intellectuals and political enemies, was jailed by the military dictatorship of Brazil. He then went to Chile, where he worked with UNESCO and the Chile Institution for Agrarian Reform. Freire has also worked as a consultant for the Harvard University School of Education and the office of education of the World Council of Churches. Freire is interested in using literacy to achieve a radical reordering of societies that depend on the ignorance of the masses to gain and maintain power.

Freire's most famous book, *Pedagogy of the Oppressed* (1970), received a wide readership in the United States and England, which enabled his ideas to be incorporated into the educational philosophies of the time, and to be applied to concepts for the education of children.

According to Freire, as the disenfranchised in a society learn basic literacy skills, they can also learn **critical pedagogy:** how to analyze their role in society, society's power structures, and the nature of inequality. He believed that every person is capable of looking critically at their world and their position in that world. Further, Freire proposed that all education has moral value: essentially students learn to accept the status quo, or they are empowered to challenge society's power structure, and the position they hold within it. This approach to education is revolutionary in two ways. First, most educational philosophies hold that children need to be taught the basics of education—including literacy, historical facts, and societal rules and laws—before they can become critical thinkers. Maslow's hierarchy of needs fits this idea, as does Bloom's taxonomy of education, which requires learning the basics before the child can engage in the higher-order activities of analysis and synthesis. Even Dewey views the uneducated as immature and needing to be led by the mature (the educated). Freire suggested that children and adults who are just beginning to become literate should engage in critical analysis and thought. Second, he suggested that the learner critically analyze what he learns for bias, omissions, and untruths.

Freire's ideas have had a strong impact on early childhood education in this country. These ideas are the foundation for much of multicultural education. Further, they have inspired U.S. educators to analyze biases within our educational system: in textbooks, in how we teach (learning styles), and in what we teach (content). Finally, the concept of anti-bias activities—children engaging in critical analysis and activities to rectify inequalities in school and society—has its roots in critical pedagogy.

Disability Rights

Schools and early childhood programs reflect the times in which they exist. The Civil Rights movement of the 1960s not only impacted our society, but had a radical effect on our education programs. Schools and early childhood programs began to change to meet the needs of all children, particularity those who had been poorly served in the past: children with disabilities, poor children, and minority children.

Individuals with Disabilities Education Act. The 1954 Supreme Court decision *Brown v. Board of Education of Topeka*, while specifically addressing the education of black children, also affected other children who historically had not had full access to public education. One of these groups was children with disabilities. In 1972 the courts declared unconstitutional a law in Pennsylvania that allowed schools to refuse to educate children they deemed uneducable. In 1975, Public Law 94-142 was signed by President Ford. Later, after several amendments, this law became known as the Individuals with Disabilities Education Act (IDEA; 1990). The specifics of IDEA are covered in detail in Chapter 6. Briefly, this law covers the following areas:

- provides free education for all children, regardless of their disability or the severity of that disability, from birth to age 21;
- requires this education to be in the least-restrictive environment (LRE);
- applies to all public schools; Head Start and other publicly funded education programs have their own, different requirements and regulations;
- does not directly apply to private early childhood programs and private schools (unless they have a contract with a public school), but children with special needs who attend private programs can receive services for these disabilities, free, from the local public school;

- control of entire process regarding serving children with special needs, from diagnosis to possible litigation if their needs are not met, by the child's parent or guardian; parents must approve every step of the way.

IDEA has revolutionized publicly funded early childhood programs because it requires these programs to provide for the individual needs of each child with a disability. It is no longer sufficient to offer the same program for each child, under the guise of equality, and then let children with disabilities fail. Children with disabilities who are younger than school age are served through a locally constituted agency called Child Find. And finally, no longer are children with disabilities—especially those with severe challenges—denied educational opportunities.

Americans with Disabilities Act. The Americans with Disabilities Act (ADA) was signed into law in 1990. This law is an update of the Rehabilitation Act of 1973 and expands civil rights protection to people with disabilities. ADA covers all places of employment that employ fifteen or more people, public accommodations, public transportation, and telecommunications.

Unlike IDEA, this law also affects private early childhood programs (preschool programs, private schools, and school-age programs). Programs cannot discriminate in hiring staff because of a candidate's disability. They also cannot deny service to a child with a disability, so long as that service does not require them to change the fundamental nature of their service. This means that a program that generally provides group education and care does not have to accept a child whose disability requires a full-time aide (unless an outside source pays for the aide). The physical premises of the program must be handicapped accessible, including ramps, wide doors, and bathrooms large enough for wheelchairs. Playgrounds must also meet specific playground accessibility requirements.

Multicultural Education

Multicultural education grew out of the ferment of the Civil Rights movement (Banks & Banks, 1997). Minority groups demanded that schools include their histories and experiences in the curriculum, hire minority staff, and tailor the programs to meet the needs of minority students more effectively. Then women's groups insisted that schools provide equal educational opportunity in all areas, including math, science, and sports, to girls. They lobbied for changes in curricular content, hiring of more female administrators, encouraging girls to succeed in math and science, and passage of Title IX. The rights of disabled students in schools—based on IDEA and ADA—are also a result of the Civil Rights movement of the 1960s.

Multicultural education has been embraced by some public schools and many early childhood programs. Celebrating cultural holidays and including the history and culture of the students' racial and ethnic groups in the school's curriculum are ways that programs address multicultural education. Other programs have taken a more in-depth approach to including diverse curricular content in all areas, teaching tolerance, respect, and appreciation for a wide spectrum of diversity, and changing the very nature of the school's climate.

The impact of multicultural education on early childhood programs is discussed in detail in Chapter 6. Implementing multicultural programs in early childhood programs is particularly challenging because many early childhood programs are segregated by income (Head Start, private programs for middle-class communities) and because small community programs reflect the homogeneous population of the community they serve. Head Start's ten Multicultural Principles (HHS, 1990), offer an example of one program's beliefs about the need for a multicultural approach.

1. Every individual is rooted in culture.
2. The cultural groups represented in the communities and families of each Head Start program are the primary sources for culturally relevant programming.
3. Culturally relevant and diverse programming requires learning accurate information about the cultures of different groups and discarding stereotypes.
4. Addressing cultural relevance in making curriculum choices is a necessary, developmentally appropriate practice.
5. Every individual has the right to maintain his or her own identity while acquiring the skills required to function in our diverse society.
6. Effective programs for children with limited English speaking ability require continual development of the primary language while the acquisition of English is facilitated.
7. Culturally relevant programming for children enables children to develop an awareness of, respect for, and appreciation of individual cultural differences. It is beneficial to all children.
8. Culturally relevant and diverse programming examines and challenges institutional and personal beliefs.
9. Culturally relevant and diverse programming and practices are incorporated in all components and services.

Contemporary Directions

Developmentally Appropriate Practice

In 1987 the NAEYC published *Developmentally Appropriate Practice in Early Childhood Programs Serving Children from Birth through Age 8* (Bredekamp). The primary purpose of this document was to provide guidance to programs seeking NAEYC accreditation for their programs, because this accreditation required developmentally appropriate activities and expectations. A second, and wider, purpose was to respond to the growing trend among early childhood programs to become more formal, and a tendency among many of these programs to teach a modified academic public school curriculum.

Developmentally Appropriate Practice (DAP) is a document that attempts to translate current knowledge about how young children develop and learn into the best teaching practices. The document supports hands-on learning, child-centered investigation, whole-child development, and the role of the teacher as a facilitator and structurer of learning and guider of behavior. Further, it is a strong indictment against rote learning, whole-group instruction, and teaching only narrow academic skills in isolation.

Since its publication, the DAP document has sold more than half a million copies, and NAEYC has distributed several million brochures that describe the approach (Bredekamp & Copple, 1997). Several state departments of education have adopted the guidelines, as have British Columbia, Australia, and New Zealand. Other national education organizations have adopted similar guidelines for teaching young children.

While **developmentally appropriate practice** soon became the preferred theoretical approach to working with children from infancy to age 8, its actual implementation has been spotty. Dunn and Kontos (1997) reported that as few as one-third to one-half of the programs they studied were developmentally appropriate. This has also been my experience in observing a variety of programs across the country (Wardle, 1999c). DAP is, however, viewed by many as the approved early childhood approach, and the approach representative of the dominant culture (Grieshaber & Cannella, 2000).

In 1997 the NAEYC published a revised edition of *Developmentally Appropriate Practice in Early Childhood Programs* (Bredekamp & Copple). The new document "represents NAEYC's current best understanding of theory and research regarding how children learn as well as shared beliefs about what practices are most supportive and respectful of children's healthy development" (p. vi). The revised edition places more emphasis on the expert role of the teacher, relationships of children and adults, the role of culture and families in children's early experiences, authentic and meaningful assessment, and use of these guidelines with exceptional children. DAP is discussed throughout this book. Critiques of this philosophy are also examined.

Janice E. Hale

Janice E. Hale is one of a new breed of African American educators. Born in Fort Wayne, Indiana, she was educated at Spelman College and has a doctorate in early childhood education from Georgia State University. She currently teaches at Wayne State University. She has written two books, *Black Children: Their Roots, Culture, and Learning Styles* (1988), and *Unbank the Fire: Visions for the Education of African American Children* (1994). In these books she presents her vision for high-quality education for African American children.

"The Visions for Children Curriculum . . . combines flexibility and structure" (Hale, 1994, p. 175). It is a program for children 2 to 5 years old. Child-directed learning occurs for an hour and a half in the morning and an hour in the afternoon. Two half-hour periods—one in the morning and one in the afternoon—are reserved for play and gross motor activities. There are also times set aside for lunch, breakfast, snacks, and naps. The rest of the day is spent in small-group activities with different teachers, who specialize in distinct areas. The curriculum includes a wide range of specific advice and instruction for the teachers. One central feature is the use of monthly themes as a way of integrating all content and skill areas. Hale has developed twelve themes: eight themes repeat each year for three years and four are new each year. Field trips and enrichment activities are driven by these themes. Each week a different African American hero is selected and profiled. These heroes are also used to introduce some of the curricular content (for example, George Washington Carver leads to a discussion

▶ *Janice Hale has developed the Visions for Children Curriculum, which targets African American students.*

of plants; Paul Robeson introduces songs and drama). Their images are placed on bulletin boards. There is a special effort to profile African American women.

Hale divides the curriculum into five broad components: physical, communicative, creative, inquiry, and cultural. These areas are then broken into smaller components, for a total of thirty-one. The thirty-one components of the curriculum are further subdivided into 120 concepts, each with its own lesson plan, standards and rubrics, and clear instructions regarding how they should be taught. Hale also provides lists of materials needed to teach each lesson.

James Comer: The Comer Process

James P. Comer is a medical doctor who is the founder and chair of the Yale School Development Program, as well as associate dean of the Yale School of Medicine. He has published six books and innumerable articles in the popular and professional press. He is another member of the group of African American educators intent on improving educational opportunities for minority children in this country. He developed the Comer Process, a model for reforming poorly performing public schools, many of which serve a disproportionate number of minority children. The Comer Process is based on six assumptions regarding what must be done to reform public schools:

1. Understand the complex dynamics that affect schools. These dynamics include the impact of parents, families, teachers, communities, income, attitude, beliefs, and institutional politics on human growth and functioning. Understanding these factors should guide reform.

2. Start where the children are. Schools must reflect the real lives and experiences of children, communities, and neighborhoods. They must be based on the real world, not someone's fantasy. (This is very much like Dewey's philosophy.)

3. Keep pace with our changing society. Society continues to change, and these changes make it more and more difficult to support each child's full development. Schools need to stay abreast of changes and respond to the needs of students and their families.

4. Focus on relationships and child development. The best instructional methods, curricula, and equipment will not produce good outcomes without good relations among teachers, parents, administrators, and students, and good relationships occur through development.

5. Develop group goals, trust, respect, and accountability to standards. Academic expectations and standards are part of the Comer Process, and grow out of the emphasis on child development.

6. Make financial commitments and policy changes. To do this we need consensus among all policymakers; to achieve consensus we need a national debate. Teachers and administrators need to be trained to implement the kind of approach used by the Comer Process. We should also create an **educational extension service** (like the highly effective agricultural extension service) to support those involved in education. Funds need to be available to pay for functional community, family, and school performance.

This process is a mechanism to implement Comer's philosophy in local schools. Once a school has contracted to implement the process, three community development teams are created: the School Planning and Management Team, the Parent Team, and the Student and Staff Support Team. These teams make decisions about how to promote student learning in the school. They work using three basic principles: consensus, collaboration, and no-fault. Student activities and performance are designed along six developmental pathways—physical, cognitive, psychological, linguistic, social, and ethical.

Figure 3.2

Model of the Comer Process

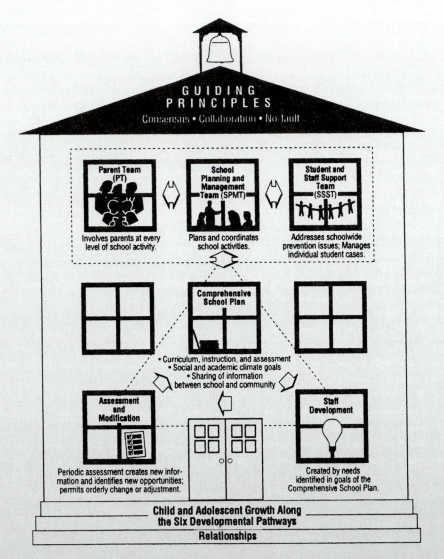

Source: © 1997 School Development Program (SDP), Yale Child Study Center. Reprinted with permission from Comer, Ben-Avie, Haynes, Joyner (1997), *Child by Child.* New York: Teachers College Press.

The School Planning and Management Team develops each year a Comprehensive School Plan, which sets the framework for the school's activities: goals and objectives, curriculum, standards, instructional practices, the academic and social climate of the school, and how to share information between the school and the community. The plan includes improvements and standards for each of the six developmental pathways.

The Comer Process is one of many models now being used to try to improve educational results in local public schools, especially for minority children. These models are popular partly because local districts are giving individual schools more autonomy, and partly because of a general recognition that the one-approach-fits-all policy of local districts has failed schools in low-income communities.

Thomas Lickona: Character Education

Thomas Lickona modified Lawrence Kohlberg's stages of moral reasoning and simplified the presentation of the stages. He added Stage Zero to the table, provided reasons to be good (why a child would strive to behave morally), and outlined ways parents and teachers can support children as they progress from stage to stage (Lickona, 1983). In Chapter 12, I cover each of these stages, and their impact on development.

Out of his work on moral reasoning, Lickona developed a belief that children learn appropriate moral behavior through three processes: being told what is right, being shown what is right (modeling), and having lots of opportunities to practice these moral behaviors. He used this concept to become a founder of the contemporary **character education** movement. As part of this effort he also created the Center for the 4th and 5th Rs (respect and responsibility) at the University of New York in Cortland.

Character education in public schools has a long history in this country, starting with the first public schools in the Massachusetts Colony, which were created in 1642 specifically so children could read the Bible. In the 1920s a large character education movement spread across the country, and in the 1960s the values clarification movement was born. The new character education movement was developed as a reaction to an increase in unacceptable behaviors in public schools and the lack of consistent moral instruction in many schools. After the Supreme Court decision of 1963 that outlawed the use of mandatory prayer in public schools, schools took a hands-off approach to activities perceived to be in any way religious or moral. The new character education movement sprang up as a reaction to this values vacuum. Lickona and other leaders of the current character education movement believe in several basic premises, which include the following (Lickona, 1987):

- Everything we do in schools and early childhood programs has a moral basis, whether we like it or not.
- There are values, or attributes, that we can all agree should be taught, and that transcend specific religious affiliations. These include loyalty, respect, kindness, responsibility, and honesty.
- For character to be taught in early childhood programs and schools, a schoolwide approach is needed. An isolated curriculum in a specific classroom will not work.
- One of the central goals of public education is to work with the community to develop citizens with the values and morals required by a free, law-abiding, democratic society.

Character education is helping early childhood programs and schools in their struggle to determine how best to develop moral individuals, to keep schools safe, and to implement conflict-resolution programs to assist in resolving problems with increasingly diverse student populations.

Technology

The personal computer has revolutionized the Information Age. The Internet, chat rooms, Web pages, immense storage capacity, CD-ROMS, and various software applications have radically changed the way we do business. Technology has also accelerated the globalization of business and information. And the personal computer has had an effect on early childhood programs.

There are several ways early childhood programs use computers. They include teaching basic keyboard skills; teaching basic academic skills and subskills, such as letter–phonemic relationships, addition facts, and multiplication; offering computer use as a reward in behavior management programs; providing a computer learning center; extending and enhancing all other learning activities; and assisting children with specific learning disabilities. Some programs view simply learning to use and becoming familiar with computers as a goal.

There are many challenges regarding the use of computers in early childhood programs. One is the technology divide. Many children enter early childhood programs with great familiarity with computers, because they have one or more at home, their parents and siblings know how to use them, and they are as much a part of the child's early learning as crayons, books, dolls, and Happy Meals. Other children have no computers at home, have never used one, and are unfamiliar with any aspect of their use. Further, even if they were to go to a library or other public place that has computers, their parents do not know enough about computers to assist them and reinforce their use. So most early childhood programs face an extremely wide range of student skills, knowledge, and familiarity with computers. Therefore, for any program to be effective, it must be highly individualized.

Another problem faced by teachers is lack of training and expertise. Many early childhood caregivers are not competent computer users themselves; and this is particularly true of programs that serve minority and low-income children, which only widens the technology divide. Additionally, many early childhood teachers have not been taught the most effective approaches for integrating computers into the curriculum and the learning environment. As a result, computer use is often offered as a reward for children who have completed other tasks; as **skill and drill** practice; and simply to learn keyboard skills—often before children's hands are large and coordinated enough to develop these skills.

Adding to the difficulties, very few early childhood programs have enough computers. *Enough* means one for every four students, because this allows students to integrate computer use with all other learning activities and experiences. Many public early childhood programs—especially schools—use the computer lab approach, in which students work at computers at a specific time each day, in the computer lab, engaged in specific skill acquisition activities. Computer labs do not lend themselves to the integration of the computer with other learning tools. For computers to be fully effective, children should be able to use them for all classroom activities: to research sail designs for a boat

▶ *The use of technology, while it has revolution-ized the way we teach, poses many challenges for educators. (PhotoEdit)*

they are building on the workbench; to learn more about the endangered species they just saw on their field trip to the zoo; to develop a newspaper that tells parents about their field trip; to graph the growth of the tomato plants in the garden; to download playground safety standards as they begin to upgrade their play-ground, and to check out tourist information in the foreign city they are studying in social studies.

A developmental curriculum and standards for technology education is lacking. Schools are not clear about what computer skills they should be teaching, at what age, and in what sequence. The state of Colorado has just implemented a law that uses the results of a literacy test to grade individual schools. As a result, many public early child-hood programs use their computers only to teach literacy.

Much of the available software for young children—up to age 8—focuses either on games or on skill and drill. Software companies are more interested in advancing tech-nology and marketing their products than in hiring early childhood curriculum experts to develop appropriate software. People who do develop software draw from two knowl-edge bases for their creation: computer games and computer-assisted instruction.

Many early childhood education programs fail to capitalize on the use of comput-ers to assist children with learning and other disabilities. Among the greatest assets of using a computer in early childhood education are its ability to individualize instruction and to assist students who have learning disabilities that make regular instruction par-ticularly difficult. It appears that computers are particularly helpful for children whose learning style is not verbal or logical-mathematical. Children who are kinesthetic, need immediate feedback, and require constant cues along the way benefit greatly from ap-propriate computer assistance. For gifted students, of course, the computer provides a wonderful opportunity for accelerated learning, enhancements, and multidisciplinary approaches. My son, who is a **twice-exceptional student** (gifted and with a specific learning disability), became very competent in computer use. Unfortunately, many early programs do not capitalize on this asset of computers, because of the lack of teacher knowledge and skills, unwillingness to let special-needs students use the computers for enough time (especially in programs where the computer is used to reward children who excel in the standard curriculum—usually not the student with special needs), and the dearth of good programs designed for these children.

Much of the software for young children suffers from being developmentally in-appropriate and using racial, ethnic, and sexual stereotypes and violence. This is a re-sult of the dominance in the field of video games—which are often very stereotypical and violent—and the lack of crucial knowledge about equity and diversity by program designers and developers.

The use of technology in early childhood can revolutionize education programs. For it do so, however, educators must focus on these ideas: overcoming the technology divide, training teachers, having enough computers for everyone in the classroom to have access (not a lab), expanding curricular approaches to capitalize on new ways computers allow us to teach, and using computer software and enhancements creatively to serve children with a variety of learning and physical disabilities.

Reggio Emilia

In 1945 a young teacher, Loris Malaguzzi, became involved with a school in Reggio Emilia, in Northern Italy, that was built and run by local parents. Malaguzzi worked with parents and teachers to fashion a radical approach to early childhood education—one that totally rejected the state-sponsored approach (much as Montessori did with her Casa dei Bambini). In 1963 the local municipality agreed to support the project financially. Today there are thirty-two children's centers in this wealthiest part of Italy. To implement their philosophy, the Reggio Emilia programs recruit young people right out of high school, match them with master teachers, and then train them in their distinctive philosophy. The philosophy is based on a respect for children's knowledge, capacities, and innate drive to make sense of their world. It is implemented through a method that includes the following steps:

- *Observation.* Teachers carefully and continually observe children to learn their interests and their experiences. They then use this information to structure and provide opportunities for learning and educational activities.
- *Representation.* Children use art to formulate their theories of how things work and how things relate to one another. In this way they create models of information and knowledge.
- *Documentation.* The child's entire learning and experiential process is documented by means of photos, tape recordings, videos, and teacher writings. This documentation is presented in huge wall-mounted newspapers and functions as a way to validate children's learning efforts and to communicate to parents children's learning activities.
- *Revisitation.* Children continually recycle back to their original experiences, creating new artwork and developing new conclusions. Projects children engage in often take weeks, even months, to complete.

Since 1981 a slide presentation about Reggio Emilia, *The One Hundred Languages of Children,* has been traveling the world, communicating to early childhood experts and practitioners alike the value and success of this unique approach.

In Chapter 4, I discuss the Reggio Emilia curriculum for early childhood in more detail. Its philosophy has had a strong influence on early childhood programs in this country and around the world, and the financial investment by the local government in Reggio Emilia is equally impressive. Eight percent to 10 percent of the town's budget is spent on the program; 42 percent of the town's 3- to 6-year-olds and 31 percent of the town's infants are served by it. In 1993 the cost per child was $880 a month, and the average fee paid by parents $119 (on a sliding scale); the cost for 3- to 6-year-olds was $600 a month, and the average fee paid by the parents was $114. Preference for admission is given to children with disabilities and children of single and working parents. By comparison, parents in the United States pay 90 percent of the cost for child care; only the poorest in this country get any kind of child-care subsidy.

Many aspects of Reggio Emilia have affected—and continue to affect—U.S. early childhood programs. Much of this approach is a reaffirmation of the best of Dewey, Froebel, Rousseau, Herbert Reid (art education), and Bruner, along with free-school beliefs in the child, Head Start early underpinnings, and Gardner's theory of multiple intelligences. But the approach is also in direct conflict with some major trends in today's early childhood programs in this country: underfunding of early childhood programs, an increased emphasis on standards and academics in both private and publicly funded programs, teaching content out of context and relying on teacher-directed approaches, and teacher preparation training that focuses more on traditional educational practices than innovative, radically new ideas.

New Brain Research

Over the past ten to fifteen years (since the mid 1980s), considerable neuroscientific research has been conducted on the human brain, specifically the brain development of infants. This research was triggered by advancements in research tools such as brain imaging technologies, and a growing concern about the status of children in this country (Shore, 1997). The research has provided knowledge about the brain and development that would have been incomprehensible ten to twenty years ago.

Human development hinges on the interplay between nature and nurture. Beginning before birth and continuing throughout development, the brain is affected by the environment—including nourishment, stimulation, responsiveness, and stressors. The environmental impact directly affects the development of specific brain circuitry (the "hard-wiring"). The brain is made up of brain cells and synapses—the connections between the cells—and the vast majority of synapses are produced during the first three years of life. Those that are used a lot—through appropriate environmental input—tend to become permanent; those not used are eliminated. Thus early childhood environmental input affects the wiring of the brain. This development is a function of active interaction between nature (genetic endowment) and nurture (environment; Shore, 1997).

Early care has a decisive and long-lasting impact on how children develop, their ability to learn, and their capacity to regulate their own emotions. A strong, secure attachment between a child and a caregiver can have a positive biological function; caregivers can provide direct mediation in helping children control their emotions.

The brain has a remarkable capacity to change, but timing is crucial. An individual's brain capacity is not fixed at birth: it can be changed by experience. During the first ten years of life—and especially the first three years—a child's brain can be changed, and problems rectified, through intensive and timely intervention. Thus there are many opportunities to support a child's growth and development. What's important to know is the crucial periods at which this support, intervention, and nurturing should occur.

There are periods when negative experiences or a lack of positive stimulation have more impact than others. For example, a mother's depression has a more negative impact on a child's development at certain ages, and early exposure to alcohol, nicotine, and cocaine appear to be more harmful than originally thought. Experiences of trauma or ongoing abuse early in a child's life can have lasting effects both on cognitive development and on depression, anxiety, and the inability to form healthy attachments to others.

Evidence points to the wisdom and efficacy of prevention and early intervention. Study after study shows that timely, intensive, appropriate intervention can radically improve the prospects of young children who are considered at risk of cognitive, social, or emotional impairments. Children from families with the least formal education derive the greatest cognitive benefit from intervention programs, and this early intervention appears to have a lasting effect.

The results of this new brain research suggest the following for early childhood practices (Shore, 1997):

- Provide prevention and primary health care for expectant and new parents and their children. Pregnant women need secure, safe homes, void of stress and abuse, and adequate nutrition.
- Promote responsive parenthood by expansion of proven approaches.
- Safeguard children in child care from harm and promote their learning and development. Most child-care centers are mediocre or poor; many family care programs—especially the unlicensed ones—are worse.
- Enable communities to have the flexibility and resources they need to mobilize on behalf of young children their families.
- Convey the new knowledge about the brain. This new information must be communicated to families and the public in a way that maximizes early support and intervention, provides continual assistance in child development, and connects the family with cultural traditions and practices.

Howard Gardner: The Theory of Multiple Intelligences

In 1983 Howard Gardner published *Frames of Mind*. In this book he proposed that our technique of measuring intelligence—IQ—is far too narrow and should be radically expanded. He subsequently defined intelligence as the capacity to solve problems or to fashion products that are valued in one or more cultural settings (Gardner & Hatch, 1989). Gardner's theory was not new; it expanded on the work of Guildford, Meeker, and others. But he was the first person to conceptualize this approach into a simple, cogent, integrated theory and to disseminate it widely to educators and experts. Initially he described seven intelligences; later he added an eighth. They are

1. *Logical-mathematical.* This intelligence includes the ability to reason logically and deductively, and to think in a linear fashion, and is most often associated with math and science.
2. *Linguistic.* This is the mastery of the use of language—both oral and written—and includes the use of language to express oneself and to structure memory. (The first two intelligences are the focus of most of our traditional educational approaches.)
3. *Spatial.* This is the ability to manipulate and create mental images to solve problems, and includes artistic and mapmaking abilities; it can also be found in blind children.
4. *Musical.* The proclivity to compose, and to recognize and use musical pitches, tones, rhythms, and patterns, is considered a musical intelligence.
5. *Bodily kinesthetic.* This intelligence involves the ability to coordinate and to excel in gross and fine motor physical activities. Children who excel in this skill are often athletes or dancers, enjoy tactile stimulation, are well coordinated, learn by doing, and move around the room a lot.

▶ *One of Gardner's 8 intelligences is kinesthetic.*

6. *Interpersonal.* Interpersonal intelligence enables one to be aware of the feelings and intentions of others and able to use this knowledge to work effectively with others. People who are strong in this area are natural leaders.

7. *Intrapersonal.* This governs sensitivity to one's own feelings and internal motivation. Children with this bent are often introspective, highly philosophical, and concerned with their role in the school.

8. *Naturalist.* A sensitivity to and appreciation of living things and the natural world—weather, plants, animals, geology—characterizes this intelligence. These children may be good gardeners, enjoy raising animals, and find great pleasure in the outdoors.

Gardner believes that these **multiple intelligences** do not operate independently: children must use a variety of them to complete tasks and achieve certain accomplishments. He also believes that different cultural contexts emphasize and cultivate different intelligences in children. The theory suggests that teachers and early childhood programs should teach to, support, and use all eight intelligences, not just the logical-mathematical and linguistic ones; and they should find ways to teach basic facts and concepts using as many of the intelligences as possible, because this approach produces deeper understanding. Children should be helped to capitalize on their strengths—their unique learning style—to learn new material. Since many special-education students are not logical or mathematical thinkers, they often can succeed as well as other students when material is presented to them in a way that matches their intelligence or learning style. The concept of multiple intelligences provides an effective way for early childhood programs to match their curriculum and teaching approaches to children with diverse cultural backgrounds.

The multiple intelligences theory is highly consistent with many of the underpinnings of good early children's programs. It can be seen in programs that stress a wide range of curricula, including dance, movement, art, blocks, play, playground, literacy, social skill development, and enhancement of self-concept; it is alive and well in developmentally appropriate practice (Bredekamp & Copple, 1997); and it is the focus of the whole-child approach. But to his credit, Gardner has taken these fundamental early childhood beliefs and done two important things with them: he has extended the philosophy not only to the entire school curriculum but to all learning, including for adults; and he has expanded our view of intelligence (an almost sacred notion of learning potential) to include vital components of early childhood curriculum: art, music, dance, movement, social skills, leadership skills, and self-concept development.

Developmentally Appropriate Practice

Bilingual Education

Bilingual education has its roots in the Civil Rights movement of the early 1960s. The topic belongs in this section because it is very relevant today and because the number of children in early childhood programs whose home language is not English continues to increase, posing a variety of challenges for these programs.

There are many children in this country who speak a variety of languages other than English. They can be grouped into three general categories: children from Native American tribes who have retained or are now preserving their own language, children from families who speak English but wish to preserve their home language, and new immigrants who do not speak English. In 1992 the Los Angeles Unified School District identified at least eighty non-English languages in their schools. It is estimated that the number of children in America between the ages of 5 and 17 who have limited proficiency in English is 3.3 million (Stanford Working Group, 1993).

In 1968, Title VII of the Bilingual Education Act recognized the challenges of non–English-speaking children in our schools and the need for special programs for them. In 1974 a Supreme Court decision, *Lou v. Nichols*, determined that preventing children from full access to a free, good-quality education based on their inability to speak English is illegal. Like multicultural education and educational equity for children with disabilities, bilingual education is based on issues of educational equity. Bilingual-education advocates reacted against a system that often placed children in special education, and suspended or dismissed them from school, simply based on their inability to speak English. This, of course, is now considered illegal. Until recently, the most popular approach to bilingual education emphasized teaching English while maintaining the use and cultural respect of the home language. This approach is based on five basic ideas:

1. Language development in the home language as well as in English has positive effects on academic achievement.
2. Language proficiency includes proficiency in academic tasks as well as in basic conversation.
3. An **ESL** (English as a second language) **student** should be able to perform a certain type of academic task in his or her own home language before being expected to perform the task in English.
4. Acquisition of English language skills must be provided in contexts in which the student understands what is being said.
5. Students who do not speak English often experience a lesser social status in their school. Therefore, English- and non–English-speaking students should be in classes together in which cooperative learning strategies are used. English speakers should be provided opportunities to learn the minority languages, and teachers and administrators should model using the minority languages for some noninstructional as well as instructional purposes (Crawford, 1987). This approach is called two-way bilingual programs.

However, there has been a radical shift in recent years in the way we teach English to non-English speakers. The state of California passed legislation to require accelerated acquisition of English by immigrants (full-immersion programs); there are several national advocacy groups supporting similar legislation in other states; and there is wide dissatisfaction with the inability of many U.S. schools to graduate students competent in the English language.

Regardless of the approach schools take to teach English, early childhood programs must address two major issues relating to this topic: how to teach non–English-speaking children (and work effectively with their parents), and how to integrate this approach with their multicultural education program. Many believe that full-immersion programs are not multicultural, deny the language diversity that exists in this country, and force language minority students to assimilate to the majority culture's values and mores (Ovando, 1997).

Another obvious challenge is that, as more non–English-speaking children enter our programs, there is an increased need for bilingual teachers and materials. Finally, there is the growing interest in providing second-language acquisition starting in the early childhood years to English-speaking students. Because of research that shows that younger children acquire a second language more easily than older children, that most other countries teach a second (or third) language at a young age, and that the global marketplace requires U.S. citizens to know more than one language, teaching a second language to English-speaking young children is gaining popularity. The foreign language taught in these programs is often a different language from the home language spoken by limited English proficiency (LEP) students, and therefore two-way bilingual programs would not always work.

Conclusion

The history of our early childhood programs follows the history of our country. As we have become more diverse and have recognized the strengths and variability of this diversity, so have our approaches to early childhood and schools. Today we see an array of programs, philosophies, and approaches that seem to have little in common. The central issues that these programs address include providing equal education for all children; supporting our country's racial, ethnic, and religious diversity; preparing children for success within traditional K–12 programs and the later school years; involving parents and local communities; and overcoming the technology divide. Additionally, we must find a way to fund all programs at a level that teachers and caregivers can receive adequate pay and benefits.

Questions and Projects

1. Why are so many people who have influenced early education white men? Does this fact make our programs culturally biased? How? What should be done about it, if anything?

2. Select one of the movements covered in the chapter and discuss what impact it has had on current early childhood programs. For example, how has the concept of free public education affected current views of early childhood education and full-day kindergartens?

3. Select one of the early childhood programs or philosophies described in this chapter (Montessori, Waldorf, Head Start, and so on). Visit a local program that uses that philosophy. Compare and contrast what the book says with what you observe.

4. Select an important person in the development of early childhood education (with your instructor's approval). Research his or her background and address these issues: racial/ethnic/and cultural background; formal education; contribution to the field; how the person's ideas were spread; and whether you agree with the person's philosophy or approach.

CHAPTER

4

Curricular Approaches

*A*ny discussion of early childhood programs and primary schools eventually focuses on the specific **curriculum** offered by the program. But what exactly is a curriculum, and where does it come from? This chapter helps students understand that a curriculum is the written plan designed to implement the program's philosophy. The kind of curriculum a program uses is more about value choices than about scope and sequence, instruction, or goals, objectives, and outcomes. This chapter also helps students understand the ways program philosophy is driven by funding sources and politics, and how a curriculum must be supported through resources, environments, parents, teachers, and teacher training. Evaluating the curriculum—determining whether it is accomplishing the results professed—is a central part of a curriculum plan; but this aspect will be addressed in Chapter 14. ■

Questions to Consider

1. What is a curriculum?

2. How is a curriculum implemented in an early childhood program?

3. Who decides on a program's curriculum?

4. What is the relation among goals, objectives, outcomes, and standards?

5. How do early childhood curricula, such as High/Scope, Reggio Emilia, and the core knowledge curriculum, differ?

6. How does a program's curriculum affect the children?

What Is Curriculum?

There are many definitions of the word *curriculum*. Some of them include "a plan of learning" (Saylor & Alexander, 1974); "a sequence of potential experiences developed by the school for the purpose of disciplining children and youth in group ways of thinking and acting" (Smith, Stanley, & Shores, 1957); "a desired goal or set of values, which can be activated through a development process culminating in experiences for children" (Wiles & Bondi, 1998); "all of the learning of students which is planned by and directed by the school to attain its educational

▶ *One goal of many early childhood curricula is to teach good nutrition habits.*

goals" (Taba, 1962); and "all of the experiences that learners have under the auspices of the school" (Doll, 1970). For this book I use two general definitions of curriculum: (1) everything each child experiences while at the school or center, and (2) a written plan describing specific series of activities and experiences designed to implement predetermined goals, objectives, or outcomes.

Philosophy

The reason educational experts' definitions of a curriculum differ so much is that all curricula are based on educational **philosophy.** What is the philosophy of the school, program, child care, or after-school program? Is it to meet the needs of the whole child; to increase children's self-esteem; to provide meaningful learning; to prepare children for well-paying jobs when they graduate or for admission to a prestigious university; or to make society fairer and less racist?

The Head Start philosophy is a comprehensive approach designed to give low-income children a "head start" in public school success. It holds that all the child's needs must be met—social, emotional, nutritional, medical, and dental needs, along with the need for parent support and school readiness. Many public preschool programs believe their role is only to prepare children to be ready for kindergarten—so they teach specific academic readiness skills.

The question then becomes, What philosophy does a program adopt? There are two ways this occurs. First, educators, psychologists, and theorists develop their own educational philosophy, which is then used to create a program, the process involved in the development of Montessori, Steiner, Hirsch, Reggio Emilia, and the British Infant and Primary School programs. For example, contrary to the official position of the Italian educational establishment, Maria Montessori believed that young children from low income families could be educated, and she also had clear beliefs about how they could be educated. As you can see, educational philosophies are about *beliefs*—about what and how children learn, what a program should do, and how resources should be used. Programs based on a particular philosophy then open their doors and attract parents who have a similar philosophy.

The second way a program adopts a philosophy is that a program's major **stakeholders** create one. Stakeholders are individuals and organizations that have a direct interest in the program. For private schools, parents are the number one stakeholders, because they pay for the school. For Head Start, the federal government is the main stakeholder, because it pays for the program. Most public early childhood and school programs have a variety of stakeholders: parents, politicians, school administrators, and special-interest groups.

A curriculum is then designed, based on the philosophy of the program. For example, if a program believes it should help children respect diversity, it will include activities, materials, and instruction relating to diversity issues. The philosophy of the Denver International School, a school my children attended, has a philosophy of teach-

Figure 4.1

From Philosophy to Classroom Instruction

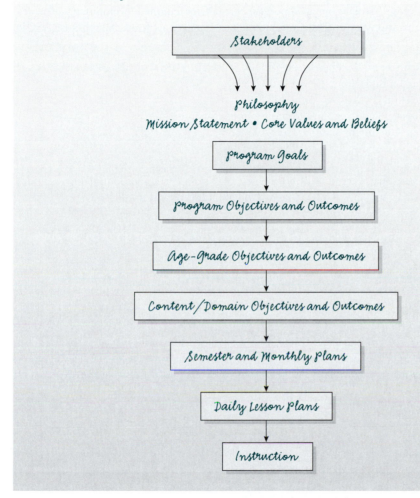

ing French citizens' children in the United States so they can reenter the French system on their return to France. Thus the French national curriculum is used.

National Philosophies

By looking at the general educational goals of several countries, it becomes obvious how these goals reflect the role of education within each society—the nation's philosophy. The main goals for Australia are fulfilling lives and active citizenship, joining the workforce, overcoming disadvantages, and achieving fairness in society. Taiwan's educational goals are the three principles—geography, history, and the economy (the meaning of *nation*)—utilization of group life (operation of democracy); productive labor; and eight moral values—loyalty, kindness, love, faith, righteousness, harmony, peace, and fidelity. China's main educational goals are to develop good moral character, to develop love of motherland, literacy and intellect, healthy bodies, and interest in aesthetics (Wiles & Bondi, 1998).

In 1982, the Association of Supervision and Curriculum Development, a professional organization, identified ten major educational goals for U.S. schools (ASCD, 1982):

- self-conceptualizing (self-esteem);
- understanding others;
- basic skills;
- interest in and capability for continuous learning;
- responsible membership in society;
- mental and physical health;
- creativity;
- informed participation in the economic world of production and consumption;
- use of accumulated knowledge to understand the world;
- coping with change.

The most recently widely accepted U.S. national goals are the six goals developed as part of Goals 2000. These are (State of Colorado, 1991):

- Goal One: By the year 2000, all children in America will start school ready to learn.
- Goal Two: By the year 2000, the high school graduation rate will increase to at least 90 percent.
- Goal Three: By the year 2000, American students will leave grades four, eight, and twelve having demonstrated competency over challenging subject matter including English, mathematics, science, history, and geography. Every school in America will ensure that all students learn to use their minds well, so they may be prepared for responsible citizenship, further learning, and productive employment in our modern economy.
- Goal Four: By the year 2000, American students will be first in the world in mathematics and science achievement.
- Goal Five: By the year 2000, every adult American will be literate and possess the knowledge and skills necessary to compete in a global economy and exercise the rights and responsibilities of citizenship.
- Goal Six: By the year 2000, every school in America will be free of drugs and violence and will offer a disciplined environment conducive to learning.

In this country, the curriculum used in schools has historically been determined by the state and local school districts. Laws regarding school curricula are based on state constitutions and are created and revised by state departments of education, which are then implemented by the local school districts. Other countries with public education use curricula determined by their national governments. In this country, the move toward content standards—as well as Goals 2000—is an attempt to create a national curriculum.

Another fundamental difference between our curricula and those of other countries is the way we envision the role of public education. In most countries, the school is a place in which children learn to become loyal, productive citizens within that country's existing social order. In this country we have viewed the role of public education from a somewhat different perspective:

- to train people to be productive participants in a democracy;
- to provide the knowledge and skills needed for citizens to improve the society;
- to enable the less fortunate to succeed. We view schools as the great social leveler. In a society in which anyone can be president, schools are where this leveling of the playing field occurs.

Early Childhood Philosophies

A variety of philosophies underpin the range of early childhood curricula used in our early childhood and school programs.

Maturational. Friedrich Froebel talks about young children unfolding like a flower. He believed that just as a flower should be allowed to bloom when naturally ready, so children should not be pressured to speed up their development. The Waldorf philosophy holds that teaching isolated academic skills, such as letter recognition, to young children is detrimental to later growth. Arnold Gesell believed that physical development followed a predetermined path and should not be accelerated. These are all examples of a maturational view of early childhood growth and development.

Maturationalists believe children's intellectual, physical, social, and emotional development will unfold along predetermined paths, provided they receive the appropriate physical and social environment (including other children and adults). Today the Gesell Institute is the foremost advocate of this philosophy and has developed a battery of assessments to determine children's developmental levels.

Developmentally Appropriate Practice. Developmentally appropriate practice (DAP) is a philosophy based on the ideas of leading early childhood experts, theorists, and research. "In a developmental approach to curriculum design . . . decisions about what should be learned and how it would best be learned depend on what we know of the learner's developmental status and our understanding of the relationship between early experience and subsequent development" (Katz, 1995, p. 109). Developmentally appropriate practice is a concept of child development and education centered on three basic interacting ideas:

- what we know about child development and learning: the body of knowledge gained through research, observation, and theory development;
- what we know about individual differences—strengths, interests, experiences, challenges—of children within overall group trends and stages;
- what we know about the relationships of individual children and the social and cultural context in which

▶ *Good early childhood curricula focus on the whole child, including physical development.*

they live and learn: how do these factors affect motivation, determine relevant and meaningful learning, and support the goals of the early childhood program?

These basic ideas are then broken down into twelve principles, which characterize the developmentally appropriate philosophy (Bredekamp & Copple, 1997).

1. *Domains of children's development—physical, social, emotional, and cognitive—are closely related. Development in one domain influences and is influenced by development in other domains.* Children don't develop or progress in just one area, or domain. For example, when a child learns to read, this accomplishment also increases the child's self-esteem. By the same token, children who are put down for struggling to read will have their self-esteem negatively affected, which in turn will hinder their reading progress.

2. *Development occurs in a relatively orderly sequence, with later abilities, skills, and knowledge building on those already acquired.* We know from extensive research and careful observation that all children follow a similar path in learning basic skills and concepts.

3. *Development proceeds at varying rates from child to child as well as unevenly within different areas of each child's functioning.* While the sequence of development is constant among children, the rate of development is prone to individual differences; further, a child might develop rapidly in one area—say, cognitively—and less rapidly in another area—say, emotionally.

4. *Early experiences have both cumulative and delayed effects on individual children's development; optimal periods exist for certain types of development and learning.* Certain tasks are learned most effectively at certain ages; for example, learning to walk and talk. Further, children need targeted experiences at specific times to support this development and learning. Without these experiences, development is delayed.

5. *Development proceeds in predictable directions toward greater complexity, organization, and internalization.* Young children are very simplistic thinkers who rely on real experiences and concrete learning. As they mature, they learn to think in more complex and abstract ways; this enables them to organize their thoughts.

6. *Development and learning occur in and are influenced by multiple social and cultural contexts.* What and how children learn depends greatly on their social environment. For example, in an environment that reinforces language, a child will learn to talk more easily than a child in an environment that punishes, corrects, or simply ignores the child's effort to communicate.

7. *Children are active learners, drawing on direct physical and social experience as well as culturally transmitted knowledge to construct their own understanding of the world around them.* Young children learn through direct, hands-on, meaningful experience with materials and important people in their lives.

8. *Development and learning result from the interaction of biological maturation and the environment, which includes the physical and social worlds children live in.* Children learn through maturation, their environment, and an interaction between both. For example, when children's maturity determines that they are ready to walk, the environment must support their efforts to walk; in order to learn to ride a bike, they must be physically, intellectually, and emotionally ready to learn to ride a bike.

   9. *Play is an important vehicle for children's social, emotional, and cognitive development, as well as a reflection on their development.* Play allows children to develop in each area and to integrate learning across domains; the kind of play children engage in is determined by their stage of development.

   10. *Development advances when children have opportunities to practice newly acquired skills as well as when they experience a challenge just beyond the level of their present mastery.* Two Piagetian concepts discussed in detail in Chapter 9 illustrate this idea: all newly acquired skills, behaviors, and concepts must be practiced and used many times to become internalized in the child's mind; and children learn most effectively when they are presented skills, concepts, and behaviors slightly beyond their current abilities, which is why multi-age groups work so well.

   11. *Children demonstrate different modes of knowing and learning and different ways of representing what they know.* Children who know the same things will demonstrate that knowledge in different ways. For example, some children can express their knowledge through writing, others through speaking, others through art, and still others by computer use and play.

   12. *Children develop and learn best in the context of a community in which they are safe and valued, their physical needs are met, and they feel psychologically secure.* While most curricula focus on specific academic and other goals and objectives, it is clear that a basic level of safety, security, trust, and sense of belonging is needed for children (and adults) to learn.

Core Knowledge Curriculum. According to E. D. Hirsch, Thomas Jefferson supported public education because he believed that children in a democratic society should be taught a shared body of knowledge. Hirsch has used this idea in developing his curriculum "to introduce solid knowledge in a coherent way into the elementary school curriculum" (Hirsch, 1996, p. 13). According to this philosophy, there is a core body of knowledge every American child should learn in school; the body of knowledge must be taught in a carefully developed sequence of activities and lessons; and all children, regardless of race, background, and so on, should learn this body of knowledge.

   To this end the core knowledge curriculum is based on a series of books, starting with *What Every Kindergartener Needs to Know* and proceeding through *What Every Sixth Grader Needs to Know.* In the core knowledge curriculum philosophy, the teacher is the agent that dispenses the knowledge, making sure it is presented in the correct sequence and assuring that it has been learned before the child progresses to the next sequence of skills and information. **Teacher-directed learning** is called **didactic.** Many educational philosophies are highly didactic, especially as children progress from kindergarten to third grade.

   While the core knowledge curriculum movement is the most obvious example of this kind of philosophy, many public school curricula are based on the belief that specific content and skills must be taught at specific ages, that knowledge should carefully build on prior learning, and that curriculum should therefore have a carefully developed scope and sequence.

Goals, Standards, Content, and Scope and Sequence

Goals, Objectives, and Outcomes

Curricula generally have goals, objectives, and outcomes. All three involve what the program intends to do. They exist to help the program translate its philosophy into a plan of instruction, which then becomes the program's formal curriculum.

Goals are general areas that the program intends to cover. They are desired areas of student learning, behavior, and attitudes, and are usually written for the entire program or school (or even school district). We have already discussed national goals. Goals are not written in measurable terms and are often more wishes than actual results to be achieved.

Objectives arise from goals. They are narrower, more specific, and often—but not always—measurable. Sometimes they are written in behavioral terms: "The child will be able to read the book with no mistakes." "The children will correctly spell 80 percent of the words on the list."

Outcomes are goals and objectives for the end of a specific period of learning—at the end of first grade; upon graduation from high school; at the completion of the character education curriculum. Some are measurable, others are not.

Standards

In recent years, U.S. educators have focused on content **standards.** These are specific goals and objectives for each content area for each grade—science, math, social studies, literacy, and so on. These standards are generally developed either by professional associations (National Association of Math Teachers), or by state departments of education, or both (often states will adopt professionally developed standards). Many of these standards are used in public elementary schools. Some states—such as Colorado—are also developing standards for preschool programs. Standards determine what should be taught at each grade level in each content area, and the proficiency each child should achieve in this content. The state of Colorado has also developed tests to determine student proficiency in these standards, including the Colorado Student Assessment of Proficiency (CSAP) for student progress in math and literacy.

Scope and Sequence

Most educators believe that skills, concepts, and content are learned in a prescribed order. For example, children should learn addition and subtraction before they learn multiplication and fractions; children should learn about themselves and their families

▶ *One outcome of many early childhood programs is for children to be able to work and play together.*

before learning about cultures and nations. The idea of sequencing learning based on what a child has already learned and experienced is called **scope and sequence.** Almost all content curricula—social science, reading, literacy, math, and others—have a carefully determined scope and sequence, developed by curriculum experts.

One problem with a scope and sequence approach is that it often ignores the child's development. Developmental psychologists believe that children learn skills and concepts most effectively at certain times—when they are ready—a concept often termed **readiness.** Readiness periods necessitate that we provide the correct teaching and assistance for particular skills at the appropriate times. Another problem with the concept of scope and sequence is that if children miss part of the sequence (through sickness, moving, inability to learn the concept) they are often penalized. Further, gifted and advanced students are often held back from moving ahead in their learning because this will destroy the carefully developed scope and sequence of the class as a whole. A scope and sequence approach ignores the individual differences of experience, learning style, cultural background, and individuality we have come to associate with a developmentally appropriate approach to learning. Finally, a strong adherence to scope and sequence often keeps a program from using an integrated curriculum approach, which is much more consistent with a developmentally appropriate philosophy.

Content, Skills, and Concepts

Returning to the idea that all curricula are driven by specific goals, objectives, and outcomes, the question then becomes, What are the skills, concepts, and content that will be taught? Many of the differences among various early childhood curricula are a result of this question. Some stress teaching **basics,** others specific content, and still others general concepts; while some, of course, attempt a combination of all three.

Whole-Child Approach. Many early childhood curricula use the **whole-child approach,** in which all aspects of the child's growth are addressed by the curriculum throughout the program—cognitive, emotional, social, moral, and physical—because the theory holds that it is just as important to help children develop fine and gross motor skills as it is for them to know the alphabet. These programs are based on the belief that a whole-child approach is the best way to lay a solid foundation for a child's later school success.

Basics. Curricula such as Hirsch's core knowledge curriculum focus on teaching skills and content determined to be needed for specific academic advancement. Skills might include adding single digits or knowing the alphabet; content might be the names of the states in the Union, and the names of animals on the farm and in the rain forest. Basics curricula are not really concerned with how skills and content are taught; and they are not concerned with other goals, such as creativity, self-esteem, justice, or solving social problems.

Concepts. One of the difficulties of designing a curriculum for young children is that basic academic concepts are not developed in a linear fashion. Theorists such as Piaget, Vygotsky, Erikson, and Lickona (see Chapter 3) have shown that concepts such as whole versus part, inclusion (I am part of a family, the family is part of a community), moral ideas, fractions, and cause and effect are very difficult to understand by young children. A curriculum based on their theories requires a scope and sequence that match the developmental stages of children. Further, a curriculum that is responsive to developmental needs will stress a hands-on, **integrated approach** to learning.

Different Early Childhood Curricula

In the early childhood field, some specific curricula have been developed that reflect specific philosophies about how and what children should learn. Some of the most popular approaches are covered here.

Montessori

Philosophy. Maria Montessori believed that children learn differently at different ages, within three-year cycles. She thought that during ages 3 to 6 children have an **absorbent mind:** a stage of development wherein children are highly responsive to learning through all their senses, and learning occurs in an integrated manner. Children this age also have an innate need to order and categorize their new and fascinating world, and they have a need to master their own emerging physical abilities—running, jumping, balancing, throwing a ball, holding a paintbrush, and so on.

At this age children do not need direct instruction. Thus a Montessori classroom is designed for children to work independently and explore their environment through touching and manipulating (Kahn, 1995). Montessori believed that such independent learning builds initiative, concentration, and self-discipline. "Our work as adults does not consist in teaching, but in helping the infant mind in its work of development" (Montessori, as quoted in Kahn, 1995, p. 4).

Classroom. In Montessori programs, 3-, 4-, and 5-year-olds are in the same classroom and usually have the same teacher for three years. Montessori believed that children learn from one another, with older children learning by practicing what they have acquired with younger children, and younger children learning by the modeling of older children. Children in Montessori classrooms also learn to care for the environment by returning materials and maintaining an orderly classroom, which is carefully arranged to support Montessori's concept that children learn independently. Classroom furniture is child-size, as are all learning materials; and the classroom is divided into four learning areas (centers): practical life, sensorial, mathematics, and language. The classroom is calm and carefully ordered by the teacher.

Practical Life. The practical life center encourages children to participate in activities of daily adult life; further, it provides an important link between home and school: the child engages in cleaning and sweeping activities using child-size brooms, mops, and other items. Children develop mastery and satisfaction in completing these tasks. Practical life experiences are broken into four areas: care of person (buttoning, zipping, tying shoes); care of environment (cleaning, sweeping, gardening, ironing); development of social relations (greeting, serving, thanking—"graces and courtesies"); and movement (balancing, jumping, dancing).

Sensorial: Exploring the World. "The sensory education which prepares for accurate perception of all different details in the qualities of things is the foundation of all observation. This helps us collect from the external world the materials for imagination" (Montessori, as quoted in Kahn, 1995, p. 14). Montessori believed very much in learning through all the senses, which develops the child's creative and expressive abilities, and also supports basic academic growth. For example, her famous sandpaper letters enable children to learn individual letters through visual, tactile, and muscle memory.

Mathematics. Montessori's concrete materials are designed to maximize young children's interest in counting, ordering, compartmentalizing, and organizing. Children learn about quantity—more, less, same as—and basic arithmetic skills—addition, subtraction, division, and so on—through the use of concrete materials specifically designed to teach each of these concepts. Like all Montessori materials, the math materials carefully build on each other.

Language. Montessori viewed oral language as the foundation for written language. Further, the Montessori approach stresses learning a precise vocabulary of labels for all activities and objects in the classroom, with an emphasis on expanding each child's vocabulary.

Instruction in written language starts with learning the alphabet and the sounds that make up our language. This knowledge is then used to construct the written language—first to form words, then to form sentences. Children learn additional new words and concepts by exploring science, geography, culture, and other subjects.

Art and Music. Art and music education are integrated into the four learning areas. Materials for art and music activities are available in each area, and are used in learning language, math, and physical movement. Montessori environments stress design, aesthetics, order, and overall beauty; to Montessori, art and music are a central part of learning.

Outside Environment. Learning outside is viewed as an extension of the classroom, providing added opportunities to learn responsibility, independence, basic knowledge, and additional language and math skills and concepts.

Montessori Materials. A hallmark of the Montessori method is the materials, which were designed specifically by Maria Montessori to implement her curriculum and to teach specific skills or concepts. For example, the **pink tower** is made up of ten pink cubes that range from large to small. They are to be stacked sequentially, thus teaching the concept of size. Because the **critical feature** of this material is size, each cube is painted the same color. Other materials teach about color, linear measurement, area, and specific geometric shapes and forms.

Montessori materials are **self-correcting.** If a child does a task incorrectly, it is easy for the child to see where the mistake lies, and then retry the activity, without adult direction or intervention. All materials can be used together and have more progressive elements that are visited later on (for example, the pink tower also teaches basic metric measurement).

Montessori materials are carefully crafted from wood and finished aesthetically. They are presented on low shelves that children can reach during their "open work

▶*Some curricula provide lots of concrete, hands-on experiences.*

time"—about three hours each day. Once children complete a task, they return the materials to their place and move on to another activity.

Role of the Teacher. Montessori believed children have an inner motivation to learn and develop. Thus, the teacher's role is to help the child use this motivation to learn, which is achieved through careful observation and setting up and maintaining the environment to maximize this growth. A Montessori teacher follows the lead of the child, providing structure, support, modeling, and a sense of calm, order, and warmth.

The original Montessori programs were for poor children under age 6. But, there are now many Montessori elementary schools around the world, which add content areas to the preschool model, such as language arts, Spanish (or English, in non–English-speaking countries), social studies, science, and computers. In true Montessori

style, these subjects are integrated throughout the curriculum. Emphasis is placed on the connections among the different areas of study (Kahn, 1995).

High/Scope

The High/Scope curriculum is an approach developed by the High/Scope Education Research Foundation of Ypsilanti, Michigan, based on **constructivism** and cognitive development theory (Hohmann & Weikart, 1995). It includes academic, social, emotional, and physical development, and stresses child-initiated learning activities (Schweinhart & Weikart, 1998). "The High/Scope curriculum is an open-framework approach in which the teacher and child plan and initiate activities and work together. Classroom activities are partly the result of the plan–do–review sequence, planned by children themselves and supported by teachers" (Schweinhart & Weikart, 1998, p. 58). The High/Scope curriculum is the approach used by the famous Perry Preschool Project.

A High/Scope classroom is set up with a variety of traditional learning centers, as well as other temporary learning areas. Children engage in active, hands-on manipulation with materials in each center, and learn through interactions with materials and their peers. In true Piagetian style, they construct their knowledge through these on-going interactions.

The plan–do–review sequence, which is the heart of the curriculum, is a child–adult framework for learning that follows this sequence:

- The teacher and child discuss and plan what the child will do in a particular learning center (plan).
- The child engages in activities in the center (do).
- The child then returns to the teacher and, before moving on to another activity, discusses what was done in the center (review). This discussion may include

whether the child changed the plan once in the center, and why, and covers both affective and academic aspects of the activity ("I really had a good time"; "Jimmy showed me what happens when you mix red and yellow paint").

When I was a Head Start director, I introduced the High/Scope curriculum to the program. We found that the plan–do–review process gave our children a sense of purpose and direction in their learning; it also enabled them to report to their parents at the end of the day what they did in school. The structure of the plan–do–review—especially the concept of planning ahead—was very powerful to our children, who come from backgrounds in which little planning and goal-setting occur. The curriculum also gave our teachers specific roles to play within a developmentally appropriate classroom, without resorting to too much adult-directed teaching. This gave them a sense of actually teaching the children, not simply watching them passively.

Waldorf Education

The Waldorf philosophy, developed by Rudolf Steiner, has three central components: Body, Soul, and Spirit (Steiner, 1926). Body is about how people learn from the external, physical environment; Soul is the way one derives personal meaning from the environment, connecting experiences to one's unique being; and Spirit is how an individual's unique personality is brought to bear on the learning situation. Education is about developing the Body, Soul, and Spirit.

Educational Philosophy. Waldorf education is the most whole-child and maturational of all the curriculum models covered in this chapter, because Steiner's philosophy divides the curriculum into three distinct stages: early childhood, middle childhood, and adolescence. When the Waldorf curriculum is carried through successfully, the whole being—head, heart, and hands—have been educated (Barnes, 1991).

Early Childhood (Body). In Waldorf education, early childhood is from infancy to first grade, with a concentration on preschool and kindergarten. This is a time to develop the body: exposing children to learning about the environment through their senses. For teachers of children this age, creating an environment that encourages exploration, imitation, and creative play is the goal, so that children can imitate their social and physical world: role-playing a parent's cooking or working, painting and drawing to describe the world, imitating language through nursery rhymes, songs, puppet shows, and creative dance. Engaging in more specific intellectual activities at this age is viewed as destructive.

Middle Childhood (Soul). At this phase, extending from first grade to puberty, children's main vehicle to learning is imagination, which allows them to learn a vast array of intellectual information in a meaningful way. Steiner held that at this age, children do not learn rationally and abstractly, but rather through emotions and feelings. Thus, learning in middle childhood should focus on whole learning—projects, legends, folktales, mythologies, art, dance, and drama—rather than intellectual information taught in isolation from their feelings and personal meaning.

Adolescence (Spirit). After the onset of puberty, the spirit of the child emerges: the child begins to develop a unique view of the world, and learns from this personal perspective. The intellect comes to the fore during this time, and is used to integrate the body and soul as children learn more about the world and their place in it.

Curriculum Elements. There are several curriculum elements that derive from this philosophy. The first is implied by the discussion of the three distinct, self-contained stages: a **spiral curriculum.** During each stage, and even within a stage, the same basic knowledge is introduced and experienced at different levels of complexity and depth, each time becoming more complex and integrated.

Each school day begins with a single lesson on one topic that lasts up to three hours and continues for several weeks. The emphasis is on exploring the topic using a variety of approaches—art, movement, language, and more. During the rest of the morning, shorter lessons are taught, such as foreign languages (which start in first grade). Afternoons are devoted to more active pursuits such as art, crafts, gym, dance, and gardening. Teachers stay with the same students through the middle childhood grades (elementary school), particularly during the initial three-hour period, which allows teachers and students to develop strong relationships that help nurture the nonintellectual aspects of the child. Waldorf education not only believes that the arts and practical skills are essential components of education, but that children who do not receive them will be emotionally and socially crippled. The goal is for each subject that is taught "to contribute to the development of a well-balanced individual" (Barnes, 1991). All learning at each age includes activities that involve all faculties.

Examples of a Lower-School Curriculum. During first through third grades, a typical curriculum might include the following:

- pictorial introduction to the alphabet, writing, reading, poetry, and drama;
- folktales and fairy tales, legends, stories, nature stories;
- house building, gardening;
- history, math, language arts, and science, taught in three- to five-week main lessons (three hours apiece);
- handiwork: woodworking, knitting, sewing;
- music: singing, recorder, brass, strings, other instruments;
- movement: dance, games, gymnastics;
- foreign language;
- art.

Because Waldorf education is maturational and integrated, it does not lend itself well to traditional testing; further, government-mandated tests make little sense within the Waldorf philosophy.

British Infant and Primary School

The Stanley British Primary School in Denver, Colorado, is an example of the British Infant and Primary School program. The mission of this school is to provide a challenging education within a diverse and supportive environment that values the distinct contributions and abilities of each child; and to encourage and facilitate the use of the

British Primary School philosophy in the larger community (as described in the 1996 parent handbook). The philosophical goals include the following (Myer, 1992):

- to create an integrated curriculum in a challenging, experiential learning environment;
- to help children develop to their fullest potential, emotionally, socially, intellectually, creatively, and physically;
- to help children learn how to learn and establish a firm foundation for lifelong education;
- to provide a nurturing, mutually respectful community;
- to help children be responsive and contributing members of the world;
- to value diversity of all kinds—racial, ethnic, and socioeconomic, as well as children with special needs and challenges;
- to actively involve parents in their children's education.

History. The British Infant and Primary Schools model comes from the British public school infant (ages 5 to 7) and primary (ages 8 to 11) schools of the 1960s and 1970s. The practices of these schools developed from the Nuffield Foundation (a hands-on approach to math) and the theories of Dewey, Froebel, and Piaget, and they encourage whole-child learning, child-directed activities, projects, multi-age groupings, hands-on learning, and an unstructured day. These ideas were brought to the United States in a series of articles by Featherstone (e.g., 1967) and led to the free school (alternative school) movement and the open classroom.

Whole-Child or Integrated Approach. The British Infant and Primary School(s) approach supports educating the whole child—social, emotional, creative, intellectual, and physical aspects—and teaching new skills and concepts using each of these aspects. The philosophy is to follow the child's interests and motivation in learning a variety of age-specific skills and concepts through the use of a variety of approaches and using various cognitive, sensory, and kinesthetic learning styles.

Emphasis on Creativity and Learning by Doing. Various forms of creativity are utilized to enable children to express what they have learned, and to support each child's development of a strong, independent, unique personality. It is believed that children learn best by immersing their whole being in the learning process: painting, writing, dancing, playing, manipulating objects.

Emphasis on the Environment. Since the British Infant and Primary Schools approach focuses on individual exploration and mastery, designing a classroom to facilitate and encourage this process is crucial. Classrooms are designed with a variety of learning centers, a library and reading area,

▶ *In the British Infant/primary philosophy children are encouraged to collaborate with each other.*

and opportunities for children to display their work. There are few chairs, no desks. Noise levels are often high, and social interaction is intense.

Reggio Emilia

Reggio Emilia schools were started after World War II in Italy by parents and educators. Today they include twenty schools, for children aged 3 to 6, and thirteen infant and toddler centers, for children aged 4 months to 3 years.

Philosophy. The Reggio Emilia philosophy is designed to bring together the three central elements of education—teachers, parents, and children—and to strengthen

Some Differences between a Traditional Program and a Britsh Infant and Primary School

Here are a few comparisons between a traditional program and a British Infant and Primary School approach, taken from a document of the Stanley British Primary School (2000, pp. 4–5):

Traditional Program	Stanley British Primary
Children are grouped according to age within a twelve-month range, in single-grade settings.	Children are grouped in multi-age and multi-grade settings.
The curriculum is presented part to whole, with emphasis on discrete academic skills.	The curriculum is presented whole to part, with emphasis on integrated learning.
Planning of curriculum and activities is based on grade level and local and state standards. Adherence to a fixed curriculum is highly valued.	Planning of curriculum is based on teacher enthusiasm and children's needs and interests.
Teachers begin with what the child doesn't know.	Teachers use children's knowledge as a springboard to further understanding, and subject matter is uncovered.
Instruction is mostly to the whole class, with small groups for reading, writing, and math.	Direct teacher instruction is focused primarily on small groups.
Children's learning is dependent on aural attention to memory.	Children are encouraged to collaborate with one another and learn through firsthand experience.
Learning is passive most of the time.	Children's learning is a result of active participation, with guidance and support from teachers.
The day is scheduled in blocks of time.	The school day allows for long blocks of uninterrupted time.
Assessment of children's learning is viewed as separate from teaching, and occurs through testing.	Assessment of student learning occurs through teacher observations of children's work, portfolios, and exhibits.

their relationships. These relationships are the foundation of the philosophy. "What is most appreciated all along is the shared sense of satisfaction and accomplishments as individuals and as a group" (Malaguzzi, 1993, p. 9). The values of this philosophy are:

- an interactive, constructivist view of learning;
- intensive relationships among all participants;
- a spirit of cooperation;
- emphasis on research by the individual and the group;
- attention to context;
- two-way communication;
- acquisition of knowledge in relation to groups.

Children are viewed as rich in potential, strong, powerful, competent, and most of all, connected to adults and other children (Malaguzzi, 1993). The overall goal of the Reggio Emilia approach is to create an amiable school—active, inventive, livable, documentable, and communicative (Malaguzzi, 1993, p. 9). All aspects of the school are strongly interdependent: carefully designed and aesthetic environments, the nature of learning, and documentation.

Curriculum. The curriculum of Reggio Emilia schools follows the child's interests, potential, and experiences—what is called an **emergent curriculum.** The content and activities are developed through children's interactions and negotiations with other children, staff, and parents, and are based on relationships: meetings with parents, teachers and students to define goals and time lines; and meetings to assure cooperation and organization for all projects.

The schedule is full-day; activities and projects are timed by children's personal rhythms and sense of time. Children remain in the same group and with the same teachers for three years, but they change environments as they mature and learn. Teachers are partners with the children in their learning, work together as a team with a group of children, and work across teams to develop the most effective ways to refine the teaching process and record children's learning. Teachers also receive input from the **atelierista** (an artist) and **pedagogista** (an educational consultant).

Teachers prepare the environment and materials; children create the content of the curriculum by developing projects and activities. Projects may take a few days or several months, and are based on student interests and experiences, theory building, and questions. Teachers help form a student's initial impetus into projects.

Each school has an atelierista and an atelier. The former is an artist; the latter, a studio. The atelierista helps children develop ways to express their knowledge and learning—what has come to be known as **the one hundred languages of children**—and enables children to present, or document, their learning continually. These documentations provide symbolic representation of their development, communicate to parents what students are doing, and develop strong self-esteem in the students.

The central organizational unit for projects is a small group (two to four children). The belief is that children gain most of their social and academic knowledge through small-group learning—through self-exploration and exploring with other children—assisted and structured by teachers, the artist, and the pedagogista. In Reggio Emilia schools teachers enter the program with very little teacher training. Most of the training occurs on site, supported by the experienced teachers and the pedagogista.

Core Knowledge Curriculum

The core knowledge curriculum, adopted by core knowledge schools (which include private schools, charter schools, and some regular public schools), is based on one simple idea: all American children should learn and know exactly the same knowledge and skills at the same grade level. It is a very specific skill and content curriculum developed by E. D. Hirsch. The philosophical base of the core knowledge curriculum is Hirsch's book *Cultural Literacy* (1987), a book that details what students in U.S. schools should know. Later books divide this knowledge into grade-specific skills and content. Hirsch believes that the purpose of education is to unite a society by teaching students society's cultural literacy: what cultured children should know. "The high mobility of our children, especially those who can least afford educational disruption, makes common learning more needed in the United States than most other nations" (Hirsch, 1996, p. 232). The argument for this philosophy is that there is a body of culturally accepted knowledge and skills (from knowing fairy tales and Mother Goose rhymes to memorizing the capitals of the world's countries). This body of knowledge is the content of the school's curriculum, and its acquisition by students is a predictor of the students' later financial success (Hirsch, 1996, p. 12).

The core knowledge curriculum is the application of the philosophy of cultural literacy. "I emphasize in this content the importance of defining content for a particular grade level, since the school year is the critical unit of curricular planning" (Hirsch, 1996, p. 28). Clearly, within our discussion of curricula, the core knowledge curriculum is fixated on content and skills, and is solidly outcome-based—requiring children to master these skills and content at each grade level. The teacher's role essentially involves leading, directing, instructing, and evaluating.

Single-Subject Curricula

Truly speaking, a curriculum is everything that goes on within a program, from literacy activities in the classroom and disciplinary policies and procedures to parental involvement and whether outdoor play is encouraged. But the term *curriculum* is also used to describe single-topic programs, usually implemented for a limited period of time and always directed at a single issue, content, or behavior. (Sometimes these are called **canned curricula**).

Character Education. A number of early childhood programs and elementary schools—both public and private—have adopted character education curricula, which are designed to bring moral behavior back to the schools and to reduce unacceptable behaviors. The Heartwood Character Education Curriculum is one such example. In Chapter 15 I discuss these curricula in more detail.

Anti-Bullying Curricula. As a result of increased school violence and the public's perception that schools are less safe than they used to be, many educational programs are instituting anti-bullying curricula. One is the Bully Proofing Program, used by a school district in Englewood, Colorado, which is designed to reduce verbal and physical intimidation of children.

Self-Esteem Curricula. Many early childhood programs have the development of a child's positive self-esteem as one of their primary goals. While some programs address this goal through their overall curriculum and the instructional approaches they use, others adopt a single curriculum to develop the child's positive self-esteem. Most educators believe a single-subject approach to developing positive self-esteem is not effective.

Multicultural or Diversity Education. Multicultural education can be addressed in two ways—including diversity throughout the program (as described in Chapter 6) or implementing a specific diversity curriculum. A unit on black history and culture during Black History Month is one example of a single-subject approach. Again, many believe this kind of approach to diversity is not really effective and can, in fact, be counterproductive. Chapter 6 provides a full discussion of how diversity may be integrated throughout the early childhood program.

Hidden Curriculum

Much more occurs in a school or early childhood program than is covered by the written plan and the educational philosophy. The **hidden curriculum** includes everything that occurs in a program that is not covered by the philosophy and curriculum. A good example of a hidden curriculum in an early childhood program is the message communicated to children about diversity in a homogeneous program with no minority staff, materials, or curriculum content. Programs that solve all social conflicts with strict rules and direct adult intervention have a hidden curriculum that supports authoritarian power and does not encourage children to solve their own problems.

When I was a Head Start director I discovered that our hidden nutrition curriculum was much more powerful than our official one. Our official curriculum based on the Head Start philosophy called for nutritional snacks and meals, classes for parents about good nutrition, books on healthy eating habits, and classroom activities supporting healthy food choices. Our hidden curriculum, however, included lots of celebrations and parties with fatty and highly sugared cookies and cakes, pop and other unhealthy drinks. Parents would also send very unhealthy food with their children for these celebrations (Wardle, 1987).

Curricula and Staff Interactions

The role of the teacher is different in different types of programs, depending on the curriculum. Curricula that are didactic—teacher-focused and -directed—obviously place very different responsibilities on the teacher than developmentally appropriate approaches—ones that expect teachers to be facilitators, structurers of learning, and scaffolders of experiences for children. Research indicates that these different teacher roles produce radically different interactions between teachers and children (Kontos & Wilcox-Herzog, 1997). And since the quality of teacher–student interaction enhances student development, this fact is of interest.

Not surprisingly, teachers involved in implementing teacher-directed curricula use more negative behavioral management techniques and lots more direct verbal instruction. Teachers in more developmentally appropriate programs use more divergent questions and expand more on children's activities (Kontos & Wilcox-Herzog, 1997). Further, teachers in more DAP programs exhibit more warmth—interactions characterized by warmth, acceptance, respect, and responsiveness to children's behaviors.

Developmentally Appropriate Practice

Teachers in didactic programs typically exhibit less warmth, sensitivity, and verbal stimulation and are more likely to use negative approaches to behavior management. Children in DAP classrooms tend to be socially competent, considerate of their peers, more communicative, and under less stress.

It seems that curricular approaches and teacher–child interactions go hand in hand—the more DAP the program, the more likely it is to encourage warm, stimulating interactions.

Implementing the Curriculum

The part of the curriculum that is meaningful to children is what they experience, which is largely composed of the activities they engage in within the child-care center or school, but also includes ways families are involved, community field trips, homework and other policies, and school–community relationships and activities. The curriculum is implemented through the environment (indoors and outdoors), learning materials and resources, teachers and staff, grouping of students, lesson planning and scheduling, use of technology in supporting the curriculum, and use of the community.

Environment

The environment is central to the implementation of the curriculum. A curriculum that includes physical development must provide adequate indoor and outdoor space for physical activities; a curriculum that includes the basics of computer usage must have enough computers in each classroom for children to use on a regular basis. In Chapter 5 I discuss in detail how environments can support or detract from the program's curriculum. For example, environments that support individual children's needs include private spaces: individual cubbies, personal lockers, and places to get away from the crowd; and programs that value creativity have lots of opportunities to display children's creative efforts, along with a variety of art materials and equipment that are placed near a water source and are easy to maintain and keep clean.

Staff

Almost all educational curricula view the teacher as the focal point for curricular implementation. Many curricula—including Montessori, Waldorf, British Infant and Primary Schools, and some Froebel programs—require that their teachers matriculate from teacher training institutes or colleges affiliated with these approaches. Reggio Emilia requires on-the-job training. Public school programs require a combination of general college teacher training (four to five years) and a practicum for teachers, but very little for paraprofessionals. Although Head Start for many years required a Child Development Associate certificate for its teachers, now it requires college degrees. The kind of educational preparation teachers receive is considered crucial for the appropriate implementation of the curriculum, and is discussed extensively in Chapter 7.

One of the greatest challenges for many early childhood programs in this country—especially family child care and many institutional child-care programs—is a lack of trained teachers. Another problem is that many public school early childhood teachers are educated as traditional elementary school teachers, not as teachers of younger children (Wardle, 1987b). The recent emphasis on standards in many states simply aggravates the problem. Other issues regarding how teachers implement curricula include the following:

- Some teachers do not always believe in the curriculum they are implementing.
- It is difficult to teach about diversity if the staff lacks diversity.
- Teachers model and reinforce personal values and attitudes they were raised with, which may or may not be consistent with the program's philosophy.
- While many early childhood curricula use an integrated approach—teaching math, science, literacy, physical skills, art, music all together—some teachers are comfortable teaching only some of these areas.

Thematic Approach

Many teachers plan classroom activities by **theme.** Particular strengths of this approach include (1) young children experience the world largely through themes, (2) an integrated approach to learning is easier through the use of themes, and (3) using themes provides needed flexibility to adapt experiences to match each child's experience and background. Typical themes include community workers, the body, home and family, pets, transportation, the rain forest, dinosaurs, farm animals, nutrition, weather, birds, how we grow, exploring the earth, bugs, friends and neighbors, all about me, reptiles, musical instruments, and the seasons.

Once a theme has been selected, various activities are chosen to explore the theme, including art, reading, writing, music, physical activities, science, social studies, field trips, and classroom visits. Further, children should learn about the theme through cognitive, physical, emotional, and aesthetic activities; and to maximize a theme, parents should be informed about it and solicited to provide resources, information about their children's interests, possible visits to the program, and field-trip ideas, including their own place of work.

Two cautions regarding theme-based curriculum planning are in order. First, for children to learn, activities must be personally meaningful to each child. I remember visiting a Migrant Head Start program in the Southwest in which the teachers were using a national curriculum to teach children about St. Patrick's Day. None of the Irish activities made any sense to Spanish-speaking Hispanic children living in the deserts of southern Arizona.

Second, avoid **curriculum by celebration.** Sometimes teachers use major holidays as their themes—Thanksgiving, Christmas (winter celebration), Black History Month and Martin Luther King, Jr., Day, St. Patrick's Day, and so on. This is poor planning for a variety of reasons—because there are far more interesting things young children can study in depth, and because this is a "tourist approach" to diversity (a **tourist curriculum** is one that teaches the superficial aspects of diversity—traditional dress, foods, songs, and dances—rather than developing a rich, in-depth understanding of different peoples—religions, histories, values, and struggles).

Bread. The base of the USDA food pyramid depicts complex carbohydrates, such as cereals and breads, that should be consumed in greater quantities than foods higher on the pyramid (thus the pyramidal shape). According to Endres and Rockwell (1994), between 25 percent and 29 percent of U.S. children between the ages of 6 and 11 are overweight. Thus a major goal for early childhood programs should be to teach young children about the nutritional value of food choice, and to expose them to new foods that are good for them. An ideal approach to achieve this is an integrated approach.

Figure 4.2

Transportation Curriculum Web

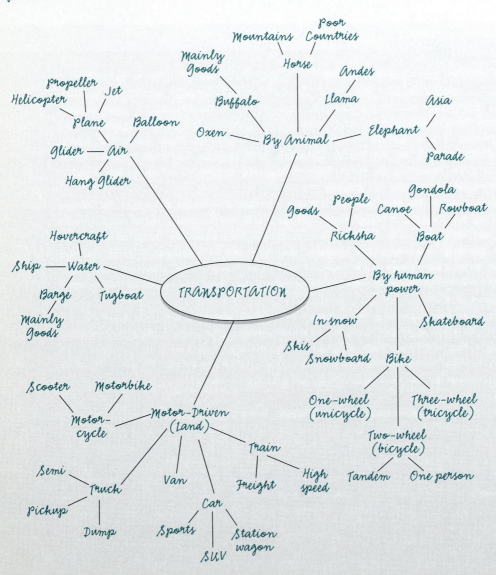

As an example, Fuhr and Barclay (1998) provide a thematic approach, called the Bread Basket. Their program involved many elements:

- *Reading.* The class read a variety of books on bread and wheat, including several versions of the *Little Red Hen* and *Bread, Bread, Bread* (Morris, 1989), set up listening centers with bread-related books, and had children bring to class empty cereal boxes.
- *Experience.* Children sampled a variety of ethnic breads; the teacher brought to class a real wheat stalk and ear for children to learn about each of its parts; children experimented with yeast in warm water, and they created their own favorite sandwiches.
- *Field trips.* Children went to a bakery to observe—and smell—bread being baked. They also visited the bakery section of the local supermarket, observing how bakery products were packaged and displayed.
- *Writing.* Each child wrote a journal detailing favorite pictures from the book *Bread, Bread, Bread*, wrote a sandwich story in the class book, wrote a thank-you note to the bakery, created their own version of the *Little Red Hen*, and wrote down a recipe.
- *Discussion.* Children discussed different kinds of bread, favorite sandwiches, and new sandwich creations.
- *Cooking activities.* The class baked whole wheat bread, painted toast (using food coloring), prepared Rudolph sandwiches (wheat bread, peanut butter, maraschino cherries, pretzels, and raisins), and made their own low-sugar cereal.
- *Mathematics.* Children measured ingredients for recipes, cut bread and paper bread shapes into a variety of fractions, graphed favorite breads, measured the amount of sucrose in one serving of each cereal, and solved bread-related story problems.
- *Science.* Children observed the chemical reaction of yeast in warm water, compared six different grains, compared different kinds of flour, examined a wheat plant, compared the amount of wheat in different cereals, and studied the nutritional analysis on each cereal box.
- *Social sciences.* Children examined different ethnic breads, determined countries of origin of various kinds of breads, and learned about children from different countries.
- *Art.* Children illustrated books on favorite sandwiches, made sandwiches using construction paper, examined cereal boxes and the packaging of cereal, created props and sets for a *Little Red Hen* play, and painted a scenery mural that illustrated the book.

To learn about nutrition, which is essential if we are going to change children's eating habits, children need an integrated approach that includes hands-on activities, eating foods, and learning about foods that are good for them; an approach that involves all their senses and produces positive emotional responses. These activities need to be repeated throughout the child's early childhood experience (Fuhr & Barclay, 1998).

Lesson Planning

The nitty-gritty of curricula is developing schedules and lesson plans. In all early childhood programs, it is the responsibility of the teaching staff to plan and implement activities and experiences that enable children to reach the goals, objectives, and outcomes of the curriculum. How this is done depends largely on the philosophy of the program and the curriculum being followed. Many curricula, such as Montessori, the core knowledge curriculum and some public school K–3 curricula, are carefully **prescribed**—meaning that many of the day-to-day decisions about what to teach and how to teach, are predetermined. In other approaches, notably emergent curriculum, Reggio Emilia, and the British Infant and Primary Schools approach, much of the planning is left up to the teaching staff, as they respond to children's needs and interests.

Clearly, the lesson planning process is "where the rubber hits the road" in the overall curriculum process. If a goal and objective are in a curriculum but there are no activities to enable children to learn them, then the goal and objective won't be met. A good example is that many American public schools expect that their children "will become productive members in a free society," yet few schools actually provide activities to teach this goal to students (voting activities, community service, decision making, and so on). Regardless of how prescriptive or nonprescriptive a curriculum is, the central task of lesson planning is the same: to assure that all goals, objectives, and outcomes of the curriculum are fully implemented within the program. Many teachers use unit plans, weekly schedules, and daily lesson plans to achieve this planning process. The goals and objectives for each of these plans must fit within the program's overall curriculum and suit the scope and sequence for the age of students in the class. In the elementary grades, content plans (science, social studies, math) are often developed on a unit and daily basis.

Adequate planning cannot take place without three essential components: training, planning time, and technical assistance. Teachers must be trained in effective ways of converting curricula into meaningful activities and experiences, and of differentiating these activities for all children. Teachers need enough time to do their planning, as well as technical assistance and support from supervisory staff.

Daily Schedules. All daily lesson plans must fit within time available. Many components of the daily schedule are determined by forces outside the teacher's control—arrival time, scheduled time to use the playground, snack and meal times, time allotted for naps, and times that visitors or experts can come to the classroom. Further, many of these events dictate additional activities—bathroom visits and handwashing before lunch, putting on and taking off outdoor clothes before and after playground time, and so on. Here is a typical daily schedule for toddlers:

▶ *Home-based programs can also implement a curriculum.*

6:30–7:30	Arrival, breakfast Greet each child and parent; ask parent for any important information As children arrive, help them select learning-center activities
7:30–11:00	Diaper check and toilet practice Selection of learning-center activities Teacher-directed activities in small groups Handwashing, morning snack Outdoor activities
11:15–2:15	Diaper check and toilet practice Handwashing, lunch, and toothbrushing Nap time Relaxing activities: music, being read to in library center
2:15–4:30	Diaper check and toilet practice Handwashing, afternoon snack Activities in learning centers Outdoor activities
4:30–6:30	Diaper check and toilet practice Dismissal of children and communication with parents Cleanup and children helping return materials Individual tabletop activities and library corner Cleanup and preparation for next day

Lesson Plans. Teachers have their own ideas about how to plan lessons, and each program has a different process teachers are expected to follow. Lesson planning is the act of translating the program's goals and objectives into age-appropriate activities for children, within the physical constraints of the program and the program day. To assist teachers, many programs provide lesson-plan formats and a teacher's guide to follow. Some daily lesson-plan formats include a way for teachers to list the specific objectives they wish to address—for example, physical, social and emotional, intellectual and cognitive, creative and aesthetic, and communicative and literacy.

For a theme-based approach to curriculum, once a theme has been selected or preselected, the teacher must then determine the desired objectives or outcomes, which come from the curriculum's overall scope and sequence and should derive from the monthly and weekly plans. There should be outcomes in all domains, such as social and emotional, physical, intellectual and cognitive, and verbal and communicative, and they should be determined before activities are chosen. For example, suppose a teacher develops a preschool lesson plan for children going into kindergarten the next year, and its objectives and outcomes are based on *Critical Skills for Kindergarteners* (Johnson, et al., 1995). According to this article, some of the skills required for children entering kindergarten are (pp. 322–325):

- *Social skills:* puts on own coat; toilets independently; attends to a self-directed task for fifteen to twenty minutes; and negotiates verbal solutions to conflict situations.

- *Readiness skills:* matches uppercase to lowercase letters; names numbers one through twenty when shown a written model; and prints the upper- and lower-case alphabet from examples.
- *Language skills:* uses, *he, him, she, her;* uses five- to six-word sentences; verbally identifies similarities; and uses *biggest, smallest,* and so on.

Say the theme chosen is transportation. The objectives to be taught for the day's plan are intellectual: matching numerals to their written symbols; social and emotional—attending to self-directed tasks for fifteen to twenty minutes; language and communication—identifying similarities and using *biggest, smallest, best, dirtiest;* and physical—putting on and taking off coat, and independently placing coat in own locker. Clearly the choice of objectives depends on the individual children's experiences and ability. If all the children can already put on and take off their coats and place them in their locker, then this objective is meaningless. Further, any objectives will need to be differentiated for children who are either more or less advanced.

For the selected objectives, under the theme of transportation, the teacher has selected the following activities:

- *A field trip to the local bus depot.* On the field trip the children will put on and take off their outdoor clothing, count the number of buses coming and going, and compare bus sizes, cleanliness, and which are their favorites.
- *Documenting the experience.* On return the children will be expected to spend from fifteen to twenty minutes reporting on the field trip in their personal journals: drawing a picture, cutting out buses and other vehicles from magazines, and pasting them into their journal.
- *A whole group discussion.* The children will be asked to describe the trip, focusing on comparative words—*favorite, biggest, dirtiest, best.* The teacher will write some of the words on a large piece of paper and hang it in the reading corner.
- *Working with classroom materials.* In the block area children will create a bus station and use miniature buses and other vehicles to represent the field trip. The focus of the activity will be on counting the number of buses and other vehicles, and matching a symbol of the correct number to the sets of vehicles.

Obviously, children will be learning much more than these selected objectives. The point of the objectives is to plan the lesson with the overall curricular goals in mind.

The Project Approach

Recently the project approach has reemerged as a significant curriculum focus. Its philosophy acknowledges children's natural dispositions, intellectual curiosity, and need to investigate the environment, and reflects a belief that young children learn best by doing (Katz, 1995). According to Katz, this approach is "an in-depth investigation of a topic worth learning more about. The investigation is usually undertaken by a small group of children within a class, sometimes by a whole class, and occasionally by an individual child. The key feature of a project is that it is a research effort deliberately focused on finding answers to questions about a topic posed either by the children, the teacher, or the teacher working with the children" (p. 1). Three general phases that occur when using the project approach are outlined on page 118.

Difference between Teacher-Planned Experiences and the Project Approach

This table outlines a few differences between teacher-planned experiences and the project approach (adapted from Helm & Katz, 2001, p. 3).

Teacher-Planned Units	Projects
Length of learning experience predetermined; usually one to two weeks.	Length of learning experience determined by the nature of the project—several weeks to sometimes months.
Topics determined by curriculum and teacher.	Topics negotiated between teacher and students with integrated curriculum goals. Children's interests important in selection.
Teacher plans, presents topic, prepares learning environment.	Teacher uses observation of children's investigations and interest to determine the next step of the project.
Objectives determined by teacher based on curriculum goals. May include inquiry experiences.	Teacher uses webs to determine prior knowledge, then organizes projects for students to learn what they don't know; integrates curriculum objectives as project progresses; always involves child investigations.
Knowledge gained through teacher-planned activities, small and large group activities.	Knowledge gained by children involved in determining activities and events to answer questions.
Resources provided by teacher and students.	Resources are brought in by students, teachers, experts, and from field visits.
A field trip may be included; if so, it generally will be near the end of the study.	Field-site visits are a central part of the project; several may occur, usually early in the project.
The topic may be taught at predetermined times or integrated into many content areas throughout the day	The project permeates the day and classroom, involving many curricular areas and skills.
Activities are planned by the teacher to learn specific concepts and skills.	Activities focus on investigation, answering questions, using resources. Teachers assist integration of concepts through discussing and debriefing.
Representations are for specific activities—drawing, creating maps, writing a play. These aren't usually repeated.	Representations (drawing, building, writing) challenge students to integrate concepts and document what children are learning. Activities are repeated to show growth.

Phase 1: Beginning the Project. A general topic is selected from child interests, teacher interests, or curriculum content. Once selected, the topic should be evaluated using these criteria (Helm & Katz, 2001):

- Topics should center on hands-on, concrete activities and provide direct experiences for children.
- Topics should easily relate to the students' prior experience.
- Topics should contain real sites near the program that students can visit and revisit.
- Topics should be chosen that allow children to do research with minimal adult assistance.
- Topics must enable children to represent what they have learned through activities and techniques appropriate for their ages—drawing, role-playing, photos, dioramas, and so on.
- Topics should relate to the program's goals and objectives.
- Topics should directly relate to children's home and community experiences. This makes them more meaningful to the students.

Once a topic is selected, the teacher should create a planning web. This **webbing** should determine a range of possible activities and concepts to be taught, and should then be grouped by curricular goals and objectives. Time is spent with the children to determine prior student knowledge and experience on the topic chosen. Books, videos, real objects, dramatic play, and discussion can be used to begin to focus children's interest in the topic; ways to involve parents in the project and ways children can demonstrate their learning are explored. Also, opportunities to document children's progress during the project—observation, checklists, anecdotal notes, products, and so on—must be determined (this topic is discussed at length in Chapter 14).

Phase 2: Developing the Project. Phase 2 has two components: reexamining the planning web and preparing for field work and expert visitors. In reexamining the planning web, the teacher needs to integrate individual children's webs with the teacher's web, and then match program goals and objectives to the revised web. Decisions must be made regarding appropriate field trips and visitors, and then all the practical planning needs to be done. A variety of tools for children to record information should be considered—clipboards, cameras, tape recorders, video camera, pens and pencils, art materials, and more—and ways found to determine how children will represent what they have learned through concrete activities—pictures, displays, new webs, lists of questions answered, dictated information, tape reports, constructions, murals, and so on.

Phase 3: Concluding the Project. In this stage children bring their work to completion and summarize what they have learned. Children take what they have learned and extend it in ways that relate to their own experiences, families, and community.

The central focus of this stage is for children to share, through individual products, what they have learned throughout the project, which can be done through exhibits, role-playing, histories of the project, plays, music, written reports, scrapbooks, open houses for parents, presentations to parents, take-home books, and community displays (exhibits, concerts, and the like). Older children might develop PowerPoint presentations, computer-generated books, presentations for city committees and commissions, and reports for the local media (radio, TV, newspapers).

Resources and Materials

No curriculum can be adequately implemented without resources and materials. A few general issues regarding resources and materials include the following:

- *Whatever the objectives of the curriculum, enough materials must be provided to teach them.* A good example is to make sure the program has enough computers to implement its technology objectives.
- *Materials and equipment must be developmentally appropriate.* For example, books written for fifth graders are not appropriate in a preschool classroom. All equipment must match (or be slightly higher than) each child's developmental level.
- *Materials should require minimal supervision for their use.* Organized early childhood programs have relatively high teacher–student ratios. Teachers need to spend most of their time in high-quality interactions with students, and should not spend lots of time showing children how to use equipment, or making sure they don't misuse or break it.
- *Materials must help develop all curriculum objectives.* For example, if a curriculum objective is to enhance children's self-esteem, then there must be materials (books, posters, artwork, puzzles, dolls, and so on) in which children can identify themselves and their families. If one objective is to teach children to make choices, there must be lots of materials that encourage this behavior.
- *Materials must communicate the values of the curriculum.* A program that has nice, fancy, new computers but few books and shoddy, unsafe playground equipment communicates to all (the community, parents, teachers, and children) that the program values technology education, but places little importance on reading and gross motor development.
- *Materials must also be available for program objectives not specifically for the children.* These include teacher morale, parent–center relationships, diversity, father involvement, and so on.
- *Materials must be safe.* In multi-age groups, safety is particularly vital. Young children can choke on small objects (pen tops, small blocks, beads, puzzle pieces, caps of all kinds) that older children may be comfortable using; older children can be strangled by long strings, neckties, and hood ties. Toxic materials should never be used.

Clearly, a central part of the curriculum planning process is making sure there are adequate and appropriate materials for the planned activities. Sometimes this is achieved by getting materials from storage, or moving them from another area in the classroom. On other occasions it requires soliciting materials from parents, purchasing resources for specific projects, or soliciting them from the community. There is nothing more frustrating to children and teachers than trying to implement activities without enough of the needed materials.

▶ *Field trips are an essential part of any early childhood curriculum.*

Field Trips

As children spend more time in early childhood programs, schools, and before- and after-school programs, the need for community field trips increases. The use of field trips as important educational experiences within the overall curriculum is discussed here. First, field trips should provide real, concrete examples of content being addressed in the curriculum. Field trips are often most effective at the onset of a theme or unit, providing experience in and exposure to the topic. Field trips should be used to expose children both to experiences in their own communities and to experiences in new, unfamiliar communities. All field trips should be as carefully planned as classroom activities, using a field trip form much like a lesson-plan form. And field trips should be carefully fitted within the goals and objectives being addressed at that time in the classroom; they should not be random, scattergun activities arranged at the whim of the teacher or administrator.

Children need ample opportunities to explore ideas and concepts presented through field trips—reading books, drawing pictures, taking photos, doing Internet searches, and so on. Further, a variety of learning should be encouraged through field trips, not just cognitive learning. Finally, students need to be directly involved with hands-on experiences relating to the field trips (depending on their age)—planning, reporting (photos, videos), interviewing, getting maps off the Internet, and providing additional information to the class.

Technology and the Curriculum

There are, of course, various ways technology can support an early childhood curriculum, depending on the curriculum used, the knowledge and competence of the teachers, and the available equipment. In an article in *Early Childhood Educational Journal* (2001), Trepanier-Street et al. discuss ways technology can be used to support long-term projects in a mixed-age (4–6 years old) classroom that uses a Reggio Emilia philosophy.

Documentation. In a Reggio Emilia philosophy, documentation of student projects serves to provide insight into the child's development and learning and to suggest ideas for teachers to web, enables children to observe and learn from their own actions, and shows other students and parents the student's progress. In the case described by Trepanier-Street et al., digital cameras were used to document projects, and images were immediately downloaded into a computer file; printed out to create books, journals, and newspapers; and then stored for later use. Photos can be used by teachers and students to discuss various aspects of a project; students can also revisit a project, or an entire documentation panel can be printed from the computer. Also, these images can be printed out onto transparencies and later used with a traditional overhead projector.

Using a computer software writing package, children can add words to photos—either creating a story, or describing the events that are represented in the photo—thus creating a classroom book.

Another way to document a child's learning is through the use of video. There are two approaches, conventional video and computer video. Conventional video can be used for teachers to review a child's activities, to plan future support and scaffolding, and to show parents and families what the child has been doing. Through the use of video, children can see a different view of their own learning and get an infusion of self-confidence. The advantage of digital video is that it can be downloaded into a computer file, and individual frames can be printed out and included on documentation panels. The video printer also allows for individual images to be printed out. Teachers can use these images to develop further activities and ask questions to provoke more learning.

Finally, the scanner can also be used for documentation purposes. Many children create original artwork as they experience new growth and development. The scanner enables these images to be placed in the computer file without having to take the original artwork. Children can add writing to these pictures and string pictures and writing together to create a book. The scanner is also great for placing original images—flowers, maps, charts, music, and more—in the computer, and for making transparencies for the overhead projector.

Using software to write and draw. Using both writing and drawing software, children can write and illustrate stories, create signs for the block and dramatic play areas, and create class newspapers. This approach is particularly helpful for children whose freeform art is severely limited, or who may have special needs that constrain their use of pens, pencils, and art materials.

Use of the Internet. The Internet is a wonderful resource for children doing projects. The teacher may need to guide children to appropriate Web sites—and may need to check them out ahead of time. There are even sites where children can consult experts, who then E-mail back answers to them. Two of these educational sites are Exploratorium and Encarta.

Another great Internet activity is for the class or project team to create a Web page. Parents find this especially useful, as they can check out progress of their child's projects on the site. The Web page can also be used to solicit parental support of projects—expertise, books, resources, and more.

Chapter 5 details how to set up technology centers and select appropriate software, and provides additional information about how to use technology with exceptional children. For the best integration of technology into the curriculum, most early childhood programs have a technology adviser who works carefully with teachers and parents to develop ways that technology will enhance the curriculum.

Mixed-Age Grouping of Students

Ever since Horace Mann returned from observing the Prussian military's approach to education in the early 1800s, American schools have traditionally segregated children by age. Many programs still do so, especially traditional public schools and back-to-basics programs. There are, however, other approaches to grouping children that are considered more conducive to the implementation of certain curricula.

Today, most children have far fewer opportunities to experience cross-age interactions than children in the past because families are smaller, more time is spent in age-segregated child-care and school programs, and there are fewer opportunities to explore activities with the extended family.

General Benefits. As would be expected, there are many social and academic benefits for mixed-age activities in child-care and school programs. Mixed-age grouping enables teachers to respond to individual differences, lessens the temptation to compare students, and is easier on teachers, because the children have a variety of needs rather than all going through the same stage at the same time (all having tantrums, all teething, and so on). Because children in mixed-age groups are at different developmental stages, teachers can respond to the individual needs of each child (say, a child might be verbally advanced and socially immature).

Clearly, teachers still have a crucial role in mixed-age groups, namely, to help children gain a perspective on their own learning and development, support young children, and develop appropriate leadership styles. These are all important behaviors for children to learn.

Social Benefits. In mixed-age groups, the older children develop leadership qualities, caring and nurturing behaviors, and scaffolding techniques; they also may assist and provide modeling. In same-age groups, these same children may compete and challenge, and show fewer of these helpful behaviors and attitudes. Mixed-age grouping is particularly helpful for older children who are less socially skilled and have difficulty regulating their own behaviors. It seems that, while reminding younger children of appropriate social behaviors, these older children also regulate themselves. Older children also learn appropriate ways to negotiate with the young children when they are available to assist them and when they need their own time.

Younger children learn from the older children appropriate nurturing and guidance behaviors, which they will use, in turn, when they become older. And, of course, younger children often look up to older children as their models and heroes.

Intellectual Benefits. Older children gain important intellectual skills by teaching younger children skills and concepts they have recently learned, by practicing new concepts, by reframing and restructuring ideas to match the young child's learning, and by adapting their knowledge to match that of another. Teaching younger children also builds the older child's self-esteem. When younger children (3–4 years old) play with older children (5–6 years old), they engage in far more complex play. The older children initiate and structure the activity and model the behaviors. Younger children are also stimulated by older children to use more complex language and problem-solving skills.

While mixed-age grouping is most often discussed in the literature for children under age 6, it is practiced for older children in Waldorf schools, British Primary Schools, Montessori, and other programs. Some small private schools mix ages purely by necessity, not having enough children for each grade. This was, of course, the basis of the one-room schoolhouse.

Looping

Looping is an approach used by some elementary schools in which a teacher is assigned to the same group of students for at least two consecutive years (Bellis, 1999). Often the classroom includes two age groups of children. Looping developed from the British Infant and Primary Schools family groupings, American alternative schools, and the one-room schoolhouse, and it is becoming more popular for a variety of reasons. Looping provides a sense of security and belonging for students, which increases academic success (Bellis, 1999). Less time is taken up at the beginning of each school year, and there is increased parental involvement. There is improved social interaction among classmates, and because teachers have two years to monitor a child's progress, there are fewer special-education referrals. Individualized instruction increases, and because students return to the same teacher, learning opportunities are extended during summer vacation. There is also a greater sense of family—among parents, teachers, and students.

Because teachers have the same children for at least two years, they have more time to get to know their strengths and weaknesses, and thus to individualize their instruction, which allows teachers to respond to the natural variability among all children. Looping is often used in public-school gifted programs and magnet schools that attract creative and advanced students. The challenge of looping, especially in traditional public settings, is the same as any other innovation. Teachers, parents, administrators, curriculum specialists, and even some students are comfortable with the one-age, one-grade, one-teacher approach, and everything that goes with it (grade-specific textbooks, outcomes, and tests, curricula created on a specific scope and sequence, and teachers who prefer to teach a specific grade). Many educators believe that education (especially starting in first grade) must be a stepwise process, from grade to grade.

Any early childhood program wishing to implement looping—especially after kindergarten—must carefully look at each of these barriers before doing so. Resistance from parents and teachers, especially those who have taught for a while, can be particularly strong.

Parents and Curriculum

Parents are major stakeholders in all early childhood programs. In tuition-based programs, they are the principal stakeholders, because they pay for the program. Further, as I discuss later in this book, active parental involvement in all aspects of an early childhood program, including curricular development and monitoring, is considered a vital component of any program. There should be continual and multiple opportunities for parents to contribute ideas regarding the curriculum, and for the program to communicate to parents details of the curriculum.

Seeking Input from Parents. There is a variety of ways programs can seek input from parents. But parental input into the curriculum is based on the understanding that the education and welfare of each child is a partnership between parents and the programs (teachers, experts, and so on). Parent meetings, official parents' groups (boards), parent committees, and parent surveys and questionnaires are all good examples of formal processes to solicit parent input. Some programs, such as Head Start, also have mandated procedures. Informal methods to collect data include parent–child conferences and one-on-one discussions between parents and teachers and the director or principal.

Implementing the Curriculum. Early childhood programs use a variety of ways to include parents in their curricular activities. Many of these are discussed in later chapters of the book. Visiting classrooms as experts or to demonstrate a skill, volunteering in the classroom, participating in various committees, communicating with teachers at conference time their children's interests and parental expectations, and using parent interactive bulletin boards are all ways for parents to become involved.

Communicating with Parents. Children's World Learning Centers developed a series of brochures for parents of particular age groups. On the back of each brochure is the program's educational philosophy; the body of the document lists themes to be covered and objectives to be addressed. For example, for older preschool during spring, the themes are Let's Create, Let's Invent; Our Friends and Neighbors; Let's Explore the Earth; Let's Look at Animals and Bugs; and Look How We've Grown. The categories for outcomes are communication, social/emotional, cognitive, and physical (CWLC, 1997). Some of the objectives covered are tells and retells stories; learns how to make and keep friends; explores concepts of weight, mass, and volume; and develops small-muscle coordination. The document clearly tells parents what their children will be doing—content and objectives. If parents believe their children should be doing something else at this age, this document provides a vehicle for that discussion between the parent and the teacher.

Modifying the Curriculum. Many early childhood programs use teacher committees to work on curricular changes. It is crucial, however, that these committees work very closely with parents and parent representatives. It is a good idea to have parents on various curriculum committees.

Conclusion

All early childhood programs have a curriculum or curriculum development approach. Further, as standards and school quality continue to be stressed, an understanding of curriculum is essential. All curricula come out of a school's philosophy, which describes what the program believes should be taught in school and how it should be taught. Because people have different philosophies about education, there are a variety of different curricula. Standards are an attempt by government to quantify the curriculum—what will be taught, and at what level. Teachers take the curriculum and implement it as activities and learning opportunities for children.

Questions and Projects

1. Select an age group (infancy to age 8). Select a curriculum for this age group. Discuss why you made this choice.

2. Visit three preschool programs (children aged 3 to 5) that use three distinctively different curricula. Interview staff and parents about the curricula. Discuss the similarities and differences.

3. Interview the curriculum specialist (or person in charge of curriculum) at a public elementary school. Ask this person to describe the process used to align the curriculum with new state standards.

4. Find a "canned curriculum" (character education, anti-bullying, conflict resolution). Write a short piece on whether you believe it will actually teach the goals and objectives it claims to.

5. Select one of the curricular approaches discussed in this chapter. Develop a brochure for parents explaining the approach. Include philosophy, goals, outcomes, and other pertinent information. Try to convince parents to enroll their child in this program.

CHAPTER

5

Environments

*E*nvironments for young children have three primary purposes, namely, to keep children safe and healthy, to implement the curriculum, and to support children's growth and development. This chapter carefully addresses each of these purposes, and the relations among them. Obviously the environment that is needed to achieve these purposes differs depending on the child's age. Infant and toddler environments are distinctively different from environments for school-age children. The vitally important relationship between the environment and children's behavior is also examined. ▪

Evaluating Child-Care Environments

I am a consultant for a national Migrant Head Start training center. In that capacity I am sometimes contracted to evaluate the physical environment of migrant programs. Recently I worked with a program in Wisconsin. As I drove through rural Wisconsin, I reflected that the long northern winter was over, and fresh wheat and corn were pushing through the dark, rich soil. Birds were migrating through the rolling countryside, which was covered with acres of different-size pine trees. My task was to evaluate the physical quality of all sites used by the local programs, which were situated in a community building, a renovated rural school, a shared space with the local regular Head Start program, a module (mobile building), and a variety of spaces connected to local churches—basements, educational outbuildings, and a combination of both. The program served

Questions to Consider

1. What should the environment for young children look like? Why?

2. What is the relationship between a program's goals and objectives and the program's physical environment?

3. Is there a relationship between the physical environment and children's behaviors?

4. What are the environmental needs of infants and toddlers?

5. Are the needs of school-age children different from those of preschool children, and if so, how? What are those needs?

6. Does the fact that young children are spending more and more time in early childhood programs change the nature of those environments?

7. What are the needs of adults who work in early childhood programs?

children of migrant families originating in southern Arizona and Mexico; the children's ages ranged from infancy to kindergarten age.

How should I go about evaluating these sites? How would you? To determine effectively whether each site met the requirements of the program, I took with me a variety of manuals, documents, and books. These included Head Start facilities documents, Wisconsin Child Care licensing requirements, **environmental checklists,** and playground safety guidelines.

When I first visit one of these sites I carefully evaluate specific aspects: safety, meeting program goals and objectives, regulations, providing the needs of children and families, and accessibility (compliance with the ADA). Clearly, all of these aspects overlap (for example, all regulations should be concerned with safety), but separating them allows me to view important components that make up the entire environment. I assess the entire program: classrooms, bathrooms, playgrounds, hallways, and the surroundings—the proximity of the building and playgrounds to busy streets and pollution.

Safety

Safety is the most important concern for any children's environment. It involves many areas, including the heat of the water, coverings of electrical outlets, strings hanging from window blinds, tripping hazards, and basic playground safety. Fire safety considerations include extinguishers, exits, and the easy removal of infants in cribs. Other safety concerns include sharp edges and hard surfaces in the classroom, potential traffic hazards, whether children can leave the site undetected, and whether strangers can easily gain access to the facility. Related safety issues for child-care environments are durability and repair. Does the building need repair? Can it withstand institutional use? Is it easy to maintain and keep clean? Buildings that need constant repair, are unsanitary, or are difficult to maintain pose a whole range of safety hazards for children.

Another safety concern involves reducing and controlling the spread of germs and diseases. A common problem with all early childhood programs is the ease with which typical early childhood illnesses spread. Almost everyone who has run an early childhood program must deal with lice. Any parent will tell you that when their children first attended a center they caught every illness imaginable. Strep throat is another infectious disease common in child-care programs. Some of the illnesses young children get simply cannot be avoided, but programs need to minimize the problem. Efforts to control the spread of germs include frequent handwashing with liquid soap by children and staff, sterilizing eating utensils and toys that infants and toddlers put in their mouths, providing an adequate supply of hot water, and good circulation of air that should be kept at a pleasant, but not too warm, temperature. Children need frequent opportunities to go outside, run around, inhale fresh air, and dissipate the germs. They need to be able to go outside year-round. Indoor surfaces should be made of materials that can be easily kept clean, washed, and sterilized (American Academy of Pediatrics, 1997).

Regulations

There are a many regulations that affect early childhood programs. These include local fire, health, and building codes; state social-services licensing requirements; and program-specific regulations, such as Head Start Performance Standards or local school district policies. Additionally, many programs adopt voluntary standards—for example, National Association for the Education of Young Children *Accreditation Criteria and Procedures* (NAEYC, 1991a), and the *Handbook for Public Playground Safety* (Consumer Product Safety Commission, 1997). Religious programs and certain public-school programs are exempt from many of these regulations, but no program is totally free of regulations.

Because different agencies and authorities create regulations, they often conflict with one another. When I was beginning to remodel a warehouse for a Head Start program, the fire inspector said we needed an automatic sprinkler system, but the building inspector said we did not. The fire marshal visiting another one of my centers required a foam extinguishing hood above the cooking range, but the marshal visiting a center twenty miles away did not. Because of overlapping local, state, and federal jurisdictions and different funding streams, conflict is unavoidable. Complicating matters further, some guidelines are not laws or regulations, while others have been proposed but are not yet fully approved. As a consequence of all these factors, it is easy to see why following regulations is rarely a simple process. When I evaluate a program, my intent is to determine whether the spirit of the regulations has been met and whether there are any outstanding issues the program needs to address. To these ends I use regulations as a guide to help me evaluate and assess the child-care environment.

Program Goals and Objectives

Program goals and objectives are the specific activities and accomplishments a program must accomplish to meet its obligations, which are usually articulated in the program's philosophy or **mission statement,** the funding document, or other program documents. Program goals and objectives cannot be achieved without environments that support them. For example, all Head Start programs require children to have many opportunities to run, climb, roll, skip, jump, swing, push, and engage in other physical activities. Thus a safe, well-equipped playground is required. Many early childhood programs expect their students to become familiar and somewhat proficient with computers. Yet without a sufficient number of computers in each classroom, this goal would be nearly impossible to achieve (Haugland, 1999).

Since Migrant Head Start is a comprehensive program with multiple objectives, the demands on the environment are complex. Classroom objectives require space, equipment, and appropriate materials. Services for parents require meeting and training rooms, accessibility, and confidential offices. Dental and medical objectives require their own unique spaces and equipment. Most programs I evaluate do a fairly good job of providing for the classroom needs of the children but lack outdoor play space, as well as adequate space for parents and support staff.

While many early childhood programs express a profound belief in the central importance of their teaching staff, these programs don't support this belief with adequate planning, leisure, or storage space. Staff members often have no private area of their own where they can get away from children and parents; other facilities have a windowless closet at the back of the building.

Needs of Children

A program that serves preschool children for only two and a half hours a day has different environmental requirements from a program that serves children from infancy to age 6 for eight to ten hours a day. For example, a playground in an all-day program must be more complex and varied than one visited by children as part of a part-day program. Infants need cribs, diaper changing facilities, crawling areas, and an infant-toddler playground. Children who attend a day-long program need a place to sleep, eating areas, and more varied play areas, both inside and outside.

A central need for children is to have an environment that matches their physical size and ability. This poses a major challenge for anyone evaluating, redesigning, or selecting space for young children, as their physical needs are simply vastly different from those of older children and adults. Other obvious needs of young children include comfort, privacy, **autonomy,** variability, a sense of security, cultural relevance, and opportunities for creativity and challenge. These specific needs of children will be continually revisited throughout this chapter.

Americans with Disabilities Act

The Americans with Disabilities Act (ADA) requires unobstructed access to all public buildings that employ more than fifteen people. For child-care purposes (other than home-based care), the provisions of this act extend to just about any program, including schools and religious programs. The act applies primarily to people in wheelchairs (thus the need for handicapped-accessible bathrooms and ramps), but also to individuals with other disabilities, including hearing and sight impairments, mental disabilities, and learning challenges. The ADA includes playground access, and specific regulations in this area have recently been approved. I discuss them in Chapter 8.

Personal Experience

We all bring our own experiences to tasks we are asked to do. And this is good! Regulations, checklists, and accreditation criteria go only so far. When I evaluated the facilities in Wisconsin, I used my own experience to determine answers to these questions:

- As a parent, does this place make me feel welcome?
- As a child, can I find what I need? Do I feel comfortable? Do I feel this place is designed for me and people like me? Do I see myself, my family, and my culture in the environment? Does it feel familiar?
- As a staff member, are there places I can get away to and be on my own? Do I feel important?
- Are there bathrooms for male staff and fathers, or do I as a male have to use a bathroom where I feel uncomfortable and where I feel I don't belong?
- Is the playground a place in which a child can make choices, enjoy peers, and have new experiences every day, or is it hot, dusty, boring—indicating a poor design?
- Does the program truly understand the distinctly unique needs of children?

A good program evaluation for children is often more a function of a person's gut-level response than an objective, systematic analysis. Of course, the evaluator needs to have extensive experience with a variety of children's programs and environments. And a person's gut instinct cannot override laws, regulations, and health and safety guidelines.

Should Early Childhood Environments Be Like Home or Like School?

What should the overall feel of an early childhood program be? Should it be like a downward extension of a school—an institutional setting with hard surfaces, straight corridors, blackboards on the wall, and harsh, neon lighting? Or should it be like home: comfortable, fuzzy, familiar, somewhat disorganized, and personalized? This is a tricky question. Those who support the idea that programs for young children should be like a home express the belief that the home provides all the developmental needs of young children (Greenman, 1988): physical, social, emotional, and cognitive growth. This view also stresses that a homelike environment is important because it supports the child's cultural identity and racial and ethnic foundation. The argument for the institutional approach emphasizes the functional nature of institutional settings, which are easier to supervise and clean and often facilitate the specific educational objectives required by the program and its funding source. Like so many either–or arguments, both approaches have merit, and both have fallacies.

The major drawback with a homelike setting is the difficulty of keeping it clean, safe, and easy to supervise. A home is simply not designed for lots of children. The central problem with the **institutional approach** is that it is simply a downward extension of school buildings, partly because many people view early childhood programs as schools for infants, toddlers, and preschoolers. Further, early childhood buildings are often designed like school buildings because builders, designers, regulators, and safety experts are familiar with building schools and with solutions developed for school-age children. But the downward school approach is problematic because young children have distinctly different needs from school-age children (Wardle, 1989).

Environments That Support Children's Early Experiences

Jim Greenman (1988) has addressed the question of providing an ideal environment for young children by proposing the question, What should the child's early experience

▶ *Should an environment be like a home or an institution? The author's first early childhood environment.*

include? Greenman maintains that the early childhood experience sets the foundation for a person's entire future: joys and fears, self-image, response to new experiences, and shyness or openness to others. In answering his own question, he identifies six primary needs for children. I will use his categories to explore how a good early childhood environment can support each child's early childhood experience.

Places Rich in Experience. Children need to be able to explore and experiment. Indeed, childhood is a time when we learn firsthand about the physical world: the wetness of water, the constant pull of gravity on a falling stone, the stink of rotten fruit, the feel of concrete to a bare knee, the beauty of a sunset. Children learn all of this knowledge through direct experience.

Places Rich in Play. In Chapter 8 I suggest that, among other things, play provides a way for children to integrate the vast quantity of new experiences with their rapidly developing minds, bodies, emotions, and social skills. New brain research supports this concept by stressing how children learn best through an integrated approach—combining physical, emotional, cognitive, and social growth (Shore, 1997), and learning new skills, concepts, and information across both content areas and learning disciplines.

Places Rich in Teaching. "Children need teachers who know that what motivates children is to have their questions answered, not the teacher's. Teachers who stimulate more questions than they directly provide are truly teaching" (Greenman, 1988, p. 33). The role of the teacher is crucial in a child's life—as a confidant, colleague, model, instructor, nurturer, guider, and scaffolder of educational experiences.

Places Rich with People. Clearly children need lots of exposure to other people in their early childhood years. One of the great weaknesses of Western society is that our children are receiving less and less direct exposure to the richness and color of the local village—baker, milker, gardener, carpenter, organ tuner, bricklayer, and painter. One of my great joys as a child growing up in communities of the Bruderhof was walking over to the woodworking shop to observe Harry, our carpenter, repairing windows, carving intricate patterns, and sawing wood. I loved the smell of fresh wood, the care and deliberation of the craft, and Harry's gnarled, kindly hands and face. In traditional villages children were exposed to a diversity of adults, not just caregivers, teachers, and heroes. Young children's lives must be rich with the variability, humanity, and culture of lots of people.

Places to Be Significant. Children need to feel important. In past eras children had the responsibility to care for animals, water the garden, do farm chores, and care for other children. Children need to feel that what they do is meaningful to someone besides themselves—to the family, community, neighbor, or grandparents—and that they are contributing to their environment, not just depending on it to meet their needs.

Places to Call Their Own. A basic human need is the need to belong. We all feel more secure, comfortable, and relaxed when we return home. Adults go back to their childhood homes to discover and reinforce their roots; we all want to know about our ancestors. Children need to feel they belong too. They need to be close to people they know, have familiar and comfortable objects, and be in settings that have a personal history. "A child who attends a child care program from infancy through young school-age years will spend more time in child care than all hours of schooling, and may spend more waking hours in child care than at home. Child care centers and homes are places where childhood happens" (Greenman, 1988, p. 34).

Considerations for Early Childhood Environments

There are a number of factors that need to be considered when planning and developing appropriate environments for young children, from infancy through 8 years old. Below are some general considerations for designing, setting up, and maintaining early childhood environments (Wardle, 2001a).

Responsive Furniture, Equipment, and Materials. Young children require lots of soft, flexible, comfortable materials and equipment that can be molded to their needs. The best environments for children are ones that adapt, respond, and conform to each child's individual physical, cognitive, and emotional characteristics, rather than environments that constantly require a child to adapt to them.

Developmentally Appropriate Physical Activities. Environments should also provide opportunities for lots of developmentally appropriate physical activities. Young children are physical beings. They both learn through total physical involvement and require a high level of physical activity, variety, and stimulus change (Hale, 1994). Many argue that one of the reasons so many boys are diagnosed with ADHD is that we do not provide the level of physical activity that they naturally need for optimal development (Wardle, 1989).

Concrete, Hands-on Activities. Young children need lots of hands-on activities—playing in water, building mud pies, making things out of wood, putting dolls to bed, and constructing towers and fantastic cities. They also need a variety of ways to represent new experiences—through dramatic play, drawing pictures and taking photographs, making recordings, and using language. Young children don't need activities that require them to be still and inactive for long periods of time.

Change and Variety. Children seek out a constant change of stimuli—scenery, textures, colors, social groups, activities, environments, sounds, and smells. The longer the child stays in a program during the day, the more variation and stimulation the child needs. Boredom kills brain development; it also gets lots of kids into lots of trouble.

▶ *The indoor environment should be responsive and flexible.*

Natural Lighting. Exposure to natural lighting is desirable for young children. Large windows in every room are a godsend. The effect of natural light changing during the day is something we simply cannot reproduce with artificial lights. Enough lighting is needed for detailed and focused work, and lighting should be used to create different areas and moods in the classroom. Reflection on glass and shiny surfaces must be avoided.

Appropriate Temperature. Child-care environments should be neither too hot nor too cold. Germs and bacteria love warm, stagnant air. Overly warm environments cause children to be lethargic, sleepy, and uninvolved, so fairly cool environments should be provided so children don't get too warm and flushed when they are active. An ideal environment allows teachers to vary the room temperature in accordance with the activities of the students in each room.

The Natural World. While children clearly need to spend part of their day outside on appropriate play equipment, ideal child-care environments also provide opportunities to interact with the natural environment. Young children should develop an emotional connection with the natural world, which enables them to learn basic scientific phenomena, to enjoy and respect the environment, and to master basic knowledge needed for later school success.

Decorations. The environment for young children should reflect the importance of children by including carefully presented examples of their work and showing images of children at the child's eye level. These images should reflect the culture of the children in the program and of children throughout the world. Bulletin boards should be interactive, encouraging children to engage with the pictures and stories, add to graphs and surveys, and incorporate the bulletin boards into their learning. Decorations should meet the needs of the children, not adults—staff, administrators, or parents.

Private Space. A central challenge for early childhood programs is to respond to the uniqueness of each child within a collective environment. Issues such as ease of cleaning, maintenance, supervision, cost, and adult aesthetics should not detract from providing spaces that children feel are designed especially for them: small private areas, individual cubbies, secluded corners, lofts, and odd-shaped areas.

Child Size and Scale. This is important for all early childhood programs, but especially in environments that were not originally designed for young children (Wardle, 1989). Toilets, sinks, windows, faucets, drinking fountains, mirrors, towel racks, toothbrush containers, and bulletin boards need to be at the child's level. Also, young children need the functional areas to be close together, including the bathrooms, eating areas, playground, and gross motor area, to encourage self-help skills, integrate learning, provide a homelike atmosphere, and ease supervision. In some programs, significant distance separates the classroom from these areas.

Challenge. Richard Dattner (1969) talks about *graduated challenge;* Elizabeth Prescott about *complex* and *super-complex units* (1994; for more discussion of these terms, see the Environments and Children's Behavior section later in this chapter). Graduated challenge is the idea that materials and equipment should be able to be used in progressively more complex ways by children; complex and super-complex units are combinations of materials that have more than one use. What both emphasize is the vital notion that children who spend most of the day in a program must have more than their basic needs met. Children in full-day programs soon move beyond initial exploration of materials and equipment, and therefore require environments that are more complex and challenging.

Storage. Early childhood programs need lots of indoor and outdoor storage space. Indoor space includes everything from kitchen space for utensils and food to closets and shelves for educational supplies. The location of storage is important—the secret is to provide storage for items close to where they will be used. Thus the best storage for classroom use is in the classroom itself. With classroom storage, teachers do not need to leave their students to get or return materials, and they can creatively extend or enhance an activity with additional materials or a piece of equipment. In one building I remodeled, we created in-classroom storage by building wall-to-ceiling storage units along an entire wall of each classroom, separating the materials from the classroom with seven-foot sliding doors. Plenty of appropriate storage is essential for any well-designed early childhood program.

Infants and Toddlers

Caring for infants and toddlers in group settings is a fairly new idea. The **Israeli kibbutzim** have been doing this since the 1930s and 1940s, but larger-scale attempts are more recent. Traditionally infants and toddlers have been cared for by the family or in extended family groups; many infants and toddlers are still cared for at home. But now, increasing numbers of infants and toddlers are in our community centers and other early childhood programs.

I have already discussed how many early childhood environments are downward extensions of traditional school programs—a problem that is exaggerated when we consider the needs of infants and toddlers. Infants are children up to 12 months of age, toddlers from 12 months to 30 months (Greenman, 1988). Infants and toddlers need environments that are carefully and specifically designed to meet their unique needs.

Setting up a Classroom in a New Community Center

I walk into the new child-care center in the Research Office Park at Penn State University. It smells like new paint, carpet glue, and cardboard boxes. The setup team from corporate headquarters of which I am a member is charged with arranging all the new materials and equipment in each of the classrooms. We must determine the location of the various learning centers and choose where to put shelves, tables and lockers, cribs, mirrors, and bulletin boards, but many other decisions have already been made: size and shape of classrooms, location of bathrooms, location of carpet and tile areas in each classroom, placement of fixed storage areas, and entrances and exits. The philosophy of the program dictates things like the numbers and function of learning centers; the type of program—full-day, part-day, school-related—dictates much of the arrangement, and, of course, the infant area is arranged very differently from the room for school-age students. All the equipment and educational materials for each classroom have already been selected and purchased for us. The community child-care center will serve children from infancy to school age of parents who work for Pennsylvania State University and its conference center.

Infants

To create programs to meet the needs of infants, we need to know what babies can do. What do infants do? First, infants use all their senses to collect information about the world around them. They watch, touch, hear, mouth, grasp, reach for and knock over, smell, and taste. Second, they use their limited skills to experiment. They squeeze, drop, move from one hand to another, clap, kick, and put in and take out. Finally, they try out and practice all the new abilities and skills they are so rapidly developing, which includes sitting and pulling up, crawling, rocking, cooing, babbling, imitating sounds, interacting with others in a variety of ways, and experimenting endlessly (Greenman, 1988).

What Infants Need. Infants need environments that support and encourage all developmentally appropriate behaviors. They also need environments that support each infant's continued mastery and progress along a unique **developmental path.** Opportunities for lots of movement are particularly important, because this enables infants to see the world from a variety of perspectives, providing stimulation and interest. Many cultures recognize the need of stimulation by placing infants on the back of their mothers, who provide stimulation and variety as they perform their daily activities. This need for movement is particularly acute before infants can crawl and walk.

Infants also need interaction with one another; moreover, because they have not learned social skills and are essentially amoral regarding responsibility to others, they require adult assistance in this effort. Encouraging infant exploration of the world around them and of one another is a tremendous challenge. An infant's relationship with safe, trusting, and consistent adults is crucial in developing healthy intellectual, emotional, physical, and social growth. Thus the human environment in infant and toddler programs is extremely important: it must be an environment that responds to the infant's needs and wishes, and places the infant in the center of the program—not adults, curriculum, schedules, policies, or older children. Infants need to have the security of a trusted adult so they can explore, take risks, experiment, and grow.

Toddlers

What can toddlers do? Toddlers are preoccupied with what they can do physically, including walking down, over, under, and through; climbing up, over, under, and on top; and sliding, swinging, hanging, jumping, and tumbling. Toddlers are also intrigued by manipulating objects. They enjoy taking apart and putting together; stacking and knocking over; carrying, selecting, and examining; and collecting and dumping. Finally, toddlers are involved in the cognitive processes of ordering and rearranging, discovering and investigating, trial and error, exploring the world with all of their senses, and imitating adult behavior (Greenman, 1988).

What Toddlers Need. Toddlers are in the process of becoming mobile, autonomous, and social. They are beginning to use language and always want to test, experiment, and declare their independence. Toddlers are a contradiction, which makes working with them both challenging and rewarding. On the one hand they are pushy, extroverted, and independent, but on the other they are dependent, shy, passive, and insecure. Toddlers continually want to create the world in their unique image. We need to create an environment that supports this fickle disposition. On top of all these challenges, toddlers must also master toilet training, a task that requires complex abilities on their part and that is fraught with cultural constraints on the part of parents and caregivers.

Environment for Infants and Toddlers

As with environments for all children, environments for infants and toddlers include two central aspects: the physical environment and the human environment. Additionally—and most important for infants and toddlers—is the inclusion of parents in the care of their children in a program.

A good physical environment allows for high-quality interaction between adults and infants or toddlers, enabling adults to stay close to children while meeting their basic needs. Adults should not have to leave a child to get a diaper, or walk across the building to find food, warm the bottle, or use sinks. The placement of all needed items and materials should be clear, logical, and convenient. Further, the sequence of routines for activities like diaper changing should be clearly listed and obvious to all.

While caregivers must maintain sanitary procedures while changing diapers and toilet training, they should concentrate on high-quality **interactions** with babies during these activities, and while preparing the child to sleep and comforting or feeding the child. Adult–child interactions must be relaxed and provide appropriate stimulation and opportunities for imitation and game playing.

When infants and toddlers are not involved in eating, diapering, or sleeping, they should be placed in an environment that facilitates autonomous actions and minimizes adult involvement. Enclosed passageways, mirrors, and responsive surfaces provide opportunities for stimulus change and encourage safe risk-taking and exploration without constant adult control and intervention.

Diapering. The diapering area should be set up in such a way as to encourage a relaxed, unhurried approach, which can be achieved by placing the diapering table in the play area or in the crib room, since infants are changed before and after naps. One diaper table for six to eight children works well. A sink and a source of running water for handwashing are necessary, as wet wipes are not sufficient. All needed materials should be within easy reach of an adult standing at the table. Babies should not be strapped to the diaper table. Instead, an adult should keep one hand gently on the child at all times. Layout of the diapering area is central to safety and health, and therefore should be carefully evaluated on a regular basis.

Bathrooms. Easy access to bathrooms is an important consideration for all child-care environments, indoors or out. Step stools empower children to use bathrooms on their own, when they are able to. Another factor to consider is whether there is sufficient space within the bathroom to allow an adult to assist a child in need with ease. Having a bathroom attached to each group area is particularly advisable for young children who can't and shouldn't have to wait to use it. Child-size stools can reduce the fear of falling into the toilet for children and lead to more autonomy. Ideally there should be a bathroom stool for every five toddlers. A bathroom should have two exits to improve traffic flow, and large bathrooms do not work well; fifteen toddlers to one bathroom is a maximum.

Bathrooms must be very easy to clean. Tile surfaces on the floor and extending at least three feet up the walls make for the most practical cleaning environment. A central floor drain and a floor faucet are also very useful. Because of fluorescent lighting and hard, glossy surfaces, bathrooms can appear to be sterile, institutional settings. Use softer, more focused lighting, ambient light from windows, plants and blue-green color schemes to provide a calmer and more relaxed bathroom environment (Greenman, 1988).

Chairs and Tables. Except for eating, there really is no need for lots of toddlers to sit around a table at one time. Large tables waste lots of space, especially in toddler rooms. A variety of tables should be provided. Flexibility is the key; small tables that can be combined when needed to make larger tables are best. Tables should have adjustable legs so children of different sizes can work at them with their feet flat on the floor.

Chairs are available in many types: some easy to clean, some easy to stack, some more secure on the floor than others. Educubes are useful as chairs, stools, tables, dramatic play props, and building blocks (especially on the outside playground). Toddler chairs need to be secure and low to the ground. The Community Plaything Me-Do-It chair is great for young toddlers, because it is very sturdy and encourages independence.

Supporting Adults in Infant Programs. A good infant environment needs to support adults and to encourage them to be effective caregivers. To do so, the environment must provide seating for caregivers that enables them to meet the needs of children constructively. While laying out seating for adults would seem like a simple enough issue, a common mistake is to cluster adult seating together. Such an arrangement encourages easy social interaction among adults but is problematic for children (Greenman, 1988). Young children need to be close to adult caregivers to feel secure and independent. I remember when my children were young and my wife and I set aside specific play areas in our home for them. To our surprise, they would leave their play areas and bring their toys to play next to us. Most young children, in fact, desire the close proximity of caregivers. When adults are seated together, a bottleneck of children forms around the adults. Placing children's needs first, the best way to prevent such bunching and to distribute children more evenly throughout the environment is to separate and scatter adult seating (Greenman, 1988). The design should encourage adult–child interaction, not adult–adult interaction.

Adults working with infants must be team players who understand that babies need consistency of care, support, routine, and activity. It is essential that infants receive support, nurturing, and bonding with individual caregivers and a seamless, consistent approach.

Working with Parents. Many parents of infants are very insecure about their role as a parent and guilt-ridden about leaving their child with someone else, especially if they are first-time parents. Further, many parents simply are not sure what their relationship should be with the caregiver, while many many infant caregivers are not very secure regarding their role with parents. In the greater scheme of things, they are often viewed as baby-sitters, as opposed to educators or teachers. Infant caregivers need to be able to work well with infants, as well as communicate effectively with and support parents; they

▶ *Sleeping is an important biological function and any location devoted to sleeping should provide a comfortable, relaxing, and secure environment.*

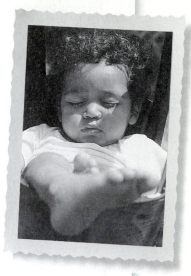

need to develop an honest and healthy partnership with the parents regarding the chlid's welfare.

Parents need to feel comfortable in the infant area. There should be a place for them to hang their coats and sit down, and a bulletin board especially set aside for parents, where they can get current information and parenting ideas. An atmosphere of welcome and inclusion is particularly vital for fathers, who usually feel alienated from the early childhood program (Cunningham, 1998–1999). Because of deep-seated cultural issues, men feel even more unwelcome in an infant/toddler area. Pictures of infants with fathers, specific ideas for involving fathers with their children, and messages for fathers (maybe even specific male-parenting classes) will help.

Sleeping. An early childhood program needs a space where infants and toddlers can sleep uninterrupted for a portion of the day. Sleeping is an important biological function, and any location devoted to sleeping should provide a comfortable, relaxing, and secure environment.

For programs that serve children of varying ages it is important to provide a separate sleeping area so that those sleeping will not be disturbed by active children, or active children will not have to be unnecessarily quiet. Separate sleep areas also allow staff to set up for the next activities while the children rest. Some programs have separate crib rooms and nap rooms; some do not. Toddlers benefit from sleeping in a smaller, more familiar space; infants excel at sleeping almost anywhere and can tune out most unwanted stimuli. Still, for programs with more than six infants, a separate crib room is a plus.

The area used should be well ventilated. Indeed, in good weather, sleeping outdoors on a transition area or under shade works well—a common practice in Europe and other parts of the world.

The surface and material children sleep on depends on licensing regulations, parental preferences, cost, and storage. A variety of cradles, cribs, and floor mats can be used, depending on the age of the children. Children should never share the same crib or mattress. Sanitation is a crucial issue, especially since young children will have many accidents while they sleep.

Toys and Learning Materials for Infants and Toddlers

In her book *The Right Stuff for Children Birth to 8: Selecting Play Materials to Support Development* (1995), Martha Bronson lists appropriate toys and materials for each age group. The book provides an extensive, even exhaustive list. I will summarize some of the general ideas, noting that each age group will add additional materials without necessarily disregarding ones by younger-age children.

Infancy through 12 Months. Infants love to follow moving mobiles with their eyes, enjoy batting and kicking at objects, and like rattles and bells. Mirrors are great because infants can stimulate themselves by moving, and a few dolls and stuffed animals work well. A collection of balls and push toys can be introduced as infants grow older.

Toddlers 1 to 2 Years Old. Added to the previous list are sand and water toys, toy cars and trucks, simple lightweight blocks, and sturdy books. Children this age love music, push–pull toys, balls and toys they can ride on—materials that capitalize on their growing mobility and expanded interests.

Toddlers 2 to 3 Years Old. At this age children are increasing their small and gross motor skills and expanding their pretend play. Add dress-up clothes and housekeeping furniture, miniature people and animals, unit block sets, and water tables. Toddlers also enjoy simple puzzles and pegboards. Simple games, stacking blocks, beads for threading, more books, and a variety of art materials should be added, along with a variety of musical instruments. However, make sure all pegs, beads, blocks, and so on are too large to choke and swallow.

Preschoolers

Developmentally, children between the ages of 3 and 5 advance in many different areas. Thus, they need an environment that provides for their social and emotional needs, their cognitive and language development, and their physical growth. Not only do preschool children learn a tremendous amount in each of these areas, but they integrate this knowledge to develop overall skills and abilities. For example, the preschool child uses newly developed physical, social, emotional, and language skills on the playground. Good early childhood environments must support this rapid, complex, and uneven development.

Environments for Preschoolers

When designing the layout of an empty preschool classroom, how should a person proceed? The list below, adapted from Olds (1982), offers some suggestions.

- Begin by identifying every permanent feature within the room—entrances, windows, sinks, bathrooms—and ask yourself how children can use them.
- List everything that will occur in the room and all the activity areas you will need.
- List activity areas that are to be multipurpose and those that are fixed—lofts, playhouses, and so on.
- Determine what changes if any will need to be made to the room during the day—for eating, nap time, gross motor activities, and other program elements.
- Determine what activities will be limited by or tied to permanent fixtures within the room. For example, since art activities are heavily dependent on water, art areas will have to be located near sinks. Consider noise from adjoining centers, traffic, messy and neat activities.

- Determine whether any considerations, such as the placement of electrical outlets and windows or the quality of lighting and flooring, make a space particularly suitable for certain types of activities.
- Place activity areas that use similar materials or have compatible requirements next to each other.
- Make sure that each activity area provides sufficient space for children. Remember that children are whole-body learners. Thus they need room to lie down and read a book, stand up and play with a newly made airplane, swing a large paintbrush, or flop onto a cushion.

As the list suggests, there is a variety of factors to consider when designing the layout of a classroom. No classroom is perfect. And good teachers will modify the layout of their classroom as they determine what works and what doesn't, and as they add new and challenging experiences for their students. The following sections further discuss some of the challenges that must be carefully addressed in setting up a preschool classroom.

Figure 5.1

Possible Room Arrangement for a Preschool Classroom

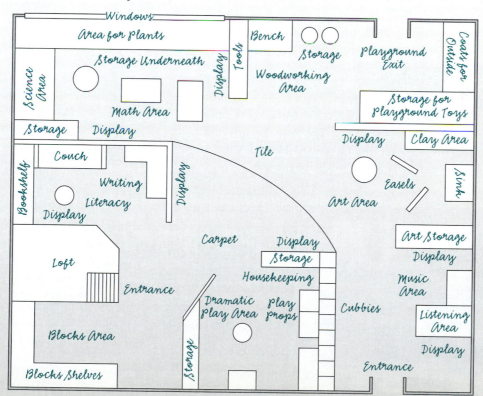

Entrances and Exits. All classrooms have entrances and exits: to the corridor, play-ground, or bathroom. Others may simply have a single entrance and a fire exit. What-ever the configuration, entrances and exits present specific challenges. Children may wait in these areas to go to the bathroom or wash their teeth, gather by the outside exit while they put on their coats, or wait by an exit to transition to another area. Areas around exits often become congested and noisy. Because of this problem, carefully de-signed displays, quiet corners, and areas where children need high levels of focus and attention should be kept away from entrances and exits. Furthermore, because exits and entrances receive heavy usage, they need to have resilient, easy-to-clean surfaces. Some programs place protective mats over carpeting by the doors.

Storage. Storage areas are a little like entrances and exits—they receive lots of traffic and are noisy, and therefore sometimes foster disruptive behavior. Storage areas need to be set up so they don't create so much congestion and noise that they disturb other children. Storage must be designed so students' materials are easily accessible by chil-dren, while materials the teacher wishes to control are stored away from children's reach. And just as storage for the staff should be close to where the items and materials will be used, classroom supplies should be close to where they will be used: art supplies near the art area; paper, pens, and crayons next to the literacy area; and blocks, trucks, minia-ture people, and animals by the block area.

Access. The classic example of access issues is the art area. Along with providing easy access to paint, easels, paper, and brushes, the art area needs to be close to a water source so paints can be mixed, brushes washed, and tables and easels easily cleaned. The closer the art area is to a water source, the better. Similarly, a woodworking bench must be close to where the wood and other woodworking materials are stored; and the reading area must be next to the bookshelves, magazine bins, and other reading supplies.

Noise. Managing noise is obviously important in a classroom. Carpet on the floor ab-sorbs noise, as does absorbent tile on the ceiling. The reading center should be next to a quiet area—say, the art center. Blocks are loud and should be located next to another loud area, such as the woodworking bench. Classrooms that have transition porches can place some of the noisier activities in these areas, which can then be moved to the out-side area in good weather.

▶ *Materials need to be easily accessible and easy to return.*

Color. There is great disagreement regarding color for early childhood classrooms. Historically schools have had drab, muted colors; I remember my high school was painted in army surplus green. Theories regarding color choices include recommending muted, neutral colors to provide even, low-key stimulation, and opposing the use of cutesy, car-toonish Disney-style decorations because these are too commercial and portray an adult's version of childhood. Some people believe the overall environment should provide a background of natural wood tones and neutral colors, to allow the children's products and activities to take center stage.

A colleague (with art and design training) and I developed an effective approach to color for a recently remodeled Head Start center. We selected a different color for each room. One wall—optimally the wall opposite the outside window—was painted in a strong, deep tone of the chosen color (blue, raspberry, aquamarine); the other three walls were painted in a very light (almost off-white) tone of that same color. Carpet and checkerboard tile in each classroom were chosen to complement the color scheme. Teachers, parents, and children really liked this solution to the color dilemma, because each classroom had an individual characteristic, and each was bright and colorful. When I left the program for a year's sabbatical, however, my boss had all the classrooms repainted in dull gray!

Bulletin Boards. Children's work should dominate all the walls of an early childhood program. The work displayed should be both finished products and works in progress, and, like the decorations in an infant and toddler area, should reflect the diversity both of students in the program and of people throughout the world. Bulletin boards in classroom musts be placed at the child's eye level; in the rest of the building they should be at different levels, depending on whether the audience is children, or parents and staff.

Cleanliness. A central concern of all early childhood environments is cleanliness. Dirty environments not only look bad but also pose potential risks for children. Bathrooms need to be easy to clean; carpeting needs to be of an industrial grade that can tolerate frequent cleaning; counter and table surfaces need to withstand a strong bleach solution; dolls and stuffed animals should be machine-washable; and plastic toys should be dishwasher-safe.

Floor surfaces also play a big part in cleanliness. For example, the entrance and exit area connecting the classroom to the out-of-doors should be constructed of durable, easy-to-clean surfaces such as tile or linoleum. The flooring area under the sand and water table, art easel, and eating areas should also be of comparable materials—or covered with a durable plastic mat. Floor space that should provide more comfort and absorb more noise must be covered in a carpet that is easy to clean and dirt resistant. Some activities, such as block play, dramatic play, and others, can be conducted on a wide range of surfaces, so long as the surface chosen doesn't trap dirt and germs and can withstand regular cleaning.

Flexibility. Teachers should be able to arrange and rearrange classrooms to facilitate the delivery of their curriculum and to personalize their learning environments as they see fit. Classrooms built as a basic shell—a generic, overall framework—easily permit teachers to modify and adapt the space to their needs. Conversely, classrooms that include permanent built-in features such as lofts, playhouses, tables, benches, alcoves, and cubbies, can severely limit the teacher's options. While built-in features can add immediate value to the learning environment, they also limit the flexibility to change (Wardle, 2001b).

Learning Centers. Many early childhood environments are organized into **learning centers** based on the program's goals and objectives. A learning center is an area designed for a few children to engage in projects and activities involving a theme or discipline. Traditionally these include art, science, writing, reading—or one literacy center—housekeeping (dramatic play), math manipulatives, sand and water table, and the block area. Some programs also include woodworking and computer learning centers. Programs need to make sure centers reflect the cultural interests of the children and that equipment in the centers includes props relevant to each child's home experiences: clothes, cooking utensils, tools, toys, artifacts, and the like. Each center is equipped with materials, tools, and appropriate furniture.

Additionally, preschool classes include activity areas—places where certain kinds of activities occur, be it play, snuggling together, listening to stories, eating lunch, doing puzzles and games, or physical activities. These areas should have clear, well-defined boundaries (fixed or temporary) and should have sufficient space for children to engage in the activity. Each area should have a particular feel that encourages specific activities and behaviors. These expectations should be reinforced through signs and pictures of appropriate behavior, lists of rules (with pictures), a system to control the number of students in an area (such as tags), and consistent reinforcement by staff.

Most of the program's planned activities are centered on these areas. A real disadvantage, however, of arranging a classroom in centers is that this approach tends to

Computer Learning Centers

As computers are being integrated into the early childhood experience, environments need to be designed and created to facilitate appropriate computer use. Haugland (1999) recommends that computers be introduced into classrooms when children are 3 years old, in the belief that computers are not developmentally appropriate for children under that age. Like other early childhood curricular issues, the environmental context greatly affects how computers will be used in the classroom.

Basic equipment. At present, standard computer configurations require a central processing unit with (sometimes) a separate monitor, mouse, speaker, keyboard, software, and appropriate desk or workstation. A large trackball-type mouse works well for younger children. A keyboard should be used only after children's hands and hand muscles become strong enough to use it. Fortunately, software for young children does not require a keyboard. Additionally, a printer and a touch screen expand the computer's use. The printer encourages children to integrate the computer into other learning center activi-

ties; a touch screen works well for students with fine-motor or eye–hand coordination challenges. With the addition of a digital camera and a scanner, children's artwork and photographs from field trips can be transferred to the computer.

Computer workstation. The computer center should be in a visible location. The monitors should be situated so they can be seen throughout the classroom (Haugland, 1997); children involved in other centers and activities should be able to interact naturally with children using the computers, while the visibility also allows the teachers to supervise the area without leaving another part of the room. Teachers should allow other children to offer assistance to a child at the computer who needs help.

The ratio of computers to young children is important (Haugland, 1999). The ratio a program should strive for is one computer for every five children. If the program has limited resources for computers, it is better to rotate two or three computers from one classroom to another each month or semester than to reinforce traditional curricular ideas of separate, unrelated content areas—language arts, science, social science, math. In Chapter 10, I provide a variety of ideas for integrating literacy activities into all the interest areas. This concept should be expanded to include all content areas and disciplines in each center. Further, children should be encouraged to integrate ideas and materials in all learning activities. For example, a child might make a sign in the writing center and use it as part of her block play; another child could build a boat in the woodworking area, then try it out in the sand and water table. The project approach discussion in Chapter 4 provides ideas for expanding beyond the learning-center focus—allowing children more input into what will be learned and experienced, and providing richer, more complex integration.

Dividers. Dividers are any physical objects that serve to delineate areas within a classroom by obstructing movement, sight, and sound. Using them, teachers can create interest areas, control traffic, and distribute children throughout the classroom. Almost anything can be used as a divider, so long as it is safe. This includes shelves, couches, easels, fabric hung from a line, streamers attached to the ceiling, folding screens, puppet stages, and more, not just equipment designed specifically for the purpose.

spread the computers out so there is only one computer in each classroom, since access to a single computer does not allow teachers to integrate the computer effectively into the overall curriculum. As with other materials and equipment, limited computer resources lead to an artificial emphasis on sharing. In such a setting, the value of a computer rises in significance within the classroom and allocating usage becomes a problem; it tends to become a reward for other activities and behaviors. A computer station should be large enough to hold all the computer equipment and to provide seating or space for at least three children. A 30-inch-long table for one computer, or 42-inch-long for two, works well. The unit must be at least 30 inches deep and its height adjustable from 18 inches to 26 inches. School-age children will require a table surface of 30 inches high. Adjustable heights are essential to prevent back pain and other physical problems. The workstation can be made of wood or steel, and requires a sturdy frame to keep from bowing under the computer's weight.

Other considerations. Computer cords should be carefully bundled with Velcro or plastic ties and kept at the back of the workstation. Locking casters allow the unit to be easily moved, while the computer monitor needs to be at the child's level. The central processing unit should be under the tabletop, preferably behind a locked door, and the unit's switch and disk slots should be protected by a locked cover or protector. Chairs should fit under the table, provide adequate back support, and enable seated children to place their feet flat on the floor when looking directly at the monitor. A separate computer lab outside the classroom, while common in schools, is not a good way to integrate the computer into all classroom learning activities.

Placement in the classroom. The computer station needs to be located next to a power source and be kept far away from water (the sand and water table, bathrooms, and so on), the glare of a window, and magnets (even those found on a science table). The station needs to be situated in a fairly quiet location that is away from heavy traffic areas.

Safety is obviously a crucial issue. Some dividers are easy to push over. The larger and heavier they are on the bottom, the safer they are, so heavy materials should always be stored at the bottom of free standing bookcases, cabinets, and storage bins used as dividers. Another solution is to attach extra legs to a divider or to fasten it securely to the floor or wall. Recently several equipment companies have introduced dividers that attach directly to storage units and furniture, providing a variety of flexible approaches to both delimiting space and providing needed storage. Ideally, dividers should be multifunctional. For example, using storage units, couches, and play furniture as dividers serves the extra function of facilitating play and learning activities. Dividers can also be used to display children's work as well as posters, pictures, rules, instructions, diagrams, and so on. Felt board, Peg-Board, and soft-surface boards that attach to the back of storage furniture, bookshelves, and block containers are also available. Mirrors can be attached in the same way.

Dividers do not need to be solid to be effective; indeed, solid dividers limit flexibility. Solid dividers or walls of more than thirty to forty inches high disrupt the circulation of air throughout the classroom and limit the supervision of children within the area beyond the divider. Latticework, fabric, blinds, wicker, bamboo curtains, and hanging plants can serve as useful dividers too. One of my teachers did a great job dividing her space with colorful fabric streamers attached to the ceiling and flowing to the floor. Fabric—like a parachute—can also be used to reduce the height of part of the room to create a cozy area.

Dividers about three feet in height are great for creating small spaces because they provide adequate separation while allowing for adult supervision. These dividers can be constructed of slotted bases of two-by-fours fastened to plywood, tri-wall, heavy cardboard, or Plexiglas; of toy chests and benches with extended backs; or of cinder-block shelving and stacked milk crates.

Lofts. Lofts are quite popular in many programs. A loft is a permanently raised area that may encourage gross motor activities with slides and a ladder, may be for quiet activities such as reading, or may be a combination of both. Some programs design and build their own, and there is also a variety of commercially available lofts. See Purchasing and Building Safe Lofts for information about loft safety issues.

In my teaching experience I have built several lofts. At PACER School in Kansas City, parents and I built a loft that was essentially a 4 × 4 × 4-foot frame covered with plywood. We cut square, triangular, and circular entrances into the cube, and children could climb in and out of it, or they could sit on the cushioned top of the big box to read or do their homework. Later I designed and built a cubical loft that was fastened to the wall using cantilever construction methods. The only entrance was by a ladder. When I taught a kindergarten class at the Bruderhof school, a parent and I built a conventional loft, with a ladder, railings, and a small lamp underneath to provide light for reading.

Tables and Chairs. Ideas for tables and chairs for preschoolers build on what I have already covered for toddlers. A variety of tables should be provided—large tables for big projects and eating; smaller tables for small group and individual activities. Again, small tables that can be combined when needed to make larger tables are best. Tables should have adjustable legs so children can work at them with their feet flat on the floor. Tables

▶ *A safe loft built by parents at New Meadow Run school.*

10 inches to 18 inches high can effectively be used by many children standing or kneeling.

Chairs are available in many types. A classroom should include a variety of chairs: stools, cubes, armchairs, rocking chairs, chairs of different heights, chairs for the computer station. Children can also sit directly on the floor or on cushions.

Bathrooms. Easy access to bathrooms is an important consideration for all early childhood environments, inside or out, and should include child-high door handles. Having a bathroom attached to

Purchasing and Building Safe Lofts

There are no federal or industry safety guidelines specifically for lofts. Before lofts are purchased or built, important safety issues should be considered. Safety guidelines can be interpreted from safety guidelines for other equipment, including those used for playgrounds (see Chapter 8).

- **Entrapment.** Any area that can trap a falling child by the head can cause **entrapment**. There should be no gaps anywhere between three and a half inches and nine inches in size. This includes steps and railings. Also, railings should be vertical, not horizontal.
- **Barriers.** The upper deck of the loft should have a barrier all the way around it except for entrances and exits. The height of the barrier depends on the ages of the children.
- **Steps and ladders.** For lofts that are more than two feet from the ground, steps or ladders should have a break or platform halfway down, so a child cannot fall the entire distance from the platform to the floor.
- **Absorbent mat.** Place an absorbent mat under the step or ladder, extending six feet in all directions, and kept clear of toys and playing children.
- **Proximity to windows.** Do not locate a loft near windows, because a child could fall out of the window.
- **Ceilings.** Lofts that are so high off the ground that tall children can push out ceiling tiles and play with electrical wires and heating

ducts are obviously unsafe. Make sure that the ceiling above the loft is solid, or too high for children to touch.
- **Supervision.** It must be easy for teachers to supervise children using a loft. Plexiglas sides or slats provide unrestricted views. The location of the loft within the room can also make a difference.
- **Durability.** Lofts need to be constructed of durable materials so that they will last, remain attractive, and not become unsafe. Carefully finished hardwoods are best in commercial lofts; softwoods can be used for do-it-yourself lofts, but they should be carefully and well finished and painted or varnished to withstand constant cleaning.
- **Furniture on the loft.** Carefully supervise children playing on furniture on the top platform of the loft, because they can easily fall over a railing.
- **Cleanliness.** Just as other toys and materials need to be easily cleaned, so do lofts. Carpeting should be removable for regular washing, and the entire loft easy to disinfect.

each group area is particularly advisable for young children, who can't and shouldn't have to wait to use them.

Most programs don't separate genders in bathrooms for children under age 5, though some ethnic and religious groups do require separate bathrooms. As I pointed out earlier, a bathroom should have two exits, to improve traffic flow, and large bathrooms do not work well. One bathroom should not serve more than forty preschoolers, or more than fifteen toddlers. If a program's objectives include toothbrushing, more bathroom space must be provided for this activity, including space for the storage of toothbrushes close to the sinks.

Bathrooms must be easy to clean. Cleanliness, lighting, and approaches to reduce the institutional feel are the same for preschool bathrooms as they are for toddler bathrooms. It is also important not to let the bathroom become a storage catchall. Avoid placing wet clothes, art materials, cleaning materials, mops and rags, poisons, supplies for the sand and water table, and so on in the bathroom.

Sleeping. Older children (preschoolers) seem to be able to sleep on almost anything: mats, molded plastic, cots, sheets on carpet, blankets on grass. Storage space for sleeping equipment is another important consideration, as is ease of cleaning. Programs that serve children who take a nap during the day must give special consideration to noise. As I discussed in the toddler section, the need for a quiet area for napping children must not infringe on other children's activities. Thus the proximity of classrooms to each other is also a crucial issue.

Toys and Materials for Preschoolers

Add to the list of materials discussed in the toddler section hand puppets, hollow (large) blocks, measuring and science materials, more materials for the sand and water table, and a wide variety of puzzles. Specific math, art, and literacy materials should be added, along with musical instruments; more complex games; a variety of gross motor materials such as beanbags, balls, and skip ropes; and fine motor materials such as strings and beads (Bronson, 1995).

Preschoolers are expanding their interests, becoming more skilled with fine and gross motor development, and are learning more specific preacademic content. Many materials are now broken into specific school-related categories: art, music, math, science, literacy, and so on.

Use of the Outdoors

In Chapter 8, I discuss the use of the outdoor playground to meet many of the developmental needs of young children. But our children need exploration and learning beyond the playground. "Two important aspects of life are shrinking in children's lives: nature, in all its transcendent, powerful glory—unpredictable, mysterious, untamed, infinite—and nearly as absent, open spaces and physically challenging spaces, places to literally take off, scale and explore" (Greenman, 1993, p. 36).

While infants and toddlers need to experience the joys and benefits of the outdoors as much as possible, preschoolers' mobility, curiosity, and cognitive abilities make outdoor activities particularly important for them. As the lives of our children become progressively more confined to classrooms and small apartments, and ever more dominated by passive TV watching and video-game playing, we need to find ways to use the environment beyond the early childhood program for children's learning.

In the past, the educational use of the community outside the school was a natural complement to schooling. Often it no longer is. Kay Stephens (1999) argues that nature is a strong contributor to a child's resilience. Children under stress often find nature to be a comforting refuge from the problems they face at home or at school. For these children nature can provide needed security, protection, peace, and quiet. Predictable patterns and cycles of nature—seasons, changing weather, cycles of growth and decline, rain and sun, life and death—relax and soothe children. They can see beauty, nurturing, and order in a world that for them has none of these. Children retreat into a world of nature and come to consider its various components as their friends. "Spending hours outdoors with nature allows children to leisurely and intimately experience nature's gifts. . . . the world of nature shelters children, blanketing them with a protective shield, helping them fend off the stress of irrational, illogical, and unfathomable adult behavior" (Stephens, 1999, p. 53).

Gardens. Gardening is a good approach to providing hands-on activities about nutrition—especially vegetables, foods many children have trouble eating. Growing and caring for vegetables in a garden develops in children an appreciation of healthy foods. At this age children are developing an awareness of food and of the relationship of what they eat and drink to their health. They begin to understand that some foods are better for them than others.

The best location for a garden is somewhere in the playground. If there is no space in the playground area, a windowsill or pot garden can be used, or the class can care for a garden in a community garden plot. A garden in the playground needs to be close to a water source, out of high-traffic areas, and away from trees that provide too much shade (most plants need at least five hours of sun each day). Raised beds work well. Leave space between gardens for children to walk; raised beds also allow children in wheelchairs to help care for the garden (Dunbar, 2001).

Soil should be carefully prepared before vegetables are planted, using a good mix of topsoil and fertilizer. Further, it is a good idea to get a local expert to help with the program—an agricultural extension professional, master gardener, or parent. Children in each class should plant seeds in seed-starter pots and place them in the sunlight to grow. The plants will sprout in a few weeks. Identify each plant with little flag, such as a picture cut out and pasted from the seed packet. The best time to transplant outside varies depending on local climate. Once the plants are transplanted, each class can take turns watering and weeding the garden. After the vegetables ripen, each class can pick enough to make a healthy snack (Dunbar, 2001).

There is a variety of easy-to-grow vegetables, and the selection depends on the geographic location of the program; they include carrots, radishes (which come up very quickly), cucumbers, green beans, lettuce, onions, peas (except in hot weather), and bell peppers. If there is enough space, corn, tomatoes, and pumpkins and other squash are also fun.

Other Outdoor Experiences. Here are a few suggestions of other outdoor experiences for preschool and school-age children:

- Firsthand exposure to wild animals carrying out their routine behaviors in natural habitats—as opposed to farms and zoos.
- Regular opportunities to interact with nature at and near the child's program, such as involvement with vegetable, flower, herb, and butterfly gardens; exploring and enjoying trees and shrubs; observing seasonal changes; watching spiders, insects, plants, decay, and the like; and experimenting with prisms and sound chimes, banners and flags.
- Parent-led interactions with a variety of local natural outdoor environments.
- Using various tools to explore the natural world: magnifying glasses, small buckets and bags, binoculars, bug cases, cameras, identification books, paper and crayons for rubbing, tools for digging, and more.

Locations for these kinds of activities may include urban walkways (Denver has a tremendous trail system that includes an irrigation canal and a river, with seasonal wild birds and animals), parks, historic outdoor museums and demonstration farms, community gardens, river embankments, and botanical gardens with trails, ponds, and various environmental zones. Wildlife refuges and bird sanctuaries are also excellent places to visit (Wardle, 1995a).

School-Age Children (through Age 8)

In some public and private schools, kindergarten children are placed with other school-age children in the "big school." These schools are often characterized by single classrooms for each age group; more institutionalized arrangements for bathrooms, hallways, cafeterias, and playgrounds; and a more structured approach to instruction. Many elementary schools, however, are adapting ideas from good early childhood programs, such as learning centers, mixed-age grouping, looping, team teaching, integration of subject matter, and creative and extensive use of the outdoors and the community. In these cases, discussions in the previous section are applicable here. The central question to be addressed in programs that serve young school-age children is whether the environment maximizes their potential learning, based on each child's development, or imposes ideas, environments, and approaches that are, at best, pushed-down concepts more effective with older children (Wardle, 1989). As states adopt increasingly rigorous standards and local districts implement those standards by pushing down academics and structure, the mismatch between what children need and their school environment increases.

Materials

Materials for this age group continue to add complexity and challenge. Additional art materials include clay and other media and a wide variety of specific skill-development materials, including printing and book-making materials. **Math manipulatives,** measuring equipment, materials for learning about money and telling time, all sorts of science materials (including those related to weather, the solar system, plant and animal

▶ *Materials in the environment need to reflect the culture of the children who use it.*

life, and basic human anatomy) and a variety of computer programs are added, along with more diverse books and literacy materials (Bronson, 1995).

Materials that enhance the development of physical skills and abilities include those required for specific sports, including basketball, soccer, and baseball, along with more challenging and advanced playground equipment.

Environments for before- and after-School Programs

Over the past ten years, programs designed to care for school-age children before and after the traditional school day have mushroomed across the country (National Institute on Out of School Time, 1998). The increase has occurred because parents are busy working or going to school themselves, and because children do not have safe, supervised places to go after school. In Chapter 2 and Chapter 8, I discuss different aspects of school-age programs.

Although school-age programs exist generally for children aged 5 (kindergarten) through 12, I will cover issues for children aged 5 through 8. School-age programs are located in public and private schools (run by the school or by contractors), child-care centers (for-profit and not-for-profit), churches, and recreational facilities, often sharing space with a variety of other, often dissimilar, programs.

School-age programs need to provide an environment that differs from the environment children left behind at school. The environment should be less structured, less academic, and less formally controlled by adults. Moreover, school-age environments should be designed to meet children's collective and individual needs and wishes, rather than the needs of teachers, administrators, and instructional objectives. The environment must appear different to children—softer, organized by interest areas, and appropriate to the children's developmental needs. Wherever the program is located, the space needs to be adapted to meet the needs of school-age children, which are very different from those of younger children. The school-age environment must receive the same level of care, attention, concern, and support given to every other environment in the building.

A well-planned environment for school-age children should be inviting, caring, organized, safe, and continually enriched with new ideas and challenges.

Creating an Inviting Space. Providing an environment that makes students feel welcome can be achieved in a variety of ways.

● Find out the interests, needs, and wishes of the students in the program by using a variety of data-collection methods, such as surveys and questionnaires.

- Collect information about students' hobbies, sports, cultural celebrations, and music preferences. Based on this information, materials, equipment, and games can be procured.
- Develop a system for students to change the environment continually to meet their needs. For example, if students need more space in the lounge area, explore how this can be achieved. A process that encourages students to bring in appropriate artwork, music, and other typical school-age artifacts should be implemented.
- Establish areas where students can influence layout and design, and other areas that will be controlled by staff only. Ask for and expect student input regularly. Fixed activity areas should also have items and materials that can be modified or changed by students. It is important for students to feel that a space is theirs and that it is responsive to their individual and collective wishes.

Fostering a Caring Atmosphere. The school-age environment can communicate to students a sense of caring, or it can communicate a feeling of neglect and inattention. Communicating a sense of caring can be done by providing the personal touch, by anything that reflects the interests or identity of the individual children—posters with children's names on them, acknowledgment of birthdays, names next to preferred activity areas, and activities that match names with interests. Preparation also communicates a sense of caring. School-age children need to have some projects planned for them every day. This should be done by asking for student input ahead of time and developing projects with the interests and ages of all of the students in mind. Since personal choice and student control are a central part of these programs, teachers must accept that not all children will choose to engage in all teacher-initiated projects.

Developing and Maintaining an Organized Environment. School-age environments need to be organized to facilitate a variety of behaviors and patterns unique to this age group, particularly an enhanced interest in social activities and group games.

Age-appropriateness. The greatest challenge for a school-age teacher is to meet the needs of a wide age range of children. The chronological age range for this group spans 5 to 8 years old; developmentally, however, this range is more like 4 to 12 years of age. The task of matching activities to such a wide developmental range is extremely difficult, but it can be achieved if the environment is carefully designed with differing developmental abilities in mind.

Materials, activities, and information for younger children should be placed at a height where children can see and reach them. Posters, bulletin boards, signs, and calendars for these children should be placed three to five feet off the ground. Bookshelves, shelves with toys and art materials, and boxes of blocks should be close to or on ground level. Moreover, because young children respond to what they see, most of these materials should be labeled with symbolic cues.

Materials, information, and interactive bulletin boards for older children should be more than four feet off the ground. Messages and signs for these children should be written in clear, easy-to-read print. Any materials or equipment not to be used by younger children should be stored high up, in cupboards with doors on them, or locked away. Because older children are bigger and need more space, make sure areas designed for older children have enough space for the activity required. An area for younger children can discourage older children's presence by placement of furniture and equipment that is too small, low, or confining for older children in the area. It is crucial that furniture in each area fit the physical size of children for whom the area is designed.

Interest Areas. We know that part of developmental growth has to do with interests and preferences. Young children like dolls, blocks, puzzles, trains, using art materials to experiment, looking at animals, and looking at picture books and simple reading books. Older children prefer to use art and craft materials to make specific things (projects), and they are very social. Older children also prefer sports, fashion, and gender-specific magazines and books.

Noise. I've discussed the issue of noise for younger children, and this issue gets more extreme as children get older (and louder). Active games cannot be placed next to homework or reading areas; the cooking area, where children argue about ingredients and what to cook, should not be placed next to an area designated for quiet and relaxation.

Mess. Cooking and art activities create lots of mess. Computers, books, homework, writing projects, and drawing activities require clean, nonmessy environments. In designing the space, make sure these issues are carefully considered.

Returning Materials. One of the best ways to keep an environment clean and orderly is to develop a system that enables children to access and return materials easily themselves. Any such system will always require some behavioral expectations of children, but layout of the environment makes it possible. First, make sure that only those materials that are actually to be used by the children are accessible to them. All other materials should be kept out of the way in an inaccessible area. Next, organize materials and equipment by activity and store them next to or in the appropriate activity area, thus eliminating the need for children to move things around to get at what they want. Equipment and material should also be stored in such a way that children won't have to disrupt the activities of others to access them. Good, clear labeling on storage areas that helps children locate and return items can make a big difference in keeping things organized. Just bear in mind that many young children cannot read well. Finally, after completing one activity, make sure children return all materials to the appropriate storage area and throw away all trash before they begin a new activity.

Creating and Maintaining a Safe Environment. Like all children's programs, school-age programs must critically address safety issues. Unfortunately, because these programs often share space with another program—say, the local school—and because they are administered by a third party, safety is sometimes compromised.

Specific environmental concerns include making sure areas are easy to supervise; providing bathrooms close to the classrooms; and assuring that playgrounds are safe, in good repair, developmentally appropriate for all the children, and contained by a fence or other barrier. While safety issues for before- and after-school programs are no different from those of other child-care and school programs, the range of children served and the diverse physical environments used for these programs make safety a particular challenge.

Keeping Areas Enriched. Here are a few tips that work to keep the school-age area continually interesting.

- Educate parents and children about items and materials that can be used in the program.
- Keep track of supplies and replace as needed.
- Set up with designated space and labeled containers for everything from table games to scrap yarn.

Environmental Checklists

There are various checklists designed to help programs evaluate their space. These include *The Early Childhood Environment Rating Scale* (1998) and the *Family Day Care Rating Scale* (1989), both by Clifford and Harms; the *School-Age Care Environment Rating Scale* (Harms, Jacobs, & White, 1995); the *Accreditation Criteria and Procedures* (NAEYC, 1991A); and *Essentials for Child Development* (1991). Below is an excerpt from a checklist for assessing space in a preschool age-program (*Essentials for Child Development,* 1991, pp. 104–107). In using the list, the observer should check "yes" or "no."

Yes	No	
☐	☐	All state and local safety requirements are met (refer to local state licensing guidelines).
☐	☐	Your space is flexible so you can meet the needs of children or adults with disabilities.
☐	☐	You can monitor children's play in an area while standing.
☐	☐	Your space is designed to encourage a wide variety of age-appropriate, culturally relevant activities.
☐	☐	Indoor areas are bright, well lit, and appealing.
☐	☐	You give each area outdoors a specific purpose: vehicle riding, swinging, climbing, sand play.
☐	☐	You assign and label each area of the room for a specific type of activity: table toys, dramatic play, blocks, reading, science, messy activities (clay, paint, water, sand), private thinking space, music, large muscle, and other appropriate categories.
☐	☐	You group quiet activities together and noisy activities together.

Yes	No	
☐	☐	You place related activities near each other: blocks and small transportation toys, for example.
☐	☐	You have enough play areas that children spread throughout the space without crowding.
☐	☐	Some areas are hard (tables, chairs, vinyl floors), while others are soft (pillows, rocking chairs, carpet).
☐	☐	You have varied areas so that some contain activities that have one use (climber and slide) while others are more complex (large hollow blocks).
☐	☐	You have made clear pathways for children to walk from area to area without walking through the middle of busy spaces.
☐	☐	Your pathways are short. You have no long hallways or empty spaces within the classroom that invite children to run and yell.
☐	☐	You frequently observe children to see how they use the space and make adjustments as children's skills and interests change.

- Establish relationships with local community businesses and solicit donations of old stock or scraps such as paper and cardboard, wallpaper, books, carpet samples, paint cards, wood, and so on.
- Keep weekly purchasing to a minimum: long-term planning is more effective.
- Get input from the children when listing needed supplies, including involving children in the budgeting process.
- Work together with other programs in the building, and check with the local licensing agency to determine equipment and materials that can be shared.

The best school-age environments provide a mixture of new, used, donated, and handmade equipment. The challenge is to keep everything organized and in good repair, and for everyone involved with the program to accept their responsibility in maintaining a safe, clean, organized environment.

Environments and Children's Behavior

When I talk to child-care workers about children who are causing problems in their class, I always advise them to examine carefully all potential environmental influences before they consider an individual child as the cause of the problem. Are there things present or absent from the environment that might trigger the child's behavior? Does the problem always seem to occur in the same place or at the same time of day or after a specific activity? The environment has a direct and powerful impact on a child's behavior.

Factors That Influence Behavior

Certain environments are more friendly to children's needs than others. Environments that match children's physical, emotional, social, and cognitive needs are much more user-friendly. Certain aspects of the environment have a direct impact on children's behaviors.

Softness versus Hardness. I have already talked about how important soft, responsive environments are for young children. A soft environment that includes such things as sand, water, grass, rugs, pillows, and the lap of a caregiver responds to a child's need. Children have more freedom of action on the yielding surfaces of a pile rug. Children can push sand around or pound clay, and these soft materials will respond accordingly. Conversely, a hard environment forces a child to adapt to its unresponsive surfaces and materials. Children who experience hard environments for a long period of time become fatigued and stressed. Furthermore, the

▶ *The environment must be carefully designed for the physical size and ability of the children who use it.*

longer children spend in such an environment, the more pronounced the negative effect (Prescott, 1994).

Open and Closed Materials and Equipment.

Open play equipment and materials are those that offer children many ways to engage with them. For example, children can use sand, water, or modeling clay in a variety of ways, depending on their maturity, ability, past experience with the material, and interest and involvement at the time. Closed materials, on the other hand, offer an extremely limited or singular mode of engagement. For example, a jigsaw puzzle has only one correct solution. Similarly, most Montessori equipment must be used in one prescribed manner. While closed equipment builds a sense of competence in children as they complete a task, it offers a very narrow range of use. Children who cannot meet the equipment's correct use requirements become frustrated, and those who can do so easily soon become bored.

The open–closed dynamics is not a fixed, either–or dichotomy, of course, but instead a continuum. Legos and Tinkertoys are a good example of material that fits in the middle of the continuum, having specific physical qualities that must be carefully followed by the playing child, but being flexible enough to encourage a wide range of creative activities. According to Prescott (1994), early childhood programs need to provide open materials, closed materials, and materials that lie somewhere between. Programs should, however, emphasize an abundance and variety of open materials and equipment because they provide children with a sense of self-control and independence in a world in which many of their actions and behaviors are prescribed for them.

Simple and Complex Units.

All toys, equipment, and materials have the potential to stimulate and maintain children's interest. Dattner has defined this impact as **graduated challenge** (1969). More recently, Prescott has used the term *complexity* (1994). Building on this idea, Prescott developed a three-tiered model for describing toys, equipment, and materials. According to Prescott, a **simple unit** possesses a single manipulative component; a **complex unit** combines two different manipulative components together; and a **super-complex unit** combines three or more manipulative components. For example, a pile of sand on its own qualifies as a simple unit. Adding a plastic shovel to the sand makes it a complex unit, and adding a bucket of water or a collection of animal figures to the sand and the shovel would create a super-complex unit. Modeling clay by itself is a simple unit; but by adding toothpicks and cookie cutters, the whole collectively becomes a super-complex unit.

Complex and super-complex units provide abundant play challenges and possibilities for individual children and groups of children. In group settings, complex and super-complex units enable all children to be involved in a variety of interesting and challenging activities without competing for the same toys and equipment. Providing complex and super-complex units challenges teachers to integrate all sorts of learning materials and equipment into children's play activities, an idea that is highly supported by the new infant brain research. Children need opportunities to use and to combine materials and equipment in a variety of ways.

Addressing Problems Environmentally

As I pointed out, lots of behaviors and other problems that surface in everyday early childhood programs can be addressed by carefully examining and then changing the environment. The following examples are summarized from the book *Planning Environments for Young Children: Physical Space*, by Kritchevsky, Prescott, and Walling (2nd ed., 1977).

Sharing. Many programs experience conflicts relating to children sharing. These are usually caused by two basic problems: not enough choices (lack of quantity) and too narrow a variety of choices (lack of quality). Prescott believes that during choice periods, there need to be about five items or activities for each child to select, and that the types of activities should differ. Variety is better than a collection of the same toy. For example, rather than provide three identical tricycles for children to play with, it is advisable to provide one single-seat trike, a two-seater, and a trike with a wagon attached to the back for carting around blocks and sand. Such a scheme promotes diversity of use.

Uninvolved Children. Bored children exhibit behavioral problems. Boredom that stems from an absence of challenge or novelty can be addressed by bringing new and more complex materials into the classroom. Boredom can also result when children are unable to focus because of interruptions or disruptions; and children can become uninvolved when the layout of their environment encourages them to float into and out of activity areas or there are large vacant spaces ideal for rough-and-tumble play. To avoid this problem, activity areas must be well defined and well protected. View the area from the child's eye level. Are there clear passageways between each area? Is each area sufficiently separated and self-contained?

Children Who Are Stuck. Some children seem to get stuck in repeating an activity and need to broaden their involvement. There are several ways to address this dilemma, including removal of the activity the child is fixated on and replacing it with another activity that is qualitatively different. For example, replace a puzzle on a table with open-ended art activities and projects from another table. A teacher can also restructure the activity: for example, if a child always plays alone in an individual activity, find ways to introduce another child into the activity in a safe and secure way. Maybe a child who plays alone with clay can be encouraged to continue playing with clay with another child or with the teacher.

Fatigue. Prescott and her colleagues have observed children who had problems after cleaning up at the end of the morning and getting ready for lunch. At the end of the morning, children often became tired, irritable, and asocial. They are also very hungry, and their blood sugar may be low. One potential solution would be to take the children to a quiet area with rugs and pillows, read to them, and let them relax before lunch.

These authors also found that children bounced back nicely after their midday nap and were ready to go for the rest of the day. They observed that adults, however, began to drag as the day wore on. To address adult fatigue, environments should provide seating for adults that permits them to continue their engagement with children without interruption (adult-only behavior and communications should be discouraged at such times). Just like children, adults in early childhood programs also need an environment that provides softness, complexity, variety, and freedom from too much intrusion.

Conclusion

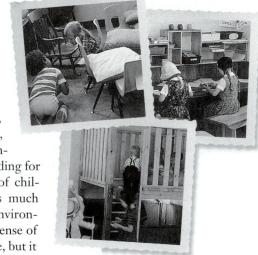

The challenge of providing environments for young children is to balance the unique and ever-changing needs of children with requirements for health, safety, and security. Laws, regulations, standards, and guidelines, along with specific program policies, exist to help programs create and maintain a level of health and safety. Providing for all the complex, developing needs of children, from birth through age 8, is much more difficult. Not only must the environments support the child's need for a sense of belonging and quest for independence, but it must nurture and challenge rapidly developing cognitive, social, and physical abilities. Further, as young children spend more time each day in early childhood programs, the need for flexibility, challenge, complexity, diversity, and responsiveness increases. Finally, because young children are so dependent on high-quality care and interactions with adults, early childhood environments must carefully consider the needs of teachers, caregivers, and parents.

Questions and Projects

1. Select a group of children between infancy and age 8—a single-age group or a multi-age group. Develop a list of appropriate toys and equipment to equip a classroom for the chosen age group.

2. Use graph paper to design a classroom environment. First decide on the ages of the children in the classroom, the length of time they attend the program each day, and the kind of program (its philosophy). Lay out learning and activity centers, tables, storage units, and other equipment based on this information. If you have access to an early childhood or school classroom (for example, a college lab program), examine its classroom for ideas. How would you design the classroom? Why? What learning opportunities do you want to enhance? Why? Maybe you could try out your arrangement in a real classroom.

3. Select a classroom equipment catalog for early childhood programs (Community Playthings, Kaplan, Environments, and Lakeshore are examples). Determine the age and number of children you are serving. Then go though the catalog and select equipment for a classroom. Include storage units, tables, chairs, cots (if needed), shelves, sand and water tables, easels, dividers, and more. While cost is important, do not consider it for this activity.

4. You are working in a low-income preschool program with few economic resources. A local business has donated one computer. Parents and teachers are enthusiastic about the children having a computer to use. What will you do? Why? How?

CHAPTER

6

Diversity *in* Early Childhood Programs

*A*merica is becoming more and more diverse. And in recent years, our view of diversity has changed. In the past we subscribed to the concept of **assimilation,** which expected all new immigrants to this country to become "American" while ignoring the uniqueness and struggles of existing minorities, such as Native Americans and African Americans. We have moved to a concept known as **pluralism,** which supports the idea that America is composed of a variety of people, each with their own values, dreams, and cultures—an approach that has forced educational programs to rethink the way they do things in an effort to ensure that every child has the opportunity to be successful. The new approach centers on the concept that a child who has a good sense of confidence and a healthy self-esteem is more likely to succeed. To this end early childhood programs are concerned with supporting each child's unique self, which includes racial, ethnic, gender, and economic status, family background, and individual strengths and personality.

This chapter explores each area of diversity—race, ethnicity, culture, gender, exceptional students, language, and socio-economic status—provides tools to help teachers meet the unique needs of these students, and discusses the role of education in providing equality for all students. Specific tools are discussed, such as an anti-bias and ecological model and a checklist for selecting educational materials. ▪

Questions to Consider

1. What are the philosophical, constitutional, and legal bases for diversity in early childhood programs?

2. What are different kinds of diversities that families and students bring with them to our programs?

3. What are different ways early childhood programs can support the unique identity of each child in their program?

4. What is a twice exceptional student, and how can early childhood programs meet the needs of these students?

5. What is diversity of diversity?

6. What procedures should be followed to make sure a student struggling in an early childhood program receives needed support and services?

7. How can technology help programs meet the diverse needs of all students?

Diversity, Equality, and Equity

As the Declaration of Independence and the U.S. Constitution reveal, questions of individual equality have concerned this country since its founding. Although equality was first reserved for white men with property, through historical movements such as women's suffrage, the Civil Rights movement, and the passage of the Americans with Disabilities Act (ADA), the concept has been expanded to include all U.S. citizens.

Traditionally, most **Americans**—both longtime citizens and new arrivals—believed that education provided the best vehicle for achieving equality. America was founded on a variety of principles, one being that success and happiness should be based not on birth or social position but on achievement. Schools are viewed as places in which all children can receive the education that will prepare them for success. Thus, diversity in our early childhood programs and schools centers on the question of equality. Does every child who enters these programs have equal opportunity to succeed? Can a poor child from the Appalachians become a lawyer? Can a recent Hmong immigrant learn the English language and American values well enough to become a doctor? What about the inner-city child, a child growing up in the Taos Pueblo in the mountains of New Mexico, or a child using a wheelchair because of cystic fibrosis?

Specific federal laws, such as the Civil Rights Act and the ADA, and Supreme Court decisions such as *Brown v. Board of Education of Topeka*, require that public schools and federally funded programs meet the needs of all children, including those with disabilities and those who do not speak English. Religious and private programs are required to meet some but not all of these laws. But beyond the law, there is our ethical responsibility to meet the needs of all of our children to the greatest extent possible.

Diversity is not only concerned with equality; it is also concerned with equity. **Equality** means that all students receive the same educational opportunities (for example, that the elementary school have a ramp for the child in a wheelchair). **Equity** means that educational programs adapt aspects of their programs to maximize the potential of every child (Banks & Banks, 1997). A program must determine the unique educational needs of each child, and then develop approaches to meet those needs. For example, for children who have a hearing disability, there should be illustrations of people using sign language in their classroom materials and on the walls, and they should be able to learn and use sign language as part of their studies. This goes beyond equality, but it is critical for the children's educational success.

Types of Diversity

Since the Civil Rights movement of the 1960s, which sought to win rights for oppressed minority groups in this country, educators have been concerned with increasing educational equity for members of a range of cultural and ethnic groups. These initial diversity efforts concentrated on children from different racial and ethnic groups, and on gender equality. Since then, however, our definition of diversity has expanded to include exceptional children (children with a variety of disabilities and gifted children), children from different economic backgrounds and religions, children whose primary language is not English, and children with different sexual orientations. Of course, there are many children in our programs who are diverse in a variety of ways.

▶*Children from diverse cultures bring a richness of arts, crafts, and music to our programs. We must find ways to capitalize on them without creating a tourist approach.*

Diversity of Diversity. Traditionally, there has been a tendency for diversity education to restrict its focus to students within each of these categories (for example, poor children, disabled children, and so on). There is tremendous diversity within each group, however—something that I call the **diversity of diversity.** Clearly, there are children with characteristics from more than one diversity areas—say, a gifted Native American girl who is poor. Furthermore, there is diversity within each category—a whole range of special needs; different kinds of giftedness; and different forms of poverty and hardships.

Under the category of racial and ethnic groups, there is also tremendous diversity. For example, within the traditional American racial category of Asian/Pacific Islanders are Vietnamese, Chinese, Filipinos, Cambodians, Hmong, Japanese, Indonesians, and Micronesians, to name a few. Historically many of the countries these people come from were bitter enemies; some still are today. A Korean student in one of my classes angrily objected to being placed within the Asian racial category because the category also includes the Japanese, a people who have traditionally persecuted Koreans. First-, second- and third-generation Americans from various nations, people with different occupations, urban and rural residents, and well-educated and blue-collar workers add to our view of diversity. Another example of diversity can be seen by looking at people who come under the black or African American category—descendants of slaves, descendants of free blacks, people with relatives from the Caribbean, recent immigrants from various African nations, and blacks from Central and South America. Maybe the group with the widest diversity is Hispanic (Latinos), who include Puerto Ricans, Argentinians, people from Central America, people who proudly trace their ancestry directly to Spain, recent Mexican immigrants, and second-, third- and fourth-generation Hispanics. And of course, all of these groups have additional diversity from a vast range of religious affiliations. While many Hispanics are Catholic, increasing numbers are not. Some American blacks are Muslims, others Southern Baptists, still others Jehovah's Witnesses, Catholics, or Quakers. Asians belong to a host of Christian, Buddhist, Hindu, or animist faiths.

Racial and Ethnic Diversity

Most early childhood teachers are white. Until fairly recently most toys and educational materials reflected white children and families in their content and pictures. For education to be equal for all children, we need to find ways to include them in everything we do. Children have to see themselves and their families in books and materials; they need to read about things familiar to them. Thus racial and ethnic diversity must be directly addressed in our programs.

Racial and Ethnic Identity.   One of the guiding principles of **multicultural education** is that children need to feel positive about their racial and ethnic heritage in order to have positive self-esteem, and children who have strong, positive self-esteem are more likely to succeed in academic pursuits and social interactions than children who don't (Ogbu, 1987). Young children, be they black, Guatemalan, or Navajo, need to develop a sense of pride and belonging in their group identity.

William Cross has studied the issue of self-esteem and positive racial identity (1987). While his work has focused on black children, I also believe his concepts work well in explaining how all children develop positive self-esteem in a world that is often hostile to them. Cross divided self-concept (positive self-esteem) into two distinct components: **reference-group orientation** (RGO) and **personal identity** (PI). Reference-group orientation includes racial identity, group identity, race awareness, racial esteem, and racial self-identification. Personal identity includes self-worth, self-confidence, personal traits, and interpersonal confidence (Cross, 1987). According to Cross, both of these components come together to make up a child's self-concept.

Although many have assumed that children with a high personal identity must also have a high reference-group orientation, Cross's studies show otherwise. For example, a black adult with a very high self-concept may not necessarily have a strong affiliation with the black race or be active in issues relating to black culture, politics, or social struggle. Conversely, a Hispanic adult actively identifying with Hispanic political and social struggles does not necessarily have a high personal identity (Cross, 1987).

What does this mean? Studies have shown that black children raised in white adoptive homes have few personal identity differences from black children raised in black homes (McRoy, 1981; Shireman & Johnson, 1980). While these children do not have a reference orientation to the black group, they have one to a different reference-group. According to Cross, a child's healthy and supportive reference group orientation—the reference group—will differ from child to child. For example, a biracial (black and white) child will have a different reference group from a black child (Wardle, 1999e); a black child in an adoptive white home a different RGO from a black child raised in a black home; and a Vietnamese child raised in America by Vietnamese parents a different RGO from that of a Vietnamese child raised in Vietnam (Cross, 1987).

Development of Racial Identity.   Diversity education recognizes that children's racial and ethnic backgrounds affect the set of experiences children bring with them to early childhood programs and require teachers to understand these differences to teach these children effectively. But how do children develop a sense of racial and ethnic identity? And how do children develop a sense of which ethnic and racial group they belong to? Finally, how do children realize they belong to a different race from other children in their neighborhood, school, and classroom?

Development of racial and ethnic **self-image** appears to be very similar to development of gender image (Aboud, 1987). Young children have to learn what it means to be a boy and what it means to be a girl, including a concept known as *constancy*, which is the idea that a characteristic like gender or race remains the same despite changes in external features such as clothes, hair length, occupation, and where someone lives. Before children learn gender constancy, they believe a woman is someone who has long hair, wears a dress, or works in a gender-specific job. A man on the other hand wears pants, has short hair, or is employed in typical male occupations. Children learn the concept of **racial and ethnic constancy** in the same way. For example, they learn that skin color does not wash off after a bath. It appears that the recognition of characteristics similar to and different from one's own occurs several years before children view themselves as members of a particular racial or ethnic group.

One interesting aspect of children's development of racial and ethnic constancy—their own and that of others—is that this identity is not always based on physical characteristics or government racial and ethnic categories. English and French Canadian children define themselves in terms of their language; black children in terms of skin color and hair; Chinese children in terms of eyes, food, and language; and Native American children in terms of possessions and activities (Aboud & Christian, 1979). Recognizing physical differences among children from different racial and ethnic groups is particularly prominent in children 8 to 12 years old, and more so for black children than for white children (Katz et al., 1975).

In viewing the development of children's ethnic and racial self-identity, it is important to recognize that as children develop their ethnic identity, it is perfectly natural for them to "try on" the identity of children from racial and ethnic groups other than their own. When I taught kindergarten in an all-white school, one of my kindergarten children painted her face brown. When asked by her parent why she did this, she said she wanted to be like RaEsa (my youngest biracial daughter). Black children in predominantly white schools and surrounded by white media images have shown a preference for white dolls. Black children adopted into white homes have said they want hair and skin like their adoptive mother's. These children are experimenting with the idea of racial and ethnic constancy, just as little boys will put on makeup, dresses, and a necklace to experiment with gender identity. Also, according to Aboud (1987), what may appear to be childhood prejudice against children who are different may be not so much a reflection of deep-seated prejudicial attitudes as it is a reflection of the cognitive and perceptual limitations of young children. Young children's ability to categorize and conceptualize is very primitive and limited.

Multiracial and Multiethnic Children. A child of two English parents, I grew up on a farm in the English border country next to Wales. I attended infant and early childhood programs provided by the religious community in which my parents were members. Later I attended the community

Development of Racial and Ethnic Identity

Learning a sense of racial and ethnic identity is a complex developmental process. In this country, children progress through the following stages (Aboud, 1987):

- **Infancy:** Children can discriminate between dark and light stimuli, dark and light faces.
- **Ages 3 to 4:** Children can recognize black and white children, but not their own racial or ethnic identity. Children are very interested in physical similarities and differences.
- **Ages 5 to 9:** Children learn to recognize their own racial identity label and develop beginning awareness of group affiliation. Awareness of group belonging comes after learning group similarities.
- **Age 7:** Recognition by white children of a black child, black children of a white child.
- **Age 8:** Recognition by children of other ethnic groups (Native American, Asian, Hispanic). Apparently, the salient features of these groups are less clear to children than those of white and black children.
- **Ages 8 to 10:** Develop racial or ethnic constancy, and a stronger sense of group belonging.

▶ *The increase of interracial marriage is resulting in more multiracial and multiethnic children in our programs. Ruth Benjamin Wardle and Francis Wardle. (K. McNeil)*

school, which focused on outdoor education, arts, and academics. In 1964 I came to the United States, where I finished high school and attended college. In 1974 I met my wife, who grew up in Kansas City, Missouri, attended Catholic schools, and spent summers in rural Oklahoma. When we met she was attending college to become a teacher and I was teaching in a small private, alternative elementary school.

Although our backgrounds are similar in many ways, most people first notice that I am white, and my wife is black. And when people first meet our children, they immediately notice

View of Race Differs from Country to Country

Jefferson Fish's daughter is black. She has a boyfriend in Brazil. When Mr. Fish's daughter travels to Brazil to be with her boyfriend, she is no longer black. How come (Fish, 1992)? Biologically, Fish's daughter is biracial—she has a black parent and a white parent. But in America, anyone with any black heritage is considered black—a concept that has become known as the **one-drop rule** (Daniel, 1992). In Brazil, however—a country with a similar history of slavery to ours but a very different approach to racial categories—Fish's daughter is considered *morena.* "A morena has brown or black hair that is wavy or curly but not tightly curled, tan skin, a nose that is not narrow, and lips that are not thin. Brazilians who come to the United States think that a morena is a brunette" (Fish, 1992, p. 1). Brazilians consider morenas to be within the government's broad racial category known as brown, which includes a range of people with mixed racial and ethnic heritage.

This story illustrates an important concept of race and ethnicity: they differ from country to country. For example, many in this country believe the Maya of Guatemala are Hispanic, because Guatemala is primarily a Hispanic country and Spanish is the official language. In this

country, Hispanics speak Spanish and have a history of oppression; in Guatemala, however, Maya speak their own language and are oppressed by the Latino ruling class. They do not consider themselves Hispanic. And—while many from the United States believe that everyone who lives in South America is Hispanic, Brazilians view themselves otherwise because they speak Portuguese; their cultural history is from Portugal; and Spain, which once ruled Brazil, is considered a historical enemy.

The point is that different societies have different ways of categorizing people, which confirms that race and ethnicity are not biological terms but social and cultural ones. One cannot ascribe unique physical and behavioral characteristics to people in specific racial and ethnic groups. There are black people with blond hair and blue eyes; there are white people with dark skin and dark eyes (Hispanic, Asian Indian, and so on). Further, as society changes, these terms will change. In the 1990 U.S. census, more than 9 million people filled in the "other" category, believing that traditional census categories did not adequately describe their heritage and identity. And in the 2000 census, 6.2 million people selected more than one racial or ethnic designation.

their mixed heritage. Other children are also confused by our children and ask questions such as, "Well, what are you, anyway, white like your father, or black like your mother?" In this country even children are preoccupied with race and racial labels (Wardle, 1999e).

Multiracial and multiethnic children are children whose biological parents cross traditional U.S. racial and ethnic lines to have children. The most obvious example of multiracial children are children with a black and a white parent; but these children embody a wide range of combinations: black and Hispanic, Native American and white; Vietnamese and black, and so on. Multiracial and multiethnic children also include foster and adoptive children, as well as children in blended and single-parent families. Finally, these children include those of parents who are themselves multiethnic or multiracial. Children of mixed heritage expand our view of diversity. What are they: black, white, Hispanic, Native American?

According to Root (1996), the numbers of multiracial and multiethnic babies are increasing faster than single-race babies in this country. Since 1989 there have been more than one hundred thousand biracial babies (black and white) born every year in this country, a total of more than one million first-generation biracial infants having been born since that date (Root, 1996). This increase in biracial children also applies to racial and ethnic combinations other than black and white.

As I have already discussed, in America anyone with any black heritage is considered black. Further, anyone with a white parent and a parent of color is given the identity of the parent of color (Daniel, 1992). Today some parents of multiracial and multiethnic children still follow this approach; others raise their children as a human beings with no racial identity, or with membership in the human race; and still others let their children decide on their racial and ethnic identity when they are old enough to choose. Additionally, a growing number of interracial parents (both biological and adoptive) are raising their children as multiracial or multiethnic.

Many psychologists believe that multiracial and multiethnic children have particular difficulty determining their racial and ethnic identity in this race-conscious society (Bowles, 1993; Gibbs, 1989). Also, more and more experts believe that children who identify with both parents' heritages at an early age will have fewer identity problems as they grow older (Cruz-Janzen, 1997). When our eldest daughter was 4 years old, she came home one day after a fight with her friend Jose, a boy whose family had just moved to Kansas City from Mexico. In the heat of the fight, Jose told Maia she was black and he was not. "How come I'm black and he's not, when he's darker than me?" Maia asked through her tears. We then realized we had to deal both with the negative stereotypes about black people that Jose expressed, and with the issue of our daughter's racial identity. We decided to raise our children with a label they could use to identify who they are (biracial or multiracial); appreciation of and pride in both sides of their background; and lots of discussion about, exposure to, and interaction with all forms of diversity.

Multiracial and multiethnic children and families challenge early childhood programs' approaches to diversity because these children cannot be placed within a traditional racial and ethnic category. Moreover, little is known about this population, so there is almost no information to help programs meet their needs. Interracial and interethnic parents are often unsure themselves about how to raise their unique children, and therefore they look to the early childhood program for help, advice, and support.

And, there are almost no commercially available classroom and curricular materials—books, dolls, people sets, family posters—to help support multiracial children's identity development.

Culture and Diversity

Culture is another important diversity issue. Culture is about values and transcends race, ethnicity, national origin, group belonging, language, or religion. Values are the rules we use to conduct our daily lives. Cultural values shape how we raise our children, expectations for boys and girls, educational goals, the importance of religious beliefs and ceremonies, and roles and responsibilities of family members and community leaders. Many of these values come from religion; others come from traditions held by a large group or subgroup of people; and still others are passed from generation to generation within individual families and extended families.

The United States is made up of many cultural groups with different values. Along with the mainstream American values of the majority, there is a host of other value systems held by members of various communities. For example, mainstream American values focus on individual rights and responsibilities, along with personal independence and aspirations. Yet I was raised in a communal religious society that stressed communal decision making, group identity and loyalty, and suppression of individual needs to the welfare of the group. This religious community also had strict rules about dating, educational expectations, and attitudes about money and private possessions. When I left the community, I struggled with conflicts between the values with which I was raised and mainstream values and attitudes.

While mainstream American values originated in the northern European traditions brought by its founders (other than the Native American nations), America has become a unique cultural entity. These mainstream American values, and the values held by any of the subgroups within this nation, are dynamic; that is, they change over time. People who belong to a distinct group within the overall American culture are, of course, also American, which means they subcribe to many of the mainstream values and may experience a conflict between some of these values and others originating in their subgroup. As a young Hmong student said, "One of the worst problems for a Hmong kid is being in a situation where you have to decide if you're going to respond as a Hmong or as an American. . . . When I go to school I am an American. But soon as I walk in the door at home, I'm in a different world" (Podeschi & Xiong, 1994, p. 9).

Teachers of children from diverse backgrounds need to be very sensitive to the values of their student's parents. What are their specific values? For example, are parents comfortable coming to the center when they have questions or concerns? Are some of the values of the center different from those supported at

▶ *Children who recently immigrated to this country experience considerable culture shock. They are not always sure where they belong.*

Developmentally Appropriate Practice

home? For example, does the center have the same expectation of both boys and girls, yet the home treats them differently? And if there is a conflict between home and school values, what should the program do? The program must decide which aspects of the program philosophy (values) cannot be changed and which ones can be adapted to match parents' values. What makes this particularly challenging is that many programs serve parents who hold a variety of values between themselves.

When conflicts between a family and the program exist, care must be taken to determine the source of the conflict. There is a tendency automatically to ascribe these differences to the race, ethnicity, language, or national origin of the family. There is also a tendency to generalize values from one family or person to all members of their racial or ethnic group. Both of these temptations are to be avoided, because they can reinforce stereotypes, perpetuate inaccuracies, and limit expectations for all of our children. I have developed an anti-bias and ecological model to help educators consider individual family's and children's values and expectations as they tailor their program to meet the needs of everyone who uses it. This model is discussed later in the chapter.

Food. One of the ways cultural differences show themselves is through food. This is probably because eating food is such a social activity. Recently my wife and I had an experience that illustrates this point. We were invited to lunch by the parents of one of our daughter's friends, a young girl enrolled in my daughter's middle school. Because she had recently come from France and therefore knew little English, this girl was paired with my French-speaking daughter as her mentor. The girl's family originally came from the island of Madagascar, which was a French colony (the two girls looked identical!). The family invited us to lunch on a Saturday. Luckily we had not overly scheduled the day with our usual soccer and track-meet appointments, as the lunch lasted three hours! There was an appetizer, a salad, several main courses, and dessert. We drank coffee, water, and wine, all enjoyed in a leisurely atmosphere of conversation about cultural differences, national customs, and family matters.

Different cultures emphasize different meals. In England, our big meal was breakfast— oatmeal, fried eggs, bangers (sausage), fried bread, fried potatoes, and fried tomatoes. In Brazil breakfast is a light meal of cheese balls, black coffee, and various fruits; the big meal there is lunch, which is followed by a siesta.

When Euro-Disney opened in France, it was very unsuccessful, partly because Disney did not take into account that Europeans sit down to eat their meals at a leisurely pace. The Disney concept requires that people be willing to stand in line to get food, eat on the run, and move through their parks in a short period of time. They make their money serving as many people as they can as quickly as possible.

Language. Cultural differences also include differences in language usage. Recently, I traveled from my home in Colorado to western Pennsylvania and West Virginia. In Colorado, mountain streams are called gulches, while in Pennsylvania and West Virginia they are called runs. In Colorado, mountaintops are called peaks; in West Virginia they are knobs. These regional differences can also be found in the Spanish language used in California, Texas, New York, and Puerto Rico. Black Africans raised in the West Indies or former British colonies in Africa have British accents and very different language usage from Africans raised in former French colonies, who have French or Creole accents. Adolescents separate themselves from adults through their unique use of language; different adolescent subgroups separate themselves from one another by using their own vernacular and slang.

Obviously, people from different countries have different languages, and ethnic groups have specific languages that are part of their culture: Hispanics, Chinese, Japanese, Brazilians, Germans, Poles, Italians, and so on. In Chapter 11 there is an extended discussion of different ways to accommodate and support children and families that do not speak English. As America becomes more diverse, issues relating to non–English-speaking children in early childhood programs will increase.

Gender

During the early childhood years, children develop gender identification: their understanding of what it means to be a boy or a girl, a man or a woman. And because young children are concrete learners, they try on these new ideas. Thus we often hear children saying things like "You can't play on the woodwork bench, because it's for boys," "Boys don't play in the housekeeping area," or "We only want boys in our game." One of our challenges is to help children develop secure gender identification without learning these gender prejudices.

There is a large amount of research showing that parents respond differently to sons and daughters, and reinforce traditional gender roles and stereotypes (Ban & Lewis, 1974; Will, Self, & Datan, 1976). Because many teachers are parents, it is logical to assume that they also reinforce these stereotypes. And because most early childhood teachers are women, they tend to feel more comfortable with girl's play, behaviors, and styles of social interaction than with boys' rough-and-tumble play and aggressive behavior (Hale, 1987; Johnson, Christie, & Yawkey, 1999). There is a temptation for programs to provide a dual curriculum: one for girls and one for boys; this results from differences in curricular materials, classroom activities, adult expectations, and the ways teachers respond to boys and girls. Girls are encouraged to talk about their feelings when depressed, seek comfort from adults, and provide support and comfort to others. Boys are expected to redirect their feelings into activities and to handle problems alone. Teachers tend to respond more negatively to boys and favorably to girls (Kontos and Wilcox-Herzog, 1997), and to communicate their expectations to the children ("Sarah, you are upset because your mother just left? So let me hold you," "Johnny, why don't you go and play with the trucks so you can forget that you are upset").

Boys seem to be harder to handle than girls. When I was a Head Start director, I struggled with the reality that my teachers, who were women, showed a preference for having girls in their classrooms. They felt boys were more difficult to manage than girls, and referred far more boys than girls to the disability coordinator for special-education screening (Wardle, 1991). Added to this dilemma, many boys in our early childhood programs come from single-parent homes headed by females, and most early childhood educators are women (Wardle, 1991). Our different expectations mean boys are allowed to fight and girls are not; girls are often expected to help clean up the classroom, while boys are excused, and teachers provide nurturing to girls, yet they expect boys to function independently.

Teachers of young children need to be very conscious of how they respond to boys and girls. They must carefully examine their expectations, behaviors, interactions, and responses. Specifically, teachers need to examine whether they expect boys to play in the dress-up area and girls in the woodworking area, and whether they are as comfortable sitting on the ground in the block area building a futuristic city as they are working with children doing a puzzle on a table. Here are some ideas to help address gender differences (adapted from Wardle, 1987):

- Add all sorts of props to the dramatic or fantasy play area, and allow all students to play out their experiences and fantasies. (I prefer the term *dramatic-* or *fantasy-play area* because I feel the term *housekeeping area* dictates the kinds of props that are included). Some of these added props include hard hats, tools—and a tool box, phone books, and a briefcase.
- Add props to the block area to increase the variety and range of play. These might be dolls, animals, miniature people to suggest miniature fantasy play, and art materials to encourage children to make doors, windows, store signs, and advertisements.
- When weather permits, move some dramatic play to the outdoor area.
- Help children select learning centers they usually avoid, for whatever reason. This might require you to model involvement and enjoyment in that center. When I was a Head Start director, I noticed that the woodworking benches in the classroom were being used for everything except woodworking. I asked teachers why the woodworking area was not being utilized, and they told me they were uncomfortable making things out of wood. So our next training day was spent learning how to make things on the workbench, which resulted in teacher involvement with children at the workbench, and more student participation in woodworking activities.
- Make sure you encourage children to use all of the learning centers and to engage in a variety of activities. For example, if a girl wants to play in the block area and another child says, "You can't play there, that's just for boys," respond with something like "No, it's not—it's for everyone, and I like to play with blocks, too!" Invite a reluctant boy to play with you in the dramatic-play area. Modeling works wonders.
- Include books, posters, artwork, and other curricular materials that challenge and contradict stereotypes.
- Challenge children's own stereotypical thinking. "Only girls play in the housekeeping area" should cause a response such as, "That's not true. My husband has great fun cooking in our kitchen."

In our society we often expect boys to be interested in science and math, and girls in art, dance, music, and literacy. Many of our teachers hold these same expectations of boys and girls. We must make sure to counteract these expectations. This starts with awareness and is followed by specific teacher behaviors and modeling. If we choose a child to show how a math problem is solved or to explain a scientific phenomenon, we must make sure we don't always call on the boys. When asking a child to read to the whole class, we must make sure we ask boys as well as girls.

Because we are products of a culture that still treats girls and boys differently, we must be ever vigilant. Certainly, girls and boys are different in many ways. But our responsibility as early childhood educators is to make sure we do not limit their learning because of our expectations and behaviors.

Exceptional Students

Gifted Students

As our concept of diversity has expanded, it has broadened to include gifted students, because these students are often very different from other students and have their own distinctive needs (Clark, 1997). Most definitions of gifted students place them in the "exceptional student" category—meaning that they have educational needs not normally met by traditional educational programs. "Gifted children mean those persons . . . whose abilities, talents and potential for accomplishment are so outstanding that they require special provisions to meet their educational needs" (State of Colorado, 1994). Gifted students exist in every racial and ethnic group.

Giftedness used to be considered a characteristic, set at birth and maintained throughout life. Many believed that gifted students did not need any specific programs—that their giftedness would enable them to succeed in any learning environment, including ones that did not meet their needs (Clark, 1997). It is now believed, however, based on extensive research and the number of gifted students who fail, drop out, or underachieve in school, that gifted students are those born with a potential that must be nurtured, challenged, enhanced, extended, and supported by their environment—both at home and in school (Clark, 1997).

Gifted students used to be considered students with high ability and potential in cognitive areas—usually standard academic subjects. The definition of *gifted* has expanded, and now the concept includes students with high abilities in one or more of these areas: cognitive, affective, intuitive/creative, and motor/physical/sensory expression (Clark, 1997).

Characteristics of Gifted Students. Specific characteristics indicate giftedness. While we look at some of these characteristics, it is important to remember that no child exhibits all of them and that there is as much difference among gifted students as there is among other students. For purposes of organization, these characteristics are placed under Clark's categories of giftedness, which she bases on functions of the brain (1997).

- *Cognitive* (makes advanced use of language, learns new information easily, understands advanced abstract concepts, is a classic linear thinker, and is concerned with justice). Such children use advanced vocabulary at an early age, talk a lot, and ask lots of questions. They also know a lot about many things, acquire new information very easily, and balk at learning by drill. They love to argue, solve puzzles, and engage in higher-order thinking activities.
- *Motor/physical/sensory expression* (shows advanced ability in physical activities, dance, and drama; uses all senses to learn about the world and to create reality). These children pick up physical and dance skills without instruction, invent new techniques, and are responsive to multisensory approaches. They also see minor details in products and performances.
- *Intuitive/creative* (is highly creative, and sees things from a unique perspective; has the ability to learn and understand entire concepts in one session). These children use all sorts of materials in highly creative ways, love variety and

▶ *Gifted students need to be encouraged to solve problems in diverse and nonlinear ways.*

novelty, and have a vivid imagination. They have a strange sense of humor and do not seem to learn in a sequential, logical pattern.

- *Affective* (has a high level of emotional and affective functioning; this category involves feelings, working with others, and learning social abilities). Leadership giftedness falls under this category. These children enjoy organizing and leading groups, take risks, and seem overly cocky. They also like to make decisions, and they synthesize diverse and complex information easily.

Needs of Gifted Students. Because gifted students have unique characteristics, they also have unique learning needs. While all students have some of these same needs, gifted students show more extreme examples. Some of these needs have to do with advanced acquisition of basic skills, but many involve different ways of accumulating information and solving problems; further, some of these areas address deficiencies of gifted students, such as their difficulty working with other children, perfectionism, and difficulty coming to grips with their uniqueness. Below is my summary, based on Clark (1997), of some of the unique needs of gifted students:

- access to challenging curricula;
- freedom to explore ideas as deeply as they wish and to discuss these ideas in depth;
- encouragement to solve problems in diverse ways and in a nonlinear, nonlogical fashion;
- opportunities to apply knowledge in real situations;
- opportunities for planning their own learning, developing frameworks and strategies for problem solving and data gathering, and devising ways to evaluate their learning;
- opportunities to know themselves and their needs, to clarify their own feelings and expectations, and to use personal values as motivation for learning;
- opportunities for integrated learning and higher-order processing of all content;
- opportunities to learn with gifted peers, and guidance in developing specific social skills and leadership abilities.

Early Childhood Programs for Gifted Students. A developmentally appropriate early childhood program that lives up to its goals will meet the needs of gifted students (Bredekamp & Copple, 1997). But many of our early childhood programs are not developmentally appropriate (Dunn & Kontos, 1997) and with an increased emphasis on standards, there is a tendency for some programs not to meet the needs of gifted children. Providing programs for gifted students does not mean simply increasing the quantity and difficulty of academic tasks, which is the easiest and most common approach.

According to Parke and Ness (1988), four ideas should be kept in mind when designing a curriculum for young gifted students: (1) activity choices should focus on explorations, manipulations, and play; (2) children should be involved in the curriculum, both in decision making and in learning to take responsibility for their learning; (3) the curriculum should focus on and reflect the unique needs and interests of each child; and (4) the program should provide for the special learning needs of gifted students, which include faster-paced learning, greater insight, and broader interests than other children their age.

Activities should be project-based, integrate information from a variety of traditional disciples, encourage extensive in-depth learning and conceptual approaches, and support problem solving and higher-order thinking. Classroom approaches must also nurture creative development—artistically, musically, and in creating cognitive patterns. Furthermore, approaches should capitalize on gifted children's need to make learning personally meaningful.

Optimally, a program for gifted students up to the age of 8 would include mixed-age groups, mentoring by experts in specific fields and older students, lots of open-ended activities, integrated and project learning, use of the community, a web approach to curriculum (often based on large thematic concepts), and interdisciplinary activities. Drill, repetition, rote learning, and learning out of context should be minimized.

Minority Students in Gifted Programs. Minority students are underrepresented in gifted programs, and there are many reasons for this inequality. Many educators believe that minority students simply won't be gifted, and parents of these children are often not aware of the characteristics that define their children as gifted or that special programs exist. Further, most schools rely on IQ tests to identify gifted children, and minority children score poorly on these tests because of a variety of **cultural biases.** Another problem is that by the time many schools identify their gifted students, some minority students are already identified as having special needs. Also, early childhood programs that serve minority students tend to use traditional, skill-based teaching methods, which don't meet the needs of gifted students. Finally, most programs for gifted students cost far more money than low-income families can afford (see Hope Gifted Program for Inner-City Children in Chapter 2).

Children with Disabilities

For most of the history of this country, children with disabilities have experienced isolation, segregation, misplacement, misdiagnosis, and poor-quality education in our schools and early childhood programs. Students with a vast range of special needs were often thrown together in one room, with minimal stimulation, programming, or instruction. More often, students were systematically excluded from regular classrooms simply because they were different from children without disabilities. In many cases, children with special needs received no education at all.

All of this changed with the passage of the Education for Handicapped Children's Act (1975), later renamed the Individuals with Disabilities Education Act (IDEA; 1990). The law covers children from infancy to age 21, emphasizes several key concepts, and, like most diversity legislation, is based on individual students' right to a free, appropriate education. One of the law's premises is that the best way to educate children with disabilities is through a concept called a **least-restrictive environment,** which means regular class placement must be considered seriously before any other placement is made for children with special needs. In this section of the chapter, the terms *children with special needs, children with disabilities,* and *children with developmental delays* will be used interchangeably.

All students with special needs must have an **Individual Family Service Plan** (IFSP; infancy through age 2) or an **Individual Education Plan** (IEP; ages 3 to 21). According to Wolery and Wilbers (1994, p. 30), the IFSP must include:

- a description of the child's present level of development in physical, cognitive, communicative, socioemotional, and adaptive behavior;
- a description of the family's resources, priorities, and concerns related to enhancing the development of the child;
- major outcomes, criteria, procedures, and timelines for the child and family goals;
- a description of early childhood intervention services necessary to meet the child's and family's needs;
- dates, intensity, and duration of services;
- the name of a service coordinator who will help families gain access to needed services;
- a transition plan to assist the child and the family in their move from infant and toddler services to preschool services;
- a description of the natural environments (e.g., homes, child-care centers) in which early intervention services will be provided.

An IEP is written for children aged 3 and older. It is far more program-specific than an ISFP, but it retains the basic focus of serving the child in the least-restrictive environment, and parental control of the process. The IEP must include (Wolery & Wilbers, 1994)

- the child's present levels of educational performance in every area;
- annual goals of educational performance to be achieved by the end of the school year;
- short-term objectives that lead to achieving the annual goals;
- the specific educational services needed, including the kind of program needed and adaptations required;
- the length of time services will be required;
- the extent to which the child will be involved in regular education programs;
- a justification for the type of educational placement the child will receive;
- those individuals responsible for implementation of the program;
- a way to determine whether short-term objectives are being achieved—at least on an annual basis.

Both the IFSP and the IEP are developed by specialists, school staff, and the parent(s). These plans are based on the student's needs—not curricular outcomes, academic standards, or school goals and objectives. A child with special needs might have some objectives similar to classmates, while others might be radically different. Of all the diversity areas addressed in this chapter, the education of children with disabilities has the most specific and clear-cut legal requirements. The courts have held educational programs accountable to fulfill the IFSP and the IEP. Central to IDEA is the role of the parents (or legal guardians). Every step of the process—from initial screening, participation, and approval of the IFSP or IEP to eventual programs and adaptations—must be approved by the parent.

When my son, Kealan, was in the early grades, we had him carefully diagnosed in an attempt to determine why he struggled with some of his academic activities. After it was determined that he had a specific learning disability that resulted in barriers to his learning to read, write, and organize material logically, we attended a meeting with his teacher and other school professionals—including a psychologist, a special education teacher, and a nurse—to go over all the test results and to develop a plan to address his academic and organizational needs. The meeting is called a staffing, and results in the IEP; an annual staffing to review the child's success, and adjust educational goals if needed, is also required.

Kealan's initial testing, staffing, and development of the IEP occurred while he attended the private Denver International School. Like most private schools, this school did not provide services for children with special needs, so we worked with the local public school to develop a plan and implement his program. Every week Kealan walked from his school to the public school to receive one-on-one help from the special education teacher. Public schools are required by law to serve the needs of all students who have disabilities, even when they attend private, religious, or home schools.

Children who are not yet school age receive services by going through a process called Child Find, which determines the child's specific disability, then recommends a community agency that can meet the child's needs. Child Find is made up of early childhood providers and special-needs experts. Young children with special needs should also receive services in the least-restrictive environment, which means that for children in a regular child-care program diagnosed with a special need, the first option is to find ways to serve them within their original program. Of course, all such decisions ultimately are up to the parent.

Definition of a Special Need or Disability. There are various definitions of special needs, depending on the program and age of the students. For example, Head Start's categories are different from those used by the public school. Public-school categories are based on whether the disability affects the child's learning; Head Start's are much broader. Severe dental problems are covered under Head Start's definition. Many states use the term *developmental delay* for preschool children, as opposed to the school term *children with disabilities* (Wolery & Wilbers, 1994). Part H of IDEA (for children 0 to 2) has different categories from those for children 3 and older. The thirteen categories for children ages 3 to 21 are deafness, hearing impairments, multiple handicaps, dual-sensory impairments, mental retardation, orthopedic impairments, other health impairments, severe emotional disturbance, specific learning disabilities, speech (language) impairments, visual impairments and blindness, traumatic brain injury, and autism. Each state has its own criteria to determine what constitutes each of these disabilities (Wolery & Wilbers, 1994).

Children with ADHD. Attention Deficit Hyperactivity Disorder is a growing concern in many early childhood programs. Technically, it is not one of the disability categories mentioned above. Nevertheless, if it affects a child's learning it can usually fit within one of the several categories. Signs of a child with ADHD include (Whaley, 2001, reporting J. Peterson):

- fails to give close attention to details or makes careless mistakes in schoolwork or other activities;
- often has problems sustaining attention in tasks or play;
- often does not seem to listen when spoken to directly;
- often does not follow through on instructions and fails to finish schoolwork or homework;
- is often easily distracted;
- often fidgets with hands or feet or squirms in seat;
- often leaves seat in classroom or other situations when remaining seated is expected;
- often runs or climbs excessively when it is inappropriate to do so;
- often talks excessively;
- often blurts out answers before questions have been completed;
- often interrupts or intrudes on others.

The most common response to a diagnosis of ADHD is medication—usually Ritalin, which can be prescribed only by medical staff. There are other approaches, including behavior modification. The use of Ritalin is controversial, especially as it butts up against teaching substance abuse prevention. While the numbers of children diagnosed with ADHD continue to increase, it is becoming very clear that many of these children have other learning disabilities and behavior challenges that are masked by ADHD. Further, as we stress standards and academics at younger ages, more and more children will exhibit these kinds of behaviors.

Identifying Children with Disabilities. Some children in early childhood programs have already been identified as having a specific disability or developmental delay, while other students have not yet been identified. Early childhood professionals are instrumental in helping to identify children with special needs. The usual progression for identifying a child is as follows: (1) parents or teachers suspect that something is preventing the child from maximizing full potential in the program; (2) a screening tool indicates a potential area of weakness in the child's development, or shows no apparent delay or learning challenge; (3) a specific series of diagnostic assessments is administered, to isolate the specific area(s) of disability; (4) a staffing meeting assesses the child, considering sources such as teacher and parent input, test results, specific physical indicators (height, weight, and so on), and other relevant information; and (5) the child's IEP or IFSP is developed. The child's parent(s) or guardian(s) must agree to each activity involved in this process, including the initial screening, and at any point the parent can request that the process be terminated. As I have already indicated, federal law requires that children with disabilities stay with their peers in normal community programs—child care, religious programs, schools—whenever possible.

Implementing Approaches for Children with Disabilities

Like all forms of diversity, there is tremendous diversity within the large category of special needs. In fact, as I will discuss in the next section, many students with special needs are also gifted, as my son, Kealan, is. Any effort to adapt the environment and teaching approach for these children must carefully address all of their needs, not simply the area that has been identified. Alterations to the environment, assistive equipment—including technology—and altering instructional approaches for children with disabilities depend on the special needs that are being addressed, and on the IEP and IFSP.

All classroom furniture, equipment, and instructional materials are designed and made for typically developing children, which means they are made for the physical development, abilities, and behavior of the average child (Wardle, 1999a). As children differ from the norm in terms of physical size, abilities, and so on, these materials are less likely to meet their needs. Thus, adaptations must be made. Sometimes only slight changes are required in one area. Other times major adjustments in a variety of areas are required. There follow a few examples of the kind of adaptations that can be made.

ADHD. Children with ADHD often are easily distracted, like to debate rules and expectations, and become bored easily. Programs should provide for these children an environment that minimizes distractions—a setting that is well defined. Provide many opportunities for hands-on, project-related activities; make sure that when a task is completed there are other activities the child can immediately select (a project box, activities on the computer, and so on). Try to make movement from one activity to another simple and clear. Post rules clearly, keep them short, and make sure instructions are simple, sequential, and easy to follow. Use multiple forms of communication: oral, written, visual symbols.

Visual Challenges. Ideas for working with children who have vision challenges include sorting activities that allow children to sort and classify by touch. All visual cues—pictures of where material is stored and so on—should have **tactile cues** as well. Make magnifiers available. Use Big Books for reading and prereading activities, offer children opportunities to feel objects that are being discussed (at circle time or group reading, during visits from a community member, and other opportunities), adapt written materials to large letters with lots of white space, and provide felt boards and other options for giving tactile information. When changes to the environment are made—such as rearranging furniture or setting up new learning centers—show these changes to the visually challenged children one-on-one, and encourage them to feel the new configurations.

Hearing Challenges. Use picture charts for directions and rules, when needed; limit noise that can interfere with a child's learning, such as traffic noise, noise made by other children, noisy activities, or a nearby phone. Written notes should be sent home to reinforce verbal instructions given to children; provide sign-language materials in the center or school, and give rules and instructions in sign language to all the children.

Physical Challenges. For children with physical challenges, specialized seating that gives the child needed support when engaging in all activities—such as water play, art, or sitting at a table—needs to be provided, which may require specially designed equipment or adaptations of existing equipment. Supply large brushes and mural paper for art projects, and offer unit and hollow block construction activities for children with fine motor challenges. Individual sand and water tubs can be provided for children who have difficulty with larger water tables. Provide bigger tools—large pencils, chalks—for children who need them. Adjust the environment so that children with physical challenges can work cooperatively with other children.

Twice-Exceptional Students

Students with special needs and gifted students are two groups of students considered exceptional students. Unfortunately, the public and many educators often believe these students belong at opposite ends of an ability continuum. We know, however, that there are gifted students within all other diversity groups (girls, minority students, and students with special needs). Whitmore (1981) suggests that there are at least half a million gifted students, K–12, who also have special needs. Gifted students with special needs are considered twice exceptional.

Twice-exceptional students are usually not identified as gifted because either their disability masks their giftedness or they use their giftedness to compensate for their disability. This is possible in part because identification of gifted students occurs in the early grades, when it is easier for children to compensate for their disability. Some twice-exceptional students fail easy identification tasks, yet pass more difficult ones (Silverman, 1989), and thus may be inaccurately identified.

Special-education efforts tend to concentrate on intervention and remediation of deficits (Karnes, 1979). Further, special-education intervention focuses on specific, manageable tasks. Because gifted students do not learn this way, gifted students with special needs often rebel against this kind of approach, viewing it as unchallenging, boring, or an insult. All gifted students often avoid repetitive, out-of-context learning. Twice-exceptional students require the same kind of learning challenges and opportunities as do other gifted learners.

To meet the needs of twice-exceptional students fully, special-education consultants, early childhood teachers, and others involved with both special education and gifted programs should receive specific training about the needs of the twice-exceptional child. Further, these professionals need to work collaboratively to develop more effective ways to identify and serve the educational needs of these children. Teachers of young children should receive training in the unique needs of the twice-exceptional child, along with in-service training from special-education experts and experts in the education of gifted students. Finally, identification materials and procedures—for gifted students and students with special needs—should be carefully analyzed to make sure they do not screen out either gifted children or special-needs children.

Responding Appropriately to Diversity

It is impossible for a teacher to know everything about each child's racial and ethnic identity, abilities and disabilities, and family background. Further, as I have discussed, diversity of diversity makes this task even more complex. The development of the anti-bias and ecological model is an attempt to help teachers understand the unique background of each of their students.

The Anti-Bias and Ecological Model

The anti-bias and ecological model of multicultural education (Wardle, 1996) proposes an approach to looking at various experiences each child brings to the early childhood program. While traditional multicultural models tend to label a child with the U.S. Census Bureau ethnic or racial label and then define that child based on that label, the antibias and ecological model proposes that each child's background should be viewed using seven distinctly different factors: race or ethnicity, culture, gender, ability or disability, community, family, and socioeconomic status. These seven factors differ in weight and influence for each child, and they interact uniquely to define each child. For example, for some children family is the most important influence on their identity; for others it is race or gender, for still others their disability, and for many a combination of several factors.

Race and Ethnicity. In America the U.S. Census Bureau has divided our population into five general categories. These are American Indian or Alaskan Native, Asian/Pacific Islander, black, Hispanic, and white. The 2000 census allowed people to select more than one of these groups to define their identity.

It has long been recognized by scientists and anthropologists that racial and ethnic categories have no biological basis. Further, there are obvious overlaps, such as some

Figure 6.1

Factors of the Anti-Bias and Ecological Model

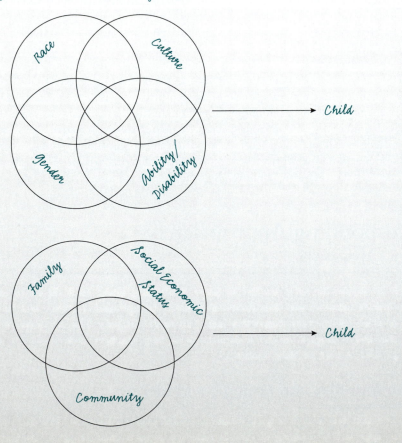

▶ *Some programs are homogeneous, some are racially and ethnically mixed. This is a Native American (BIA) school.*

Puerto Ricans who fit in both the Hispanic category and the black category. The Hispanic category specifically emphasizes Spanish culture and Latin American origin, yet 50 percent of South Americans are residents of Brazil, whose primary cultural influence comes from Portuguese traditions (National Geographic Society, 1993). And there is no place in these broad groups for people of multiracial and multiethnic heritage, including African Americans with significant Native American or Asian heritage, Hispanics with Korean or Japanese heritage, and the newer population of biracial and multiracial children.

Despite these problems with the concepts of race and ethnicity, they are still very powerful concepts for America in the twenty-first century. The racial or ethnic group a family belongs to has a profound impact on a child's experiences. Factors for a child and family based on belonging to a racial or ethnic group include a common history, including a history of persecution, oppression, stereotypes, and personal degradation; a position within our country's mainstream; or a specific government status, such as membership in a protected class, qualifying for affirmative action or scholarships, or membership in a tribal nation. Belonging to a racial or ethnic group also includes certain expectations, both from within the group and from without.

Families within these groups may tend to exhibit certain characteristics that differ from those of other groups. For example, many Hispanic families speak Spanish and are large and religious; Asian families tend to be extended, teach respect for elders, and show respect for others by averting their eyes; Native American families also teach respect for elders, and for cultural values and traditions; black families often have considerable extended-family support, and some are quite religious; and many white families place a great deal of emphasis on education. But we must be very careful about these generalizations, because there are always small-group and individual examples that don't fit the norm, and because values, attitudes, expectations, and behaviors continually change. Finally, each member of these groups is also a member of the larger American culture.

Culture. Some thinking suggests that race defines culture. This concept holds that racial differences cause cultural differences. I have a good friend from Sierra Leone, in Africa, who was a member of her country's 1996 Olympic team. The other day she told me that she cannot return to her country because she belongs to the lower class, and even though she has lived in the United States and France and has a computer science degree, she will never be accepted by the upper class of her country. The separation between these two classes is so great that marriage between members of the two different classes is taboo. The ruling class of Sierra Leone is made up of descendants of black former slaves from the United States; the lower class, native Africans who never left their country. While these two groups are viewed as both belonging to the black racial group, they comprise two distinct social and cultural groups in her country.

Having a separate cultural category in the anti-bias and ecological model allows a distinction to be made between American blacks and first-generation blacks from Africa and the Caribbean; among Spanish Americans living in the mountains of northern New Mexico who are direct descendants of original Spanish settlers, Puerto Rican immigrants in New York, first-generation immigrants from Brazil, and mestizos from Mexico; or among third-generation Chinese Americans and first-generation Hmong, Cambodians, and Vietnamese. It also allows us to appreciate the rich differences of customs, religions, art, dances, houses, and languages among various Native American nations in this country and throughout Central and South America (Sample, 1993).

A central component of a child's cultural experience can be religion, depending on the way the members of the family choose to practice it and how actively involved they are. Do they attend a synagogue, mosque, or church regularly? Are they active members in their religious community? Do they send their children to religious early childhood programs?

Culture really addresses those parts of a child's experience that frame the way the child views the world. This includes childrearing practices within the family, ideas, expectations, beliefs, different groups the family associates with, involvement in local and national politics, and more. Of the seven categories in this model, culture is probably the most important. Talking to an Amish child about the importance of a college education will not be effective, because the Amish finish school at the end of eighth grade. Trying to use rap and hip-hop music with a young gifted black student studying the cello at a local college may not work, either.

Gender. The gender category is obvious. What is not so obvious, but very powerful, is how schools, early childhood programs, parents, toy and materials marketers, and teachers respond to children based on gender. The category is also very important in relation to other categories, such as ability or disability (more boys are in special education than girls), culture (some cultural groups raise boys and girls with distinctively different roles and expectations), and family. Sexual orientation is also covered under this category.

Ability or Disability. A child's unique strengths and challenges are covered here. Strengths include artistic and musical abilities, excellence in dance and physical activities, specific academic strengths, and other unique abilities covered by Gardner's eight intelligences (1983). A child might be learning ballet and gymnastics, or be on a soccer team; or maybe identified through a gifted and talented search. Challenges include diagnosed special needs, potential special needs, and behavioral and social problems that might pose difficulties for the child at school.

Community. The category of community includes small college towns, suburbs, inner cities, Native American reservations, small rural communities, segregated and integrated neighborhoods, ethnic sections of town, and religious communities like the Amish. The influence of community also addresses movement between communities. For example, many low-income families move from one community to another within a school year. Some families, such as the new Maya immigrants in Houston and recent Mexican immigrants, have two communities—in their native country, and in the United States.

Communities include a variety of components that directly affect families. These include opportunities available for children, including schools, early childhood programs, club activities, and recreational centers. They also include services and support for the whole family, such as health clinics, bookstores, and playgrounds. Additionally, communities include a variety of different media outlets and services. And, of course, religious institutions are a vital part of each community.

Family. The family is the most crucial influence on young children. Family diversity includes two working parents, teen parents, adoptive parents, foster parents, single parents (male or female), blended families, interracial and interethnic families (including transracial adoption), families that combine divergent religious beliefs, grandparents raising grandchildren, gay and lesbian families, and the level of extended-family support. Parenting styles—authoritative, authoritarian, or permissive—and various forms of family challenges (alcoholism, domestic violence, drugs) also influence a child's family experience. And, of course, all these configurations interact with and overlap one another. For example, a child might come from a white teen family with lots of extended family support, a permissive parenting style, and a hardworking, motivated single parent.

The family component also includes media and computer use at home. Homes in which TV is used as a baby-sitter are very different from homes in which TV viewing is carefully monitored, or in which there is no TV at all. Not only do homes that have computers and Internet access enable their school-age children to do sophisticated homework projects, but parents in those homes often pressure their children's programs to provide computers and computer access.

As I have already said, religion is a very strong component of a child's experience. Although religion is part of the culture category, the family is the primary place for children to experience religion: traditions and celebrations, practices, values, attitudes about gender roles and people who are different, and views of history, science, and society.

Socioeconomic Status. Socioeconomic status has a powerful impact on the development of children. Lack of health insurance, poor nutrition, homelessness, welfare, crime, poor-quality educational programs, and lack of recreational choices are all results of it. Even the kind of child-care program a child will attend is largely a function of the family's income. Poor families use subsidized nonprofit programs, Head Start, relative care, or home-based care. Middle- and upper-class children will stay at home with a parent or nanny, or attend university lab programs, commercial child care, home-based programs, or public or private tuition-based school programs. A family's early childhood choices are not just a function of tuition cost, but are also determined by availability, location, transportation, hours of service, and whether parents feel comfortable with these programs. When my son was in first grade, he attended an expensive private gifted program on a scholarship. It was a very negative experience for us, because we felt we could not voice concerns and were looked down on by many of the paying parents and viewed as less than full participants in our child's education.

In this society we tend to segregate children by family income at a very early age— segregation that continues with poor children attending low-quality city public schools, and wealthy, white children attending an array of religious, private, and high-quality suburban schools that most low-income families cannot afford or access.

Using the Model as a Guide. The use of the anti-bias and ecological model requires the early childhood program to know the children, communities, and families they

▶ *The use of the anti-bias and ecological model requires teachers to know their children, communities, and families before they purchase materials and decide on instructional strategies.*

serve before they purchase curriculum materials and decide on instructional strategies. Further, because curriculum materials still tend to support broad social categories (often stereotypically), programs must be very selective in their purchasing, and may have to make some of their own materials. I have often tried to get educational supply companies to provide materials for multiracial families and children, but their representatives always tell me there is not a great enough demand for such materials.

Curriculum materials, classroom activities, and community outings must address all seven factors of this model in a way that teaches children that diversity is normal and appropriate and that all aspects of each category are valued. They must help children construct their own unique identity. Early childhood programs cannot ever convey the idea of one correct or preferred point of view (for example, professional occupations being the best, suburban single-family homes the preferred place to live, white people the norm, or boys the preferred gender). Also, teachers must be careful not to imply that characteristics common to families served in the program are better than those of families not served. For example, if the children served are primarily Southern Baptist, the program cannot communicate that this religion is better than other religions. The exploration of each factor's variability must be supported in the program, regardless of whether the program is homogeneous or diverse.

A Case Study Example. Joao Meira, father of first-grader Isabella, complained to the principal that his daughter was very unhappy in her public-school classroom. She had few friends, disliked the teacher, and was struggling with reading and math. Isabella complained that the teacher used her as an example when teaching some Spanish words and expected her to be friends with the Hispanic girls from the neighborhood. The teacher gave Isabella basic instruction in computer use, and seemed confused when Isabella asked the teacher if she could do a computer Internet search for a project. Isabella could not find books of interest to her in the classroom. She was looking for books about female doctors, dentists, and lawyers, but could only find ones about famous athletes and African American and Hispanic American heroes. And she was very upset that the teacher limited her time painting and drawing, her favorite activity. A student could use the art area only when she finished her academic subjects, which Isabella had a difficult time doing.

Because Isabella is dark-skinned, in a school that served primarily children from a low-income Hispanic area of town, the teacher made some inaccurate assumptions about her. Here is a brief use of the model to help the teacher more effectively meet Isabella's educational needs.

- *Race or ethnicity.* The teacher assumed Isabella was Hispanic; the reality is that she is Brazilian, speaks Portuguese, and has a Portuguese colonial heritage.
- *Culture.* Again the teacher assumed that the child came from a low-income, Hispanic background and spoke Spanish. The reality is that she is from a Brazilian professional cultural background.

- *Gender.* The teacher assumed Isabella's role models for women were mothers, aunts, and elder sisters who primarily care for children—an inaccurate assumption even for the other children in the class. The reality is that Isabella comes from a home that expects girls to become professionals.
- *Ability or disability.* The teacher believed Isabella was not good at anything in particular. In reality she is quite competent in computer skills and gifted artistically. Unknown to the teacher, she has a learning disability that hinders her learning reading the way it is being taught in the classroom.
- *Community.* Unlike her classmates, Isabella comes from a middle-class, integrated community.
- *Family.* Isabella comes from a professional family in which education is stressed and children are expected to go to college. Homework is more important than any other expectation or activity.
- *Socioeconomic status.* Isabella's father is a doctor who recently immigrated to this country. He teaches at the local university hospital.

Clearly Isabella is going to continue to struggle in school, and may even drop out, if the teacher does not change her instruction, expectations, and approach, based on the components of the anti-bias and ecological model.

Technology and Diversity

Computers provide an effective way to help programs diversify to meet the extensive needs of different students, students with specific disabilities that act as barriers to traditional learning, and gifted students. In particular, computers allow students to demonstrate their intelligence and knowledge in a more realistic and favorable light. This means, for example, that children who can write but do not have the fine motor control and skill to hold a pencil can still demonstrate their ability using the computer keyboard; children who have trouble distinguishing the sounds of the spoken word can use a visual display on the computer to break down these sounds. Another advantage of using a computer for children with specific learning challenges is that students can control the speed at which the activity is learned, speeding up or slowing down specific lessons to suit their own learning needs.

Computers assist students who may not be successful learners in the traditional verbal and mathematical intelligences (Gardner, 1983), which dominate most educational approaches. Computers work well for the visual learner, hands-on learner, and spatial-temporal learner, and for those students who enjoy taking things apart—cutting, pasting, copying, editing, and so on. Assistive technology is one of the ways schools can meet the legal requirement of serving students with disabilities (Behrmann & Lahm, 1994). The kinds of assistive technology devices or services used by a program depend on the individual child's IEP, and can be used both to assist students in basic instruction and to help with the regular curriculum. Part of my son's IEP was to use a specifically designed computer program to help him break down the phonetic elements of words, which he could not naturally discern.

There are several things that need to occur for computers to be used effectively to assist students with diverse needs in the classroom. Early childhood computer software must be carefully selected so that it supports the forms of diversity that we have discussed. Further, computers must be used as an integral part of the everyday curriculum, not simply as an enhancement or add-on, a reward system for behavioral or academic accomplishment, or a way to practice skill and drill activities. Staff training must help all teachers understand that students who learn in nontraditional manners are not deficient, and that adapting to their needs is not changing program standards, expectations, or outcomes. Teachers also need to understand that expanding the way traditional subjects are taught increases the educational quality of the entire program.

Children should be encouraged to work together on the computer, thus capitalizing on different developmental levels and encouraging social-skill development—especially for children who may be socially immature. Computer programs should capitalize on the computer's ability to teach things in new, exciting, and innovative ways, and should be incorporated into the early childhood program's overall educational philosophy.

Program Considerations

There are many things early childhood programs can do to respond to all sorts of diversity, as many programs already do. Most important, diversity should be woven into the fabric of the program, not just added on in a token or "tourist" manner (Derman Sparks, 1989). Children and families of all backgrounds need to be brought into the mainstream of the program and kept there year-round to feel fully accepted and worthy participants. Here are a few ideas to consider.

Families and Children in the Program. It is vital all students and their families see themselves reflected throughout the program. They need to see other children and families like themselves in books, puzzles, doll sets, posters, pictures on the classroom walls, textbooks, games, videos, computer programs, and other classroom materials. They need to see these visual messages in the overall school or child-care program: artwork, bulletin boards, parent boards, newspapers and magazines offered to parents, and the lending library. Materials the program uses to communicate to its stakeholders—parents, politicians, community members—must reflect the diversity of every family participating in the program. These materials include newsletters, parent education materials, policies and procedures manuals, and program announcements.

Staff Training. There should be continual staff training on diversity issues covering a variety of areas, starting with opportunities for staff to explore their own biases, prejudices, and assumptions. The training should also include information about different learning styles, working with diverse parents, use of the community, and the history, art, music, and political struggles of all segments of the American population.

American children develop many attitudes based on the media. Staff training should help teachers explore inaccurate views of history and provide approaches for teaching children correct information. For example, traditional depictions of the old West are counteracted at the American Cowboy Museum in Denver, which presents a live demonstration about the role of the black cowboy in the West and a display of the buffalo soldiers. There are other presentations around the country showing the significant roles played by various minority heroes and groups.

Training should also explore assumptions and stereotypes. For example, investigate the common assumptions that Asian children are good at math and science, black boys are all athletes, and all girls are preoccupied with their appearance. Finally, training should cover any new diversity issue that presents itself in the individual program. The populations we serve change all the time, demanding new information and methods.

Staffing. Modeling is a very powerful teaching tool for all values of the early childhood program. It teaches behavior, character, attitudes, and morals, and it works to teach diversity. (Chapter 9 covers this learning method in the discussion of social-learning theory). Any program seeking to be responsive to the diversity of the families and children it serves must strive to provide a diversity of staff and volunteers in the program. Clearly it is not possible to match the diversity of staff with that of children and families—and, in a homogeneous program, it is not desirable. But programs should strive both to have policies and procedures that encourage hiring employees with racial, ethnic, special-needs, gender, and other diversities, and to make sure diversity exists at every level of the organization. It does little good if a program has lots of diversity, but all of the minority staff hold positions at the bottom of the organization.

Diversity in early childhood programs also includes men (Cunningham, 1998–1999), which poses many challenges to our programs. In early childhood programs, men are a distinct minority, and as such often feel unwelcome, unwanted, and powerless (Cunningham, 1998–1999). Fathers in our programs often feel the same way. Not only do boys need male models in our programs—especially boys from female-headed, single-parent homes—but girls also need strong male models.

Individual Diversity. As I have already mentioned, traditional approaches to diversity in this country have focused on group differences. While it is important to continue to address the contributions, strengths, viability, and value of ethnic, racial, and other groups in the lives of families and children served by early childhood programs, it is paramount to respond to individual families and their children, because of the tremendous diversity within each larger group, overlap between groups, and the psychological need of each of us to be treated as individuals. Programs must also carefully guard against stereotypical responses, unnecessary categorization, and labeling. Avoid staff training, selection of curricular materials, cultural and ethnic celebrations, and classroom activities that assume that group membership is more important than individual personality, family, learning styles, needs, and abilities.

Developmentally Appropriate Practice

Use of the Community. All early childhood programs and schools continually need to explore ways to work closely with their community and use its resources to enrich the complex fabric of the program. Effective use of the community is one way for programs to expand the diversity of adults in the program.

Invite interesting people to visit your program; take field trips to exciting businesses and activities; create mentor programs with local colleges, high schools, and businesses; develop partnerships with local companies; form a relationship with the community senior center; work closely with museums, cultural centers, and community experts. My father, who is nearly 80 years old, is invited weekly to participate in a nature walk with the Spring Valley School preschool children, so he can convey his considerable knowledge about the history of the area, and its flora and fauna, to the children. As a past teacher, my father communicates information and his love of the local lore to the preschoolers in a way that they can understand, while enjoying their company and the beautiful countryside of the Pennsylvania Appalachians.

Working effectively with the community takes time and effort (which is why many programs do not do it well). Two general ideas are essential; first, the educational philosophy of the program must be clear to everyone who volunteers; and second, the use of the community should increase the programs' exposure to diversity, not to stereotypes.

Visits by minority sports heroes do little to expand students' views of successful minorities, while having women and disabled individuals who are successful in law, business, politics, and the arts come to the center or school and work with the children has great value.

Avoid Diversity by Celebration.   Some programs use holidays and celebrations to include diversity in the curriculum. Martin Luther King, Jr.'s birthday, Cinco de Mayo, Chinese New Year, September 15, and St. Patrick's Day are examples. This approach is very problematic. In Chapter 4 I discuss the ineffectiveness of teaching diversity through a single-subject curriculum. There are other problems with teaching diversity through celebrations:

- To teach about Hispanic culture and history only at Cinco de Mayo and on September 15 shortchanges the important contributions of Hispanic people, histories, and culture to this society. Further, children with a Hispanic background need to see themselves in the program all the time.
- It's a "tourist" approach—communicating to children that diversity consists only of dance, food, costumes, and that we can learn about diversity like tourists.
- It is not an integrated approach. Diversity should be woven richly throughout the entire curriculum, in every subject area, and throughout the entire year.
- It tends to segregate the program and its families—Hispanic families celebrate Cinco de Mayo, black families Martin Luther King Day, and so on.
- It reinforces a group approach to culture, which teaches that everyone from the same group is the same. As I have said, we need to stress diversity of diversity, as much as diversity from group to group.
- Celebrations in early childhood programs often focus on food and drink, as well as a high level of activity. Not only are the foods and drinks served usually inconsistent with good nutrition for young children, but the atmosphere teaches children that the only way to have a good time is to drink and eat. Goals for many early childhood and school programs include developing healthy nutritional food choices and eating habits, developing behaviors in children that resist substance abuse, and learning in low-stress, nurturing environments.

Authentic, Nonstereotypical Materials

I have talked about how important it is that all children and parents see themselves in a variety of materials used in the program. These materials must support individual children's self-esteem, expand their view of the world and the choices it offers them, and in no way communicate to them that they are somehow inferior because of skin color, gender, eye shape, hair texture, language spoken, or disability. It is equally vital that nobody be omitted or invisible, including interracial families and children in transracially adopted families. Reflecting the lives of all our children requires careful assessment of books, learning and curricular materials, products for communicating

▶ *Authentic artifacts representing families included in the program should be displayed throughout the school or center.*

with parents, and teacher training materials. Of particular concern are computer programs, Internet sites, and the content of some popular songs and radio stations. It is not good enough for materials to be an authentic expression of a culture. As M. I. Cruz-Janzen points out, all cultures, nations, and groups of people have biases, prejudices, and stereotypes. Many non-Western countries also have deep prejudices, for instance, about women and dark-skinned people (Cruz-Janzen, 1998).

Materials and Activities Checklist

This is a partial checklist I developed to use in selecting materials and activities that support diversity. It is understood that these materials and activities must be developmentally appropriate. For the first section, a "yes" answer is required.

☐ Do the materials and activities enhance children's self-acceptance, knowledge, and understanding of their heritage and identity by showing their culture in a positive way?

☐ Do the materials and activities enhance children's understanding and acceptance of people and cultures different from them by showing those cultures in a positive manner?

☐ Do the materials and activities expand the children's view of the world by exposing them to new ideas, people, and viewpoints?

☐ Are the materials carefully designed with sensitivity and respect toward children and diversity through the use of acceptance and understanding?

☐ Do the materials and activities address several areas of diversity in a positive manner?

☐ Are the materials and activities part of the overall curriculum and classroom materials, and integrate naturally into classroom activities and experiences?

☐ Does the activity require children to face prejudices, stereotypes, labels, assumptions, and misconceptions that they are developing, by challenging their thinking and behaviors?

☐ Does the activity show diversity in realistic, contemporary settings (for example, Native Americans doing real jobs in contemporary clothes, rather than dancing in headdresses)?

The following questions should be answered with a "no."

☐ Is the material or activity a token? (for example, one minority doll; one book representing each traditional racial group, one day a year to celebrate Asian cultures)?

☐ Do the materials and activities emphasize differences among groups and cultures without addressing common bonds, histories, and aspirations (e.g., collaborations between blacks and Native Americans; black–Jewish cooperation)?

☐ Do the materials or activities convey that people who belong to the same ethnic or racial group are all the same (no diversity of diversity)?

☐ Does the activity stress membership in a particular cultural group at the expense of each child's total and unique background, including language, culture, family, nation of origin, community, religion? Does it imply that racial and ethnic diversity are the most important, or the only, areas of diversity?

☐ Does the activity force multiracial and multi-ethnic children either to be invisible or to choose an incomplete identity? Must they select only one of their backgrounds?

☐ Do the activities and materials indicate in some way that one group, culture, religion, language, or art form is the best or better than another (for example, the preferred jobs are held by white men, the less-preferred by women and minorities)?

The Hmong in America

A closer look at the Hmong will help us understand unique cultural values of a group existing within the larger American culture.

History of Hmong Immigration to the United States.
"Well over a hundred thousand Hmong are now in the United States, some living where they first settled with their sponsor assistance in the late 70s and early 80s, others changing locations to join family or to better their situations" (Podeschi & Xiong, 1994, p. 3). The Hmong came to this country as refugees because they were allies of the United States during the Vietnam War. As part of their agreement to fight with the United States against the communists, the United States promised to protect them whatever the outcome of the war. When South Vietnam fell, the Pathet Lao of Cambodia attacked the Hmong. Many fled to Thailand, and then were given asylum in this country.

Hmong Culture.
The Hmong are a hill people from Southeast Asia who were concentrated in Laos before the Vietnam War. They have neither a country nor official symbols (flags, money, and the like), but they have their own culture, traditions, heritage, and language. They supported themselves by means of primitive agriculture. "They came to the United States as one of the least educated groups of Asians. Having primarily an oral tradition, and little of a written literacy, the Hmong must struggle doubly hard for self-sufficiency and acceptance" (Podeschi & Xiong, 1994, p. 1). Original Hmong immigrants are poorly educated and don't speak English. Hmong children struggle to take full advantage of American education. "An overriding aspect of Hmong life is their clan social structure. Clan plays various roles in Hmong society—for example, each clan has its own religious taboos that shape its traditional religious activities, and each clan determines lineage and Hmong groups which can intermarry" (Podeschi & Xiong, 1994, p. 6).

Cultural Value of Education.
The Hmong still hold many of their original values, along with new values they have learned in adapting to this country. The differences between the old and new values often cause tension, conflict, and anxiety, especially for the younger generations, who are caught between determining which of the old values they wish to retain and which new ones they want to embrace.

Hmong traditional values stress interdependence, reliance on the group, and communal survival. Children learn to do what is best for the group, not the individual. A Hmong child is motivated by group success and believes in sharing schoolwork and helping colleagues on tests and assignments. The Hmong culture respects formality and authority. Teachers are highly respected. Hmong parents are reluctant to question what teachers do, and the American concept of parental involvement in schools is foreign to them. They view the educator's role as transmitting skills and knowledge; they believe all other issues, including misbehavior, school problems, parental concerns, and child care (also school-age care) are the responsibility of the extended family and clan leadership. Hmong students are reluctant to discuss any personal matters with the school.

Clearly Hmong children who attend our programs live in two cultures. They are part of a new generation torn between the security, loyalty, and respect of the old ways and the freedom, fashions, music, independence, and money of the American lifestyle. For educators working with Hmong students, the challenge is to support the child's pride, belonging, and identity within their own cultural context while helping them to function productively within the larger society. To help these students, early childhood programs need to communicate constantly with families and community leaders, respect the different values of various cultural groups, understand the tension children often experience, and help children integrate the values of the greater American culture with those of their family and community.

Conclusion

Early childhood educators are becoming increasingly aware of the diversity of students they serve and the need to adapt programs, curricula, and teaching approaches to meet the needs of these students. Traditional categories of diversity include race, ethnicity, gender, and special needs. But diversity also includes gifted and twice-exceptional students, multiracial and multiethnic children, students from a variety of family structures, and sexual orientation. Further, diversity includes the range of student experiences within each of these groups, the fact that many children belong to more than one group, and the unique experiences each child brings to the early childhood program.

Questions and Projects

1. Select a learning materials catalog for children of the age you teach or intend to teach. Select materials from the catalog that you believe support children's individual diversity: gender, race, ethnicity, abilities, special needs, unique experiences, and more. Explain how each of your choices supports diversity.

2. Suppose you have a very bright 7-year-old in your class. She has an IQ of 155, yet she cannot read. You don't understand what is going on. What should you do to help this child progress?

3. Use the seven factors of the anti-bias and ecological multicultural model to map out your own strengths, challenges, culture, and individuality.

4. Suppose you work in a public-school early childhood program in a suburban district. The families you serve, and the staff at the school, are overwhelmingly white and middle-class. What can you do to expose your children to diversity without resorting to a tourist approach?

5. A parent wants to enroll her 5-year-old child in your preschool program. The program is part of a public elementary school. The child has cerebral palsy. Your principal has informed you she does not want a child with CP in her building (this is a real-life example). What do you do?

6. Create a twenty-item list of local diversity resources for an early childhood program in your area. Use the phone book, local contacts, Web pages, diversity coordinators at local schools, ethnic stores, libraries, national groups and any other sources you can think of.

CHAPTER

7

Teachers *as* Professionals

*T*his chapter is about what each of you is currently doing—preparing for or already engaged in a profession working with young children. As such, it is more directly applicable to you than any other chapter in the book. Further, your approach to reading the chapter will be different from that of reading the others—more introspective, and involving self-evaluation. I hope this chapter expands your knowledge of the field while enabling you to begin to evaluate both your preparation for working with children and your educational institution's role in that process. Various terms are used to describe people who work with young children: *providers, caregivers,* and *teachers.* Unless another term is essential for discussing a specific topic—say, discussing paraprofessionals—I will use the term *teacher* to describe professionals who work with young children. ■

Who Becomes a Teacher?

Characteristics

Both my mother and my father were teachers, my three sisters all teach, and I am a teacher. Many of us enter the profession because it's part of our family tradition or heritage; others enter because they like working with children, or want to make a difference in the lives of children. Regardless of motivation, it appears that good teachers have a variety of similar characteristics. These include (Wardle, 1991; after Feeney & Chun, 1985):

Questions to Consider

1. Why have you chosen to work with young children? Where do you expect to be, professionally, in five years? Ten years?

2. What should teachers of young children know?

3. What constitutes professionalism in the early childhood field?

4. Why is knowledge of family involvement crucial in preparing teachers of young children?

5. Should programs like the CDA and paraprofessional training constitute the first rung toward a teaching degree?

6. Is child care fundamentally different from early childhood education? And should teachers receive different preparations depending on whether they provide child care or education?

7. How would you solve the crisis of low pay and benefits for child-care workers and early childhood teachers?

- patience;
- energy, coordination, and physical strength;
- self-understanding, continually learning, and a high ability to abstract;
- genuine respect for children and ability to support growth (even when their behavior is not acceptable);
- sense of humor, positive attitude;
- a child-centered perspective, and ability to play and work with children;
- formal training in child development;
- curricular approaches that include many experiences related to children's interests, and innovative use of materials;
- flexibility (less structured, less punitive, values mistakes as a learning opportunity);
- interpersonal competence, emotional stability, emotional warmth, sensitivity, and involvement;
- ability to observe and interact individually with children and accept individual differences, read individual cues, and encourage individual responsibility and activity;
- verbal interaction skills.

According to Cartwright (1998), a teacher of young children should have these characteristics:

- good physical health, because of the activity of young children and the requirements of the job;
- emotional maturity, including an inner sense of security and purpose, an ability to provide discipline yet encourage spontaneity, and a warmth based on an inner sense of security;
- integrity, both a true sense of self-knowledge and honesty toward others;
- self-awareness, using self-evaluation and introspection to become knowledgeable about oneself, one's strengths, weaknesses, and unconscious behaviors;
- theoretical grounding—a thorough background and knowledge in the field, especially in the developmental-interaction approach to learning;
- warm respect for and courtesy to all children, and ability to work with individual children to support their development of self-disciplined learning;
- trust in children, belief in their growth and ability to fulfill their potential, desire to support growth and allow for individual differences;
- discretion, especially respect for the privacy of the child and her family.

Teachers as Learners. As part of my father's teaching approach, he was always involved in a variety of projects. At one time he trained a group of homing pigeons. As these pigeons learned to return home, school groups would take them on their field trips, and then release them to return, carrying messages of the class's progress and interesting details of the field trip. Later the students plotted the pigeons' routes on the map and calculated the increasing distances of their flights. He also studied Ewell Gibbons's books on natural edible plants, found these plants with his students, and made salads, desserts, and other concoctions. On another occasion he grew rye with his students; harvested, shucked, and ground it; and baked rye bread with his class. Another project he undertook involved Braddock's Trail, a significant route in the Revolutionary War. First, he

▶ *Teachers are also learners: New Meadow Run school enactment of Braddock's campaign against the Americas, based on personal research by Derek Wardle, teacher.*

studied the trail in great detail, including conducting several excavations and charting the route. Then one day he had the school principal dress up as General Braddock, mount on a beautiful white stallion, and lead the whole school on a crisp winter morning on a march along the trail.

My father's insatiable interest in the world around him—nature, history, industry, social movements, and local points of significance—contributed greatly to his teaching (Jones, 1998). While these activities were of intrinsic interest to him, he always found ways to include them in his teaching. Some years ago I ran into one of my father's past students and asked her about her favorite memories of the school. Without hesitation she replied, "Your father's projects!"

Teachers as Role Models. My first teaching experience after college was in a small alternative school in the beautiful mountain town of Taos, New Mexico. As part of the physical education curriculum, I introduced the students to folk dancing, one of my favorite pastimes. As my students became more competent, we created a performance group, which then presented demonstrations at local community events, parks, schools, and BIA (Native American) schools. The students obviously enjoyed both learning the new dances and performing them in front of an audience. Thirty years after teaching at Da Nahazli school, I received an E-mail from one of these students, who told me how much she enjoyed the dancing. She believed the performance activities taught the students responsibility and how to solve their own problems. Of most surprise to me, however, was that she continued to study dance in college, and participated in a number of community dance events.

Teachers are very powerful forces in the lives of their students, going far beyond instruction and implementation of the curriculum. Teachers are models, guides, structures of experience, and confidants. But maybe most powerfully, students seem to remember teachers' infectious enthusiasm, joy in learning, and delight in the world around us.

Teacher–Student Interactions. The basis for the relationship that develops between teachers and children is in the interactions between them. Research suggests that these interactions need to be warm, nurturing, supportive, and sensitive to student needs. Further, research suggests that the most important factor is the quality of teacher–student interaction, not the frequency (Kontos & Wilcox-Herzog, 1997). Teachers tend to use lots of language in their interactions, and enjoy socializing with children. Time is also spent on monitoring children's behaviors and on behavior management.

Teachers, however, must be very conscious of their interaction patterns. For a variety of reasons discussed in Chapter 6, teachers are more supportive and nurturing of girls, and more harsh but more verbal with boys; they spend more time with children who seek out their attention, both because of discipline issues and with children who are fun to be around (Kontos & Wilcox-Herzog, 1997). Teachers must make a concerted effort to interact with all children, especially those who are shy, self-directed, or simply easy to overlook.

Teachers' Role in the Classroom

Teachers have a variety of roles to play, and must balance many demands. These include ensuring the health and safety of the children, making lesson plans that implement the objectives of the curriculum, managing the activities in the classroom, observing the children and evaluating their performance, collaborating with parents, and keeping the children challenged and occupied.

Implementing Health and Safety Procedures. A vital role for teachers is implementing a program's or school's health and safety policies and procedures—everything from handwashing, toothbrushing, and using universal precautions when responding to cuts and bruises, to bleaching tabletops and practicing fire drills. Teachers are responsible for making sure children don't leave the classroom or playground unnoticed. They must follow safety procedures when taking the class to the playground or on a field trip, and monitor the general safety of the classroom—watching out for broken toys, carpet trip hazards, long cords on window blinds, choke hazards, and uncovered electrical outlets; making sure fire routes are posted; and rigidly following diaper-changing procedures. All the health and safety procedures are too numerous to list here, but they constitute a central responsibility for the teacher. The teacher must also make sure children are picked up from the home, school, or program only by an authorized person.

Planning. Throughout the book I talk about a myriad of things young children should experience in early childhood programs, including activities that promote language development, and math and science skills and concepts; knowledge about the real world and social world; and opportunities to use art, music, dance, and drama in their development. The child's experiences need to include learning basic social skills, developing a secure and positive identity, and having many opportunities to explore the world through play and field trips. Further, children need to learn to take care of themselves, to develop positive dispositions, and to engage in lots of physical activities. It is the teacher's responsibility—with the guidance and structure of the curriculum, books, lesson plans, and so on—to plan a program in which all of these things take place. Teachers also need to plan how to implement IEPs and IFSPs (plans for children with disabilities), how to involve parents, and when to do evaluations, screening, and assessments. For new teachers, planning is often very deliberate and laborious; more experienced teachers plan in a more wholistic, flexible, and multidimensional way.

Implementing the Curriculum. Implementing the curriculum involves two major areas—setting up and maintaining the environment, and providing activities, choices, and possibilities for children to meet the curricular goals and objectives. Providing a stimulating and challenging environment requires obtaining equipment, setting up and rotating learning centers, and making sure the classroom is organized in such a way that children can easily find and return materials. Setting up the environment also requires providing images for environmental print (see Chapter 10), putting a variety of artwork and children's work on walls and bulletin boards, and making sure there are ample multicultural materials. Children need to feel the classroom is theirs; they also need to be relaxed and stress-free. Since young children are concrete learners, activities for implementing the curriculum must focus on hands-on activities, field trips, visitors to the classroom, choice, individualization, and self-directed learning.

Observation and Assessment. Observation of children is a central role of the classroom teacher. How can we plan activities that match a child's development if we don't know what that development is? Observation enables us to gain this important information. Much observation is informal—how well is Johnny reading? Is Yvette progressing in her ability to share? How is Juan's writing coming? Chapter 14 discusses more formal ways to collect information. Other assessments enable the school to know how each child is progressing on competencies or standards—often calculated by means of tests—some required by the state at specific grade levels. And there are checklists and assessments to determine whether a child can benefit from specific services, such as a gifted and talented program or special education, or whether a different program would better match the child's needs. Authentic assessment of children's products can be used with parents at conferences, and help determine their overall progress.

Managing the Classroom. The teachers are the bosses of the classroom—they keep things moving, make sure snacks arrive on time, and help children get their coats off in the morning and find them in the evening. They tidy up, keep the playground sand from messing up the carpet, and return the books to the reading corner. They manage both the physical and the social environment. Is the class ready for the guest speaker? Does everyone have a library card? Has the pet bunny been fed? Good teachers develop a relaxed, but very efficient, ability to manage the classroom.

Working with Parents. As the head of the classroom, teachers function directly with parents in a variety of ways. They must make parent volunteers feel welcome and appreciated; they must encourage and support parents who come to the class to demonstrate a project, lecture on a topic, or be a role model. Further, teachers need to be open and nondefensive in communicating to parents what they are doing in the classroom and why. Parent–teacher conferences are also part of the teacher's responsibility.

Teachers' Role in the Center or School

Teachers have a variety of essential roles they perform outside the classroom but within the overall program. It is impossible to cover all these roles, but some include being on committees, mentoring and training other teachers, working collaboratively with other building staff, and working with professionals from outside the building or program.

Implementing Policies and Procedures. Every school and early childhood center has official health and safety procedures, developed from state licensing requirements, as well as fire and building codes, playground safety guidelines, state immunization laws, and school- or program-specific procedures (often required by their funding sources)—including medication and discipline policies, policies regarding who is allowed to pick up a child from the building, field trip procedures, pet-care policies, and transportation procedures. Teachers are on the front line of implementing all health and safety policies and procedures throughout the center or school.

Committees. Early childhood programs and schools establish a variety of committees to address specific issues. While some of these are **standing committees** (they exist all the time), most are **ad hoc committees** (designed to address specific issues and then disband). Examples of committees are diversity, curriculum, career development, new playground, orientation, and celebrations. These committees really have two purposes: to get teacher input into crucial decisions and activities, and to accomplish important tasks that otherwise would not get done. For example, at Adams County Head Start, a committee made up of community representatives and teachers planned and staged the annual Adams County Children's Festival.

Training and Mentoring. Many states require new public-school teachers to have a mentor on the job, and some large early childhood companies have developed procedures for the mentoring of new staff. Mentoring has been a very effective training approach in the business world for years, and it is especially popular in businesses that are committed to cultural diversity (Thomas, 1991). As staff become proficient and progress through the developmental stages discussed later in the chapter, they are expected to provide training to other staff. All teachers have areas of strength and expertise, and the field benefits immeasurably when teachers share their knowledge.

Working Collaboratively with Other Staff. Early childhood teachers must be good team players. Teachers need to be able to share information about children, discuss scheduling of the playground, arrange field trips, solicit needed advice from one another, and capitalize on a collective approach. One of the skills college preparation programs try to teach—through projects, assignments, presentations, and practicums—is the team approach. And, of course, teachers have to learn to work effectively with colleagues in the classroom (whether it be a teacher, assistant teacher, or volunteer). Teachers must be able to use differences—teaching styles, age, culture, language, and more—to enhance teamwork.

Working with Other Professionals. Teachers work on a regular basis with nonteaching professionals who have input into the classroom, be they a supervisor, principal, or director; special-education and gifted specialists; or social-service workers, psychologists, or counselors. A teacher's role is to maintain leadership of the classroom while working professionally with these specialists for the good of each child. Working with other professionals presents a unique challenge because specialists see the classroom from their particular focus, while the teacher must be a generalist. Teachers must learn procedures to follow when they disagree with other staff or need more input and assistance than they are getting.

Working with Parents. Good early childhood programs and schools work effectively with parents. They welcome parents into the building at all times, ask parents for input and ideas, treat parents who are on various committees as equals, and provide resources and support to individual parents who need or request them—agency referrals, reading materials, community contacts, and so on.

Teachers' Role in the Community

Early childhood professionals are seen as experts by the community. As such, their community roles, while overlapping, involve conferences, committees, and advocacy.

Conferences and Committees. All early childhood organizations provide regular local conferences—some for classroom teachers, others for specialists such as special-education, reading, and bilingual teachers. These conferences provide the newest information in the field, along with an opportunity for participants to learn from one another and to gain support. Organizations such as Head Start, as well as large early childhood chains, conduct their own regional and national conferences. Conferences are important ways to communicate information and build a sense of solidarity within the field. As teachers become more proficient, they are invited to make presentations at these conferences.

Community committees are very much like building committees, except they involve representatives from various sectors of the community and have a wider scope. Community early childhood committees are involved in a variety of activities, including organizing conferences, developing local legislation and standards, and coordinating festivals and advocacy activities.

Advocacy. Members of professions are expected to be advocates. NAEYC's code of ethical conduct speaks to this expectation: "We acknowledge an obligation to serve as a voice for children," and "to support policies and laws that promote the well-being of children and families" (NAEYC, 1998, p. 10). The statement of commitment says, "To the best of my ability I will . . . serve as an advocate for children, their families, and their teachers in communities and society" (NAEYC, 1998).

Advocacy in our field generally involves supporting policies, approaches, and laws that enhance the lives of children and families, improving the status of early childhood education as a field, and having a positive impact on the lives of early childhood professionals. How this is done is, of course, open to individual interpretation. While it is clear that increasing salaries and benefits for early childhood teachers is positive, as is expanding Head Start, it is not equally clear that allowing vouchers to fund public schools would improve the lives of children, families, and educators. And what happens when proposed legislation enhances the lives of children but may be negative for teachers—for example, allowing uncertified teachers in public schools, in order to reduce class and group size?

Working with Parents. Teachers must develop a fine balance in their relationships with parents in the community. Clearly, the more teachers understand the dynamics, culture, and climate of the community, the better they can support their children's growth and learning. It is crucial, however, to keep personal and professional relationships separate.

Becoming a Teacher

Paraprofessionals

Paraprofessionals are used extensively in public early childhood programs at every age level. **Paraprofessionals** are staff members working with children in a public school,

Head Start program, or other educational program who have only a high school diploma or GED and no formal teacher education. The use of paraprofessionals started to grow in the 1960s, with the creation of Title I and Head Start. Paraprofessionals were hired by these programs to employ the poor; to bring cultural, ethnic, and linguistic diversity into educational programs; and to enable minorities and low-income people to enter the teaching profession, specifically because there were so few cultural, linguistic, or ethnic minority teachers. (This is one reason Head Start was established outside of the traditional public-school structure.) Universities and school districts established partnerships to educate paraprofessionals, and the Child Development Associate (CDA) program was established to give Head Start teachers formal teacher training. The inclusion of paraprofessionals led to an influx of historically underrepresented people into our schools and early childhood programs.

Unfortunately, in almost all cases the training mechanisms for paraprofessionals have disappeared, because of lack of funds. Further, Head Start employees with CDA training have tended to stay in the local program, rather than move on into the general teacher population.

Use of Paraprofessionals. Today, paraprofessionals are attractive to schools because they match the linguistic, cultural, ethnic, and racial diversity of our ever-changing school population, while teachers are still predominantly white, middle-class, monolingual English speakers (Harper, 1994), and because they are paid less than certified teachers. They are often entrusted to teach minority children basic skills, as well as being the main bilingual or ESL instructors in the classroom and often the school's primary contact with minority families (especially those that do not speak English). Training that paraprofessionals receive within the schools is directed at skill building, use and preparation of materials, and recipe approaches to instruction (Apple, 1986). This training is often separate from regular teacher training. Paraprofessionals generally lack adequate preparation and in-service training to meet the needs of the students with whom they are entrusted.

Career Path for Paraprofessionals. There is no systematic career path by which paraprofessionals can become teachers, and those who wish to must do so on their own. In one project designed to provide training for paraprofessionals, within three years only 3 percent of the 150 participants had enrolled in a program to pursue a college certificate, citing a lack of social and emotional support, career advice, and, most important, financial support (Harper, 1994). Wages for paraprofessionals are quite low, and many are the significant wage earners for their families. Because of the current teacher shortage, some school districts are developing programs to assist paraprofessionals to offset these educational costs.

A clear, well-defined career path is needed to enable paraprofessionals to become certified teachers. According to Harper (1994), it is crucial that paraprofessionals be given the skills and training to meet the educational needs of children and families they serve, that career paths be developed so paraprofessionals can move up levels based on formal preparation, and that these paths lead directly to full teacher certification. As paraprofessionals move up these levels, their pay must increase proportionally, rewarding additional responsibilities and paying for their continued education. An example of this concept follows (from California, which requires a four-year degree plus an additional year of graduate teacher preparation; Harper, 1994):

- *Level I, Teacher Assistant.* High school diploma or GED. Paraprofessional could help prepare materials and supervise activities.
- *Level II, Teacher's Aide.* Completion of general college requirements with two years of college preparation. In addition to tasks already mentioned, the aide would supervise students working on assignments, and tutor individual and small groups of students under the direction of the teacher.
- *Level III, Teacher in Preparation.* Completion of baccalaureate degree program and admission to a credentialing program. Additional responsibilities would include working with small groups of students in enrichment and reinforcement activities, and lesson-planning activities for small groups under the teacher's direction.
- *Level IV, Student Teacher Intern.* Completion of teacher credentialing program course work and advancement to student teaching. Additional responsibilities include planning, teaching, and evaluating of whole class under the supervision of the teacher and college supervisor, and moving toward full, independent responsibility.
- *Level V, Credentialed Teacher.*

Child Development Associates

As a result of the creation of Head Start and the increasing number of child-care programs throughout the country, a need to train early childhood caregivers and teachers became apparent. In 1970 a group of early childhood leaders developed the concept of a national program that would identify the basic **competencies** needed to provide quality care and education; provide training in each of these competencies; and evaluate caregivers based on the competencies, then award a national credential. Out of this concept the **Child Development Associate** (CDA) was developed, which is fundamentally a **field-based program**—activities, knowledge, and a credential based on what teachers do in a program's classroom, not the college classroom. Many Head Start staff are low-income parents who often feel alienated by traditional college settings; further, many local Head Start facilities are far removed from colleges and universities. In 1975 the CDA program was implemented for teachers working with children aged 3 to 5; in 1989 a bilingual (English–Spanish) specialization was added, and later a certificate for teachers working with infants and toddlers was introduced.

The CDA program is run by the Council for Early Childhood Professional Recognition, a branch of NAEYC. By 1997, almost one hundred thousand people had received a CDA credential, and forty-seven states plus Washington, D.C., use the CDA as part of their child-care regulations. Some colleges and universities also give credit to degree applicants who have a CDA. The credential is available for teachers in center-based programs (preschool or infant/toddler endorsement) and family child care, and for home visitors. The bilingual specialization is available for each of these settings.

There are two paths a caregiver can follow to receive a CDA: the CDAP3 program, and the regular CDA. In the CDAP3 process, training is provided by the Council, using the *Essentials in Child Development Associates Working with Young Children* curriculum. For the regular CDA program, training, collection of needed materials, and preparation for assessment are provided by colleges and universities nationwide, the U.S. military, some Head Start programs, and some private child-care providers. This regular CDA

▶ *CDA candidates must learn 6 basic competencies, including "to support social and emotional development and provide positive guidance."*

approach works in one of two ways: either a program contracts with a local college to teach the content, observe the fieldwork, and prepare the candidate for the assessment; or a program—Head Start, child-care chain, military program—uses its own curriculum and provides a trainer, who makes sure the candidate meets all the CDA requirements.

Competencies. The CDA has six competency areas, which are themselves divided into functional areas. A **CDA candidate** must be able to demonstrate mastery in all of these areas:

1. *To establish and maintain a safe, healthy learning environment.* The functional areas are safe, healthy learning environments.
2. *To advance physical and intellectual competence.* Functional areas are physical, cognitive, communicative, and creative. The candidate must provide a variety of activities that promote growth in each of these areas.
3. *To support social and emotional development and to provide positive guidance.* Self, social, and guidance are the functional areas.
4. *To establish positive and productive relationships with families.* The one function area is families, and it requires the candidate to work closely with each child's family.
5. *To ensure a well-run, purposeful program responsive to participants' needs.* The one functional area is program management, and it involves planning, organizing, record keeping, communication, and working as a team player.
6. *To maintain a commitment to professionalism.* The one functional area involves knowledge of early childhood theories and practice, promoting quality, and lifelong learning.

Requirements. To apply to receive a CDA, a caregiver or teacher must be 18 years old or older; hold a high school diploma or GED; be able to speak, read, and write well enough to fulfill all the responsibilities required of a CDA candidate; and sign a statement of ethical conduct. Further, a candidate must have completed at least 120 clock hours (classes) in child development, based on the six competency areas, and which can occur through the CDAP3 process or other formal instruction. To receive a CDA, the candidate must present the following documents:

- *A professional resource file.* This is a working file that includes an autobiography, a statement of competence (how the candidate meets each competency area), and a resource file, which includes specific items such as the phone number to call to report suspected abuse, contacts for family counseling, lists of songs and books, and so on.
- *Parent opinion questionnaires.* These are confidential questionnaires given to every parent of a child under the care of the CDA candidate, and they assess

the candidate's ability to work with parents, support parents' efforts to assist their child's development, and provide communication.

- *CDA Assessment Observation Instrument.* This form rates the teacher's skill and performance while working in the setting and is administered by a professional adviser.

A CDA representative conducts an assessment and interview when the teacher has completed the course work and collected all the listed documents. In the oral interview, the CDA representative uses pictures with written scenarios of specific activities with children and asks questions based on these scenarios. For example, the picture might show two 4-year-old boys fighting over the use of a swing. The representative might ask, "What would you do if this occurred on your playground?" In the written part of the assessment, the CDA representative administers the Early Childhood Studies Review, a sixty-item multiple-choice test. Based on these items, the Council determines whether the candidate should receive a CDA.

College Degrees for Teachers

Associate Degrees. Associate (AA) degree programs are often the first exposure prospective teachers have to formal education in early childhood preparation. AA degrees are awarded by a variety of institutions, including community colleges and technical schools. States define their own criteria and standards for these programs, and determine the extent to which the AA aligns with the state's four- or five-year degrees. College programs must also meet the accreditation requirements of the National Council for Accreditation of Teacher Education (NCATE). The NAEYC has developed guidelines for institutions offering an AA for early childhood professional development (1996a), and the Division for Early Childhood/Council for Exceptional Children provides additional standards for professionals working with children with disabilities from infancy to age 8. Guidelines developed by professional associations are an effort to guide state requirements for preparing early childhood professionals; they reflect the latest knowledge, based on research and best practices. They include curriculum content, recruitment of candidates,

T.E.A.C.H. Project of North Carolina

"The T.E.A.C.H. Early Childhood Project is a statewide program designed to provide educational scholarship opportunities for child care center teachers, directors and family home providers who work in regulated settings" (Day Care Services Association, Inc., n.d.). The program provides scholarships at all community colleges, as well as universities offering four-year degrees, in North Carolina. Courses that lead to the North Carolina Early Childhood Credential, CDA, AA, or bachelor's degree in early childhood education are funded.

Scholarships provide for tuition, books, travel, paid release time (from work), and bonuses for completing the program—or a raise in the recipient's current position. This bonus or raise is contingent on the beneficiary committing to stay at their current position for a minimum of one year.

The program also funds training for experienced early childhood teachers who wish to become mentors of new teachers. Additionally, the experienced teacher receives a $700 bonus during the first year of mentoring and a 3 percent salary raise at the end of the second year of mentoring. Finally, T.E.A.C.H. provides financial awards to full-time undergraduate students in child development, contingent on their commitment to teach in a licensed or registered child-care program in North Carolina at the completion of their degree.

methods of assessing proficiency, and qualifications of instructors. The NAEYC guidelines for the AA college curriculum include (1996a):

1. *Child development and learning.* This criterion requires graduates to be able to use current knowledge and research to have a positive impact on a child's physical, social, emotional, linguistic, cognitive, and aesthetic development; to individualize instruction; to modify environments; and to support a child's and family's unique cultural context.

2. *Curriculum development and implementation.* Graduates can plan and implement activities that match individual student needs, are developmentally appropriate, and respond to children's cultural uniqueness and special needs. Students can manage classrooms that develop each child's pro-social behavior and self-esteem, and that integrate special-needs students' IEPs and IFSPs. Teachers can also establish and maintain a safe, low-stress environment and know the procedures for recognizing and reporting suspected child abuse and neglect.

3. *Family and community relationships.* Teachers receiving an AA should be able to establish positive, collaborative relationships with families by sharing information about their children, and be able to involve the family in planning for the child. Teachers should be able to work with other professionals in the community to meet the needs of the children they serve.

4. *Assessment.* Teachers should be able to use informal assessments to tailor activities to meet the needs of each child, and use formal procedures to develop the most effective programs for the children, including students with special needs.

5. *Professionalism.* Graduates should continually adjust their approaches to benefit children and families; remain up-to-date with research, laws, and best practices; and understand the history, philosophy, and current trends in the field. They should know and support the Code of Ethical Conduct, continually grow professionally, work together with colleagues, and be an advocate for young children, their families, and other early childhood professionals.

6. *Field experience.* The student must work effectively during a three hundred clock-hour direct experience requirement, supervised student teaching, or practicum with children of diverse ages, abilities, and cultural and linguistic backgrounds.

Baccalaureate Programs. There are many early childhood teachers with a variety of four-year educational backgrounds, including psychology, child development, elementary-school education, human services, and more. There are several ways to qualify for a public-school teaching credential: candidates can receive an infant to grade three certification, a K–6 certification, and in some states, a license to teach children aged 3 to 8 (third grade)—four- or five-year degrees with a practicum requirement. The NAEYC guidelines for institutions offering the early childhood credential build on the criteria just covered:

1. *Child development and learning.* The graduate will understand factors that affect a child's learning, including risk factors, developmental variations, and specific disabilities, and will develop environments to respond to these factors. The graduate will understand the relationship of culture, language, and thought on the child in the program; support a child's cultural and linguistic diversity; preserve non-English home languages; and promote anti-bias activities.

2. *Curriculum development and implementation.* The teacher will be able to implement the appropriate use of technology, including assistive technology for children with disabilities; develop concept learning approaches and opportunities; and adapt instructional practices to address the learning diversity of all students. Also, the teacher will understand how to use the physical environment, schedules, routines, and transitions to enhance children's learning.

3. *Family and community relationships.* Teachers should be able to assist parents in making decisions about their children's education and their own parenting skills. Further, they should be able to help families receive community services, based on their unique needs, and work with families as a dynamic human system.

4. *Assessment and evaluation.* This area is greatly expanded from the AA guidelines and includes being able to collect a variety of data on each child's progress to use to plan future experiences; to use authentic assessments to check each child's progress and communicate to parents; to work with other professionals to evaluate the needs of families; to use standardized assessments, along with authentic assessments, to check the progress of each child; to help in the development and implementation IEPs and IFSPs; and to use evaluations to monitor the quality of the program continually.

5. *Professionalism.* The teacher should understand basic program administration and operation, including supervision of staff and volunteers.

6. *Field experience.* The student should be able to evaluate field experiences, including those that involve working with parents and working with teams of professionals.

Which Certificate Is Best?

As I have often mentioned, the field considers early childhood to cover the ages from infancy to 8 years old (third grade). In many states, however, there are two degrees that prepare students to work with young children—infancy to third grade, and K–6—and other states provide a 3 years to third grade certification. With the increase in early childhood programs across the country, one would expect a growing popularity of infancy to third grade and 3 years to third grade preparation programs. The reverse, however, is true. Public schools generally prefer hiring teachers with K–6 certification because it provides them with more flexibility. Further, in some states teachers with K–6 credentials can teach 3- and 4-year-olds if they are part of a class that includes kindergarten in the title (e.g., kindergarten for 3-year-olds and junior kindergarten programs; Silva & Johnson, 1999).

Whether those teaching our young children have an early childhood or a K–6 certification is crucial because teachers who do not have a solid background in early childhood development and practice will not support developmentally appropriate practice, along with a child-centered and family-centered approach to learning. Many public-school early childhood programs tend to suffer from the "elementary school teacher fallacy" of too much subject matter emphasis at the expense of child-centered learning (Silva & Johnson, 1999).

Silva and Johnson recently conducted research to determine the preferences of Pennsylvania principals regarding hiring staff with an early childhood degree or a K–6 certification (1999). The study determined that principals have become more accepting

▶ *Teacher-child interaction is at the heart of growth and development.*

of the early childhood certificate and that, while they preferred K–6 staff for the primary grades and N–3 for transition, kindergarten, and junior kindergarten classrooms, they were more likely to hire K–6 teachers. Although they saw the value of the early childhood certification, fiscal and organizational concerns were the main reasons they preferred to hire teachers with the K–6 certification. It seems that staffing decisions in schools are made primarily for organizational efficiency, rather than for the needs of children (Silva & Johnson, 1999). As we increase publicly funded early childhood programs, states need to create credentialing options that do not compete with each other and that focus on the needs of the children to be served— especially young children.

Relation between Education and Quality. The state requirement that teachers in public schools have a minimum of a bachelor's degree, and salary increases in many school districts being based on teachers taking graduate work, supports an assumption that teacher education translates into quality of instruction. While the current teacher shortage is pushing this idea to the limit, many early childhood teachers do not have college degrees. In fact, most states still do not require child-care staff to have specialized training. The evidence, however, strongly suggests that teachers with more education provide higher-quality teaching—at least in the area of teacher–student interactions (Kontos & Wilcox-Herzog, 1997). The more education early childhood teachers have—everything else being equal—the more responsive, attentive, nurturing, and sensitive they are in their interactions with students. Further, where states have increased the educational requirements for licensing child-care providers and provided additional training, the quality of teacher–child interaction has increased (Hayes, Palmer, & Zaslow, 1990). This correlation between teacher education and quality of interaction is true of teachers in both center-based programs and family child care: "Research consistently shows that training is an important predictor of involved, sensitive teacher–child interactions" (Kontos & Wilcox-Herzog, 1997, p. 8).

The quality of teacher–student interactions is crucial because research consistently shows a positive link between high-quality interactions and low student stress, increased verbal ability and intelligence, and higher social and socioemotional development (Kontos & Wilcox-Herzog, 1997).

Developing Teachers

When we consider teachers and their skills and abilities, we immediately think about how to prepare teachers: What training do they need? What is the best way to prepare teachers to work with young children? And, how do prospective teachers learn best?

Approaches to Teaching Teachers. The traditional model of teaching college students is that of the expert (instructor and textbook) imparting knowledge to students. This model is based on several assumptions:

- there is a **body of knowledge** that students must learn;
- the instructors—along with the textbooks—are the source of this body of knowledge;
- students need to acquire this knowledge (listening to lectures and doing assignments) and prove they have learned the knowledge (through testing);
- students best learn the knowledge through passive listening and learning.

According to Jones (1993), however, the traditional teacher preparation approach does not match how adults optimally learn, which is through the use of their inherent curiosity, intrinsic motivation, and self-directed study in a supportive environment. Further, people do not absorb knowledge, they construct it in their minds through mental processing, emotion, and social interactions. Information needs to be manipulated, banged about (debated), and processed. Learning also takes place within a social context—classroom, conference, child-care center, school staff training. Finally, all learning has a political context: we teach the curriculum because the state will pull our funds if we don't, we do not teach our 4-year-olds a second language because our program philosophy does not support bilingual education, and so on (Jones, 1993).

Developing teachers is very similar to developing children: it requires empowering teachers to direct, evaluate, and embrace their own learning; an institution to offer a certain body of knowledge; and teachers to progress through specific stages (Katz, 1972). The main differences between children's and adults' growth and development is that adults have a lot more past experience (positively and negatively affecting learning), and they are more cognizant about their motivation to learn (to get a job, make more money, pursue a dream). Accordingly, adult learning theory is based on these basic realities (Knowles, 1980):

- an adult learner is an independent, self-directed human being;
- adults have an extensive body of experience that provides a learning resource;
- adults' readiness to learn is tied to their social roles—spouse, parent, breadwinner, head of the household, and so on—which affects how the adult learns;
- the adult's perspective on learning is based on an immediate need to apply what has been taught.

Based on adult learning concepts, early childhood teacher education should include the following:

- Students in early childhood education programs need to be empowered by the instructor to evaluate their strengths, weaknesses, and professional goals, and then plan their learning.
- A variety of methods should be used by the instructor to enable students to evaluate their experiences critically and to grow from them in working with children, families, and communities.
- Learning should be planned around the specific tasks early childhood professionals face—planning, working with parents, discipline issues, managing the classroom, and so on.

- The content of the curriculum must start with the immediate professional concerns of the early childhood educator, not with abstract concepts of theory, psychology, or history.

Adult education approaches require college instructors to establish a risk-free, collegial environment and to promote a free exchange of ideas. They require students to take responsibility for their own learning, and for being a responsible part of a learning team (the classroom). Some specific suggestions to implement an effective program for early childhood teachers are outlined below (Jones, 1993).

1. *Create lots of opportunities for students to make choices and direct their own learning.* This requires trust, autonomy, and a baseline of knowledge and skills on the part of the student. I have also found it very difficult to use this approach with students who are used to being told what to do, how to get a grade, and how to do the minimal amount of work needed to pass a class.

2. *Introspection.* Throughout my years of teaching teachers, I have been continually surprised at the answers I get when I ask the question, "Why do you do . . . ?" Usually I get "because I always have," "because the previous teacher did," "because children need to know this," "because this is what I learned when I was in school," and "because children need to learn to follow directions." Introspection requires teachers continually to question what they are doing, to have a rationale for their practice, and—most important—to be comfortable with their rationale for what they are doing with children, families, and colleagues. Teachers also need to be open to others—including parents—questioning what they are doing.

3. *Make sure the body of knowledge is learned.* It is the responsibility of the instructor to ensure that a certain crucial body of knowledge is learned by the students, which can be conveyed in a variety of ways—short lectures, readings, research, group projects, visiting experts, and the like—and can be evaluated through a variety of authentic processes.

4. *Provide lots of direct experience.* Knowledge is meaningless unless the learner can immediately try it out to determine if—and under what conditions—it works. Students need to be able to try out ideas on each other, children, families, and others.

5. *Minimal standards must be set and adhered to.* Providing a diversity of ways to learn (including lecture, direct experience, readings, reports) and a variety of ways to demonstrate what has been learned should never be seen as a way to reduce standards. Standards for classroom conduct, group activities, and presentations of materials must be established and maintained.

6. *Have lots of ways to "mess around" with new information.* This can be done through debates, open classroom discussions, challenging knowledge and information (not only that of the student but also of the instructor, the book, and the body of knowledge), and inviting visiting experts with an opposing point of view. To be able to do this effectively, a college classroom must be a secure place, students must respect one another, and a Socratic climate must exist.

7. *Know and understand the politics of education.* Education is a political process—especially if it is funded with public money. We cannot make the mistake of teaching our adult students that early childhood education is somehow a professional process driven only by good intentions and caring for children, and void of the political realities of money, power, and special-interest groups.

Developmental Stages. Lillian Katz has defined the developmental process teachers go through after they start working with children (1972). These are:

- *Survival.* New teachers experience a sense of inadequacy, being poorly prepared for all their challenges, so they simply try to survive.
- *Consolidation.* During this stage the teacher learns to focus on specific tasks in her role, discovers she does indeed have the ability to affect individual children, and knows more and is capable of more than she thought.
- *Renewal.* The teacher is now able to move outward, exploring new and innovative approaches, working with other staff, and beginning to reflect on her teaching and profession.
- *Maturity.* At this stage the teacher is ready to expand outside the classroom—in-service training opportunities, becoming a mentor for new teachers, attending and presenting at conferences, and so on.

Professionalism

What It Means to Be a Professional

According to the National Council for the Accreditation of Teacher Education (1994), a professional teacher does the following:

- provides frequent information to families about student learning and achievement;
- engages parents and families in the educational process;
- participates in professional organizations;
- volunteers to contribute in school and community projects;
- identifies and uses community resources to foster student learning;
- establishes a system for maintaining information on student progress;
- regularly serves as an advocate for all students;
- is able to assess own professional growth and seeks out opportunities for professional development;
- works as a team player within the school community.

As mentioned before, the sixth competency goal of the CDA standards is "to maintain a commitment to professionalism." CDA's definition of professionalism includes knowledge of child development, promotion of high-quality care and education, and improving one's own personal and professional competence (Council for Early Childhood Professional Recognition, 1991). Professional responsibilities are included in many of the tasks, areas of knowledge, and skills I have already discussed. They involve knowledge and support of the field, confidentiality of student and family information, advocacy, and working with other professionals.

Code of Ethics. All professional organizations have ethical codes of conduct, which provide broad guidelines for members of the profession. The purposes of a professional code of **ethics** are (Corey & Corey, 1998).

- to educate the professionals to the nature of sound ethical practices, so professionals can apply these guidelines in specific situations;
- to provide a vehicle for professional accountability—ultimately, these codes exist to protect the organization's clients (in our case, children and families);

Organizations and Publications

Administration for Children and Families (ACF). The division of the federal government that administers all three Head Start organizations (regular, Migrant, and Indian) and block-grant child-care funds. Publishes *Children Today.*

The American Montessori Society (AMS). Spearheads the implementation of public- and private-school Montessori programs in the United States (www.amshq.org).

Association for Childhood Education International (ACEI). Addresses issues relating to the care and education of children, infancy through early adolescence (www.acei.org). Publishes: *Childhood Education.*

Association of Latin American Professionals in Child Care and Education. A nonprofit organization that provides training in Spanish to early childhood teachers and caregivers.

Association of Supervision and Curriculum Development (ASCD). A national organization that covers all grade levels, focuses on formal education, and publishes a vast array of books (www.ascd.org). Publishes: *Educational Leadership.*

Center for the Study of Biracial Children (CSBC). An international organization that provides support and training for teachers, social workers, and psychologists who work with multiracial children and families (www.csbc.cncfamily.com).

Center for the Child Care Workforce (CCW). Advocates for better conditions, compensation, and professional growth for child-care teachers and providers (www.ccw.org).

Child Care Action Campaign. Educates and lobbies for better and more affordable child care (212-334-9595).

Children's Defense Fund (CDF). Leads a natioal effort to increase government support for children and families, especially low-income families (202-628-8787). Publishes the annual *The State of America's Children.*

Child Welfare League of America (CWLA). Leading national organization dedicated to children in adoptive and foster care (202-638-2952). Publishes *Child Welfare.*

Council for Exceptional Children. The leading national organization dedicated to meeting the needs of students with disabilities, along with providing support and guidance for professionals working with these students (www.cec.sped.org). Publishes *Journal of Special Education.*

Council of Early Childhood Professional Recognition. The part of NAEYC that administers the CDA program (800-424-4310).

Ecumenical Child Care Network (ECCN). A national interdenominational organization that works with church-based child care and early childhood programs (www.eccn.org).

Educational Resources Information Center/ Elementary and Early Childhood Education (ERIC/EECE). Federal clearinghouse for a vast range of early-childhood–related materials. There are various other ERICs (urban education, disabilities/gifted, teacher education, assessment and evaluation, technology, etc.) around the country (http://ericeece.org).

- to serve as a catalyst for improving practice; the codes force the field to examine critically the letter and spirit of ethical principles.

Ethical codes offer general guidelines that require individual professionals to make ethical decisions in specific situations; they identify ethical principles and standards for a profession to aspire to and be judged by, but do not guarantee ethical behavior or prescribe solutions for all ethical issues. Using ethical codes requires sound individual ethical judgment.

National Association of Child Care Professionals (NACCP). Works with both for-profit and not-for-profit programs nationwide, with an emphasis on improving management capabilities (www.naccp.org).

National Association for the Education of Young Children (NAEYC). The national association of local chapters of AEYC, this organization addresses issues of care and education for children, infancy to age 8. Hosts a large annual conference (www.naeyc.org). Publishes *Young Children.*

National Association of Child Care Resource and Referral Agencies (NACCRRA). A national association of resource and referral agencies, which provides information to parents about available child-care and education options in their communities (www.naccrra.net).

National Association of Early Childhood Teacher Educators (NAECTE). A membership organization for early childhood faculty at four-year colleges and universities who are concerned with early childhood teacher education (www.naecte.org).

National Association for Family Child Care (NAFCC). This association provides technical assistance to family child-care associations nationwide, through professionalism and accreditation (www.nafcc.org).

National Black Child Development Institute (NBCDI). A national organization that focuses on child care, health care, education, and child welfare for black children. Offers an annual conference (www.nbcdi.org).

National Child Care Association (NCCA). Assists private, licensed providers of child care with technical and professional support (www.nccanet.org).

National Coalition of Campus Child Care Centers. The national umbrella organization for campus child-care centers (www.campuschildcare.org).

National Head Start Association (NHSA). The national—nongovernmental—association dedicated to supporting Head Start programs nationwide, serving children from infancy through age 5 (www.nhsa.org). Publishes *Children and Families.*

The National Program for Playground Safety. Provides national advocacy and training on playground safety (800-554-PLAY). Publishes *Playground Safety News.*

Ounce of Prevention. Provides training, research, and advocacy for parents of young children in the areas of child-abuse prevention, assessment, and education (www.ounceofprevention.org).

Southern Early Childhood Association (SECA). Covers fourteen states; gives a unique southern perspective, along with a national viewpoint (www.SouthernEarlyChildhood.org). Publishes *Dimensions in Early Childhood.*

Stand for Children. National organization that supports local efforts on the part of children and families (800-663-4032).

Other early childhood publications. *Scholastic Early Childhood Today, Early Childhood News, Child Care Information Exchange* (www.ccie.com), *Early Childhood Educational Journal.*

NAEYC Code of Ethical Conduct. The NAEYC's code of ethical conduct (1998a, p. 3) is built around six core values:

- appreciating childhood as a unique and valuable stage of the human life cycle;
- basing our work with children on knowledge of child development;
- appreciating and supporting the close ties between child and family;
- recognizing that children are best understood in the context of family, culture, and society;
- respecting the dignity, worth, and uniqueness of each individual (child, family member, and colleague);
- helping children and adults achieve their full potential in the context of relationships that are based on trust, respect, and positive regard.

The code then describes teachers' responsibility to various groups involved in early childhood care and education: the children, their families, colleagues, and the wider community and society.

Children. Our chief responsibility is to provide safe, responsive, healthy, nurturing settings for children, and not to participate in any activity that causes harm—psychological or physical—to a child. This principle has precedence over any other principles in the code. Ethical practices include being cognizant of the current early childhood knowledge base and using this knowledge to design and implement programs; creating and maintaining safe and healthy environments; respecting the special vulnerability and uniqueness of children; and supporting inclusion of children with special needs in our programs. Further, we have a responsibility to report suspected child abuse and neglect, as well as any other practices or situations that we believe endanger the health and safety of children.

Families. We recognize the central role of families in the education and healthy development of their children. To this end we should develop open, trusting relationships with families, provide information regarding the progress of their child, and respect each

family's culture and childrearing values. Further, we should work closely with families to improve their parenting skills and provide advice to help them support their child's growth and education. We must inform families of the program's philosophy, and make families welcome in the program at any time. We must provide confidentiality for family information and not use our professional relationship for personal gain. We must be knowledgeable about community resources that support families, and use them as needed.

Colleagues. These fall into three categories: coworkers, employers, and employees. Our responsibility to one another as coworkers involves a relationship of trust, cooperation, sharing of

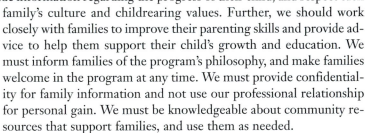

▶ *NAEYC's Code of Ethical Conduct is built around 6 core values including appreciating the close ties between the child and family.*

resources, mutual team building, and professional recognition. Concerns about professional behavior of colleagues are first addressed with that person; gossip and rumors about colleagues are not acceptable. Criticism of a colleague should be based on fact and motivated by our interest in what is good for the child and program.

Our responsibility to our employers requires assisting them in providing high-quality services, upholding the program's reputation, trying to provide change—if needed—from within the program, and speaking on behalf of the program only when authorized to do so.

Early childhood programs have a responsibility to promote working conditions that enable their employees to work collegially to provide what is best for children, families, and the field. Employers also have a responsibility to train staff and to provide sound and ethical management practices for hiring, supervision, evaluation, and termination. Finally, employers have an obligation to try to provide an adequate livelihood for staff.

Community and Society. Our primary responsibilities to community and society are to provide the services they need, work cooperatively with other community agencies, and advocate for children everywhere. We have a responsibility to the goal of giving all young children access to high-quality early childhood programs, and the goal of supporting the well-being of children and families. We should work together with other organizations toward these ends. Further, we should support the field of early childhood education and its further professional development.

Ethical Decision Making. One of the functions of a code of ethical conduct is to help guide professionals in making decisions. One model for doing so is (Corey & Corey, 1998)

1. Identify the problem. Gather data to help clarify the exact problem, and the nature of the problem.
2. Apply the Code of Ethics. If you cannot do this, continue to the next step.
3. Determine the nature and dimensions of the dilemma, and seek consultation. Talk to more experienced teachers, a supervisor, maybe a college professor, or a member of the AEYC governing board in your area.
4. Generate possible sources for action. Brainstorm a variety of solutions.

Statement of Commitment

The NAEYC statement of commitment, published* in 1998, articulates that teachers will, to the best of their ability,

- ensure that programs for young children are based on current knowledge of child development and early education;
- respect and support families in their task of nurturing children;
- respect colleagues in early childhood education and support them in maintaining the NAEYC Code of Ethical Conduct;
- serve as an advocate for children, their families, and their teachers in community and society;
- maintain high standards of professional conduct;
- recognize how personal values, opinions, and biases can affect professional judgement;
- be open to new ideas and be willing to learn from the suggestions of others;
- continue to learn, grow, and contribute as a professional;
- honor the ideas and principles of the NAEYC Code of Ethical Conduct.

Reprinted with permission from the National Association for the Education of Young Children.

5. Consider the possible consequences of all options and determine a course of action. Eliminate those that don't provide an ethical solution, and determine which of the remaining ones offer the best solution.
6. Evaluate the selected course of action. Make sure it does not pose an ethical dilemma.
7. Implement the chosen course of action.

Early Childhood Teachers in Society

Teachers of young children have a crucial role in our society: They care for and educate the next generation. Despite this critical role, we provide teachers—especially those of very young children—with minimal benefits, and we really do not treat teachers as true professionals. "Anyone can teach" is an accepted belief of many. Because of this, it is difficult to attract and retain teachers. Yet we know the quality of care and education received by our children depends to a large extent on the quality of teachers and caregivers.

Respect

The early childhood field has always been made up of two overlapping activities: educating children, and caring for children. Teachers are not valued as much in this society as they are in Europe and Asia, and the field of child care is even less respected. Many view child care as simply baby-sitting. In my graduate education classes, I am ashamed to admit, many of my teachers view their job as vitally important, and the job of caring for children as being of much lesser consequence. Many recent initiatives at the federal and state levels have been in early childhood education (see Chapter 2), but not in child care. Politicians seem to believe that the public is willing to pay for high-quality early childhood education programs (often as preparation for traditional K–12 programs) but not for high-quality child care. This lack of respect translates into poor benefits. While public-school teacher salaries are not great, they are fantastic compared to those of child-care providers and teachers. Public-school teachers receive health benefits and retirement programs, and their salaries are significantly higher than those of child-care workers. One reason that Ziegler has proposed that all early childhood programs be sponsored by the local public school system is to provide these teachers the same benefits and salaries as their public-school counterparts (Ziegler & Matia Finn-Stevenson, 1996).

Regardless of program type, philosophy, or funding, however, the most important factor determining the quality of a child's early childhood experience is the quality of adult–child interaction (Krajec et al., 2001). The expertise, passion, and involvement teachers bring to their interactions with children provide an experience children will remember all their lives.

Teacher Shortage

Nationwide there is a general shortage of K–12 teachers partly due to a lowering of respect for teachers as professionals. In fact, the early childhood field has been experiencing a shortage of crisis proportions for more than a decade (Krajec et al., 2001)—a condition that is a direct result of low pay, low status, poor working conditions, few benefits, and very few opportunities for advancement (Ripple, 2000; Whitebook et al., 2001). Nationally, the average pay for child-care teachers is $15,430, and only one-third of child-care centers provides health insurance (Center for the Child Care Workforce, 2000). While many child-care providers care for children of poverty, the providers themselves struggle with many of the same survival issues. Not only do child-care programs hire people with minimal training in child development, but many of these teachers also have a poor work ethic and communication skills. Part of the cause of the teacher shortage is the inability to retain teachers and caregivers. Of all teaching staff employed in centers in 1996, 76 percent were no longer on the job in 2000. Nationally, annual turnover rates are about 30 percent for teachers working in child care (Center for the Child Care Workforce, 2000). Even the fast-food industry has better pay, working conditions, and benefits than are offered to many child-care workers—and less stress.

The teacher shortage poses a huge dilemma for our field. First and foremost, the high rate of turnover of teaching staff negatively influences the quality of care provided—especially regarding children's social, emotional, and linguistic development (Phillips et al., 2001). Further, as more of our children come from homes that lack a stable adult presence, and research continues to show the crucial importance of stable, emotionally safe environments for optimal development, the problem becomes more extreme.

Cost and Quality

Many believe a central reason early childhood teachers receive little public respect, along with abysmal wages and benefits, is the lack of quality standards in the field. In most states, the department of social services enforces child-care licensing designed to protect the health and safety of young children. There are no uniform federal standards for early childhood education and care. This lack of quality standards has resulted in a system that provides a vast range of quality for our nation's most precious resource—our young children. And—as I discuss in many places in this book—research on optimal brain development shows how crucial the first ten years of life are. According to the 1995 Cost, Quality, and Child Outcomes study, 14 percent of centers studied were considered good- or high-quality, 74 percent mediocre to average. According to a Families and Work Institute study of family child care—much of which is unregulated—9 percent of those studied were good, and 35 percent could result in harm to a child (1994). It is very clear that high-quality early childhood programs are good for children, while poor-quality programs can be detrimental (Krajec et al., 2001). There is a clear need to provide higher, consistent standards across the nation to protect children and provide an environment that maximizes a child's development.

But what, you might ask, have quality and standards to do with teacher respect, pay, and benefits? Below are the components needed for a high-quality early childhood experience, according to Krajec et al. (2001):

- small overall group size and low adult–child ratio;
- organized and safe environment;

- responsive interactions between teachers and children;
- a well-planned, integrated curriculum;
- experiences that develop children's cognitive, social, emotional, and physical development;
- consistent, well-trained, and well-compensated staff;
- parental involvement;
- strong leadership and management skills of the director;
- supportive work environment and ongoing professional development.

Clearly a stable, educated, satisfied staff—teachers and administrators—affects every one of these areas. A variety of initiatives nationwide designed to increase the training, benefits (both pay and health insurance), and opportunities for promotion of child-care teachers are currently in place. Programs like T.E.A.C.H. (see T.E.A.C.H. Project of North Carolina in this chapter), which provide scholarships to help teachers receive formal education in early childhood education, and receive pay increases based on that education, exist in more than 14 states. All these programs pay supplements to teachers, directors, and family child-care providers based on formal education. Rhode Island provides health insurance to early childhood family child-care providers and center providers who serve poor children. Programs like the California Early Childhood Mentoring Program provide mentoring and stipends for novice teachers. Head Start has increased its average teacher's salary from $14,600 to $17,800 (many Head Start teachers don't teach during the summer) and provides health insurance to all teachers and increased retirement benefits (Whitebook, 1995).

Men in Early Childhood Programs

The early childhood field has historically been dominated by females—particularly teachers and caregivers, but also elementary-school principals and child-care administrators. Today, less than one in twenty workers in child-care centers is a man (Neugebauer, 2000). In 1977, 6 percent of child-care center staff were men; in 1988 that number dropped to 3 percent (Whitebook, 1989). In Illinois, 98 percent of teaching staff in non–public-school programs—including Head Start—are women; 96 percent of administrators are women (Krajec et al., 2001). The figures are somewhat better, however, in elementary schools, for both teachers and administrators. Reasons that there are so few men in early childhood programs include:

- *Low pay.* While the low pay and compensation in our field are unacceptable for anyone, men have been raised in this society to earn enough to support their families. Men simply expect to get paid more. Of course, women should also.
- *Bias against hiring men.* This bias includes a belief that women are naturally disposed to nurture young children, while men are not. Many directors expect higher levels of education for men in the same position compared to women; men are not allowed to change diapers or toilet-train toddlers; men are believed to play too roughly with children; and many directors believe men are more likely to molest children than women (Neugebauer, 2000).
- *Hurdles after being employed.* Once men are employed, they face suspicion from parents of their motives for being in early childhood programs, resulting in re-

▶ *Many people believe it is critical we increase the number of men in the field. Both boys and girls benefit from male teachers and care givers.*

quests to remove children from classrooms that have a male teacher. Further, many in society believe that men select a job in early childhood education because they are incapable of getting "a real job." Men in early childhood programs are often expected to do all the physical work—take out the trash, shovel snow, bring in the milk for the cooks, and so on. But men also report being singled out for what they cannot do. "Men cannot change diapers"; "Male teachers cannot take children to the bathroom"; "Men cannot be left alone in charge of a classroom" (Neugebauer, 2000).

- *Men feel isolated.* Because there are so few men in the field, and because those who are experience society's, parents', and directors' mistrust, men often feel very isolated and feel they have no one to support them.
- *Men are not always welcome.* While much of the public supports the presence of men in elementary schools, especially in certain roles—gym teacher, principal, math or science teacher—there is a strong bias against men working with children of kindergarten age and younger—from other teachers, administrators, advocates, and politicians.

Increasing Numbers of Men in Early Childhood Programs. Many people believe it is vital that we increase the number of men in our field, especially in early childhood programs that serve children who do not have a stable male model in their lives. Specific suggestions provided by Neugebauer and others for directors, principals, and administrators of school-age programs to increase the numbers of men in their programs include (Cunningham, 1998–1999; Neugebauer, 2001):

- *Examine your own attitudes.* Do you really want men? Once you get men in the program, are you open to the diversity they bring (which may challenge the ways you have always done things)?
- *Be an advocate for men.* This should include working proactively with parents to convince them of the value of having men in the center. It is easy for a director, principal, or female teacher to hide behind the reticence of parents in order not to hire men. But this does not change the situation.
- *Provide numbers.* We are all familiar with tokenism when it comes to hiring minority staff, or women in predominantly male businesses. The same concept holds for hiring and retaining men: they need other men in the program so that they don't become the "symbol of manhood" (good and bad) in the program.
- *Spread the word.* Men—like anyone else—want to work in a place that supports and appreciates them. A center that wants to hire and retain men must be

proactive—hold workshops about the value of including men, seek publicity for their efforts, highlight their success.

- *Advertise in the right places.* Programs seeking men should advertise in publications men are likely to read and use words in these advertisements that attract men—such as *recreation, activity, leadership,* and the like.

- *Treat all employees the same.* Men should not be expected to do all the stereotypical male activities—playing sports with the children, fixing the bus; further, personnel policies should not separate men and women. They should be general enough to cover both.

- *Involve fathers.* Find ways to improve father involvement in programs. This provides a more comfortable environment and a sense of comradeship for male teachers.

- *Help men find support.* Retaining men is largely contingent on their finding support with other men. Help create men's caucuses, attend conferences that address male issues, create a regional male support group and give conference sessions.

- *Provide good working conditions.* Like women, men want competitive salaries, benefits, opportunities for advancement, and a professional environment in which to work every day.

Working with Parents

Teachers of young children have always recognized a need to work closely with the child's family. However, as families become more and more diverse, and as a larger variety of children attend early childhood programs, this need has increased. Further, the early childhood field now strongly believes the teachers and parents must work together in a partnership to most effectively benefit the child.

Working with Families

Working closely with parents and families has always been a central component of early childhood education. Friedrich Froebel developed activities for mothers to do with their children at home; mothers' day out programs and parent cooperatives were developed by parents to meet their children's and family needs; and Head Start has always insisted on parental involvement. Head Start regulations require staff home visits on a regular basis. Furthermore, as early childhood programs are viewed by the public and politicians as a major way to address school failure among minority and low-income children, parental involvement has been targeted as central to this effort.

Various studies show that parental involvement improves students' academic performance. This includes higher grades, higher scores on achievement tests, better student behavior and attitudes, and more effective schools (Henderson, 1988). Further, when teachers actively involve parents in teaching practices, parents increase interactions with their children at home, feel more empowered to assist their children, and rate their teachers more highly (Jones, 1993). According to the Northwest Regional Educational Laboratory, parental involvement at the school level is crucial to school success (NREL,

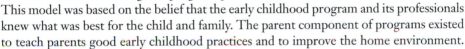
▶ *Teachers must consider the child's home culture and environment, including extended family.*

1990). The National Council for the Accreditation of Teacher Education standards (NCATE, 1994) require beginning teachers to be able to work closely with families in support of student learning.

While nonschool early childhood programs have embraced the parental involvement concept—with a range of effectiveness—public schools have often struggled with this concept, a struggle that has increased as the demographics of public-school families have radically changed.

A Paradigm Shift. The traditional parental involvement model for early childhood programs and schools was a professionally driven parent-education tradition—educators trying to improve the child's home environment and using the parent to implement what the educator believed to be good program practices (Powell, 1998). This model was based on the belief that the early childhood program and its professionals knew what was best for the child and family. The parent component of programs existed to teach parents good early childhood practices and to improve the home environment.

The current view of parental involvement is different. "Evolving over the past three decades is the image of early childhood programs as family support systems that function as modern-day versions of the traditional extended family" (Powell, 1998, p. 60). Parents are now viewed as equal partners in the education of their children. Programs now work closely within family and community contexts, because of changing family demographics, the ecological view of child development (Bronfenbrenner & Morris, 1998), the fact that many more children are being taught by teachers from radically different backgrounds from their own, and an appreciation of the power of good home–program collaboration.

Parents' and Teachers' Views of Good Early Childhood Programs. Parents and early childhood staff differ on their views of good early childhood practices. Many parents support teacher-directed practices of rote learning, memorization, and drill and practice, while early childhood teachers emphasize play and self-directed learning (Dunn & Kontos, 1997). Emphasis on teacher-directed learning of academics is especially strong among low-income parents. Further, parents tend to select programs for their children that professionals view as mediocre (Powell, 1998). Parents select programs that provide the kind of early childhood program they want for their children: those that want teacher-directed instruction in academics put their children in programs that provide this; those that prefer play and self-directed learning choose programs that provide this kind of approach.

Another factor that affects family–program collaboration is whether the home and the program see eye to eye on the individual child's abilities and proposed classroom experiences. Congruency in this area produces children who are more successful in their later school experience.

Parent–Staff Confidence. Parental involvement increases if parents and staff have confidence in each other. Mutual parent–staff confidence is crucial, even when their views differ (Powell, 1998). Both parents and staff view collaboration as an important factor. Parents view good staff as those with knowledge and skills, and as caring people. Parents consider their caregivers' experience with children, concern for safety, and discipline style as essential factors. Friendly communication is also considered important by parents. Staff view good parents as those with open communication and good knowledge and childrearing skills. Many teachers judge parents to be poor in their parenting skills. Studies indicate that teachers have less communication with parents they judge to be poor at child raising than with parents they judge to be adequate, and children of these parents are lower in cognitive, linguistic, and social development (Dunn & Kontos, 1989). In an extensive study on parent–teacher relationships in elementary schools, Epstein (1984 and 1985) found that teachers who did not emphasize parental involvement expected more parental help and support at home from single parents, poorly educated parents, and low-income parents, as compared to two-parent homes. These same teachers also viewed single and low-income parents as less helpful and responsible in supporting the children's schoolwork at home. Teachers who emphasized parental involvement, however, made equal demands on all parents, regardless of the parent's marital status or education, and rated single parents just as helpful with the children's education as married parents.

A central challenge with program–family communication is language. While we serve more and more families who don't speak English, few programs employ staff that speak the non-English languages of the parents (Chang, 1993). Language is not a problem with family child care, however, because parents purposely select providers who speak their language.

Responsive Environments. Traditional activities involving parents—volunteering in the classroom, parenting workshops, and home visits—do not work with many of today's families and programs. To engage parents, programs need to match what they provide to the needs of families. High-risk families need child care, transportation, and personnel who understand their unique needs (Powell, 1998). This can be very expensive for a school or program.

While it seems obvious that parents who believe they can have an impact on their child's development will become involved in a program, we often ignore this concept. "Perceptions or beliefs then appear to be among the important factors that may contribute to parents' decisions about participating in a workshop" (Powell, 1998, p. 64). Three factors that affect whether parents become involved in their child's education are the parents' understanding of their role in working with their child's program; the parents' belief that they can, in fact, have a positive impact on their child's education; and whether the program really wants them involved or is simply following policies and procedures (Hoover-Dempsey & Sandler, 1997).

Individual involvement with parents—through a primary child-care worker and tailored around the individual needs of each family—have more lasting effects on children's academic success than group approaches to family involvement (Seitz & Apfel, 1994). The individual relationships, and the responsiveness to the unique family issues, are essential.

Family Engagement. According to Powell (1998), some specific ideas can help programs develop effective program– or school–family partnerships. These include:

- *Programs must serve families, not just children.* Policies, procedures, and practices must consider how they affect the family and how they include the entire family.
- *Programs need to respond to the demographics of their families.* Staff must speak the language of the parents and understand their values and traditions.
- *Parents and staff must have confidence in each other.* Parents need to know the staff are skilled, knowledgeable, and caring. Thus, they need opportunities to get to know staff, and staff need training to be able to include the family's perspective and see the parents' strengths.
- *Parent communication must be individualized.* Each child should have a primary caregiver who communicates frequently and consistently with the parents. There should be opportunities for parents and staff to develop shared goals for the child. Staff need to be available when parents are most visible in the program.
- *Programs should view parents as individuals.* Parental involvement increases when parents are seen as more than just "Jaime's father"—as whole people with unique needs and interests.
- *Supports—such as child care and transportation—and parents' beliefs are important.* Recognizing the way parents feel about their involvement is as important as program support. A program must find ways to help parents see their importance to their child's success.
- *Definitions of quality early childhood programs must place a higher emphasis on the family component.* Quality indicators must reflect the crucial nature of family involvement.
- *Education preparation programs should emphasize working with parents.* Teacher credentialing and continuing education must provide added focus to developing skills to communicate with parents, and to appreciating individual family perspectives.

Working with Diverse Families

Much has been said and written about the shift from the two-parent home, with husband working and mother staying at home (the traditional family), to contemporary family structures, which are extremely diverse. For early childhood programs and teachers to include parents and families effectively in their children's education, working with diverse families must be a central part of teacher preparation. Specifically, teacher preparation programs should meet the following goals (Jones, 1994):

- help teachers become sensitive to diverse family structures;
- help teachers become knowledgeable about the value of parental involvement in the educational process for all students, not just middle-class students;
- gain practical experience working with diverse families, including communication, at-home reading projects, and parent–teacher conferences;
- learn various approaches that work effectively with diverse families.

Barriers to Working with Diverse Families. Students who learn about working with diverse families begin to understand the needs of those families: single parents and poor parents have little time to work with schools because they juggle many roles, and are trying to stay financially afloat; poor parents and parents who were not successful in their own school experience (dropped out, punished for speaking another language, relegated to self-contained special-education classrooms) are reluctant to work with teachers and other school staff; single parents, fathers, and families in which both parents work cannot participate in school-based activities during working hours; and blended families, noncustodial parents, and extended family members need to be considered in scheduling conferences, communication, and family involvement. Students learn why many parents do not initially see their child's early childhood program as positive.

Including Diverse Families. Once students have learned about issues facing diverse families, they need to learn and try out ideas that effectively increase parent involvement of these families. This often requires extra effort and resources—involving the whole family, making transportation available, providing child care, sending personal invitations, and making individual phone calls (Jones, 1994). Students can learn about schools that successfully include families, try out a variety of activities, and learn from one another. Programs that effectively include parents do things like operate family centers, provide workshops to help parents with children's math and science assignments, provide home book bags, provide a telephone contact person, offer family activities once a week, and provide transportation to school activities. Home visits are also conducted when parents cannot get to the program (Jones, 1994).

Helping Parents Help Their Children. Programs should empower parents and other adults to work with their children on school-related issues at home. Ideas that work include activity calendars for parents and children, creative homework assignments that require parent–child interactions, and read-at-home programs (with parent communication, calendars, daily sign-off by parents, classroom goals, and victory parties; Jones, 1994). Parent–teacher conferences are crucial opportunities for programs to find ways to work with parents. Prospective teachers need to learn how to conduct effective parent–teacher conferences. One goal is to establish a positive relationship with the parents and to plan ways cooperatively for the parent to become involved. Teachers learn effective parent–teacher conference approaches through role plays, enacting possible scenarios, using written tips and guidelines, and working in small groups to develop approaches to possible problem situations.

Working with Fathers

Historically, early childhood programs have viewed parent communication and involvement as mother communication and involvement; fathers have been ignored. Even when fathers attempted to become involved—or were forced to because they were single parents—they experienced considerable frustration. Some fathers still report that staff use them simply as a link to their wife and show a decided preference for communicating with the mother.

The Importance of Father Involvement.

Today there is an increased awareness of the importance of father involvement in the lives of children. Children whose fathers participate in school activities (as volunteers, attending parent–teacher conferences, and so on), are more likely to receive As and participate in extracurricular activities (U.S. Department of Education, 1997). Children whose fathers are directly involved in their school are less likely to repeat a grade or to be expelled or suspended; they do better on academic tests, are less likely to engage in violent behavior in school, and stay in school longer (Horn, 1998).

Barriers to Father Involvement.

There is a variety of barriers that make it difficult for working fathers to become involved in the care and education of their young children. A central problem is work schedules, which necessitate that programs provide opportunities for involvement after traditional working hours. Another challenge is that programs and specialists are simply more comfortable communicating with mothers. While many women now work full-time, the image of the mother as the child's caregiver and liaison with her child's program continues. Further, men and women have different styles of relating to each other. Since almost all teachers and special-education professionals are women, this can pose a communication conflict. Historically men were the authority in the family, and they still are in some families and cultures. Today, many women who have experienced abusive relationships with men resent the presence of men in their programs, an issue that appears to be particularly pronounced in Head Start programs, where many of the staff are single mothers (Turbiville et al., 2000).

What Fathers Want.

Research shows that fathers, like the rest of us, should be treated as individuals when encouraging involvement in their child's programs (Turbiville et al., 2000). Programs need to talk with fathers and find out their interests and how they would like to be involved with their child's program. A form or questionnaire should be given to fathers at the time the child enrolls, and additional efforts to collect information should occur throughout the child's attendance.

Men prefer program involvement when the entire family is involved. They want activities that respond to their family's unique needs, not father-only programs. Research on a variety of early childhood programs shows this to be the number one preference, probably because in so many homes both parents work, and therefore they value any time the family can be together.

▶ *Fathers are a central part of the child's life, and need to be supported and encouraged by the program or school. (Ruth Benjamin-Wardle)*

According to the same same research, fathers did not view the lack of male staff or volunteers in a program as detrimental to their involvement. In some programs fathers enjoyed working on maintenance-type activities; in others they did not (Turbiville et al., 2000). Fathers in typical community-based child-care programs preferred these kinds of involvement activities: family activities, Daddy and me activities, opportunities for both parents to learn about their child's future, opportunities for both parents to learn about child development, and sports activities.

Conclusion

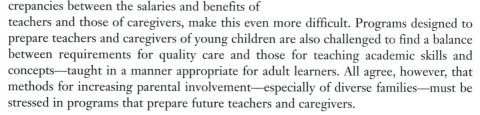

The early childhood field in this country is composed of a collection of diverse programs and providers—with a vast range of philosophies, practices, and sponsors. Consequently, staff who work with young children also make up a diverse profession, with a variety of education, skills, and experiences. They range from young people just out of high school to credentialed teachers and a variety of specialists. Combining this diversity into one profession is challenging; further, the difference between child care and education, and the discrepancies between the salaries and benefits of teachers and those of caregivers, make this even more difficult. Programs designed to prepare teachers and caregivers of young children are also challenged to find a balance between requirements for quality care and those for teaching academic skills and concepts—taught in a manner appropriate for adult learners. All agree, however, that methods for increasing parental involvement—especially of diverse families—must be stressed in programs that prepare future teachers and caregivers.

Questions and Projects

1. Briefly rate yourself on each of the six CDA competencies. How could you improve in areas where you are weak?

2. Write a short paper about where you would like to be, professionally, (1) when you finish this program, (2) in five years, and (3) in ten years. Describe degrees or certification and the kinds of positions you would hold, and discuss how you will achieve these goals.

3. Look at the characteristics of good teachers, and rate yourself on each of these.

4. Why are you preparing to be a teacher of young children? Write a short essay on factors of your childhood and life that have influenced you to become a teacher.

5. Should more men be involved in working with young children, or is it "only natural" that women dominate this field? Write a short paper.

6. Contact two professional early childhood organizations, have them send you their materials, then provide an oral presentation of the organizations to the class.

CHAPTER

8

Play *as* Curriculum

*P*lay is synonymous with early childhood. Most early childhood theorists include play as a central part of their approach; early childhood professionals talk a great deal about play. Even so, the inclusion of play in programs for young children faces two strong challenges: first, there is a great deal of debate about what actually constitutes play; and second, many politicians and educational policymakers believe play is off-task behavior that does not contribute directly to the acquisition of important educational skills and concepts. As the use of educational standards sweeps this country and as teaching academics is pushed down to younger-age children, the inclusion of play in early childhood programs becomes more and more controversial.

What exactly is play? Why and how is play important to the healthy development of children? And how does play translate into important academic outcomes and educational growth? This chapter explores all of these areas and hopes to provide enough information to enable education students to develop their own opinion regarding play—both indoors and outdoors—for children 0 to 8 years old. ■

What Is Play?

All young children play, as do adults and many animals. Many believe playing is an absolutely crucial part of the early childhood experience. Some go so far as to say children who do not play (for whatever reasons) are likely to become criminals (Brown, 1994). But what is play?

Questions to Consider

1. Why is play important in the healthy development of young children?

2. What are the different kinds of play?

3. What is the relationship between play, learning, and education?

4. What are gender differences evident in play? What are the causes of these differences?

5. Why are good outdoor playgrounds needed more today than in the past? Why are infant and toddler playgrounds needed?

6. What is the role of adults—parents and teachers—in play?

While most of us know play when we see it, academics have trouble defining it (Johnson, Christie, & Yawkey, 1999). Play involves a free-choice activity that is nonliteral, self-motivated, enjoyable, and process oriented. Central to this definition is **nonliterality**—the nonrealistic aspect of play. This means that the external constraints of time, use of materials, rules of the play activity, and roles of the participants are all determined by the children. They are based on the children's sense of reality. To put it another way, children define play; and the nature of play changes depending on the children involved. What may be play to one child at one time may not be play to another child at another time.

I observed Guatemalan girls in their colorful traditional clothes gleefully throwing soap at one another while washing clothes in mountain streams. They seemed to be playing. Yet an American child washing clothes in the family's washer, preparing for the next school day, is probably not playing. Guatemalan boys energetically run after an old soccer ball on a water-logged highland field. They rambunctiously push the ball toward the goal, appearing to all to be playing; American children practicing a complicated soccer drill, under the watchful eye of their strict coach, may not be. A 2-year-old sitting on the kitchen floor, banging away on a collection of pots and pans while his father does the dishes, is clearly playing. And some Amish children engaged in a frantic game of tag during recess are also playing.

Animals and Play

Many scholars have carefully studied the play of animals. They have been particularly fascinated by the play of young animals, believing that through play young animals learn and practice social and fighting skills, and develop the physical strength and endurance needed to survive as adults (Brown, 1994). The social skills learned include developing social bonds and teamwork, and recognizing the hierarchy of power within the group. Through play, young animals also learn flexible behavior that prepares them to be resourceful in dealing with the unexpected. Many play theories postulate that humans use play in a very similar manner: to develop skills, attitudes, and abilities necessary to function successfully as adults within a society and a culture.

Additionally, in a 1994 article in *National Geographic*, Stuart Brown, a physician, makes a strong case that animals also play "just for the fun of it." In his article Brown remembers a polar bear playing with a dog (usually sworn enemies). The dog "wagged his tail, grinned, and actually bowed to the bear, as if in invitation. The bear responded with enthusiastic body language and nonaggressive facial signals. These two normally antagonistic species were speaking the same language, 'Let's play' " (Brown, 1994, p. 7). Every evening for a week the bear returned to play with one of the dogs.

Other examples in this article about animals playing for sheer joy and pleasure include a raven in Wales that slid down a ten-foot snow embankment on its back, then stood up, walked back to its starting point, and repeated the activity several times; dolphins leaping and cavorting with humans; and young Japanese macaque monkeys creating snowballs by rolling snow along the ground the way children do, then proudly displaying their snowballs to other monkeys.

I have a dog, Ginger, who loves to play. Actually, she loves three kinds of play. She likes the traditional retrieving of a ball, which she brings back, expecting it to be thrown again. But she plays this game only when she chooses. Sometimes I will pick up the ball and throw it, and she just stands there, looking at me in puzzlement. She also loves to play hide-and-seek with my children. They go downstairs, hide, and then yell, "Find." She then races downstairs to find them. Finally, Ginger loves to play tag outside. Being part grayhound, she is very fast. She seems to love challenging me to tag her, and then racing off. When I tire of the game and turn to work on my garden or to clean up the yard, she jumps up and places her front paws on my back, as if to say, "Come on, let's keep playing."

Characteristics of Play

As I mentioned earlier, children's play includes certain essential characteristics: it must be chosen freely, be undertaken for its own sake and not have as its purpose an end goal, and be pleasurable to the children. In *Play and Early Childhood Development* (1999), Johnson, Christie, and Yawkey elaborate on these ideas.

Nonliterality. In play, children create their own reality. While it may be ten o'clock on a hot June morning, the children may pretend they are building an igloo in the middle of winter. They may use a unit block to represent a shovel. And they may build an igloo ten feet tall. In one of my Head Start classrooms, a group of children built a casket out of unit and hollow blocks, placed a child in the casket, covered it up with boards, said a service, and then "buried" the child!

Intrinsic Motivation. Play is undertaken for the sake of the play itself. When children no longer want to play, they leave. It has no other reason—to solve a problem, get a grade, satisfy the teacher, or earn tokens or money.

Process Oriented. A group of children loves to build a fort, but shortly after it is finished, they tear it down to build something else. In play, the children enjoy the activity of playing: it is not goal oriented. This lack of emphasis on product provides a low-stress atmosphere that allows children to experiment, risk, and be flexible.

Free Choice. Children view the same activity as play or not play, depending on whether it was chosen freely by them (King, 1979). And free choice is defined by the child, not an adult.

Positive Affect. Children enjoy playing! This is illustrated by their continual choice to do so, whenever possible. Playing children often show great pleasure on their faces.

Theories of Play

Philosophers and academics have been fascinated with play for a long time. A theory is an attempt to place a phenomenon or concept within a larger framework. In the case of play, theorists have attempted to place play within the frameworks of development, knowledge, education, and culture.

Classical Theories of Play

Some of the older theories of play are summarized in the following table (Johnson, Christie, & Yawkey, 1999). Many educators and much of the public still support some of these classical theories.

Name of Theory	Originator of Theory	Purpose of Play
Surplus energy	Schiller and Spencer	Eliminate surplus energy
Recreation	Lazarus	Regenerate energy expended in work
Recapitulation	Hall	Eliminate ancient instincts
Practice	Groos	Perfect instincts needed for adult life

Surplus Energy. This theory proposes that animals and people have a specific amount of energy that can be used to meet their need to survive—hunting, defending territory, fighting, and so on. The energy that is left over must be dispensed with somehow: this is the role of play. People who believe that children who have been cooped up all day in a classroom need to let off steam support this theory.

Recreation Theory. Based on the ideas of German poet Moritz Lazarus, the recreation theory states that play exists to reenergize people. Thus, people who have worked hard all week need to play hard on the weekend, to recharge their batteries. To be effective, the play activity must differ greatly from the work activity. To a degree, this theory is the opposite of the surplus energy theory. People who believe in the need for children's days to be broken up into periods of instruction and active play, or recess, would seem to support this theory.

Recapitulation Theory. Developed by the American psychologist, G. Stanley Hall, **recapitulation** theory argues that children's play develops through the same stages as the development of the human race: animal, savage, tribal member, hunter, and so on. Climbing trees (primate behavior) occurs before group play (tribal behavior). For Hall, the purpose of play is for children to experience these primitive stages, thus eliminating them from adult behavior.

Practice Theory. According to practice theory, play provides the opportunity for people and animals to practice skills and behaviors needed to survive. For example, young animals engaging in play-fighting are practicing the physical and social skills needed to be effective hunters. For children, playing in the sociodramatic play area enables them to practice being a doctor, parent, teacher, and so on.

Modern Theories of Play

More contemporary theories of play come out of more recent theories of development, research in children's behavior, and a combination of both.

Psychodynamic Theory. Freud, the father of psychoanalytic theory, believed that play enables children to eliminate the effects of a traumatic experience before that experience is placed in the child's subconscious. Thus, a child who has experienced domestic

▶ *Making things with materials is called constuctive play, a form of cognitive play.*

violence, or observed a tragic accident, should be encouraged to reenact these experiences in a play situation, for as long as needed to work out the trauma. Freud believed that experiences that find their way into the subconscious influence future behavior, unless dealt with through therapy.

Erik Erikson, a later psychoanalyst who developed a psycho-social theory of development (see Chapter 9), believed children use play to enable them to progress through his developmental stages.

Cognitive Theories. Jean Piaget viewed play as a central part of his theory of cognitive development (see Chapter 9). For Piaget, play enables children to practice and internalize newly acquired skills and concepts. A child who has just learned that a large ball always bounces in the same manner when dropped on concrete will practice bouncing the ball—play with it—to internalize this new concept, until the knowledge becomes automatic.

The Russian psychologist Lev Vygotsky believed that play is the way children learn to represent real experiences when those experiences are not actually present: for instance, a girl uses the doll she is playing with to think about her new baby brother. And play provides a structure children use to assist in social and cognitive development—the **scaffolding** needed for them to advance. Playing children can practice good behavior, experiment with new words, and try out more complex social interactions.

The contemporary American psychologist Jerome Bruner has suggested that because play is not controlled by the pressure of producing results or trying to meet external goals, it allows children to develop new, creative, and flexible ways to solve problems. Children then use these methods to solve real-life situations. Bruner believes play teaches flexibility, creativity, and outside-the-box thinking strategies. For Sutton-Smith, play enables children to prepare for adult life—what he calls adaptive variability, the ability to adapt behavior to meet new situations in adult life. But because adult life changes and is not predictable (note the advent of the computer), play teaches children the flexibility and adaptability they will need as adults to change with the times. Sutton-Smith also believes that play provides protection for children against the negative effects of structure, goals, and the stress of the adult world.

For the husband-and-wife team of Jerome and Dorothy Singer, play is a positive, creative force in the total development of children—fostering divergent thinking, self-control, and empathy. Play provides a way for children to control internal (mental) and external stimulation. Children use this ability to create pleasurable experiences: a child who is bored at home can go to the back yard and have fun playing with her dog; a child who is bored waiting for her mother in the dentist's waiting room can have a pleasurable daydream.

Developmentally Appropriate Practice

Arousal-Modulation Theory. Developed by Berlyne (1960) and Ellis (1973), the **arousal-modulation theory of play** states that play is the way humans maintain arousal (stimulation) at an optimal level. Research has shown that humans need a consistent level of stimulation—not too much and not too little (which must account for the popularity of commercial TV!). According to this theory, when children are bored or understimulated, they seek out play opportunities to raise their level of stimulation; when they are overstimulated, they use play to reduce the tension.

Bateson's Theory. To Bateson (1955), play is a rule-governed activity in which all participants must understand the rules or "play frames" in order to play. Everyone involved in play-fighting knows that it is not for real. And if someone forgets, the other children exit the play momentarily to remind the erroneous player. The Mayan girls throwing the soap while washing clothes in the stream know that the rules of the game require that the clothes still get washed. Amish children playing jump the stick all understand and agree to the frame of taking turns and exiting the game when they are out. Children communicate to each other in a variety of ways the expectation of the play activity.

Bateson and colleagues have shown that playing children will constantly shift between the play frame—their role in the play activity—and their real selves. They do so in a variety of ways to set up, maintain, and terminate the play activity. Bateson is particularly interested in how children shift back and forth between play and reality, and how a child's immediate surroundings affect the child's play (Bateson, 1955).

Wardle's Theory. While I am not recognized as having a specific play theory, I want to present my perspective within this broader discussion. First, children progress through stages of play and through levels (complexity) of play. As children master new concepts and practice them through repetitive play, they progress to the next level. In essence, children create their own curriculum. Because children like to learn new information and want to master new tasks (ever watched a child persist in learning to ride a bike?), and because they hate to be bored, children self-diagnose what they know and what they can learn next. Play provides the ultimate curriculum for social, physical, and cognitive advancement. Second, by using materials, interactions with others, and mastery of tasks and skills to progress through levels of play, children develop a sense of control over their environment and a feeling of competence and enjoyment. And play provides a natural integration among all the crucial brain functions and learning domains, an integration that is often missing in teacher-directed instruction. Research shows that integration is very important to brain development (Shore, 1997).

Play is also a very effective way for children to accumulate a vast amount of basic knowledge about the world around them—knowledge needed in language arts, math, science, social studies, and the arts. When playing with sticks in the sand, a child learns about the properties of sand, how posts are used for building, erosion by water, the effect of moisture on materials, the impact of the wind, and the nature of gravity. A child playing with tadpoles in a pond learns about the cycle of life, the properties of water, and concepts related to water safety and drowning. In sociodramatic play, children experiment with words, phrases, and idioms they have heard, and learn more complex ways to express themselves and relate to others.

Why Play?

Why is play critically important for the development and education of young children? Here are a few of the reasons.

Abstraction. Our world is filled with abstract symbols; words are abstractions for things and ideas; letters for sounds; numerals for quantities. *Three* can mean three apples or three wars. Young children live in very concrete worlds: *mother* is their mother; *dog* is the German shepherd down the street. Playing is the process children use to move from reliance on concrete objects in their thinking to manipulating abstract ideas.

Practice. Basically we learn by discovering new concepts and skills, and then practicing them until they are fully internalized in our minds. The process of practicing is as important as the process of discovering. Play provides a self-motivated, enjoyable way to practice.

Control of the environment. Central to the concept of play is the child's control of the activity— choosing the materials, deciding on the level of complexity, adjusting the challenges, and deciding whom to play with. This sense of control gives children a feeling of empowerment about their world and their learning.

Social skills and moral rules. When children engage in dramatic play, they often select roles that are outside their own direct experience. By doing so they learn about someone else— a vital skill in learning social and moral behavior. In social play children also learn to control their egocentric wishes for the good of the group. Later, children play games with rules they learn to follow for the good of the game, but not made up by them—much as all people must learn to follow the laws of society for the good of everyone.

Flexibility and creativity. In play, children use objects and toys to create stories, build constructions, and engage in a fantasy world. The use of materials in flexible and creative ways teaches children to be creative and flexible thinkers with abstract ideas and concepts.

Risk takers. Learning requires a great deal of experimentation and trial and error. When children learn to talk, they try out new words, grammatical structures, and expressions. When children experiment with scientific ideas, they must try something many times to develop a theory (the steeper the angle of the board, the faster the toy car goes). Experimenting and risk taking require an environment that doesn't punish every mistake or correct every experiment. Play is such an environment.

Physical activity. More and more research indicates that U.S. adults, and many children, are overweight. Active physical play is a good way to address this problem because children choose to be physically active because it's fun, and physical play in childhood develops a disposition toward voluntary adult physical activities and active lifestyles (Wardle, 1987b).

Play and How Children Learn

Psychologists and early childhood educators believe that children's play includes all of the forms of the learning that take place at this age: physical development, cognitive growth, emotional maturity, and development of speech all occur though play. Maybe this is why I believe play is crucially important for the healthy development of young children.

Types of Play

In examining the development of children's play from infancy through 8 years old, it is helpful to break play down into three general types: **motor or physical play, social play, and cognitive play.** Children obviously do not restrict themselves to only one type of play at any particular time; further, children develop through various stages of play within each of these categories. Until recently, researchers viewed this play development as a linear progression from simple, unidimensional play toward more complex, multi-dimensional play (Johnson, Christie, & Yawkey, 1999). From the current information about individual differences and cultural influences, it is clear this linear approach is overly simplistic. It is a helpful perspective, however, especially in Western societies that require young children to progress rapidly from simple childlike play to a highly complex, abstract world of digital information, while at the same time requiring children to move from solitary play to an ability to function effectively in a free society of social contracts, laws, moral expectations, and complex social interactions.

Physical or Motor Play. When we think of play, physical or motor play usually first comes to mind: climbing a piece of equipment, playing catch, and riding a bike. Most outdoor playgrounds focus on children's motor play needs. And an emphasis on teaching very young children specific sports skills—soccer, gymnastics, baseball—places a strong focus on children's early physical development. The increased concern by doctors and educators over the poor physical health of our population is resulting in more organized physical activities for young children in early childhood programs and recreational centers.

Clearly children's motor play is directly tied to their physical development—in fine motor skills, gross motor skills, and overall body coordination. A child who has not learned to walk cannot engage in play activities that require mobility; a child who is still mastering the ability to catch a large ball with two hands will have trouble with ball games that require this skill. And development in these areas is a direct result of a combination of factors, including diet, genetics, environment, and level of activity.

I was quite surprised to observe the advanced physical development of Mayan children in Guatemala. I played soccer with the boys, and walked with different children over the treacherous, narrow dirt pathways, jumping streams and scaling mountainsides. I observed them run between the corn plants, climb the limbless trees, and walk with their parents ten kilometers each weekend to the local market. They also helped pick corn, carry water from the well, wash clothes in the stream, and build the daily cooking fire. They were physically advanced and well coordinated.

I also experienced the same phenomenon when I visit the religious school and early childhood program in Pennsylvania, where my sisters teach. Because the program's educational philosophy includes extensive use of the outdoors, dance, games, and working in the communal gardens; and because families engage in hikes, games, gardening, and picnics and don't have TV or computers, their children are physically advanced.

Knowledge about children's physical and motor development is essential for educators. It enables us to make sure we don't expect certain abilities that are inappropriate for a child's age (for example, computer keyboard use before full hand development), while helping us provide adequate and appropriate ways to support and challenge their

▶ *Play teaches children important social skills.*

physical development. Knowledge of children's physical needs also motivates us to advocate for physical activities, both inside and outside, in our programs. The importance of whole-body movement and **kinesthetic** activity cannot be overemphasized. Physical play provides an avenue for children to integrate, practice, and display their rapid physical development.

Social Play. As children develop, they progress from solitary play to play that involves interactions, taking turns, starting and ending play with others, and use of language to guide the play activity. Mildred Parten's classic observational studies (1932 and 1933) created a well-accepted general progression of social development stages in play. These are:

- **Solitary play** (2–2½ years old). A child plays alone and independently, engaged in different activities from those of other children in the vicinity. The child essentially ignores other children while playing.
- **Parallel play** (2½–3½ years old). Children still play independently, but near or with other children. Children play with the same or similar toys or activities—such as digging in the sandbox with sand tools. But they still don't play with each other.
- **Associative play** (3½–4½ years old). Children play together, using similar toys, engaging in similar activities, and interacting with each other, but they never truly cooperate by discussing the activity, working together, or ignoring their own interest to serve that of the other child. Individual interests and needs still dictate the play.
- **Cooperative play** (4½ years old and up). In cooperative play, children truly play as a group, often setting aside individual needs—at least for a while—for the good of the group. Children might assign roles in a dramatic play activity, they might work together to build a fort, or they might build a town in the sand together. The ability to set aside personal needs and wants for the good of the group characterizes cooperative play.

Parten's stages provide a helpful way to view the development of children's play from individual, solitary activity to an ability to enjoy playing with a group of other children—with the necessary social skills of give and take, sharing, and communication. It seems clear, however, that unlike with Piaget's stages of cognitive development, children can—and do—go back to earlier stages in social play. I have observed my 12-year-old daughter engaged in hours of solitary play building complex houses with Lego blocks.

It is also clear that the ability to progress through these stages is somewhat dependent on learning specific skills—social behaviors and language skills (Johnson, Christie, & Yawkey, 1999). Today many elementary schools around the country are eliminating recess because children are unable to play appropriately together. Maybe as a result of TV watching, limited outdoor play opportunities, and busy parents, children haven't developed the specific social skills and language needed to play together.

Cognitive Play.   All children use objects in much of their play—blocks to create a city, a piece of wood to represent a phone, or a bat and ball in baseball, cricket, and rounders. Children also use their bodies in different ways—climbing, jumping, somersaulting, skipping, representing a doctor in dramatic play, or playing in a soccer game. It is clear that children progress through various stages as they use objects, materials, and themselves in more and more sophisticated ways. These stages are functional play, constructive play, symbolic play, and games with rules. Cognitive play describes how children use materials, objects, and people.

- **Functional play.** Essentially functional play involves using objects or the body in ways dictated by the physical characteristics of the object or body: stacking blocks, splashing water, digging in the sand, doing somersaults, jumping off a log, throwing a stone. Functional play is often repetitive, like bouncing a ball. Functional play decreases with age.
- **Constructive play.** Constructive play is organized, goal-oriented play and increases in frequency as the child matures. Constructive play involves using materials and objects to make something: digging sand in the sandbox to build a castle, using paint to create a picture, or building a fort with sticks, materials, and rope. The material or toy is used to create something else.
- **Symbolic play.** Symbolic play involves using oneself and objects in a representational way. Examples include a child using a block of wood to represent a phone, a child saying she is a doctor and Juan her patient, or a child throwing a ball on the playground and declaring, "John Elway throws a touchdown!" The power of symbolic play is that it allows children to use materials in nonconcrete ways. We know young children are concrete learners, and to an extent we all are. Yet in Western society, education and culture stress representational processing. Math, reading, and writing are symbolic systems: the numeral 5 represents the abstract quantity of five of something; the letter *a* represents an abstract sound that, combined with other sounds, creates a word—which is, in turn, an abstract symbol for an idea or thing. Symbolic play is vitally important in helping children move from the concrete to the abstract.
- **Games with rules.** We have all observed a young child playing a game of baseball who, when tagged out, declares, "This time let's say you have to be out twice to be out!" Or a child who says, "Give me another chance." What's happening is that young children want to stretch the rules of the game to meet their individual needs—to stay in the game, have fun, and be the center of the activity. These children have not fully learned that in games with rules, the rules must always be enforced, regardless of individual needs, otherwise the game simply falls apart. Games with rules are exactly what they imply—group play activities that require that externally imposed rules be followed. These rules are imposed by the game itself, and are not arrived at by a consensus of the children playing. As children get older and enter the **concrete operations stage** of thinking, they are more able to play complex games with rules.

Combining Two Play Categories: Sociodramatic Play. As I pointed out earlier, physical or motor play, social play, and cognitive play do not occur separately from one another—they occur in a variety of different combinations. One of the most popular and frequent examples is **sociodramatic play,** "when two or more children adopt roles and act out a story or situation" (Johnson, Christie, & Yawkey, 1999, p. 230). Thus, sociodramatic play involves children who are playing cooperatively (at the social stage) and symbolically (engaged in cognitive play) at the same time.

Sarah Smilansky (1968) has extensively studied children's sociodramatic play. She has developed a Sociodramatic Play Inventory—five categories of high-quality group dramatic play. These categories are role playing, make-believe transformations, social interaction, verbal communication, and persistence.

Role playing. In their play, children adopt roles (mother, teacher, doctor) and communicate these roles to other children ("I'm the doctor"). They then play with role-specific behavior.

Make-believe transformations. Symbols are used for real objects and actions. For example, a block of wood is used as a phone, moving the hand up and down is used to symbolize hammering, and the setting is defined: "This is a doctor's office."

Social interaction. At least two children are engaged in the play, and all are using the agreed-upon roles and transformations.

Verbal communication. Children use language while involved in dramatic play. They use language to set up the play, define roles, define the environment, set the story line or drama, keep other children in line ("Doctors don't do that!"), and use language appropriate to their assigned roles.

Persistence. Children engage in the activity for quite a while, depending on their age—preschoolers for at least five minutes; kindergarteners for ten minutes. Persistence is dependent on giving children enough time to set up their sociodramatic play activity (Smilansky, 1968). Several studies have shown that children from low-income backgrounds engage in less sociodramatic play than their middle-class counterparts (Feitelson & Ross, 1973; Rubin, Maioni, & Hornung, 1976). The assumption of these and other studies is that children who lack sociodramatic play are often delayed in their cognitive development and education, and that learning the important symbolic systems of the child's culture—such as math, words, and the alphabet—is crucial.

Smilansky's research shows that low-income preschool and kindergarten children's sociodramatic play can be increased through **play training** (the teacher either coaching children how to engage in dramatic play or actually becoming part of the play activity) and direct experience. She provided direct experiences to the children, such as going on a field trip to the zoo, then returned to the classroom and encouraged dramatic play by modeling the activity.

Designing Play into the Curriculum

An ideal curriculum for young children should carefully integrate play throughout. Because of the different developmental needs of children and the developmental progression of each kind of play discussed in this chapter, play involvement in the curriculum looks very different for infants, toddlers, 3-year-olds, 5-year-olds, and 8-year-olds.

Here are a few ideas for including play in a curriculum, based on the underlying assumption of this chapter: that play is crucial for the healthy educational, social, moral, and emotional development of all young children. Remember that a curriculum includes program goals and objectives, activities, resources, time during the day, the environment, and teacher interactions and involvement.

Encourage All Forms of Play, Indoors and Out. Programs should provide a balance of indoor and outdoor play, including programs for infants and toddlers, and should provide environments that encourage each type of play discussed in this chapter. All play environments should be well maintained and replenished with necessary materials. Teachers should be actively involved in children's indoor and outdoor play—providing, changing, and enriching materials; modeling play behaviors and offering coaching strategies for social play; adding props; developing scripts; and exposing children to new ideas through field trips and visits of interesting people to the program.

Provide Enough Time to Play. Children need enough time to play. Research has shown that children need a minimum of thirty minutes to set up their play and progress to more complex and higher-order play (Christie & Wardle, 1992). Periods of about forty minutes to one hour allow enough time for children to become fully engrossed. Children should be encouraged to integrate toys and materials across different learning centers. For example, a child takes a doll from the dramatic-play area and puts it in a bed she made in the block area; a child paints a picture of the main character in the story the teacher just read, and then puts the picture up in the reading area; a child mixes a soup of water and food coloring to give to his sick doll in the dramatic-play area.

Stress the Importance of Play. Play should receive as much weight as other activities in the curriculum: in time, materials, teachers' attention, in-service training, and so on. Teachers should not always be pulled away for other duties during the children's playtime; and not all of the in-service training should be about academics. Provide specific staff training in play activities staff members may be uncomfortable with. Many female staff do not feel comfortable at the woodworking bench; some do not choose to play with children in the block area; a person with limited Spanish ability will be frustrated reading stories to the children in Spanish. Also, find ways to encourage children to play in the play areas they try to avoid. Typically, girls avoid the block area and woodworking bench, boys the dramatic play area.

Include Diversity in Play Environments. Examples of diversity should exist in every play area: pictures of female construction workers over the woodworking bench; dolls representing a variety of races and ethnicities; cooking utensils and other props in the dramatic play area; and pictures of igloos, hogans, yurts, kivas, adobe pueblos, sod houses, and gypsy caravans in the block area.

Communicate the Value of Play to Parents. Programs need to find many ways to explain the value of play to parents. Post explanations about the skills and concepts children learn in each play area: for example, in the block area, list that children learn to share, cooperate, build; children learn size, shapes, relationships, gravity, and the post-

and-lintel construction system; children learn to be creative and flexible problem solvers. Also develop brochures and pamphlets to send home, provide in-service training to parents on the value of play, and train staff just how to respond to a parent who says, "What is my son learning? All he does is play all day!" A center could also purchase or create a simple video that explains to parents the value of play (*Children Come First*, produced by Community Playthings, and *Linking Literacy and Play* by the International Reading Association are two examples.)

Integrate Play throughout the Day. Play should be integrated throughout the day, not just after a strenuous educational activity so the children can relax and recharge. Also, schedule play opportunities for children to practice and explore new information after a book has been read, after a field trip, after a traumatic personal experience at home, and after a new skill has been taught.

Programs need to appreciate that play, by definition, tends to be messy and disorderly—at least from an adult's perspective. Play is child-initiated and -controlled, which means that children use materials in unconventional and sometimes unorthodox ways. This does not mean, however, that they should be allowed to engage in unsafe activities or destroy materials. It does mean they may be messy and use materials in ways adults never thought would be possible!

Since play is such an integral part of every aspect of young children's growth and learning, it should also be an integral part of every aspect of the curriculum.

Play Materials

As we all know, play often involves objects. When I worked in the Guatemalan highlands, I observed Mayan children playing with bottle caps, soap, and sticks. We have all seen children play with a variety of common objects: banging on kitchen pots and pans, making intricate art with flower petals and grasses, damming a stream with sticks and stones, and creating exciting patterns with different-shaped stones in the sandbox.

An entire industry has grown up around the need for children to have play objects—what most of us call toys. A secondary market has developed around the creation of educational materials, or educational toys. Probably the first educational toys were Friedrich Froebel's gifts (1832; see Chapter 3). His ten gifts were a collection of balls; wooden blocks; wooden cubes, rectangles, and pyramids; mosaic tiles; sticks and rings; and colored beads. These toys were designed to achieve specific goals consistent with Froebel's educational theory. Educational curricula are characterized by the use of materials and teaching strategies to achieve specific educational goals, objectives, or outcomes (Wiles & Bondi, 1998). Thus, any toy or material that can be said to assist in this effort can arguably be called educational.

The idea of educational toys, or learning materials, is very popular today. In fact, Froebel's gifts are now being made and marketed by a toy company (Uncle Goose Toys, 1999). But what exactly makes a toy educational? There is so much emphasis today on teaching specific academic and educational outcomes during a child's early years that we now expect all learning materials and "good" toys to further these outcomes. "These materials are designed to teach specific skills and concepts. They are more didactic (teacher directed), structured, and outcome oriented than other types of play materials"

(Johnson, Christie, & Yawkey, 1999, p. 288). Essentially, educational toys and learning materials are those that meet (or claim to meet) adult educational outcomes. As was discussed in the definition of play, children (not adults) define play for themselves. Thus, there is a central conflict in the very concept of educational toys.

A good toy or educational material challenges, involves, stimulates, and engages a child's imagination (Wardle, 1999b). Good toys encourage complex play—used in a variety of ways, combinations, and more sophisticated play—not simply motor or functional play. The best example of a good toy is blocks. Crayons and paints are other good examples. Children use these materials to create, build, construct, move, restructure, replicate real experiences, and invent new ones. Other good toys encourage complex

Selecting Toys and Play Materials

The following checklist is based on an article I published in the *Child Care Information Exchange* (Wardle, 1993).*

Does the toy have high initial interest?
Initial interest is created by novelty, attractive physical characteristics (color, shininess, frills, strange noises, etc), and interest to the child (matches likes, friends have one, saw it on TV).

Does the toy have high prolonged interest?
Everyone knows the story about the attractive Christmas gift that was eventually ignored by the children for the box it came in. The box had high prolonged interest. Toys that have high prolonged interest include blocks, crayons, balls, Duplos, dolls—they are flexible enough that children can use them in a variety of ways.

Can the toy be used with minimal adult supervision?
Toys should not use adult rules, need constant attention to solve conflicts among users, or require close adult supervision to prevent misuse or breakage.

Does the toy strengthen self-concept?
Dolls that reflect the child's cultural and physical characteristics are a good example. Can the child positively identify with the toy?

Does the toy strengthen the child's respect for others?
Does it expose children to diversity in non-stereotypical ways?

Does the toy teach alternative ways to solve conflicts and arguments?
Many video games and other toys teach children that force is the way to solve problems. Good toys provide a different approach: teamwork, give-and-take, and so on.

Is the toy durable?
Will it withstand constant, active use by children; will it last over time; if designed for the outside, will it last outside; can it be easily repaired?

Is the toy versatile?
Can it be used in many ways; can children impose their own meanings on it? Examples are blocks and dress-ups.

Is the toy adaptable and progressive?
Can it be used by children at a variety of different levels; can one child use it in progressively more complex ways? For example, Lego blocks can be grouped by color, used to build simple constructions, and used to construct a futuristic space vehicle or a replica of a complex castle from a book.

Is the toy easy to keep clean?
Can it be sterilized in the dishwasher; can the cloth components (such as dolls' clothes) come off to be washed; does it absorb and "attract" dirt?

*Reprinted with permission from Child Care Information Exchange PO Box 3249, Redmond, WA 98073. (800) 221-2864. www.ChildCareExchange.com

language usage, the development of abstract thought, and imagination. Dramatic play develops these skills. Toy cars and trucks, dolls, dress-up props, child-size furniture, and large cardboard boxes encourage dramatic play. These toys are effective because they require children to add detail, meaning, context, and function to their play activity. In addition, good play materials match and enhance a child's social development. Balls, blocks, dolls, wagons, and play on playgrounds are more fun when children play together. And when children play together they learn a variety of social skills—give and take, helping each other, sharing, and teamwork. Good play materials also teach a variety of complex problem-solving skills, help children enjoy physical activity, and encourage complex language usage and forms of representation.

Does the toy encourage large and small muscle development and eye–hand coordination?
Because fine and gross motor development are occurring rapidly at this age, toys and play materials must encourage and support this development.

Does the toy strengthen social relationships?
Balls are usually more fun when played with by more than one child, as are large blocks. A swivel swing requires more than one player to be fun.

Does the toy arouse imagination and creativity?
Dramatic play materials are a good example. Enough toys must be provided, and the environment needs to encourage creativity and imagination.

Does the toy encourage intellectual development?
Is language, grouping of similar objects, labeling, or comparing shape, size, weight, and color encouraged? Is basic knowledge taught?

Is the toy safe, and can it easily become unsafe when broken?
Safety, of course, is the number one criterion for selecting toys and play materials. A variety of factors determine safety, chief among them are the child's age, durability, and absence of sharp points and edges.

Can the child easily replace the toy in its correct storage place?
Toys with lots of little parts are difficult to re-store.

Is the toy developmentally appropriate?
Children develop progressively though physical, social, and cognitive stages. Toys should match these stages.

Does the toy encourage constructive play?
Constructive play involves making things: blocks, woodworking, painting, crafts.

Does the toy convey to the child a sense of quality?
Is it well made, does it feel solid when picked up, does it look as if someone took care in making it, and does it keep its appearance over time?

While all toys in a program won't meet every criterion, all should be developmentally appropriate, safe, durable, and easy to clean, and should minimize supervision. Other criteria encourage more extensive use of toys and self-concept development. Make sure the program has toys that cover all the other criteria. Don't overemphasize one area.

▶ *One criterion for selecting toys and equipment is whether it sustains prolonged interest. Will it hold a child's attention over time?*

So toys and materials do teach important developmental goals and objectives. The problem is, as Johnson, Christie, and Yawkey suggest, that educational toys are "designed to teach specific skills and concepts"—and these are usually discrete academic skills. Maybe the way to look at this dilemma is to suggest that good play materials teach to **developmental goals and outcomes;** while educational toys teach to **educational goals and outcomes,** which are much more narrow.

How do we know if toys and materials actually encourage play? What criteria should we use for their selection? What makes a good plaything? I have seen children playing with old tires, children involved in a soccer game in the middle of the town plaza, children jumping off a table into a pile of leaves, and children using sticks in a pretend fight. Children use bottle caps, stones, sticks, balls, blocks, water, sand, soft wax, paints, food colors, dolls, old cloths, hard hats, and rope to play.

In selecting toys and play materials, educators must be very careful. In general, good toys and play materials can be used for more than one activity, match the child's developmental age, do not require constant adult involvement, are durable, are simple, and encourage children's play and fantasy (*Children Come First*). Educational materials should implement the program's overall philosophy (Greenman, 1988); further, these materials should withstand constant use and encourage learning.

Toy Safety.   Children can be injured by unsafe toys. Safety hazards include choking, cuts from sharp objects, and poisoning by lead paint. Here are a few overall toy safety guidelines adapted from the National SAFE KIDS Campaign.

- When selecting toys, consider the child's age, interests, and skill level. Be especially careful when selecting toys for children under age 3. Toys with small parts, including small balls, pose a choking hazard.
- Avoid toys with sharp points or edges.
- Avoid toys that produce loud noises which, in some cases, can permanently impair a child's hearing.
- Strings, straps, or cords on toys should be shorter than seven inches. Long strings or cords pose a strangulation hazard.
- If purchasing an electric toy with a heating element such as batteries or an electrical plug, be sure it is for children older than 8 years old. These toys are a potential burn hazard for younger children.

- Be sure propelled toys such as arrows or toy darts have blunt tips with rubber or flexible plastic suction cups, cork, or other protective points. Check to see that tips are attached securely to shafts.
- Check to make sure a toy does not contain lead-based paint. Exposure may result in lead poisoning.

Block Play

Playing with blocks has been synonymous with early childhood education for as long as we have had early childhood programs. As I have already discussed, Froebel developed blocks to implement his kindergarten philosophy. Caroline Pratt revolutionized American early education with the development of the basic unit block, and with her philosophy regarding the role of blocks in children's early learning (Pratt, 1924; 1948; 1973). Today, all early childhood supply companies sell unit blocks. *The Block Book* (E. S. Hirsch, 1996) offers an excellent discussion of the powerful contribution block play makes to the total development of young children—in creativity, dramatic play, math, science, social studies, and school readiness.

Blocks are an important learning material for a variety of reasons. As children play with blocks they master new skills and building techniques, engage in more complex and detailed play, and become active, independent learners. Block play allows children to organize and express their experiences, and to expand their creativity and fantasy. Block building activities can easily be scaffolded by a competent teacher to enrich, lead, and extend the play.

Stages of Block Building (Johnson, 1996). All children progress through specific stages as they use blocks in play. This is also true for older children who have not previously experienced block play (except for stage one, which is omitted by older children), although older children progress through the stages much more quickly. Knowledge of these stages will help teachers better support children's block play.

- *Stage One.* Blocks are carried around but are not used for construction (very young children).
- *Stage Two.* Building begins. Children mostly make rows, either horizontal (on the floor) or vertical (stacked). There is much repetition in this early building pattern, which is basic functional play with blocks.
- *Stage Three.* Bridging: children create a bridge (or portal) by using two blocks to support a third. In architecture this is known as the post-and-lintel system.
- *Stage Four.* Enclosures: children place blocks in such a way that they enclose a space. Bridging and enclosures are among the earliest technical problems children have to solve when playing with blocks, and they occur soon after a child begins to use blocks regularly.
- *Stage Five.* With age, children become steadily more imaginative in their block building. They use more blocks and create more elaborate designs, incorporating patterns and balance into their constructions.

- *Stage Six.* Naming of structures for dramatic play begins. Before this stage children may have named their structures, but not necessarily based on the function of the building. This stage of block building corresponds to the "realistic" stage in art development.
- *Stage Seven.* Children use blocks to represent things they know, like cities, cars, airplanes, and houses. They also use blocks to stimulate dramatic play activities: zoo, farm, shopping center, and other locations.

Water Play

Water is one of the most versatile of play materials; it is a very flexible substance that fosters curiosity, imagination, and experimentation in children (Crosser, 1994). All children love to play in water, regardless of age, language, culture, education, physical disability, or special need, and this seems to be one of those experiences that all young children need to have. Several years ago I volunteered to teach art to a gifted 10-year-old. When I got to the lesson on mixing colors, adding black and white paint to provide shading and a three-dimensional effect, the student spent the next several lessons simply mixing colors. He was truly fascinated and engrossed by the process, and apparently never had the chance to play with water when he was young.

Opportunities for water play should be provided inside and outside. The easiest way to do this inside is with a water table. Outside there are many options, such as bringing the water table outside; using buckets and other containers; adding hoses, sprinklers, and wading pools; or installing sand and water tables in the playground. Outdoor water activities include having a car wash of all the wheeled playground equipment; giving all the dolls' clothes a good washing; and painting the sidewalk, fence, and play equipment with water (Crosser, 1994). The great advantages of conducting water play outside are that children can make a lot of mess, there is more space, and cleanup is easier.

Cognitive Learning. Children learn a rich variety of cognitive concepts through water play. They learn a myriad of math concepts, including more and less, addition and subtraction, liquid measurement, classification, counting, equality, heavy and light, sets (all floating objects in one group, all sinking objects in another), consistency, and thick and thin.

Because playing with water allows children to learn fundamental properties of liquids, water play teaches a variety of science concepts and basic knowledge. Some of this science information includes flow, pressure, displacement, hydro force, erosion, floating and sinking, ripple effect and waves, absorption, mixing with other materials (such as oil), gravity, suspensions, and the effect of water on other materials.

Children playing in water will also learn the language needed in the various activities and materials they use, and develop important social skills. But maybe most important, they will get to mess around with such a fascinating, flexible, and versatile natural material. In messing around with water they can also learn about the **conservation** of liquids (Piaget, 1954). Children can learn that water poured from a tall, narrow glass onto a wide, flat pie dish has not changed in amount, even through it appears to be far less.

Some Ideas for Promoting Discovery Learning in Water Play. Here are some ideas for activities using water, adapted from S. Crosser (1994 [Reprinted with permission from the National Association for the Education of Young Children]):

- Punch a row of holes from the bottom to the top of a two-liter soda bottle.
- Attach funnels to each end of a length of flexible tubing.
- Put salt in the water, then try to float and sink objects.
- Substitute snow for water in the water table.
- Place a large chunk of ice in the water table. Provide safety goggles, rubber mallets, popsicle sticks, and rock salt.
- Make a water lens by dropping water on a newspaper that has been placed inside a zipped food-storage bag.
- Give children heavy aluminum foil to shape into boats.
- Suspend a pulley from the ceiling just above the water table. Thread a rope through the pulley and attach a bucket to one end of the rope.
- Offer a variety of cloth squares (canvas, oilcloth, cotton, leather, silk, nylon netting, vinyl, wool, polyester) and see which float in water.
- Experiment with all kinds of paper and cardboard.
- Experiment with varying the amounts of water and air inside zippered sandwich bags.
- Try making a siphon with flexible plastic tubing and a bucket.
- Predict which of a variety of seeds will float and which will not. Use nuts in shells, milkweed, maple seeds, cottonwood, coconuts, buckeyes, and others.
- Challenge children to create a boat from found objects, then move it from one end of the water to the other without using hands—blowing through straws, and so on.
- Challenge children to make a bridge over a portion of the water, using scraps.
- Let children have fun mixing water, salad oil, and different food colors.

Working with Parents. Some parents do not believe their children should play with water at home or in the early childhood program. They see water purely in functional terms: to drink, wash dishes and clothes, and wash children's hands. They believe children who play in water are confusing the important task of keeping themselves clean with playing, and that children who play with water in school are not learning anything (Crosser, 1994). Teachers need to communicate to parents the values of play—both in the early childhood program and at home—which can be done in a variety of ways, including inviting parents to the center to observe children playing, providing simple brochures and newsletters that explain the value of play, and conducting parent training on water play. Caution must be taken to explain the value of water play in language that is familiar to parents, not using educational jargon, complicated words, or language that talks down to parents.

▶ *Playful behaviors are important between parent and child.*

Play and Culture

Children from different cultures play differently. These different play patterns depend on the child's culture, including the influence of TV and videos, the quantity of commercially available toys, the involvement and support of adults in the play of children, the active inclusion of children in the community, and the access children have to natural environments and materials.

One evening after a communal supper at the Spring Valley Bruderhof, a father read the familiar fairy tale *Billy Goats Gruff*. The Bruderhof is the religious community where my parents live and my sisters teach. In this community, most meals are held communally, and include the young children. At this supper of about 150 people, a father read the fairy tale for all of the children, and four other fathers enacted the story. They used a large dining room table as the bridge, and the billy goats walked over the table while the giant threatened them from underneath. The fathers wore their everyday clothes and used no props (though it helped that men in the community traditionally wear beards). They used large gestures to give a very active enactment of the struggle.

As this activity was going on, I carefully turned to watch the expressions of all the children in the audience. They were absolutely spellbound: standing on their chairs among their families, their attention focused on the presentation. They were enthralled. Children in this religious community have no access to TV; and are entertained by one another and members of the community.

When I lived in the highlands of Guatemala in the summer of 1976, I had the opportunity to observe young indigenous Mayan children in their home setting. The young boys played a game with pop-bottle caps. Children as young as 5 and 6 years old delighted in this game, in which they threw caps against a wall and scored points depending on where the caps landed. Maya children have no TV or commercially made toys. I also played soccer with the boys of the small mountain village. Often, after a long day, the village men and older boys joined the younger children in soccer games. I marveled at the skill, knowledge, and simple teamwork of even 6-year-olds. Anyone who has traveled in developing countries has seen youngsters playing soccer in empty lots, plazas, streets, and

Gender Issues in Play

"By the time children enter the preschool classroom or child care center, they show extensive gender differences, as well as similarities, in play behavior" (Johnson, Christie, & Yawkey, 1999, p. 90). Anyone who has taught young children knows that gender differences in play are a fact. The discussion—often a heated debate—is why this is true. How much is biological, how much cultural, and how much a response to the environment? Every culture has distinctive roles for men and women, and starts to train girls and boys for these roles almost immediately after they are born. For example, Carol Gilligan (1982) believes that in our culture girls are raised to be nurturing, supporters, and team players, while boys are raised to be aggressive, dominant, independent, and decision makers. We also know that a major developmental task of all children, both during early childhood and then later in adolescence, is gender identification—the process of internalizing their gender as a crucial component of their identity. Children back yards. Soccer is a universal game that has been passed on from generation to generation, younger boys learning from older boys and men.

While the Maya boys in the small village were helping their fathers in caring for the corn or playing soccer on the highland field, the girls were usually washing clothes in the stream. The girls would make a game of it, though, by laughing and giggling, splashing each other, and throwing the soap. I also observed young children accompanying their parents to work: the local form of child care. In every instance, the children would develop a game to play while their parents worked: splashing the water, using sticks for swords, drawing in the dirt, or playing with the leaves of the bean plants on the dirt floor of the meeting house.

When I taught kindergarten students at the New Meadow Run Bruderhof School in rural Pennsylvania, I had a young student from Lake Titicaca, Bolivia. She spoke no English but soon became fully immersed in all the classroom activities. Her favorite learning-center choice was the dramatic-play area, where she usually played by herself or with one other student. She spent lots of time caring for a large doll by dressing her, combing her hair, and putting her to bed. She then wrapped the doll in a big blanket, tied it on her back, and carried her around the classroom, just as women carry their children in Bolivia.

On another occasion when I visited my home in Pennsylvania, we went to see some of my parent's Amish friends. They took us to their school, where we listened to the children sing Christmas songs. I was surprised to see no playground equipment on the small patch of grass outside the school, not even old pieces of farm machinery, tires (they don't have cars or use rubber tires on farm equipment), or tree stumps. *What did the children do at recess?* I wondered. Then I watched the children run out of the classroom onto the playground. One small group of children played a game with a broomstick. Two children held the stick at each end, parallel to the ground. Each child in the group, both girls and boys, jumped over the stick. Then the stick was raised. The object of the game was to see who could jump the highest. The lack of equipment did not deter the Amish children's outdoor play.

use play to implement this progress. Some anecdotes will illustrate ways that our culture both reflects and reinforces gender identification.

When I worked for a national child-care company, I participated in an annual presentation from representatives of Dacta (the educational arm of Lego and Duplo). At one of these meetings, the salesperson discussed the company's attempt to sell more Lego and Duplo sets to girls. She then showed us examples of new products for girls—blocks in predominantly pink, green, and purple—and the marketing materials for these blocks, which included pictures of dollhouses, kitchens, and large fantasy mansions.

One of my first tasks as a new Head Start director was to determine a process for assigning students to their respective classes. I soon discovered that my staff already had a system: boys were always last to be assigned, because teachers felt they were more difficult to manage than girls and were more likely to have behavior problems.

When my children were quite young, our family attended an Evangelical Friends church in Denver. As was our custom, we would get dressed up for church—especially our four children, three girls and a boy. On one particular Sunday, my 3-year-old son got ready for church like any other Sunday. But this time he dressed like his three sisters: in a white lace dress, with lots of ribbons and barrettes in his long, carefully brushed curly hair. Needless to say, many in the congregation were shocked! I wondered to myself if a 3-year-old girl wearing pants and short hair would have received the same reaction.

Toy Preference.
Toy preference by many girls and boys is well established by age 3 (Sutton-Smith, 1979). Beginning with Parten's studies in 1932, the research literature has shown that boys and girls prefer different toys: girls tend to play more frequently with dolls and art materials, boys with blocks and wheeled toys. Girls are more likely to use both girl's and boy's toys, boys only boy's toys (Liss, 1981). Gender play differences are reinforced by cultural expectations, and they begin with the parents' response to the gender of their newborn infant, as illustrated by radically different ways parents decorate their children's bedrooms, and the different interaction patterns between parents and their children. Many parents are still uncomfortable letting boys play with dolls and have different gender expectations regarding pain, disappointment, and emotional hurt. Fathers tend to play much more roughly with their sons than they do with their daughters. Certain cultural differences accentuate these gender differences.

As children move into organized child-care programs, gender preferences in toy and material selection are reinforced by peers and teachers. And, of course, manufacturers of toys, books, magazines, educational materials, and computer software further this differentiation.

Motor or Physical Play.
By the time children are 4 to 5 years old, we begin to see a marked gender difference in physical play. Boys tend to be more active and boisterous than girls and engage in more physical contact (Johnson, Christie, & Yawkey, 1999). Given a choice, boys choose to play outside on gross-motor equipment, girls inside in the dramatic-play area and on craft tables (Harper & Sanders, 1975). In outside play areas, boys use between 1.2 and 1.6 times as much space as girls. Boys also engage in far more rough-and-tumble play (play-fighting) than girls (Carlsson-Paige & Levin, 1987) and seem to gravitate to larger play groups and more organized games.

When children move from child care to grade school, they progress into more organized sports, such as soccer, gymnastics, and ballet. While these sports tend to follow the same gender tendencies—boys into more aggressive activities, girls into more graceful and aesthetic ones—the increase in numbers of girls playing baseball, hockey, and soccer is challenging this trend.

Social Play.
While Parten (1933) found the age-related social play differences I have already discussed, she found no gender-related differences regarding social play. Other research has shown that preschool children prefer to play with children of the same sex (Fishbein & Imai, 1993), a preference that increases during the early childhood years. When preschool children do engage in mixed-gender groups, boys tend to dominate and there is more conflict than in same-gender play groups. Boys are more assertive and dominant, girls more compliant and less disruptive, in their social play.

Use of Play Materials.
There is a distinctive difference in how girls and boys play with materials. Girls prefer to use objects according to a plan that has a purpose (construc-

tive play), such as completion of a puzzle or coloring a page. Boys are more likely to use objects in more functional ways: pushing a small vehicle or stacking blocks. Boys play on the floor, with wheeled toys and blocks; girls sit at tables or play with dolls while seated in a chair. When children enter school the trend continues, with girls preferring arts and crafts, boys woodworking and gym.

Symbolic Play. Girls and boys do not differ in total amount of symbolic play during the preschool years. Given a choice, boys and girls tend to select gender-stereotypical subjects: boys choose to play the roles of husbands, fathers, sons, firefighters; girls select mothers, daughters, wives, babies, and brides (Grief, 1976). They also choose different kinds of activities during pretend play based on their different interests. When I taught kindergarten I successfully increased the amount of time the boys played in the dramatic-play area by adding hard hats, toolkits, fireman's hoses, and other typical male props. The boys who played there still engaged in typical male-role activities.

As children mature and enter the early grades, their symbolic play becomes more complex and sophisticated. But girls still prefer to engage in symbolic play that primarily reflects their concerns and interests relating to nurturance and relationships with others, while boys are still involved with autonomy and power. As our society increases choices of adult professions for both men and women, I expect to see young children begin to blur these gender roles in play. At the same time, many of the new immigrant groups entering this country have highly structured gender roles.

Outdoor Play

The Purpose of Outdoor Play

In less hectic, less modern times, young children spent a great deal of time outside—climbing trees, feeding farm animals, damming streams, picking flowers, playing hide-and-seek among the stones, bushes, and buildings, and catching frogs. Young children's outdoor activity was considered a natural and normal part of childhood, and children across the country—from New England to California—enjoyed a natural exposure to the outdoors. While the exploration of nature was never planned, directed, or systematically supervised, it provided lots of important developmental opportunities. Children learned about how plants grow, what is needed to care for farm animals, the joy of jumping across a stream, how to climb trees, and concepts such as a cloud building in the sky to the west in the morning would mean a rainstorm in the afternoon. Certainly life during those times was not all rosy. Children had chores to perform, conditions were often harsh, they were exposed to various risks, and many family farms depended on children's labor to survive.

As life for American families has changed, so too has the way we raise children. Most children today are raised in cities and small towns; few are raised on farms. Further, most parents are now employed away from home, and their young children must be cared for by others (Willer et al., 1991). The concept of nonfamily or extended-family members caring for young children is fairly recent in this country, and is still foreign in some cultures.

▶*Soccer is a global game: Mexico City plaza.*

As we began to provide programs for young children away from the family, educators developed ideas about how best to meet children's needs. Head Start was developed to provide the solid foundation for young children to succeed in their formal school experience. Other programs developed with various philosophies and focuses. But because traditional schools are associated with development of specific academic skills—learning to read, learning to write, social studies, math, science, and so on—many early childhood programs gravitated toward teaching academic, or preacademic, curricula. And K–12 schools themselves shifted from being multi-age, one-room schoolrooms to being divided into single-age grades, with specific kindergarten entrance requirements.

Fairly recently, educators and psychologists have come to the realization that an emphasis on preacademic learning and the behaviors associated with that learning (sitting still, functioning in large groups, being quiet, always listening to the teacher), is not necessarily good for young children. We also know that many children have few outdoor opportunities at home because of busy parents, small apartments, and unsafe neighborhoods. We now recognize that the many hours young children used to spend outdoors were very important for their development. As young children spend more and more time in early childhood programs, the need for appropriate, challenging, and interesting outdoor opportunities becomes more evident.

It's clear, then, that providing high-quality outdoor experiences for young children is a crucial responsibility for early childhood programs. Often outdoor play time is the only opportunity children have to enjoy a range of important developmental activities— running; jumping; making lots of noise; messing around with natural materials; observing animals, birds, and plants; climbing; hiding; and digging in the ground.

What Should a Good Outdoor Playground Include?

A good outdoor playground is a safe replica of the outdoor environment many of us enjoyed growing up—nature, variety of textures and materials, gardens, streams, loose parts, places to get away from adults and other children, opportunities for experiencing weather changes, and the joy of having lots of responsive materials to manipulate, create, and play with (Greenman, 2000; Rivkin, 1995). Richard Dattner's playground criteria (1969) provide a helpful guideline in determining what should be in a good playground. Another helpful approach is to determine how the playground can be used to extend the indoor environment and to provide opportunities that cannot be provided inside. Extension activities include sand and water equipment, painting sidewalks and fences, using chalk to draw murals, and creating a woodworking area. Examples of activity opportunities that are difficult to provide indoors include swinging and climbing; riding trikes, bikes, and scooters; and playing physical group games.

Does the Playground Meet All the Children's Needs?

How do we know whether an outdoor playground is meeting the needs of children? Dattner (summarized here) has developed criteria to help us answer this question (1969).

- *Experience.* Does the playground provide a vast array of experiences for the children?
- *Control of experience.* Are there opportunities for the child to control experiences—build, roll, collect, spill, dig, and so on?
- *Graduated challenge.* The playground must provide a range of old and new experiences, practice play, and new challenges.
- *Choice.* This allows children to control the environment, to select the level of risk they are prepared to handle, such as sliding from a high slide or jumping off a small step.
- *Fantasy.* Young children have active imaginations. Their imagination needs to be encouraged by providing very general-looking structures—houses, forts, tunnels, and the like.
- *Separation from adults.* Children need to be allowed to make mistakes, stumble, fall, delight in freedom, and create their own laws of order. Minimize rules and adult supervision.
- *Durability.* Will the playground withstand heavy use by normal children? Will it withstand the local weather conditions?
- *Interest.* A playground must provide for both kinds of interest: initial and prolonged. Initial interest is caused by physical characteristics that attract children: color, size, newness. Prolonged interest is the ability to hold a child's interest over time, because of complexity, challenge, and the like.

- *Adaptability.* The equipment should have more than one use, so that it can be adapted and redefined by children in a variety of ways.
- *Encouraging large and small muscle development and eye–hand coordination.* Overhead bars encourage large muscle development; weeding the garden develops small muscles; and painting a mural on the sidewalk or filling a cup with pebbles develops eye–hand coordination.
- *Strengthening social relationships.* Does the playground encourage social play, dramatic play, games with rules? Children need to learn to play together, reciprocate, and play games with rules. Swings, wagons, and waiting for a turn on the slide teach social skills; games like red rover, drop the hanky, and follow the leader all are games with rules.
- *Encouraging intellectual development.* Does the playground encourage language development, class inclusion, labeling, abstract thinking, and acquisition of basic knowledge? Caring for plants in a garden teaches about weather, life cycles, and pests. Playing in the sandbox with a friend and talking to them about the town they are building, the houses in the town, and where people work increase verbal skills. Predicting what will happen to the sand castle after the rain is abstract thinking.

Location and Components of a Playground

Specific playground designs differ, depending on space availability, geographic location, age and number of children, resources, and the type of program served. Here are some general suggestions for designing a playground for young children, aged 3 to 8.

Location. Locations of playgrounds for schools and child-care centers are usually not ideal. If a building is being designed from scratch, however, the playground site must be an integral consideration in the design. The ideal playground is on the northeastern side of the building in hot climates (for shade) and on the southwestern side of the building in cold climates (for maximum sunlight). The playground should connect directly to the main building, so children can easily and safely gain access from their classrooms. It should have running water (for gardens, sprinklers, and drinking fountains), some hills and flat areas, a large storage shed, and a variety of safe trees and shrubs.

Surfaces. At least three surfaces should be provided on the playground: fall-zone surface (under all equipment), hard surface (for balls, wagons, hopscotch, art activities, bringing indoor equipment outside, pathways), and grass (for picnics, games with rules, and sprinklers in hot weather).

Areas. Provide areas for gross motor play (climbing equipment and swings); an area for dramatic play; an area for games with rules; areas for constructive play (sandboxes, places between equipment); and a place for wagons, bikes, trikes, and big wheels.

Sand. Sand is one of the best play materials available. If sand is not used as a fall-zone material, provide large sandboxes for children to play in.

Water. Water can be provided in wading pools and buckets, and from hoses and sprinklers. Water is a fabulous play material and, when combined with sand and other materials, provides endless learning.

Garden. Tending a garden is a wonderful way for children to learn basic scientific facts about seasons, growth, sun and water, and where vegetables come from. It's a great learning experience for young children, and an opportunity for children to bring ideas to the center from home.

Infant and Toddler Playgrounds

Until fairly recently, outdoor playgrounds were designed and built for school-age children (6–12 years old). These playgrounds were designed to meet the physical-education philosophy of most schools—which concentrated on physical exercise, especially upper body activities. As younger children began to be served in a variety of programs in this country and around the world, playgrounds designed for school-age children were modified for younger children. Unfortunately, many designs were not appropriate for the developmental level of these children. So new, more developmentally appropriate playgrounds were designed and built for children aged 3 to 5. But now we have programs that serve even younger children, from infancy to age 3, that need playgrounds.

In examining the issue of playgrounds for infants and toddlers, there are several developmental aspects that separate this age from preschool children, including the small size of the children, the basic needs of infants and toddlers that require specific design features (access to water, changing tables, and more), and the need for constant, close, and careful adult supervision. Thus play equipment, pathways, and the overall area are quite small, and adults spend more time sitting with infants, holding an infant on the lap while swinging on a porch swing, and observing children while they are playing. Infant and toddler play is more dominated by the sensory part of sensory-motor play: textures, sounds, smells, light patterns, shadows, and reflections in water.

Location. The infant and toddler playground should be as close to the building as possible, and close to the infant and toddler classrooms. It should have places for teachers to sit with the infants, areas in which an infant can lie on a blanket on the grass, and lots of shade. The playground needs to have a variety of safe textures, surfaces, smells, and sounds: sand, wood, stones, bricks—as well as smooth, coarse, soft, and hard surfaces. Hard surfaces include wood, half logs, cobble, brick, patterned rock, concrete blocks, and more. Grass should include gentle hills, to allow for rolling and attempts at walking up and down graded surfaces. There should be large, rounded stones, and a variety of flat surfaces. Wood makes a good flat surface for the sand-and-water area, as well as for other areas that need good drainage. Children need shady spots, sunny spots, hideaways, and open area. The infant and toddler area should be physically separated from the preschool area, protected by some form of barrier—a wall, fence, or hill.

Design. An infant and toddler playground has various unique design components.

- *Areas.* Bushes, rocks, low barriers, gardens, and other natural features, should be used to create semiprivate areas for infants and toddlers to get away, and feel enclosed and secure.
- *Pathways.* Pathways for crawling and walking make infants and toddlers feel as if they are going somewhere. Have them meander with no specific direction; provide lots of different surfaces, and a variety of materials to delineate areas: rope, chain, poles, iron, pipe, wooden railings, and so on.
- *Texture, color, and sound.* Provide a variety of textures for children to touch: smooth, round boulders; rough bark; soft pine needles; wood of various textures. Provide safe trees and shrubs that change with the seasons; with flowers, leaves turning colors, cones, and the like. Banners, parachutes, and low tree branches that move in the wind add sound and visual stimulation. Different wind chimes provide additional sounds.
- *Shade.* Shade is essential, both for the infants and toddlers and for the adults caring for them. Trees provide the best shade, but lawn umbrellas, canopies, and awnings can also provide adequate shade. Use low barriers to protect children from the wind.
- *Sand and water.* Sand provides a great medium for the tactile stimulation that infants and toddlers need. Provide

▶ *Children need to be able to get away and be alone on the playground—while still being supervised.*

both large sandboxes for groups of children to play in, and small ones (a tire is ideal) for solitary play. Water provides sound, touch, and visual stimulation. Combining the two creates a wonderful super-complex unit (Prescott, 1994). Kompan markets a nice variety of sand and water tables for this age child; other providers have different options.

- *Places for adults.* Adults need spaces to interact with and supervise children: benches; porch swings; large, comfortable logs; wide sides on the sandbox.

Equipment. Groups of tires sunk halfway into the ground provide interesting tunnels; short plastic tubes work well too. Infants and toddlers like a sense of enclosure but don't want to be totally contained. Anything with a roof suggests a house to these children. If you have a cube, keep the top off; tubes and tunnels should be short. Provide old trees and climbers to pull on, straddle, climb. Never provide any climbing platform or surface higher than two feet.

Children this age like simple combinations of playground equipment, such as a slide and tunnel. Infants and toddlers are learning to crawl, pull themselves up, stand, step one foot in front of the other, walk up and down steps, walk up and down ramps, and go down a slide without falling over. Playground equipment for this age group needs to support and encourage this kind of physical development: small steps, slight inclines and declines, and places for children to sit and play individually and in small groups. Slides must be short and low, and have adequate sides to support the child's body. Panels that reflect the child's image or can be manipulated also meet their needs. The equipment needs a fall zone, but because infants and toddlers are smaller than preschool children, the fall-zone surface does not need to be as deep or as large as on a preschool playground.

Because infants and toddlers do not play together cooperatively, equipment for children this age should allow solitary play (playing by oneself) and parallel play (playing next to other children with the same toys), not actually playing together.

Toys. Provide sturdy toys for children to sit on, place both feet on the ground, and propel themselves forward. Young children have to build muscle strength on these toys before progressing to pedal toys. Wagons and wheelbarrows are also excellent as the children grow older. Sand and water toys, balls, loose junk (safe), smooth wooden boards, parachutes, plastic rings for throwing, short movable tunnels, and plastic tubes should be provided. New materials can be added on a regular basis to keep children from becoming bored. Some of these can be brought from the inside.

Playground Safety

Playground safety has become a very important issue, both in the United States of America and around the world. In August 1999, an international playground safety conference was help at Pennsylvania State University. The reasons for this concern are many. Many children are injured—and some die—on playgrounds (Frost & Sweeney, 1996). An additional concern, especially in this country, is the cost of liability to cover playground accidents. The United States, Canada, Australia, and England have official playground safety guidelines.

Figure 8.1

Preschool, infant, and toddler playground designed for a Migrant Head Start program in Texas, by F. Wardle

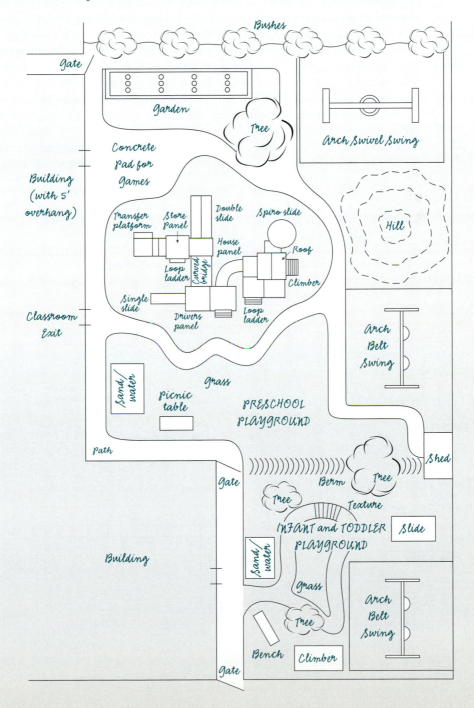

Playground Hazards to Avoid. There are various playground safety guidelines available for professionals working with young children. I have included (and adapted) a brief list from the National Playground Safety Institute (n.d.):

1. *Improper protective surfacing.* The surface or ground under and around the playground equipment should be soft enough to cushion a fall. Improper surfacing material under playground equipment is the leading cause of playground-related injuries, with more than 70 percent of all accidents on playgrounds caused by children falling. Hard surfaces such as concrete, blacktop, packed dirt, or grass are not acceptable under play equipment. Many surfaces offer protection from falls, including hardwood fiber or mulch, sand, and pea gravel. These surfaces must be maintained at a depth of twelve inches and not become compacted. There are also synthetic or rubber tiles and ground up rubber that are appropriate, but expensive.

2. *Inadequate fall zone.* A fall zone or use zone is the area under and around the playground equipment in which a child might fall. A use zone should be covered

Figure 8.2

Swings require a very large use zone area, because a child could fall or be thrown out of the swing seat.

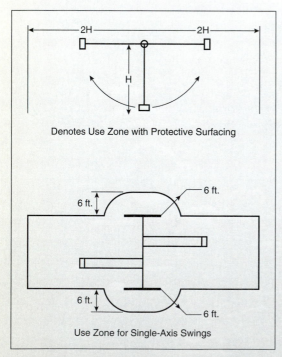

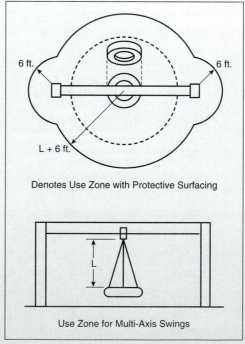

Source: Handbook for Public Playground Safety. Washington, DC: U.S. Consumer Product Safety Commission, 1997, p. 7.

▶ *Safe playgrounds require no protrusions on equipment.*

with appropriate surfacing materials and extend a minimum of six feet in all directions from the edge of the play equipment. For slides higher than four feet, the surface should extend the height of the slide plus four feet. Swings require a much greater area for the use zone. The use zone should extend two times the height of the swing, both in front of and behind the swing.

3. *Protrusions and entanglement hazards.* A protrusion is something on the equipment that could impale or cut a child if a child should fall against it. Some protrusions are also capable of catching strings of clothing worn around a child's neck, which is especially hazardous because it can result in strangulation. Examples include bolt ends, open S hooks, and open chain links. Rungs and handholds that protrude outward are also dangerous. Special attention should be paid to the entrance of slides.

4. *Entrapment in openings.* Children often enter openings feet first and attempt to slide through them. Because children's heads are the largest part of their bodies, an opening that is not large enough will allow the body to pass through and entrap the head. Generally, there should be no openings on playground equipment that measure between three and one-half inches and nine inches. This includes openings at the top of the slide, between platforms, between railings, and between the rungs on climbers and climbing nets.

5. *Insufficient equipment spacing.* Improper spacing between pieces of play equipment can cause overcrowding. A minimum of twelve feet should exist between two play structures, providing room for children to circulate and preventing the possibility of a child falling off one structure and striking another structure. Swings and other pieces of moving equipment should be located in areas away from other structures.

6. *Trip hazards.* Exposed concrete footings, abrupt changes in surface elevation, tree stumps, and rocks are all common trip hazards that are often found in play environments.

7. *Lack of supervision.* A play area should be designed so that it is easy for a parent, caregiver, or teacher to observe the young children at play. It is estimated that more than 40 percent of all playground injuries are directly related to lack of supervision in some way. Constant supervision is needed on all playgrounds.

▶ *Active supervision in outdoor play is needed to assure safety.*

8. *Age-appropriate activities.* Children's developmental needs vary greatly from infancy to age 12. In an effort to provide a challenging and safe play environment for all ages, it is important to make sure that the equipment in the playground is appropriate for the age of the user. Areas for preschool-age children should be separate from areas intended for school-age children and for infants and toddlers.

9. *Lack of maintenance.* In order for playgrounds to remain in safe condition, a program of preventive maintenance must be employed. There should be no missing, broken, or worn-out components. All hardware should be secure. Wood, metal, and plastic should not show signs of fatigue or deterioration. Surfacing materials must also be maintained.

10. *Pinch, crush, searing, and sharp-edge hazards.* Components in the play environment should be inspected to make sure that there are no sharp edges or points that could cut skin. Moving components such as suspension bridges, merry-go-rounds, and some swings should be checked to assure that there are no parts that might crush or pinch a child's finger.

11. *Platforms with no guardrails.* Elevated surfaces such as platforms, ramps, pathways and bridges should have guardrails that prevent accidental falls. Equipment should have guardrails on elevated surfaces higher than twenty inches off the ground, including steps.

Other Common Safety Hazards.   There are several other common safety hazards that should be avoided in playgrounds. These include ropes, cables, and wires that could trip or strangle a child. Poisonous and prickly plants—especially in infant and toddler playgrounds—metal slides and other equipment that can get hot and burn children, and areas that retain water for a long period of time (thus creating the health hazards that come with stagnant water) should be avoided. Adequate shade is becoming a crucial issue for all playgrounds.

The Role of Adults in Play

Many of our young children simply don't know how to play; those who do often do not engage in complex play—higher forms of social and cognitive play. Further, as I have already discussed, this lack of prolonged, sophisticated play is detrimental to students' further academic, social, and moral growth. So children who don't know how to play need to be be taught how to do so.

Encouraging Free Play

Adult involvement in play has always been controversial (Johnson, Christie, & Yawkey, 1999). When I talk about adult involvement, I am not discussing the adults' role regarding safety and supervision, but rather, adult involvement in what some people call *free play.* Adults have long had a tendency to impose their own will on play, keeping children from determining the form and nature of their own activities. In response to this tendency, some teachers provide truly free play, a totally hands-off approach to play in the classroom and on the playground. This is unfortunate, because teachers can be very instrumental in helping children play. The crucial variable is *how* adults become involved in children's play. The trick is to allow children to select and control their play, without imposing adult goals (improving vocabulary or introducing academic labels like numbers and colors), and to let children direct the activity. Following are some appropriate ways for adults to support children's play (based on Johnson, Christie, & Yawkey, 1999).

Setting up the Environment. In Chapter 5 I discussed the powerful impact of the environment on children's behavior. With this in mind, it is clear that adults should arrange environments carefully to encourage and support children's play. A central role of teachers is to change, adjust, and improve the environment continually—in this case the play environment.

Providing Encouragement. Adults who participate in children's play should let children know that play is an important, worthwhile activity, not a waste of time or off-task behavior. This requires specific training for some parents and teachers, who have been taught to view play as meaningless behavior that does not support academic growth.

Modeling Play Behavior. By playing together with children, adults teach children more complex forms of play—socially, cognitively, and linguistically (Sylva, Roy, & Painter, 1980). And when adults are actively involved with children in their play, the children tend to play for longer periods of time.

Teaching Appropriate Peer Interactions. Adults can coach children to use appropriate conflict resolution strategies, along with other social skills—an essential task, as an increasing number of children do not have the appropriate social skills to solve interpersonal conflicts.

Scaffolding the Play Activity. Adults can operate as resource people within the play activity—adding suggestions, ideas, possibilities, and more complex plots that expand the play and make it more educational. And adults can further scaffold all sorts of activities in play that allow children to develop within their zone of proximal development (Vygotsky, 1978). Thus children can explore new and more complex play possibilities.

Increasing Verbal Skills. Adults can model new and more complex verbal skills—vocabulary, sentence structure, and sentence complexity. Because of the low-risk, stress-free environment of play, children are free to experiment with new words and verbal expressions.

For teachers to support children's play effectively, they must believe in the value of play to enhance social, moral, and academic growth; understand the intricacies and fine points of play; and enjoy playing themselves. Playful teachers make the best play models for children!

Conclusion

In this chapter I have explored a variety of concepts regarding play and young children. Play is a very complex phenomenon, and its relation to the overall growth of children is multidimensional. For politicians, educators, and teachers to make intelligent decisions regarding the kind and amount of play to include in early childhood curricula, they need to understand play. And to understand play, they need to know where play fits within the theoretical models of growth and development. Crucial to the discussion of play is the ever more tenuous divide between educational goals and outcomes on the one hand, and growth and developmental goals and outcomes on the other. As we provide more organized educational opportunities for young children, this debate will increase. The role play we should have in our early childhood programs needs to be aggressively included in the debate.

Questions and Projects

1. Take one sheet of 8½ × 11 paper, fold into thirds (making six panels), and create a parent–communication pamphlet describing the value of play to parents of young children. Keep the language simple. Use graphics—drawn freehand or using a computer. Your job is to convince parents to increase the amount of time they spend playing with their children at home and in the community.

2. Recall your favorite play activity as a child. Describe the kinds of play you engaged in, and how you feel they helped you develop as a person.

3. Use the playground safety guidelines (National Playground Safety Institute) to evaluate a local playground for young children. Write a one- or two-page paper summarizing the results of your examination.

4. Using graph paper, design a playground for a child-care center that serves children aged 2 to 5.

5. In a classroom a teacher has noticed that the boys never go into the housekeeping area, and rarely engage in sociodramatic play. If you were the teacher, what changes would you make to increase the dramatic play activities of boys in the classroom?

6. Develop your own theory of play. What is its purpose? Should it be encouraged and developed in young children? Why?

Resources

Children come first: Selecting equipment for early childhood education. Community Playthings. 359 Gibson Hill Rd., Chester, NY 10918. www.communityplaythings.com

Consumer Product Safety Commission. *Handbook for public playground safety.* 1997. Washington, D.C.: Government Printing Office.

Early Childhood Outdoor Institute 1313 N. Bellevue Blvd. Bellevue, NE 68005-4012 Publish *Earthworm*

National Playground Safety Institute

National Program for Playground Safety. *National action plan for the prevention of playground injuries.* Cedar Falls, Iowa: University of Northern Iowa. 1-800-554-PLAY.

National Recreation and Park Association 22377 Belmont Ridge Road Ashburn, VA 20148-4501

National SAFE KIDS Campaign 1301 Pennsylvania Ave., N.W. Washington, D.C. 20004

CHAPTER

9

Child Growth *and* Development

For a long time scholars and practitioners have been interested in how children develop, and in the factors that influence human behavior; they have created theories to try to explain these two phenomena. In this chapter I describe many of these theories, research that tries to explain how children develop and some ideas and concepts about teaching and learning. There is also a section on typical development—designed to give the student information about the general profile of children's growth. This chapter is very eclectic, and is probably more effective used as a resource than being read straight through. ■

Typical Development

Children develop along a developmental path—they roll over and crawl before they walk; they giggle, say "da da," and use incomplete sentences before engaging in sophisticated language. Here I briefly outline these developmental pathways. It is important to remember while studying this section that there is a great deal of individual variation within these overall trends, much of it a function of individual differences and cultural variations. Therefore, early childhood professionals must be very careful before deciding a child is not typically developing.

The discussion of typical development is divided into physical, social and emotional, and cognitive and linguistic domains; and within each domain into infants (aged 0–12 months), toddlers (aged 12–36 months), preschoolers (aged 3–5 years), and early elementary-school children (aged 6–8). Grouping

Questions to Consider

1. Why isn't there one theory that explains all human development?

2. Does human development progress in a straight line, or do children develop in a more irregular fashion?

3. Why do children at a certain age believe four quarters are more than five quarters?

4. What does a 5-year-old believe happens to the sun during the night?

5. Can a child who is scared and hungry learn effectively?

6. How do we store information in our memory?

Developmentally Appropriate Practice

▶ *At different ages children develop socially, physically, emotionally, cognitively, and morally.*

development in this way aids in studying typical development, but progress in one area greatly influences development in the other areas. For example, before they can learn to speak, children must be physically able to form their lips and tongue in the way required to make the required sounds. The information in this section is adapted from the work of Allen and Marotz (1994).

Physical Development

Three principles control the process of physical development in children: cephalocaudal and proximo-distal development, and refinement. **Cephalocaudal development** is the development of muscles from the head to the toes. Infants first learn to control muscles around the head and neck, then the trunk, and then the arms. Muscles for standing and walking develop later. **Proximo-distal development** is the development of muscle control starting at the center of the body and progressing to the extremities of arms and legs. And **refinement** is the progression from overall gross motor control—sitting, walking—to fine motor control—use of fingers to hold a paintbrush, filtering sand between toes, holding a ball in one hand.

Infants. Between birth and 12 months of age, babies go through a series of stages.

Newborns. The newborn arrives with a series of *survival reflexes*, which provide crucial survival behaviors: swallowing, sucking, gagging, blinking, rooting to find the nipple, and the startle reflex. The *moro reflex* is triggered when the infant is quickly lowered onto her back—the arms are thrown out, then brought back over the chest. The *grasp reflex* occurs when an object—say, a mother's finger—is placed in the infant's hand. The infant will step in a walking motion when held upright with feet touching the ground *(the stepping reflex)*. The newborn prefers the fetal position—especially when sleeping.

Ages 1–4 Months. At this age, many of the reflexive behaviors are either replaced with learned behaviors or simply disappear. The rooting and sucking reflexes are well developed; when babies are held facedown, they hold their head upright with legs fully extended. Infants now grasp objects with the entire hand, without holding them. Infants wave their arms, clasp their hands above their head, and reach for objects, but movements are jerky. When in a face-up position, babies turn their head from side to side; they can roll from front to back to front. By the end of this period, infants can be placed in a sitting position, head steady, with support, such as on an infant seat or caregiver's lap. They enjoy this newfound perspective.

Ages 4–8 Months. Reflexes continue to be modified: the blinking reflex is well established, the sucking reflex is voluntary, and the parachute reflex develops (children held facedown will throw out their arms when lowered suddenly). Infants will reach for objects—first with both arms, later one at a time; they pass objects from one hand to another, and hold objects with the whole hand (palmar grasp) and use a pincer grip (finger and thumb). Infants at this age place everything in their mouth. They lift their head when placed on their back, roll over at will, can pull themselves into a crawling position, and can sit alone without support. They like to be held in a standing position, to flex their legs, and to jump up and down.

Ages 8–12 Months. Infants continue to develop their ability to grasp objects one hand at a time, move them from one hand to another, pick up objects with the pincer grip, and let them go by dropping or throwing them. They can stack a few objects. At this age infants can pull themselves up to a standing position and stand alone, using furniture for support, as well as creep on hands and knees and crawl up and down stairs; they can walk with adult supervision.

Toddlers. Between the ages of **1 and 2 years,** toddlers' ability to move—first through skillful crawling, then by unsteady walking—adds a whole new dimension to their lives (and requires careful safety-proofing of the environment). Toddlers can get to their feet, carefully stand alone, and—at the end of the period—walk unassisted, though they often fall and don't know how to stop. They push or pull toys as they walk. Toddlers crawl up and down stairs in the same position. They repeatedly pick up and throw down objects, carry toys from place to place, and help to turn book pages. They use full arm movements to draw, and love to help self-feed.

Age 2. Older toddlers are becoming more mobile—walking erect, walking around objects, and running with fewer falls. Also, they can balance on one foot and jump up and down on two feet. Many children this age—especially girls—become toilet trained. Improved fine motor control allows children to hold a cup, throw a ball underhand, unbutton large buttons and zippers, and grasp large crayons and pencils to scribble. Toddlers love pouring and filling sand and water, and stacking four to six blocks. They can propel wheeled riding toys with their feet.

Preschoolers. For the next several years, growth is much slower and more even, and development occurs on a variety of levels.

Age 3. At this age, children's posture becomes more erect, their tummy doesn't stick out, and they have a full set of baby teeth. They work on mastering a variety of physical activities. Preschoolers can walk up and down stairs using alternate feet; they can jump in place, feed themselves without assistance, throw and catch a ball with arms extended, and enjoy swinging. A preschooler can hold crayons and markers with a tripod grasp (between first two fingers and thumb) and enjoy drawing and painting. Preschoolers can stack eight or more blocks, love to play with clay, carry liquids without much spilling, and pour liquids from one container to another. They wash and dry their own hands and brush their teeth. They usually achieve complete bladder control during this time.

Age 4. Four-year-olds are full of energy and physical activity. They can walk in a straight line, hop on one foot, pedal and steer a tricycle, climb all sorts of playground equipment, and jump over objects. They can run around objects, changing speeds; can build a tower with ten or more blocks; and can reproduce some letter shapes. The 4-year-old can sit with legs crossed (but not for long), is more accurate when hitting nails and pegs with a hammer, and can thread small wooden beads.

Age 5. Children this age are constantly practicing to master their newfound physical skills and abilities. They can walk unassisted up and down stairs, walk backward in a straight line, learn to turn somersaults, walk on a balance beam, and skip using alternate feet. They can ride a trike skillfully (and some learn to ride a bike), balance on either foot with good control, and copy basic shapes and uppercase letters. This age child has good control of a pencil or marker, cuts along a line with scissors—sort of—and has developed hand dominance—preference for their right or left hand.

Primary School Children. From 6 to 8, children are integrating all their newly achieved physical mastery into increasingly more complex tasks.

Age 6. Physical growth itself slows down, and the body takes on a more lanky appearance as arms and legs grow longer. Muscle strength increases, and both large and fine muscle movements improve along with eye–hand coordination, resulting in lots of running, jumping, climbing, bike riding, swimming, soccer, gymnastics, and T-ball. Children this age love to create using all kinds of art media; they can also write numbers and letters—though still may reverse certain letters and numbers. They can fold and cut paper in simple shapes, and tie their own shoes.

Ages 7–8. At 7 and 8, children continue to enjoy mastering physical challenges and using these skills in competitive and group games and activities. Endurance has increased, along with agility, balance, and control; they have good control of a pencil and can create uniform letters and numbers.

Social and Emotional Development

Children learn to relate to others—first their mother and primary caregivers, later other adults and children. As they grow older they also begin to control their emotions, learn appropriate responses to the environment, and learn to communicate their needs and wishes with more precision.

Infants. The newborn is totally dependent on the mother or primary caregiver. However, the caregiver's response to the newborn also depends on the child's personality. Thus, an important relationship develops between the infant and the caregiver.

Newborns. Initially, newborn babies sleep seventeen to nineteen hours a day, and like to be held close and cuddled when awake. Each newborn has a distinct personality. They express their needs using different cries, and are developing a sense of security and trust with parents and caregivers. They usually stop crying when held.

Ages 1–4 Months. Infants make eye contact with people and situations, and respond to adult voices differently, including expressing fear and anxiety, but smile in response to friendly voices and expressions. They like to be held and cuddled, and coo and gurgle when awake. Infants entertain themselves with their fingers, hands, and toes; enjoy bathing, diaper changing and tickling; and reach out to familiar people. If crying, they will soothe when a parent or caregiver comes close.

Ages 4–8 Months. At this stage infants are more outgoing, enjoy people and activities around them, smile, coo, and reach out. They can discriminate among different people in their environment, and by 6 months they show preference for a caregiver—usually their mother. They begin to develop stranger anxiety. Infants at this age imitate and respond to facial expressions, actions, and sounds made by others. They like to be held, make noise and move their body to get attention, and get upset if their toys are removed.

Ages 8–12 Months. Toward the end of their first year, children do not like being separated from their parents or caregiver, and have developed stranger anxiety. They like being involved in the activities of family and friends, and will become assertive by kicking, screaming, or lying on the floor. Many develop a favorite blanket or toy. Infants this age will respond to hearing their own name, and they will carry out simple requests if they choose to.

Toddlers. Toddlers are more friendly toward others and less anxious about strangers.

Ages 1–2 Years. Children in their second year help pick up and put toys away, enjoy adult attention—being held and read to—and imitate adult behavior in play. They recognize themselves in the mirror, and are becoming independent by saying no and refusing to do things that they used to do willingly, resulting sometimes in tantrums. Their high degree of curiosity can lead to tragic results, if not carefully supervised.

Age 2. The 2-year-old is very impatient and bossy, has difficulty making decisions, and wants things to be done in a certain exact way, which leads to frustrations, defiance, temper tantrums, anger, and physical aggression. "No" becomes the favorite word; at the same time, they begin to show empathy and caring, especially to children who are hurt or in distress.

Preschoolers. The preschool child is gaining new social skills, including understanding taking turns, enjoying group activities, and playing with other children. All these activities are still quite limited, however.

Age 3. The 3-year-old is eager to please, seems to enjoy life, joins in simple games with other children, and uses objects symbolically. Preschoolers still have nightmares and fear of the dark, may be aggressive in possessing toys, and engage in make-believe play—alone and with others. They may still have a favorite blanket, toy, or stuffed animal. They show affection to younger and vulnerable children.

Age 4. The 4-year-old is very outgoing, but shows extremes of emotions. They have imaginary friends who are very important, cooperate well in activities with other children, and usually can resolve disagreements verbally. They tend to be selfish and seek adult approval, and they want to do things independently but often get frustrated because they do not know how. Four-year-olds begin to spend lots of energy making friends and excluding others; they engage in role playing and make-believe activities.

Age 5. By this age, children are more able to enjoy group activities and games, share toys, play cooperatively, and engage in complex dramatic play activities, though they occasionally revert to selfishness. They care for younger children, have one or two special friends, follow adult directions, and still need adult approval—while exhibiting fewer mood swings.

Primary School Children. The early primary school child integrates skills and abilities from each area of development, is competent in the care of his or her own needs, and can engage in a variety of activities with adults and other children. However, while appearing competent and savvy, this age child still needs lots of opportunity to play, engage in hands-on learning, and learn social skills.

Age 6. For children entering elementary school, friendship takes the place of dependence on parents, but parental approval is still needed. Six-year-olds are highly competitive, invent rules for games, let their ego determine moral standards, and are very self-critical. They can shift rapidly from loving and helpful to obstructionist. They are very inquisitive and enthusiastic, and concerned about being good and not being bad.

Age 7–8. By this age, children are very social, especially with same-gender friends; outgoing, cooperative, and affectionate; like to be the teacher's helper; and can be trusted to carry out responsibilities and chores. They are into belonging to a group, and worry about not being liked, so they often tattle to adults.

Cognitive and Linguistic Development

Infants. Recent research has documented the tremendous cognitive and language development that occurs during this period. The newborn infant is processing a huge amount of information and building a fundamental foundation for language development, including the use of communication to get basic needs met and to engage in social interactions.

Newborns. Newborn infants' hearing is very good, and they can discriminate their mother's voice, for which they show a preference. They use their limited vision to track a moving object with their eyes if it is ten to fifteen inches from their face; and they study their own hand. Infants' sense of smell is good, and they can discriminate some flavors. They use all their senses to gain information from the environment. Crying, other vocalizations, and fussing are used to communicate; newborns show a preference for human voice and music; react to sudden, loud noises; and turn their head to a voice.

Ages 1–4 Months. Infants track objects—including their own hands—more skill-fully, move eyes from object to object, look at objects and then reach out to them, and believe that what is "out of sight is out of mind." At this age they can localize the source of a sound, move in tune to music, and imitate modeled gestures. They can distinguish their parents' faces from others, if nonvisual cues are also present. They like to mouth objects. Infants listen to a voice, rattle, and so on, and can follow and lead in a "con-versation" face-to-face with a parent. They babble and coo in response to speaking and to their own sounds, and they can produce single vowel sounds.

Ages 4–8 Months. By now, infants can turn and locate familiar sounds; imitate movements like pat-a-cake and waving bye-bye; use hands, mouth, and eyes together to explore the environment; and love to throw objects onto the floor and watch the care-giver retrieve them. They search for objects that have been hidden under a cloth. They can reach with both hands, play with small toys, bang objects together, and bang on ob-jects, but things still go in the mouth. They have developed full attachment to their mother or single caregiver. They begin to respond appropriately to familiar words, in-cluding their own name; they imitate nonspeech sounds, produce a full range of vowels and some consonants, and use sounds to express emotions. Infants at this stage babble by repeating the same syllables, such as "da da da da," and respond to simple commands.

Ages 8–12 Months. As they approach one year, infants carefully observe people and activities in the near environment, follow simple instructions, reach for toys they see even when beyond arm's length, imitate activities (playing pat-a-cake), delight in re-peatedly dropping objects to be retrieved, and use everyday objects, such as cups, cor-rectly. They are beginning to understand relationships between objects, such as putting a spoon in the mouth and brushing hair with a brush. Children this age will initiate a conversation by babbling, jabbering, or shouting; they respond when their name is called; and they babble in sentence-like vocalizations. They say "da da" and "ma ma." They enjoy rhymes and simple songs, vocalize, and move to music.

Toddlers. Language acquisition, object permanence, and the ability to move to inves-tigate and experience are all milestones that greatly increase toddler's cognitive and lan-guage development. Thus, both language development and cognitive development advance rapidly, yet unevenly, during this age.

Age 1 year. One-year-olds enjoy peekaboo activities with an object; move a toy from one hand to the other when they get a second toy (crossing the midline); can man-age three to four objects at a time by placing some to the side; and put objects in their mouth less frequently. At this age toddlers understand relationships between objects—such as spoon and bowl, doll in a crib, cup on a saucer—enjoy looking at picture books, and place small objects in a container and then dump them. They can name everyday objects. They continue to string sounds together into speechlike forms, use holophras-tic speech (one word conveying an entire idea) and some two-word sentences, and fol-low simple directions. One-year-olds will point to familiar persons and toys, and will respond to questions with "yes," "no," or shaking the head. During this time children acquire between five and fifty words—mostly for animals, food, and toys. They still enjoy participating in rhymes and songs, and engage in more turn taking—reciprocity—in conversations.

Age 2. More sophisticated eye–hand coordination enables toddlers to put together and take apart objects, and to put large pegs in a pegboard. They can classify simple objects using one physical dimension; self-chosen activities are given longer attention; they discover cause and effect; and they find hidden objects by looking in the last place they were left. Two-year-olds name objects in picture books, like to participate (point, talk) while being read to, and use from fifty to three hundred different words, stringing three- to four-word pronouncements together. Receptive language (what is understood) is much greater than expressive language (what is produced)—which is true throughout a child's development. They use *me* and *I*, as well as some plurals, and they begin to talk about things not immediately present. The two-year-old repeatedly asks, "What's that?"

Preschoolers. Preschoolers use language both to communicate to others—peers and adults—and to represent ideas and experiences in their minds. They are becoming more flexible thinkers, but are still limited by concrete thinking. Language ability—number of words and correct grammar usage—takes off at this age.

Age 3. Three-year-olds listen attentively to stories, make comments during stories, and like to look at books and "read" them. They like books with riddles, guessing, and real information; play with materials symbolically; and can place eight to ten pegs in a board or six blocks in a square board. At this age children can copy circles, squares, and letters while drawing; they can sort objects by a single physical characteristic, usually color or size. Conceptually, they understand size relationships, along with more and less, and can arrange cubes in a line on the floor or tabletop. They have a primitive concept of time and length of time—all day, two days, and so on.

Children age 3 use language to represent objects, events, actions, and people that are not present; ask more and more questions; and answer simple questions correctly. They use different methods to keep a conversation going. While 3-year-olds talk about themselves, they also engage in social rituals—"hi," "goodbye," and so on. They can recite nursery rhymes, sing songs, use verbs with *-ing* endings, and use *s* to denote plural. They put *no* and *not* in front of nouns or verbs to indicate negative.

Age 4. Four-year-olds can stack five blocks in order of size; some children this age begin to read very simple books—with lots of visual cues. They like stories about how things grow and work; enjoy wordplay and silly language; understand *same, biggest, tallest,* and *more;* and comprehend the sequence of daily events (such as schedules), but have no real sense of time. Children this age can use the words *on, in, under, hers, baby's, can't,* and *don't,* and answer *why* and *how many?* They begin to use the past tense correctly. The 4-year-old completes complex sentences and recites simple songs and rhymes.

Age 5. Five-year-olds sort objects by color or size, build steps with small blocks, sort items using one criterion (all that float; all with two legs). They can place objects in order from shortest to tallest, smallest to largest; understand *first, second,* and *last;* and can match clock time with daily activities, though their concept of time is still primitive. Children this age still ask lots of questions and want to learn many new things.

They use fifteen hundred words or more, tell stories while looking at picture books, like jokes and riddles, use irregular past-tense verbs—*went, swam, dug*—and understand the singular and plural of verbs.

Primary School Children. Primary age children use language in social situations, to solve problems, and to represent experiences. They discover language can be used for humor and put-downs. Cognitively, this age child is moving from preoperational thinking to concrete operations, which allows them to think more abstractly with less reliance on real objects and perceptions.

Age 6. Six-year-olds have a much longer attention span, when interested; they begin to understand some forms of conservation (for example, liquid); they like puzzles, counting and sorting activities, and matching objects and pictures. They enjoy being read to and making up stories, recognize some words by sight, and still believe in the tooth fairy and Santa Claus. Six-year-olds love to talk a lot—sometimes without stopping—ask many questions, and can carry on an adult conversation. Their vocabulary is now between ten thousand and fourteen thousand words. They usually solve problems and express emotions with language. They use self-talk to guide simple problem-solving activities and are experimenting with all sorts of things, including slang and bathroom talk, which they find very funny.

Ages 7–8. By this age children collect, organize, and display objects using complex classification processes. They are interested in what others do and think—friends, cultures, places—understand cause and effect, and can use complex logic to explain daily events. Some children still produce letter reversals and sound substitutions. At 7 and 8, children like to read alone and write imaginative tales; they can recall accurately what has been read, and often exaggerate their own accomplishments—in minute detail. They love jokes and riddles, use adultlike sentence structures in conversation, and like to praise or criticize others.

Theories of Development

What Is a Theory?

A theory is a way of organizing data, ideas, and concepts to provide a more complete understanding of what the information means than would be gained by viewing it in a piecemeal fashion (Dworetzky, 1995). A theory is a system of rules or assumptions that predict or explain phenomena. A good theory provides accurate predictions; if correct, it will predict all possible behaviors and situations. But if a piece of data that logically should fit into a theory doesn't, then the theory must be changed or abandoned. There are many theories that try to explain human development: none is totally correct, and many contradict one another. Theories are developed based on people's knowledge of human behavior, and their cultural context. Thus, Europeans have created theories of human development that emphasize the relation between the environment and a person's inherited predispositions (Piaget, Erikson, Vygotsky, Froebel) because European culture stresses family inheritance and genetic endowment; U.S. theories tend to focus on the power of the environment because we believe that each person, regardless of family background, is created equal and can succeed—"Anyone can become president" (Dworetzky, 1995).

Regardless, developmental theorists in any culture face a daunting task: human behavior is extremely complex, with many variables. A variable is a force or factor that can affect an outcome. Some variables that affect human development include genetics, genetically transmitted diseases, accidents, the environment, developmental stages, nutrition, attachment, family dynamics, and culture. Because of this complexity, creation of a single overarching theory to explain human behavior is impossible, and theorists have focused on segments of human behavior and learning. Erikson studied psychosocial behavior, Piaget cognitive behavior, Chomsky language development, and Gesell physical development. The hope is that eventually all these theories will come together to present a full picture of human development.

Power of a Theory. All human-development theories must have power. The power of a theory is like the engine in a car—it makes it go. For example, the power behind Piaget's theory is the constant tension between accommodation and assimilation; the power behind operant conditioning is our biological need for food, shelter, and love, and our desire to avoid punishment. Power moves the theory forward, keeping a person from becoming stuck. For example, a person who is punished for a specific behavior will learn to avoid that behavior. If people did not mind punishment, they would not learn to avoid that behavior (say, jumping into a deep pool).

Critical Periods. In 1937 Konrad Lorenz reported a study he conducted on newborn ducklings. He made sure he was the first moving object the ducklings saw after they hatched from their eggs; they then followed him wherever he went—including swimming—as if he were their mother. It seems the ducklings were programmed to accept the first moving objects they saw after their birth as the object to follow—their "mother." Lorenz called this phenomenon **imprinting.** Through further studies Lorenz discovered that imprinting would occur only during a very short period after the ducklings hatched, and if it did not occur then, it would never do so; further, it can never be reversed (unlearned). Periods of development during which learning must take place or will forever be left out are called **critical periods.**

Attachment. There is a critical period for bonding in humans. According to Bowlby (1982), humans are preprogrammed to engage in specific behaviors to try to create an **attachment**—usually, but not always, with their mother during their first year of life. If attachment does not occur, Bowlby and others argue, humans will have problems with intimate relationships later in their lives and will engage in asocial behavior such as juvenile delinquency and abusive sexual behaviors.

Sensitive Periods. **Sensitive periods** are times during an organism's development in which a particular influence is most likely to have an effect (Dworetzky, 1995). Sensitive periods differ from critical periods in that behaviors that have not been acquired during the period can be acquired later on, but with much more difficulty. During sensitive periods, humans are genetically predisposed to learning certain behaviors—talking, sexual attraction, sexual identity development, walking, and so on. Chomsky's concept of a language acquisition device (see Chapter 10) is a language development theory based on the concept of sensitive periods. According to Chomsky, humans in all cultures are preprogrammed with all the necessary structures to learn all languages that exist in the world. During a sensitive period they interact with the environment to learn their culture's language. It also appears that learning a second language is most effective during the sensitive period of 3 to 10 years of age.

It is not clear, however, to what extent a child's prior experience influences these sensitive periods. For example, is the preadolescent's sudden interest in the opposite sex partly due to exposure to a sexually charged media culture? Further, we don't know what learning and behaviors are most affected by these periods—or their exact time frame. It would be extremely helpful if we did. Are children at certain ages more vulnerable to substance abuse, violent tendencies, or developing healthy relationships with members of the opposite sex? Knowing this would be very helpful, because we could then target our teaching and limited resources to maximize these opportunities.

Invariant Stages. As a trained biologist, Piaget was fascinated by the stages of a butterfly's development: it starts with an egg, which hatches into a caterpillar; then, after eating a great deal and getting quite large, the caterpillar forms a chrysalis, which eventually opens up and a butterfly emerges. Piaget was particularly struck that at each stage in this metamorphosis, the organism is completely different, and that once the organism completes a stage it cannot return to an earlier stage. Piaget's theory of cognitive development is based on this concept: his four stages must be followed sequentially, and they cannot be revisited once left. While these stages are not strictly based on a time (age), they must occur in a specific order. For example, a child must complete the sensorimotor stage (infancy to about age 2) before moving to the preoperational stage; and once that stage is achieved, the child cannot return to the sensorimotor stage.

Maturational Theory

It is common knowledge that humans develop in a certain sequence—along a developmental path. Children crawl before they walk, scribble before they draw, babble before they speak, and are egocentric before learning to share. This seems to be true of all children in all cultures. Thus the sequence of children's development is preset in their genes: it is inherited. **Maturational theory** holds that this programming is the most important determinant of development. Arnold Gesell carefully documented maturational physical development; the Gesell Institute still provides detailed age-related charts and books. While maturation theorists believe development to be highly predictable, they also believe it's uneven. At certain times in a child's life, growth spurts occur; at other times, little seems to be happening. Thus development—in all areas—will be accelerated at certain times and slower at others.

Not only do maturation theorists believe that children's developmental progression is preprogrammed, but they minimize the importance of the environment, being strongly opposed to attempts to accelerate a child's development—physically, intellectually, or emotionally. They believe this effort produces negative results in a child's later life.

▶ *Gesell was interested in the natural development of children—what he called maturation.*

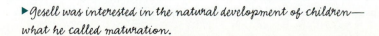

Stage Theories

It seems that certain periods in a child's life are critical for development in specific areas. We know that all normally developing children learn to speak between 12 and 36 months old. A few exceptional children can learn before this age, but a child who has not done so by age 3 will have great difficulty speaking later on. Theorists believe that infants who don't experience bonding with a significant adult within their first year to develop a secure attachment will experience difficulty developing important relationships later in life. Erikson's psychosocial theory, Piaget's cognitive theory, and Kohlberg's and Lickona's moral development theories are all stage theories.

Cognitive Theories

How do children think? How do they take information from the environment and their experiences and place it into their minds? How do children construct their image of the world? And, how do children use their knowledge to solve problems and predict results? These are fundamental questions cognitive theorists set out to address. They attempt to describe these and other complex ideas about how the mind works and how we use our minds in daily tasks and activities.

Piaget

In Jean Piaget's theory of cognitive development, the tension between assimilation and accommodation provides the driving force. According to Piaget, a child is continually trying to resolve this tension, which facilitates the child's progress through four distinct stages: sensorimotor and preoperational stages, concrete operations, and formal operations. *Operations* are central to his stages, because Piaget is interested in how children solve problems, determine cause and effect, and figure out how the world works. As children use the tension between accommodation and assimilation to make sense of the physical world, their cognitive abilities develop from simple, impulsive responses to the environment by all senses to a sophisticated ability to reason, communicate, think, understand cause and effect, and predict future events and results.

Accommodation and Assimilation. According to Piaget, children actively process information they receive from the environment. From birth (actually, before birth), children take in stimuli from the environment—light, smell, taste, sound, and textures. Piaget claims that children process this information in two distinct, but related, ways. **Assimilation** is the process of taking in information and matching it to a **schema** a child already has—an internal concept of an object or phenomenon. For example, if children have learned that balls bounce, when they see a cannon ball they will assume it bounces, too. Even if they see the cannonball dropped and it doesn't bounce, they will still maintain the schema that all round objects bounce. **Accommodation** is the process by which the child changes or creates new schemata to match new information from the environment. It takes many examples of contradictory information before the child will accommodate. The more actively children are involved in the environment—playing, manipulating, using all their senses—the more quickly they will change the incorrect schema. For example, a child may have developed the idea that all objects thrown in a pond float: water physically keeps everything up. It will take lots of actively playing in water with many objects in water to change this view. Then the child will construct a new schema—maybe that large, heavy objects sink, and small, light ones do not. While this is a more accurate concept, it is still not totally correct. The child will have to accommodate several more times before developing an accurate view of floating and sinking.

As children resolve the continual tension between their internal vision of the world and reality, their thinking becomes more complex, sophisticated, and accurate. Because it is based on a process of actively constructing one's internal view of reality, Piaget's theory (and others that have a similar concept) is called a constructivist theory. The basic concept of constructivism is that children construct their knowledge, through active interaction with the environment. This is the opposite of the idea that children simply absorb information given them by a teacher or observed from the environment. Constructivism requires active manipulation and processing of the environment. For example, for children to learn that the color green is produced by mixing yellow and blue, the constructivist approach requires them to mix a variety of paints in different amounts and combinations. As they do this, they construct basic ideas in their mind: mixing different colors produces new colors; mixing certain combinations produces orange, purple, and so on; and mixing yellow and blue produces green. Children then repeat the action to make sure the theory holds up, and under what conditions it does (how much blue and yellow, how thick the paint, and the like). Through a combination of manipulating the environment and constructing theories about mixing colors, and then testing those theories by mixing a variety of paint combinations, children construct their view of how green is made. Central to the process are active manipulation of the environment, constructing a theory in the mind, and constant revision of the theory.

Growth and Practice. While Piaget's theory is progressive—starting at a fairly unsophisticated level of cognitive ability and ending with the highest level of adult intelligence—it is not linear. In other words, Piaget does not believe development follows a straight line. His stages are more accurately conveyed in a stepwise fashion, which not only illustrates the abrupt shift from stage to stage but also describes smaller advances within each stage. For example, a child might discover that a nice big rubber ball bounces. This is an example of acquiring a new concept. Once the child has gained this knowledge, it is necessary to play a great deal with a variety of balls to internalize the idea that balls bounce. Piaget calls this activity practicing the new concept, and it is equivalent to the horizontal part of a step. After lots of practice, the child then discovers that the amount of a ball's bounce depends on certain characteristics—size, materials, and how well it is inflated, which is equivalent to the vertical part of a step. According to Piaget, the activity of internalizing through practice is as important as the acquisition of new concepts.

Sensorimotor Stage. The **sensorimotor stage** takes place between infancy and age 2. Infants learn about their world through direct use of their senses—smell, hearing, sight, touch, and taste (especially the latter). Children respond reflexively to outside stimuli, then begin to create schemata using this information. For example, a child reflexively looks at a moving mobile, then maintains eye contact with it because it is interesting. The next time the child begins to look for the mobile in order to track its path. While infants investigate the world by putting objects in their mouth, tracking movement, and responding to their mother's voice, they cannot think symbolically about these objects or activities. When an object is placed out of an infant's view, the infant forgets it ever existed. For the sensorimotor child, out of sight (or other sense) is out of mind.

Once a child has achieved **object permanence**—knowing that although an object is placed out of sight, it still exists—the child has moved to the preoperational stage.

Preoperational Stage. When I was a Head Start director I used to conduct training for other teachers. On one occasion I presented Piaget's cognitive theory to the staff of another Head Start in La Junta, Colorado. I took my daughter Eirlys—a beaming, independent, opinionated 4-year-old—with me. As part of training about preoperational children, I demonstrated the concept of liquid conservation to more than a hundred teachers. I poured water from a large glass jug first into a tall, narrow glass tube, so that the participants could clearly see that the tube was full. I then poured the water into a flat glass saucer. I turned to Eirlys, who was standing next to me and had been carefully observing the demonstration, and asked her, "Which container has the most water in it, the tall glass tube or the plate?"

Without hesitation, she loudly replied, "Oh, daddy, you are so stupid! The tube has the most—can't you *see*?"

Children in the **preoperational stage**—which goes from age 2 to age 6 or 7—believe what they see. Preoperational children have not learned what we call *conservation*—the concept that objects do not change in volume, mass, length, number, weight, or area simply because they appear to change. Thus the water I used, while physically appearing to change in amount, actually did not. A round clump of clay does not change size when flattened into a pancake, yet children this age believe it does.

Arrange two rows of quarters on a table, one with four quarters, the other with five. Make the row with five quarters the shortest row. Then ask 5-year-olds to choose the row of quarters they wish to take to the store to buy whatever they want. They'll choose the four quarters because the row is longer, and to them *longer* means more. Even after they count the quarters in each row, they'll still pick the longest row: the physical evidence outweighs the symbolic evidence, that five is greater than four.

Nevertheless, preoperational children do think symbolically. They represent objects, ideas, feelings, and experiences with words; they represent amount with numbers; and they can represent relationships through pictures and dramatic play. The chapters on play, literacy, and math and science explain this symbolic representation in more detail. The point here is that unlike the sensorimotor child, the preoperational child can represent ideas, experiences, objects, and feelings not immediately present; further, they can use these symbols to think about their experiences. But the preoperational child is still subject to the power of direct perception.

Preoperational children are also **egocentric.** A researcher was interested in determining what preschool children know about the relationship between the sun and the earth, the creation of day and night, and the four seasons, so she asked preschoolers, "What happens to the sun at night?" One little boy who had recently moved from New England to Atlanta responded by running to the window, looking out at the rising sun, and declaring, "The sun followed me to Atlanta!" When I picked up my daughter one winter evening from the baby-sitter, it was already dark, with a full moon shining. As

▶ *Where does the sun go at night? According to the preoperational child, it follows the child!*

we walked to the car I pointed out the moon to her. She smiled, her eyes lit up, and she proudly proclaimed, "Look, daddy, there's *my* moon!"

Also at this age children attribute human characteristics to inanimate and nonhuman objects. Because clouds move, children believe they're alive. Animals, dolls, puppets, and miniature people are all given human qualities. Stories such as *Peter Rabbit*, *Winnie the Pooh*, and *The Wind in the Willows* (toads, muskrats, and so on)—along with Mickey Mouse, of course—illustrate this point. Monsters are also prevalent. When my son was about 3 years old, he would not take a bath unless we chased away his monsters, And yes, he was convinced there were two monsters!

Concrete Operations Stage. Between the ages of 6 or 7 and 11 or 12, children can think logically about almost everything. They can think backward and forward, expand ideas, and engage in all sorts of manipulation of symbols they have developed. **Concrete operations stage** children can think about more than one piece of information at a time, are less egocentric in their thinking, and can consider other people's perspectives, feelings, and points of view. Even so, children at this stage have extreme difficulty thinking about abstract concepts they have not personally experienced—especially results of personal problems or dilemmas. They cannot comprehend the results of substance abuse or irresponsible sexual behavior. "It won't happen to me" typifies the concrete operations child's view of the world.

Formal Operations Stage. This stage rarely occurs before a child is 11 or 12 years old, and it continues to develop for several years. The **formal operations stage** is characterized by the ability to think abstractly, logically, and mathematically—all the skills needed in higher math and complex science classes. For example, children who have achieved formal operations can test a hypothesis by examining one variable at a time, while keeping the others constant. Even if the result is something they have never personally experienced, they can project the result of allowing a bunch of teenagers—some smoking, some drinking, and all fooling around—to drive a car on the safety of each person. While Piaget suggested children develop formal operations sometime after age 11–12, it seems clear that it does not occur until much later. Many high school students have not fully achieved formal operations.

Vygotsky

Vygotsky's cognitive theory is known as a **sociocultural theory** because he believed that children's cognitive development is largely predicated on their social interactions and context. He believed children develop their cognitive structures through individual interaction with the social environment, and that each culture provides a different social

Figure 9.1

Vygotsky's zone of proximal development is the dynamic area in which instruction and learning take place.

Child can ride the
bike with assistance
from her father

Vygotsky's
Zone of Proximal
Development (ZPD):
The area between
what a child can do
on her own and what
she can do with expert
support

Child can sit on bike
and place feet on the
ground

environment for their children. While some of these acquisitions are universal—all children everywhere learn to be social, become highly skilled in language, and learn the rules and mores of their society—the specific nature of this knowledge is defined by each child's culture.

The central way children develop cognition is through language, and since language grows out of a culture's social interactions, expectations, and values, children's cognition reflects their culture. Initially, infants and young toddlers use language as a social teacher—they respond to the language around them: directions, nurturing, stimulation, soothing, and so on. As children begin to internalize language, however, it is used to structure their internal reality: they talk to themselves to structure learning, to place new experiences in their mind, and to order these experiences. Children first talk aloud to themselves as they think things through; eventually, they talk internally to themselves— what Vygotsky called **private speech.**

Zone of Proximal Development. As a learning theorist, Vygotsky was less concerned with what children can do and know than with their learning potential. To address this idea, he developed what is called the **zone of proximal development** (ZPD)—the distance between what children can do independently in a specific area or skill, and what they can achieve in the same area and skill with expert guidance (Berk & Winsler, 1995). The zone of proximal development is the dynamic area in which instruction and learning take place.

An example can be seen in teaching children how to ride a bike. It is impossible to teach them to ride a bike before they are "ready"—before they have the physical ability to sit on the saddle and reach the pavement with their feet, the ability to turn the handlebars in the direction they want to go, the desire to learn to ride the bike, the skill of integrating and using incoming information to direct the bike, and a lack of fear. This is the baseline of the ZPD; the top of the ZPD is the ability to ride the bike—albeit with their father puffing away behind, holding the seat.

Once a new skill or concept has been mastered to the extent that it can be achieved independently, the zone is shifted upward moving children ever forward in their learning. The zone of proximal development is very helpful for teachers because teaching children something they already know is a waste of time, while teaching them beyond the zone will frustrate both the child and the teacher. It helps teachers understand the value of targeting assistance within the zone, and it provides a distinct role for the teacher in children's learning processes.

The motivation to learn within the zone must come from children, who need to be actively involved, to lead and direct the activity. Anyone who is more advanced than the students in the skill or task can be the teacher, including other children. In fact, in many cases other children are more effective teachers, because they know how to provide the most helpful guidance. Teachers should support and guide children from behind—either literally, as with parents teaching children to ride a bike, or in terms of supporting, suggesting, and structuring.

Scaffolding. The concept of scaffolding developed from Vygotsky's work; he did not actually use the term. The word is a metaphor describing a process of assisting children in learning, and is based on the scaffolding used to construct a building: a framework that is required to assist in the building process, which is then removed once the building is built. In learning terms, scaffolding includes ideas, techniques, and methods provided by teachers (or peers) that help children learn within the zone of proximal development, and that are eventually internalized by children. For example, everyone who does jigsaw puzzles uses unique scaffolding—such as first collecting all the edge pieces starting with the corners, completing all the edges, piecing together the bottom of the picture, and finally completing the main objects and characters. This approach was originally taught to the puzzle maker, who now uses it automatically.

To scaffold learning, teachers and peers should help children stay within the zone of proximal development, provide less assistance and support as children move toward doing the activity independently, and promote self-regulation. In other words, instructors should provide strategies that children can use to scaffold their own learning. Other obvious ways the teacher can scaffold activities include:

- *setting the scope or parameters of an activity.* For example, start painting with just one color, so children learn to use a brush, and then add other colors later.
- *urging children to progress to the next stage when ready.* For instance, suggest a child is ready to take the training wheels off the bike when the child appears ready.
- *controlling the setting.* An example would be limiting toddler activities to the small playground, where equipment is safe and challenging to the toddler.

● *arranging activities to show the child an effective sequence.* For example, when planting a seed, first fill the pot with soil, then plant the seed, water the pot, and finally, place the pot in a sunny area.

Teaching children a sequence can be done by telling them the sequence, modeling it, or both. A teacher can also break down large, confusing activities into smaller, manageable parts. And if a task is too easy, the teacher should add complexity, change the goals, and expand the zone.

Private Speech. The goal of scaffolding is for children to be able to scaffold their own learning. According to Vygotsky, this occurs through private speech. For example, once the jigsaw activity has been scaffolded by the teacher, further independent jigsaw activities should be controlled by children saying to themselves, "First, I need to collect all the edge pieces and do the edge of the puzzle." Once this is complete, they say to themselves, "Now I need to do the bottom of the puzzle." Eventually, they will follow this sequence without talking to themselves. To maximize the use of private speech, teachers need to ask questions, provide statements that help the child see the scaffolding, and solicit suggestions—"What would happen if . . . ?" Teacher-directed instruction does not help children develop their own private speech to use in directing their further learning.

Information Processing

Suppose you are teaching a second-grade class, and midway through the year a new student enrolls. To determine his math knowledge, you give him a simple paper and pencil test with addition, subtraction, and multiplication problems. You sit him at a table to complete his work. After half an hour you pick up his paper and correct the work. He has done very poorly. Why? The most obvious reason is that he hasn't learned basic math. But there could be various other reasons. Maybe he did not adequately hear or understand your directions; perhaps he was distracted by the children playing at the computer next to him; possibly in the new environment he was so nervous that he could not focus on the task; or he knew how to do the math but had problems writing the answers quickly enough. Finally, he might have known how to do the math problems, but in the past had relied on a teacher or peer to give him a specific cue to get started.

There are many tasks and activities children must master to be able to accomplish simple school-related problems, and there can be a whole host of reasons why a student might struggle with these problems—some not immediately evident. **Information processing theory** describes the entire learning process, and therefore can help us isolate where a child might be struggling. Furthermore, this theory provides knowledge about children's progress through each step in the learning process. If we know the steps by which children learn, we can find ways to improve our teaching. While information processing describes this learning activity for a person of any age, each step in the process is influenced by developmental stages. For example, information that is personally meaningful to a 5-year-old will not be meaningful to a 15-year-old.

Perception. All learning starts with perception. Of course, we perceive with all of our senses—smell, taste, touch, sight, and hearing. We use our senses to take in information from the environment so that we can process it in our minds. To maximize our ability to take in information, our senses need to work well; therefore, it is vital that children have periodic expert sight and hearing tests. A child whose hearing or sight is limited will struggle to learn unless modifications are made. Also, children need to learn to use their senses to discriminate important information—to hear instructions carefully, follow written words on the page, and feel the sandpaper letters.

Attention. Lightning and thunder always get our **attention.** They attract our attention because they are bright and loud, respectively. Adding to this effectiveness is that storms often occur at night, so lightning is a strong contrast in the dark sky; and storms often occur after very calm weather, making them seem much louder and wilder. We attend to—focus on—the parts of our environment that capture our senses because there is too much in the environment for us to take in. The aim is to attend to the important information and ignore the rest.

A familiar college example illustrates my point. A professor enters her classroom carrying a huge block of ice—say, two feet square—which she places in the corner. She then proceeds to give a standard psychology lecture while the ice slowly melts, creating puddles of water on the ground and seeping into the carpet. At the end of the lecture the professor gives a brief quiz on the material she covered, which every student fails. Why? Because the students were all attending to the melting ice block in the corner, and not to the lecture.

What we attend to depends on two basic factors: the environment and how it is arranged, and the way our minds work. I already mentioned that loud sounds and bright lights attract our attention. Novelty, salience, incongruity, and repetition, emotion, and meaningfulness do so also. *Novelty* means new, different, unusual; *salience* means something that stands out—color, size, shape, taste, smell, sound, and so on. A bright pink car is salient, a whistle blowing is salient, and the smell of a sewage plant is salient. *Incongruent* means unexpected: the TV commercial of an NBA star knitting is a good example. Clearly, any stimulus that is continually repeated will get our attention—recall those car alarms? *Meaningful* and *emotional* characterize things that we attend to because they relate to our experiences, or because they cause an emotional reaction—fear, love, joy, excitement.

Our minds respond to the environment by tuning out information that we don't need. This is called **habituation.** For example, in most college classrooms there is a low buzz from the air conditioner, which we are unaware of it until it turns itself off. This change reminds our brain of noise that is in the environment. And all of us have tuned out our teacher at one time or another! Because our minds tune out boring information, teachers need to use a variety of attention-getting devices to get children's attention, and continually change the environment to maintain their attention. A child who does not attend to crucial information will not learn.

Working Memory. A child who has learned to kick a soccer ball will be able to repeat that feat at a future time; a child who has learned the alphabet will be able to recite it later on. In other words, learning involves memory. But we don't simply put information into our memory the way we experience it—we process it first. Information must be processed in our working memory, then stored in our long-term memory.

Our **working memory** is very short (five to twenty seconds), and it is very limited; it can hold only five to nine units of information at any one time. Any new information we want to place in long-term memory must be processed very quickly, or we will simply lose it (forget it). For example, when trying to remember a new phone number, we must either write it down or find a way to put it into our long-term memory, or we will

▶ *Information processing is a theory that explains how children take information from the environment and store it in their minds, and then retrieve it when needed.*

forget it. Alternatively, we can repeat it in our mind until we find a way to remember it; but we are unable to learn anything else until we have dealt with the number. There is a variety of ways to process information in our working memory. The most obvious but least efficient is repetition—or memorization. Other, more efficient methods are

- *Tie the new information to something we already know*—that is already in our memory. For example, I might remember the name of someone important I met at a party by noting that his name is the same as my father's middle name.
- *Pick out crucial features to remember.* A Mercedes Benz is defined by the distinctive three-pronged emblem, a Rolls-Royce by the flat grille with RR on it. I remember the waiter because he has an accent.
- *Use elaboration.* Actively add information to what we want to learn to make it easier to learn. For example, some children add their own words to the pledge of allegiance to make it easier to remember.
- *Use meaningful learning.* We remember things based on what we know and experience. Teachers need to find ways to tie new information to what children already know.
- *Use visual imagery.* As it suggests, this involves creating visual images of something to remember. These images are fairly accurate.
- *Use heuristics*—an aid, cue, or shortcut to remembering information in processes, such as "the order of information is the same as the alphabet."

Since the working memory is the bottleneck of the system, teachers must introduce new information slowly, find ways to use the different methods for putting information into long-term memory, and limit their use of rote learning and memorization.

Long-Term Memory. In **long-term memory** we store everything we have done, experienced, learned, and imagined. It appears to be limitless (we never really forget anything), and all stored information is connected to other stored information. The secret to using long-term memory effectively is to find ways to retrieve stored information, including remembering how we put the information in, recognizing that each individual's method of processing information is **idiosyncratic** (unique to that person), knowing that children tend to store information with pictures while adults do so with words, and remembering that we store information in the context in which we learned it. Thus we remember the elephant in the zoo—not in the pizza parlor or on the street. How we put information into long-term memory, and then how we retrieve it, are two sides of the same coin. For example, in helping a student remember what a zebra looks like, the teacher might say, "Remember when we went to the zoo last week? Remember those animals we saw that looked like horses? Remember what Johnny said they looked like?"

Figure 9.2

Sequence of Information Processing

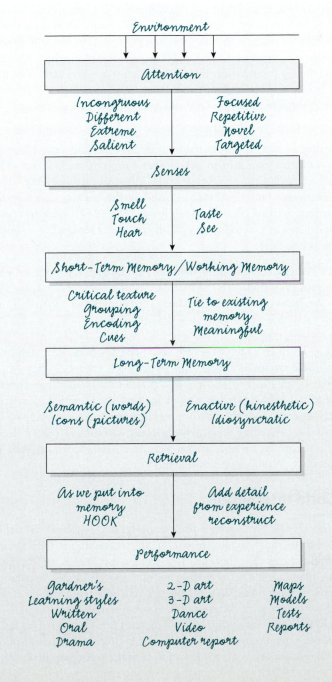

Environment

Attention

Incongruous	Focused
Different	Repetitive
Extreme	Novel
Salient	Targeted

Senses

Smell	Taste
Touch	See
Hear	

Short-Term Memory / Working Memory

Critical texture	Tie to existing
Grouping	memory
Encoding	Meaningful
Cues	

Long-Term Memory

| Semantic (words) | Enactive (kinesthetic) |
| Icons (pictures) | Idiosyncratic |

Retrieval

As we put into	Add detail
memory	from experience
HOOK	reconstruct

Performance

Gardner's	2-D art	Maps
Learning styles	3-D art	Models
Written	Dance	Tests
Oral	Video	Reports
Drama	Computer report	

Retrieval. Information placed in our memory is useless unless we can get at it when we need it. Placing lots of information in our memory that cannot be retrieved is a waste of time. Apparently everything in our long-term memory is connected to another piece of information in a giant web. The secret is to find what is connected to it.

One way to look at this is to use the computer as a metaphor. To place something in your computer's memory, you create a file with a name, then place the file in a folder. When you want to retrieve the file, you can do a search, but it is much easier to remember where it is (in which folder) and how you labeled it (which filename). The same is true in retrieving information from your memory: if you can remember where you filed it (my recent trip to England) and what you named it (Shakespeare play at Stratford), you will retrieve it. Some ways we retrieve information are

- based on how we put it into long-term memory;
- according to how it's connected to other information (since I learned the new number by hooking it to an old number, I must go back to that old number first);
- based on the last time we brought the information from long-term memory (my memory of my first house is based on the last time I remembered it);
- according to the context in which it was learned (if I want to remember the person I met at a birthday party, I should try to remember as much about the party as possible).

Once we remember something, we then elaborate it, meaning we add details. Let's suppose we recall our friend's red Mercedes. When we retrieve it, we add our general image of a Mercedes car—expensive, shiny, elegant, and so on. In fact, our friend's car needs a wash, is a little old, and has a few dents in it!

Performance. In an episode of the TV show *The Simpsons*, Bart demonstrates that he understands the French and Indian wars by telling his teacher about the battle at Fort Necessity, but he gets an F on a paper and pencil test. He has a performance problem. Children need to be able to demonstrate what they have learned. Teachers need to help children demonstrate what they know and also help them discover the best way to do so, and in the best way they know how. Students demonstrate what they know differently: write a report, take a test, draw a picture, create a video, present a play, develop a 3-D model, give an oral presentation, and more.

Teacher–Child Interaction

Cognitive theories of development place considerable emphasis on children's interaction with their environment. But teacher–child interaction is viewed as crucial to the implementation of cognitive theories. Teachers are involved in socializing with children, encouraging play, setting up activities, monitoring children's behavior, and helping children manage their misbehavior. Effective teachers tend to be warm, sensitive, involved, and not harsh with children. The most frequently observed teacher–child interactions are praise or nurturing, redirection, and limit setting. The least frequent are divergent questioning (questions that expand thinking) and elaboration. The quality of teacher–child interactions is more important than the frequency. Even so, teachers must make a conscious effort to provide high-quality interaction with all of the children under their care and education because they tend to interact with children who seek their attention, need their attention due to behavioral issues, or are fun to be around (Kontos & Wilcox-Herzog, 1997).

Research suggests that the quality of teacher–child interaction has a positive impact on children's development. Children who receive sensitive, responsive involvement from teachers tend to exhibit less stress, are more competent socially, are more intelligent and task oriented, and have better linguistic development. "There is consistent evidence that teachers who are sensitive to children's needs and who engage, encourage and verbally communicate with children, nurture more optimum cognitive, language and socio-emotional development" (Kontos & Wilcox-Herzog, 1997, p. 11).

Behaviorism

Behaviorism is a concept that explains the role of the environment in shaping behavior. Here I review the basic concepts of classical conditioning and operant conditioning; in Chapter 12, I cover basic behavioral techniques used in early childhood programs.

Classical Conditioning

Ivan Pavlov discovered through his experiments that when he repeatedly fed his dog immediately after he rang a bell, the dog would eventually salivate every time he heard the bell, even when he received no food. Thus Pavlov got the dog to salivate to a new stimulus (the bell)—what Pavlov called a *conditioned stimulus.*

Classical conditioning occurs when two stimuli are presented at approximately the same time, and the neutral stimulus eventually produces the response. The response—in this case salivation by the dog—is involuntary: the dog does not make a conscious choice to salivate, which is why classical conditioning is so powerful.

What's particularly interesting is that one can now take the sound of the bell and pair it with, say, a flash of bright light, which then becomes conditioned to produce the salivation. Then we might match the bright light with getting up and moving across the room, and so on. The cumulative addition of conditioned stimuli is called *higher-order conditioning.* My dog, Ginger, loves to run with me during my daily exercise. Initially, her leash became the conditioned stimulus that produced the behavior of excited running to the door, panting. After considerable higher-order conditioning, however, Ginger now gets excited and runs to the door every time I sit down to put on my shoes!

People and Classical Conditioning. When John goes to school for the first time, he gets into a fight; the next day his teacher shouts at him; and during the third day he is falsely accused of hitting a classmate. He quickly associates school with punishment and develops a very strong school phobia. Not only can children—and adults—be classically conditioned, but it is very easy to do so, and very difficult to undo. Clearly we can be conditioned both negatively (fear, dislike, a sense of failure) and positively (high self-esteem, dispositions, enjoyment).

Extinction. When Pavlov kept ringing the bell without giving his dog any food, the conditioned response (salivation) became weaker and weaker. Eventually the conditioned response died out. This is called *extinction*. Conditioned behavior in humans can also become extinct. John can overcome his school phobia if subsequent school experiences are generally positive. The problem is that this does not always occur. If John always remembers the negative experiences, this acts as a means of continuing to condition his negative association with school, thus preventing extinction.

Spontaneous Recovery. Even though John may have totally extinguished his school phobia, it may return. Maybe he moves to a new school and finds, unconsciously, that he is suddenly afraid of school again. Pavlov called this phenomenon *spontaneous recovery*, the reemergence of a conditioned response after it appears to have been extinguished. Even though it does reappear, however, it is less powerful the second time around.

Stimulus Generalization. Sarah has become very scared of her mean uncle, who mistreats her every time he visits. When Sarah discovers her first-grade teacher is a man, she is terrified. Then she is taken to the principal, and when she discovers he's a man as well, she becomes totally unreasonable. What has occurred is that Sarah has generalized her fear of her uncle to similar stimuli—well-dressed men in their mid-forties. Called *stimulus generalization*, this response is more likely to occur the more similar the new stimuli are to the one that initially caused the reaction.

Stimulus Discrimination. When Pavlov conditioned his dog to salivate at the sound of a bell, he also conditioned the dog to salivate at the sound of a high-pitched tone, but not at the sound of a low-pitched tone. He did this by feeding the dog after the high-pitched tone but not after the low-pitched one. This is called *stimulus discrimination*. If Sarah had had lots of positive interaction with men of slightly different physical description from her uncle during the same time as her negative experience, she probably would not have generalized her fear.

Classical Conditioning and Education. Classical conditioning has huge implications for teachers and schools. We all know children who say, "I can't draw," "I hate math," "I hate school," and "Teachers don't like me." These are all classically conditioned behaviors that have a powerful impact on our children's learning. One reason classical conditioning is so powerful is that the behavior is involuntary—we don't think about it. To reduce the negative power of classical conditioning, we need to make sure that early childhood programs and classrooms are positive experiences, stress the importance of warm, supportive teachers, and make all learning pleasurable—especially during the early years. We should also try to minimize situations in which children become conditioned to associate school and learning with failure: tests, intimidating situations, and activities that inspire fear.

▶ *To reduce the negative power of classical conditioning, we need to make sure all learning is pleasurable—especially during the early years.*

Operant Conditioning

Operant conditioning is made up of positive reinforcement, negative reinforcement, and punishment. All are produced by following a behavior with a reinforcer or punishment. While B. F. Skinner and other psychologists developed the theory of operant conditioning, they did not advocate its use in educational settings. Most early childhood educators believe, as I do, that operant conditioning is overused in many early childhood education programs, and that we should be helping young children develop internal control and self-discipline instead of relying on external control. I include this discussion on operant conditioning because I have discovered that many teachers don't fully understand how it works—and doesn't work.

Positive Reinforcement. A positive reinforcer is praise, candy, self-congratulation, grades, money, or other pleasing stimulus that—when used immediately after a particular behavior—increases the frequency of that behavior. For both positive and negative reinforcement to work, certain things must occur:

- *The reinforcer must follow the behavior.* Reinforcers that come before the desired behavior do not work.
- *The reinforcer must follow immediately.* Because a reinforcer changes the behavior that occurred immediately before it, a time lapse between the behavior and the reinforcer could result in reinforcing the wrong behavior. A child who returns from washing his dirty hands by running back into the classroom and causing a commotion, and solicits the teacher to say to him, "Well done, Johnny," is receiving positive reinforcement for running, not for washing his hands. The more a reinforcer is delayed, the less effective it is—particularly for young children.
- *The reinforcer must be based directly on the behavior that is being changed.* Any exception weakens the whole process—and maybe even enforce the idea that teachers won't keep their word. It is vitally important for teachers carefully to think through ahead of time the behavior they intend to reinforce, and what they intend to use as a reinforcer.

Negative Reinforcement. With negative reinforcement, the behavior is increased by removing a stimulus—something unpleasant or undesirable. Examples include removing children from being grounded after they have come home on time three nights in a row, or removing children from time-out after they have settled down and expressed remorse.

Primary and Secondary Reinforcers. There are two kinds of reinforcers that work to shape behaviors: primary and secondary. Primary reinforcers are those that meet basic human needs: food, water, warmth, physical affection, attention, and love. Secondary reinforcers are those that children have learned, through association, to be rewarding: praise, stickers, grades, and money. Primary reinforcers are more effective for people who lack basic needs; secondary reinforcers work better for people whose basic needs are already met.

When Do Reinforcers Work? Teachers and parents are well aware that not all reinforcers work with all children. The three crucial factors needed for reinforcers to increase the targeted behavior are timing, size or attractiveness, and schedule of reinforcement.

As I have already said, for positive and negative reinforcement to work, immediate reinforcement is vital. When this is not possible, teachers should let students know immediately after the behavior what and when the reinforcement will be given. For example, after a student has completed a math assignment, the teacher might say, "That was a great job. Because you did so well, you can have free play time after lunch."

The larger and more attractive the reinforcer, the more effective it is. Unfortunately, what might be attractive to one child might be meaningless to another child. Cookies might work for a child who rarely gets cookies, but not for a child who dislikes them. The relative size of a reinforcer is more important than the actual size—increasing the length of time a child gets to spend on the computer works better than starting with a large amount of time. Reducing the amount of time (or other reward) actually acts as a punishment to the child.

When teachers first try to change a child's behavior, they need to reinforce that behavior each time it occurs. Once the behavior has fully changed, it does not need to be reinforced every time, and the intervals between reinforcements should be lengthened.

All of these considerations illustrate why behaviorism is a poor technique to use in the classroom. With the number and the diversity of children in a classroom, a teacher simply cannot provide the consistency required to make the process work. And, as I have discussed in other places, free play and computer use should not be used for rewarding behavior, because all children need these experiences, not just those who are good.

Punishment. Punishment is distinctly different from positive and negative reinforcement. While positive and negative reinforcement increase the likelihood and frequency of the behavior, scolding, spanking, and time out are designed to reduce or eliminate a certain behavior. Punishment is also the removal of something pleasant with the goal of reducing or eliminating a negative behavior. Examples of this kind of punishment include reducing children's allowance because they have misbehaved and loss of a privilege ("You can't go on a field trip because you did not clean the art area"). Punishment must occur immediately after the negative behavior.

Social Learning Theory

Social learning theory attempts to explain how humans learn from one another—through observation, imitation, and modeling. Its discussion belongs here because other humans are part of the environment. Albert Bandura of Stanford University is a leading researcher in this area. Some of the key concepts of this theory are (Ormrod, 1999)

- *People learn by observing the behaviors of others and the results of those behaviors.* Thus, a child who sees another child jump off the high platform on the playground without hurting himself, and gain lots of approval from his peers, will imitate that jump.
- *Learning can occur without a change of behavior.* People who learn something this way don't necessarily exhibit that new learning; further, it may show up in later behavior. For example, a 6-year-old who has watched a World Wrestling Federation match on TV may indicate no change of behavior; but later, at school during an argument over the swing, he body-slams his antagonist.
- *The consequences of the behavior affect how well it is learned.* A behavior that a child learns through imitating another child or TV personality is more likely to con-

tinue if reinforced—by other children or adults. For example, a child who begins to speak and behave like a cool character on a TV show will continue to
do so if his friends also find it cool; he will stop this behavior if his friends
think he's a dork.
- *Cognition plays a role in social learning.* Unlike behaviorism, in which the new behavior is automatically produced in the animal or child, in social learning cognition—thinking about the activity—is a vital component. In the example of
the student imitating the TV personality, the student thought about the positive results he hoped to achieve from his peers by acting and speaking a certain
way. This is a cognitive process.

Modeling. Bandura believes that many behaviors people learn are acquired through
modeling. For early childhood teachers, this concept is crucial because we talk so much
about positive role models, the impact of TV and videos on our children, and so on.
There are two types of models: live models—teachers, parents, coaches, athletes, and
peers—and symbolic models—persons or characters in books, on TV, in cartoons, and
so on. For many young children, the latter form of modeling is very powerful. Examples of children learning through modeling include (Ormrod, 1999):

- Children whose parents model reading at home are better readers.
- Children are better at doing math problems when they observe others model
  the correct method of solving a problem.
- Children are less likely to engage in risky behavior after seeing a peer model
  refusal skills.
- Children are more likely to challenge gender-role stereotypes when they see
  others behaving in a non–gender-stereotypical fashion.
- Children are more likely to be intolerant of racist statements when their peers
  refuse to tolerate such statements.

Among the mistakes we often make about models are assuming that anyone can act as
a model, and that a model will automatically have a positive influence on our children.
I remember one time the governor of Colorado brought some role models to my daugh-
ter's elementary school to support his anti-drug campaign. He brought members of the
Denver Broncos football team—one of whom was a well-known convicted wife abuser.
Obviously these men were not positive role models for my daughters.

For either live or symbolic models to be effective, they must have certain characteristics:

- *They must be competent in the area they are modeling.* Someone who models
  reading must be a good reader; someone who models staying in school must
  be a successful school graduate. Thus a professional athlete who dropped
  out of school or college is an ineffective model for teaching children to stay
  in school.
- *The model must have the respect of and stature in the eye of the learner.* High-school
  football players and other popular students will effectively model appropriate
  (or inappropriate) behavior toward less-successful students in school.
- *The model's behavior must fit what the learner wants.* Children who like a certain
  musical artist might imitate the way he dresses to make themselves cool in the
  eyes of their peers, but ignore the artist's message about drugs because they
  don't want to hear it.

- Children tend to imitate the model's behavior that meets their needs at the time. Young girls into fashion will imitate the latest teen idol, while boys into aggressive behavior will imitate a WWF wrestler.

Parents and teachers are very powerful models if viewed by children as being competent, respected, and powerful.

Social and Emotional Theories

Erikson's Psychosocial Theory

Erik Erikson developed a stage theory to explain a person's development within the context of family, peers, society, and culture—called a **psychosocial theory.** Essentially, Erikson recognized that people are social beings who must develop, thrive, and live within a variety of social settings.

The stage nature of his theory is far less rigid than Piaget's cognitive theory: a person can regress (go back to previous stages), and a person who does not successfully complete a stage has opportunities to do so later in life. Unlike Piaget and several other stage theorists who only described development during childhood, Erikson created a life-span theory. While the first four stages cover the early childhood time frame (and are described in more detail in Chapter 12), all of the stages are briefly presented here because early childhood professionals work with colleagues and parents at different stages. For example, teen parents struggle with issues at the identity versus role confusion stage, even though they have children; grandparents will be confronting ego integrity versus despair.

Trust versus Mistrust (Infancy). During this stage, infants need to learn to trust the world around them—both human and physical. Basic needs must be met, and the environment must be predictable enough for the infant to feel safe and secure.

Autonomy versus Shame or Doubt (Ages 1–3). Children must develop a level of independence. The challenge for parents and caregivers is to provide the support and nurturing children need—especially regarding toilet training—while encouraging a healthy attitude about independence. At this age children are coming to terms with their own uniqueness in the world.

Initiative versus Guilt (Ages 3–5½). During the preschool years, children are moving away from the direct control of the parent or caregiver and must be encouraged to do so. An appropriate environment encourages risk taking, initiative, experimentation, and exploration. Again, the challenge is to support this risk taking with-

▶ *Erikson developed a life-span theory that provides 8 stages, starting at infancy and continuing to old age.*

out endangering a child's safety, which is a particularly difficult challenge in early child-hood programs, where safety is vital, and discipline can easily punish a child's exploration and initiative.

Industry versus Inferiority (Ages 5½–12). During the elementary-school years, chil-dren master so many skills—riding a bike, learning to read, swim, play soccer, dance, speak a second language, perform gymnastics, and more. The challenge is to learn to feel competent, especially in relation to one's peers. A child who does not learn this will de-velop a sense of inferiority, which will have an obvious impact on future school success.

Identity versus Role Confusion (Adolescence). It is not surprising that middle- and high-school students are preoccupied with joining groups in which they feel they be-long, wearing clothes that define their individuality, and struggling to define themselves vis-à-vis their parents and the greater society. To Erikson this is a manifestation of their need to define their identity and their future role in life. Identity includes gender, race, and value identity (thus group membership), and role has to do with selecting a future career and vocation.

Intimacy versus Isolation (Early Adulthood). At this period most Americans marry and begin a family. The ability to establish healthy sexual relationships and develop close and mature friendships is crucial at this period. In our culture this involves monog-amous sexual relationships, as well as workplace, professional, and social friends.

Generativity versus Stagnation (Middle Adulthood). During middle adulthood peo-ple must find ways to pass on their culture and traditions to children—as parents, coaches, teachers, foster parents, mentors, and so on. Transferring values to the next generation is essential to the survival of a society.

Ego Identity versus Despair (Later Adulthood). As adults age, they look back on their lives and their accomplishments, and reflect on the number of their youthful goals they were able to achieve. Adults who complete this task satisfactorily—look back with fond-ness and a sense of success and achievement—gain ego integrity; those that don't turn to despair.

Emotional Intelligence

Emotional intelligence (EI) is a set of abilities that differ markedly from IQ, our tra-ditional way of assessing a child's potential for future success. Also, according to Gole-man (1995), EI is as powerful as or more powerful than IQ in determining a child's future success. Goleman believes that people with a high EI are more successful than people with a low EI. Emotional intelligence includes "abilities such as being able to motivate oneself and persist in the face of frustrations; to control impulse and delay gratification; to regulate one's moods and keep distress from swamping the ability to think; to em-phasize and hope" (Goleman, 1995, p. 34). Men and women with high EI differ from each other. Men with a high EI are outgoing, comfortable in social settings, and don't worry endlessly. They commit to people and causes, accept responsibility, are ethical and caring. They are comfortable with themselves and others. Women with high EI are as-sertive, express their feelings, and feel positive about themselves. They are outgoing, comfortable in social settings, and handle stress well. They are spontaneous and playful.

According to Goleman, the main components of emotional intelligence are

- *Self-awareness*. Knowing your feelings and their relation to your behavior; seeing your own strengths and weaknesses; accepting; being able to laugh at yourself.
- *Personal decision making*. Knowing how you make decisions—based on reason or feeling—and using this knowledge in making future decisions.
- *Managing feelings*. Finding ways to handle anger, fear, and stress constructively, and to redirect negative self-talk.
- *Empathy*. Understanding other's feelings—especially if they are different from your own.
- *Communication*. Accurately talking about feelings; listening, not blaming, separating another's behavior from your reaction to that behavior.
- *Self-disclosure*. Being realistically trusting; knowing when to reveal yourself, when not to.
- *Insight*. Recognizing patterns in your own emotional life and in the lives of others.
- *Personal responsibility*. Taking responsibility for your own actions and decisions.
- *Assertiveness*. Expressing your wants and feelings without anger or being passive–aggressive.
- *Group dynamics*. Being able to follow or lead, depending on the situation.
- *Conflict resolution*. Effectively solving conflicts at home, in the workplace, and elsewhere; knowing how to negotiate win-win solutions.

Teaching Emotional Literacy. Goleman believes it is as important to develop EI in young children as it is to develop intellectual skills and abilities. Essentially, children should be taught the main components listed above, in order to develop what Goleman calls **emotional literacy,** which is the ability to master the emotional domain. To learn emotional literacy, students engage in games that encourage cooperative activities and capitalize on conflict and disagreements, rather than punishing or ignoring them. Children are encouraged to come to grips with their feelings, and to resolve disagreements and resentment in a win-win manner. The curriculum for emotional literacy includes recognizing one's own feelings and learning the vocabulary for them; seeing the connections among thoughts, feelings, and actions; assessing the consequences of an action before taking it; recognizing one's strengths and weaknesses; and learning to manage feelings—to handle anxiety, anger, and sadness. Other content includes learning empathy, taking another's perspective, being assertive, being a good listener, and learning how to be cooperative and resolve conflicts.

Clearly, part of the approach to teaching emotional literacy involves teaching teachers new approaches to discipline—approaches that rely on negotiation, conflict resolution, and understanding the causes of children's anger and frustration.

Goleman believes the best way to develop emotional literacy is to integrate the emotional literacy curriculum into every aspect of a child's education program. Further, he feels the best approach is to start learning emotional literacy in early childhood, because emotional skills and dispositions provide a solid foundation for the acquisition of school-related academic skills. Teaching emotional literacy must match children's development—their cognitive development, and the maturation of brain cells and nerves. A child who is not cognitively able to take another's perspective will be confused by an activity that teaches empathy. An example of an age-appropriate activity to teach emotional literacy, which is used in many elementary schools, is the stoplight approach to controlling one's behavior (Goleman, 1995, p. 276):

Red light	1. Stop, calm down, and think before you act.
Yellow light	2. Say the problem and how you feel.
	3. Set a positive goal.
	4. Think of lots of solutions.
	5. Think ahead to the consequences.
Green light	6. Go ahead and try the best plan.

To a great extent, teaching emotional literacy is like teaching character: it argues that a central role of our early childhood programs is developing attitudes, behaviors, values, and dispositions outside of the standard academic curriculum, and it challenges the current national and local trend toward standards, tests, and academic accountability (see Chapter 14).

Other Learning Theories

Metacognition

Lev Vygotsky explained how children use private speech to structure their learning, an activity that is a form of **metacognition**—knowledge people have of their own learning and approach to memory, and the way they use this knowledge to help them learn. The more people understand how they learn and use the knowledge, the better learners they become. We all learn in different ways, and as I have discussed in the section on information processing, memory is highly idiosyncratic. Talking to oneself and using words to structure learning is a form of metacognition. Other forms include (Ormrod, 1999):

- being aware of one's own ability to learn and memorize, and using those abilities;
- knowing learning strategies that work and those that don't (for example for most of us, meaningful learning is far more effective than rote learning);
- planning an approach to learning that will maximize its effect (I learn best with good classical music in the background; my son learns with alternative rock and the TV on);
- monitoring learning: know when you have learned something, and when you need to relearn it;
- knowing the most effective way to retrieve information already learned.

Metacognition is based on two important concepts: first, learning is a complex process; and second, each of us learns differently. As teachers we must help children understand how they learn most effectively, and then teach them to use this knowledge to structure and maintain their learning.

Meaningful Learning

Meaningful learning involves experiences, tasks, and contexts that make sense to the individual child. They make sense to the child because they relate to something the child already knows. In meaningful learning, new information is placed in the memory much more quickly and is remembered (retrieved) more easily (Mayer, 1996). It is clear that if new material—whatever children are learning—makes sense to them, it can be learned. If it does not—let's say, capitals of countries—it is extremely difficult to learn.

Meaningful learning is an important concept for early childhood educators. Ways to use meaningful learning to teach children include:

- *Provide a rich experiential context.* Teaching about jungle animals by visiting the zoo is much more effective than reading about them in books.
- *Provide lots of rich, interesting, and varied experiences.* Many children we serve have had limited experiences before entering our programs. Field trips are very important for young children (Wardle, 2000a).
- *Never teach concepts, tasks, and skills in isolation.* Always teach in context, and help children remember the context.
- *Find ways to relate what is being taught to what children already know.* "Remember the elephant in the zoo we saw last week? It comes from a continent called Africa." "You live in Denver. Denver is the city in Colorado where important laws are passed. This is called a state capital. Every state has one."
- *Understand children's contexts and ways of learning.* Since each child has a different body of experiences, we need to individualize all teaching, provide choices, and know the backgrounds of all our children.
- *Make it personal.* Help each child find a personal hook in connection to what is being taught.

As our programs and classes become more diverse (racially, ethnically, linguistically, economically), individual children's experiences will be more varied. We must find ways to make learning meaningful to each child, not just children of middle-class backgrounds or those whose experiences are similar to ours.

Representation

In memory we represent things not immediately present. According to Jerome Bruner, we do this in three different ways. **Enactive representation** is muscle memory—riding a bike, swimming, doing a complex dance, remembering a difficult gymnastics routine. **Iconic representation** is memory through pictures and images—the arches of McDonald's, the swoosh of Nike, icons on computers, and the picture a child draws of a dog. **Symbolic representation** is words and numbers. Enactive representation lasts a very long time. As the saying goes, "It's like riding a bike—you never forget it." Iconic representation is very powerful, which is why major corporations rely on it for selling products. And symbolic representation is highly flexible—it is used to create the Declaration of Independence, Shakespeare's plays, and the Big Bang theory.

Many parents become very excited when they discover that their 3-year-old can read *McDonald's* and Toys "Я" Us. Actually, this is not reading; the child has remembered the icon of the yellow arch and the backwards *R*. Bruner suggests that children's memory progresses from enactive, through iconic, to symbolic; and that teachers should spend more time developing enactive and iconic representation in our children—through dance, rhythm activities, games, art, using a camera on field trips, illustrating journals, and so on. Further, we should find ways to tie symbolic learning to enactive and iconic knowledge: learn numbers through marching, hand clapping, and skip roping; have children draw, paint, model, and build constructions of their experiences, and then write about these experiences under the artwork.

▶ *According to Gardner's theory of multiple intelligences, some children are particularly skilled at relating to others.*

Multiple Intelligences

In several chapters I have discussed Howard Gardner's eight intelligences, or learning styles—a theory that suggests each person has preferred ways of learning, which are as valid as all other ways of knowing. Gardner argues that the tendency of traditional educational programs to teach only in the logical-mathematical and verbal styles shortchanges many of our students. Gardner believes that students should learn to use all the intelligences, while capitalizing on their preferred styles. For example, even though I am a teacher and writer, my preferred learning styles are visual, kinesthetic, and naturalistic.

Implications of Gardner's theory for early childhood educators are extensive. Because traditional school instruction is designed for children who are logical-mathematical and verbal, we must be sensitive to students who are not strong in these areas, make sure we use a variety of styles to teach our students, and be careful how we assess (test) children and refer them (for other services). Most assessments favor children who are logical-mathematical and verbal. In the past, early childhood programs often discriminated against students who had other kinds of strengths, an approach that is no longer acceptable. Four general approaches can help us teach according to each student's learning styles:

- Recognize that children do have preferred ways to learn, capitalize on these styles, and provide opportunities for children to learn in their preferred style.
- Piggyback skills and information that do not match a child's learning style to their preferred learning style. For example, teach a child to write who is a visual learner by encouraging the child to draw in a journal, then write about her drawings.
- Help children learn their preferred style and ways to adapt materials and tasks to capitalize on that style.
- Help children to develop high self-esteem for their ability to perform in their own style, especially if it is a style other than logical-mathematical or verbal.

Hierarchy of Needs

At the beginning of this chapter I discussed the power behind a theory—what drives it and makes it work—and showed that one source of this power is our basic needs. Maslow proposed that we have five basic sets of needs (1959; 1973):

- *Physiological needs.* These are food, water, oxygen, sex, exercise, lack of boredom, and so on. One reason many public schools provide free breakfast is to satisfy the basic need for food.
- *Safety.* We like to feel safe and secure. Most students feel safe in a program that has predicable yet flexible routines, which give them a sense of security.

- *Love and belonging.* People need comradeship and belonging. Elementary-school children want friends; adolescents want to belong to one of the many school groups.
- *Self-Esteem.* We need to feel good about ourselves. Johnny's proud of the castle he made with blocks; Antonia feels good that she can read a book in the reading corner. Self-esteem in young children is demonstrated by their ability to master new tasks and challenges: climbing, talking, painting, reading, kicking a ball, doing gymnastics, and so on.
- *Self-actualization.* People want to become "all that they can be." We pick hobbies because they are fun, we read books to gain more knowledge, we learn about other cultures and countries because they fascinate us. We have a need to get better and better.

Maslow places these five types of needs in a hierarchy, believing the lower needs must be met before people can move to the next level: children who are hungry, cold, or frightened in school will not learn; children who do not feel they belong in school will not perform well; and students won't study simply for the sake of knowledge (self-actualization) until their other needs are consistently met.

Maslow's theory provides great insight into how young children learn. Further, understanding the needs of children, and the hierarchy of needs, can help teachers work more effectively with children from diverse backgrounds. As I said earlier, for some children, grades, promises of a successful future, and threats of punishment don't work. One child's sense of self-esteem might be linked to playing basketball well; another's, performing a gymnastics trick.

Taxonomy of Educational Objectives

Benjamin Bloom has proposed another form of hierarchy—his *taxonomy of educational objectives*, which is a breakdown of cognitive processes into six levels, starting with basic information (facts) and moving to complex critique and evaluation. According to Bloom, children should learn basic knowledge before moving to the next higher level. Teaching children new vocabulary before reading a story is an example of this theory—vocabulary being basic knowledge. The taxonomy's hierarchy is

- *Basic knowledge.* Basic facts, definition of terms, multiplication factors, capitals of states, and the like. These are often learned through memorization.
- *Comprehension.* Understanding information; being able to rephrase it in one's own words.
- *Application.* Using the information in new and different situations. A child who knows that all plants need water will water his plants when the soil dries and his plants begin to wilt.
- *Analysis.* Breaking down an argument into its component parts, and determining logically whether it is correct or not by doing so.
- *Synthesis.* Taking ideas, concepts, facts and putting them together to create something new and different; for example, creating a new society, or developing rules for a school that address a variety of issues.
- *Evaluation.* Providing a critique of knowledge. For example, determining whether and how a curriculum meets the needs of all the students in the program.

Unfortunately, many programs stress only the basic-knowledge level of the taxonomy. Further, many teachers believe in the hierarchical nature of the model, even though it has been questioned (Krathwohl, 1994). Many special-education interventions focus just on the basic-knowledge level; gifted students often get bored because they thrive on the upper levels of the taxonomy (Clark, 1997).

We should attempt to engage children at every level of the taxonomy in all of their cognitive activities. Children can be asked what's fair and not fair in a story (evaluation), to express what they experienced on the field trip (comprehension), to suggest how an idea could be used to create new class rules (application), to hypothesize why dinosaurs became extinct (analysis), and to use what they saw at a construction site to build an imaginary city with blocks (synthesis). We should be very careful not simply to stay at the basic-knowledge level—for any of our students—because, as we have seen with other theories, memorization is the least efficient way to learn new information. And besides, children get bored, and bored children don't learn.

Conclusion

Theories that describe human growth and development, and different ways children learn, are very helpful to early childhood educators. They help to guide and support our teaching, and to provide the best possible care and education for our children. Our knowledge of growth, development, and learning defines the field of early childhood education and gives us credibility.

Questions and Projects

1. Write a short paper describing your own theory of development. What's more important, nature (biology) or nurture (environment)? What are the important influences to development?

2. Observe an early childhood program. Based on your observations, determine the theories that are the basis of the program.

3. Think about all the ways this society uses behaviorism—rewards, punishment, classical conditioning. Give examples. Is this good?

4. What theoretical approaches should public-school elementary programs use? Why?

5. Design a brochure by folding a single sheet of 8½ × 11 paper into three equal sections. Develop a brochure to convince parents that it is important for them to pick up their infants when they cry. Illustrate the brochure.

CHAPTER

10 Language *and* Literacy

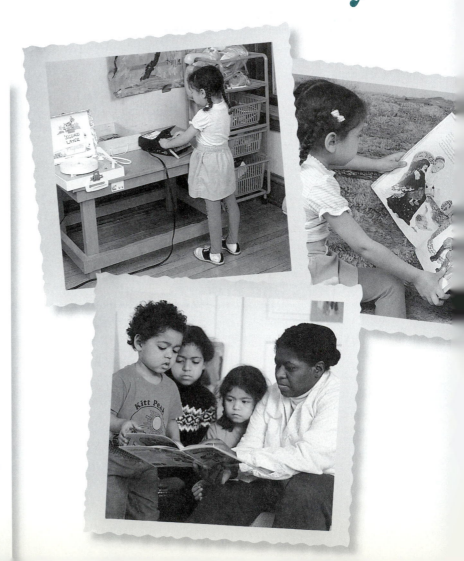

*D*uring the early years, almost all children master the incredibly complex task of learning to speak. At the same time they are establishing a solid foundation for reading and writing—two extremely important skills required to function successfully in school and in life. The foundation of these vital and complex human tasks is developed during the early years. A child who reaches age 8 and has trouble with any of these areas will continue to struggle during his or her school experience. And because each of these areas is so important for a child's future, methods and applications supporting children's development and learning in each area generate considerable debate and conflict. Just one example is the conflict between whole-language and skill-based (phonics) reading instruction. This chapter explores how the areas of reading, writing, and oral language are interrelated and provides ideas for supporting their development, including ways the family and community can assist in this important task. Finally, the chapter discusses bilingual education and second-language acquisition. ■

Oral Language Development

Literacy development in young children is composed of three interrelated components: speaking, writing, and reading. These three areas develop in relation to one another, and the ability of children to develop in one area—or their struggle in that area—affects their ability in the other areas. Additionally, children develop listening skills that help them with these tasks. Children who have difficulty hearing the distinctly different components

Questions to Consider

1. What is the relationship among oral language development, development of reading, and development of writing?

2. What is emergent literacy, and how can it be promoted?

3. Why is storybook reading such an important literacy activity?

4. What is the best approach to meeting the needs of non–English-speaking students in early childhood programs?

5. What are the developmental stages of learning to speak, read, and write?

6. How can emergent reading and writing activities be encouraged at home and in the early childhood program?

Developmentally Appropriate Practice

of words will find reading difficult. My son had this problem, and he struggled with reading during most of his school experience. In this chapter I will first address oral language development, but this approach is not meant to suggest that one skill must be fully developed before another: all occur simultaneously in the child's development.

From the moment of birth, humans seem to be programmed to communicate (Christie, Enz, & Vukelich, 1997). Infants a few days old can distinguish their mother's voice from other voices and can respond through vocalization and movements. Between birth to 4 months of age, babies are already capable of producing and distinguishing all of the 150 sounds that make up human speech—in all languages (Kuhl, 1993).

We know the general progression of language acquisition and the approximate time new stages should occur. And we know why children learn language. Clearly, talking—communication—is an essential activity of all human beings. "Children and adults, with varying degrees of sophistication, use language to express or assert their needs, connect with self and others, and create, comprehend, and expand their knowledge of the immediate environment and the world at large" (Christie, Enz, & Vukelich, 1997, p. 24).

Language Development Progression

The progression of children's linguistic development follows a highly predictable course for almost all typically developing children, but the rate at which it is accomplished may vary greatly from child to child (Copeland & Gleason, 1993).

Age	Language Skill
3 months	Makes cooing sounds
7 months	Makes sounds such as "giving a raspberry"
10 months	Single-syllable babbling ("ma," "da," "ba")
11 months	Multiple-syllable babbling ("mama," "dada," "baba")
14 months	Uses "mama" and "dada" (or similar sounds) to call parents
16 months	Uses some words besides "mama" and "dada"
22 months	Has a vocabulary of four to six words
	Can express some wants
	Can be understood by strangers about half the time
23 months	Can form two-word sentences
26 months	Has a fifty-word vocabulary
29 months	Uses "me," "you," and "my"
34 months	Uses prepositions
	Can carry on a conversation
	Can identify and use "cup," "spoon"
37 months	Can be understood by strangers about three-quarters of the time
47 months	Can be understood by strangers most of the time

A few children fail to follow this sequence successfully within a normal time range. These children need expert assessment and intervention. The challenge is to know when a child is within the normal range of variability and when a child is obviously delayed.

While children are developing their language abilities to accomplish these purposes, they are also developing cognitively, physically, emotionally, and socially—which skills, in turn, affect the complexity and sophistication of their language development.

Theories of Language Acquisition

There are several theories that explain how children acquire language. In Chapter 9, I covered a variety of theoretical approaches to learning, including behaviorist, social learning theory, constructivist, maturational, information processing, and significant periods. Theories of how children learn a language fall within these overall approaches. Here I will discuss behaviorist, linguistic nativist, and social-interactionist theories.

Behaviorist. **Behaviorist theory** holds that children learn new skills and behaviors by having their behaviors reinforced by the environment. Behaviors that are reinforced will continue; those that are not will disappear. "Behaviorists suggest that through operant conditioning (rewarding desired behaviors) infants gradually learn expressive language by being rewarded for their imitation of the sounds and speech they hear" (Christie, Enz, & Vukelich, 1997, p. 21). For example, after accidentally saying "mama," an infant is rewarded by the mother's facial expression and words. Thus, infants will continue to say "mama," and will associate this word with their mother (classical conditioning). As children grow they try out new sounds and word combinations. Those that are reinforced continue; those that are not, disappear.

Linguistic Nativist. **Nativism** is a belief that infants have an innate capacity to learn language: they are preprogrammed to do so. This preprogramming is a container, or rule-bound structure, through which language develops—what Chomsky (1972) calls a **language acquisition device.** Nativists believe that this predisposition to learn language is much stronger than other forms of learning. The role of the environment is simply to activate the preprogrammed capacity—much like turning on a computer and activating a specific program—and to provide minimal support for continual language growth. According to this theory, all children are preprogrammed to learn any language.

Social-Interactionist. Social-interactionists combine the behaviorist and nativist approaches, while also adding a constructivist perspective. Thus they suggest that children are born with a genetic predisposition to learn languages, but that the environment—especially the infant–parent interaction—is crucial, and the children's own construction of knowledge is essential to language learning. Central to the social-interactionist perspective is the parent's (or caregiver's) role in matching children's level of language development with the appropriate environment, and continually increasing their interaction as children progress, from repeating coos and gurgles to labeling objects and asking questions. Providing environmental stimulation at the optimal level for children's progress is known as scaffolding within the zone of proximal development (Vygotsky, 1962; see Chapter 9).

Language Terms

To further the discussion and understanding of oral language development, it is helpful to know some of the terms used for various components of language.

Phonology. **Phonology** is the sound system of a language; **phonemes** are the individual sounds that make up that system. In English there are two kinds of sounds, consonant and vowel sounds. Part of the phonology of English are the stress and intonation we place on words and sentences. Where the stress is placed in a word or sentence can change its meaning (for example, RECord as opposed to reCORD; IS she coming? or is SHE coming?)

Morphology. **Morphemes** are the smallest units of meaning in oral language. They are composed of one or more phonemes. There are several categories of morphemes, which can be used in a variety of combinations to create new meaning.

Idioms are expressions that carry a meaning very different from the literal meaning of the words in them—"carry a conversation," "hit the road," and the like. These differ by language and culture.

Syntax. **Syntax** is the system of rules by which morphemes are combined to create meaningful sentences and expressions: grammar, punctuation, and so on.

Semantics involve the various contextual variations of meaning the same language can assume. Culture plays a role in creating subtle variations in meaning. Many words and phrases have different meanings in the United States and England; some even differ in different parts of this country. All languages have these semantic variations.

Pragmatics. **Pragmatics** is the use of language to communicate the speaker's intent in realistic situations—the use of formal language plus a whole range of cues, including body language, voice inflection, and facial expression. The literal meaning of words can be enhanced or even contradicted by the way they are said. Pragmatics also involves ways to use all the component parts of language in realistic settings—the give-and-take of conversations, culturally appropriate use of expressions and idioms, asking questions, and speaking on the phone.

Supporting Language Development

Language develops through complex interactions between children and their parents and other caregivers. There is a variety of ways adults support this development. One way is to respond to the infants' vocal attempts—coos, gurgles, and so on. Another is to talk to children while engaged in everyday activities, such as feeding, diaper changing, bathing, and dressing. As children grow older, the complexity of these conversations should increase. Because of hectic schedules and other demands, many parents do not talk enough with their children, especially in give-and-take conversations (as opposed to reprimands or instructions). Other approaches include:

- singing to infants a variety of songs, especially ones meaningful to the family's culture;
- taking children on a variety of shopping trips and visits to friends and family (while on the trip, engage in conversation about what the children see and feel, and what they would like to do);
- listening carefully to children's conversations: language development requires careful and responsive listening;
- reading a variety of books to children, and encouraging others—at home and in the program—to do so;
- supporting children's dramatic play: in dramatic play children are free to try out new words, experiment with complex sentences, and express new ideas;
- severely limiting TV watching (be concerned if your child's early childhood program uses TV and videos; research shows that an elementary-school student watches TV an average of twenty-five hours a week; Neuman, 1988).

▶ *Listening activities reinforce auditory discrimination, the sequences of stories and scripts, and the structure of communication.*

Oral Language, Reading, and Writing

Although many assume that learning to read starts with formal instruction during kindergarten and the early grades, it actually begins much earlier. Children who do not receive important literacy knowledge and skills before the initiation of formal instruction struggle after instruction starts. According to Schickedanz (1999), there are three myths associated with learning to read and write: (1) oral language must develop before written language; (2) children learn oral language naturally, but they acquire literacy-related knowledge only through direct instruction; and (3) children must achieve a certain level of physical and mental readiness before written language can occur.

Oral and written language development occur simultaneously, each supporting and enhancing the other. Just as oral language occurs through interaction between infants and important adults, adults scaffold infants' responses to the written word through reading to them, developing the infants' interest in books, and modeling reading behaviors. The level of reading readiness of children entering school is directly related to the quality and quantity of literacy experience they have, and the role of parents and caregivers is central in providing this literacy experience. Parents and caregivers who use language rarely—and then primarily for instruction, direction, and verbal punishment—do not provide the necessary environment for language development.

Development of Emergent Writing

As children master the complexities of oral language, they are also developing the foundation for learning to write, which also follows a predictable developmental path, beginning long before the inception of formal writing instruction and following a series of progressively sophisticated forms of writing. Painting, drawing, and attempts at creating specific symbols are the first stage of this progression. Children need to progress through the specific developmental stages, and should be encouraged to experience each stage fully before moving to the next. The general process of emergent writing follows this progression (Sulzby, Barnhart, & Hieshima, 1989):

- pictures;
- scribbles;
- random letters;
- random and initial letters;
- copying from environmental print;
- invented spelling;
- conventional writing.

Figure 10.1
Emergent writing follows a predictable progression,
according to Sulzby, Barnhart, and Hieshima (1989).

STAGES IN THE DEVELOPMENT OF LEARNING TO WRITE

All children pass through predictable stages as they master the skills involved with writing. It is impossible to place a direct age guide next to each stage, because each child is unique. However, we can approximate the age at which these stages occur. These predictable stages are:

1 <u>Pictures</u> (3-5 years)

In this stage children draw pictures and give labels like, "This is my house", "This is my dog", "This is a picture of me at the zoo".

Pictures

(This is my house.)

2 <u>Scribble</u> (3-5 years)

In this stage children do a scribble immitation of writing. The scribble looks nothing like a word with letters, but the child believes she is writing.

Scribble (Approximation)

(This is my house.)

3 <u>Random Letters</u> (3-5 years)

This is a string of letters that have no relationship to the words represented. The child understands letters are used to create words, but doesn't know which letters.

(This is my house.)

Random Letters

4 <u>Random and Initial Letters</u> (4-6 years)

The child begins to use some letters that accurately reflect the sounds of the word, but also uses some that do not correspond to the words he is trying to represent.

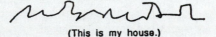
(I have a dog.)

Random and Initial

5   <u>Initial Consonants</u>   (4-6 years)

The starting sounds of words are the most obvious phonetic sounds for children. And since consonants create the most easily recognizable sounds, they are used first.

I L M B
(I like my bike.)

Initial
Consonants

6   <u>Initial and Final Sounds</u>   (5-7 years)

The most important sounds of any word are the initial and final sounds. At this stage the child correctly uses letters representing the initial and final letter sounds of the words she is trying to write.

I lk mi Bk.
(I like my bike.)

Initial and
Final Sounds

7   <u>Vowel Sounds Appear</u>   (5-7 years)

At this stage children begin to include the vowel sounds in their writing.

I lik to pla with my cat. (I like to play with my cat).

Vowel Sounds
Appear

8   <u>All Syllables Represented</u>   (6-8 years)

Every syllable of every word used in the idea being communicated is represented by letters. Often the words are misspelled or sounds of combined letters are misinterpreted in a particular word.

My favorit dinosor is the stegosorus.
(My favorite dinosaur is the Stegosaurus.)

All Syllables
Represented

9   <u>Multiple Related Sentences and Many Words With Correct Spelling</u>   (7-9 years)

Many sentences, punctuation, and many (but not all) correctly spelled words.

Today I am going to the stor with my mothr. I am going to by a present for my brothrs brthday. He is thre yers old.

Multiple
Related
Sentences
and Many
Words with
Correct
Spelling

Source: From J. Mason (Ed.), *Reading and Writing Connections.* Copyright © 1989. Reprinted by permission of Allyn & Bacon.

Typical "Mistakes" Children Make on Their Way to Learning to Write

Since children naturally omit letters from words, concentrate on the beginning and ending sounds of words, and try to be phonetic spellers, their first attempts to spell a word are usually incorrect. Various "mistakes" are evident in the normal developmental progression. These include reversing letters, repeating letters, omitting letters, mirror writing (writing an entire word or sentence backwards), omitting silent letters, and invented spelling. Children should not be discouraged from writing because of these various mistakes. Only later should they begin to edit their work for spelling and grammar.

Encouraging the Development of Emergent Writing

There are many ways early childhood programs can encourage the development of emergent writing. Of most importance is to provide opportunities, materials, and support for the natural attempts by children to represent their experiences, thoughts, feelings, and imaginings in pictures and writing attempts. Here are just a few ways to accomplish this:

- Provide lots of meaningful opportunities to write: letters, greeting cards to parents and friends, sign-in sheets and boards, chalkboards, writing and drawing in sand, writing with glitter, using stencils, making posters, and engaging in all sorts of art projects.
- Acknowledge and support children's efforts as they progress through the seven stages of emergent writing listed above. Do not push children to advance to a stage before they are ready.
- Don't correct children's written words or spelling until they are able to understand the structure of words or they request your help.
- When requested by children, provide specific help in writing, spelling, capitalization, and so on.
- Provide opportunities for children to "read" back to you things they have written, even though you cannot read the words.
- Have children dictate the story or narrative behind a picture, map, or other art project. Write this dictation on the picture.
- If children want to copy environmental print and different words, encourage them to do so; but don't insist that they do.

Journal Writing

Journals provide a wonderful opportunity for children to record their lives, experiences, hopes, and fantasies—a process that helps children to understand that events can be recorded, and then reread in the future. Preserving experiences for future use is a central concept of writing. Most children will start their journals with pictures before graduating to writing. Journals can take a variety of physical forms, including bound journals, three-ring binders, pieces of paper stapled together, and pre-made books brought from home. Before you start, explain to children that the purpose of the journal is for them to record their experiences, thoughts, ideas, and stories in something they can keep for themselves. Help children write their journals by writing down dictated stories and by encouraging children to put something in the journal at least once a week—a drawing, some writing, a photograph from a field trip, a picture cut out of a magazine of an animal they have seen. Try to meet with two to four children each day to talk with them about their journals and to plan and scaffold their work. Don't force reluctant children to write; if they wish to draw, or paste in pictures, that's fine.

Children should be supported at their developmental level of writing. Help them appropriately move to the next level. You can encourage very expressive children to record their stories on a tape recorder, which can be played back later. Parts of these recordings can be written into the journal. Encourage children to sign and date their journal every time it is used. Journals should be kept in an accessible but quiet location, where children can work in them as they choose.

Writing Workshops

Writing workshops are another opportunity to support young children's writing development, an approach that works particularly well in the early elementary grades (starting in kindergarten). The philosophy of writing workshops is based on our current understanding of emergent writing.

Writing workshops were described by Donald Graves in his book *Writing: Teachers and Children at Work* (1983). These workshops require blocks of time for children to focus on writing. Scheduling three to five workshops each week, lasting from forty-five to sixty minutes, is ideal. Writing workshops require a writing center, lots of materials, an individual folder for each child, and clipboards for writing in various locations.

Much of the writing workshop involves children working together on writing activities, because at the early elementary age, writing is a social act (Christie, Enz, & Vukelich, 1997). Rules must be established, however, for the interaction to remain focused on writing.

To start the workshop, students should be told what it is like to be a writer (from books read to them during oral reading time), that they will be authors, and that they should begin to think of topics to write about. The teacher should model topics she would write about, emphasizing familiar subjects. Rules should be established for the

Approaches to Teaching Writing

These recommendations are based on Christie, Enz, and Vukelich, *Teaching Language and Literacy* (1997).

- Children should write on topics of their own choosing.
- Children should write for real audiences—peers, parents, overseas pen pals, and so on.
- The writer should, in sequence, (a) decide on content and presentation of content, (b) make sure the writing says what he or she wants it to, and (c) edit for mechanical correctness.
- Children should write as many drafts as needed.
- Children need time to write, and to consult with peers and teachers about their writing.
- Writing skills should be taught within the context of the child's writing.
- Some children write better alone; others with interaction with peers and the teacher.
- Helping children convey specific content is a crucial writing objective.
- Children should learn different kinds of writing: narrative, persuasion, informational.
- A variety of strategies should be used to plan writing pieces: webbing (see Chapter 4), charts, writing a draft, thinking out loud, brainstorming, and more.
- Writing takes time; each piece must be worked and reworked.
- Children need to be taught how to write.

workshop: focus on the writing, don't worry about spelling initially, no talking for the first five minutes, behavioral expectations for the group sharing time, and so on.

The specific components of each workshop are (Atwell, 1987)

- *mini-lesson:* five to ten minutes to teach children a specific aspect of writing, based on their needs;
- *status-of-the-class report:* a five-minute quick check of what each writer plans to do during that particular workshop;
- *writing:* thirty minutes of writing and talking to peers and the teacher about the writing;
- *group share:* ten to fifteen minutes of one or two children responding to questions from others about their writing projects.

The nature of teacher input during these workshops changes as students advance in their writing and editing skills. Teachers should devise a variety of ways to track student progress using reports or forms. Information from these reports provide direction for future mini-lessons. As children progress during elementary school, the quality of writing ability improves, editing procedures become more detailed and advanced, and children gain expertise in each form of writing: narrative, persuasion, informational (how-to).

Publishing. Since writing is to be read by others, finding ways to publish children's work is important. Children's work must be carefully edited, through a search for mechanical errors by students. Only work to be published needs to be edited; editing can begin at first grade. During mini-lessons, teachers show students how to go about this editing process, then assist the students by conferring with students one-on-one.

There is a variety of ways to publish children's written work: framing and displaying the work on the wall, different binding, laminating, making a class newspaper, and creating a multimedia presentation using scanners and the computer. Again, these should gain sophistication as children advance.

Young Children and Books

As I have already mentioned, children who have lots of experiences being read to before they enter school are much more successful when formal reading instruction is introduced than children without these experiences. Being read to teaches children about vocabulary, sentence structure, plot design, and the sequencing of ideas; it also teaches them about book language, which is different from conversational language.

Early childhood programs should encourage parents to read to their children at home, and to provide regular opportunities for children to be read to. Exposure to books during the preschool years increases a child's linguistic knowledge, which itself produces better readers in the early grades (Wells, 1985; Synder & Downey, 1991). Two kinds of books are read to children at this age—predictable books and expository books. Predictable books have lots of repetition, allowing children to read along, thus gaining habit and confidence in the reading process. Expository books are nonfiction books that are informational—about houses, different parts of the world, animals, how things work, and the like. A good reading program for preschoolers should have a nice mix of both kinds of books. Some books include both approaches.

▶ *Children should be encouraged to read any time and any place.*

Developmental Progression of Using Books for Infants and Toddlers

Schickedanz (1999) details the progression of important experiences with books, summarized here.

Birth to 3 Months. Ideal books for this age have simple, large pictures or designs with a contrasting background. Stiff cardboard books that open up to create a panel and stand on their own work well. The book should be placed in such a way that babies can view it when they choose, but can also choose to look elsewhere. Babies this age enjoy having parents and caregivers sing lullabies and recite nursery rhymes and other repetitive verse. Infants love repetitive sounds and rhythms. Traditional and cultural lullabies are great to use for this age. Paul Robeson, the great African American actor and singer, sings a variety of international lullabies from all over the world in their native languages, and many other recordings are available.

Ages 4–6 Months. Cloth and soft vinyl books are ideal for this age because they are easy for babies to grasp and pick up, they don't disintegrate in babies' mouths, and they can be washed. Sometimes babies will chew on a toy as you read to them and show them the book. Simple, bright pictures against a contrasting background still work well. Infants between 4 and 6 months of age still love to hear adults sing and read poetry and rhyming text to them. The more familiar infants are with the material, the more they enjoy it.

Ages 7–9 Months. The pincer grip enables infants this age to handle books with cardboard pages, which are better than soft, vinyl pages. Cardboard or block books—especially the books known as Chunky or Chubby—fit into a child's hands, are easy to hold, are virtually indestructible, and have pages with a spring device that makes them easy to turn. These books should have bright, bold illustrations of things the infant is familiar with and adults can name. Reading to children at this age involves holding them while reading to them—labeling the pictures, and reading rhymes and rhyming language. Infants are not interested in stories. Sometimes infants are satisfied to sit on an adult's lap and simply play with the book.

Older Babies. Books for children nearing 1 year need to be of cardboard, though now regular cardboard books are fine. The book's content begins to capture their interest. When reading to older babies, many adults follow a certain progression in reading: (1) Get the child's attention by pointing to a picture and saying, "Look at that." (2) Ask questions, such as, "What is it? What do you see?" (3) Respond to the infant's response and keep the conversation going (Schickedanz, 1999, p. 21). As infants grow older, they will become more involved in this give-and-take. Older babies move a lot when they are being read to. They might actually get out of the adult's lap and demonstrate something from the book, or go and get a toy the book reminds them of. At bedtime children are more likely to sit quietly in an adult's lap and listen to a book.

Ages 12–18 Months.

Children up to age 1½ enjoy books about familiar characters (TV characters, animals, children like themselves, objects, events); they also like books with songs and repetitive verses, as well as books that use pictures, with a few words, to depict a theme: for example, a simple story of a child eating supper, having a bath, dressing for bed, and then being tucked in (Schickedanz, 1999). But they are not ready for stories with plots.

Children like to hear lots of descriptive talk about objects of interest in the book, which should be named. They might look at a book and babble away, as if reading it. And they love nursery rhymes and other predictable text, because they can join in. They are still very active while a book is being read.

Ages 19–30 Months.

During this age, many parents engage in discussions with their children about shared experiences. "Remember where we went yesterday?" "You petted an animal, remember its name?" "Did you like the elephants?" Initially children say little, but by about 24 months, they begin to answer more questions, though the adult still dominates the conversation. By about 27–30 months, children begin to ask questions. These parent–child discussions are called personal narratives, and they are similar in structure to stories children read in storybooks later on; this activity of relating personal narratives to each other prepares children to understand and enjoy storybooks.

Discussions and stories in books for this age group begin to include emotion, feelings, motivation, and cause and effect. Why was the child upset? Why did the frogs argue? Why did the neighbors help build the house? These elements are crucial components of a story with a plot.

Ages 30 Months and Older.

Toddlers love actual stories about familiar experiences: children missing their parents when they travel, not liking a new food, hurting oneself, going to bed, or forgetting a favorite toy somewhere. Illustrations can now include more information and action. Books for this age should have a picture and a small amount of related text on each page. The information in the picture fills in information left out of the text.

Toddlers might still want to play while a book is being read. They enjoy longer stories at bedtime and still love predictable books. At age 2, the child can talk with the adult about the content of the book. Parents ask questions about the book and its relation to their life. "Do you have a dog like Jake?" "Do you feel sad when your father has to leave for a trip?" Again, though, adults still lead the way. They engage in what is called scaffolding—structuring and maintaining the activity. By about age 2½ to 3 years, some children take more initiative in discussions based on the book's content.

The advancement a child makes regarding interest in and involvement with the text and pictures in the book being read depends largely on the quantity and quality of the adult's reading involvement. Some parents engage the child actively in looking at books and asking questions about pictures and text. An important role of early childhood programs for young children is to educate parents in this interactive approach to storytelling and overall language development. Clearly, children who receive appropriate language stimulation at home and in the center will progress well.

Use of Books to Teach Specific Language Concepts

Books can be used effectively to teach specific language components. Specific methods for using stories to teach new words include pointing to illustrations at key points during the reading, providing a simple definition when a new word is introduced in a book, and using vocal sounds to indicate the meaning of the word, for example, "pop," "scratch," and "shriek."

After the book has been read, go back over the illustrations and use them to generate further discussion about the story, thus reinforcing the words used in the text. On successive readings of the text, additional words can be defined. Don't quiz children after the end of the story on the meaning of words from the book. Explaining the meaning of words should be done in the spirit of wanting children to understand the story.

Story reading in the early years produces children with better language development (Chomsky, 1972; Wells, 1985). Storytelling promotes **decontextualized language** learning: the use of cues that help in understanding oral language are missing—the

---

Progression of Story-Reading Behaviors

This is a summary of the stages children go through when learning to read (Schickedanz, 1999, p. 34 [Reprinted with permission of the National Association for the Education of Young Children]).

1. Vocalizes (unintelligibly) while pointing at pictures (7–10 months).
2. Labels pictures in familiar books (10–14 months).
3. Uses book babble (that is, nonsense jabber that sounds as if the child is reading rather than conversing with someone; 13–14 months).
4. Fills in the next word in the text when the adult pauses, says the next word before the adult reads it, or reads along when a highly predictable text is read (15–28 months).
5. Pretends to read to dolls or stuffed animals and to self (17–25 months).
6. Notices print rather than just pictures. For example, the child points to labels under pictures as the pictures are named (15–20 months).
7. Shows some familiarity with the text. For example, says a word or phrase that goes with a page of text as soon as the child sees the illustration (17 months).
8. Recites part of a story's text outside of the story—reading content, for example, when swinging in a swing (21 months).
9. Recites whole phases from favorite stories as the adult pauses at opportune times (24–30 months).
10. Asks to read books to the adult and may be able to recite several books fairly accurately, especially if they are simple and predictable (28–34 months).
11. Protests when an adult misreads a word in a familiar, and usually predictable, story. Typically offers the correction as well (25–27 months).
12. Moves a finger or whole hand across a line of print and verbalizes what the text says. The rendition may be the exact text or an accurate paraphrase (32 months).
13. Reads familiar books aloud, rendering the text very accurately, particularly when a book is predictable (30–36 months).

speaker's facial expressions and tone of voice, and the activity the speaker is engaged in. With oral language the speaker can also be asked to repeat or expand on what is being said. These cues are not available to a child listening to a book, so the child must pay much closer attention to the spoken language.

Story reading also promotes adult–child discussion. The more parents and teachers talk with their children about stories being read, the more story reading improves language development. Adult–child discussion includes analyzing events and characters, asking children to predict what will happen next in the story, helping make connections between the story and the children's lives, summarizing sections of the text, and explaining new words.

Stories have a specific structure, with a plot and a theme, but with specific episodes differing from story to story (Schickedanz, 1999). **Expository texts** are organized differently from stories. What children learn about the framework of books will help them understand the content of each new book, much as what we know generally about maps (top is north, bottom south, there is a legend to explain symbols and scale) helps us read new maps.

Children's books are written in such a way that they enhance the relationships of individual sounds of words: rhyming texts, juxtaposition of different sounds, alliteration, and so on. In normal conversation we are not interested in the sounds of words, we are interested in their meaning—the information they convey. It requires specific attention and learning for children to switch from attending to the meaning of words to awareness of language at the phonemic (sound) level. Specific activities and experiences are necessary for children to concentrate on the phonemic aspect of language, which is important in learning to read. Many books for young children are written in verse, which teaches children rhyming and alliteration. Adults should help children discriminate the various sounds of words, ask them to come up with new rhyming words, and eventually play rhyming games with them.

Children bring a body of knowledge to each reading experience, which helps them understand what they read and assists them in sounding out new words. It's difficult for children to sound out words that they have never heard and that have no meaning to them. For young children, real experiences are the primary source of background knowledge. Books add to this store of knowledge—broadening, enriching, and further developing it. Books should be selected to expand a child's firsthand experiences from field trips, classroom presentations, family outings, the neighborhood, and visits to the zoo.

Reading at Home

An analysis of twenty-nine studies of parents reading to their preschool children at home shows that reading helps children with specific language development, emergent literacy skills, and actual reading achievement (Bus, van Ijzendoorn, & Pellegrini, 1995). Other studies show that parents who read to their children at home provide access to good children's books, develop positive attitudes toward books and reading, and model how books should be held. Reading to children at home also provides assistance and feedback in how to read, supports independent engagement in reading by familiarizing children with stories, and encourages children to read on their own (Christie, Enz, & Vukelich, 1997).

▶*Parents should read to their children on a regular basis, to enhance literacy skills.*

All cultures have a rich tradition of telling stories to young children. A good storyteller will freely adapt, change, and enrich the story. A strong reader will also engage the children in talking about the story—adding to it and encouraging them to provide their own interpretations. Reading to children is a very powerful experience: sitting with an individual child, and having the child turn the pages, develops a warm, positive relationship between parent and child.

Parents and grandparents who don't speak English should be encouraged to read to their children in their own language. Almost all of the skills children learn from being read to are learned in any language. Early childhood programs should do all they can to encourage parents to read to their own children by giving parent workshops on the importance of reading to children, providing a take-home library of children's books, covering the vital importance of this activity in newsletters for parents, visiting libraries so children can sign out books, and sponsoring various activities that stress the importance of reading at home.

The negative effect of TV on home reading is becoming ever more apparent. Early childhood programs should help parents find ways to reduce TV watching by their children. Sponsor a day a month or an hour each evening when the TV is off in the house. Discourage parents from putting a TV in children's rooms; distribute the American Pediatric Association's recommendations for the amount of TV time that is appropriate for children to watch; and provide parent meetings, in-service training, newsletters, and experts to discuss this important topic. Parents need to understand that TV is far more destructive than just a passive entertainer: it keeps children from reading.

Selecting Books to Read

Clearly it is important to choose books carefully for reading to young children. Choose books you like, but ones that are also enjoyable to young children and that capture their imagination in the first couple of pages. The text and illustrations must work together on the same page, must be free from any stereotype or bias, and be absent of violence. The story should stimulate the child's imagination, and a wide range of family lifestyles and cultures should be included in the books selected (Curry-Rood, 1999).

As I have already discussed, stories with minimal text are preferable for young children, and stories with repetitive phrases, rhyming words, and crisp dialogue are often favorites. Illustrations should be of the highest quality, with good color, sharp line drawings, and superior photographs. A variety of artistic styles should be covered in a good-quality picture-book collection. Stories should encourage independence and celebrate competency in children. They should affirm the value of each child (Curry-Rood, 1999).

Reading Books to Young Children

Because reading to children before they enter formal (K–12) education is so vital to their school success, early childhood programs should make this activity a priority. Take time to talk with each child in your class. Use these conversations to find out their interests, experiences, and fantasies, which then should be used to select books for group reading. Also, encourage children to share their favorite books with the rest of the class. You might even read a child's selected book to the whole group.

Once a selection is made, practice reading the book ahead of time: turning the pages, holding the book so the children can see the illustrations, maintaining eye contact, and being expressive. You might want to practice in front of a mirror. It is quite an art to be a good reader to young children, because young children are so egocentric, yet love to be read to in a group. Each child understands and experiences the story from a limited range of experience, and needs to make sense of the book from that experience. And—as we know—children at this age experience with their entire being. Most important, remember that bored children get into trouble. If lots of children seem uninterested and uninvolved, they probably are. A few cautions about group reading are needed before I give specific suggestions. First, it is essential always to remember that the main objective of group reading is to help children learn to read. Thus, it should be a pleasant experience that teaches the positive value of reading. Sometimes other objectives get in the way: teaching specific words, multicultural concepts, group social skills, and moral values. If these occur naturally and interactively in the overall reading process, good. But they must never become more important than helping children learn to read.

Select a book that can be completed in one sitting. After you have had a field trip, classroom visitor, or other experience, read a book that relates directly to that experience. Provide real props related to the book that students can touch, smell, hold, see, and experience. For example, for the book *The Empty Pot* (Demi, 1990), a flower in a flower pot is a great prop. A bicycle bell or helmet works well for the book *The Magic Bicycle* (Doherty, 1995). Seating is important for a group of young children listening to a book. Create comfortable seating for students—carpet squares or mats that delineate the circular seating area—or other ways to establish visual cues that define the circle. Make sure each child has a clear sight line to the teacher, book, and prop. Select a consistent cue to let children know it's circle time. A method that uses more than one of the senses works the best.

The way the teacher reads the book helps hold children's attention. Express your feelings, and use lots of expression and emotion. Pace your reading—slow down, and adjust your pace to fit the different parts of the story. Make the story fit the needs of the children you are reading to, changing, editing, and providing enhancements. Involve children by asking questions: "What do you think will happen?" "What do the pictures mean?" "Have you had the same feelings as the boy in the book?" "Would you like to grow a plant, like the girl in *The Empty Pot*?" As the children become more familiar with the story, the complexity of these questions increases. "Do you ever . . . ?" "Would you like to . . . ?" "Would you have done the same thing? Why?" "Where do you think she was going?" (Lewman, 1999). Children need to be actively involved in the story.

After telling the story, leave the book in an area where children can go over it individually or in small groups. Set up props in the dramatic-play area so children can further extend the ideas in the book. Provide materials in the art center and book area, and at the woodworking bench to encourage activities related to the book.

Children love to hear the same story over and over again. It seems this assists in their ability to understand the structure of the story, the meaning of new words, the security of the plot. Repetitive reading also improves language and recall skills and increases attention span. To capitalize on this need for repetition, one suggestion is to select a story a week and read that story every day. As children become more and more familiar with the story, they should be encouraged to engage actively in its reading: repeat sections aloud, predict what will happen next, and participate in physical activities that mirror those in the story.

Have a regular guest reader time when parents, volunteers, and important people visit and read to the children. This not only provides a new and different approach (children love novelty) but also models the value of reading to the children.

The Great Debate: Whole-Language versus Phonics

How do children learn to read? Maybe, more important, what's the best way to teach children to read? Over time the answer to this question has fallen into two highly polarized and heated camps: the whole-language approach and the phonics or skill-based approach (Edelsky, 1990; Christie, Enz, & Vukelich, 1997). To understand the debate, it is important to look at both sides.

Whole-Language Approach. The term **whole language** is really a misnomer. This is a constructivist approach that argues that children should learn to read by constructing meaning through interaction with written materials; it is based on the belief that a child's interest in the material is crucial. According to Sweet (1993, p. 4), a constructivist reader:

- uses prior knowledge to gain information from new materials;
- uses a variety of skills in a strategic way to gain information independently;
- is internally motivated to read for information and pleasure;
- interacts socially to make gains in literacy development.

Children learn to read by reading lots of authentic materials—literature and informational pieces, along with their own and other children's work. Children should have many choices in what they read, with reading integrated across all curricular areas, and children reading for content and meaning. Children also switch between reading and writing, taking ownership of their progress and using writing in a variety of ways—journals, reports, labels, personal messages, and more.

Materials used to teach reading should differ from child to child, depending on their interests and abilities. Needed skills—such as phonemic awareness or word attack—should be taught in mini-lessons as needed by each student. *Phonemic awareness* is using knowledge of letter sounds as one of many strategies to read (Christie, Enz, & Vukelich, 1997). In this approach, no teaching manuals or basal readers are used, and teachers provide skill instruction and scaffolding to enable children to become independent readers. Advantages of this approach include the following:

- all teachers and all curricular areas are used to teach reading;
- meaningful instruction builds a student's motivation;
- the approach stresses the importance of environmental print, both at home and in the early childhood program;
- it is based on children's needs and interests.

Skill-Based Teaching (Phonics). In the skill-based approach to learning to read (popularly called **phonics**), children are taught all the subsets of skills needed to learn to read. Further, they use an extensive basal reading system that includes flash cards, charts, computer software, vocabulary lists, and teacher instruction manuals. Skills are carefully introduced and reinforced in a sequence calculated to be best for learning the skills; and basal texts, supplemental texts, and assessments are carefully selected to support this sequence. Reading is taught in isolation from other subjects, including writing. The advantages of the skill-based approach include the following:

- it meets the political need to teach the basics;
- it teaches skills that are measured on standardized tests, and thus can be improved;
- the outcomes are clear and easy for all to understand;
- children can be expected to follow the scope and sequence easily, even when they move from school to school;
- it provides a systematic approach that is attractive to those who want a clear, well-articulated method.

Disadvantages include the following (Christie, Enz, & Vukelich, 1997):

- too much emphasis is placed on skill and drill, often leading to knowledge about single letters and vocabulary, but not reading comprehension and fluency;
- texts are boring, because they are written to use only the words in the sequence and to repeat the words often, which turns children off from reading; children don't read for meaning;
- reading is taught in isolation from writing and other subjects;
- reading is not taught as an enjoyable or meaningful activity;
- assessment is based on isolated word recognition and recall of text, not reading strategies, fluency, and analysis of what has been read.

Two Approaches to Teaching Reading

This summary is based on the arguments of Christie, Enz, & Vukelich (1997).

Skill-Based Approach (Phonics)	Whole-Language Approach
Teacher chooses materials	Child chooses most materials
Basal readers are used	Materials are authentic—literature, own works, others
A rigid set of scope and sequence skills	Skills taught as needed in context while reading
Lots of independent reading	Independent and social reading
Assessment via tests	Ongoing assessment based on active reading
Taught separately from other subjects	Reading across the curriculum

A Combined Approach. Many excellent reading teachers use a variety of techniques from both of these methods to teach reading to young children. While there is considerable debate—and will continue to be—over what a reading program should include, Diegmueller (1995) suggests that a good program should include a balance of oral and written language; an organized skills program that includes phonemic awareness, phonics, and decoding skills; ongoing diagnosis and assessment to let teachers and administrators know each child's progress; and early intervention for children who struggle. In addition, Adams (1990) believes that children should read books made up of their own oral language; teachers and children should read—as a group—the same books over and over; and children should individually read books that are clearly structured and illustrated to assist in the reading process.

Reading is one of the school-based skills that is central to later school success. Teachers must find ways to utilize every tool in their arsenal to teach a child how to read. Invariably, they will pick tools from both sides of the debate.

The Crucial Role of the Family in Language and Literacy Development

Developmentally Appropriate Practice

The foundation of literacy development occurs at home, and the parent is central to this development. There are various ways families can encourage language and literacy development. Parents should talk with and listen to their children as they play and do daily activities together, and read with their children at a regular time every day, whenever they ask, and anytime, anyplace. Parents cannot read to their children too much! Toddlers and preschoolers should visit the library on a regular basis to choose books to check out and read at home, and parents should use their library's special services, such as children's reading groups.

Parent should set up a quiet, comfortable place at home for reading and looking at books. Display books so children can see the covers. Include magazines, pictures, and wordless books. Also include comfortable furniture and soft pillows. Use a special bookshelf or plastic crates to store children's books, and store books and other reading materials where children can reach them. Add new books often. Also, give children books as birthday and Christmas gifts.

Writing materials such as washable, nontoxic crayons and markers; paints and brushes; different kinds of paper; and envelopes of different sizes should be kept where children can reach them and use them easily. Their use should be encouraged and modeled: write a list before shopping, write on the calendar your children's sports activities and your appointments, and write cards, letters, and a journal.

Parents should take books and writing materials for their children whenever they leave home, so they can read or write at the doctor's office, on the bus, and in the car. Have a box of books in the car, and change them often: books both for parents to model reading while waiting at the office or getting the car fixed, and for your children (Curry-Rood, 1999). A specific period of time every day should be set aside for personal reading and writing: books, writing and reading letters, reading the newspaper and magazines, and using recipes and manuals.

Age-Specific Suggestions

The U.S. Department of Education has created a package to encourage families to support literacy development in children called *America Reads Challenge: Ready*Set*Read* (1998), which includes growth charts, developmental activities, and a calendar with daily ideas. Some of these age-specific ideas are summarized in the following sections.

Babies (Birth to 8 Months). Some things that babies do related to language development: they listen and respond to voices and sounds around them, and respond to their name. They coo, gurgle, laugh, and babble to themselves. They enjoy listening to stories. And they take turns while singing and playing with another person.

Katie's father helps her learn about language: he talks with her during a daily activity—bath time. He says her name again and again so that she will learn to recognize it. He serves several turns in their verbal game and then encourages her to take a turn. He responds to her babbles as if he knows what she is saying.

Crawlers and Walkers (8–18 Months). During this period, children use sounds and gestures to say hello or get attention; say a few simple words; and point at things they want. They like rhymes and simple songs, and enjoy reading with a favorite person. They are able to turn the pages in sturdy cardboard books, hold large crayons, and make marks on paper.

Marcus's sister, Maria, helps him learn about language: she responds to his sounds and actions as if he were saying words. She lets him turn the pages of the book. She talks to him about what he seems to be saying. Just as important, she lets him find something else to do when he has lost interest in reading.

Toddlers (18–36 Months). During this dynamic phase, children learn new words every day. They speak using groups of words ("Ned go out"), and ask many questions ("What that?"). When talking with people, they take turns; they join in when a book has rhymes and repeated words. They are able to name objects in picture books ("Ball"); they look at books on their own. They say "no" and "not." And they scribble with crayons and washable markers.

Rosa's caregiver helps her learn about language in a variety of ways: she responds to Rosa's requests by answering with a group of words. She describes what she is doing. She asks simple questions that Rosa knows how to answer. And she sings with Rosa, then congratulates her on learning the song.

Preschoolers (3–5 Years). Preschoolers listen to stories and conversation, and make up silly words and stories. They talk to adults and to other children in complex

▶ *Early childhood literacy activities must be reinforced at home.*

sentences, mastering many rules of grammar. They use language to think, to share ideas and feelings, and to learn new things. Like younger children, they still enjoy the same books over and over, and retell familiar stories to themselves and others. Their comprehension deepens, as they are able to think about what the characters in a book might feel or do. They draw and write with pencils, crayons, and markers.

Gina's family helps her learn about language: They have a regular story time every day. Grandpa offers to write with her; and Mom talks to Ms. Jenkins (her child-care provider), so that Gina can begin to write at family child care and at home.

Kindergarteners (5–6 Years). By this age, children can recognize and reproduce many shapes and numbers. They are gaining control over writing and drawing tools. They write words using invented spelling, and they like to dictate stories for others to write.

Parents and other adults can support this development by making sure the child sees them write every day. They can also talk with children about their writing; give children a box of writing materials that they can easily use—with pencils, paper, crayons, clipboard, and markers. They can participate in the developmental process by asking children to read back what they have written.

First Graders. By the time regular classroom instruction begins, children should be able to read and retell familiar stories, as well as use strategies to break down a passage, and identify an increasing number of words by sight. They can write about topics personally meaningful to them, are beginning to use capitalization and punctuation, and are beginning to use reading and writing for their own purposes.

Parents can talk with their children about favorite storybooks; read to them and encourage them to read on their own; suggest that they write to friends and relatives; and encourage children to share what they have learned about reading and writing.

Second Graders. As they near age 8, children can use strategies more effectively—rereading, questioning, and so on. They can write about a range of topics, use common letter patterns to spell words, and punctuate simple sentences. They should spend time reading daily.

Parents can encourage their ongoing development by continuing to read to children and have them read, as well as visiting the library regularly. Parents should become involved in school activities. They should come up with nonschool activities that require reading and writing. It is also important to read materials about children's interests and hobbies.

Third Graders. Children this age enjoy reading. They use a variety of strategies when reading, and make connections between texts. They should be able to write in many forms (story, poem, report), and to revise and edit their own work, spelling correctly in the final draft.

Parents can take them to the library and bookstores. They should continue to find ways to support children's progress in reading and writing—encouraging children to use and enjoy print for a variety of purposes (games, directions, and so on)—and engage children in conversations about what they read.

Environmental Print

Environmental print provides all sorts of examples and models of writing for children. **Environmental print** is defined as all the words and writing that surround us on a daily basis: street signs, billboards, newspapers, calendars, posters, awards, food containers, magazine covers, packages, mugs with writing on them, phone books, greeting cards, and so on. The amount and variety of environmental print creates a **print-rich environment,** which reinforces the importance of reading and writing; illustrates how words are written, spelled, and combined into meaningful sentences; and displays a variety of writing fonts, from print to cursive to fancy.

Signs and Symbols

The first words children "read" are actually symbols they have memorized: McDonald's arches, Toys "Я" Us, the name of their early childhood program, and traffic signs. The child has learned a symbol that represents one specific product or place (a one-to-one relationship). Children learn only signs that are meaningful to them.

There are many ways to capitalize on children's use of signs as part of their emergent reading skills. For example, children can create shopping lists by cutting products out of catalogs and pasting them on a piece of paper. When my children were young, they created lists for Christmas and their birthdays. On field trips, take a simple camera; ask children to point out signs (stop signs, street names, store names, billboards, advertisements, and more), then take pictures of them. Once the photos have been developed, help the children create a picture map on butcher paper, and glue the photos on the map. Talk with the children about what the signs represent. Photos from a digital camera can be downloaded into the computer and then used for a variety of activities.

Create signs in your program and on the playground: traffic signs, safety signs, labels for storage and activity areas (coats here; put dishes here; water fountain). For younger children, use simple pictures paired with words.

Environmental Print in the Classroom

Provide lots of examples of different words and numbers, both in the classroom and in the center. The overall purpose of a print-rich environment is to show children the value of the written word and to encourage them actively to create words, sentences, and stories. Place charts, posters, a large model of the daily schedule, and a list of classroom rules on the wall. Students' names can go above their lockers; large calendars and wall newspapers in progress can be attached next to appropriate centers. Place "For Sale" signs in the math learning area; enlarged copies of book covers, Big Books, and so on, in the reading corner, and blueprints and housing advertisements in the block area. Some other ideas for creating a print-rich environment include the following:

- Label all learning centers with words and pictures (block area, dramatic-play area, woodworking area). Use lowercase letters.
- Place a notepad and pencil or felt pen on the wall next to the toy telephone.

- Ask children to help add print-rich materials to each center, both brought from home and made by the students.
- Write song lyrics on large lined paper, have children illustrate them, then attach the paper to the classroom wall.
- Help children create a variety of personal journals, books, records, correspondence, greeting cards, and other documents.
- Create a wall newspaper with children's daily dictated and original contributions and art.
- Post signs for specific classroom reminders (handwashing instructions, rules for each learning center). Accompany these written signs with visual symbols.
- Post daily snack and lunch menus with words and pictures.
- Display children's names throughout the classroom (for young children, their names are the most meaningful words)—on cubbies, birthday charts, help charts, growth charts, matrixes, lists of personal opinions (likes ice cream, doesn't like apples, and so on). Place a photo or a self-portrait next to each name, whenever possible. Provide sign-in sheets for learning centers, classroom chores, and other activities of the day.

Use of Environmental Print in Specific Learning Centers

In addition to these ideas for making a classroom a print-rich environment, there are many things that can be created in each specific learning center. The following sections offer a few ideas for each area.

Reading Center. Provide displays of different books that can be easily reached and returned by children. Include in these rotating displays the book being read aloud, books brought from home, and books being sent home as part of a library sharing program. Also include books that support and extend a classroom theme or project, and copies of books created by children and the whole class.

Provide a listening area with books on tape and blank tapes so children can create their own stories; also include posters, copies of pages from books, charts, and sign language illustrations on the wall. Include copies of children's magazines and newspapers—*Big Back Yard, Ranger Rick, Ladybug*—and display examples of children's writing efforts.

Writing Center. The writing center should provide a variety of ways to encourage writing: a range of different papers; a variety of shapes, textures, and thicknesses; envelopes; sticky pads; old checks and checkbooks; menus; message pads; and a variety of writing materials, including magnetic letters and numbers (with a metal board on which to use them), a felt board with cutout letters, stencils of different-size circles, french curves, rulers, and drawing triangles. Place large lined paper on the wall for children to write on. You might create a continuous newspaper with different themes and focuses. Opportunities to copy, trace, and try out letters and numbers—stamps, word and letter stencils, typewriter, cookie cutters in letter shapes—should exist throughout the writing center. Provide a variety of book-making materials that children can use anytime. Have children make individual mailboxes for each child.

Science Center. Provide labels for various objects in the science area, and place on the wall charts, graphs, and visual displays of scientific experiments and phenomena (weather changes, seasonal characteristics, growth stages of a plant). Write up science experiments and attach them to the wall; keep updated growth charts, and convert them into graphs. For older children, provide a card box with simple projects inside. Explain the instructions for the projects carefully, using simple words and visual symbols.

Children can create charts of positive instances and negative instances—for example, things that float and don't float; things that fly and don't; animals that eat grass and animals that don't. Add children's books about science and nature.

Dramatic-Play Center. Add the following materials to the dramatic-play area: a phone book, telephone message pad, shopping lists, newspapers, magazines, catalogs, cookbooks, coupons, notepads and pencils, children's books, date books, maps, order forms, wall calendars.

Art Center. Ask children questions about their artwork; write down their comments, and encourage them to tell stories. Label the paint containers with the color of the paint in the container. Along with obvious art materials, include tracing templates (all kinds, including numerals, letters, different-size circles, french curves, animals, plants, cars), a variety of magazines, greeting cards, and stamps and stamp pads.

Dramatic-Play Activities to Promote Literacy

Emergent literacy can be encouraged by creating temporary activities in the classroom. Some ideas for short-term projects and supplies for them that promote literacy are detailed here (Christie, Enz, & Vukelich, 1997).

- *Home center.* Notepads, Post-It notes, babysitting instruction forms, telephone books, message pads, message board, children's books, magazines, newspapers, junk mail, cookbooks, recipe box, and product containers from children's homes.
- *Business office.* Notepads, telephone message forms, calendar, typewriter, order forms, letterhead, envelopes, stamps, file folders, wall signs.
- *Restaurant.* Notepads, menus, wall signs ("Pay here"), bank checks, cookbooks, product containers from children's homes.
- *Post office.* Stationery and envelopes, stamps, mailboxes, address labels, wall signs ("Line starts here").

- *Grocery store.* Notepads, bank checks, wall signs ("Supermarket"), shelf labels for store areas ("Meat"), product containers, coupons.
- *Veterinarian's office.* Appointment book, wall signs ("Receptionist"), labels with pets' names, patient charts, prescription forms, magazines (in the waiting room).
- *Airport and airplane.* Tickets, bank checks, magazines (on board the plane), air sickness bags with printed instructions, maps, signs ("Baggage claim area"), safety cards.
- *Library.* Books, shelf labels for books ("ABCs," "Animals"), wall signs ("Quiet, please"), library cards, checkout cards, computers, typewriters.

Block Center. Place pictures of buildings, vehicles, and the community, with labels under them, in the block area; provide large paper and markers to encourage children to make road maps. Cardboard and poster board, scissors, markers, and rulers should be available for making signs to go with buildings. Street signs, road maps, building blueprints, and photos of buildings under construction all add a sense of reality to the block area. Also include brochures for trucks, cars, earth movers, and road graders.

Use of Technology to Support Emergent Literacy

Technology should be integrated within the literacy curriculum. Computers can effectively complement, support, enhance, and **differentiate** the program's overall emergent literacy effort—depending on the age of the children, the availability of software, and the expertise of teachers. Most important, the computer program should be integrated with all other classroom activities. Computers should not be used for specific drill activities; they should also not be used to reward children who have completed more traditional writing tasks. Computers are particularly powerful in assisting children who struggle with conventional literacy efforts. Their hands-on applications, self-paced learning, and visual appeal are very effective with these children.

Software chosen to support literacy efforts should be interactive and based on the child's interests and experiences; it should also be able to be used in connection with activities in other learning centers: art, science, reading. Through the use of scanners, publishing software, and digital cameras, field trips, personal journals, individual pictures, and more can be integrated into larger writing projects on the computer. Students can create stories by cutting and pasting clip art, sounds, music, different noises, words, and drawings. They can create stories to be read in a group, and create classroom and programwide newspapers, menus, and announcements. For older children, access to Web sites can augment research and other literacy activities.

Teachers need specific training and continued support to integrate technology effectively within the overall curriculum, to learn how to use the computer like any other classroom material, and to learn how to support the program's philosophy and curriculum. And they need to learn new ways the computer can be used to enhance and differentiate the program's overall literacy effort.

Selecting Software for Young Children

Parents and educators carefully select toys, learning materials, and books for their children. Various criteria are considered in making these selections—including safety, durability, cost, interest, and meeting children's developmental needs (covered extensively in Chapter 8). Selecting appropriate computer software for young children is an equally important task. But because computer software is comparatively new, and much of it is aggressively marketed to parents as an academic learning aid (Haugland, 1999), particular care is required in this activity. Lots of software is at a skill level too high for the children for whom it is marketed and concentrates on skill and drill learning activities.

In a study evaluating children's computer software, only 25 percent was found to be developmentally appropriate; further, children who used the skill and drill programs for forty-five minutes a week experienced considerable losses in creativity (Haugland, 1992). Also, learning from these skill and drill activities did not translate into improved performance on academic tests.

Good software must match children's individual interests and developmental level, and teach concepts in a variety of real-life situations (Haugland, 1999). In an effort to assist teachers and parents in selecting appropriate software for young children, the Haugland Developmental Software Scale (1999) has been developed. The criteria for this scale include child control, age appropriateness, clear instructions, expanding complexity, independence, nonviolence, process orientation, real-world features, and technical features (color, design, and so on). Software that includes people should represent diverse cultures, people of differing ages and abilities, and diverse family structures. To use software that simply reinforces skill and drill activities and does not expand the child's learning in a variety of directions and at a variety of places is simply underutilizing this tremendous technology.

The Role of Teachers in Literacy Development

In any educational endeavor, the teacher is the crucial component. The role of the teacher in literacy development includes setting up, arranging, and rearranging the environment; developing and introducing literacy activities; and engaging in interactions with students that encourage, scaffold, and extend the literacy development of young children. The following are some age-specific ideas for teachers working with young children as summarized from the document, Continuum of Children's Development in Early Reading and Writing (*Young Children*, 1998).

Preschool

During preschool, children explore their environment and build the foundation for learning to read and write. To support this stage, teachers should share books with children, including Big Books; model reading behavior; and reread favorite stories. They should talk about letters by name and sound, establish a literacy-rich environment, engage children in language games, and promote literacy-related play activities. Further, teachers should encourage children to experiment with writing by supporting art activities using a variety of media, writing dictated stories and accounts in journals and on pictures, and introducing students to specific writing and publishing software.

Kindergarten

Kindergarten children develop basic concepts of print and begin to engage in and experiment with reading and writing. Teachers can encourage children to talk about reading and writing experiences, provide many opportunities for children to explore and identify sound–symbol relationships in meaningful contexts, and help children segment spoken words into individual sounds and blend those sounds into whole words. They should frequently read interesting and conceptually rich stories to children, provide daily opportunities for children to write, help children build a sight vocabulary, and create a literacy-rich environment for children to engage independently in reading and writing.

First Grade

Children begin to read simple stories and can write about a topic that is meaningful to them. Teachers should support the development of vocabulary by reading daily to children, transcribing their language, and selecting materials that expand children's knowledge and language development. They should model strategies and provide opportunities for identifying new words.

Children should be given opportunities for independent reading and writing practice, and should be encouraged to read, write, and discuss a range of different text types (poems, informational books, and stories). New words should be introduced, and children should be helped to build lists of commonly used words from their writing and reading. Strategies should be taught for learning to spell new words. Teachers should demonstrate and model reading strategies to use when comprehension breaks down.

Second and Third Grades

Children aged 7 and 8 begin to read more frequently and write various text forms using simple and more complex sentences. Teachers should create a climate that fosters analytical, evaluative, and reflective thinking. They should teach children to write in many ways, and ensure that children read a range of texts for a variety of purposes. Teachers should teach revising, editing, and proofreading skills, as well as more strategies for spelling new and difficult words.

Children continue to extend and refine their reading and writing to suit varying purposes and audiences. Teachers should provide daily opportunities for children to read, examine, and evaluate narrative and expository texts; they should continue to use a curriculum that fosters critical reading and personal response, teach children to examine ideas in texts, and encourage children to use writing as a tool for thinking and learning.

Children's knowledge of correct written conventions should be extended—grammar, spelling, and punctuation. A climate that engages all children in lots of reading and writing activities should be established and supporting materials created. Teachers should also encourage children in all forms of conversation, and build a love of language in all its forms. Reading and writing activities should be integrated across all disciplines.

Failure to Learn to Read and Write

Even when we provide all necessary assistance to support children in developing literacy skills and knowledge at the right time in the correct sequence, some children still experience problems learning to read and write. And as the population of children we

▶ *There are complex reasons some children—*
especially boys—struggle to learn to read.

serve becomes more diverse, the number of those who do not follow the "normal" progression will certainly increase. I was one of these children; my son was also.

As a child, I struggled to learn to read and write. At age 12, I was still struggling; I believe I read my first book from cover to cover when I was about 13 years old. Consequently, my writing and spelling suffered. I am still an atrocious speller (thank goodness for Spell Check!). But this inability to read and spell did not keep me from succeeding academically—ultimately getting a Ph.D., teaching at the college level, and writing for national magazines.

Why was I such a poor reader? In looking back at my childhood and in observing my own son struggle with reading, I believe it was caused by a variety of factors. I was an outdoor child who loved our farm on the border country between England and Wales—animals, birds, trees, and especially wildflowers. I also enjoyed art, woodworking, and folk dancing. While I experienced lots of oral literature and folk singing at home and in my early childhood program, I saw little environmental print because I lived on a very isolated farm, with minimal interaction with the outside world. As a result, I developed no interest in books. I also had so many opportunities to enjoy hands-on learning that books always seemed to be a second best.

My teachers did not know how to use my interest in the countryside, art, music, and dance to teach emergent literacy skills. Reading and writing were viewed—as they were in all schools at that time (Christie et al., 1995)—as a discrete discipline. I also probably had a specific learning disability. In many ways my son is like me: very active, artistic, athletic. Through the special-education diagnostic and staffing procedure, it was determined that he has difficulty with auditory discrimination—the ability to isolate the various sound components of speech. Obviously, this specific learning disability makes learning the phonemic components of reading and writing a problem.

Two major reasons for students' school failure in this country are poverty and not speaking English. When these two factors are combined, the effect can be devastating. A variety of programs and efforts have been developed to address the impact of poverty and non-English speaking on academic success. Increasingly, the divide between the poor and middle classes—education, access to technology, high-school graduation and beyond—are a serious concern for educators and politicians.

Interventions

There are many programs designed to work with students who are behind their peers in language development, reading, and writing: Child Find, reading recovery, special education, Title I, Head Start, and so on. Some school districts adopt national programs, while others mix and match various approaches. It is essential that children who are struggling with any aspect of literacy development be diagnosed and receive remediation. Some educators argue, however, that labeling children and isolating them from their peers to provide the special services can be very destructive. The legal requirement to serve children in the least-restrictive environment is one attempt to reduce this impact of labeling children.

Public schools receive federal funding for each child identified as a special-education student; other funding sources, from Title I and bilingual programs to state-funded preschool programs, are targeted at children with a deficiency of some kind (low income, delayed development, lack of skills). The term *at risk* is a popular label for these students. Unfortunately, this approach to funding programs isolates children who struggle academically and rewards schools for identifying large numbers of "at-risk" students. Title I has moved in the right direction, from funding individual students to funding the entire school.

I believe I succeeded academically despite my early dislike of academic subjects, my delayed literacy development, and my apparent learning disability because of the approach my family and teachers took to my education. I was never labeled as having any needs different from those of my peers, and I never personally believed I had a problem. I knew I couldn't read, and I knew writing was difficult for me, but I believed all children had these kinds of struggles in one way or another. I continued to enjoy art, dance, soccer, hiking, and nature throughout my early school life. Teachers never said, "You cannot go and play until you have finished reading the book," or "You must finish writing before you can paint." Although I struggled, I developed positive self-esteem through my art, woodworking, and dance activities. Eventually I leaned to read, and I learned to cope—and, most important, I learned to feel proud of my academic effort.

Impact of Intervention Approaches. As I discussed in detail in Chapter 6, the sooner children with a disability are identified and a program developed to meet their unique needs, the more likely the child will be to achieve success in school. Nevertheless, we must carefully examine the impact of intervention approaches on children. Some of my concerns regarding these programs include the following:

1. What is the negative impact of labeling a child as deficient in some way? At what point does a child begin to live out this label—to believe in it—and to what extent does the system begin to treat the child as a label? How many of our children say to themselves, "I cannot succeed because I have a special need . . . I cannot succeed because I'm poor . . . I cannot succeed because I'm at risk"?

2. What is the impact of teacher's lower expectations of children with a special need or challenge?

3. Why is it more boys and more minority students have these labels and are in programs for at-risk students? This is a major concern.

4. Many children are placed in special programs inappropriately, for a variety of reasons including behavioral problems in the classroom, the bias of an administrator, and tests that are incorrectly administered and inappropriately interpreted.

5. At what point does the natural variability of students, and the biological needs we all have, become a cause for intervention? For example, is the reason so many

boys are diagnosed with ADHD because our school expectations do not match boys' natural need for activity, space, stimulus change, and excitement (Hale, 1994)?

6. To what extent are intervention programs institution-driven rather than student-driven? Are children placed in special education because they have a special need or because the program needs the federal money?

7. Some methods used to teach students who are placed in special programs do not meet the needs of these children. Twice-exceptional students (gifted students with special needs) often get bored and drop out of school because the most popular approach to remediation emphasizes repetition and practice.

Children who struggle academically in programs have the same needs as other children: self-esteem, confidence, peer acceptance, a belief that important adults in their lives have faith they can succeed, and to be treated as whole, competent human beings.

Bilingual Education and Second-Language Acquisition

Language acquisition and emergent literacy activities initially focus on a child's first language. But soon after children learn their first language, many learn a second language. In most countries around the world, except the United States, young children are expected to learn at least two languages.

The children of Panimasiguan, the small village in the highlands of Guatemala in which I worked for a time, first learn Cakchiquel, their native Maya language. In first grade they are taught in Cakchiquel, as they begin to learn to read and write. But in second grade they are also taught Spanish, the official language of Guatemala, and all their educational materials are in Spanish. The children from this impoverished mountain village who continue their education beyond sixth grade also learn English, thus becoming trilingual.

Three of my own children attended a bilingual French school in Denver. This school, whose French teachers are French citizens, start English-speaking children in a full-day preschool program in which they are taught in French, in a full-immersion approach. As students progress each year, more English is added to the curriculum: 80 percent French to 20 percent English, then 70 percent French to 30 percent English, until instruction is balanced at 50 percent French and 50 percent English. One of my daughters, who entered the school at age 4, now speaks French so fluently that, according to native French speakers, she speaks French "better than some French children."

In America (the United States) we have historically focused on teaching English to children who do not speak it, in an attempt to mold all newcomers into a new American identity. Children who spoke a language other than English, including Native American children, were punished. In the past few decades, however, our approach changed as educators recognized the value of teaching children basic academic concepts in their home language before teaching English. Teaching children in their home language also validates children's cultures. But the pendulum has recently swung again, with new laws in California, Arizona, and Colorado requiring the teaching of English to non–English-speaking children as quickly as possible.

Window of Opportunity to Learn a Second language

One reason teaching English-speaking children a second language is important for early childhood educators is that research shows that the ideal time to learn a second language is between ages 3 and 10, during a significant period in development (see Chapter 9). Children who learn a second language during this early time frame often become highly fluent; those who learn a second language after age 10 often struggle with the language throughout their lives. It is clear that if we want our children to learn a foreign language, we should provide intensive instruction within this window of opportunity.

Bilingual Education

Bilingual education in this country has become a highly emotional issue. Actually, the debate is not about bilingual education; it's about what kind of bilingual education to use. *Bilingual* simply means "relating to two languages"; and in this country *bilingual* is used to mean English and another language—often, but not always, Spanish. Clearly, teaching children English is an important issue, because children who do not speak English struggle to succeed in school and to graduate from high school. The questions that surround this debate include the relation between children's first language and their culture; the connection between children's first language and their self-esteem; and whether children's acquisition of nonlinguistic concepts—math, social studies, science— is delayed if children first must learn English. Further, people are concerned that if the majority of instruction in school is in the child's own language, and the child's classmates, family members, and people in their neighborhood don't speak English, they may never really learn English.

Supporting Children Who Don't Speak English

An early childhood program that serves a non–English-speaking population needs to balance several factors in providing a bilingual program for these children. First, the program must be responsive to parents' needs and wishes. Some parents want their children to learn English as quickly as possible; some do not. Second, English must be taught in a way that never puts down children's home culture, by providing classroom materials and content that reflect their culture. Children who do not speak English need to maintain a close affiliation with their home culture, and be able to communicate effectively with their non–English-speaking parents. The purpose is to teach the language, not to change or challenge children's backgrounds. Third, it is important to find ways to teach the English-speaking students in the program a second language, thus validating second-language learning.

Bilingual education should never be equated with remedial education or special education; students in bilingual programs should never be viewed as incompetent or inferior to other students regarding their scholastic development. It is essential to hire competent second-language teachers, which is often difficult because people who speak a second language can find more lucrative jobs in the private sector. Bilingual education should be provided for all students in the program who do not speak English. Further, while it is important to support a child's home language, we cannot forget that a central purpose of education is to teach children to speak, read, and write in English.

Non–English-speaking children's parents should receive program communication in their native language, along with parent training and other services for parents. This should be done through newsletters, pamphlets, meetings, personal communications, videos, radio and cable TV shows, festivals, and programwide activities.

Second-Language Acquisition

Clearly, with the window of opportunity for second-language acquisition being between 3 and 10 years old, children should start instruction in second-language learning in the early grades. Unfortunately, there is a strong bias in this country against teaching

NAEYC Position Statement: Responding to Linguistic and Cultural Diversity

This document is summarized here; the full document is published in *Young Children* (1996b).

Early childhood programs should foster the development of children's home language and the development of English. To minimize disruption between home and the early childhood program, the program should find ways for families to bring their home and culture into the program.

The Challenge

Approximately 9.9 million of the estimated 45 million school-age children in this country live in homes in which a language other than English is spoken (Waggoner, 1994). Responding to this linguistic and cultural diversity can be very challenging.

A. Recommendations for Handling this Challenge

- Recognize that all children are cognitively, linguistically, and emotionally connected to the language and culture of their home.
- Acknowledge that children can demonstrate their knowledge and capabilities in many ways. Children who speak a language other than English should have opportunities to demonstrate their abilities and be valued for them. Children should be given opportunities to demonstrate what they know and can do, not what they don't know and can't do.
- Understand that without comprehensive input, second-language learning can be difficult. In learning a second language, it is far more difficult to be academically proficient than simply to be fluent. It is easier to learn

complex cognitive concepts in the child's first language, and then to transfer that knowledge to the new language.

B. Recommendations for Working with Families

- Actively involve parents and families in the early learning program and setting. Efforts should be made to involve parents in the education of their children in the center or school. The program should also learn about the community children live in, and include aspects of that community in the program.
- Teach parents the value for children of knowing more than one language, and provide strategies to preserve their first language. Early childhood programs should help parents of children who don't speak English understand that a second language is best learned within the context of natural interactions that occur within everyday settings. Help these parents understand the value of preserving the child's first language.
- Recognize that parents and families must rely on caregivers and educators to honor and support their children in the cultural val-

young children a second language. A young French teacher from the school my children attended was asked by his barber what he did for a living. When he replied that he taught French, the barber indignantly replied, "Why? In this country all you need to know is English!" Many educational professionals don't believe young children can handle two languages at one time—especially children who might have specific educational challenges (Hakuta, 1986).

As we enter a global economy, all U.S. children need to learn a second language—in the early childhood years. Because many other countries have included teaching a second language in their schools for many years, they can provide ideas, models, methods, and approaches to effectively accomplishing this important task. For example, Canada

ues and norms of the home. Programs need to develop communications that are in the family's language.

C. Recommendations for Professional Preparation

- Provide professional preparation and development to early childhood educators in the areas of culture, language, and diversity. Content to be covered in this preparation should include language acquisition, second-language learning, working with diverse families, cross-cultural communication, and issues pertaining to race, language, culture, and community involvement.

- Recruit and support early childhood educators who are trained in languages other than English. Staff members who know a variety of languages and have exposure to various cultural and economic settings can be a tremendous asset to the program, and can provide training and leadership in working with families who don't speak English.

D. Recommendations for Programs and Practice

- Recognize that children can and will acquire the use of English even when their home

language is used and respected. Bilingual children have cognitive advantages. Non–English-speaking children should have opportunities to learn advanced concepts in their own language, while also learning English.

- Support and preserve home-language usage. Use of the child's home language should be clearly evident in all aspects of the program's environment and communications with parents. Community members should be recruited to assist in the programs, and the early childhood staff should attempt to learn each child's home language. Teachers should also model appropriate use of English. All students should be given daily opportunities to develop complex concepts and higher-level thinking in their own language.

- Develop and provide alternative and creative strategies for young children's learning. Teachers should provide a variety of ways for all children to demonstrate their knowledge, learn new concepts, and work interactively with other children.

▶ *Family exploration into the community becomes a source for later discussions, writing, and story telling.*

has pioneered programs for teaching French to English-speaking children. They start at age 4 with a full-immersion program, and at the end of the program the children are as proficient in French as native French Canadian speakers. The same bilingual program has also demonstrated that children who learn French starting at a young age improve their English proficiency. Learning grammar, spelling, and writing in one language improves a child's ability in those areas in another language.

Combination Programs

Another approach to bilingual education and second-language acquisition is emerging: programs that combine teaching English to non–English-speaking students with teaching English-speaking students a second language. These programs are sometimes called 50:50 programs, or dual-language programs. Half the day is taught in English, the other half in the second language. Thus, all children receive 50 percent of their instruction in English, and 50 percent in a foreign language. The equal weight given to both languages avoids the perception that non–English-speaking students are inferior. For these programs, qualified staff need to be found, second-language learning should be started in the early years, and the dual program should be continued through middle and high school.

Conclusion

Early literacy development is essential for a child's future school success. Literacy involves speaking, listening, writing, and reading. While we have historically thought of writing and reading as beginning later than listening and speaking, all four skills develop at the same time. Further, the foundation for these crucial skills starts in infancy and is molded by parents' and caregivers' verbal interaction with the child. Early childhood programs can provide a vast array of activities to assist children in their continual development of essential literacy skills. Programs also are challenged to support the literacy development of students whose home language is not English. And as we move into a more global society, we must consider whether our literacy should also include teaching all children in our programs a second language.

Questions and Projects

1. Select a child you know between the ages of 1 and 5 years (from the neighborhood, from a program, or elsewhere). Observe the child on three separate occasions, at least once when the child is interacting with an adult. Observe the child's language development, and then write a one- or two-page paper on this development.

2. Compare a program in your community that teaches English as a second language with a program that teaches young children a foreign language. What do they do the same? What is different? Why?

3. Select a typical learning center (math, writing, and so on), other than the reading center, and design a literacy activity for children aged 3–5. Describe how you would include environmental print, specific materials you would include, activities the teacher would introduce, and the role of the teacher.

4. Design a small brochure communicating to parents the value of literacy activities, suggesting things they can do at home and in the community with their children to promote literacy. Pick the targeted age of the students (between infancy and third grade). Use a computer if you have access. Make it attractive. Alternatively, you could create a short video for parents.

5. Select a writing software program for second- and third-grade students. Evaluate the program for developmental appropriateness, integration of learning centers, lack of violence, and diversity.

Resources

1998. *America Reads Challenge: Ready*Set*Read.* A joint project of the Department of Education and the Department of Health and Human Services.

Computers and Young Children Web site: http://cstl.semo.edu/kidcomp

Haugland, S., and J. Wright. 2000. *Young children and technology: A world of discovery.* Boston: Allyn and Bacon.

International Reading Association. 1995. *Linking literacy with play.* Tape, guide, and reading materials. Newark, Del.: International Reading Association.

CHAPTER

II Encouraging Creativity

The arts in early childhood programs usually include painting, drawing, working with clay and other three-dimensional materials, music and movement, singing, and creative dance and drama. In this chapter woodworking and folk dance have also been included. The challenge for early childhood educators is to understand the vital role the arts play in the total development of the child, the need for arts to be integrated throughout the early childhood curriculum, and the struggle to balance the arts with the current trend toward specific academic instruction. This chapter addresses each of these issues, while presenting a strong argument for the importance of the arts in early childhood programs. ■

Questions to Consider

1. Is there value in singing to infants?

2. Is there any relationship between movement activities and learning to speak and read? What is it?

3. Is there a place for technology in early childhood arts programs?

4. How can the arts be used to explore diversity and multi-culturalism?

5. Should the erosion of the arts in some early childhood programs be a concern? Why?

Why Creative Activities Are Crucial in Early Childhood Programs

As many schools and early childhood programs in this country focus more on standards, the basics, and accountability, the question is whether the arts are critical to a quality early childhood program, and, if so, what the rationale is for including them. What is the value of the arts—both for their own sake, and as a way of supporting and enhancing teaching of the basics?

Theoretical Underpinnings

The arts have always had a central place in early childhood programs, from Froebel's belief in art and dance to the Waldorf emphasis on the arts. In this country, John Dewey was the first strong proponent of incorporating the arts into universal public education. Contemporary advocates include educators who support Howard Gardner's approach to visual and kinesthetic learners, and theorists who believe the arts to be the best foundation for later academic growth.

John Dewey and Progressive Education. Dewey believed art should be experienced by every child in the schools. Further, he saw the arts as a fundamental form of expression and communication—of equal value to all the other subjects in the curriculum (Dewey, 1934). "Children's art was taken seriously, regarded as authentic, worthwhile, and valued on its own terms" (Engel, 1995, p. 8). One of the central functions of art, according to Dewey, is to allow children to express their deepest thoughts and feelings. Dewey believed that intellect and emotion are interconnected. "Many a person is unhappy, tortured within, because he has at command no art of expressive action" (Dewey, 1934, p. 65).

Freud and Psychoanalysis. For psychoanalysts, the arts in education provided the outlet for repressed feelings, which would become destructive without such an outlet. The use of art throughout the curriculum was encouraged—with no set art lessons—and teachers were reluctant to judge or critique the work of children. For psychoanalysts, "art as therapy came first and art as aesthetic experience second" (Engel, 1995, p. 10).

The Avant-Garde in Art. The movement away from realism in the art world, which started at the turn of the twentieth century, and toward art that more closely reflected emotions, psychology, and state of mind, had an influence on the arts in schools. This change led to an appreciation of art that was direct, spontaneous, inventive, and lacking respect for rules of gravity, perspective, and accuracy of color—very much like children's art. Artists such as Klee, Chagall, Picasso, Miró, Kandinsky, and Marc painted in this fashion. I remember, as a budding young child artist, being enthralled by Marc's blue horses and Klee's wonderful childlike compositions. These avant-garde artists established the aesthetic value of children's art in its own right, as opposed to children's art simply being a preparation for adult aesthetics.

Cognitive and Developmental Psychologists. Cognitive psychologists began to look at the development of art as closely related to the development of cognition—as evidence of cognitive development. From this perspective, art gained added importance as being intimately tied to intellect, and was taken more seriously. In 1943 English educator Herbert Read wrote *Education through Art*, in which he argued that art activities are an essential component of a child's education. He also believed that the developmental progression children experience in their art activities, from broad scribbles to approximation of reality, is not simply a progression to adult art performance, but an expression of the way a child feels and experiences the world at each developmental stage.

In 1947, Victor Lowenfeld created a developmental-stage theory of art, which Lowenfeld viewed as the expression of children's combined development in emotional, intellectual, physical, social, and aesthetic areas. Like the psychoanalysts, Lowenfeld believed that any adult control of the artistic process—imposing standards, grading, using coloring books—was highly detrimental to children's development. Lowenfeld's stages are (Engel, 1995):

- scribbling (ages 2–4)
- preschematic (ages 4–7)
- schematic (ages 7–9)
- drawing realism (ages 9–11)
- pseudo-naturalistic (ages 11–13)
- crisis of adolescence (ages 13–17).

Contemporary Approaches. Rudolf Arnheim sees art as visual thinking—a way children take information in from the environment; sort, classify, manipulate, and enhance this information; and then use it to store information, solve problems, and advance cognition. For young children, a shape drawn on a piece of paper can represent a number of things with a similar structure—a visual **prototype.** Children use visual images to help them perceive information in the environment more accurately and in more detail. Arnheim believed the skills learned in this activity transfer to other cognitive processes—promoting flexibility, creativity, problem solving, and more (Arnheim, 1969).

Gardner, who is discussed at length in other chapters in the book, furthers Arnheim's ideas by viewing the arts as a way children manipulate materials in the service of their ideas (1980). Art provides the most easily accessible medium for children to work through feelings of aggression, violence, love, conflict, and confusion, and to come to grips with their own feelings of anxiety and helplessness (1980). Further, Gardner considers the arts the principal way kinesthetic and visual learners process information.

The Arts for Their Own Sake

As the early childhood education community becomes more and more engulfed in the trend of standards and accountability sweeping the country, the question of where the arts fit into our programs becomes more and more important. In many states, school success is being defined by scores on math, reading, and writing standardized tests. Creative endeavors are, seemingly, unimportant. While it is fairly easy to argue that the arts are needed to assist students in learning the basics of math, reading, science, writing, and social studies, it's an entirely different issue to argue that the arts should be taught for their own sake. Do the arts, as Read suggests (1956), have their own specialized characteristics, laws, and skills that should be taught and encouraged in our schools? And when Dewey argues that education is experience (1934), is he also arguing for the experiences learned through the arts?

Children learn a variety of skills, concepts, dispositions, and attitudes through arts activities that they cannot learn elsewhere in a program. Some of these are outlined below.

The arts provide a unique way to process new information. As discussed at length in Chapter 9, many theorists believe that learning involves taking information from the external environment and matching it to existing internal mental structures (Piaget, 1952; Vygotsky, 1978). Artistic activities provide an ideal medium for manipulating concepts, putting ideas into reality, creating images that represent thoughts and emotions, and making tangible new concepts for all to see. Art is the medium through which young children work; artistic experiences add personal feelings and record solutions to dilemmas (Engel, 1995).

The arts teach children how to evaluate their own growth. Ultimately, children produce art to meet their own standards: build a boat on the workbench that floats; make a birthday card they believe their father will like; and create a dance that expresses the anger they feel. The child decides when the song sounds right, whether the clay pot should have thinner sides, how large to make a wooden sculpture, and how to dramatize Billy Goats Gruff. A central component of growth is developing standards and living with those standards.

The arts teach children how to create their own reality. To handle the constant bombardment of the external environment—from peers, teachers, parents, books, TV, videos, films, and so on—children must be able to create an internal reality into which they can retreat, a secure, friendly, consistent world that forms an anchor for them. Art activities provide a great vehicle for children to create, extend, and reaffirm this internal reality. Children paint pictures of the way they see the world, do clay models of their ideal family or imaginary pet, and make music that takes them to a peaceful place.

The arts empower visual and kinesthetic learners. As Gardner has shown through his theory of multiple intelligences, many of our students are not verbal-linguistic or mathematic-logical learners, but are visual and kinesthetic learners. Visual arts provide a legitimate avenue for visual thinkers to excel; dance, drama, folk dance, and woodworking provide acceptable avenues for the kinesthetic learner to succeed, and to avoid behavior problems caused by too many passive activities.

The arts develop enactive and iconic memory. Jerome Bruner believes that all of us think enactively (muscle memory), iconically (pictures and visual images) and symbolically (words and numbers). Further, he believes that children use enactive and iconic memory with more ease than they do symbolic memory. Artistic activities in early childhood programs help children focus on developing these memories before concentrating on symbolic memory.

The arts teach children to be creative and innovative. Art is about pushing boundaries, using materials in new and unique ways, not accepting limitations, and finding alternative solutions. For minority and low-income children, who continually experience the constraints of racism and poverty, the ability to push further and to challenge limitations is a tremendous asset.

The arts encourage messing around. Piaget believed young children must actively manipulate the real world in order to learn (1952). They must have lots of real experiences with the concrete world at their level of experience and understanding. A child who, while messing around with sand and water to make interesting and unusual patterns, discovers that the water erodes sand, learns far more about ecology than reading about erosion in a textbook. The arts involve hands-on interaction with the environment: bodies, props, paint, water, chalk, wood, play dough, clay, dried leaves, wax paper, dress-ups, glue, and so on.

The arts develop self-esteem. My son struggled through his school years because he did not excel academically. Nevertheless, he developed great joy in art activities and a tremendous sense of accomplishment. Art activities are processes in which children direct the entire activity—from selecting the kind of medium and subject to deciding when the project is complete. With art children create a little world of their own—something that is theirs and that they can feel proud of.

The arts develop creative thinkers and problem solvers. Intelligent, successful thinkers are creative thinkers and good problem solvers: they have learned to think outside the box. The creative process is a continual problem-solving activity: "How can I make my song sound like a lullaby?" "How can I make the dog in my picture look mean?" "How can I make my clay person stand up?" The arts teach creativity because they teach trial and error, testing alternative solutions, and experimenting in a risk-free environment.

The arts help children deal with their emotions. My son has a very deep sense of justice, fairness, and student rights, which he felt were consistently violated in his high school. He was able to use his art to explore these feelings—to put into form abstract ideas about equity. As a child I was extremely shy and did not like school, but I found a sense of belonging in the arts—woodworking, folk dance, painting, and drawing. They became my home. Children need outlets as they struggle to handle a world that often makes little sense to them and seems unkind and unfair. The arts provide this place.

Providing art activities in schools develops in children a lifelong appreciation for all the arts. One of the richest rewards of life is a joy in and appreciation of the arts—plays, concerts, art exhibits, music festivals, cultural concerts, and dance presentations. Children who are exposed to a rich variety of the arts in their early childhood programs develop this sense of lifelong appreciation.

An Integrated Approach

The most common approach to curriculum and instruction in U.S. schools is to divide instruction by subject matter or traditional content areas—science, math, music, art, writing, reading, social studies. The opposite approach is the integrated curriculum, which teaches skills and content in an integrated matter—usually centered on a single theme, project, activity, or field trip. Tied closely to an integrated curriculum is an integrated approach, which emphasizes teaching skills and content across the curriculum.

An example of an integrated approach—both curricular and instructional—involves creating a classroom garden (Dunbar, 2001). Content covered in this activity might include:

- planting seeds, growth of plants from seeds;
- the weather, the seasons;
- preparing the ground to plant, and using organic fertilizers;
- impact of pests;
- nutritional value of vegetables, eating fruits and vegetables every day, the USDA food pyramid;
- sun and shade, the movement of the sun;
- measuring plant growth;
- preparing vegetables to eat.

▶ *Children learn to appreciate the beauty of the natural world.*

Some of the skills learned might include

- reading, writing labels for each plant;
- writing numbers (prices for selling plants to parents);
- planting;
- drawing, printing;
- preparing the soil;
- learning a harvest or spring dance, and learning about various Native American spring and harvest dances and songs;
- working together;
- listening to and reading books about plants and gardening;
- writing and illustrating journal entries about daily progress;
- determining when the vegetables are ready to pick;
- comparing market prices to the cost of growing food;
- creating a calendar of events and progress;
- graphing procedures (rainfall, the number of plants picked each day, and so on);
- creating posters advertising vegetables for sale;
- making a book about the project for the community, or writing and illustrating an article for the local paper;
- making a book about the project for younger children in the program.

The objective of an integrated approach is to teach the skills and content specified in the curriculum in a way that makes sense for the children, and through projects, activities, experiences, and challenges that are of interest to students.

The arts lend themselves naturally to an integrated approach to curriculum and instruction. The use of the arts also helps in integrating other content skills. Young children love to experiment with paint, glue, clay, wood, photography, printing images, and creating murals; they enjoy moving to music, making up dramas, simple role-playing, and learning folk dances; and they love to "make music." Thus, arts education benefits greatly from an integrated approach.

Art as a Means of Supporting the Basics

Many skills and dispositions children learn through the arts assist them in learning math, science, writing, reading, and social studies. There are too many to cover completely, but a few examples of using the arts to support learning the basics are outlined here.

Making learning meaningful. For many children, representing and processing their thoughts and experiences through art makes the learning process more meaningful to them, by enabling them to place what they learn within their own personal, family, and cultural experience (Engel, 1995).

Developing eye–hand coordination. Many art activities, from drawing, painting, and woodworking to holding a rhythm stick and clapping a castanet, develop fine muscles and the eye–hand coordination required in writing, using the computer, reading (tracking with the eyes), manipulating math materials, drawing maps for social studies, developing graphs, and other skills. Art activities also help the integration of the nerves, muscles, and various parts of the brain needed to perform academic activities.

Developing essential reading skills and spelling. All music activities teach skills related to reading: rhythm, rhyme, repetition, phrasing, auditory discrimination, phonemic patterning, learning to hear the sound structure of words and phrases, and more.

Learning cultural knowledge. In art activities, children learn everything from the names of colors, woodworking tools, musical instruments, and famous composers to the use of different dances for specific ceremonial occasions, names of artists and art styles, and knowledge of various cultures. For example, knowledge of classical music teaches about the world's religions, dance forms around the world, and how music forms like jazz influenced Western music.

Providing access to ways to learn the basics. For students who struggle with academics, the arts can provide a wonderful entry point. For some students it is easier to draw a picture of their trip to the zoo than to write about it; for others, creating a drama representing a historical event is much easier and more fulfilling than writing a paper on the event. Art allows these students a legitimate way to express what they have learned, plus an entry into learning the basics—for instance, the child who drew a picture of the zoo can be helped to write comments about her picture.

Keeping children in school. Few preschool and elementary-school children drop out, but much of what we do for children of this age lays the foundation for keeping them in school later on. Many believe that children who are actively engaged in extracurricular art activities are more likely to stay in school. The foundation for these dispositions is developed in early childhood.

Using enactive and iconic representation to learn the basics. I talked about these forms of memory in the previous section; enactive and iconic representation also assist students in learning the basics. Skip-rope routines, rap songs, clapping, chants, and other kinesthetic and rhythmic activities are used to teach multiplication tables, to spell words, and to develop other basic academic skills. Visual imagery works well for remembering important information and is much more powerful than rote memorization. Iconic thinking also assists in computer learning, since many processes are represented in icons. One of my graduate students used action research to show that basic multiplication facts can effectively be taught through various kinesthetic activities.

Providing a break from academics. All children need a break from intensive academic pursuits; young children, who are physically active, need constant change, and are still developing their ability to attend to important information (stay on task); they require lots of physical and artistic breaks throughout the day. Art activities enable children to concentrate on the basics.

Providing a connection to the child's culture and heritage. Art is one of the best ways children can develop a strong attachment to their cultural heritage—through stories, plays, visual symbols, music, dance, and creative activities that use tales, myths, and symbols of the culture, allowing children to bring their culture, family, and community into the school.

Arts versus Craft

After four years of studying the creative process of art development at Pennsylvania State University (the home of Victor Lowenfeld), I was suddenly thrown into my student-teaching experience in a suburban district of Pittsburgh, Pennsylvania. Every day I traveled to a group of elementary schools with my teacher-mentor—a friendly lady with a flock of little kids at home. We'd go from classroom to classroom, providing "art lessons." While some of these activities matched what I had been taught in my university art classes, much of it felt like a well-scripted dog-and-pony show.

Developmentally Appropriate Practice

Then Easter came, and my mentor presented a lesson that involved every child making an identical cute rabbit, with large ears attached with paper clips and a cotton-wool tail—precisely what I had been taught was totally inappropriate. I was so confused I did not know what to do, my relationship with my mentor deteriorated, and my carefully crafted GPA plummeted!

The essence of the arts as an education process is their creative element. And for this creativity to occur, the children must control the process: select the materials, choose the colors, decide on the technique, select the subject, and use their own internal standard to determine the aesthetics (Szyba, 1999). Any artistic endeavor in which an adult controls most of these activities is not a creative process.

Children need to be in charge of the artistic process because the very nature of making these decisions not only teaches them how to make decisions but develops a sense of confidence, a feeling of empowerment, a sense of accomplishment—"I made it"—and positive self-esteem. Further, when children make choices—even ones that don't work out—they learn about the world. A child who chooses to make something from a piece of wood, only to find that the wood splits each time she tries to nail it, learns a great deal. If a teacher, knowing this would happen, selected another material, the learning opportunity would never have occurred.

Recipe Art. Adult-prescribed and -controlled art activities are very common in many early childhood programs (Szyba, 1999). Reasons are that they are teacher-controlled (thus teachers feel comfortable), teachers tend to do what they did when they were young, teachers are often unclear themselves about the value of open-ended activities, and some teachers believe only a few gifted students are creative (Szyba, 1999). But maybe the main reasons for cute, recipe-oriented activities are that they are not messy and that they produce nice results that adults (parents and administrators) love to see. After all, some parents find it easier to feel proud of a cute cut-out Mickey Mouse attached to the fridge than a montage of paper, colors, and scribbles that seem meaningless.

The Place for Crafts. Every culture has a rich history of crafts, be they quilts, straw stars, prints made from wooden stencils, beautiful ceramic pots with stylized patterns, rugs decorated with ancient motifs, or dolls. The nature of these crafts—color, design, images, method of construction, materials—are all predetermined by cultural tradition. Thus they are not creative activities in the sense discussed here. Nevertheless, they do have a place in early childhood education (Wardle, 1999f). Craft activities are valid when (1) they are distinctively different from creative activities, and the children know it; (2) there is an abundance of open-ended creative opportunities in the curriculum; and (3) the crafts are culturally meaningful to the children who make them. For example, when I taught kindergarten children in a religious school, they sometimes copied and illustrated the religious and folk songs that are a central component of the Bruderhof culture (Wardle, 1999f). These children, however, also experienced a rich array of open-ended activities. Hmong children might learn Hmong embroidery; Amish children quilting, and Native American children from certain tribes sand-painting motifs and kachina-related crafts.

Coloring Books. Even coloring books have a place in young children's development—to help them master eye–hand coordination, develop fine motor skills, and prepare for handwriting activities. But since coloring books seem the favorite way many businesses, agencies, and community organizations communicate their message to children, there is no need to provide them in a program. Further, as we continue to move toward standards, tests, and uniform approaches to education, we must support every opportunity for children to engage in open-ended, creative activities (Szyba, 1999).

Technology and the Arts

A vast array of ways exist to use technology with the arts. And as technology advances and is affordable for more early childhood programs, additional uses will be discovered. The challenge is to use technology to enhance and enrich the artistic endeavors of children, and not as a substitute for them. Since computers are particularly good at reproducing visual images and eliminate the need for children to master the use of different materials and muscle control, the temptation that computers will replace concrete, hands-on activities in the visual arts is a particular concern. Computers can automatically reproduce a wealth of visual images—and if one is not careful, these images become the norm or standard, depriving children of their own creative genius. We should never get to the point that a child says, "I can't draw, so I'll use the computer to do it for me!" Further, as I have already discussed, the manipulation of concrete objects and materials that occurs when children engage in the creative process is crucial to their overall development—intellectual, emotional, physical, and social. Nevertheless, there are numerous ways technology can enhance the creative process; it can, for instance,

- combine original artwork, text, and formatting to make books, individual journals, brochures, greeting cards, announcements, and labels;
- be used to conduct research on artists, musicians, composers, playwrights, artistic and musical movements, and influences in society;
- provide labels for art exhibits, playbills for drama and dance activities, and announcements for exhibitions and performances;
- scan a variety of children's original art to store for later use in projects and portfolios, or display in parent conferences;
- be used to download masterpieces and classical music to match the curriculum or enhance a **teachable moment** with a child—for example, "Wow, that picture of yours reminds me of a Diego Rivera painting. Do you know his work? Let's see if we can find some on the computer";
- provide creative opportunities for children whose disabilities keep them from holding a brush, standing by the easel, or doing a dance. There are also programs that allow children with other disabilities—say, ADHD and cerebral palsy—to engage in the joys and benefits of artistic expression;
- facilitate the creation of books, newspaper articles, reports, and studies: students can take digital photos and make audio recordings in the community, and then combine them with texts to make different products;
- be used to store digital video that records dances, field trips, and other activities, which can later be viewed by parents at a parent night or during parent conferences;
- assist children in creating films, from simply recording basic drama activities to writing scripts, developing costumes, and creating an entire film;

- create PowerPoint presentations that include original art, poetry, 3-D structures, and more;
- help children learn animation by using animation software;
- help the class develop a musical slide show using original art and original music;
- be used to download a variety of music—classical, folk songs, oldies, contemporary, gospel—for use in creative dance activities;
- enable creation of a mural over a time period: children develop art images and then store them in the computer; when enough are collected, the photos are downloaded to create a huge wall mural.

The possibilities are endless! The limitations are having the equipment—computers, printers, software, cameras, recorders, and scanners—and the knowledge of the teachers—or student experts.

Open and Closed Activities for Preschoolers

Closed Activity	**Open Activity**
Clay	
"Use the clay I gave you to make frogs."	"What does the clay feel like? What can you make with it? Take a try and see what you can make."
Coloring	
"Color the people in the picture."	"Here are some crayons and paper. Choose any color you wish. Experiment with making different marks with the crayon—the side, tip, edge—also with mixing different colors. Make a picture of something from our field trip to the zoo."
Collage	
"Here are some pieces of construction paper cut to make a flower. Use the model I made to make your own flower, by pasting it onto the white paper I gave you.	"Here are some pieces of different-colored paper, some glue, and a sheet of white paper. Create some pictures by cutting the papers and pasting them onto the white paper I gave you."
Painting	
"Paint a nice picture of a car for a Father's Day card."	"Use these different colors to paint with. What size paper would you like—and what kind of brushes?"
Cutting	
"Here are some shapes on construction paper. Cut out the shapes and paste them on the piece of paper."	"Here are some magazines with animals, a piece of paper, and glue. Pick the animals you like, cut them out, and then glue them on the paper to create a picture. You can add a background with crayons or paint."

The Visual Arts

Stages of Art Development

As children develop through physical, cognitive, and social-emotional stages, they also progress through specific art stages. These stages are a function of both their overall development and their increased experience with various art-related materials, instruments, and opportunities. The art sequence is invariant: it follows the same progression for each child. Individual differences exist, however, regarding the age a child enters a stage, based on the individual's maturity and exposure to artistic activities. The following summary is based on C. Cherry, *Creative Art for the Developing Child* (1972).

Scribble Stage (Ages 1–3). Young children begin their artistic expression by experimenting with producing images on paper. They progress through distinct stages, until they can represent their unique view of the world.

Figure 11.1

Stages in Art Development

Scribble stage

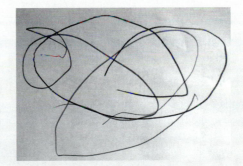

Basic forms

Later pictorial stage

Basic Scribbles. During this stage children make random marks on paper (or other surface) with anything that makes a mark. Children will hold the marker in a variety of ways, and the result is unorganized and uncontrolled, because they have not actually developed the skills to control and direct the marker. Children love the feeling of pushing the instrument around and leaving an image on the paper. The shapes that result are created by the children's muscle movements.

Controlled Scribbles. These scribbles result from children's realization that they can, in fact, influence the scribbles they are making: that what they do and the resultant images are connected. This is a wonderful realization on their part! Thus, children at this stage make the same images time and again, proving to themselves this connection. The images are those that are the easiest for a child to make at this developmental age: circles, zigzags, and lots of lines.

Basic Forms (Ages 3–4). As children's eye–hand coordination and muscle control improve, they begin to create more controlled shapes and lines. They also have a greater sense of intention.

Early Basic Form Stage. Children now create pictures with lots of basic shapes in them, deliberately directing the process. The shapes of this stage are circles, ovals, and arcs or rainbows (because this is the movement that is easiest to make with the whole arm). Pictures appear more organized than before.

Developmental Continuum in Children's Drawings

B. Engel (1995) has created a developmental continuum that progresses into the primary years, outlined here.

Preschoolers (Ages 2–5). Scribbles—often off the edges of the paper. Changes forms or shapes. Experiments with different effects—color, motions—to see what happens. Art reflects the motion of the hand and arm. Makes circlelike shapes, combined straight and curved lines. First schematic images.

Early Primary-School Children (Ages 4–6). Combines shapes to create pictures of things. Has favorite images to draw. Begins representing things—usually people. Creates basic shapes—houses, boats, letterlike forms. Subjects become more literal (what children see in their environment). Begins to develop an individual style. Each image is separate—not related to others. The size and detail of an image is based on its emotional significance. Uses the same concept, or prototype, to draw similar objects—all four-legged animals, all birds, all people—then adds details.

Middle Primary-School Children (Ages 5–8). Repeats the same image a great deal. Details of pictures often stereotypical—houses with chimneys and smoke, girls with dresses and long hair. Uses images to create narratives and illustrate ideas. Often a different baseline is used on the same picture; figures never overlap, houses are see-though. Moving toward diversity within types—different flowers, buildings, cars. Has favorite subjects, and will add props to figures to designate roles—farmer, bus driver, policeman. Moving toward more naturalistic colors.

Later Basic Form Stage. To the forms already discussed, children add shapes that involve straight lines: squares, rectangles, circles with lines through them, and so on.

Pictorial Stage (Ages 4–5). Preschoolers can now use their skill in drawing basic forms to create pictures that represent familiar objects—people, houses, cars, and so on.

Early Pictorial Stage. During the pictorial stage, children might also make pictures of things they want to see or experience. These pictures are drawn very quickly, and usually in isolation. Thus the objects drawn don't relate to one another—each is a different size and may be drawn differently, as children continue experimenting with different ways to create images that represent what they know.

Later Pictorial Stage. Children eventually move on to having created a symbolized form for each object—tree, person, house, and so on. Each looks just like the others of the same type (though sizes may differ). Now the entire picture is organized, the objects relate to one another, and an entire idea is presented—family, zoo, farm, construction site, house. At this stage, however, the sizes of objects are not proportional, because for children this age size is based on emotional importance. Thus people are usually the biggest objects in the picture, and the child the biggest of all.

Teaching Art

The secret to teaching art is to encourage, support, and scaffold art activities without imposing an adult judgment on the child's artistic expression. To an extent, we adults are obsessed with the art product, while the child should focus on the art process. The added challenge, of course, is that many teachers don't feel they are artistic or creative. To teach art effectively, we must address all these issues, always providing an environment that is conducive to the creative process—open-ended, lots of materials and choices—and messy!

Setting up the Environment. In Chapter 5, I discussed at length appropriate environments for encouraging art activities. The art activity should occur near a water source, plastic should be placed on a floor that isn't concrete or tile, children need to wear smocks, and the activity should not be close to other materials and equipment that could get damaged. Many art activities work best outside, or in a transition area between the inside and the outside. Another requirement is to have easy access to all the materials needed for the particular activity. You don't want a child wandering across the classroom with a brush dripping with red paint because she needs to find another piece of paper. And the children need a place to put their completed work to dry.

For preschool-age children, an art center should always be available. Materials, projects, ideas, and models in the center should be rotated on a regular basis. When older children have a choice of activities, art should always be an option, and a variety of art materials should also be easily accessible whenever children are working on projects.

▶ *There are lots of opportunities to engage in art activities outside.*

Training and Support of Staff. As with other creative endeavors, most of our staff don't feel they are visual artists. Teachers need ongoing training to help them find the "artist within," and to allow them to experiment with new, open-ended approaches and techniques. Regular art training also communicates to staff that the program or school considers art of equal importance to subjects such as literacy, math, and science. Artists on the program's staff should be supported and encouraged, be they photographers, sculptors, water colorists, oil painters, pastel artists, woodworkers, illustrators, or others, by displaying their work and using them to teach their art. These artists model to the children the value of using their artistic talents as a form of expression. The Reggio Emilia model embraces the role of an artist in the early childhood curriculum.

Encouraging the Development of Art in Children. Children are naturally disposed to engage in the artistic experience: they love to experiment, make things, try out new ideas, create a mess, and design new shapes, colors, textures, and patterns; most of all they like to see how they can change and affect their environment. As soon as children can enjoy finger painting, making handprints and footprints on butcher paper, and scribbling with crayons and chalk, we should provide a range of art experiences for them to explore on a regular basis. Below are just a few ideas to help teachers nurture this process in young children.

Understand that art activities are, by definition, messy. Because the art process involves pushing the limits, trying new materials, experimenting with approaches, and stretching the rules of physical laws, a mess usually results—certainly more so than with activities like reading a book or filling out a work sheet. This is the price we must pay for encouraging such a worthwhile activity.

Emphasize the process, not the product. Art is about doing things—with materials, ideas, emotions, and dreams. For young children, the product is always secondary. Art activities that have no product include mixing food coloring, water, and salad oil in a water table; drawing with colored chalk on a sidewalk, and then pouring water on the drawing to create interesting patterns; and use of a prism to create light combinations on a wall.

Encourage creativity by providing supersize materials—including large brushes, large chalks, big pieces of paper, and large sidewalks to draw on. A child who is more concerned with staying on a small piece of paper, or within the lines, will not be very creative. Also, all children need enough time to finish their activities. One of the realities of art experiences is that they cannot be bounded by time.

Find ways to encourage three-dimensional art. As adults, we tend to be focused on flat art; but children need all sorts of opportunities with 3-D art materials: wood, clay, play dough (made of flour and salt), wood-scrap sculpture, tongue depressors, stones glued together, cardboard tubes and boxes to make big sculptures, plaster of paris, papier-mâché, and so on.

Provide lots of art materials and choices: paint on the easel, felt pens, crayons, chalk, shapes to trace around, various print stencils and pads, glue, yarn, construction paper, carpet scraps, wallpaper samples, shiny and textured paper, wood shavings, pastels, and more. Also provide a balance of activities, from ones that require fine motor skills, such as painting and drawing, to activities that involve larger movements, using mural paper, collage, painting on a wall or fence in the playground, or tie-dyeing. As children become more sophisticated and skilled with various media, expose them to more challenging techniques: collages, photography, making transparencies, computer graphics, watercolors, acrylics.

If children want to tell you about their art, be all ears. But don't expect them to do so, and don't expect the art to look like anything conventional, though it usually looks like something very important to the child!

Put up examples of children's work throughout the center, including the boardroom. When I taught at the Bruderhof religious school, I saw children's work in the toy factory, offices, corridors, laundry room, principal's office, and maintenance shop. Use student images in newsletters and parent information pamphlets; present regular art shows; join with other programs to find ways to acknowledge and support the arts. An art festival on the outside playground can be great fun. Also, display examples of well-known artists' work, representing a variety of cultures. The art should be of high quality, present a range of styles and periods, and connect with the children and families in the programs. Expose children to aboriginal paintings, religious icons, the great Mexican muralists, African American quilts, Pueblo kachinas and silver jewelry, the baroque churches of Brazil, and Caribbean art. I recently visited the campus of an early childhood program in Southern California that displayed beautiful, nicely framed photos of Amish children; unfortunately, the children attending the program were from Mexico.

Emphasize that everyone can be an artist. This is particularly important for students who have a disability. All children can find ways to express themselves artistically.

Provide art activities that minimize adult control and involvement. Many projects must be set up and initiated by the teacher, but then children should be able to assume full control. Also, avoid activities that are highly predetermined, require adult judgment, or use an adult standard to define success: coloring books, kits, craft activities, following the teacher's model.

Integrate art into all other learning centers, and integrate all other learning centers into art. Make covers for journals, paint a picture to music, make puppets to go with a script that illustrates a story, use the woodworking bench to create kites for a science project.

Don't use art as a reward or as punishment. Never, ever, withhold children's art activity because they have not finished their academic work, or because they are disruptive. Often the children who benefit most from art are the those who struggle with traditional academic activities and have problems conforming to behavioral expectations, so punishing children in this way will give them the message that what they enjoy and are good at is not important.

Art Projects. Children's art experiences during the early childhood years involve primarily personal experimentation and expression. Even so, group projects and direct teacher instruction should also be included—especially for elementary-school students. Many cultures, especially non-Western ones, engage in a variety of collective art endeavors. Find ways to create classroom, program, and even citywide projects. Wall-size murals on butcher paper, daily wall newspapers with illustrations, a photo mural of everyone's family, an intricate sidewalk or wall display of patterns and symbols, a large quilt, and a tabletop papier-mâché model that portrays the setting of the book being read in class are some examples. Invite teachers, visiting parents, visiting artists, and students from nearby art schools regularly to introduce students to new techniques, materials, approaches, and methods. Students should be given lots of opportunities after the lesson to explore the technique, and to find unique ways to apply it.

Woodworking

Woodworking activities are wonderful for children aged 3 through 8, because they provide a variety of opportunities children enjoy and need. Starting with the toddler gaily banging away on kitchen pots and pans, young children thrill at making a noise by hitting something. With woodworking, they also learn that this hammering can have a purpose. And young children delight in mastering their rapidly developing muscles, fine motor development, eye–hand coordination, and integration of senses, muscles, and nerves. Early childhood educators often stress the value of teaching the whole child, yet we often provide limited opportunities for this to occur. Woodworking develops the whole child: creativity, learning new skills (nailing, sawing, drilling, smoothing wood with a sure form and sandpaper), mastery, development of self-esteem, fine motor skills, and meaningful learning.

And children this age love to make things. Once they have fully explored the processes of banging nails, sawing, drilling, and smoothing wood, they will want to make something. Woodworking is a basic constructive play activity. By integrating this newfound knowledge to create something, children develop a great sense of accomplishment.

Setting up the Woodworking Center. Woodworking makes noise, so it needs to be set up away from quiet activities or used only during certain times—such as free-choice time. Woodworking activities work well in indoor–outdoor transition areas and covered outdoor spaces. Otherwise, a corner of the room near other noisy activities, and bordered by dividers or a hallway, works (Huber, 1999).

While a large tree trunk works well when children are practicing nailing, eventually a solid workbench, with a vise, is needed. The workbench should be placed on a flat surface, and should be the height of a child's waist. There is nothing more frustrating than trying to nail on a table that bounces around. Tables that are not built for woodworking don't work. Basic

▶ *Young children love woodwork.*

tools include hammers, C-clamps (4-inch and 6-inch), 14-inch crosscut saws, Sure Forms, a hand drill (with bits), a trisquare, rulers and measuring tapes, Phillips and regular screwdrivers, pliers, rough sandpaper, and eye goggles. Later a brace and bit (large drill), coping saw, backsaw, and keyhole saw can be added. School equipment companies provide kits, or you can go to the hardware store and assemble your own. They should be real tools, not toys, but small and fairly light. Older elementary-school children—especially in school-age programs—can begin to use electric drills, screwdrivers, and sanders. A toolbox cabinet nearby is required. Silhouettes painted on the cabinet in the shape of each tool make it easy for students to return the tools.

Nails, screws, and a collection of hardware (eye-hooks, casters, bolts, hinges, and so on) should be stored within reach, in cans, plastic containers, or wooden crates (but not glass). Tape a sample of the item to each container. Use nails with big heads (roofing, box, and wire), long enough that a child can hold them between thumb and finger, but not so long that they bend easily when hammered. Additionally, provide lots of other materials—yarn and string, dowels (from ¼-inch to 2 inches, for masts, axels, flagpoles, and, when cut in thin sections, for wheels), Elmer's glue, wood staples, lids, 35-mm film container lids (make great wheels), bottle caps, and more.

Wood should be selected carefully. While new wood should be used, in many cases it can be obtained free. When I was a Head Start director, I enjoyed regular visits to the local lumberyard, where I carefully selected scrap wood for my classrooms. Occasionally I would purchase wooden dowels and a few pieces of clean 1-inch pine. These regular visits established a great relationship between our program and the local business. The best woods to use are white pine (2 × 4, 2 × 2, and 1-inch boards), redwood and cedar scraps, and other soft pine. Sections of plywood and Masonite (fiberboard) provide nice flat surfaces, and dowels and scraps from custom projects add variety. Do not use splintered wood, treated (CCA) lumber, hardwoods, or wood with nails in it. Store wood in baskets, boxes, or bins near the workbench.

Teaching Teachers. Teachers who don't know how to do woodworking won't be very helpful teaching children. While parents can come in and help students, it's also good if each teacher is familiar with woodworking. Maybe a parent or someone from the board can provide a staff training session. In my program we devoted half a training day for me to instruct our teachers—all of whom were women. They made whatever they wanted to, and in so doing learned basic carpentry skills. They became comfortable and confident working at the workbench.

Teaching Woodworking. When woodwork is introduced, allow children to simply enjoy the process—banging in and pulling out nails, cutting wood, drilling holes with different-size drill bits, sorting the pieces of scrap wood, and sanding a piece of wood. Next, children like to attach pieces of wood together, and to nail, screw, or glue things to a piece of wood. They will try all sorts of ways to do this. Finally, once children have come this far, they will try to make things—first very simple, later more complex.

Children as young as age 3 enjoy sorting different sizes of wood, returning nails to their correct containers, banging in nails, and making wood sculptures by gluing scraps of wood together, and then painting their artwork. They also love exploring the physical properties of wood—the smell, feel, and appearance. Older children will soon go beyond these activities, and learn how to use each tool correctly. Introduce one tool at

▶ *It is important that tools are stored carefully next to the work bench.*

a time; don't introduce another until the child is proficient with the first. Once children begin to make things, their imagination is their only limit: boats, cars, flags, houses, boxes, games, artistic items, animals, birdhouses, and bird feeders. Encourage children to take what they have made to other areas in the classroom: the block area, sand table, housekeeping area, and so on. They can make all sorts of sand toys, a variety of boats to float in a nearby puddle or little pond in the playground, and a variety of objects and instruments for science experiments and nature activities.

Multicultural Visual Arts

Since all cultures express their deepest beliefs and values through art, the visual arts are an obvious place to imbue the curriculum with diversity. While programs must be careful not to create a tourist approach to diversity (addressed in Chapter 6), they should capitalize on ways to use rich multicultural art throughout the program.

Safety Tips for Woodworking

- No more than two students should work at the workbench at one time.
- Provide enough tools for each student doing woodworking.
- Make sure the workbench is secure and steady: it must not rock or bounce.
- Provide constant adult supervision.
- Keep the workbench surface clear of tools, wood, nails, and other supplies that are not being used.
- When a child is drilling or sawing, the piece of wood must be secured in the vise or with a C-clamp.
- Children working at the bench should be totally concentrating on what they are doing— remove a child who is tired, distracted, fooling around, frustrated, or fighting.
- Use eye goggles.
- Have a well-equipped first aid kit on hand.
- Make sure tools are only used appropriately (don't use hammers to break stones, saws to cut apples, and so on).

Art in the Center. Because art expresses deep personal feelings, each of us has developed our own tastes and preferences, which are reflected in the art we select for our homes, as well as the center, classroom, boardroom, and training area. Artwork displayed throughout the center should include three general categories: children's own work; work representing the cultural backgrounds of all the families represented in the program—not just the majority; and a rich diversity of other cultural art—fine arts, folk art, and crafts, rugs, pottery, wood carvings, quilts, and more.

Multicultural Fine Arts. There are two ways to represent a multicultural perspective through fine art: work by individual artists from diverse cultural backgrounds; and Western art that has been influenced by other cultures. Examples of the former are the powerful art of the wonderful Mexican artist Diego Rivera and the exquisite women of Navajo artist R. C. Gorman; an example of the

▶ *One of Diego Rivera's famous murals in Mexico City.*

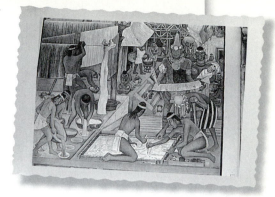

latter, the influence of African art on Picasso and other cubists and modern artists. Both types of art should be in ample evidence in the programs—in books about famous artists and their work, pictures and posters on the walls, and curricular activities about artists and artistic styles and periods.

Art Visitors. When I worked at the Greeley Head Start Program, we arranged for Native American artists and performers to visit the program. The group included a storyteller, an Aztec dance group, a mother-and-child weaving pair from Guatemala, and a group of Guatemalan marimba players. The storyteller spun his tales to the children by a fire in a tepee, the weavers demonstrated in one classroom, while the marimba players played in another, and the dancers gave a performance for everyone. We brought students and parents from all our centers to enjoy the visiting group. The children loved this approach because the activities were geared to their level, included opportunities for hands-on child involvement (weaving, telling their own story about an animal, playing the marimba, and attempting a few dance steps; Wardle, 1976).

Bringing art to the program is one of the best ways to expose children to multicultural art, because a community can provide a much wider variety of cultural knowledge and performance than any program can. Artists, dancers, photographers, musicians, weavers, ceramicists, piñata makers, poets, oral historians, and others should visit the center on a regular basis.

Music and Movement

Music and movement have always been synonymous with early childhood education. And for good reason. Here we discuss the value of music and movement for young children, describe the various approaches to teaching music by several well-known music educators, discuss the role of singing in early childhood programs, and explore several approaches to movement education including folk dance.

New Research

Ironically, as standards, accountability, and an increased academic focus take control of our early childhood programs, current research indicates a need for music and movement activities for young children. One source of this research is the new data we have on brain development; the other is mounting evidence that many young children today are not receiving opportunities needed to support healthy and developmentally appropriate physical growth and integration (Weikart, 1998). To address these two areas, early childhood programs must provide high-quality, consistent, well-developed

▶ *Music activities provide a foundation for reading and language skills.*

music and movement programs for all children, from infancy through elementary-school age.

Brain Research. During the first ten years of life, children are developing the basic hardwiring of their brains. After age 10, the pruning of this wiring occurs (Schiller, 1998). To support the development of this extensive neural network, we need to provide numerous ways to help children develop connections, patterns, and relations between information, and give children many opportunities to create connections between what they already know and what they are learning. We know many of the factors that increase learning—many of which are developed through music and movement activities—including the following (Schiller, 1998):

- *We remember things that have a strong emotional meaning to us.* Since music and dance involve the affective domain, they are emotionally meaningful.
- *The more ways we can connect new information to what we already know, the better.* Enhancing new concepts through dance, movement, and repetitive patterns and sequences is a great way to increase these connections.
- *We learn best within meaningful contexts.* One of the best ways to create meaningful contexts is to start with the whole and work to the parts. Music and movement can be contexts for basic knowledge, vocabulary, historical events (songs of the Revolution, freedom songs of the slaves), time, math, science (weather, seasons, life cycles), and other curricular areas.
- *Revisiting information often increases learning.* The structure of music and dance is based on repetition—rhythms, phrases, melodies, instrumental solos and full orchestra reply, patterns with tempo, and changes in emotions. Children learn to anticipate these repetitions.

According to Schiller (1998), there are specific music and movement activities that strengthen brain wiring:

- *Sequencing.* This means activities that establish order—first, second, last, and so on.
- *Patterning.* This includes routines, life cycles, ABAB structures of music, and so on. Clearly music and dance contain lots of patterning.
- *Sensory experiences.* Ninety-five percent of incoming information to the brain is from seeing, hearing, and touching. Music and dance clearly involve hearing and touching.
- *Cause and effect.* Children need to find the relationships between cause and effect, and be exposed to other examples that have similar patterns of cause and effect. Why does dancing exhilarate and tire at the same time? What other activities cause these same responses? What about the relation between

the mood created by the music and the dance movements you create? How does the music tempo affect the way you feel?

The new brain research has reaffirmed what traditional early childhood professionals have always known—that high-quality early childhood experiences focusing on whole-child activities and connections between different domains are crucial to the success of all children.

Lack of Adequate Motor Development Opportunities. Some recent studies indicate that many young children entering our schools have not gained the basic motor skills that children of the same age used to possess. Specifically, more and more young children seem to have particular difficulty with purposeful movement and steady beat independence. It appears these problems are due to a combination of factors, including too much sedentary TV watching, too much time on computers at the expense of active play, lack of space for outdoor playgrounds, and "fear of stranger" attitudes leading to overly adult-controlled programs for children (Weikart, 1998). Poor diets appear to contribute to the problem.

Purposeful movement is movement undertaken with conscious thought and intent, which gives children a sense of control and awareness. Programs need to help children describe what they are doing, and then plan ahead: "That dance was fun—I jumped so high, and then bent down so low. Next time I am going to make movements like I am a snake."

Steady beat timing is being able to keep an independent steady beat. Steady beat is important because it helps children develop inner control, enables them to develop coordinated physical competence, and teaches children how to match their inner rhythms to external sources—drumbeats, music and dance tempos, the rhythm of languages, and more. Steady beat timing is an essential skill young children need to develop. Research has constantly shown a positive correlation between the acquisition of steady beat independence and attention span, on-task behavior, and math and reading performance (Weikart, 1998). Thus, early childhood programs need to provide regular opportunities for young children to develop steady beat independence. Weikart (1998) suggests some ideas for doing this:

- lots of opportunities to hear rhythms, songs, and music in which children can hear the beat;
- rocking infants to a lullaby, having a toddler walk on an adult's feet while the adult speaks in rhythm or sings, walking with an infant and singing to the rhythm of the walk;
- opportunities to pat, clap, stamp, and engage in full-movement beat activities;
- skip-rope activities;
- reciting poetry, chants, and raps;
- opportunities to bounce and dribble a variety of balls, from jacks and Ping-Pong balls to basketballs;
- singing lots of simple songs;
- using clapping, stamping, jumping, and dance activities to keep time to music.

"Daily music experiences in child care (and school) can make many valuable connections to our children's language capabilities, memory, physical activity, creative thinking, emotional stability, discipline, and emerging academic success. As brain research begins to support the importance of learning through music, we must continue to find useful ways to make the gifts music provides essential in our daily routines" (Carlton, 2000, p. 56).

Music Educators

Since the late 1800s, music education has been the focus of several prominent educators and composers. While none of these methods of teaching music to young children originated in this country, they have, and continue to have, a profound impact on the way we include music in early childhood programs. No doubt you may have heard of some of these approaches; some of you may be currently teaching one.

Émile Jaques-Dalcroze. Émile Jaques-Dalcroze was a Swiss music educator who lived from 1865 to 1950. Initially, he worked with adult performers, whom he believed should develop their technique and their musical faculties. He developed exercises in which students would combine singing and keeping beat to the music, thus creating movement education. He later adapted his approach for children, and started programs to teach teachers in 1906. Still later he further refined these methods to work with children with disabilities—especially blind students. His method was brought to America in 1913.

The basis of the Dalcroze method is eurythmics, though it also includes ear training (learning to sing by ear) and improvisation (improvising on the piano). **Eurythmics** is a whole-body physical response to music, and focuses on the rhythmic understanding of music through running, skipping, jumping, and moving the arms. For example, one exercise has children march around the room, beating in time with the music with their arms while stepping with their feet to the time value of each note (Mark, 1996). These activities become very complex, involving being on the beat with the feet and off-beat (syncopation) with the arms.

Children as young as age 4 move around the room to the music, freeze when the music stops, speed up to faster music, and then become more graceful with arms and feet to flowing music. The music and body movements are integrated together, as a way to combine the intellect and the emotions. When I was a preschooler, my school used a radio program called *Music and Movement*, based on many of these activities.

Carl Orff's Schulwerk. Carl Orff (1885–1982) was a famous German composer who wrote a considerable body of work, including a humorous opera, *The Moon*, which includes a "snoring chorus." Today his *Carmina Burana* is by far his best-known work. Not surprisingly, since his compositions stress rhythmic complexities and variety, Orff believes rhythm to be the fundamental musical element, and the basis for melody. His approach to music education, called Schulwerk (schoolwork), is described in a five-volume set he published between 1950 and 1954. Orff believed the development of music education should follow the development of music in history (what we call a **recapitulation theory**). He believed that rhythm should evolve from dance movements, and melody from speech rhythms. He based these original rhythms on patterns children already know—their speech, games, chants, and vocal sounds.

Based on his belief in rhythm, Orff recognized the need for a variety of percussion instruments for children, and developed a series of child-size instruments, including xylophones, glockenspiels, drums, cymbals, wood blocks, rattles, and lutes. Schulwerk provides a variety of activities in which children use the instruments, including improvisation—inventing their own rhythms, melodies, and accompaniment. Melody is built onto rhythm, and the first melodies are chants of children's names and familiar words to simple tunes. Melodies then become more intricate and sophisticated, emphasizing repetition, chorus–solo–chorus structure, and canons (rounds).

In 1967 the first International Symposium of Orff-Schulwerk was held in California. The Orff approach has also been adapted for music therapy. Today, fifty-three colleges in this country provide approved Orff-Schulwerk music-education classes.

Zoltán Kodály. Zoltán Kodály, also a famous classical music composer, was born in Hungary in 1882, and was a contemporary of Béla Bartók. Both were committed to the collection and preservation of the national folk music of Hungary. To this end they collected a body of authentic music. Kodály believed that his beloved music would survive only if it became part of the public-school curriculum. Since much of his own music is based on Hungarian folk songs, it is no surprise that his approach to music education stresses the folk song. The Kodály method starts with 3-year-olds learning a variety of folk songs by singing, clapping, and moving to the rhythms of the songs. Hungarian folk melodies contain no half-notes (from the chromatic scale), only whole intervals. When Kodály's approach was adapted for this country, it was discovered that many of our folk songs, especially those of African Americans and from Appalachia, use this same whole-note scale structure. Kodály developed a series of hand gestures to represent both the rhythm of the music and the notes. Each note has a different hand sign, thus helping children to learn to read music by translating sounds into body motions. All children who use the Kodály method learn to read music. Musical instruments, usually the recorder, are introduced after vocal skills have been developed.

The Kodály method was brought to the United States in 1968 by several of his students, who adapted the approach for American students. The Organization of American Kodály Educators was established in 1974, and today several U.S. colleges grant a Kodály teacher certificate.

Suzuki Talent Education. Born in 1898 in Japan, Shinichi Suzuki was the son of a violin factory owner. He developed his approach, called Talent Education, to help his son learn to play the violin. He called the method he developed the mother-tongue method, because he believed that learning to play the violin should follow the same approach all children use to learn their own language—their mother tongue. Thus he developed a method that uses observation, imitation, repetition, and a gradual development of musical awareness.

Talent Education begins in infancy, when children listen to lots of recorded music. At age 3, children start learning the violin (adapted for their size) by rote and imitating the playing of their teachers and advanced students. Children learn to play melodies by rote, and progress through the same sequence of songs, exercises, and musical material. Techniques are introduced as they become necessary to play the music. Children learn individually, and active parent involvement is crucial—including attending each lesson and supporting practice. Special musical recordings accompany the first several volumes of exercises, serving as a model for tonality and expression. Even when a child begins to read music—after two years of exercises—rote learning and repetition are continued. For Suzuki, it is essential for the students continually to hear music performed in tune, and to be aware of good intonation.

All Suzuki students play the same material, which makes festivals very easy to arrange. At performances the most advanced students play first, then each progressively less skilled group joins in, as everyone plays more and more simple music. Talent Education was introduced into the United States in 1958. A number of private Talent Education schools have been established, and some public schools now use the method. Talent Education has been adapted for cello, piano, flute, harp, guitar, and double bass.

Teaching Music in Early Childhood Programs

Clearly the new brain research provides a strong rationale for teaching music to young children. But even before we had this research, there were many advocates for teaching music in our early childhood programs. Some further arguments for the inclusion of music are that music develops listening skills and helps develop auditory discrimination (vital both in learning to talk and in learning to read and write); children respond very favorably and intuitively to music, and thus it should be part of their early experiences; music creates strings of memory—songs, melodies, and recurring themes that are great vehicles to attach to new things we want to remember, like the alphabet; music helps children speak clearly and pay attention (through use of a steady beat); it makes classroom transitions easier; it helps develop social skills and problem-solving skills (games, dances, and so on); and, finally, it provides an introduction to basic musical knowledge—instruments, tone, pitch, forms of music, and more (Carlton, 2000).

Developmental Milestones. As I described in the discussion of typical development in Chapter 9, newborns have good hearing ability. They turn to sounds they like and respond to loud, angry, or high-pitched sounds. There are other music-related developmental milestones (Gordh, 1996):

- *Ages 2–3.* Children love upbeat rhythms and simple movement, playing with percussion instruments, and experimenting with sounds—including their favorite pots and pans! Children ages 2 and 3 need variety, including time to relax.
- *Ages 3–4.* At this age, children can march and play instruments at the same time, understand loud versus soft, fast versus slow, and high versus low pitch. They enjoy using instruments and voices to accompany music, live and recorded.
- *Ages 4–5.* Preschoolers like to combine chants with movement, can repeat various rhythmic patterns, and can keep time to music with clapping, tapping, stamping, and so on.
- *Ages 5–8.* This is the ideal time to learn simple folk dances, and the time to start learning an instrument. School-age children understand repeat sequences of songs and dances—choruses, verses—can sing rounds ("Row, Row, Row Your Boat"), and begin to learn music that has parts (at the end of this age range).

Listening. A central purpose of including music in a curriculum is to develop good listening skills, and to help children discriminate a whole range of sound fluctuations—high–low, long–short, loud–soft, sharp–soothing, repetitive–one long sound, and others. When I taught my kindergarten class, we developed a tape recording of familiar sounds we experienced on our walks and daily routines—a truck speeding along the highway next to the program, chickens being fed by the students, rain dripping in a gutter, and a child's father using an electric ratchet in the toy shop. We then played the tape back in the classroom to see which sounds we could recognize. There are lots of opportunities to listen to the "music" in the environment. The weather is one instance—the rustling of the wind in the leaves, thunder, rain pinging on a metal surface, and birds screeching at each other. As children and teachers listen to sounds and music, teachers should help children describe the sounds: "Boy, that was loud," "That sound is so high I can barely hear it," "I love the dance because it's so fast," and "This music makes me feel sad."

Percussion Instruments. The first instruments children use are ones that let them pound out the beat of the music. But first, let them use their bodies as instruments— lightly hitting their thighs, arms, and tummies; stamping; clapping; and snapping their fingers (Smith, 2000). Then, before introducing "real" instruments, see what ideas they might have for the use of common objects to accompany music, such as two pieces of wood, a dowel and a cardboard box, a dried gourd (maraca), a baby rattle, or a piece of wood and sandpaper. Real percussive instruments that young children love include drums, rhythm sticks, shakers, jingle bells, tambourines, blocks, triangles, and a resonator bar (Smith, 2000).

Any music that provides a clear beat and changes tempo often works well for children to play along to. Dance music is particularly appropriate—folk dances, ballets, and dance sections in symphonies.

Singing

My favorite memories of my early childhood experience on a farm in Shropshire, England, are singing songs. Every year I would excitedly anticipate spring because then we would sing my favorite spring songs from around the world. I also enjoyed singing about the harvest, the storms of winter, and the pleasures of summer. But I liked the spring songs the best—about lambs in the fields, ducks on the pond, primroses opening by the swiftly flowing stream, and sweet-smelling apple blossoms. I think I enjoyed these songs the most because for me they captured what I enjoyed about spring—new growth, new colors and smells, exciting anticipation, and the peace of the countryside. I learned lots of new words from these songs, such as *garrulous* (ducks), *emerald* (green), *slender* (daffodils), *twilight*, *swiftly* (stream), *bloom*, *cocoon* (caterpillar), and *fragrance*, not to mention some German, French, and Spanish words.

One year the kindergarten and preschool class I taught presented a Posada to the whole community. (A Posada is a traditional Hispanic Christmas activity.) All of the songs the children sang as they followed Mary and Joseph to look for a place to stay, and when they celebrated with a traditional piñata, were in Spanish. They delighted in singing songs from around the Americas—the United States, Mexico, Colombia, and Paraguay.

"I can only think of music as something in every human being—a birthright. Music coordinates mind, body and spirit . . . the greatest service to any society would be if every school day began with singing" (Yehudi Menuhin, as quoted in Swinger, 1999). All young children love to sing; all cultures have a special place for their lullabies. Like visual arts, there is a tendency to think only certain children can sing, but that's not true. And every teacher can sing as well.

The Value of Singing. Including singing in the early childhood curriculum teaches many of the skills and concepts discussed under the value of teaching music. Additionally, teaching songs helps children remember; develops in children a sense of patterning, phrasing, and the repetition of language; teaches children to sing tunefully; provides for meaningful learning; and is simply enjoyable to children. When children learn to sing together, and engage in call-and-response singing, they are learning social skills. And learning a variety of songs teaches both cultural knowledge and information about a variety of subjects and phenomena—weather, seasons, colors and shapes, emotions, and moral values.

Singing with Babies and Toddlers. In an article in *Scholastic Early Childhood Today*, Alice Honig provides ideas for singing with infants and toddlers (2000). Here are some of her suggestions. Newborn babies are soothed if you hold them and sing cradle songs, which are rich in soothing melodies and words. At 3 weeks of age, infants respond to the human voice with obvious gurgling delight. Caregivers should sing soft songs to the youngest of babies, especially when changing diapers; and an infant in distress can often be soothed if you hold the child, hum wordlessly, and dance slowly. Sing songs to infants, using a familiar tune but changing the words to include the child's name and to sing about what they are doing and feeling. Infants love songs with lots of rhyming words; use made-up alliteration to repeat sounds often, and use a variety of songs that involve physical activity and games—"This Little Piggy," "Pat-a-Cake, Pat-a-Cake," and the like.

Toddlers like to hear their name in the song, and to hear songs about what they are doing. The familiar "BINGO" song can be used to spell out the child's name. Repeat songs often, and use songs with repeated phases, choruses, and concepts that keep recurring. Encourage toddlers to join in the parts they remember. Use—and invent— transition songs, to help toddlers move from one activity to another—something they struggle with! Then move on to songs that include specific body movements—"The Wheels on the Bus Go 'round and 'round"; "Row, Row, Row Your Boat"—requiring a rowing motion—and "Ring around the Rosy," in which everyone loves to "fall down."

Singing should occur as often as possible with infants and toddlers, as they love to hear familiar tunes and learn new words and melodies, and they find great security in hearing and participating in songs they already know.

Ways to Include Singing in the Program. Using greeting songs, name game songs (using the child's name in a song), and call-and-response songs are easy ways to include singing in a curriculum. **Call-and-response**

Resources

There are many recordings of songs for children, as well as songbooks that include CDs. Ella Jenkins, Hap Palmer, Thomas Moore, Ruth Seeger, and Jackie Silberg have recordings, and children love many of Pete Seeger's renditions. Books include *Where Is Thumbkin* by T. Moore (Gryphon House), *Sing through the Day* and *Sing through the Seasons* edited by Swinger (Plough Publishing), and the teachers' guidebook *Music and Movement: The Cycle of Seasons* by Heyge and Sillick (Music Matters). MusikGarten has a specific music curriculum.

songs are songs in which the teachers—or a recording—sing out a question or statement, and then the children respond, making it possible for children with no prior singing experience to get immediately into singing. Easy-to-sing songs, such as "If You're Happy and You Know It, Clap Your Hands," "Aiken Drum," "Old MacDonald's Farm," "It's Raining," and "Dinah" (Smith, 2000), are easy for children to get into right away, as are "Farmer in the Dell," "Paper Bag Boogie," and "Twinkle, Twinkle, Little Star" (Moore, 2000). There are similar songs in every language. Don't be afraid to repeat songs as often as the children want to. Adults get tired of the same songs very easily (especially ones we have heard since we were young), but kids love repetition. Songs that are also games and ones in which children can act out are great fun. There are many songs about the seasons and different kinds of weather (Inca Harvest Song, the Mitten Song, "Hi Thunder, Lo Thunder," the Japanese Rain Song, and more; Swinger, 1999; 2000).

Music in Motion

Creative Dramatics. **Creative dramatics** is the improvisational communication of an emotion, an expression, a character, or a story (Church, 2000). In an article in *Scholastic Early Childhood Today*, Ellen Booth Church provides a stepwise approach to getting children involved in creative dramatics.

1. When you read a story, invite children to provide sound effects.
2. Introduce pantomime. Encourage children to act out the story as you read. They can act out the Big Bad Wolf huffing and puffing; the Old Woman Who Swallowed a Fly running around, catching all the various creatures.
3. Use props to initiate a performance. Give children a prop—a funny hat, a hard hat, a toy phone, a scarf, and ask, "What can you do with this?"
4. Have adults do a pantomime. Read a familiar story and have parents and other adults act it out (model). Then have the children act out the story for the adults.
5. Introduce improvisation. Read a story up to a certain point, then have children continue the story, with actions and words.
6. Share a "character bag." Fill a bag with a collection of puppets and stuffed animals. Pick an item from the bag, and say, "Once upon a time." Children then take turns selecting items and continuing the story.

Movement. Children naturally move to music. Further, music seems to reflect closely the way children feel. Start movement activities by playing a variety of music, and say, "How does this music make you feel? Move your bodies to the music" (Church, 2000). Respond verbally to what the children do, legitimizing their attempts while acknowledging that each child will respond differently: "I see you are stretching high." Encourage variation: "Can you express yourself with your whole body, just your arms, lying on the ground, standing on one foot? Can you find another way to respond to the music? How about using just your eyes?"

Add props—scarves, flags, balloons, fans, feathers, streamers attached to a stick—and ask the children, "How does this make you move—what kinds of movements does it suggest?"

Folk Dancing

Teaching folk dancing to young children provides fun and developmentally appropriate ways for them to develop physical abilities and coordination, and to get physical exercise. Folk dancing also presents an excellent outlet for active children and kinesthetic learners, desperately needed as children engage in predominantly passive activities. We need to provide a variety of appropriate physical activities for our quickly developing, naturally active young children (Gallahue, 1993). Folk dancing teaches basic concepts of rhythm, repetition, sequencing, patterning, phrasing, predictability, anticipation, musical cues, auditory discrimination, and counting. And it's very multicultural—exposing children to dances from around the world, to dances representing different historical and social times, and to a variety of cultures. For example, American square dances and contradances are based on French dances; Israeli dances include steps, formations, and music from around the world; and Mexican dances are influenced by Spanish flamenco, native cultures, and dances from the Caribbean and Africa. Teaching folk dances to young children at an early age is a fun-loving way to create a disposition toward life-long physical activity and exercise.

Teachers Learning to Dance. It's very difficult to teach folk dancing unless you can do it (and enjoy it) yourself. Many cities and universities have folk dance groups that meet on a regular basis and teach beginners. High/Scope provides a training program, Education through Movement, which is offered across the country. Performance dance groups in some communities provide instruction in African, Mexican, Polish, English, American, Scottish, and Appalachian dancing. Join one of these groups, learn the different dances, and then adapt and simplify them to meet your children's ages and abilities. Also, invite dancers to your program to teach other teachers, and to work with the children. When an outside teacher is invited to teach your children, make sure the visitor understands the developmental level of your students and is comfortable simplifying the dances for them.

Teaching Folk Dancing. The best way to start to teach young children folk dancing is to use singing games, such as "Ring around the Rosy," "BINGO," "Hokey Pokey," "London Bridge Is Falling Down," and other activities in which a group of children do specific movements to music or chants, and often sing along. Again, if you have children from other countries, a vast array of recordings is available from around the world. Every culture has some form of singing games, and there are several sources for learning new ones. Another fun introductory activity is a grand march—a parade of children dancing to rhythmic music that changes tempo and emotion frequently. The teacher should initially lead the line, modeling a variety of simple steps and formations to the music (skipping, two-foot jumps, high steps, making an arch so every-

▶ *Folk dancing provides an excellent combination of physical, musical, and social activity.*

one can go through, and so on). Then various children can take turns as the leader. Grand marches can be danced inside or outside, on a nice day—with a good sound system (or live music). Use a variety of music, and start introducing specific folk dance tunes: "La Bamba," "La Negra," "Virginia Reel," "Irish Washerwoman," "Jesusita en Chihuahua," "Mayim," "Circassian Circle," "Twelfth Street Rag," "Jarabe Tapatio," Russian troikas, and African dances.

Progress from singing games and grand marches to simple circle, square, and two-line dances: "Seven Steps," "Little Shoemaker," "La Raspa," "Circassian Circle," "Virginia Reel," "Gustaf's Skoal," "Kinder Polka," and the American squares "Red River Valley" and "Pop Goes the Weasel." There are many other simple dances that use walking, running, or simple skip steps and very simple formations. Initially avoid dances that require changing partners, intricate footwork, complex formations, or knowledge of right and left hands and feet. Remember, the purpose of folk dancing with young children is for them to have fun, dance in time and tempo to the music, and develop a love of dancing. Everything else is secondary. Children do not get bored by repeating the same dance formations. Keep the dances simple so they can learn to use the music as a cue to know what to do next. Initially you can call the instructions over the music, but eventually expect the students to remember the sequences and use the music as cues for their private speech. When children master the basics of folk dancing, they can move to more complex and interesting dances.

Using Folk Dance in the Curriculum. Folk dancing can be easily used in a variety of curricular activities, such as inclusion in units being studied, social studies activities, celebrations, and festivals. Children who learn dances from specific countries and areas of the world can learn a great deal about the world. For example, most Israeli dances concern water (waves, springs, and so on) because water is such a vital element in a desert country; "Gustaf's Skoal" (Sweden) illustrates peasants imitating (and making fun of) royalty, and "Jesusita en Chihuahua" tells of the joyful return of Mexican revolutionaries to their village (Wardle, 1975). Some Mexican dances show the influence of bullfights, English sword dances have formations that symbolize repairing fishing nets by coastal fishermen, and maypole dances celebrate the return of spring, as do many Native American ceremonial dances.

In most cultures, folk dancing is used for recreation, performances, and to preserve the culture. In a few situations, however—for example, Native American tribes—certain

Sources of Music

A central value of teaching folk dancing is to expose children to the rich variety of national, ethnic, and regional music, from the Purcell's Renaissance music for England's "Hole in the Wall" and "Gathering Peascods" to the trumpets, accordions, and strings of Mexico's "Jesusita en Chihuahua." The more authentic the music you use for the dances, the better. Find out from dance groups in town the sources of the music they use; ask parents if they have recordings of folk dances; visit ethnic shops in town (for example, many Mexican stores have good CDs of popular folk dances). And buy from educational supply companies, including High/Scope Educational Foundation, 600 N. River St., Ypsilanti, MI 48198; Educational Activities, Inc., P.O. Box 392, Freeport, NY 11520; Educational Record Center, 3233 Burnt Mill Dr., Ste. 100, Wilmington, NC 28403; and Melody House, 819 W. 92d St., Oklahoma City, OK 73114 (Worlds of Fun Series—a great collection of folk dance tunes).

dances have deep spiritual meaning and are used as part of their religious expression. These dances should not be performed just for fun. Be sensitive to this distinction, and ask individuals from specific native tribes if you have a question regarding the appropriateness of certain dances. Also, do not accept the idea that dances can be performed only by certain people; the purpose of folk dancing is to expand inclusiveness, and to show how art is influenced by a variety of cultural sources.

Multicultural Music and Dance

Classical Music. Classical music takes on a multicultural aspect in three ways: compositions by composers from diverse cultures; the influence of distinct cultural idioms, styles, and instruments in classical music; and the performance of traditional Western classical music by musicians from a variety of backgrounds.

Composers like Carlos Chavez and Manuel Ponce (from Mexico), Heitor Villa-Lobos (Brazilian), William Grant Still and William Dawson (African American), Samuel Coleridge-Taylor (English composer of African heritage), Chevalier de Saint-George (Guadeloupean of African heritage), Alberto Ginastera and Roberto Williams (Argentine), Ernesto Lecuona (Cuban), and Joaquin Rodrigo (Spanish), bring the distinct flavor of their culture to their music by incorporating folk melodies, styles, themes, and unique, authentic instruments.

Throughout the history of classical music, European and U.S. composers have included distinctive elements from other cultures in their music. In *Porgy and Bess*, George Gershwin uses styles from African American spirituals and jazz; he also used jazz extensively in *Rhapsody in Blue* and Concerto in F (for piano). Other composers, including Igor Stravinsky, Aaron Copeland, and Darius Milhaud, used jazz extensively in some of their work, while the great American composer Louis Moreau Gottschalk included Cuban and other Caribbean melodies, rhythms, and authentic instruments in his music. Even Dvořák included Native American songs in his *New World* Symphony and *American* Quartet. Milhaud's orchestral work *The Bull on the Roof*, based on a Brazilian folk melody, is a great piece of music for inspiring children to draw or paint to music; his *Creation of the World*, heavily influenced by jazz, would work well for a creative dance activity.

Multicultural Performers. There are performers from a variety of backgrounds who give classical music a multicultural flavor and help children learn the universal nature of music. These include Yo-Yo Ma (cellist), Paul Robeson (African American singer), Kathleen Battle, Silvia McNair, and other African American opera singers, Marian Anderson, who sings Bach and other classical music (as well as spirituals), and a variety of violin and piano soloists from all over the world. Hearing Paul Robeson or Kathleen Battle sing German *Lieder*, Yo-Yo Ma play a Haydn concerto, or Sarah Chang play a Beethoven violin concerto is just as much a multicultural experience

▶ *The more we know about the arts, the clearer it is that they must be central in our early childhood curricula.*

as the same singers performing African American spirituals, Wynton Marsalis playing jazz, or a group of native drummers playing for a Pow Wow social dance.

Conclusion

In this chapter I have attempted to provide a strong argument for the need for a high-quality, integrated arts program throughout a child's early childhood years, and to warn the reader of the threat to such programs from the increasing emphasis on academics in many early childhood and school programs. The irony is that as more and more children enter our early childhood programs without rich arts experiences, programs are moving away from these activities to focus on specific school-related academic lessons. Many educators and artists have always advocated for the arts in early childhood and school programs, and the new brain research has simply reinforced their beliefs. The more we know about the arts, the clearer it is that they must be central in our early childhood programs.

Questions and Projects

1. Develop a short presentation to the parents' board of a school or early childhood program, arguing for a strong arts component for the students (up to third grade).

2. Find an artist in your community (painter, dancer, musician, or other) and bring him or her to your class to give a presentation. Include hands-on activities for the students in the class.

3. Call a community arts center (museum, dance company, or other) and find out the kinds of programs they provide for young children. Do these programs include the level of hands-on activities that young children need?

4. A parent of a 4-year-old in a program has complained to the director that her child gets paint on her clothes and in her hair. The parent wants her child not to paint. Prepare a letter to the parent trying to convince her that her daughter should be allowed to paint.

5. You have set up a woodworking area, and the kids love it! But only boys use it. What are ways you can encourage girls?

CHAPTER

12 Guiding Behavior

A central concern of all early childhood programs is discipline. Everything from toddlers who bite and preschoolers who destroy other children's projects to a second grader who cannot behave appropriately on a field trip is part of discipline. This chapter presents the concept of discipline within the framework of a child's natural development of a positive self-image, a process more appropriately termed *guidance*. In exploring this development, I cover Erikson's psychosocial stages and explore the development of moral reasoning. The concept of social competence is explored, along with the delicate balance between the development of individual self-control in children and the need for group compliance in classrooms, child-care centers, playgrounds, and field trips. I also discuss behaviorism and social learning theory as foundations for classroom guidance, then provide a variety of specific classroom-management techniques and ideas for working with children in early childhood programs and schools. ■

Children's Self-Image

Children who feel good about themselves usually are not discipline problems in an early childhood program. The question is, how do children develop a strong and secure self-image? Early childhood educators have for a long time been very interested in supporting the development of a positive self-image in young children. Unfortunately, this interest has often resulted in very negative practices—"showering praise and rewards on children

Questions to Consider

1. What is the difference between punishment and guidance?

2. Does time-out work as a classroom management approach?

3. What is moral reasoning?

4. How is self-image related to classroom discipline?

5. What are effective classroom management techniques?

6. How does social competence relate to school success?

at every turn; believing a single program, book, poster, phase, pamphlet, or activity can inoculate a child with a positive self-image" (Wardle, 1995b, p. 44). Self-image is developed though children's interactions with their environment, the environment's response to them, and then their response to that response.

For example, an infant who has colic and is very fussy will have a negative effect on his mother, who may then respond to her infant with frustration. A preschool child who is always in trouble will solicit a different response from the teacher compared to a child who is compliant, easy to work with, and fun to be around. So a crucial part of children's self-image is determined by how the environment responds to them, their behaviors and actions. Another aspect of self-concept is how children interpret the response of the environment. We know that children interpret the same things differently; for example, when a child fails at building a tower with unit blocks, one child may say to herself, "Here I go again—a total failure," while another says, "That was fun and interesting— I wonder how I should change what I do so that next time it doesn't fall." This talking to oneself is called **metacommunication**—a kind of private speech—and has a lot to do with how we react to the environment.

In Chapter 6, I covered the two-factor theory of self-image (Cross, 1987), a theory that states a child's self-image is composed of two distinctive factors: *personal identity*—the way the world responds to the child and the child to the world—and *reference group orientation*— the various groups a child belongs to: gender, race, ethnicity, religion, family, income level, politics, school, and neighborhood. A child's positive self-image is based on both of these factors, and it is essential that early childhood programs help children develop positively in both of these areas. Personal identity is the way children feel about what they can do: build a block tower, sing a song, read a book, score a goal in a soccer game, and make lots of friends. For teachers and parents, what is vital is "positive, meaningful response to the individual child, not the group the child belongs to. A girl who builds a fantastic structure in the block area is competent as an individual, not as a girl" (Wardle, 1995b, p. 7).

Reference group orientation is developed by supporting children's home experiences at the center or school, assisting children in the process of gender identification, and nurturing their gradual recognition and full acceptance of their racial, ethnic,

Developmentally Appropriate Practice

Figure 12.1

The relationship of self and environment (based on Curry and Johnson, 1990).

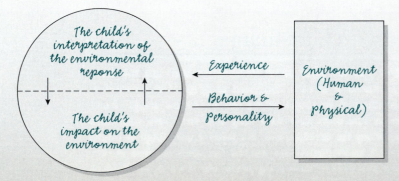

national, and cultural identity. Positive reference group orientation is developed by children seeing themselves and their families throughout the center, using their home language, providing a positive connection between home and school, and—as they get older—learning about positive contributions of people like them in the nation's and the world's history, arts, and politics.

Curry and Johnson (1990) have studied specific ways teachers and parents can enhance the self-image of young children. These are love and acceptance, power and control, moral value, and competence.

Love and Acceptance

Children need to feel they are accepted and appreciated for their unique identity. Teachers can support this feeling by:

- providing unconditional support and nurturing;
- providing age-appropriate and consistent limits;
- providing praise for accomplishing specific tasks;
- acknowledging to children that you enjoy them ("It's always fun when you are in class," "I love playing in the water table with you," "My nature walks are so much more fun when I talk to you");
- participating with a child in projects you both enjoy;
- giving each child as much individual attention as possible.

Power and Control

Children need to feel they have some control over what they are doing and where their life is going. Teachers can develop this sense of power and control by:

- providing meaningful projects and activities for children;
- providing many opportunities for children to choose;
- providing many opportunities for children to develop conclusions, solutions, and answers on their own, and to develop alternative solutions to problems;
- helping children evaluate their own performance—so that they depend less on others' praise and approval, and more on their own self-evaluations;
- developing problem-solving techniques that do not involve adults;
- providing high expectations, lots of challenges, and a belief in each child's success;
- helping children develop reasonable rules—within their abilities—to control activities.

Moral Value

All children need to feel they are a good person, and that they are being treated fairly by those around them—teachers, parents, and other children. Do they feel, deep down, that they belong? Teachers and parents can help develop these feelings by:

- making sure interactions with important adults are characterized by mutual respect, cooperation, fairness, and understanding;
- limiting **extrinsic rewards** (money, stickers) because these reinforce external judgment and do not develop self-evaluation skills;

- helping children deal constructively with failures and disappointments;
- providing opportunities for children to work together cooperatively, and to pursue long-term projects meaningful to each of them;
- supporting opportunities for children to engage in activities that connect them with the school and community: recycling, cleaning the playground, contributing to a food bank, and more;
- criticizing a child's specific behavior, but not the child (never say, "You are a bad child"; rather say, "Throwing the block is unacceptable because . . . ");
- helping children feel an important part of any group effort—team, choir, projects.

Competence

All children need to feel they can accomplish tasks children their age should be able to do: ride a bike, climb a tree, read a book, use a computer. Ways teachers can help develop competence in children are:

- basing expectations on the child's age and the child's unique strengths and challenges;
- providing lots of opportunities for children to do things—build a dam in a stream, mail a picture to grandma, talk on the phone, have a garden next to their parent's garden;
- supporting risk taking and efforts to complete tasks and solve problems;
- expecting and helping children continually to expand on their skills and knowledge, and to challenge themselves within their own capabilities.

Self-image is the result of ongoing interactions between the way children view themselves, and the way the world—including adults and children—views them. Thus what children can do themselves, how they feel about what they can do, and how important people around them feel about it all contribute to their positive self-image. It's a fluid and dynamic process, constantly changing and shifting.

Social Competence

Socially competent children are those who function successfully with adults and other children. "Socially competent young children are those who engage in satisfying interactions and activities with adults and peers and through such interactions further improve their own competence" (Katz & McClellan, 1997, p. 1). Research has consistently shown that socially competent children not only function well in schools but are also more successful in school. A central goal of guidance in early childhood programs is to support children's development of social competence, assisting children who, for a variety of reasons, struggle in this important area of development.

Research suggests that developing social competence during the early years is crucial to future school success—in fact, the ability to get along with peers in a positive manner is considered a much better predictor of future school and life success than IQ, grades, or classroom behavior. Furthermore, children who do not develop minimal social competence during the early years are at risk of a variety of problems during later school and life (Parker & Asher, 1987). The likelihood of academic failure, dropping out, suspension, crime, and health problems are greater in children who are unpopular and asocial (Kupersmidt, 1983; Parker & Asher, 1987). Teenagers who attended early childhood programs that emphasized caring and **prosocial behaviors** had lower rates of juvenile delinquency, and provided more family support and closeness, than children from a control group who attended early childhood programs that did not emphasize caring and prosocial development (Lally, Mangione, & Honig, 1988). Clearly, one of the principal roles of early childhood educators must be to help children overcome social difficulties and develop social competence.

In their book *Fostering Children's Social Competence: The Teacher's Role* (1997), Lillian Katz and Diane McClellan provide a detailed discussion of this important area, and offer specific ideas teachers can use to assist children to develop social competence. The components that make up social competence include:

- *Regulation of emotions.* Children need to learn to control emotions when needed, and to be spontaneous when appropriate. Some children let emotional responses interfere in their relations with peers; others have control over their responses. Teachers need to help children learn appropriate and constructive emotional responses to typical situations (anger, frustration, fear, confusion, excitement), through interactions and guidance.
- *Social knowledge.* Children need a sufficient mastery of language, and must know social norms and customs: share a common understanding of stories, TV programs, film scripts, and so on to participate fully in social activities with peers. Competent children know how to negotiate, communicate verbally, and resolve problems. These children usually can communicate to adults and children their needs, feelings, and wishes.
- *Social skills.* Specific social behaviors are used by children to enter group activities, approve of one another's company, request information, engage in nonaggressive play interactions, and take turns.

Common Social Challenges

Certain children appear to possess specific prosocial dispositions—they are accepting, friendly, empathetic, generous, and cooperative. Others have antisocial dispositions—they are argumentative, bossy, antagonistic, and self-absorbed (Katz & McClellan, 1997). Teachers in early childhood programs need to find ways to develop social competence in the latter. Children who are shy, aggressive, or lonely have a particular need for careful assistance and guidance.

Factors that Influence the Development of Social Competence

Children develop social competence within significant contexts. These contexts include their family, community, and peer interactions.

Family. The kind of nurturing, reciprocity, love, intimacy, and support a family provides has a tremendous influence on children's social development. *Family* includes both the nuclear and the extended family. An intricate interaction of support, love, control, and communication is needed. M. Baumrind's research (1967) shows that an **authoritative**

▶ *Part of guidance is helping children with basic skills—eating, putting on clothes, etc.*

parenting approach is most effective in developing socially competent children, as opposed to permissive or authoritarian parenting. Authoritative parenting is characterized by a combination of high control with nurturing, warmth, and good communication (Katz & McClellan, 1997). Parents who develop socially competent children also praise positive behavior, provide positive interactions between parents and children, and have a responsive approach to children's needs (Dumas & LaFreniere, 1993).

Other family factors that contribute to social competence are siblings, other caregivers in the home, and exposure to adult anger and family dysfunction. Important social experiences children have when they are young correlate very strongly to their later social relationships and commitments (Rudolph, Harmen, & Burge, 1995).

Community. A sense of belonging to a community creates a sense of well-being in children. Children whose families move a lot, as well as homeless children, often have difficulty developing social competence. Additionally, children whose parents have very few important social contacts may have trouble developing strong relationships.

Peers. Peers teach a child the basic social knowledge and skills needed to interact prosocially. Children who for whatever reason are denied this peer interaction suffer. Young children accompanied by a peer also seem to experience less stress in unfamiliar and anxiety-producing situations than children who experience the situations alone. Obviously, satisfying involvement with other young children is an important component in the development of social competence.

Nine Ways Teachers Can Help Develop Social Competence

In their book, Katz and McClellan provide nine general ideas to help teachers with the task of developing social competence in their children. They are outlined here.

Children's Feelings Deserve Respect. Children come to a program with their own set of experiences, fears, and expectations, which are based on their family and community background. Sometimes these match well with the routines, expectations, and culture of the program, and children are seamlessly absorbed into the program. More often, however, children will experience various forms of dysfunction as they move from their understanding of the social world into new situations and expectations. The teacher must respect where children are coming from but also demonstrate the knowledge needed to function in the new environment.

Nevertheless, a teacher should not condone children's misbehavior. The teacher should sensitively show empathy, and provide a clear understanding of both classroom expectations and how to meet those expectations. Also, since functioning prosocially within a classroom environment is crucial to children's future school success, teachers need to support their social development carefully.

Social Competence Is Culturally Defined. As early childhood programs serve a more diverse population, we need to understand how social competence reflects a child's cultural background. All cultures socialize children into the norms of their culture. Problems occur when children's home cultural expectations conflict with those of the school or early childhood program.

When I worked in the highlands of Guatemala after the 1976 earthquake, a team of Canadians helped local residents build replacement houses. The Canadians set up a factory in which local farmers were expected to work hard eight hours a day to help construct their own house. The Canadians were dismayed at what they perceived as the local men's lack of punctuality and unfocused work habits. The local farmers, by contrast, were used to starting work when the sun rose (a different time each day) and methodically hoeing corn for fourteen to sixteen hours a day (Wardle, 1976).

In early childhood programs, conflicts arise in the areas of discipline, gender expectations, use of language to direct and instruct children, integration of activities, and age-appropriate expectations. All of these conflicts affect social competence. Teachers cannot be aware of all different cultural values, but they need to be aware of their own values and behaviors and to work closely with parents to provide a seamless transition between home and school.

Social Difficulties Are Teachable Moments. Social competence is learned behavior, so social problems children have within an early childhood program should be seen as learning opportunities. Teachers need to help children learn the specific skills and behaviors needed to enjoy the company of and interactions with other children successfully and competently. As I have said, learning these skills is as important to future school success as learning academic skills.

Social Behavior Develops in Cycles. A child who enjoys being around others, is likable, and is appreciative will receive positive feedback from others, which reinforces this behavior. By contrast, a child who is destructive, mean, selfish, and difficult will elicit negative responses from others, which will result in further negative behavior. These behavior cycles develop during the preschool years, and then follow a child through their school years (Ladd, 1983). Children take their style of social interaction with them into new school situations, so it is important that early childhood educators intervene appropriately with children who are developing negative behavior cycles.

Direct Adult Communication Assists Children. Because the culture of the early childhood program will, to a greater or lesser degree, differ from that of the child's home, teachers need to communicate the program's rules and expectations directly and sensitively. Direct, straightforward communication to students about expected, appropriate, and inappropriate behavior is often effective in redirecting students—a method that is particularly effective for preschool and elementary-school children, whose verbal and reasoning skills enable them to understand direct, consistent expectations.

Meaningful Relationships Require a Context. One problem with children who misbehave is that the child and teacher end up spending all their energy on the behavior, which then becomes an ongoing power struggle. This is unfortunate, because the teacher–child relationship should be primarily about learning: planning, thinking, discovery, and creating.

Teacher Intervention Should Be Optimized. Guiding children's development in social competence is best achieved through optimal teaching intervention: "teacher intervention should not be so frequent that children have few opportunities to solve their own problems, but it should be frequent enough to ensure that no child falls into a negative recursive cycle" (Katz & McClellan, 1997, p. 59).

Adult Expectations Shape Children. Adults who work with children tend to label children early on—"the creative one," "the difficult one," "the quiet one," "the bright one." The danger here is that we then reinforce these labels, and children begin to try to live up to adult expectations (Miller, 1995). In Chapter 6, I discuss how this affects gender expectations. Adults' negative response to unpopular children can be particularly destructive, because the children begin to live up to their label in their home and early childhood program. Teachers must continually examine the way they think about and respond to individual children in their care, and continually challenge the mental labels they have for children.

Teachers' Interactions with Children Are Models for Behavior. In the section on social learning theory later in this chapter, the powerful impact of modeling is described. Teachers must carefully model appropriate behaviors in resolving conflicts: listening, patience, tone of voice, providing options, and so on. Other appropriate behaviors to model include soliciting suggestions from the children involved in conflict, providing ample opportunity for the children to solve their own problems, and using rules and expectations that children have helped to develop.

Erikson's Psychosocial Stages

Eric Erikson viewed human growth and development from the perspective of a person's psychological and social development (1963). From his observations he developed a life-span theory, dividing a person's entire life into eight stages. Erikson believed that a person must resolve a specific conflict, or challenge, at each stage before being able to move on to the next stage of development. He believed failure to resolve a challenge would result in difficulties in future development. The stages from birth to age 8 are: basic trust versus mistrust (infancy), autonomy versus shame or doubt (ages 1–3), initiative versus guilt (ages 3–5½), and industry versus inferiority (middle childhood; ages 5½–12). The role of parents, teachers, and other caregivers during this time is to help children resolve these conflicts and move from stage to stage. To provide assistance and support in helping children develop socially and psychologically, teachers should know the stage a child is experiencing, the stage a child is moving into, and the conflict the child is struggling with.

I discussed all of Erikson's psychosocial stages in Chapter 9; here I will cover the first four stages (up to age 8) in more detail.

Figure 12.2

The First Four of Erikson's Psychosocial Stages

STAGES	ONE	TWO	THREE	FOUR
STAGE I Birth to 1 year	Trust versus Mistrust			
STAGE II 1–3 years		Autonomy versus Shame		
STAGE III 3–5½ years			Initiative versus Guilt	
STAGE IV 5½–12 years				Industry versus Inferiority

Trust versus Mistrust (Infancy to Age 1)

Infants are totally dependent on their parents, extended family members, and caregivers to meet their basic needs: food, comfort, attention, diaper changes, stimulation, security, and sleep. According to Erikson, if these needs are met in a consistent, nurturing, responsive manner, the infant will develop a sense of basic trust. If not, the child will develop mistrust. Thus infants should be picked up when they cry, held when being fed, and responded to when they are bored, scared, tired, or upset. According to Erikson, infants need to learn to trust that the world is responsive to their individual needs.

Children who have not bonded with a parent or caregiver often do not develop this sense of trust (Bowlby, 1969). Many children who spent their first years of life in an orphanage in Russia or eastern European countries, as well as children shuttled in and out of foster homes within our foster care system, have not developed this trust.

Autonomy versus Shame (Ages 1–3)

A major developmental task for children is to create a sense of self-identity and self-control—the awareness that they are physically and psychologically separate from people around them. This is the first milestone of toddlerhood, when children learn to control their bowels and bladder, begin to walk, and begin to talk—fantastic new tasks, skills, and accomplishments that each child must master and feel proud of. This is the age when tantrums abound, and many programs struggle with children biting—symptoms of children struggling to master new abilities and developmental milestones.

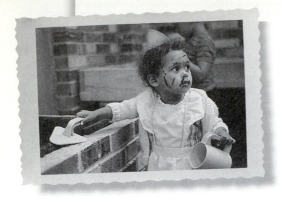

▶ *Children who are allowed to explore the environment learn they are competent and can be trusted.*

The role of parents and caregivers during this stage is to support children's attempts to develop this autonomy, by carefully encouraging and helping children learn the relation between cause and effect and by providing an environment that supports their development. Further, parents and caregivers need to provide a secure and nurturing environment for children to retreat to when their attempts at autonomy fail.

Initiative versus Guilt (Ages 3–5½)

During this stage, children move from the confines of the home, the security of their parents, and the familiarity of what they have known all their life to the new, different world outside the home. Anyone who has children knows the constant questioning at this age: "Why is the sky blue?" "Why does it rain?" "Why is the snow cold?" And children this age get into everything! The challenges for parents and caregivers at this stage are many: on the one hand, we can't allow curious children to fall down steps, run into the street, put their hands on a hot stove, or play inside a used refrigerator; on the other hand, it is essential that we nurture and support their natural inquisitiveness about the world. Not only is this important for all future learning, but according to Erikson, children not allowed to use initiative develop a sense of guilt regarding their desire for independence and an overdependence on others (first adults, then peers).

Industry versus Inferiority (Ages 5½–12)

The elementary-school child is interested in mastering physical, social, and intellectual tasks: making friends, solving problems, reading a book, figuring out a game, winning a race, climbing a tree. It's all about accomplishments. At this age children see the world as something to be mastered and controlled, and their sense of worth is based on tasks they accomplish, and on their parents' and teachers' view of their ability to master these tasks. Five-and-a-half- to twelve-year-olds need lots of opportunities to be successful, to be challenged, and to stretch their abilities and mastery. Children who do not develop a sense of mastery of their physical, social, and intellectual world will develop a feeling of inferiority. Children need help to evaluate their own skills and abilities, and to avoid depending totally on the judgment of others, adults or peers. Teachers need to be careful to minimize situations where children this age are constantly competing with and comparing themselves with others.

For each of these psychosocial stages, the adults' role is a careful balance between protecting children from physical and psychological harm and supporting their forays into an ever wider and more challenging physical, psychological, and social world.

Moral Reasoning

Piaget's and Erikson's developmental theories are based on the idea of a developmental progression: every child progresses—with some individual differences—through distinct stages, starting initially with primitive skills and abilities, and moving toward more sophisticated concepts and mastery. At each stage children respond a certain way to the world, which is different from their response at a lower or higher stage. For teachers and parents, knowing the stage a child is in helps them provide the best possible developmental support. Lawrence Kohlberg (1976) and Thomas Lickona (1983) have applied the concept of developmental stages to children's ideas about morality: good and bad, right and wrong, loyalty, friendship, justice, equality, respect, and honesty.

The development of moral reasoning is a central issue in all early childhood programs and schools. It is also a major concern in today's society, as we seem to have lost our moral compass, and as more crimes are committed at earlier ages. Even so, discussing the moral development of children can be difficult. I remember a training I did on developmental stages for a Head Start staff. I sailed through Piaget's cognitive stages with little difficulty; the idea that children develop through distinct cognitive levels seemed reasonable to teachers who work with young children every day. But when I presented the concept of moral stages—that children's ideas about morality develop over time, and change with age—I totally lost them! Almost all of the people at the training were Hispanic, and many were raised in Catholic homes. They were taught from a young age that morality is simply a matter of being told what is right and wrong, and being punished for any transgressions. They believed that teaching morality is a matter of telling a child what is right and what is wrong, and continually reinforcing the concept as the children mature. The idea that morality develops throughout childhood, and that a child's view of right and wrong changes with age, was unimaginable to them.

Lawrence Kohlberg's Stages of Moral Reasoning

Kohlberg used Piaget's stages of cognitive development to create a six-stage theory of moral reasoning. He postulated that if children think differently and process information differently at various ages, they probably think about issues of right and wrong differently also. For example, a 4-year-old boy is very concerned with fairness but views fairness only from his (egocentric) point of view. He'll say, "It's not fair, your cookie is bigger than mine," but he will never say, "It's not fair, my cookie is bigger than yours!" By contrast, an 8-year-old girl may well say, "I got more than you did—here, have some of mine." This is because the 8-year-old can see fairness from another child's point of view.

Kohlberg developed a series of moral dilemmas that he gave to children of different ages to solve. An example is a scenario in which a poor man needs a drug for his dying wife, but cannot afford it, and the pharmacist won't give it to him even though the pharmacist was charging far more than the drug cost him to buy; so he steals it. Kohlberg asked the children whether this was morally acceptable behavior. He was not interested in the answer; he was interested in how children of different ages justified their answer—what has come to be called *moral reasoning*. Based on this research, Kohlberg developed the stages of his theory.

Kohlberg believed that children progress from one stage to the next, with each stage built on knowledge gained from the previous stage, and that children cannot skip a stage. Some children (and adults) never achieve the top stages in Kohlberg's theory. Because Lickona's work is a further refinement of Kohlberg's theory, including a stage for preschool-age children, and because Lickona has adapted his stages to be easier for teachers and parents to use, I have chosen to present Lickona's adaption of Kohlberg's stages of moral reasoning in more detail. Kohlberg's work was used extensively in the **values clarification** movement of the 1960s and 1970s, which is discussed in more detail in Chapter 9.

Lickona's Stages of Moral Reasoning

Thomas Lickona expanded on Kohlberg's stage theory of moral reasoning, and based his theory on the understanding that children's concepts of morality closely follow their ability to think and reason about good and bad, right and wrong, and fairness. Children can understand moral reasoning at a higher stage than their behavior actually reflects, which causes parents and teachers a great amount of confusion, because a child will say all the right things about honesty, fairness, and sharing, and then turn around and appear to do the opposite.

Lickona's theory of moral reasoning has 6 stages, starting with Stage 0, and progressing to Stage 6. Stages 1–5 are adapted from Kohlberg's stages. For each stage Lickona profiles children's moral reasoning, explains the reasons children use at this age to justify their moral behavior—why they should be good—and then gives parents and teachers advice regarding how best to guide children through each stage (Lickona, 1983). Lickona also provides suggestions that help children begin to move to the next level, or stage.

Stage 0: Egocentric Reasoning. This stage occurs at about age 4. Preschool children begin to talk about fairness, but to them *fairness* means getting their own way. In conflict situations, they see things only from their point of view. Their reason for being good is that it will get them what they want and help them avoid punishment. Because children this age are so egocentric and curious about the world, they may cheat, lie, break the rules, or change the rules of the game or social situation to meet their individual wishes. Preschool-age children can be compassionate and helpful to others, so long as this does not conflict with their own wishes and needs.

Supporting Moral Development at Stage 0. Lickona suggests that parents and teachers take a developmental perspective: this too will pass! Preschoolers want to feel that they make the decisions—this is one of their basic ego needs—so offer choices, but make sure all the choices are acceptable. In *Raising Good Children*, Lickona gives the example of crossing the street with his son. For safety reasons he insisted on holding his son's hand, but each time his son would fight this demand. Finally Lickona turned to his son and said, "Which hand would you like me to hold?" and his son willingly offered one of his hands (1983).

Provide appropriate rewards, especially words and hugs, when a preschooler is obedient, helps others, shares, and is considerate to others.

Lickona believes that one way to respond to children at a specific moral reasoning stage is to help them move to the next stage. Ways to help preschool children move from Stage 0 to Stage 1 include requiring them to give better reasons for their behavior than simply "because I want to"; assigning chores at home and school; and playing simple

Figure 12.3

The Stages of Moral Reasoning

(Ages indicate reasonable developmental expectations for a child of normal intelligence growing up in a supportive moral environment.)

Stage 0: EGOCENTRIC REASONING (preschool years—around age 4)	What's right: Reason to be good:	I should get my own way. To get rewards and avoid punishments.
Stage 1: UNQUESTIONING OBEDIENCE (around kindergarten age)	What's right: Reason to be good:	I should do what I'm told. To stay out of trouble.
Stage 2: WHAT'S-IN-IT-FOR-ME FAIRNESS (early elementary grades)	What's right: Reason to be good:	I should look out for myself but be fair to those who are fair to me. Self-interest: What's in it for me?
Stage 3: INTERPERSONAL CONFORMITY (middle-to-upper elementary grades and early-to-mid teens)	What's right: Reason to be good:	I should be a nice person and live up to the expectations of people I know and care about. So others will think well of me (social approval) and I can think well of myself (self-esteem).
Stage 4: RESPONSIBILITY TO "THE SYSTEM" (high-school years or late teens)	What's right: Reason to be good:	I should fulfill my responsibilities to the social or value system I feel part of. To keep the system from falling apart and to maintain self-respect as somebody who meets my obligations.
Stage 5: PRINCIPLED CONSCIENCE (young adulthood)	What's right: Reason to be good:	I should show the greatest possible respect for the rights and dignity of every individual person and should support a system that protects human rights. The obligation of conscience to act in accordance with the principle of respect for all human beings.

Source: "The Stages of Moral Reasoning/Chart," from *Raising Good Children* by Thomas Lickona, Ph.D., Copyright © 1983 by Thomas Lickona. Used by permission of Bantam Books, a division of Random House, Inc.

games through which children can begin to understand the value of following rules, even when they can't initially see the personal advantage of doing so. Children at this stage also need lots of opportunities to play and solve problems with their peers, so they will begin to realize that if everyone gets their way all the time, there will never be group consensus or cooperative activities.

Stage 1: Unquestioning Obedience.

Around kindergarten age, children are less egocentric and have a deep respect for authority—especially parents and teachers. They believe that adults are always right and that if they are good, they will avoid punishment, because it is adults who determine what is good and bad. Their motivation to be good is to stay out of trouble. Children at this age believe they should do what they are told to stay on the adult's good side. But because kindergarteners are still preoperational thinkers, they can handle only one piece of information at a time and become easily confused. Thus parents and teachers need to be very consistent.

Because adults are viewed as the enforcers of moral behavior, children at this stage often don't follow rules of good behavior when adults are not present. They won't get caught! This is, understandably, the age at which tattling about others to teachers and parents is at its height.

Supporting Moral Development at Stage 1.

To help children at this age, parents and teachers should provide strong and consistent guidance, provide rules (but only a few), and enforce those rules consistently. Since children this age want to obey the authority figure, parents and teachers should reinforce (with reward-praise, smiles, hugs) children's appropriate behavior.

Parents and teachers can help Stage 1 children move to the next level by giving reasons for rules and directions. Avoid responding with "because I said so"; rather, "I said so because you could get hurt if you jump off the swing." Help children understand why certain behavior is wrong, while still not allowing that behavior to occur, and help children view fairness as also being fair to the other child.

Stage 2: What's-in-It-for-Me Fairness.

In the early elementary-school years, the reason children want to be good is to make sure other children like them. To get children to like them, children believe they must be kind to others, not for altruistic reasons but to get kindness back in return. The stage is characterized by a swing back to independence and a sense of enlightened self-interest: I'll be good to others so that they will be good to me. Children this age believe they have rights, and that adults can be wrong; an eye-for-an-eye approach to fairness is the rule. Stage 2 children obey adults who treat them well but have little respect for adults who don't; and they continually compare their status (regarding fairness) with that of others.

▶ *Mixed-age activities teach the older children to be responsible role models; the younger children learn from their older models.*

Because children view right and wrong according to the results of specific behaviors, if they cannot see the negative results of the behavior—say, lying—they don't consider it bad or harmful. Their approach to fairness leads them to believe they must retaliate when they are victims of injustice.

Supporting Moral Development at Stage 2. To support children at this age, adults should understand why they continually back-talk (to justify their behavior), should appeal to their sense of reciprocity (if you clean your room, we can go to the playground), and should be willing to negotiate until children see the fairness of the solution for both you and them.

To help move a child toward Stage 3, adults should help children become more sensitive to the feelings of others, help them try to live up to an adult's expectations rather than always getting rewards and punishments, and nurture a relationship with them so they will care about the adult's wishes. Also model acceptance of appropriate behavior, and help children feel like an important part of a group, classroom, family, or team. Membership in a sports team at this age can be very effective in developing moral behavior.

Stage 3: Interpersonal Conformity. Most 8-year-old children have not yet achieved Stage 3, which continues through the upper elementary-school years. It is important, however, for teachers to know about Stage 3, so they can assist children in moving upward. At Stage 3 children's reason to be good is to live up to the expectations of other people they care about. They reason that if other children and adults are good to them, they will think well of themselves. At this age children want to fulfill the image they have of themselves, want to get approval from peers, and believe in treating others the way they wish to be treated.

Because children now have achieved the cognitive stage of concrete operations, they are more flexible thinkers when considering moral issues. They can understand and appreciate the way others feel, and their view of adults has shifted to seeing them as usually wise and good. Stage 3 children understand their role as a member of a group; they have a clear sense of who they are and of their own values. But they are very open to peer pressure, especially peers they respect or whose approval they need. Peers are becoming the central component of their moral code.

Working with Children within Each Stage. To support children's healthy progress through each of these stages, Lickona recommends a balance of allowing children to behave naturally according to the characteristics of the stage, helping them understand their own moral reasoning (why they do what they do), and expecting appropriate behavior even if it seems to contradict the behaviors typical of that stage. He advises: respect children, and require respect in return; teach by example (modeling); teach by telling (pass on the culture's moral code); help kids think about their behavior; give children real, meaningful responsibilities; and help them develop a strong, positive self-concept (Lickona, 1983).

For teachers, these ideas reinforce many of the approaches we know work well. These include modeling the behavior you expect (everything from sharing to not yelling in the classroom), creating classroom rules and other responsibilities with student input, developing each child's positive self-image (and understanding that each child is different, with unique strengths and experiences), and talking to children about the reasons to be good (including using books with moral messages, talking about expected behavior, and having good role models visit the classroom).

Critique of Moral Reasoning

Piaget, Kohlberg, and Lickona are, of course, white men (and two of them are dead). Further, Piaget's studies were based on his own children, and Kohlberg's work was based on moral dilemmas given to groups of white boys in the United States. As I have already discussed, the foundation of our early childhood knowledge is based primarily on the writings and research of white European and American men. Many believe this places in question whether our knowledge about young children is relevant to all children in all cultures, or just to white, middle-class European and U.S. children. This criticism has been leveled against Kohlberg's and Lickona's stages of moral development.

Carol Gilligan, a student of Kohlberg's, has suggested that the stages of moral reasoning described by Kohlberg and Lickona are based on the way men and boys think, which is different from how women and girls think about morality (1982). Gilligan believes that women are more concerned with interpersonal relationships and minimizing suffering. Women, she states, focus on caring and mercy, which means they care about who is being hurt as a result of their decision and behaviors, and how to get people to help resolve the problem. Gilligan believes women in this society are raised to be more caring than men, and to be considerate and supportive of others. And thus, she believes, girls develop through distinctly different stages of moral reasoning than do boys.

Behaviorism

Behavioral techniques are used, in one form or another, a great deal in early childhood programs. As with other theoretical foundations to classroom guidance and discipline, behaviorism is covered in much more detail in Chapter 9. Behaviorism is a complex and intricate system of shaping behavior, and can only be touched on here. Of the two kinds of behaviorism—classical conditioning and operant conditioning—operant conditioning is used most as a disciplinary technique in early childhood programs. Three forms of operant conditioning are used in classrooms—positive reinforcement, negative reinforcement, and punishment. Because the use of behaviorist methods in classroom management are dependent on the teacher, they do not develop children's ability to control and guide their own behaviors or to direct their own learning. Programs that follow a developmentally appropriate philosophy try to deemphasize behaviorist methods.

Positive and Negative Reinforcement

Both positive and negative reinforcement involve following a behavior with a reinforcer. A reinforcer is a stimulus that increases the frequency of a response it follows (Ormrod, 1999). In other words, a *positive reinforcer* is praise, candy, self-congratulation, grades, money, or other desired thing that, when used immediately after a particular behavior, increases the frequency of that behavior. With *negative reinforcement* the behavior is increased by removing a stimulus—something unpleasant or undesirable—say, removing children from being grounded after they have come home on time three nights in a row; removing children from time-out after they have settled down and expressed remorse.

Classroom Reinforcers. There are a variety of reinforcers that are used in the classroom. Unfortunately, they are often overused and misused.

- *Material reinforcers.* Tangible reinforcers like food, candy, toys, and trinkets are effective reinforcers. They should be used only as a last resort, however, because children need to learn to behave appropriately without always depending on tangible rewards (they often come to expect rewards for appropriate behavior).
- *Social reinforcers.* Praise, smiles, kind words, a pat on the back, and a hug all work well as reinforcers. It is crucial, however, that the teacher praise a specific behavior, not the child in general. It's the behavior that is being modified, not the child. Teachers' attention, approval, and appreciation also work well.
- *Activities.* Children will do what they consider unpleasant or undesirable activities in exchange for the reward of engaging in what they perceive to be pleasant activities. Many teachers use the computer and free play in this way—although, as I have discussed, this is often not a good approach.
- *Intrinsic reinforcers.* Children like to master new tasks, achieve new goals, and overcome new challenges. They feel good about these accomplishments. This internal motivation is called an intrinsic reinforcer.
- *Feedback.* Providing feedback to students regarding their progress is a reinforcer, because it satisfies their need to feel successful. This is one of the ways grades work, as feedback to children that they were successful in a particular area—and which is why older children sometimes say, "I don't care about getting a C in that class, because I don't like the class."

Tokens. Tokens are very popular in some early childhood classrooms. Tokens are items that are given when a child meets a certain expectation; they are collected by the child, then redeemed for a real reinforcer—treats, candy, free time, favorite activities, or lunch with the principal. A discipline method using tokens is called a **token economy,** and should include the following conditions:

- clear understanding of the specific activity, task, or behavior that will be rewarded;
- the particular token, which must be awarded immediately after the task, activity, or behavior is completed;
- a variety of real reinforcers for which the tokens can be redeemed;
- a "store" in which tokens can be redeemed (for young children, this redemption needs to occur each day; for older children, once or twice a week).

▶ *Real accomplishments of real tasks develop a secure sense of self-worth.*

Again, rewarding expected behavior and outcomes with tokens and rewards is viewed by many as a questionable way of developing appropriate behavior and encouraging learning.

When Reinforcers Don't Work. Reinforcers often do not work, for a variety of reasons:

- *The reinforcer isn't.* What works for one child may not work for another child. This is particularly true when the child gets the reinforcer (food, attention, time to play) somewhere else, and therefore doesn't need it in the classroom.
- *Reinforcement is inconsistent.* It is very difficult for teachers with lots of children to reinforce children immediately after they engage in the desired behavior—one reason that behaviorism is difficult to use effectively in a classroom. The problem is particularly true for young children and others who cannot delay their reinforcement.
- *The cost is too high.* Children change behavior only if the reward they receive is more attractive than what they have to give up to change behavior. The class clown who receives teacher attention and lots of peer approval for his antics is not easily going to give up these strong reinforcers for something the teacher devises. Peer acknowledgment is a very strong reinforcer!
- *Teachers want too much too soon.* Modifying behavior through operant conditioning takes a long time—it is tedious, deliberate, and time consuming, and must be done in little steps. Thus it is difficult for teachers to be successful, so they usually take shortcuts, which reduces the impact.

Punishment

Punishment is distinctly different from positive and negative reinforcement. While positive and negative reinforcement increase the likelihood and frequency of a behavior, **punishment** is designed to reduce and eliminate a certain behavior. Punishment is also the removal of something pleasant with the result of reducing or eliminating a negative behavior: reducing a child's allowance because she misbehaved; loss of privilege ("You can't go on a field trip because you did not clean the art area"). Punishment must occur immediately after the negative behavior to be effective.

Guidelines for Use of Punishment in the Classroom. Punishment is often overused and incorrectly used in the classroom. If you use punishment—albeit sparingly—there are some guidelines that should be followed.

Punishment must punish. By definition, punishment is something that reduces a behavior. If the punishment does not reduce or eliminate the behavior, it isn't punishment, it's something else—sometimes even a reinforcer. What works for one child may not work for another child.

Punishment cannot be severe. A great challenge in using punishment is to select a punishment that is on the one hand effective, while on the other hand not so severe that it causes anger, resentment, or hostility. Harsh punishment also is counterproductive because it doesn't work when the person giving the punishment—the teacher—is no longer present. Punishment that destroys the relationship between the teacher and student is ineffective as a disciplinary method.

A child should be warned once before punishment is used. A child needs to know ahead of time that a specific behavior will lead to a punishment. More than one warning becomes an idle threat that communicates that no punishment is forthcoming. Thus it is essential for teachers only to warn of a punishment that they are prepared to deliver. Threats don't work.

Punishable behavior should be communicated clearly. Teachers should specifically tell children the behaviors that are unacceptable. Instead of telling Johnny he will be punished for being too loud, a teacher should say, "You are shouting and banging the blocks together, which is unacceptable in the classroom." Children need to know the specific unacceptable behaviors.

Punishment must be consistent. Consistent punishment reduces or eliminates the targeted behaviors; inconsistent punishment does not. But it is often difficult to be consistent in a classroom.

The classroom environment should be changed. In Chapter 5, I discussed how an environment can encourage undesirable behaviors, and why it is important first to assess the environment in response to a child's negative behavior. It is more effective to eliminate the cause of the behavior than to punish the behavior.

Alternative behaviors should be taught and reinforced. When punishing a child, the teacher should provide examples of acceptable responses to the situation, and then reinforce the child's appropriate behaviors.

Explain why the punished behavior is unacceptable. This works because it helps children to generalize the effects of the punishment to apply to similar unacceptable behaviors; it causes the behavior to be reduced even when the punishment is not present, and children expect to know the reasons why they should not engage in certain behaviors. Giving children reasons reduces their anger and defiance.

Some punishments don't work and should not be used. Punishments that should not be used include physical punishment, psychological punishment, extra schoolwork, and suspension from school. Physical punishment does not work because it models inappropriate behavior to the children. Psychological punishment, such as embarrassing or insulting a child, reduces a child's self-esteem, which in turn produces negative behaviors. Extra schoolwork is usually an ineffective punishment unless it is a natural consequence (children have to redo the work because they were lazy or sloppy). It is ineffective because it teaches children to dislike schoolwork, when we should be teaching young children to enjoy learning. And finally, suspension from school does not work because it is often viewed by the child as a reward, and because children who are not in school do not learn appropriate prosocial skills to change their behaviors.

Punishment should be used sparingly. Punishment can be an effective tool for managing behavior in the classroom; however, it loses effectiveness when used frequently.

Social Learning Theory

Social learning is about how people learn from each other. The principal theorist associated with social learning theory is Albert Bandura (1965; 1973; 1989). The theory uses ideas from behaviorism and cognitive theory. An example of social learning theory is a child who decides to imitate his favorite basketball hero, because he respects the player's accomplishments and because he wants his friends to like him. His friends then reinforce this choice of behavior by congratulating him and wanting to be like him.

Modeling

The most common example of social learning theory is **modeling.** Modeling occurs when children observe the behavior of a model and use that observation—either immediately, or at some time in the future—to influence their behavior. Models can be either live—an actual person doing something—or symbolic—a person or character on film, TV, or video, or in a book. We know that modeling works to help children learn. Here are just a few examples (Ormrod, 1997):

- children are better readers when their parents read frequently at home;
- children reduce their fear of a certain situation when they observe a model acting fearlessly in that same situation;
- children are more intolerant of racist language when they are around other children who do not tolerate such racist statements.

Aggression. Many studies have shown that children exposed to models involved in aggressive behavior increase their own aggressive behavior (Bandura, Ross, & Ross, 1961). Further, children who watch aggressive behaviors by characters on TV and in TV cartoons also increase their aggressive behavior (Bandura, Ross, & Ross, 1963).

Moral Behavior. By the same token, there have been various studies that show children learn appropriate behaviors from observing models engaged in moral behavior. Stories that illustrate specific moral behaviors lead to children using the reasoning of the characters in the books to solve their own moral dilemmas (Bandura & McDonald, 1963). The media—TV, videos, film—can also be effective in modeling appropriate behavior for children.

How Modeling Works. Modeling influences children's behaviors in three different ways: first, it teaches new behaviors. Children can learn completely new behaviors by simply watching someone else. Second, modeling reduces or increases existing behaviors. A child who observes another child being punished for a certain behavior is less likely to engage in that behavior; further, a child is more likely to engage in a behavior other children are rewarded for. Finally, modeling teaches similar, though not necessarily identical behaviors. A child who admires his father's basketball abilities may, because of his own unique skills, strive to be successful in soccer. My two eldest daughters excelled in gymnastics; my youngest decided to join the lacrosse team because she admired her sisters but also wanted to be different.

▶ *Our children need positive male role models.*

Characteristics of Effective Models. One of the things that frustrates U.S. parents and teachers is that children often choose the wrong models. Then, after they pick these models, they learn the wrong behaviors from them. Who becomes a model to our children, why, and how do children choose which behaviors to learn from these models? For people or characters (in a book, movie, video, TV program, or music video) to become models, they should have one of more of the following characteristics (Ormrod, 1999):

- *Competence.* Models need to be perceived by the learner as competent in the area being modeled. A child will view a professional basketball player as being competent in basketball, a novelist as competent in writing.
- *Prestige and power.* Models have to have status either within society as a whole or within a small group. This is why punk, rock, and rap stars are role models to many adolescents.
- *Stereotypical gender behavior.* Boys are more likely to imitate aggressive behaviors demonstrated by models; girls are more likely to imitate what they perceive as female behavior.
- *Relevance to the child's social context.* Children will pick and choose the behaviors they learn from models. If it suits their social context, they will imitate it; if not, they will reject it, because the social context reinforces the new behaviors. Certain behaviors—such as clothes, hairstyles, body piercing—are copied by adolescents who hang around peers with similar tastes, thus reinforcing each other's choices.
- *Familiarity.* Parents and teachers are frequent models for young children, especially when viewed by children as competent, respected, and powerful within a context or group.

Application of Social Learning Theory to Education

Modeling is a very powerful tool for teaching children. Research has shown that modeling works very effectively in teaching moral behaviors. Important factors relating to social learning theory in the classroom include the following:

- Children can learn moral values and appropriate classroom and school behaviors simply through observation. Thus classroom management must be very consistent, and teachers need to provide good modeling regarding expected behaviors.
- Modeling provides a faster and more efficient means of teaching new behaviors to children than does behaviorism (Ormrod, 1999).
- Teachers need to expose children to a variety of positive role models, which can be done using classroom visitors, films and videos, and books.
- Children will display new behaviors learned from models only if they are encouraged and motivated to do so, and if these new behaviors are reinforced.
- Children learn only from people they view as models, not necessarily people adults choose as models.
- Children learn the appropriateness of behaviors by observing how teachers respond to other children who engage in those behaviors. Are they rewarded, punished, ignored, praised?

- Children need help in setting realistic behavioral expectations. The best way to do this is through modeling of what constitutes appropriate classroom and school behavior.
- Peers can also act as very powerful models. Teachers need to be very careful about whom they give respect and status to, and which children they choose to model behaviors in the classroom.
- Children pick and choose the behaviors of the models they wish to emulate. Thus it is important for adults in a child's life to model appropriate behaviors consistently all the time (not just in school, or when they feel like it).

Discipline

Managing behavior in a child-care or school environment is very challenging. And it is becoming more and more challenging as children from a broader diversity of backgrounds and experiences attend early childhood programs, as children spend more time in programs, and as more programs increase the academic expectations of their children while reducing time for play, outdoor activities, and meaningful field trips. The challenges are many, including helping children who are by nature egocentric learn to function effectively within groups of children; having children listen to and obey their teacher; and molding each child's sense of responsibility, independence, and citizenship.

Guidance versus Punishment

There is a difference between guidance and punishment. **Guidance** is the attempt to help children develop internal controls so they can function appropriately within all social settings—home, field trips, classrooms, playgrounds. It is based on the idea that guidance must be tailored to help children form their own self-image and to help them learn that ultimately they need to be responsible for their own behavior. A central part of guidance is to teach children the consequences of their behavior: what happens on a field trip if you do not listen to the teacher's instructions? What happens to a game if you are so selfish that the other child can't play? The ultimate goal of guidance is to help each child learn the rules, self-control, and social competence to function successfully around other children in learning settings.

Punishment, on the other hand, is a punitive approach to a child's behavior. It is characterized by the need to make children mind, and it tends to be practiced to meet the needs of the adults and the program, rather than those of the children. Punishment as a component of behaviorism is a legitimate form of molding behavior, as has been discussed. The problem with punishment is that it so easily shifts the purpose for teaching appropriate behavior from helping children learn self-control and social skills to arbitrary rules and actions that promote conformity.

A guidance approach to early childhood discipline has several essential components. These include the physical environment, transitions, special-needs plans, adult behavior, classroom rules, and specific classroom management techniques.

Environment

In Chapter 5, I discussed how the way environments are designed and arranged can assist in managing appropriate behavior or in encouraging inappropriate behavior. If there are too few blocks in the block area, children will continually fight over them; if children have to walk through the dramatic-play area every time they need to go to the bathroom, this will cause conflict and disruption; and if balls from a gross motor area continually bounce into the reading corner, conflict and a need for constant adult interference will result.

Teachers should continually review their classroom arrangements to make sure they support positive behaviors. A teacher should also automatically review an area of the room in which lots of behavior problems seem to occur. Another important link between the environment and children's negative behavior is boredom. Children who are involved, interested, challenged, and absorbed tend not to get into trouble. It is essential that children have plenty to do. They need developmentally appropriate materials, choices, and enough variety to keep them involved.

Transitions

Children find transitions very difficult. A **transition** is a move from one activity or place to another—from classroom to outdoors, classroom to classroom, learning-center activities to group reading, and the center or school to a field trip. Children find this time very difficult for a variety of reasons: often it involves lots of standing around with nothing to do; sometimes it requires developmentally inappropriate behavior, such as standing in a line; and children may feel they have lost control because they are interrupted while doing something that is very important to them. Young children's sense of time is based on activities, not specific linear sections of real time. They believe they are ready to move on when the activity is complete. Also, a transition may cause a sense of fear and anxiety in children, as they move into a new and different experience or activity.

Because of all these factors, children often become disciplinary problems during transitions. I remember observing an early childhood program in South Dakota. It was in the winter (and they have long, cold winters!). To the program's credit, they had the children play on the playground every day, but as they put on hats, coats, gloves, and boots, the two teachers struggled to help children who had difficulty dressing themselves in all this clothing, while the children who dressed themselves efficiently and quickly had nothing to do while they waited. Needless to say, these eager and bored children got into lots of trouble while waiting to go outside to the playground.

There are many things teachers can do to reduce the potential for discipline problems during transitions. Some of these are outlined below.

- *Ten minutes before the end of an activity, warn students.* Ask them to begin to bring their activity to a close. Repeat this warning five minutes before the transition is to take place. Provide adequate time to clean up and to return all materials and equipment to their rightful places.
- *Provide activities for children who get ready quickly and easily.* Children should never be expected simply to do nothing while waiting for the rest of the class to be ready. This often happens at the end of the day, when children wait to be

picked up by their parents. Provide a few activities that are nonmessy and easy to put away for children to do while they are waiting. If the children who never seem to get ready get all the teachers' attention and those who get ready get none, the slow children are being reinforced, while those who responded competently are punished.

- *Provide activities for children to do while in transition.* Examples include songs, marches (to the playground), finger games, counting activities, being a dragon, and holding a rope. The crucial concept is that children in transition are doing something that has meaning and is familiar to them. Children should not be expected to stand in line, sit and wait for lunch, or wait as a group until the teacher is ready; this simply invites problems. (Some argue that young children need to learn how to do this because, as adults, they will have to stand in line and wait. But adults can leave the line if they choose, they can chat with each other, they can daydream, or they can talk on their cellular phone.)
- *Manage activities with individual differences in mind.* Once children have finished lunch, have them put their dirty plates away and then move on to to another activity.
- *Keep transitions as short as possible.* Most children can stay focused and stay on task only for short periods. The longer the transition, the more difficult it becomes.
- *Model good transition behaviors.* Try not to get distracted by other adults— teachers, directors, parents—and activities (picking up your mail, getting the phone) during transitions.
- *Maintain your approach to discipline and guidance during the transition period.* It is important to view transitions as a continuation of classroom behaviors and expectations—albeit with certain additional restrictions. They should not be viewed as isolated activities with new and different behavioral expectations.

Special-Needs Plans

Early childhood programs are serving more and more students with a variety of special needs, including learning disabilities, emotional and behavioral problems, ADHD, and physical challenges. This integration of students with special needs into the overall program fits the goals of exposing children to diversity and providing the least restrictive environment for children with special needs and is covered extensively in Chapter 6. What is important here is that there be a clear plan for each child with special needs, and that teachers know how best to address the child's needs and are comfortable and confident with the child in their classroom.

Teachers need to work closely with the program's special-needs coordinator, or the staff person in charge of students with special needs. Teachers must have adequate information, training, and support to meet the needs of these children fully in their classroom. Children with special needs are often a positive addition to the early childhood or school program, especially when teachers are adequately prepared to work with them.

Adult Behavior

Obviously, the teacher's behavior in the classroom sets the tone for guidance and classroom management. Specific classroom management skills used, responding appropriately and consistently to the unique needs of each child, providing appropriate and challenging activities, and modeling expected behaviors are all examples of good teacher management.

Central to teachers' skills in the classroom is the ability to provide a range of ever-changing, developmentally appropriate activities. If activities are too easy for students, they become bored, and then seek out ways—usually inappropriate—to stimulate themselves. If activities are too difficult, they continually seek adult help and guidance, get frustrated, and may regress into difficult behaviors. Good teachers find a balance of activities that are familiar to children and those that challenge, change, and stimulate; good teachers also have developed skills that enable them to respond to children's unique needs without making children dependent on them. Children who are overly dependent on the teacher cause disciplinary problems because they continually seek guidance, directions, and limits, placing too much strain on the teacher who has many children to work with.

Adult modeling includes showing respect both for all the children in the classroom and for parents and other staff. It includes using appropriate vocal tone and volume, giving reasons for expectations (other than "because I said so"), having high expectations for all children, and modeling specific classroom behaviors that are vital to the management of the classroom: putting toys away, cleaning up at the end of an activity, respecting students' space and projects, and sharing.

Classroom Rules

Classroom rules are important tools to help the smooth management of early childhood classrooms. A few ideas regarding classroom rules are enumerated here.

- *Make sure children help develop the rules.* This is especially true for children of preschool age and older. It makes them feel part of the classroom community. Obviously, the older the children, the easier it is to include them in the process.
- *Keep the rules simple, and don't have too many.*
- *Write as many as possible in a positive way.* Instead of "No running in the classroom," write "Walking softly only" or "Walking with soft feet." Instead of "No disrupting other projects," maybe write "Respect other children's projects."
- *Write up the rules and place them in a prominent place on the wall.*
- *Remind children on a regular basis of the rules.*
- *Try to create symbols or pictures that represent a rule.* That way, children can check on them without an adult having to read them the list.
- *Use the rules when working with students.* It is also important to explain carefully when you are applying a rule.
- *Use the rules consistently.*

Specific Classroom Management Techniques

Obviously, working with a group of young children in a classroom, on the playground, and on field trips requires a variety of skills and techniques—not to mention patience. Below are some techniques that are used to manage children in early childhood settings.

Ignoring. Behaviorism tells us that children like attention, especially from the teacher, and often will do anything to get the attention they enjoy. Sometimes the easiest way

▶*Children occupied in developmentally appropriate activities are less likely to pose discipline problems.*

to get attention is to engage in disruptive or inappropriate behavior. Some children have learned from experience that it's easier and quicker to get attention this way. One approach to reducing these negative behaviors in the classroom is simply to ignore the behavior. This works even better if you can reinforce (pay attention to) an appropriate behavior of the same student. Of most importance is to be aware of children who seem to get your attention only when they are using destructive or inappropriate behavior, which may simply be their way of seeking your attention. Of course, there are some behaviors—such as racist comments to other children—that cannot ever be ignored.

Distraction and Redirection. Sometimes a destructive child can be simply redirected or distracted. For example, two toddlers fighting over one ball might be easily redirected if another ball is provided. At that age it is far more effective to introduce the second ball than to try to explain to the fighting toddlers that they should share. Another example is two children arguing over the only spare swing on the playground. A teacher could suggest that one of the children play on the trike until another swing is available. One reason this method works is that preoperational children are very single-minded and very egocentric, so they are often unable to entertain choices and alternative ways out of conflicts. It often helps for teachers to show the two children that instead of fighting over one swing—in which case no one wins—one could be on the swing, the other having fun on the trike. (By the way, once on the trike, the child often forgets about the swing). This approach also teaches children that there are choices and alternative solutions to problems, a crucial social skill to develop.

Verbal Intervention. Verbal intervention is a technique in which a teacher directly intervenes and tries to help a child handle a problem appropriately. When Johnny starts fighting because Jimmy destroyed his **marble rollway,** the teacher helps Johnny verbalize his frustration and anger. The teacher can assist Johnny and Jimmy to work out a solution. "You help me rebuild my marble shoot, and then you can play with me." By using this technique the teacher explains to the child the important lesson that using words to work out problems is more effective than hitting, fighting, or tattling.

Logical Consequences. A fundamental idea behind the concept of guidance and helping children develop social skills and self-control is to help children understand the results of disruptive and inappropriate behaviors: certain behaviors are not acceptable in the classroom because of their negative consequences, not because they are bad or the authority figure does not want them. **Logical consequences** is an approach that makes the punishment the consequence for the action. For example, a child who spills a cup of milk must clean up the mess; children who throw things in the dramatic-play area should be excluded from that area until they can demonstrate that they can play without throwing; a child who is disruptive on a field trip should be left out of the next field trip. For this method to be effective, the consequence of the undesirable behavior must be logically connected to it and, more important, the child must see the connection. I have often witnessed preschool children who, as a result of disrupting the classroom, are punished by not being allowed to go outside to play with the other students. Not only is this not a logical consequence, but a child running around a classroom needs to get outside and let off lots of steam and frustration.

Time-Out. Time-out has been used and misused in early childhood and other children's programs for years. Almost everyone has an opinion about time-out, and there are several conflicting theoretical underpinnings for this technique. I remember as a graduate student conducting a study on the use of time-out in an early childhood program. During the days I observed the program, a 5-year-old boy spent most of his time every day in time-out. Every time he did something wrong, he was automatically placed back in time-out: in the classroom, in the center, and on the playground. Almost as soon as he got out of time-out, he was placed back in. Not only did this approach not teach him appropriate behavior, it also involved lots of time, energy, and emotion on the part of the teachers. And, of course, a child who spends most of his days in time-out does not learn to feel good about himself.

The basic purpose of time-out is to reduce stimulation of children by removing them from the environment. The belief is that the stimulation of the classroom, activity, or other children is simply too much for the child, which then causes the negative behavior. The child needs to relax, regroup, and refocus; any potential victims need time to get away from aggressive children, and the teacher needs time to disengage and refocus. The time-out allows the situation to defuse, and children to regain control of their emotions.

In strictly behavioral terms, however, time-out is punishment. It is a response to a negative behavior enforced by the authority figure, and to the child it is aversive. When my wife and I used time-out at home—sending children to their room—our children would burst into tears, even though their room was a warm, attractive place, with toys and books. But since they viewed this action as punishment, they cried.

Time-out can be an effective part of a disciplinary approach. If it is used, it should be used sparingly (remember the discussion on punishment), and it should never be used for children younger than 2. Suggest that a child take a break from the conflict situation, and place the child in a neutral area, away from other children. After you have done this several times, children will automatically know where to go; a child might even volunteer, "I need a time-out!" The child in the area should have something to do, and should be left there until able to reenter the activity appropriately.

The Friendship Table. The friendship table, or talk-it-over table, is a version of peer mediation that works for younger children. In this technique, a teacher removes children involved in a conflict to a neutral area, such as a friendship table, where they sit and try to solve the problem quietly. The teacher provides active listening—including allowing an opportunity for the children to give their side of the problem, uninterrupted, using "I" statements, and rephrasing the problem. The teacher should also ask students to suggest solutions to the problem, then help them negotiate a solution they can both live with. The role of the teacher is to defuse the situation by removing the children to the neutral site, to help them clarify the specific issues of conflict, then to provide a forum for solutions.

Developing Prosocial Behaviors in Young Children

Alice Honig and Donna Wittmer discuss a variety of ways to assist young children in developing prosocial behaviors (1994; 1996). These ideas are summarized here.

Focus on prosocial behaviors. Teachers should emphasize the importance of children helping others, model prosocial behaviors with children, label and identify prosocial and antisocial behaviors, acknowledge children's social behaviors when they assist or support other children, and notice and reward positive social behaviors—with words, hugs, and smiles, but not with stickers or other material reinforcers.

Encourage children's understanding of their own feelings and the feelings of other children. Children need help in identifying their own feelings, especially frustration, anger, tiredness, and a sense of powerlessness. They also need to learn how to gain perspective and the ability to understand and empathize with the feelings of others. These can be achieved through role playing, reading books, using puppets, and acting out stories. Teachers also need to help children understand the consequences of their behaviors—other children become hurt, upset, and sad and don't want to be your friend. Finally, children need to be taught to be assertive in their prosocial behavior—to be able to do or say something about it.

Encourage children to problem-solve and plan. Children need help in determining alternative solutions to their conflicts—both to develop alternative solutions and to imagine the results of each solution, thus being able to select the best one. Ask children to contemplate how their behavior is affecting other children and the whole class; use pictures showing children helping each other and sharing, and ask them to describe these scenarios; and teach children specific social skills such as listening, saying thank you, offering help, and taking turns.

Use positive disciplinary approaches. Teachers should use reasoning, positive reinforcement, empathetic listening, clear rules and expectations, and a positive regard for each child. Offer children alternatives to aggressive behaviors (throw the ball outside, bang on the woodworking table), and offer them choices. Choices allow children to accept responsibility for the choice, because they made it. Obviously, teachers must select these choices carefully.

Pair prosocial children with children who struggle. Shy children, and children who struggle with prosocial behavior, learn by being paired with socially skilled and assertive children.

Emphasize cooperation, and teach conflict resolution skills. In a cooperative classroom, the emphasis is on working together to achieve goals, not against each other in competition. Cooperative classrooms engender more prosocial children. Children also need to be taught how to resolve conflicts peacefully.

Use children's literature. There is a wealth of children's literature that tells stories and provides examples of prosocial behaviors—helping, sharing, empathizing, being generous, and so on. The entire Heartwood Character Education Curriculum is based on these kinds of children's books. After a book is read, children engage in discussions to

▶*Empathy toward animals leads to empathy toward people.*

help them understand the actions and motives of the characters, and how they can learn from them in forming their own behaviors.

Lead discussions on prosocial behaviors. Teachers should engage children in talking about prosocial behaviors and why it is important—why and how to share, what is fair and not fair, and moving toward the concept that the unique needs of others should be taken into account in determining fairness.

Develop class and social projects. Projects that involve both caring for the classroom and school and caring for children or people less fortunate teach altruism. Projects might include cleaning up the schoolyard, writing to children in troubled lands, collecting toys or food for those in need, and making friends with senior citizens. Children can also decide to be helpful at home and in the classroom.

Use prosocial media as a model. Children should regularly watch media programs like *Mister Rogers' Neighborhood* to see prosocial behaviors modeled. By the same token, of course, children should not watch aggressive programs or play aggressive video games.

Invite moral mentors. People from the community who have demonstrated service and altruism to others should be invited to the classroom—a person who visits people at the old-age home; someone who takes meals to a shut-in; a grandparent who volunteers in a Head Start program.

Work with families. Let parents know that developing prosocial behavior is an integral part of the curriculum, and that they can help reinforce lessons learned in the classroom. Provide techniques parents can use to help their children verbalize their feelings and provide appropriate, positive discipline.

Encourage children to care for others who need help. Children should be given responsibilities they can handle to care for and aid younger children or those who need extra help.

Include prosocial curricular components in the overall curriculum. There is a variety of prepackaged curricula that, when carefully integrated into the overall program, effectively teach a range of prosocial behaviors.

Implement a comprehensive, schoolwide prosocial program. An entire school or child-care program should develop and implement a schoolwide approach that communicates prosocial expectations and supports children's prosocial learning. These programs are often called character education curricula, and are discussed in detail in Chapter 15.

Train older children to be peer mentors.

Working with Parents

Early childhood programs must work very closely with parents in the area of providing discipline and guidance for their children. Included in this partnership must be a discipline policy, open communication between the program and parents, parent training opportunities, and the use of books, articles, and newsletters that explain the program's philosophy.

Discipline Policy. A program should have a written policy that clearly outlines disciplinary approaches it uses (and those it will not use), when and how the program will seek additional assistance in addressing problems (such as special-education options and outside consultants), suspension procedures, and even asking a child to leave. Parents should be involved in helping to write this policy, and it should be reviewed and revised periodically, with parent input. Some early childhood programs have new parents read and sign the program's discipline policy.

Open Communication. Because children in early childhood education programs often experience conflicting behavioral expectations at home and in the program, and because these children are struggling to learn appropriate social skills in a variety of settings, it is important for parents, teachers, and the program to talk to one another often about expectations, frustrations, conflicts, and disagreements.

Training and Newsletters. Programs should use every possible opportunity to provide skills, approaches, and new ideas to parents that help them develop prosocial skills and social competence in their children. Because the very parents who need this information the most often do not attend program training (lack of time, or negative association with educational programs), creative ways need to be explored to educate parents. Newsletters is one good approach; others include meetings with parents away from the program, and sending home brief, program-made videos to communicate to parents.

Libraries for Parents. Lending libraries provide books, magazine articles, videos, cassette tapes, and other parenting material that parents can borrow. As the Internet becomes more popular, programs and schools should develop Web sites that include on-line advice columns to which parents can send questions that the program will answer. Programs must realize that most working parents are far too busy to read entire advice books and magazines.

Peer Mediation

A fairly new way to address student disruption and misbehavior is peer mediation. Peer mediation provides a structured forum for the resolution of in-school disputes by using students as **peer mediators.** These mediators provide practice in critical thinking, problem solving, and self-discipline (McWhirter et al., 1998). Peer mediation programs are based on the premise that getting children to help children is an effective way of resolving conflicts. Peer leaders have credibility among peers and also serve as role models—both for their ability to help resolve problems and by modeling appropriate alternatives to conflictual behaviors. Peer mediators also benefit from the training required of the programs, the behaviors required of mediators, and their important status in the school. Because of the skills required of peer mediators, these programs have been implemented in elementary schools but not in preschool programs. The friendship table is a variation that works with preschool children.

Peer mediation programs have been shown not only to reduce conflicts in a program but also to teach peer mediators prosocial responses to conflicts. Many of these mediators themselves changed their own antisocial behaviors (McCormick, 1988).

Training

Peer mediation is not effective unless it is a schoolwide effort that has the full support of all the staff. Before a peer training program is implemented in a school, the entire school staff should receive training, which should include communication skills—active listening, message clarification, body language, giving "I" messages, questioning, and problem solving; further, role playing is used to familiarize mentors with expected behaviors.

After a schoolwide kickoff, student mediators should be nominated, selected, and trained. Nominations should come from teachers, administrators, and children, including self-nominations. Typically, students are trained by the school staff, and maybe by community consultants. The training takes five half-days, and the students should be trained in the four stages of peer mediation. At the end of the training, the peer mediators receive schoolwide recognition and some form of acknowledgment from other students (T-shirts, hats, and the like). Once the program is initiated, peer mediators meet twice a week with the school's staff coordinator to learn new skills, troubleshoot, and provide support for one another.

Introduction. This first stage of an actual mediation intervention involves the mediator asking the children involved in a conflict whether they need a mediator, and then removing them to a neutral physical location, reviewing the rules of the process, and getting the children to commit to the process.

Listening. For this stage, the peer mediator listens to each child involved in the conflict. The children relate the incident in turn, with no interruptions allowed. Each child is expected to listen carefully to the other child's account.

Wants. Here each child in the conflict expresses what he or she wants. The mediator helps the children clarify these wants by restating them. Hidden agendas are explored, and wants clarified.

Solutions. Each child involved in the conflict is asked to contribute ideas regarding ways to solve the problem. The mediator clarifies suggestions and checks for balance. Each child is then asked if the solution is acceptable, if the conflict is solved, and asks for ideas about how future conflicts can be avoided. The mediator also asks the participants to tell their friends that the conflict has been resolved, so that peers won't try to reignite the problem. The mediator then congratulates the children for solving the problem, and writes up the required report.

Peer Mediation Programs that Don't Work

Many of these peer mediation programs have been very successful; but I have observed several programs that were not successful. Some of the reasons these programs failed include:

- inadequate training of the peer mediators;
- peer mediators who were nominated and selected by the adults but were not respected and had no credibility with the other students;
- a process (especially detailed written reports) that required skills mediators did not possess;
- lack of ongoing staff support, training, and revitalization;
- the person who instituted and supported the program (usually the principal) left the school;
- lack of an evaluation to trouble-shoot and help improve the program.

Conclusion

Addressing issues of guidance and discipline in young children begins with helping children develop a positive self-image. Part of each child's self-image is social competence—the ability to function effectively with adults and peers in a variety of settings—which includes special prosocial skills and behaviors. Theories of learning—including behaviorism, social learning theory, Erikson's psychosocial stages, and moral reasoning—can provide a framework for teachers. But teachers also need to use specific classroom-management techniques to work effectively with young children, while programs like peer mediation can also help provide a schoolwide framework. Finally, staff must work very closely with parents so that they effectively support each child's ability to function successfully within a program or school.

Questions and Projects

1. What discipline methods did your parents use with you at home? Did they work? Did they cause resentment or anger in you? When you have children (or if you currently have children), what discipline methods will you employ?

2. Discuss the relationship of a child's social competence with the child's later school success.

3. Where do you stand on Lickona's stages of moral reasoning? Do you believe children go through distinct stages that are characterized by how they think about right and wrong? Do all children go through these stages? Give clear arguments for your point of view.

4. How does a child's opportunity to make choices, and to engage in student-directed learning, produce secure children with a positive self-image?

5. Design a parent communication document (newsletter, brochure, video, Web page) that communicates to parents a program's discipline approach. Use an existing program you know, or make up a program's discipline procedure.

CHAPTER

13

Science *and* Math

Mathematical and science learning have often been neglected, or at least underemphasized, in early childhood classrooms. As we move into a more technologically advanced world, and a world of global competition and business, the need for future citizens skilled and knowledgeable in mathematics and science is great both for the future of this country and for the success of individual citizens. The challenge for early childhood directors, teachers, and curriculum specialists is to develop approaches to science and math that set a solid foundation, while also developing in all of our students a desire for future math and science exploration and learning.

Early childhood educators need to find ways to capitalize on young children's natural inquisitiveness to prepare them for an ever more technological world. To do so we have to reconstruct the very way we teach math and science, and we have to focus on teaching math and science at the early childhood age. An additional area of concern is that we must be able to prepare all students to be successful in math and science, including minority students and girls, who are usually underrepresented in higher-level math and science classes in their later school experience. This chapter addresses ways to lay a solid scientific and mathematical foundation, focusing on the concepts that build math and science literacy: observation, questioning, measuring, comparing, ordering, analyzing, projection, and estimating. ■

Questions to Consider

1. What is the best way to increase science and math learning for young children?
2. How important is math and science learning during the early years?
3. To what extent can young children learn complex math and science concepts? How?
4. How should classrooms be arranged to encourage math and science learning?
5. What is developmentally appropriate math and science learning for young children?

Theoretical Basis for Math and Science Education

With my kindergarten class we often went on long nature hikes through the Pennsylvania woods and wetlands. On returning to our kindergarten classroom, we placed all our found objects on the science table. After one such trip, these might include a well-preserved animal skull, feathers from several different birds, an old nest left over from the previous year, and some blue eggshells. Stanley poured his pond water from the pail into a large, clear bowl; tadpoles at different stages of development started swimming around in the clear water. Heather put her red F (a kind of salamander) in the aquarium. Two girls started cutting out egg-shaped pieces of brown construction paper to glue onto our egg graph, which tracked the egg production of the hens our class cared for.

Before we left on our walk, Jared read the thermometer hanging outside and recorded the temperature on a chart. Anna added a new bird to the list of birds that came to our classroom feeder, after identifying it in the bird book. After snack, the children dispersed into various learning centers. Two girls sat under the loft with a book about geese and their young—on our walk we had stopped for our daily observation of a Canada goose nest. Heather and Jared went to the woodwork bench, making boats to sail on the newly unfrozen wetlands. Because they had noticed the way the wind blew at their jackets, they decided to build sailboats. And Wendy studied various Easter egg decorations in her book before copying some of them onto the eggs we had collected.

Young children are natural scientists and mathematicians. They observe everything around them; they want to know how things work, and they want to know why: "How deep is the pond?" "How many eggs did we collect today?" "How big will the tree grow?" "How many baby Canadian geese will there be?"

The U.S. Department of Education and the Natural Science Foundation endorse mathematics and science curricula that promote active learning, inquiry, problem solving, cooperative learning, and other instructional methods that motivate students (Lind, 1999). As children explore their environment, they actively construct their own knowledge. Many early childhood theorists provide insight into the ways young children learn the basic concepts of math and science. A detailed discussion of these theories is presented in detail in Chapter 9; here I simply touch on them to frame our discussion on the development of science and math knowledge.

Constructivism

The constructivist approach to teaching science and math is based on the work of Piaget, Kamii, DeVries, Vygotsky, Bruner, and others. The basic concept of constructivism is that "learners do not acquire knowledge that is transmitted to them; rather they construct knowledge through their own intellectual activity and make it their own" (Chaillé & Britain, 1997, p. 11). Further, children construct knowledge by having lots of opportunities to manipulate real objects in the real world, to discuss and reflect on what they are doing, and to represent their newfound knowledge in a variety of ways. For example, consider how a young child learns about a wooden cube. Initially the cube changes its physical appearance, depending on the angle at which the child views it (everything from a two-dimensional square to a cube in three-dimensional perspective). It may also appear to change size, depending on its relation to other objects and distance from the child. By manipulating the cube and experiencing its physical consistency—regardless of what it looks like—drawing and painting cubes, playing with cube blocks, and discussing the idea of cubes, the child gains knowledge of the physical aspects of all cubes.

For children to learn about science and math through a constructive approach they must be actively involved in manipulating real objects in an environment that encourages their ability to discover the scientific and mathematical properties of these objects and their interrelatedness. Constructivist math and science education capitalizes on the way young children think as they interact with the world. To constructivists, the essential scientific educational activity is what goes on in children's heads as they construct their knowledge about math and science.

Jean Piaget. Most young children are functioning within what Piaget called the pre-operational stage, which extends from age 2 to age 6 or 7. Children in this stage are egocentric, which means that almost everything they do and think is in some way related to them. The preoperational stage is also characterized by an emphasis on the physical attributes of the world, a very primitive ability to manipulate symbols, and the domination of a single idea at any particular moment, at the expense of all other concepts or information. As children shift to different concepts—say, from shape to color, then to volume—each factor in turn dominates their thinking, obscuring or eliminating the other characteristics. Preoperational children have not grasped the concept of conservation. Once children understand that quantity does not change with a change of physical appearance (or volume, length, or mass), they have learned conservation and have moved into the stage of concrete operations (ages 6–7).

Preoperational children need lots and lots of opportunities to have hands-on experience with real materials: playing with sand and water; building with unit blocks; playing in the dramatic-play area; serving food to their classmates at snack time; and counting marbles, beads, blocks, film containers, nails, sticks, and more. By pouring water from a wide, short container into a narrow, tall container, then back into the short container, children can see that the volume does not change—nothing is added, and nothing is taken away.

According to Piaget, once children have learned a new skill or concept, they need opportunities to practice what they have learned. In early childhood programs, practice usually exhibits itself in play. Children need lots of opportunities to play with math and science ideas.

Early elementary-school children are moving from the preoperational stage to the concrete operations stage. This means they have grasped number, volume, linear, and mass conservation. Abstract concepts can hold their own against contradictory physical evidence. Three is always three, whether it is three Nintendos or three hamburgers. Elementary-school children are capable of handling more than one piece of information in their mind, and are somewhat less egocentric. Children can now do mathematical and scientific activities not tied to concrete materials: adding, subtracting, learning scientific theories, and predicting results; but the manipulation of real objects is still very helpful, and practice is still essential.

Lev Vygotsky. Vygotsky's zone of proximal development (ZPD) is the range between what children can do by themselves, and what they can do with expert assistance from another child, teacher, parent, or volunteer (Berk & Winsler, 1995). Children who are taught outside the ZPD will either be bored because it is too easy, or frustrated because it is too difficult.

Within the concept of the ZPD, the teacher's role is one of supporting, suggesting, questioning, encouraging, and enhancing rather than providing direct instruction. A teacher working within the ZPD might observe a child building with unit blocks, and counting the blocks up to five. The child seems to have a fairly good grasp of numbers up to five. The teacher decides that the child probably can learn to go further than five with expert help, so engages the child in what happens when you add one to five; when you add one to six; and so on.

Scaffolding—an idea based on Vygotsky's work—is a mental structure that assists children in learning new concepts; once the concept is learned, the scaffold is no longer needed. Teachers can help children develop procedures, techniques, and strategies that facilitate learning math and science. Using the scientific method to gain information—form a hypothesis, collect data, prove or disprove the hypothesis—is a way of scaffolding science learning. Another approach is to make activities continually more challenging and complex, as children's knowledge develops. Vygotsky also developed the concept of private speech—children talking to themselves to direct their activities, control their behaviors, and provide verbal hints and cues. As teachers of children learning science and math, we can help children develop helpful and constructive learning strategies that they can internalize into private speech.

Children's increasingly sophisticated language and representational skills help them scaffold their own learning, and teachers should provide more complex verbal instructions for scaffolding children's learning.

Jerome Bruner.   Bruner made famous the statement, "A hole is to dig." What he meant was that young children define things by what they do—their activity—rather than by what something is called. For a young child, a hole dug in the ground is not defined as a thing—a hole—but rather as an activity—to dig. When my first daughter, Maia, was young, I built her a climbing play area in our apartment. Part of the play area was a slide. She just loved the slide, and every time she went down it, she exclaimed "Whee!" in delight. When she wanted to play on her slide, she would ask, "Whee?"

As Maia grew to be a young preschooler, I created a weekly calendar for her. It did not use months, dates, and days of the week, but was a seven-day chart. For each day we glued on or drew pictures of the activities she would do on those days. On one day was a gymnast, another day a ballet dancer, and still another a picture of someone painting a picture. Daily and weekly schedules in an early childhood program should stress activities: snack (image of eating), free play or outdoors (children playing outside), and so on, which is a much more effective approach to teaching time than the traditional calendar activity (Swartz, 1994). The idea of stressing activities also emphasizes how young children learn through doing things, rather than by learning labels for objects and ideas.

Bruner and other information processing theorists also inform us that children must pay attention to what they are learning; they need to make sense of a new concept in order to learn it; and information that has meaning to children is easier for them to learn, store in their memory, and retrieve than information that has no meaning. Using these ideas to teach math and science, we must make sure the activity is interesting to each child, at the child's level, and meaningful (Bredekamp & Copple, 1997). As children grow older (early elementary-school years), they begin to move from an action concept of

Developmentally Appropriate Practice

learning to more conventional labels (they move from action labels to object labels). Their interests and what is personally meaningful change rapidly because of new and more complex experiences (Ormrod, 1999). Teachers of early elementary-school children should carefully help them connect new learning to past knowledge and experience.

Erik Erikson

Most young children are in what Erikson calls the Initiative versus Guilt stage, which extends from about age 3 to age 5½ (Erikson, 1963), and is characterized by children's natural exploration into the social and physical world away from home. Teachers and parents should encourage children this age to explore, risk, try new things, and order the world in a way that makes sense to them. They should also realize that these children move quickly from independence to dependence, and vice versa.

Older children are in the Industry versus Inferiority stage (ages 5½–12), characterized by the need to master new challenges, tasks, projects, activities, obstacles. For math and science education, this is a wonderful stage. Children love to accomplish tasks, create projects, and complete activities. We must provide all sorts of challenging projects, must integrate math and science activities across all other learning opportunities, and provide lots and lots of opportunities for children to experience success in these areas: grow a garden, make racing cars, launch weather balloons, graph the progress of their favorite sports team, do a survey of classmates' attitudes about school lunch, observe and record weather patterns, develop hypotheses to predict results, and more.

Although children aged 6 to 8 have progressed into Piaget's concrete operations stage and Erikson's Industry versus Inferiority stage, they still need lots of real materials, problems to solve, and authentic activities. We are all partly enactive and iconic learners; so learning must be meaningful for learners, and all math and science phenomena are based on nature and real laws, structures, and concepts.

How Fundamental Math and Science Skills Develop

The best way to learn math and science is to do math and science (Lind, 1999). With young children this means having them study natural phenomena over a period of time. "Active, hands-on, student-centered inquiry is at the core of good science education (Lind, 1999, p. 74). The same can be said of math education. During early education, young children acquire both fundamental science and math concepts and fundamental processing skills. In addition to doing, children acquire math and science knowledge through asking, reflecting, discussing, observing, investigating, listening, and reasoning (Copley, 2000).

Children learn scientific concepts starting in infancy. Babies explore the world with their senses. They look, touch, smell, hear, taste. Children are born curious. Infants learn about size, weight, shape, time sequence (they cry before they get fed), and space. Piaget called this process of constructing mental relationships—including size, number, color patterns, sets and groups, and so on—**logical-mathematical learning.** Children must manipulate (order, sequence, group, and so on) real objects to develop the abstract

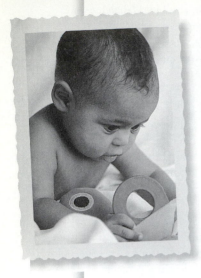

▶*Even infants are learning math and science knowledge through their senses.*

concepts of number, hierarchy, order, pattern, and more. Children use science observation skills to learn basic math skills, such as

- one-to-one correspondence (pegs in holes, one cookie for each child);
- counting (straws needed for the class, numbers of seeds needed to plant pumpkins);
- classifying (color, size, shape, texture, function, type);
- measuring (pouring sand, water, rice, and other materials from one container to another);
- the concepts of more (by adding to) and less (by taking away from).

Toddlers sort things; they put them in piles by size, shape, color, function, and likes and dislikes. Toddlers also learn about measurement by pouring sand, water, and other materials from one container to another. For the first two years, children learn through exploration all sorts of physical knowledge: taste, color, shape, smell, function (roll, fall, stack). They also learn specific skills they will use later for further learning, such as observing, describing, talking about, comparing, measuring, sequencing, and the like. Preschool and kindergarten children begin to apply basic skills of counting, measuring, comparing, predicting, and interpreting to observe scientific phenomena. For example, in the scientific activity of watching beans sprout, children will add water each day, dictate observations about what is occurring, chart the growth of their own bean sprout, and compare the time their seed sprouts to that of their classmates'. In this scientific endeavor children are counting and using one-to-one correspondence, time sequences, and comparison between groups. During preschool years, young children learn basic math and science concepts, and learn processes to help them use and expand these concepts. From grades one through three, children apply these early concepts and skills in more abstract ways.

Children develop mathematical knowledge by progressing from determining quantity by simple observation (looks more, looks bigger, feels heavier) to actively counting or measuring the quantity, length, or weight of something (Ginsburg, 1977). Children develop logical-mathematical thinking by manipulating objects and then abstracting a basic mathematical feature of the relations between objects—three apples, pencils lined up by length, the distance between each number is the same. Children must learn these mathematical concepts through interacting with the environment in mathematical ways. As children engage in math activities in early childhood programs and schools, they move on to the stage of formal knowledge. At this point they learn the meaning of a variety of symbols (−, +, =) and numbers (6, 4), and the functions and operations they represent (Ginsburg, 1977).

Math and Science Are Naturally Integrated

Fundamental math concepts include counting, classifying (by a variety of criteria), measuring (linear, liquid, solid, area), sequencing, and matching. When applied to science problems, these math concepts are called **process skills**—those skills required to solve science problems. Other science process skills are observing, communicating, inferring, hypothesizing, and defining and controlling variables. All of these process skills are used to solve both science and math problems.

For example, in an activity with balls and ramps, children are given balls of different sizes and weights, and ramps of different angles. The children might then observe differences in speed and distance contingent on the size and weight of the ball or the height and length of the ramp. In this example, children use mathematical concepts of measuring speed, distance, height, length, and counting (how many blocks are supporting each ramp?), while engaging in scientific observation (Lind, 1999).

Math and science concepts are acquired by children as they engage in traditional early childhood activities: with blocks, sand, water; manipulation; dramatic play; cooking; gardening; woodworking; block play; and more. Building this basic science and math understanding both provides basic knowledge and develops in children a vital interest in future learning—a disposition to science and math study.

How to Teach Young Children Math and Science

Teaching science and math requires us to match very carefully the way young children learn with the content, processes, and approaches we use. This is the secret of any good early childhood curriculum, as described in detail in Chapter 4. Matching curriculum with each child's developmental level is especially important in math and science teaching because, in their highest form, math and science require highly complex and abstract thought processes. Further, traditional math and science curricula have tended to concentrate on the abstract, rather than hands-on, aspects of these disciplines. Young children simply are not abstract thinkers; thus we must find ways to introduce children to science and math phenomena at their developmental levels.

Mismatching content and developmental levels leads to misconceptions and frustrations for teachers, parents, and children (Lind, 1999). The result of this mismatch is that children are not able to extend, apply, or interpret deeper meanings of the content, and their interest in and positive attitudes to science are likely to diminish. To assure a match, teachers should include certain activities in teaching:

- *Observe children.* Teachers must carefully and constantly observe how children learn, and then use this information in teaching math and science. Not only does this remind teachers of what is developmentally appropriate for the children, but it continually alerts us to just how differently individual children learn.
- *Recognize the limits of young children's learning capacity.* Young children think on a simple level, and they think concretely. Math and science use many different levels of thought and abstraction. There are certain math and science concepts and facts that cannot be taught to young children.
- *Answer children's math and science questions at their level of understanding.* One approach is to turn children's questions around to see how they would answer them.

As I have already discussed, young children are predisposed to learn about the scientific and mathematical aspects of the world. Elkind argues (1999) that young children possess two fundamental motivation strategies at this age: the need to master new tasks and challenges, and the desire to please teachers and parents. Further, Elkind reiterates what we have already discussed—that effective math and science education of young children requires a match between children's conceptual abilities and the ways they are taught, and the child must be motivated to learn.

Obstacles to Teaching Math and Science to Young Children

According to Elkind, three obstacles face those teaching young children (up to about age 7) math and science (1999). The first is that young children do not use reflective or logical analysis. For example, young children use numbers in three different ways: to label, to rank, and to count. Labels would be "five apples"; rank would be "I am the biggest," "You came home last," or "He ate the most." Higher math uses only the intervals of numbers—the idea that the distance between numbers is the same, whether it be 1–2 or 10,006–10,007. Young children don't learn this concept until they achieve concrete operations. Another example of adult math activity that is inappropriate for young children is the popular activity of learning the calendar (Swartz, 1994).

The second obstacle arises from the fact that young children are **transductive** thinkers, as described by Piaget and Inhelder (1958): young children think from object to object and from event to event. By contrast, adults use **inductive** thinking, which is using abstract criteria to think, and **deductive** thinking, which is applying general principles to specific facts in order to reach a conclusion. To young children, if two events occur together, one must cause the other; if two objects occur at the same time and place, they must be related logically in some way. "If I eat spaghetti, I must be Italian" (Elkind, 1999, p. 64).

The third obstacle is that preschoolers have their own learning goals, which tend to conflict with a program's curricular goals. For example, it isn't until age 7 or 8 that children have a good sense of clock time; and maps and geographic space do not become comprehensible until children are in later elementary grades. So to make these concepts part of the curriculum makes little sense. Young children's curriculum should focus on sensory properties and spatial and temporal relationships: color, height, texture, sound, smooth, behind, in front of, last, before, next to, huge, and so on. These are concepts that exist at the same level, and that can lay the foundation for future, more abstract concepts.

Elkind reminds us that while teaching math and science at this young age is essential, we cannot do so the way we teach math and science to older children and adults.

Teaching Math to Young Children

According to Copley (whose 2000 work is based on the *Principles and Standards for School Mathematics* published by the National Council of Teachers of Mathematics), teaching math to young children can be broken into three areas: curriculum principles, instructional principles, and assessment principles. Curriculum and instructional principles are covered below, assessment principles are in Chapter 14.

Curriculum

A math curriculum for young children should cover content, process, environment, and child-centered choices. The content of math programs for children up to age 8 should include number and operation; patterns, functions, and algebra; geometry and spatial sense; measurement; and data analysis and probability. See the chapter feature on NCTM for specifics of each of these areas. As Copley points out, to know mathematics is to do mathematics (2000). Children need lots of opportunities to use symbols, make connections among various kinds of math, communicate mathematically, solve problems, reason and think, and use mathematical operations across the curriculum. These processes include interacting with peers, investigating, interacting with materials and the environment, and constructing knowledge.

An appropriate environment for math learning includes three main types of materials. There must be concrete materials—blocks, pattern blocks, counters, attribute

Partnerships to Promote Math and Science Education

One way to address the shortage of quality math and science activities for young children is to create community and family partnerships (Weiss, 1999). These partnerships must actively include parents. Further, simply providing materials and activities to parents will not work; they need training, resources, specific instruction in math and science teaching techniques, and ongoing support. Parents must also be involved in planning the community strategy. Community agencies that need to be included are child-care centers, family child-care networks, child-care information and referral agencies, kindergarten and preschool programs, Head Start programs, parent organizations, family resource centers, family support programs, service centers, nature centers, museums, libraries, health clinics, public health agencies, schools, cable and public TV stations, volunteer groups, and Web sites, newspapers, and other media.

Additionally, money is needed simply to develop these collaborations and community programs. There must be a national and state infrastructure to help create and support local efforts. These federal and state programs should be clearinghouses for positive models and approaches; should provide grants to stimulate community-based efforts to support math and science education for children under age 5; and should actively include parents and relevant institutions. Math and science activities must be free or low-cost. They must be developmentally appropriate and help parents and caregivers gain access to a variety of community agencies and resources.

Communities need to find ways to provide collective training and funding opportunities, and to conduct needs assessments that reveal gaps in service. Further, collaborative efforts require better coordination between preschool programs and K–12 programs.

Research clearly shows that young children learn math and science concepts and facts through interactions with their environment, rather than by studying discrete academic skills. Children learn to enjoy math and science through interactions with parents, family members, caregivers, and classroom visitors, as well as by experiences like visits to the zoo and museums. "Children's early learning . . . including the precursors for learning science, mathematics, and technology . . . occurs through a dynamic process involving child, family, and community influences" (Weiss, 1999, p. 134).

blocks, objects to count (miniature people, animals, beads), and measuring cups. In addition, there should be symbolic materials—dice, number lines, graphs, computer programs, dominoes, cards, measuring tapes, thermometers, weight scales, and real and play money. Finally it is important to provide abstract materials that represent mathematical concepts—plastic numbers, stencils of numbers and functions, price tags for store items, shopping lists, phone books, adding machines, phones, and so on.

For a math curriculum to succeed, it must offer child-centered choices. Activities for children must be based on children's developmental age, their individual mathematical knowledge and skills, and their own rich personal experience. Children's dispositions at this age to explore, experiment, and theorize about the nature of things and actions should be capitalized on.

Instructional Principles

There are four fundamental instructional principles in teaching math (Copley, 2000): planning experiences, interacting with children, orchestrating classroom activities, and facilitating family–school relations. Children learn math as they do all other areas—by constructing knowledge (Bredekamp & Rosengrant, 1992). They follow a four-part process, which repeats cyclically as they learn new concepts and knowledge: awareness, exploration, inquiry, and utilization. *Awareness* is introduction to the environment or materials; *exploration* is free investigation and trial-and-error experimentation with the materials and the setting; *inquiry* is pursuing a set, goal-oriented problem, challenge, or task; and *utilization* is representing and describing the solution to a problem similar to the one they have been involved in (Copley, 2000). Teachers should plan activities and experiences that allow children to work their way through all four parts of this process. Unfortunately, there is a tendency to rush to the utilization part before all the other components have been fully explored.

Teachers must consider carefully when to get involved with a child's mathematical struggle, and how. Teachers' interactions and decisions about interaction are crucial to the instructional process. Vygotsky's ideas of ZPD, scaffolding, and private speech are particularly helpful in teaching math. Additionally, teachers are responsible for implementing the math curriculum by orchestrating activities, projects, environments, and materials to enable each child to progress toward the programs' curricular goals.

It is also important that family and school work together to support math learning. Many parents have negative feelings about learning math because of their own school experience. Teachers need to work closely with parents to help them understand how young children learn math, and to provide ideas for parents that will encourage their children's math learning at home. Of particular concern is to help parents understand the logico-mathematical thinking process—that children need to manipulate, order, and sequence materials, and talk to people (and themselves) while they are engaging in math activities. Many parents also are unaware of the positive value of using concrete math manipulatives.

Ideas for Teaching Math

There are a variety of activities and experiences teachers can use to help children develop early math concepts and skills. It is important children learn these concepts and skills before they engage in more traditional activities of counting, adding, subtracting, and multiplying.

Patterning. A repeating sequence of colors, shapes, sizes, sounds, movements, objects, or other characteristics is a pattern. A blue, red, green, blue, red, green sequence of beads in a necklace is a pattern; a row of bikes made up of first a bike with training wheels, then an adult sports bike, then a mountain bike, repeated several times, is a pattern; a daily schedule that always starts with group time, then snack time, then free play, is a pattern. As you can see, patterns are everywhere! Visual patterns are on sidewalks, soup cans on a store shelf, and shirt graphics; auditory patterns are found in dances, melodies, skip rope routines and singing games, along with words, poetry, chants and songs. Common **patterning** activities for young children are:

- recognizing existing patterns (alternating white and brown eggs);
- matching existing patterns (James creates a pattern of unit blocks on the floor; Sarah then creates the same pattern next to it);
- copying a pattern (a child paints a girl with a dress that has the same pattern as her dress);
- extending a pattern (a child has created a pattern of different-size sticks in the sandbox; you ask her to repeat the pattern several times);
- creating a new pattern (a child playing with colored pens finds out that a green, yellow, red, blue, series repeated several times creates an interesting pattern).

Some kinds of patterns are simple and some are more complex, but children don't necessarily learn them in this order. Rhythms and sounds also offer a range and variety of patterning activities.

Sorting and Classifying. Children love to sort and classify: all the black buttons in this corner, the red ones over here, and the white ones in this pile; the pictures of toys for children my age on this page, and those for older children pasted over here. Children sort and classify by shape, color, size, function, preferences, and other criteria. Sorting and **classifying** help children develop good observation skills and help them understand the mathematical concepts of grouping by tens, hundreds, thousands; by criterion (for instance, all triangles are different from all squares because of number of sides); and by type (whole numbers, fractions, and prime numbers).

There are lots of opportunities in a classroom, on the playground, and at home to encourage children to sort and classify. Children can collect all the sand toys, or all the water toys. They can put gardening tools at one end of the storage shed, return unit blocks by shape and size to their proper shelves, and sort paints, crayons, colored pencils, and markers by color. At home my wife and I often encouraged our young children to sort the clean socks into same-color pairs.

Find out from children the schema or criterion they use to sort objects. It may be different from one you would use. Maybe it is foods rabbits will eat; foods I like to eat; or clothes that are party clothes. Help them select one criterion and stick to it. A fundamental math concept to learn is that the criterion used to group objects does not change. A triangle is always different from a square based on the number of sides of each shape. Preoperational children have great difficulty sorting by more than one criterion. Do not expect them to use two or more criteria—say, fruit that is red and tastes good, or children who are boys and friends—until they have mastered sorting by one criterion.

Ordering. **Ordering** is an activity that naturally builds on classifying—arranging blocks from smaller to bigger and biggest, lining up beads from pink to bright red. Start with three objects and, like classifying, make sure you understand what criterion the child has selected for ordering the objects. Auditory ordering should also be encouraged: soft to loud foot stamps; long to short hand claps; slow to fast skip-rope rhythms; dances and music that start slow and progressively speed up (like Ravel's *Bolero* or many traditional folk dances).

Children learn to order objects by size, intensity of color, intensity of sound, speed (toy cars), weight (pulling children in wagons), sharpness, and size (for example, the various heights of children in a class). Ordering is obviously an essential mathematical concept: the basic number system is an order, from least to most; all measurement systems are based on this idea; the color wheel is based on ordering primary colors by intensity. There are lots of materials that encourage ordering, including different-size cups, cups with different amounts of water in them, paint chip samples, crayons, nails from the woodwork bench, seeds, bottle caps, and children in the classroom. Size, color, texture, length, or weight can be used as the criteria. A subsequent activity would be to graph these objects, so children can see the trends.

Children should be helped to use words that describe ordering activities: *smaller, brighter, louder, taller, thinner, stronger, harder, heavier, more vivid, clearer, longer, shorter, tastier, fatter.* Not only does this help children learn the mathematical concepts of ordering and sequencing, but it helps them learn complex language usage.

Basic Number Concepts. On one of my visits to an early childhood program, I listened carefully to a group of 5-year-olds proudly counting by rote to two hundred. They were very impressed with themselves! But understanding true number concepts is much more difficult than simply rote counting. Number concepts include counting, one-to-one correspondence, and understanding the meaning of numbers. Children must come to understand that numbers are abstract concepts that do not change depending on the physical things they are attached to. In other words, in looking at two apples and two countries, the concept *two* is the same number; five parties and five hamburgers are the same number.

Counting numbers by rote is a little like saying the alphabet. Children who can say the alphabet usually do not know the sounds of each letter; children who can count by rote often do not know that 201 is one more than 200, just as 2 is one more than 1. Children do not learn the meaning of numbers by counting; they learn it by using numbers paired with objects in everyday activities. How many blocks are needed to finish the tower? How many plates are needed for the whole class? How many seats are needed in the van so everyone can fit (don't forget the teacher)? And, since Susie is sick today, do we need as many napkins as yesterday?

One-to-one correspondence is matching one set of objects to another: plates to children in the classroom; toothbrushes to hooks in the bathroom; dolls to doll beds; swings to the number of children who want to swing. It's a skill that is required as the basis for understanding the math concepts of matching, greater and less than, equal to, and eventually addition and subtraction (how many more are needed?). When children

▶ *Children can learn beginning number concepts in many ways, including counting eggs.*

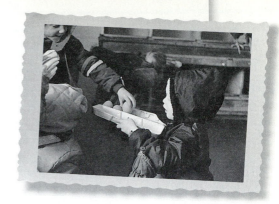

count they are using the concept of a **numeral** as a label or symbol: 5, 25, 125. When children know the actual quantity or value of a numeral, they are using a **number.** Children develop an understanding of number concepts by having lots and lots of opportunities to manipulate real objects.

Problem Solving. All children solve problems, and they do so in a variety of ways. Part of problem solving is to develop a disposition to problem solving—a positive attitude and methodology for the process. Problem solving usually includes four steps, but often these steps follow a variety of sequences: understanding the problem, planning how to solve the problem, carrying out the plan, and reviewing or reflecting on the solution (Polya, 1957). Children need help following these steps. Using math to solve problems teaches children the utility of math—that it is a practical skill used to produce important results. As children grow older, they often come to believe math is an abstract, meaningless activity with no real purpose. There are infinite opportunities for children to use math to solve problems: "How many apples do we need for our class?" "I will pick carrots for the teachers. I wonder how many I will need?" "Do we have enough trikes for everyone who wants to play on them?" "Are there enough days left in the week to finish the story?" Teachers and parents should help children solve these problems; they should not do it for them.

Reasoning. Reasoning is the process of determining the rationale for something—an action, result, purpose, cause and effect, and so on. To help children reason, teachers need to ask questions such as How do you know? What would happen if? Why do you think it does? What else works like this? What if? and, I wonder why? (Copley, 2000, p. 37).

Communicating. Children need lots of opportunities to talk about mathematical ideas—to clarify, articulate, organize, and consolidate their thinking (Copley, 2000, p. 38). Talking about math allows children to figure out what they know and how to use words to help solve problems; teachers find out what children know, and children learn math concepts from each other. To support children's use of communication in learning math, teachers should be a model in verbalizing and restating math concepts, should ask questions, and should describe what children are doing in mathematical terms.

Connecting. There are two basic areas of connections: (1) the connections between what a child intuitively knows about the world in mathematical ways ("She got more cookies than me," "We don't have enough plates for everyone," "The more sugar I put

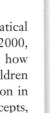

Developmentally Appropriate Practice

Expectations for Prekindergarten through Second Grade, from NCTM's *Principles and Standards for School Mathematics*

Number and operations standard

Instructional programs from pre-kindergarten through grade 12 should enable all students to—

Understand numbers, ways of representing numbers, relationships among numbers, and number systems

Expectations for grade pre-K–2

In prekindergarten through grade 2 all students should—

- count with understanding and recognize "how many" in sets of objects
- use multiple models to develop initial understandings of place value and the base-ten number system
- develop understanding of the relative position and magnitude of whole numbers and of ordinal and cardinal numbers and their connections
- develop a sense of whole numbers and represent and use them in flexible ways, including relating, composing, and decomposing numbers
- connect number words and numerals to the quantities they represent, using various physical models and representations
- understand and represent commonly used fractions, such as $\frac{1}{4}$, $\frac{1}{3}$, and $\frac{1}{2}$

Understand meanings of operations and how they relate to one another

- understand various meanings of addition and subtraction of whole numbers and the relationship between the two operations
- understand the effects of adding and subtracting whole numbers
- understand situations that entail multiplication and division, such as equal groupings of objects and sharing equally

Compute fluently and make reasonable estimates

- develop and use strategies for whole-number computations, with a focus on addition and subtraction
- develop fluency with basic number combinations for addition and subtraction
- use a variety of methods and tools to compute, including objects, mental computation, estimation, paper and pencil, and calculators

[Patterns, functions, and]
  algebra standard
Instructional programs from pre-
  kindergarten through grade 12
  should enable all students to—

Understand patterns, relations, and
  functions

Represent and analyze mathematical
  situations and structures using al-
  gebraic symbols

Use mathematical models to represent
  and understand quantitative
  relationships

Analyze change in various contexts

Expectations for grades pre-K–2
In prekindergarten through grade 2 all students should—

- sort, classify, and order objects by size, number, and other properties
- recognize, describe, and extend patterns such as se-quences of sounds and shapes or simple numeric pat-terns and translate from one representation to another
- analyze how both repeating and growing patterns are generated

- illustrate general principles and properties of opera-tions, such as commutativity, using specific numbers
- use concrete, pictorial, and verbal representations to develop an understanding of invented and conventional symbolic notations

- model situations that involve the addition and sub-traction of whole numbers, using objects, pictures, and symbols
- describe qualitative change, such as a student's growing taller; describe quantitative change, such as a student's growing two inches in one year

Geometry standard
Instructional programs from pre-
  kindergarten through grade 12
  should enable all students to—

Analyze characteristics and properties
  of two- and three-dimensional
  geometric shapes and develop
  mathematical arguments about
  geometric relationships

Expectations for grades pre-K–2
In prekindergarten through grade 2 all students should—

- recognize, name, build, draw, compare, and sort two- and three-dimensional shapes
- describe attributes and parts of two- and three-dimensional shapes
- investigate and predict the results of putting together and taking apart two- and three-dimensional shapes

(continued)

Expectations for Prekindergarten through Second Grade, from NCTM's *Principles and Standards for School Mathematics* (continued)

Specify locations and describe spatial relationships using coordinate geometry and other representational systems

- describe, name, and interpret relative positions in space and apply ideas about relative position
- describe, name, and interpret direction and distance in navigating space and apply ideas about direction and distance
- find and name locations with simple relationships such as "near to" and in coordinate systems such as maps

Apply transformations and use symmetry to analyze mathematical situations

- recognize and apply slides, flips, and turns
- recognize and create shapes that have symmetry

Use visualization, spatial reasoning, and geometric modeling to solve problems

- create mental images of geometric shapes using spatial memory and spatial visualization
- recognize and represent shapes from different perspectives
- relate ideas in geometry to ideas in number and measurement
- recognize geometric shapes and structures in the environment and specify their location

Measurement standard

Instructional programs from prekindergarten through grade 12 should enable all students to—

Understand measurable attributes of objects and the units, systems, and processes of measurement

Expectations for grades pre-K–2

In prekindergarten through grade 2 all students should—

- recognize the attributes of length, volume, weight, area, and time
- compare and order objects according to these attributes
- understand how to measure using nonstandard and standard units
- select an appropriate unit and tool for the attribute being measured

in my juice, the sweeter it gets") and formal mathematical knowledge taught in schools; and (2) the connection between math and all other school subjects—art, music, reading, dance, gym. "Students' ability to experience mathematics as a meaningful endeavor that makes sense rests on these connections" (NCTM, 2000, p. 132).

There are many ways teachers can build connections between intuitive and formal math—"Sketch a picture of your block building before you destroy it" (geometry); "Put the cookies into groups of three for each child"; "Measure the distance the marble rolls"; "How many brothers does the man in the story have?" And, of course, teachers must find ways to integrate math knowledge across the curriculum.

Apply appropriate techniques, tools, and formulas to determine measurements

- measure with multiple copies of units of the same size, such as paper clips laid end to end
- use repetition of a single unit to measure something larger than the unit, for instance, measuring the length of a room with a single meterstick
- use tools to measure
- develop common referents for measures to make comparisons and estimates

Data analysis and probability standard

Instructional programs from pre-kindergarten through grade 12 should enable all students to—

Expectations for grades pre-K–2
In prekindergarten through grade 2 all students should—

Formulate questions that can be addressed with data and collect, organize, and display relevant data to answer them

- pose questions and gather data about themselves and their surroundings
- sort and classify objects according to their attributes and organize data about the objects
- represent data using concrete objects, pictures, and graphs

Select and use appropriate statistical methods to analyze data

- describe parts of the data and the set of data as a whole to determine what the data show

Develop and evaluate inferences and predictions that are based on data

- discuss events related to students' experiences as likely or unlikely

Understand and apply basic concepts of probability

Representing. Children represent their mathematical knowledge in a variety of ways—pictures, concrete objects (including fingers), diagrams, tallies, symbols, and a variety of language. **Representation** is the way children begin to abstract mathematical concepts. Dominoes, cards, pictures and photos of objects, and clusters of dots are all representations, as are numbers and words for numbers (numerals). Teachers should help children use a whole variety of representations—concrete, iconic (pictures, photos, diagrams), and symbolic (numerals). Teachers should avoid jumping too quickly into using just numbers and names for numbers. Young children must use lots of concrete and iconic representation in their math learning.

Figure 13.1

Math and Science Representations

Using representations. Multiple representations are essential for understanding number and developing number sense. Representations for 11 include the following.

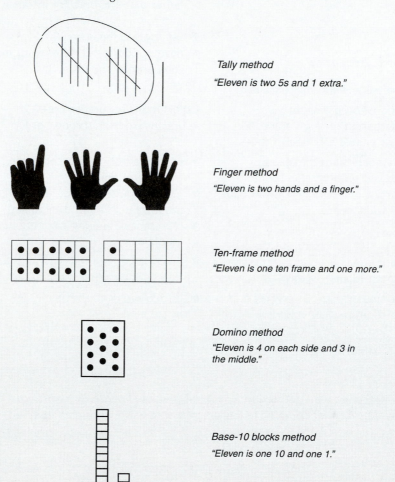

Tally method
"Eleven is two 5s and 1 extra."

Finger method
"Eleven is two hands and a finger."

Ten-frame method
"Eleven is one ten frame and one more."

Domino method
"Eleven is 4 on each side and 3 in the middle."

Base-10 blocks method
"Eleven is one 10 and one 1."

Real-life example
"There are 11 players on a football team."

Children represent number quantities in a variety of ways. The sample below shows three different representations by 5-year-olds.

This real-life picture was drawn by Chad in response to the teacher saying, "There were nine baseball players on the team. Four got sick and had to go home. How many were left to play the game?"

Stephanie used a modified tally method to express the number of pennies she had.

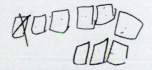

Juan used a ten-frame representation to show the number 8. He said he crossed out one box because "I got too many in the top line. There's supposed to be only five."

Source: Copley, J. V. 2000. *The Young Child and Mathematics.* Washington, DC: NAEYC. Reprinted with permission of the National Association for the Education of Young Children.

Measuring. Measuring physical phenomena is a central part of math in our society, and children are surrounded by measuring devices: clocks (time), thermometers (temperature), spoons and cups (food), gas pumps (liquids), coins (money, allowances), rulers (length), scales (weight), and measuring containers for laundry detergents. For young children any single unit can be used as a unit to measure, depending on the activity. How many pails of sand do I need to make my castle? How many unit blocks, placed end to end, are needed for my road?

A natural part of measuring is estimating. "How many cookies do we need?" "It's nearly full, so how much more water will I need?" "I wonder how much wood I need to make my train?" Estimating teaches the use of measurement, and helps children break down the environment into quantifiable amounts. It helps children order their world.

Young children need concrete units of measurement that are meaningful to them: footsteps, hand widths, book lengths, cup amounts, soup-can amounts. Children should be actively involved in all sorts of measuring activities in order to understand the importance of measuring and how different systems are developed for different purposes.

Spatial Observations. Another foundational math concept is the sense of space, understanding size relationships: position of objects (below, above, next to, after, before, in the middle, on top of), different shapes in the environment (windows and doors are rectangles; tops of cups, glasses, and pop cans are circles), straight lines, curves, perspective, and comparative size (the playground is much bigger than the classroom, which is much bigger than my room). These skills are essential foundational skills for reading (direction), geometry, writing letters and numbers, and language development.

Drawing and other art activities, playing with unit blocks and tabletop block sets, making models, woodworking, and movement activities such as folk dancing and creative dance all help the development of these important spatial skills. Some children are intuitively good at this way of observing the world. But all children need to develop foundational skills in this area.

Setting Up a Math Environment

In Chapter 5, I discussed general considerations for developing environments for young children. In Chapter 10, I also covered designing environments that encourage early literacy development. Here I will address setting up environments to encourage mathematical learning, within the broader framework of good environments for early childhood education.

It's clear from my discussions in this chapter that math learning occurs in every environment the child experiences—home, playground, field trips, store, and classroom. A good early childhood environment has materials, activities, and ideas that encourage math learning in each learning area, and also has a learning center carefully designed to encourage specific math activities. The math manipulative area should contain a large variety of concrete materials for children to use various math activities.

Developmentally Appropriate Practice

Math Materials

Children need lots of high-quality math-related materials. These should be attractive and simple to use, and should invite student participation. Whether found, purchased, or made, they must be safe—no sharp edges and no places to collect lots of dirt—they must pass the choke tube test, and they should be kept clean and well maintained at all times. Children need variety, so materials in all areas need to be changed and rotated constantly, with never too many materials in one area at a time. New materials should be added based on students' interests, and teachers and volunteers should model enthusiasm for these new materials and what they can be used for.

Materials should be selected and presented in a way that encourages students to manipulate and use them, with minimal direct adult involvement or supervision. The autonomous use of materials is enhanced if students know where materials are stored and where to return them once they have finished working with them. Cooperative learning and learning from each other can be encouraged by having enough room in each area, and by having enough equipment and materials for several students to use at one time.

There are various common materials that can be used for math activities. These include acorns and seeds, ice cream sticks, plastic jars and lids, plastic bread tags, old marbles, old buttons, shoestrings, number cubes (dice), poker chips, wooden blocks in different shapes and sizes, clothespins, wooden beads and pegs, locks and keys, nuts and bolts, measuring cups and spoons, and film containers. There are, of course, many commercial materials that can be purchased for math activities. These include wooden puzzles, geoboards, pegboards, Cuisenaire rods, pattern blocks, Unifax cubes, pattern cards, attribute blocks, Legos, Lincoln Logs, Duplos, pan balance scales, tape measures, and board and card games.

Creating a Math Center

The math center should be designed to encourage all sorts of math activities and should include activities that are tied to projects, books, field trips, visitors to the classroom, and community activities. It should be changed frequently. Guidelines for setting up a math center include the following:

- *Place the center away from noisy and active centers.* Store materials on low shelves easily accessible to students. Use bins for loose materials. Place pictures of the materials both on the outside of the bins and at each bin's position on the shelf.
- *Provide lots of working spaces for students to play with blocks and puzzles.* This can be achieved with one large table, several small tables, or low shelves with available top surfaces. Children can also work directly on a carpeted floor, which is often more convenient.
- *Provide a range of puzzles for children.* Start with puzzles that have finger grips and a few pieces. Add simple jigsaw puzzles for older children.
- *Memory games and board games that require advancing one token along a numbered board are good to include.* Also include materials for patterning and sorting, ordering, counting, spatial understanding, and measuring.

Supporting Learning in the Math Center. Children should be actively encouraged to use materials in the math area, and they should be given plenty of time to do so (Christie & Wardle, 1992). The teacher's main roles in assisting math learning are to provide an exciting and appropriate range of materials, and then to scaffold more and more advanced and complex learning by asking questions, suggesting new combinations of materials, helping students represent and record their learning, and continuing to support further manipulation and exploration.

Block Area

Unit blocks are among the best materials for learning math concepts, and I discussed their use in detail in Chapter 8. *The Block Book* (Hirsch, 1996) discusses many ways blocks can be used to teach math and other important concepts. A few examples follow:

- *Classifying.* Children can sort blocks by size, shape, and color. Children should discuss which characteristic of the block they are using to classify them.
- *Comparing.* Use blocks to learn comparative terms such as *more, less, longer, shorter, bigger, smaller, heavier, lighter, steeper, rougher, thinner,* and *the same.*
- *Patterning.* Have children create a pattern with several blocks. They then can copy the pattern, and later extend it.

- *Ordering.* Children can order unit blocks by size (short to long) and by quantity (many to few or few to many), in piles.
- *Measuring.* Select a block as a unit, then use it to measure things in the room: children's height, size of tables, and distance to the bathroom. The blocks can be stacked on top of each other or laid end to end. Record the results on a large piece of butcher paper.
- *Shape and space.* Use blocks to introduce and practice shape and space vocabulary: "Put the round block onto the square one"; "Look, by creating a fence around your farm you have made a rectangle"; "Can you build a road that goes around the whole town?"

Parent Information: Teaching Time to Preschoolers

Children need to learn about time, but their concepts of time are very different from ours. It is important to teach them in a developmentally appropriate manner.

Traditional calendar activities are inappropriate for children under 7 years old. The reason is that they are not capable of putting one concept (say, day of the week) within another concept (month, year). Further, young children view time in relation to meaningful activities, such as when my daddy picks me up, the week we go on vacation, the day I went to the zoo, or the weekend I will celebrate my birthday. Here are some ideas parents can use to help their children develop important time-related skills and concepts.

- *Create a visual, weekly calendar of events that occur the same day every week.* Use pictures of the activities on the calendar (a picture of a family going to church on Sunday, a picture of a swimmer for the day your child has swimming classes).
- *Use a variety of time words when you speak with your child.* These include *after, before, tomorrow, yesterday, next month, next week, last week, last year, before lunch,* and *after you finish doing the dishes.*
- *Count down to significant events in your child's life.* How many days to your birthday? is a good example. Create a number line, and check off each day as you get closer to the birthday.
- *Make a weekly chores list.* Make chores repeat on the same day of the week (Danny does dishes on Tuesdays and Thursdays each week).
- *When children want to do something that is scheduled for some time in the future, tell* them the events—and their sequence—that must occur before the activity. "First we will have breakfast, then do the dishes, then go to church, and after church we will go to the zoo."
- *Read books that talk about past and future, discuss the linear nature of time, and provide a time perspective.* "Now you are 6, but when you were 2, our family moved to Denver."
- *Make a ritual of seasonal activities.* These include planting a garden in the spring, building snow people in the winter, harvesting the garden in the fall. Talk about these activities with your children so that they can anticipate them and learn about the seasons.
- *Look at family photo albums and discuss the passage of time.* "Remember when we took our vacation to Disneyland?" "Remember when Sarah was born?" "This photo was taken before you were born."

▶ *A weekly activity line is a better way to learn about time and schedules than a traditional calendar activity.*

- *Problem solving.* In the block area children can use math to solve problems. "What size block do I need to finish the wall?" "How will I build a roof on my house?" "How can I make it so my tower does not fall down?"

Playground

The playground is a great place for math activities. There are limitless ways to use this outdoor environment to teach a variety of math skills and concepts. Below are just a few ideas.

Sundial. Create a sundial with children by selecting a flat area that is away from foot traffic and in the sunlight all day. Place a five-foot pole in the ground in the middle of this area. The pole can be a broomstick, a two-by-four, a 1½-inch dowel, or another type of straight stick. Observe the shadow the pole casts every hour, then mark the concrete or surface in some way. Make sure the marks cannot be destroyed by rain or playing children. Write in the hour of every position. Then have children "tell the time" when they come out to play, or during their play time.

Shadows. When the sun is low and casting long shadows, have children stand somewhere their shadows will fall on a flat, solid surface (concrete, grass, wooden fence). Measure the length of their shadow with a tape measure, and record it on a sheet of paper. Repeat the activity the same time every day for a week, and graph the results.

Velocity. Have children select a variety of things that roll on an incline: small cars, balls, cotton spools, round blocks, beads, and the like. Take these objects and toys to the slide in the playground, and have children roll them from the top of the slide in pairs. For each "race," have the children at the bottom of the slide first estimate which will be the fastest, then declare the winner. By a process of elimination, determine which of the objects and toys goes the fastest. Have children speculate why certain toys and objects are fast, others are slow.

Collecting Stones. Children collect as many stones on the playground as they can find in ten minutes. Help students count the stones to see who has the most. Help students line up their stones according to size, from smallest to biggest. Then have the children put their stones in two groups, big stones and small stones. They can also fill pails to see how heavy the stones are.

Hopscotch. Draw a hopscotch design on the concrete or asphalt with chalk. Draw numbers in the squares. Teach children the traditional hopscotch game.

Traffic Signs. Have children help make speed-limit signs for the bike-trike-wagon path. Use dowels, old mop handles, or existing signs (covered with paper). Make speed limit signs for 5, 10, 15, 20, and 30 m.p.h.

Chart Growth of Tomatoes. Create a chart for each tomato plant (one that won't wash off in the rain). When the plants begin to bear fruit, record each plant's yield by drawing a small tomato (or using a sticker) on each chart. As you add tomatoes, you begin to create a bar graph next to each plant. Based on this graph, determine which plants produce the most.

Market. On a parent day, create a market to sell produce and flowers from the garden. Have children help create price tags, advertisements (with prices), and so on. You can give out paper money, or have parents use real money to purchase products from the children's garden.

Measuring Rainfall. Buy a rainfall measuring tube and container from a science supply company or weather store. Set it up in the playground away from activity (in fact, you could set up an entire science center in the playground). After a heavy rainfall, check the amount of rain in the container with the children. Help the children understand that the more rain falls, the higher the water in the container. Later graph the daily results.

Sand and Water Table

The sand and water table is an ideal place for all sorts of math learning to take place. Provide containers of different sizes and shapes: tubs, cups, cartons, cans, spoons. Have some containers of the same shape in several different sizes, to demonstrate their obvious relationships. Provide some containers that enable students to create solid shapes with wet sand. Store these objects on a pegboard, at the children's height and next to the table. Paint the shape of each container on the pegboard.

Dramatic-Play Area

In the dramatic-play area, math concepts can be developed by having plates, spoons, knives, and forks for one-to-one correspondences. Each pan should have a lid; each shoe a mate; each brush a comb and hand mirror. Use play money, prices on items, and simple scales to encourage buying and selling activities. Small jar lids encourage matching, and props like tape measures, adding machines, and shoe-size measures encourage play with numbers.

Cooking

Cooking activities encourage all sorts of math learning. Children use math when they measure the ingredients, follow the steps of a recipe, and watch the timer as the food bakes in the oven (an egg timer is a great tool for learning about time). Children also learn counting and quantity when they determine the number of apples and eggs needed for a recipe, when they double or halve a recipe, and when they estimate how much is needed for the whole class.

Art Area

Activities in the art area teach matching (by color and shape), spatial awareness, patterning (paint a peacock's feathers), and volume and solid shapes (when children play with clay and wood). Grouping pens by color, sorting wood by size, and counting all the brushes to make sure none are lost are other math activities.

Field Trips

Field trips provide a great opportunity for all sorts of math learning, including shapes of traffic signs, numbers on street signs and houses, and prices at the gas pumps. Children can also look for the biggest tree, the best playground, the fastest slide, the muddiest pathway, or the longest walk. Older children can go on walks and do rubbings of different objects, bring them back into the classroom, and then display them ordered by shape, texture, category of object, and symbol—numbers, pictures, letters, and so on. Older children can make picture maps of the route to and from the playground or field trip destination. On neighborhood walks, children can see how many different shapes of windows can be found; the largest number they can find on a house in the neighborhood; the lowest gas prices; or the narrowest sidewalk.

Graphing

Graphing is a way to order the child's world in mathematical terms. Anything from the environment that can be sorted and counted can be graphed: people, animals, sunny days, number of dolls in the dramatic-play area, number of field trips planned. The process of graphing emphasizes basic number concepts and the mathematical concept of comparing: differences, similarities, and more and less. Graphing should not be done to compare students' ability to do a task, discipline problems, or other aspects of individual children's worth. Things like eye color, hair color, and favorite foods are all good to graph. The first graphs should use pictures (cut or drawn) or real objects, such as leaves, attached to paper. Later you can place a picture to designate the category, then use check marks for the number in that category.

Start with the Children.
As we know, children this age are very egocentric. So it makes sense to graph information about the children in the classroom. Some ideas:

- the type of transportation children use to get to school;
- children's clothing—long- or short-sleeved shirt, long or short pants, color of clothing, color of socks;
- gender;
- children's names—the number of letters in each name, the names that include a certain letter;
- children's favorite things—colors, TV shows, toys, activities, food;
- number of siblings children have, also gender and age of siblings.

School Building.
Once you have exhausted graphing information about students, you might graph information about the school. These are things that might be graphed:

- number of windows, doors, classrooms, stairs, downspouts, and drains;
- trees in the school grounds—graphed by size, leaf color, deciduous or evergreen;
- number of toilets, number of sinks;

- number of different kinds of light fixtures;
- number of sections of fencing on the playground, and number that need repair.

Classroom Materials. In the book area, choose three or four of the children's favorite books. Then have each child vote on a favorite—one vote for each child. In the house-keeping area, you can graph the number and types of dolls, or the number and types of dishes. In the science area the number and types of leaves collected, days of cloudy weather, and amount of rainfall collected on the playground can all be graphed. Children can also estimate or guess their prediction for a particular experiment, record those predictions, then compare them to the actual results. (For example, "How tall will the plant be?" "How long will it take for the seeds to germinate?") In the block area you can graph the number of blocks of each shape; the number by size, the types of toy cars, the types and number of animals in the animal sets. And in the math area you can graph materials by size, shape, color, and length.

Teaching Science to Young Children

What do I mean when I talk about teaching science? "The scientist is involved in the process of inquiry—of raising and trying to answer questions about the world in which we live. In fact, anyone who is studying anything in a methodical way is a scientist" (Chaillé & Britain, 1997, p. 15). Thus science includes activities and experiences that involve experimentation, creativity, and problem solving, with a strong dose of observing phenomena and with the goal of understanding the world. Clearly almost everything we do in early childhood programs either is scientific or has a scientific component. What makes activities more scientific is the way we help children take information from these experiences to formulate ideas about how the world works—how things move, mix, grow, interact, fall apart, rot, procreate, run downhill and speed up, and so on. Science has to do with a methodological seeking of scientific principles in the real world.

A high-quality science program for children up to third grade should be based on four basic understandings about young children: young children are theory builders; they need to build a foundation of physical knowledge; as they mature, young children become increasingly autonomous and independent, both intellectually and morally; and they are social beings (Chaillé & Britain, 1997, p. 5). As I discussed in Chapter 3, Piaget argues that children create schemata in their minds to which all new information must adapt (assimilation). When this new information constantly contradicts these schemata, children will create a new or modified schema (accommodation). For example, after a child has played with a tennis ball and a soccer ball, she creates a schema (theory) that all solid round objects bounce. Only after she drops a round wooden ball on the ground, discovers marbles don't bounce, and sees a round Christmas ornament get smashed when it hits the ground does she begin to modify her schema to suggest that only certain round objects bounce.

Children are continually theorizing and retheorizing about the way the world works. To maximize the process, they need lots of experiences with objects, and they must be flexible thinkers—willing to change their theories when overwhelming evidence suggests the necessity to do so. As science educators, we need to encourage exploration, interaction, and manipulation of the physical world, as well as flexible ways of thinking:

"I wonder why," "Could it be because," "Do you think that," "Maybe if we do so and so," "Is there another way we could try?"

As children develop, they move from dependence on significant adults to independence—autonomy. An approach to science learning as one of inquiry, experimentation, trial-and-error, and making choices capitalizes on children's natural movement toward autonomy, and makes science learning fun and interesting because it makes children feel independent and competent.

Not only do children learn from manipulating of physical objects, but they also learn from other children and adults—they are social learners. This occurs in two general ways. First, children learn when others question or contradict their basic concepts and ideas. If a child believes that all objects float in water, and his buddy challenges him with "No, I bet they don't; let's try my car in the water table," the child will be in cognitive conflict. This is good, because it is how children progress in their scientific thinking. Second, children and adults can model examples of scientific activities, a scientific approach to knowledge, and enthusiasm for that approach. "What do you think will happen when I put the car in the water?" "What will happen if I put the car on a piece of wood that is in the water? Why?" Children enjoy each other's company and learn from this company. The power of social learning is the reason that so many early childhood educators support mixed-age grouping: mixed-age groups produce a maximum of different ideas, concepts, developmental levels, and cognitive conflict.

Additional Theories for Science Learning

In the beginning of this chapter I covered several theories that help us understand how children learn math and science. Kamii and DeVries, and Forman provide some additional ideas. Kamii and DeVries divide a child's understanding of physical knowledge into two parts: actions and observations (1978). Children construct scientific knowledge by specific actions they make on objects—for example, by bouncing a variety of balls to learn about the properties of bouncing. They also use observation to construct knowledge—such as the effect in the playground of the eroding sand as water flows through the sandbox. In both methods, Kamii and DeVries believe, four criteria must exist to maximize the child's learning:

- Children must produce the movement by their own actions, and the relation between their action and the response of the object should be as direct as possible.
- Children must be able to vary their own actions.
- The reaction of the object to the action must be observable.
- The reaction to the action must be immediate. If it is not immediate, children may believe the reaction was caused by something other than their initial action on the object.

Forman and colleagues (Forman & Hill, 1984; Forman & Kuschner, 1984) believe children can learn a great deal about science if they can observe what he calls transformations and representations. **Transformation** is "the process of change," and Forman suggests that we help children understand this change rather than simply understand what an object is like before and after a change. For example, it is important to observe rain while it is raining, not just view the ground before and after it has rained. And he believes that children can understand transformations by using the concept of representation. In this case, representation is the way the scientific activity is recorded. For example, a ball that is dipped in paint and then rolled down a paper-covered incline will leave a trail marking its path—a representation of the activity of the ball moving from one place to another. Another idea of representation is to help children see the **continuum of change,** rather than simply two opposite examples. In other words, instead of simply dropping a highly inflated rubber ball to show bounce and a metal ball to show a spherical object that does not bounce, children should have experience with plastic balls, tennis balls, golf balls, baseballs, and super balls—to see the continuum of balls bouncing.

Using the ideas discussed above, children can begin to understand the complex nature of how things move in the environment. In understanding the scientific principles behind how objects move, children progress through three different approaches. First, they become involved in altering one variable of the physical world to change the result. In an activity involving balls rolling down a ramp, they might change the height of the ramp, the type of ball, or the surface of the ramp. Or they might create waves in a water table that has food coloring and cooking oil in the water, to see how the patterns of oil change with the waves. Second, they find ways to change the direction of objects in the real world. They can do this by using cardboard tubes to create different routes for marbles, create a draft to move sailboats on the water table, or create channels, dams, and diversions in the sand to direct the flow of water. The third way children observe the movement of objects is through the idea of representation I just discussed: they find ways to show the route the object takes as it moves through space. Allowing water to run across the sandbox and to the ditch leaves a line of where the water went; objects that have been dipped in paint and rolled down a ramp leave a trail of their progress. For example, a spool that is larger at one end will leave a curved representation.

Materials

There are, of course, thousands of materials that can be used to help children construct scientific knowledge. Selecting these materials requires the use of the criteria I discussed in Chapter 8 and Chapter 5, which include safety (no sharp edges, nontoxic finishes, not passing through the choke tube, and no acids or chemicals), age appropriateness, matching each child's individual level of knowledge, competence, and experience, and inviting. Additional criteria for scientific materials include: it must lend itself to isolating one variable at a time, it must be easy for children to see what is going on, children must be able to manipulate it (interactive), and children must be able to extend it to make the activity and learning more complex. Look for materials that children can influence, and materials that children can use to create variations. A good example is a marble rollway made of clear plastic, which children can set at different angles (not preset angles) and in which curves can be created (Chaillé & Britain, 1997).

▶ *Lifting a stone tells a child a great deal about mass and the energy needed to carry it!*

Provide lots of balls, in a continuum of sizes and a variety of materials of varying densities and finishes (tennis, table tennis, plastic, baseball, soccer, basketball, metal ball bearings). Plastic, rubber, and cardboard tubing is very useful. Solicit items from parents; some factories and labs have useful materials too. Many good science activities involve hanging ropes, pulleys, and objects from the ceilings, so it is useful to have one or more hooks on the ceiling of your classroom: a wooden beam with several hooks and holes in it works well. Boxes of different sizes and shapes can be used for all sorts of movement activities, such as inclines, angles, and velocity and distance experiments. And various unit and large blocks, with boards of various sizes, lend themselves to leverage, inclines, post-and-lintel construction ideas, and cantilevers.

General Materials. General science materials include Plexiglas tubes, small Plexiglas sheets, and a large framed Plexiglas sheet; clear, opaque, and cardboard tubing of different lengths and diameters; a variety of round and square boxes; sand and water tables; play dough, blocks; and pulleys and hooks.

Materials that Teach about Movement. Materials that lend themselves specifically to learning about movement include marble rollways, gears, balls of varying sizes and densities, and surface materials of various textures.

Materials that Teach about Transformations. Materials that are particularly helpful in showing transformations are Lego and Duplo sets, Tinkertoys and flexi-blocks; large sheets of vinyl; art supplies, including powered and liquid tempera, clay, sand, flour, salt, cornstarch, shaving cream, soap flakes, all sorts and types and sizes of paper, glue, yarn, paintbrushes, and paint rollers; string; clear containers; sieves and funnels of different sizes; and medicine droppers.

Materials for Observing the Natural World. Materials that can be used to assist children learning about the natural world include cages, bug catchers or homes, ant farms, aquariums, cameras, videotape, resource books, rainfall measurement devices, cloth to create flags and wind measures, magnifying glasses, binoculars, butterfly nets, and measuring tapes.

Arranging the Science Environment

An ideal classroom for science learning should provide a specific science center, plus science activities in each of the other learning centers. And, of course, science activities should also occur frequently around the building, on the playground, and on field trips.

Curiously, learning centers that offer the most science learning opportunities are also the centers that are particularly difficult to manage—because of mess, materials, noise, space needs, and numbers of children. These centers include the woodworking area, the sand and water table (or tubs), the art area, and the block area. Because these areas pose significant challenges for early childhood teachers and programs, they are sometimes eliminated, made available only on very limited occasions, or severely controlled (through rules, limited space, and limiting materials). These limitations often make these learning areas almost useless for learning science. Earlier I discussed how some of these areas seem to attract mainly boys, or mainly girls, and provided suggestions for offsetting this problem.

All the woodwork benches in my Head Start program were used for teachers' desks, aquariums, art projects, eating, and piling books on; none was used for woodworking activities until I insisted that they be! This is not unusual in early childhood programs.

Since science learning is centered on children's hands-on exploration of materials to construct scientific knowledge and principles, children must have lots of opportunities to handle materials. And by definition, this means noise, mess, cleaning up, and dirt and paint in hair and clothes. Programs need to accept this as a given, provide ways to minimize the disruption and mess (classroom management, storage, smocks, and so on), and be very open with parents about their children's need to be fully involved in exploring the scientific world. Specific parent training and parent communication pieces may be required to help parents understand this point. Here are just a few suggestions that illustrate how science can be encouraged in specific learning centers.

Block Area

This area lends itself to the scientific activities of studying movement. I remember when I was a child we created fantastic marble rollways (what we called marble chutes). We built them with several sets of unit blocks. Some got so big they touched the classroom ceiling! We also built marble rollways with straight exits that delivered the marble onto the classroom floor, and would then take turns to see whose marble would go the farthest.

Movement activities with toy cars—maybe even making cars in the woodwork area, varying the angle of an incline, and then seeing whose car will go the fastest—are fun science activities in the block area. Children can experiment with different kinds of wheels, to see which car will go the fastest (provide the least resistance). They can also experiment with different ways to get the cars to go faster: using wax, soap, and other materials to reduce friction. And representational activities can be explored in the block area. A cardboard box or an angle block taken from the hollow block set can be covered with plastic or butcher paper, and then cars, balls, spools, dowels, film containers, and more can be dipped in paint and rolled down the incline. Different colors of paint can be used to track different kinds of objects.

Sand and Water Table

This is an extraordinary environment for science activities. In it children can construct concepts relating to liquids, solids, volume, conservation, floating, mixing (sand and dirt in water), gravity, physical properties of sand, water pressure, waves, and the force of winds. Food coloring and salad oil in water provide the opportunity to see how oil floats on water. Placing a plain piece of white paper in this mix, then letting it dry, produces old-fashioned wrapping paper.

Making simple sailboats at the woodwork table, then placing them in the water table and blowing through straws onto the sails to make them go is a great activity. The children can even pair off boats and have races until the fastest boat is determined. Later these boats can be taken outside on a windy day.

An ongoing fun activity is to see which objects float, and which sink. Children should be encouraged to guess (estimate) the results before the activity. Then the results should be graphed in two categories: floats, sinks. Extend this activity to find ways that items that originally don't float can be made to do so, and vice-versa.

Art Area

The most obvious science activity in the art area is mixing: mixing paints with water (makes the powder a fluid, and gives clear water a color), mixing paints with each other (makes new and different colors), mixing colors with white paint (makes the colors lighter), and mixing color with black paint (makes them darker). As a child I was very fascinated when I discovered that mixing all colors together produces gray!

Children in the art area also experiment with liquids, gravity, and flow. I've seen children spend hours putting paint on a piece of paper attached to an easel and watching the paint run down the paper. How can they keep the paint from running? What happens when the paint runs into paint of another color on the paper? What does the running paint look like when it has dried? What happens if you take the paper off the easel and turn it upside down?

Another whole area of experimenting in the art area occurs when different media and materials are combined. Painting black paint on a picture made with crayons, and then scratching through the dried paint to reveal the crayons' patterns underneath the paint, is an example of this approach (eggs can be decorated in this manner too). For older children, batik is another example of combining materials. String tied to a roller, then soaked in paint, then rolled across clean white paper, creates great wrapping paper. What happens when you paint on wood, clay, aluminum foil, or waxed paper?

Photographic paper is used to create a variety of images when exposed to light and by placing opaque and solid objects on it. Simple cameras can even be made and used by elementary-school children. The study of light is, of course, an important scientific activity.

Any program that kiln-dries pottery offers a wonderful opportunity to explore what happens when clay is heated and how the color and texture of different slips and glazes change under extreme heat. Students can try to predict the color of their finished, kiln-glazed works of art, and also discover how glass is made.

Woodworking Area

A variety of boats can be constructed in the woodwork area. Which boats float the best and which are the easiest to direct in the water? Can children load up the boats with toy animals, toy people, and other cargo without the boat capsizing or sinking? Whose boats will take the most people and cargo? What can be done to stabilize the boats? Why is a keel needed on boats that have a sail?

While birdhouses and bird feeders are not strictly scientific objects, observing birds feeding, nesting, and feeding their young certainly is science. These objects can be made carefully on the woodwork bench or the art area, then placed in appropriate places on the playground and school or center grounds.

Science Area

The science learning center in the classroom should serve three functions: first, it should provide a display area for new inventions, discoveries, and objects picked up on nature walks and field trips. Second, it should provide easy access and storage for specific

▶*Found objects from a nature walk end up on the science table.*

science tools: magnifying glasses, binoculars, bug cages, tubes, water gauges, tapes, prisms. Finally, it should be a place for rotating science projects and experiments, such as bean sprouting, wind chimes, butterfly metamorphoses, charts of the evolution of the moth, and more. Displays should be changed often and should be related to other projects, activities, or units: field trips, books being read in the group, current natural phenomena such as an eclipse or El Niño.

Outdoor Play Area

Again, there are countless ways the outside play area can be used to learn science phenomena. Some are outlined here.

Weeds. Weed the entire garden. Then select a square section of the garden (you might want to use a square marked off by two-by-fours) where you let the weeds grow. Keep weeding the rest of the garden, and have children observe the different areas of the garden and the effect of weeds on the flowers and vegetables.

Birds. Place a bird feeder away from playground noise and traffic (preferably near trees and close to open space, if your playground faces open space). Select seeds that will attract the wild birds in your area. Help children enter the playground quietly and observe the birds feeding. Note the different birds on the feeder. Use bird identification books. You can also grow certain varieties of bird seed in your garden, such as sunflower seeds.

Planting Vegetables and Flowers. Planting, caring for, and harvesting flowers and vegetables in a garden is a wonderful scientific activity for young children. They learn about the need to care for plants; the effect of weeds, birds, and animals on the plants; and the effect of the passage of time. They also learn about the seasons and the effects of sun, water, and wind on plants. As children care for flowers and vegetables, teachers can help them:

- observe the initial shoots as seeds germinate;
- notice how plants grow from day to day;
- examine why it's important to weed the garden;
- talk about the need for water;
- notice the first leaves—and talk about how plants use leaves to collect the sun's rays to make chlorophyl (thus plants whose leaves are eaten by pests do not grow and eventually die);

▶*Many tools are instruments that help teach science and math.*

- notice the formation of buds and flowers;
- observe holes and bite marks in leaves from various birds, pests, and possibly rabbits;
- notice the development of seeds and fruits, in both vegetables and flowers;
- talk about how we know when it's time to harvest vegetables;
- stress careful observation in these activities, and enhance this observation with materials in the classroom—books, magazines (*My Big Back Yard*), charts, seed and flower catalogs, displays from the garden, and displays for parents to see.

Math for Elementary-School Children

Math curriculum in elementary schools is determined by the schools, school districts, educational and textbook companies, or religious organizations that run schools. Further, math for the K–12 program is coming more and more under the umbrella of national standards (National Council of Teachers of Mathematics, 2000).

As children gain the cognitive stage of concrete operations (between ages 6 and 7), they are much more able to handle ideas and concepts representationally—with words (spoken and written), pictures, and numbers. Children this age also have greater listening skills, social skills, and ability to follow directions. These new skills and abilities mean they can do math from workbooks, worksheets, and direct teacher instruction. Some elementary-school math approaches are based on these abilities.

But as Elkind pointed out, just because children have the capacity to do something does not mean that they should do it (1999). Math experts believe that the most effective way to continue a child's math development at this age is to provide lots of hands-on exploration and manipulation of real objects and problems. Most of these math activities will be extensions and more complex applications of the range of activities already discussed. Here are a few examples.

developmentally Appropriate Practice

Comparing

Children can move from making one-to-one comparisons of real objects to making representations of those objects, and then to comparing representations with representations. They can match the five children in the dress-up area with the five tokens on the Velcro board outside the area used to designate whether the area is full; the five dots on a large die with the five spaces a child can advance on a game board; and the five diamonds on the playing card with the number five in the corner of the card. Children can also compare things that are larger or smaller than these sets ("I got one more card than you did," "You can go one more space than me").

Ordering

Elementary-school children now truly have the skills to order things by size, height, color, sound, speed, attractiveness, preference, and so on. This concept of ordering takes off at this age. Children are also learning the labels for the ordering sequence, at this age: *first, second, third, fourth, last.* Obviously these names derive from the names of numbers (*four—fourth; five—fifth*), but note that *first* and *one* are not related, and neither are *second* and *two,* and *last* has no connection with any number. Children need help learning these labels, and their relationship with numerals and numbers.

Measuring

Children can move from their own personalized measurement system (feet, hands, bodies, blocks, and pencils) to more generally accepted measurement systems (feet and inches, pounds, yards, gallons, cups). Children will be fascinated to find out that some of these culturally accepted units are actually based on personal units: feet, yards, and so on.

Graphing

Graphing should continue to be used to record a variety of events, and to record events over a period of time (every day for a week, scores of ball games over several weeks, and the like). Graphing can also be used to plot predictions (those children who believe it will snow tomorrow, those who think the tomatoes will be ripe before the end of the school year), to record preferences, or to track attendance.

Numbers

At this age children learn the names of the numbers, learn to label numbers (the number of ducklings in the picture in the book), and begin to record these numbers using the correct symbols. They are also learning to read numbers: "That's a six, like my age." Other number activities for this age include the following:

- Children can bowl over milk cartons or plastic bottles, then count the number of bottles knocked over and the number remaining upright—handling two number concepts at one time.
- They can play dominoes, matching the correct number of dots.
- They can read simple books that include number concepts and math activities.
- Children can play "go fish" (matching) with cards—matching numbers with pictures of numbers.
- They can play board games that use dice.
- Children can create number lines, time lines, and other numerical charts.

Children are also learning how to write numbers, and to do simple addition and subtraction of whole numbers. They are also continuing to develop ideas regarding greater than and less than. When they do these activities, they still need to use real objects (fingers, blocks, beads, buttons) to help them see the concrete results, because young children first learn to add by adding individual items, and to subtract by removing individual items. They only learn math facts (subtracting 3 from 7 is 4) later on. Teachers should avoid the temptation of expecting children do addition and subtraction in their heads, and of teaching math facts, until the children have had lots of opportunity to practice adding and subtracting with real objects.

At this age it is important to encourage math learning in all sorts of new, different, and more complex and abstract directions. But it is also important to remember that we are still building the foundation of a wide area of skills and concepts, and that the best way to do so is through the real manipulation of concrete objects and through real representations (drawings, graphs, block buildings) of mathematical events. Teachers should also find a variety of ways to incorporate kinesthetic activities into learning number concepts—skip rope, chants, marching, movement activities, and more.

Science for Elementary-School Children

As children move into the elementary grades, learning becomes more structured, less integrated, and more specialized. This is also true of the teaching of science.

The goals of the science program during the first three grades depend on the school's science curriculum. School districts, private schools (independent or part of a larger educational organization), religious schools, and even home schools all have their own science curricula. In Chapter 4, I address the issue of curriculum, and the relationship of curriculum with educational philosophy and instructional practice. The point here is that, especially as we move into the formal school years, learning activities in the classrooms are driven by curricular goals and objectives.

Science curricula—especially in public schools (and public charter schools)—are established from national and state standards. These standards are initially developed by national science educators, and then translated into state policy by politicians. Most local districts then align their local standards with these state standards. (In America, local states have far more authority in direct educational policymaking than does the federal government.)

Traditionally, K–12 science programs break science down into its classical disciplines and isolate science from other subject areas. Biological sciences (plants, animals, insects) and physical sciences (astronomy, meteorology, chemistry, and physics) were each taught separately, with their own goals and objectives. Often these areas were taught through worksheets, workbooks, direct instruction, and rote memorization.

The new emphasis in science education at this age is to extend many of the behaviors and approaches that characterized science instruction at the younger ages into the elementary grades: hands-on learning, exploration, predicting, projects, manipulating variables in real settings, careful observation of real and contrived situations, and exploring the scientific world beyond the classroom.

▶ *Children observe, collect, and interpret scientific information from the natural world.*

Another focus of this new direction is integrated science: looking at science across disciplines and across categories of science. Thus a class might study the impact of the change of the jet stream caused by El Niño on plants growing in the garden (biology and meteorology), or the positions of the stars (astronomy) on cultures (social sciences and history).

Still crucial to teaching elementary-school children science is to stress causal relationships, and to emphasize discovering the scientific rules of the world around us. Thus, scientific curiosity is still the center of science learning, and the focus of a science curriculum (and its teachers) is to nurture, expand, and support that curiosity in more and more challenging and complex ways.

Conclusion

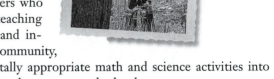

In this chapter I have covered math and science learning for young children. In an ever more technological and competitive world, American schools need to prepare citizens to be skilled, competent, and successful in science and math. To do so, our early childhood programs need to explore ways to introduce young children to these disciplines and to develop in them a desire for future math and science learning. To achieve this we need to train teachers who are confident and competent in teaching these subjects, solicit the support and involvement of parents and the entire community, and integrate exciting, developmentally appropriate math and science activities into everything we do in our early childhood programs and schools.

Questions and Projects

1. Design a math activity for typical 5-year-olds. Define your goals and objectives. Make sure the activity is hands-on, developmentally appropriate, individualized, and interesting.

2. Design an activity for the playground that illustrates incline and velocity. Think about using trikes, slides, and swings. Remember, children need hands-on, real experiences.

3. Contact community agencies—science museums, children's museums, zoos, community gardens. List at least five science and math activities community agencies provide for children aged 5 and younger, and five activities for children aged 6–8. Include the agency's name, phone number, contact person, and activity.

4. Develop a simple parent communication piece (written or video) that describes how parents can teach their children basic math foundation skills. Use illustrations, and include resources.

5. Develop a project that uses the idea of transformational representation to teach a science concept to young children. Describe the activity, concept to be taught, and target age.

CHAPTER

14

Observation, Assessment, *and* Evaluation

*M*uch of what we know about how children develop and learn has come from careful observations of children; good screening instruments are needed to detect young children who could benefit from early intervention, and good assessment tools tell us whether a program is working the way it should. Parents want to know if their children are spending their time effectively and developing a solid foundation for future success. Teaches need good assessments to determine whether their students are responding to the curriculum and instruction. And students need to know how well they are doing, how much they know, and whether they are being successful. Further, administrators and politicians require ongoing assessment methods to determine how well the program is doing and whether their investment is paying off. This chapter discusses the wide variety of assessment tools and approaches, covers the strengths and weakness of various methods, and outlines the attraction and dangers of high-stakes tests. It also gives the reader lots of advice regarding use of assessment in the classroom and program. ▪

Purposes of Assessment, Observation, and Evaluation

Learning about Children

Jean Piaget carefully studied his two children. He posed problems for them, and then observed their responses; he asked

Questions to Consider

1. What are the various purposes of observations, assessments, and evaluations?

2. What are the differences among tests, assessments, samples, scales, observations, checklists, portfolios, and program evaluations?

3. Why are many tests and checklists standardized?

4. What can assessments tell us about a child's development and progress?

5. Are assessments needed to assist normal development, accountability, or both?

6. What is test bias, and why can it be a problem?

7. Can the use of assessments be detrimental to a child's development and education?

8. Should students be involved in developing their own assessment process?

them how they saw the world, and recorded their answers. And he gave them toys and other materials, then observed how they played with them and what they said to each other as they did so. From his careful observations of, interviews with, and recording of his children, Piaget built his developmental theory. Arnold Gesell filmed many children involved in a variety of physical activities, then used the analysis of the films to develop his theory of maturation. And Lawrence Kohlberg gave groups of boys of different ages a series of moral dilemmas to solve. Based on the boys' responses to these dilemmas, Kohlberg constructed a theory of moral development. Careful observations are used by researchers to learn about children, and then to develop theories that predict children's behavior and development.

Research. Much of what we know about an infant's capacity to see, hear, feel, and taste has been determined through a variety of **laboratory studies** conducted in universities around the world. What we know about the impact of TV on children is from controlled studies of children watching hours of TV (Wright et al., 1984); our knowledge of the impact of violence on children, the power of role models (real and symbolic), and how young children respond to a variety of stimuli are all based on these kinds of studies. The advantage of research conducted in a controlled setting like a university laboratory is that the results can be directly attributed to the specific variables being studied; the disadvantage is that the laboratory is not the same as a classroom, home, or community—and the results might be different in those settings. Various observation methods and procedures are used to conduct research in the laboratory settings, including video-taping, interviews, providing specific tasks for children to complete, and observing children.

Child Development. What happens when a child enters kindergarten for the first time? What is the impact of divorce on young children? How do fathers' and mothers' interactions with children differ? What do adolescents think about their parents? The answers to these and other important questions about child development are answered through careful observation and data collection. What we know about how children learn and develop is either from theories based on information collected using these methods or from direct observation and assessment. Thus, a primary purpose of observation and assessment is to collect data to build on our body of knowledge about how children learn and develop.

Cause and Effect. There are many ways to construct research to find out specific information about children's development and learning. One of these is to study the relationship of cause and effect, which is very helpful because it enables us to narrow down positive and negative impacts on children's development. For example, what is the impact of early childhood experience on later learning?

▶ *Play scales that combine levels of social play (Parten) and levels of cognitive play (Piaget) have been used for research and to determine the level of an individual child's play.*

Do children from single-parent homes learn important survival skills that children from two-parent homes do not? Does too much TV watching interfere with school achievement? Through carefully designed research, using observation and assessment, or both, we can find answers to these questions.

The importance of this kind of research is obvious in helping to meet the needs of our children. Another advantage is that it replaces **subjective** information—say, a belief that all children from single parent homes suffer—with more **objective** information—for example, under certain conditions children from single-parent homes thrive.

Planning Activities

The philosophy of developmentally appropriate practice calls for teachers of young children to match the curriculum and classroom activities with three factors: (1) overall knowledge of the child's developmental stage (based on age); (2) the child's individual developmental progress; and (3) the child's unique set of cultural experiences (Bredekamp & Copple, 1997). Vygotsky's zone of proximal development—the window in which children learn most effectively—is between what children can do independently and what they can do with expert assistance (Berk & Winsler, 1995). And traditional curricula have a predetermined scope and sequence—the order through which a child should progress in learning a predetermined set of tasks and knowledge. All of these approaches to working with children require teachers to possess information about children's unique backgrounds, things they like to do, what they know and don't know, and what they can and cannot do. Teachers obtain this information from careful and continual observation and assessment.

Developing Individual Plans. Individual Program Plans (IPPs), Individual Learning Plans (ILPs), and Individual Education Plans (IEPs) organize data collected through observation and other assessments into specific learning plans (Martin, 1999). Children diagnosed with a specific disability or special need must have an IEP; many schools and early childhood programs—such as Head Start—are now requiring IPPs for all their children. Also, individual plans for gifted students require the collection of important information. Even if a program does not require an official IPP or ILP, for teachers to meet the needs of every child fully, an informal plan based on recently collected data should be developed.

Determining Learning Styles. Howard Gardner's theory of multiple intelligences is popular in many early childhood programs. Gardner believes that children prefer to learn new information predominantly using several of eight different learning styles or modalities (see Chapter 9 for a full discussion). While programs that use Gardner's ideas do not advocate that children should learn only by their preferred approaches, they do believe students should know their learning styles and develop approaches to capitalize on how they learn most readily. For students to use their preferred learning styles and for teachers to teach to students' strengths, assessments must be conducted that can determine each student's intelligences, an approach that illustrates using assessments to plan instruction. Another approach involves giving gifted students tests to discover what they know, thus enabling the teacher to develop enrichments and differentiations that will challenge these students.

Adapting Curriculum and Instruction. Children learn most effectively when we match activities to their background knowledge and their interests, and build on what they already know and can do. A curriculum is a general design to teach certain skills and knowledge, but teachers must expertly adjust, adapt, reconfigure, and redesign instruction based on their knowledge of the children in the class and how they learn. Teachers must base the what, how, and when of the next steps in the curriculum on what they have learned about the children through observation and assessments (Hills, 1993). Thus it is essential that teachers continually collect information about each child's progress, and then carefully tailor their classroom activities to this information. If a child has already mastered basic phonemic knowledge, it makes little sense to teach this skill. A student who recently had a baby born into his family would benefit from a unit on family, community, and culture. And if a child is struggling with English, she may need a different approach to her writing instruction than the method called for by the curriculum.

Communicating to Parents

According to Hills, any assessment program must provide to parents what they need to know about their children's progress (1993). Parents want to know several things, including whether their children are where they should be regarding learning basic skills and concepts, whether the program will provide the skills and concepts their children need to be successful in school, and whether the program philosophy matches what they want for their children (Hills, 1993). Most important, parents need information that makes sense to them—not information couched in professional jargon or school rhetoric.

Conferences. Parent–teacher conferences have two primary functions: to communicate to parents their children's progress, and to solicit information from parents that enable the program to better meet the needs of their children. **Assessments** help us to do a good job of reporting children's progress. They provide information for parents beyond simply the teacher's opinion. We can provide data about what children know, show examples of what they can do, and solicit support from parents for the next curricular and developmental stage. Maybe of most importance, good assessment data show parents how children are progressing over time. This gives parents a sense of the progressive nature of learning and lets them view their children's own growth, rather than in comparison to that of other children. A sense of overall progress is particularly helpful for parents of children who may be struggling at school. Thus good child assessment must be conducted periodically to provide the information parents need and deserve.

Assessments should not be deficit driven—focused on what children cannot do; by the same token, conferences should not be, either. Tasks, skills, and concepts that children are learning should be presented as current developmental activities, and parents should be solicited to help their children master these tasks. Concerns a teacher might have regarding a potential problem should not be brought up in regular conferences, unless they are raised by parents. Conferences must never be dominated by problems, particularly for the parents of children who are struggling.

Home–School Communication. Assessments provide a focal point for home–school communication. As such, they can add to a parent's sense of importance and responsibility, or they can create a feeling of frustration and disconnect with the program. It is vital that parents believe that the observations and assessments conducted on their children are done to benefit the children first, and the parent second (Hills, 1993). Any communication with parents regarding assessments must stress this perspective—assessments are to benefit the child and parent. The results must be easy to interpret, and it must be clear how these results can be used to benefit the children. Communication regarding assessments needs to give parents a sense of confidence in their parenting abilities and a faith in their ability to assist their children in learning. If assessments are used only to address children's problems and deficits, this will not occur.

A Set of Guiding Principles

Stiggins has presented five principles, summarized on the next page, that should be kept in mind when considering effective classroom assessments (2001).

Questions Based on NAEYC and NAECS/SDE Guidelines for Appropriate Assessment

The following set of questions is adapted from Hills, "Assessment in Context" (1993).

1. Are the assessments based on the goals and objectives of the program?
2. Are the results of the assessment used to benefit children—create plans for individual children, improve instruction, individualize instruction, and so on?
3. Does the assessment address all domains—social, emotional, physical, and cognitive—as well as students' feelings about learning?
4. Does the assessment provide useful information to teachers to improve their teaching?
5. Do the assessments rely on teachers' regular observations and record keeping of children's everyday activities and performance, reflecting behavior over time?
6. Do the assessments occur as part of the ongoing life of the classroom?
7. Is the assessment performance-based, not just testing skills in isolation?
8. Does the assessment use multiple sources of information about children—teacher interviews, children's work, and observations?
9. Do the assessments reflect individual, cultural, and linguistic diversity?
10. Do children appear comfortable and relaxed during the assessment?
11. Do the assessments support parents' belief in their children and their ability as parents?
12. Does the assessment focus on children's strengths and capacities, not just weaknesses?
13. Is the teacher the primary assessor, and is that teacher well trained?
14. Do the assessments involve collaboration among teachers, children, administrators, and parents? Are parents informed about the results in a meaningful way—not simply a letter grade?
15. Are children given opportunities to evaluate their own learning?
16. Do assessments determine both what children can do independently and what they can do with constructive support (to place them in the zone of proximal development)?
17. Are assessment results used to assist in instructional planning?

Students Are the Key Assessment Users. Students use assessment results to set expectations for themselves; assessments have more impact on student success than any other school factor. Students look to assessment results as evidence of their own accomplishments. Classroom assessment information powers the students' learning, and if the results tell students they are being unsuccessful, their motivation will decline. If students continue to fail, teachers need to adjust their approach so students can succeed.

Clear and Appropriate Targets Are Essential. Targets of achievement must be clearly defined. What, specifically, am I assessing? Further, what is the standard or criterion for doing well in the area I am assessing? Finally, what are the specific steps along the way to proficiency that I expect students to achieve?

Accurate Assessment Is a Must. Teachers must be able to define clear and specific achievement expectations—what the specific knowledge, reasoning, skills, and product expectations are. Further, we must be clear why the assessment is being given. Users of assessment results include students, parents, teachers, principals, curriculum personnel, support teachers (special education and others), superintendents, board members, and politicians. Whose needs will the assessment meet? A proper method of assessment must be used—the assessment must accurately measure what it's supposed to. I always get very frustrated when my daughter's French (she is fluent in the language) is assessed only through a writing test. This is clearly not a proper method for assessing her ability to speak the language. Finally, a proper method must include sound sampling—assessing all the skills and content that the teachers expect children to know, not isolated skills or concepts that might produce distorted results. If sound sampling is used, then a teacher can accurately assume that the results on a test represent what students know in a given area.

Free from Bias and Distortion. The purpose of an assessment is to get accurate information on each child's achievement. A biased test is one whose results do not accurately reflect students' achievement. Bias can occur because of individual teacher bias, test item bias, and bias in other areas. Teachers need to make sure that all possible sources of bias are accounted for.

Effective Communication. Results of assessments must be clearly communicated to those who need the results. While we have traditionally communicated test results through numbers, there are other approaches—words, pictures, illustrating examples, and more. Whatever we use must be very clearly defined. What does an A mean? What does "high achievement" mean? What does "needs improvement" mean? We must make sure the users of the tests have the same understanding of the meaning that we do.

Finally, students should be full partners in the assessment process (Stiggins, 2001). Here are some ways students can become involved, from the least to the greatest involvement:

- Offer ideas to the teacher about how to improve the test.
- Suggest assessment exercises.
- Develop some of the assessment exercises.

- Help develop the scoring rubric (a rubric is the criterion used to evaluate the results and the form the results should take—the standard to which the results will be compared).
- Create their own scoring rubric.
- Use their own scoring rubric to assess their achievement.
- Consider how to use assessment results to improve their own academic success.
- See the correlation among self-assessment, teacher assessment, and their own success.

Determine Program Effectiveness

Accountability is a powerful word in education today. Everyone wants to know that their money is being used responsibly—that it is producing the expected results. One way to achieve accountability is through the use of a form of program evaluation. There is a variety of methods used to determine program effectiveness.

Outcomes. Educational outcomes are the knowledge, skills, and dispositions that will be gained from the program, curriculum, or activity. Outcome-based assessment measures whether these outcomes have been met, based on some outside standard, after a given period of time (Martin, 1999). Outcomes can also be determined for noneducational areas, such as counseling, parent involvement, and community participation. For true program evaluation, all components of the program must have written outcomes, approaches to collect data for each outcome, and a standard to which the outcome is compared.

For example, one objective for the family component of Head Start is "to strengthen families as the primary nurturers of the children"; the outcome statements for this objective are that (1) Head Start parents demonstrate improved parenting skills, (2) Head Start parents improve their self-concept and emotional well-being, and (3) Head Start parents make progress toward their educational, literacy, and employment goals (Community Development Institute, 2001, p. 4). The outcomes in these three areas have to do with how well each is occurring, and a standard needs to be set. What is meant by *improved* and *make progress?* Data must be collected—parent interviews, surveys, questionnaires, and the like—that document progress and its extent. Outcomes must be measurable and time-specific (after one year, at the end of the program). To measure program outcomes, data should be collected on an ongoing basis.

As the preceding example indicates, the new Head Start performance standards (HHS, 1999) require specific outcomes for children and families. Further, each Head Start program must develop methods to assess whether it is meeting these outcomes. The educational outcomes include student performance in areas such as letter–word recognition and knowledge of book and print conventions, as well as gains in writing skills and vocabulary (HHS, 1999).

Program Evaluation. A school has an anti-bullying program. Does it work, and how will we know? Another school has just instituted a character education program, and needs to know if it is worth the money and time the teachers are spending on it. Maybe a child-care center has introduced a series of training sessions for staff and would like to know whether the training has a positive impact on the quality of classroom instruction. All these efforts can be assessed through the use of program evaluation, which involves collecting, analyzing, and interpreting data to make or support decisions about a program (Hadley & Mitchell, 1995). For example, program evaluation can be used to do the following:

- Answer specific questions about a program (How many parents are involved? How well do we retain teachers? Do men stay in our program?).
- Determine strengths and weaknesses of a program.
- Determine whether a new program should be developed.
- Determine the relationship of one program to another.
- Determine whether a program is cost effective (in terms of time, money, or staff resources).
- Determine the reputation of a program (What do parents, the community, and programs our children move into think of the program?).

Improve Programs. Almost all education programs can be improved. But it's difficult to improve without defining the areas in which the program needs to be improved. It's not good enough simply to say, "We want it to be better"; rather, a program might want to improve parent involvement, increase staff–child interaction, or improve math and science achievement. Clearly, the direction in which a program wishes to improve determines the method used to ascertain if it is successful. If a program wants to become NAEYC accredited, receiving the accreditation is the sole evaluation. If, however, a program wants to increase the number of staff who have child development knowledge, they might need to look at the classes staff are taking, the degrees they possess, and whether the program's personnel policies support retaining staff with child development knowledge.

Accreditation. In this book I have already discussed accreditation; it is presented here as one kind of program evaluation. A program that receives accreditation has passed a specific evaluation. But it must be clear that this evaluation is based on quality indicators that are in turn based on a certain philosophical perspective. A religious program that stresses obedience to authority and teaching both academic basics and the basics of a particular faith may not view accreditation as a valid measure of program quality.

State Standards. In Chapter 4 I discuss national and state goals and standards. To assure accountability and control over curricula, states have developed and continue to develop standards that define what students should know in each subject area and at each grade level. Some states have also developed standards for preschool and kindergarten children. Once standards have been developed, the logical—and political—next step is to create ways to determine whether these standards are being met. While assessments for these standards are always conducted on individual students, their purpose is to determine the quality of a school's overall performance. In Colorado, the Colorado Student Assessment Process (CSAP) is a series of pencil-and-paper tests given to students in third, fifth, seventh, and ninth grades in reading and writing and math. These tests are not typical standardized fill-in-the bubble tests; however, they are a good example of very high stakes criterion referenced tests (see below, Standardized Tests) given to all students at the same time. Results of these tests are used to grade individual schools—

and to a lesser extent school districts. Later in the chapter I discuss some of the dangers of high-stakes testing. The central problem is that the needs of the school (to look good in the eyes of the public) and the needs of politicians (to show the public they care about educational quality) take precedence over the needs of children and their families.

Satisfy Specific Funding Sources. Clearly, much of the accountability movement is aimed at satisfying a program's many funding sources—parents, politicians, voters, and others. But there are also educational programs that stipulate specific results as a condition of funding. These are usually federal, state, or foundation grants or subsidies. All federal grants such as Head Start and Title I must have an evaluation component, and often these include evaluating children's progress in target areas. Some funding sources require programs to be accredited or to achieve a certain score on an environmental rating scale (see Chapter 5). Grants for math and science programs expect to see student improvement in math and science; monies targeted for technology must be applied to increasing technology in schools (computers and Internet access), more training of teachers, and increased use of technology by students. And programs targeted to reduce bullying in school need evaluations that record a reduction of bullying behaviors. Thus each funding evaluation differs, depending on the goals and outcomes of the specific program.

Determine Special Needs of Students

Assessments are conducted on children to determine whether they have special needs or may potentially have them—including children who might be gifted and talented students. Kindergarten screening and Head Start screening are partly used to identify children with potential learning problems. Screening can determine whether a child may need additional testing in a specific area; but screening is a "quick and dirty" process and should never be used to determine whether a child has a disability. Efforts to ascertain whether a child may have a disability are needed because many learning challenges can be reduced if they are detected early. Another reason, however, for early intervention is that regulations require at least 10 percent of the children each Head Start program serves must have a disability, and because local schools receive federal funding for every child identified with a special need.

Determine Areas that Require Intervention. Based on screening results, a child may be given a variety of other, more specific assessments to isolate a potential barrier to learning. Even results of Apgar and Brazelton Neonatal Behavior Scales given to newborns can alert physicians to the need for additional assessments. Disabilities can be anything from sight and hearing impairments, to poor sensory integration, behavioral and emotional challenges, Down syndrome and cystic fibrosis, developmental delays, and a range of learning disabilities. Once a child's disability has been carefully diagnosed, an Individual Family Service Plan or Individual Education Plan must be carefully written to address the child's need, and appropriate placement determined (see Chapter 6).

Place Children in Specific Programs. Assessments are used to place children in a variety of programs—not just special education. Kindergarten screening is used to place children in remedial, regular, or advanced kindergarten. As children grow older, assessments are used to track them into various programs, classrooms, and schools. Many magnet schools require students to pass an assessment to be eligible; some charter schools and many private schools have entrance exams, and assessments are also used to determine which children can benefit from gifted and talented programs. Tracking children based on test results goes against most early childhood and early education philosophies. Children benefit from being in mixed-age, mixed-ability, and diverse population groups. Further, teachers need to develop the ability to differentiate instruction to meet the needs of all children in the classroom. Finally, children who are placed in lower-level and remedial programs based on test results soon develop a sense of failure and a feeling of inadequacy in academic activities.

Types of Assessment

Because assessments are used for so many different purposes, there are many different types of assessments. While these run the gamut from program evaluations to screening tools and IQ tests, it is important to recognize that appropriate assessments must be carefully selected, and the results obtained must be judiciously interpreted. Assessment results should be used in conjunction with other information.

Program Evaluations

Program evaluations differ from other kinds of evaluations in their focus on the entire program, or on a part of a program. While observations, tests, portfolios, and the like tell us about individual children (and, collectively, about the program itself), program evaluations focus on the bigger picture. A variety of data collection methods are used for program evaluation, depending on the nature of the activity. Usually a combination of methods is used—interviews, checklists, environmental rating scales, and more. Some program evaluations also use data the programs collect for internal program matters—such as attendance, discipline, and suspension records; parents meeting attendance records; days teachers take off for personal leave.

A program evaluation must first clearly and specifically define what is to be evaluated, determine what data are needed to answer the question and how it will be gathered, and then detail how the data will be analyzed. A report of the program evaluation is given to the people who need the report—decision makers, funders of a specific part of the program, parents, or government agencies.

Action Research. Action research is a participatory program evaluation activity. It involves the study of some aspect of an early childhood or school program by a person who works in the program, with the intent of improving part of the program. Characteristics of action research are:

- the researcher is involved in the program (teacher, administrator, or other);
- the intent is action—to do something to improve the program;
- the activity focuses on a small, manageable part of the program;
- results of the activity should be evident in a fairly short time period.

Action research is data driven. In other words, instead of saying, "We need to improve parent involvement in our program because it's not very good," action research might say, "Based on attendance records of parent activities over the past six months, we have only 10 percent attendance. We want to develop approaches to increase this number to at least 50 percent." My analysis of the discrepancy between the number of boys versus girls identified as special-education students in my Head Start program that I discussed in Chapter 6 is an example of the first part of action research (Wardle, 1991). It would only truly be action research, however, if I had developed ways to reduce this discrepancy, and then documented whether this goal was achieved.

Environmental Rating Scale. Environmental rating scales are used to assess the quality of early childhood environments. I discuss them in more detail in Chapter 5. The best known of these rating scales are Harms and Clifford's Early Childhood Environmental Rating Scale (1998); Harms, Cryer, and Clifford's Infant/Toddler Environmental Rating Scale (1989), and Harms and Clifford's Family Day Care Rating Scale (1989).

Rating instruments are easy to use and can be administered by teachers and other educational staff. The scale is divided into several major categories, which are then subdivided. Each item is rated on a scale from 1 to 7. Information is gathered both by staff and from parents on each item. A place is also provided for comments.

Accreditation. Accreditation is an evaluation of a program that carries with it the authority of the accrediting body. Colleges, schools, counseling programs, and early childhood programs are all accredited by different organizations. Specific accreditation is required for a program to give college credits; accreditation is required for a program to receive certain kinds and categories of funding; and other accreditation simply tells the world—including parents—the quality of a program. Most serve a combination of these purposes. All accreditation processes use a variety of methods to collect data on a program—checklists, interviews, rating scales, self-assessment scales, review of records, and more—but each does so in a different way, depending on its purpose. Accreditation of early childhood programs uses indicators of quality: teacher–child ratios, teacher–child interactions, teachers' early childhood knowledge, and a checklist of the environment. The process of early childhood program accreditation includes interviews, observations, completing checklists, and reviewing paperwork. A group of people then analyze the data and, based on certain criteria, make the decision whether to accredit the program.

Is Your Program Brain Compatible?

Pat Phipps, in an article in *Child Care Information Exchange* (1999), describes an evaluation used to determine whether a program is compatible with current brain research. A program that is "brain compatible" is one in which "the classrooms, curriculum, and instruction fit the way the brain learns and develops best" (Phipps, 1991, p. 55). Phipps proposes an evaluation that assesses the environment, solicits opinions regarding the program, and uses a checklist of general brain-research–based criteria.

The article is an excellent example of a program evaluation that focuses on a particular aspect, perspective, or orientation of an early childhood program. Other examples could be an evaluation of multicultural emphasis, openness to parent involvement and input, responsiveness to the community, or use of a second language in the program.

Environment. The environment is a central part of brain-based programs. Observations can be used to determine if the environment looks, sounds, feels, smells, and tastes right:

- *Looks right:* the environment is open and stimulating, and invites children to explore; bulletin boards are interesting and changed often, natural light dominates, and plants abound.
- *Sounds right:* music exists to soothe, calm, and relax, and is also used in a variety of classroom activities, transitions, and rituals.
- *Feels right:* the environment must be safe, secure, and emotionally warm; room temperature is not too hot or cold; and there is a variety of warm and soft textures and surfaces.
- *Smells right:* various interesting and pleasant scents—lemon, rosemary, orange, chamomile, lavender, and the like—exist, to soothe and stimulate.
- *Tastes right:* children need nutritious foods—eggs, fish, turkey, pork, yogurt, nuts, fruits, and leafy dark green vegetables—and lots of water.

Personal and Professional Opinions. Lots of information about a program can be gathered through interviews. Five groups should be interviewed: children, teachers, parents, administrators, and external professionals.

- *Children:* Ask children questions related to brain-compatible program elements, such as "Tell me what you did today that was fun."
- *Teachers:* Ask teachers about planning, teacher approaches, and interactions with children, then compare the responses to brain-compatible elements.
- *Parents:* Ask parents their opinion of the program—and let them know about its brain-compatible elements.
- *Administrators:* Ask how they assess whether the program is brain compatible— or do they? What do they look for, and what have they seen?
- *Outside professionals:* Ask knowledgeable people who are not affiliated in any way with the program to come into the program and view it from the perspective of brain compatibility. Then ask them their view of the program.

Use of Checklists. A checklist can be divided into five categories: environment, curriculum, materials and equipment, assessment, and scheduling. These assessments can be obtained from outside sources, such as the one developed by Phipps (1999), or can be created by the program. For each category, observers will check off whether the statements such as "A variety of aromas is evident," "Music is used throughout the curriculum," or "The schedule balances active and passive learning experiences" "are evident, need improvement, or are not evident" (Phipps, 1999, p. 56).

Standardized Tests

Standardized tests are assessments that ask a large number of students to respond to the same or similar sets of exercises under approximately the same conditions; all of these factors are standardized across all people who take the tests. As a result, these tests can be used to compare the results across students and classrooms. The classic standardized test is the IQ test, in which a score of 90–110 is average, and the distribution of scores falls nicely within a normal curve.

▶*Standardized tests require children to take tests in a very controlled, artificial environment. They tend to record what a child cannot do, rather than what they can do. (Bob Daemmrich, Stock Boston)*

Some of these tests are **norm referenced**—enabling the user to compare the child's score with those of other children who took the same test—resulting in a ranking and percentiles. Others are **criterion referenced**—comparing a child's score to a predetermined standard of acceptable performances—such as kindergarten readiness criteria. The question in the latter case is not how the child's score relates to other children's scores, but how it relates to a set criterion: is the child ready for kindergarten?

Screening and Assessment. According to Martin, screening is "a process of reviewing and evaluating behaviors or characteristics of individuals across a population or group in order to identify those who are in need of a more thorough assessment or specific support" (1999, p. 307). Screening is a form of assessment that has a very narrow objective. It can also be used to identify students for gifted and talented programs. Screening procedures use a standardized test. Key features of screening tools (Martin, 1997) are that they:

- use standardized procedures to evaluate the health and development of a large number of children (kindergarten screening, screening for behavior problems, sight screening, and the like);
- identify children in a special category or need;
- are usually nonparticipatory (the child is passive);
- usually take place in a testing location (as opposed to naturalistic observation).

Assessments, by contrast, include a variety of methods, including checklists, self-evaluations, observations, medical diagnosis, informal observations, standardized tests, and teacher appraisals—or a combination of two or more of these. Key features (Martin, 1999) include that they:

- evaluate the behavior of a child in a specific domain;
- compare a child's score to that of a norm or criterion;
- are valid and reliable (though there is sometimes a question about exactly what is being assessed);
- often require specially trained teachers, at least for some of the instruments.

Examples of screening and assessment instruments for preschoolers include the Battelle Child Behavior Checklist, DIAL-R, Miller Assessment for Preschoolers (MAP), Peabody Developmental Motor Scales, and for infants, the Bayley Scales of Infant Development and the Denver Developmental Screening Test. Obviously, there is overlap between screening and assessment, and the name of an instrument does not necessarily designate its function. In general, screening instruments are short, quick, and easy processes that the average teacher can perform; assessments are more multidimensional, take longer to administer, often require specialized training—at least in part—and provide much more information on individual children.

Ability Tests. The California Achievement Test and Terra Nova, the Iowa Test of Basic Skills and Iowa Test of Educational Development, and the Metropolitan Achievement Test and Stanford Achievement Test are very popular standardized ability tests used by schools, school districts, and testing companies across the country. They are normed in such a way that a wide range of people (parent, teacher, tester, special education and gifted expert, and so on) can get each child's results by subject area and within subject area (for example, in math, word problems, computation, basic algebra, and more), and then compare the child's results to national norms by grade level (the grade the child scored at), and percentile (the percentage of children of the same age who scored below the child).

IQ Tests. Intelligence quotient (IQ) tests are used for a variety of purposes, including placing children in gifted and talented programs, and determining children's academic potential. The most commonly used intelligence tests are the Stanford–Binet Intelligence Scale and the Wechsler Intelligence Scale for Children (WISC). Standardized on the general population, the tests are set for 50 percent of the population at any age to have an IQ of 90–110 (Clark, 1997). On the Stanford–Binet, an IQ of 132 and above is in the upper 2 percent of the population; below 68 IQ is in the lower 2 percent. The Stanford–Binet Intelligence Scale has developed over time since its original creation in 1906 by Alfred Binet and Théodore Simon. The test was designed to measure general intellectual ability—especially in verbal and mathematical areas. It does, in fact, do this quite well, and is a fairly good predictor of success in school for those who take the test after age 5 (Clark, 1997).

The WISC, developed in 1949 by David Wechsler, is the most commonly used IQ test in schools, and has both a verbal and a performance scale. It was standardized on one hundred white American (U.S.) boys and one hundred white American (U.S.) girls, aged 5–15. WISC III was developed in 1991, and normed on children representing the same demographics as the national census figures. Other IQ tests include the Leiter International Performance Scale, the Peabody Picture Vocabulary Test, and the Slosson Intelligence Test.

Problems with Standardized Assessments. Specific issues regarding standardized screening and assessments (including IQ tests) include the following (Hills, 1993):

- They are usually administered out of context. Children are often unfamiliar with the environment, testers, and general environment.
- Children cannot really show themselves at their best. They may be nervous, stressed out, shy, or disoriented. This is particularly true for young children and children not accustomed to the testing environment.
- Comparing children to other children is not always helpful—for many reasons.
- Such tests measure children's reactions, not purposeful action, initiative, creativity, or spontaneous problem solving.
- Many tests, including almost all screening tests, focus on what children cannot do.

▶ *While standardized assessments use averages to determine growth and development, we cannot forget our concern is with individual children.*

- The predictive value of standardized tests is questionable, and what they predict may not be very helpful. For example, a test may predict that a child will succeed in the early grades, but we are much more interested in how to tailor the education program so that the child will graduate from high school.
- Children who do poorly on these tests may be labeled for their entire school experience by teachers and parents, which could affect the way teachers interact with them, as well as the confidence parents have in their ability to parent successfully, thus contradicting the goal of assessment to increase parent effectiveness and empowerment.

High-Stakes Standardized Tests. Standardized tests used to evaluate the performance of schools, teachers, and administrators are called **high-stakes tests.** These are currently very popular, having been legislated into the federal educational reform effort. They are, however, very destructive for children, and to some extent for teachers, because they are not based on developmentally appropriate ways to determine exactly what children know and can do. Further, they can retard children's learning and enjoyment of learning.

An Example of a Screening and Assessment Tool

The Devereux Early Childhood Assessment (DECA) is an example of a standardized screening and assessment tool. "The three primary purposes of the tool are (1) to identify children who are low on the protective factors so that targeted classroom and home-based strategies can be implemented leading to the strengthening of these abilities, (2) to generate classroom profiles indicating the relative strengths of all children so that classroom design and instructional strategies can build upon these strengths to facilitate the healthy social and emotional growth of all children, and (3) to screen for children who may be exhibiting behavioral concerns so that these can be addressed before they become entrenched and possibly develop into behavioral disorders" (LeBuffe & Naglieri, n.d.). The instrument was standardized on two thousand preschool children in twenty-eight states, including poor children and children of similar racial and ethnic distribution to the overall U.S. population. Thus the norms represent the diversity of preschool children within the United States.

Programs developed to address the factors isolated by this instrument include (1) DECA itself, which assesses each child on three protective factors—attachment, self-control, and initiative—and also provides a behavioral-concern scale, indicating potential emotional and behavioral disorders. Children who score high on this scale need additional assessments. (2) A classroom strategies component provides direct ideas for ways teachers can increase these protective factors in each child, through the classroom environment, activities and experiences, interactions, and family partnerships. (3) A booklet for parents that provides ways to increase their children's emotional and social protective factors.

Concerns Regarding DECA. Like other normed assessments, this assessment presents several concerns. It is normed on figures that represent nationwide racial and income demographics, but most early childhood programs do not include this range of students. For example, Head Start's populations are almost exclusively low-income (by legal mandate at least 90 percent of those served must be from families below the poverty level) and are disproportionately minorities. Thus, Head Start children may score poorly on this instrument. Another problem is that while the assessment and the parent guide are available in Spanish, the other components are not. (How will a Spanish-speaking parent understand the results?) The instrument is not available in any other language, even though language diversity is a reality in many of our early childhood programs. If we expect parents to be involved with the assessment of their children, we must provide this material in the parents' primary language. Finally, while the assessment claims to look at children's strengths, the inclusion of the behavioral concern scale means it can easily be used for what Hills calls a **deficit model of assessment** (1993). (The blame for this might be better placed on Head Start, which requires screening for potential problems—deficits.)

Observations

Observation is a form of authentic assessment. Observation of children can take many different forms. Teachers are making informal observations of their children all the time. Prewritten checklists, charts, and scales are also forms of observation. All of these methods focus on individual children functioning within groups. Advantages of observation methods include the following (Martin, 1999):

- they focus on what children can do;
- they allow for individual variation within a group;
- they can be tailored to support any philosophy, program, or curriculum;
- they do not compare children to a national standard and are therefore less biased;
- they evaluate a child's actions in context;
- they empower the adults in charge of the children;
- they are often quicker and cheaper than other methods.

Role of the Observer. The person who conducts the observation may be a nonparticipant observer or a participant observer. The **nonparticipant observer** is not directly involved with children. Student teachers, and regular teachers on an intermittent basis, should try becoming nonparticipant observers, allowing for a more objective, uninterrupted opportunity to observe the children and providing a new and different perspective on children in the classroom or on the playground. **Participant observers** are teachers who record their observations while actively involved in their teaching role. Because many observations are done by participant observers, the instrument used must be very user-friendly.

Anecdotal Records. In the 1920s, Piaget recorded anecdotal observations of his own children. Anecdotal records are short narrative records of a child's behavior; they can be made at any time by the teacher and are easy to use. They can be recorded shortly after the behavior has occurred and are used for record keeping, communicating with parents, to document individual children's development, and to identify potential problems or challenges. To be effective, teachers must record the most significant behaviors, have a good memory, and be clear about which behaviors they wish to record. Some programs require teachers to use anecdotal records on a regular basis and to use them as the foundation for parent conferences. An accident report is a form of anecdotal record—documenting the behavior that occurred at the time of the accident.

Running Record. A **running record** is an unbroken form of narrative observation. It is conducted by a nonparticipant observer and records exactly what a child says and does, in sequence, as it happens (Martin, 1999). To use the method effectively, the observer needs practice in observing and writing at the same time. Further, the observer must be able to use clear, descriptive language. Using running records is a highly naturalistic approach to collecting information and is used primarily for research on children. Analysis of the information must occur after the observation; judgments should not be made at the time of the observation. The great advantage of this approach is that it records all behaviors—not just those preselected.

Marie Clay (1985), an expert in reading and reading recovery programs, developed a specific form of running record to use in assessing children's reading behavior. It is used by classroom teachers in one-to-one settings with a student reading a brief passage of age-appropriate text. The teacher uses checks for each correct word read, and a series of symbols for errors. These are recorded on a blank piece of paper.

After the observation session, the teacher calculates the student's reading ability based on the percentage of words the student reads accurately. A score of 95 percent to 100 percent classifies the text as independent reading—suitable for the child's reading for pleasure. A score between 90 percent and 95 percent means that the work being read is instructional-level material—suitable for instruction; 90 percent and below means the material is too difficult for the child.

Event Sampling. **Event sampling** is an observational process that is focused on a preselected event or behavior. The method can be used to observe one child or a group of children. Event sampling enables the observer to evaluate the following (Martin, 1999):

- *Frequency*—how often does the behavior occur?
- *Duration*—how long does the behavior last?
- *Causality*—what is the cause of the behavior?
- *Severity*—how severe is the behavior?

The purpose of event sampling is to get specific information about a specific event (not a child). One formula of event sampling is to record the antecedent event—the behavior before the targeted behavior—the actual behavior, and the consequent event—the effect or result of the behavior. This is called an ABC format for event sampling. To be effective, the targeted behavior must be clearly defined, so it's easy for the observer to recognize the event when it occurs. Event sampling can be used to observe behaviors such as biting, hitting, not sharing, creating, initiating, fighting, helping another child, asking questions, and many more. I used event sampling when I studied the use of the time-out in a child-care program. Every time a child was placed in a time-out, I recorded a variety of details, including the name of the child and the teacher, the behavior that triggered the time-out, and the length of time the child stayed there. I then analyzed my results to determine how disciplinary procedures were used in the program. When I did research on the quality of play of children on a playground, I recorded every time a child engaged in different kinds of play behaviors—physical, social, and cognitive— and different levels (complexity) of play.

Time Sampling. Time sampling is very similar to event sampling, except that **time sampling** focuses on units of time. Regular intervals are determined ahead of time, and during these intervals information on one or more children is recorded. This method can be used by a participatory or a nonparticipatory observer, and is a way to observe a pattern of behavior over a period of time without continually having to observe and record behavior. Time sampling is particularly useful in these areas (Martin, 1999):

- learning about sequences of development;
- learning about the behavior of a single child;
- looking at the behavior of a group of children;
- collecting information to plan an intervention or improvement of some kind;
- evaluating the impact of a new program, policy, or initiative.

Event sampling and time sampling can be used together. For example, when I studied children on the playground, I observed them at five-minute intervals, and I observed the play events they were engaged in during those intervals, placing them on a chart that described variations of two levels of play—cognitive play (Piaget) and social play (Parten). As a result of this time and event sampling, I could determine the quality of preschool play on the playground (Wardle, 1983).

Mapping. Mapping of an environment enables us to see its flow and usage, be it a classroom, playground, or other area. Mapping also can be used to record a single child's use of space. Does Johnny use the block area, sand and water area, and dress-up area in equal amounts? Does Sarah really flit from one center to another without any in-depth activity, as her teacher suspects? Does Maia ever use the block area? And is Jose's mother's complaint that he never uses the library corner accurate? Use of mapping techniques can determine mobility in an area, individual attention span, interests and motivation, child–child interactions, child–adult interactions, and use of specific areas in a classroom or playground. It can effectively show the use of the environment, and potential or actual traffic problems. Obviously, mapping does not explain why various routes and relationships occur.

▶ *Mapping is a way of recording a child's movement within an environment: Where does she play? Where does she not play?*

Checklist Observations. Checklists are predetermined lists of skills or behaviors that are used to determine presence of absence of those behaviors. They might be used to observe and record the following (Martin, 1999):

- physical skills (fine and gross motor);
- self-help and social skills;
- emotional and temperamental styles;
- cognitive skills;
- language and communication.

Checklists can be homemade or prepared by experts and educational resource companies. Checklists are designed to record developmental information about an individual child, list expected behaviors that are checked off when observed, and provide guidance in ways to determine evidence of a behavior. These checklists are usually used to record naturalistic observations by participant observers. There are many commercially available checklists that document specific tasks, skills, or behaviors. In selecting a checklist, these things should be considered:

- The checklist must target the area that you wish to observe.
- The items covered on the list must provide a broad enough range that the child is exhibiting some of the items (not all of them, and not none of them).
- The combination of behaviors checked (not just the individual items) and not checked must provide a trend or pattern. For example, on a good checklist to identify gifted children, a potentially gifted child should receive a "yes" on at least twenty of twenty-five items.
- The checklist must fit the specific purpose you intend—planning, identification, record keeping, and so on.

Checklists are very effective to use in conjunction with other methods. For example, in *Growing Up Gifted*, Clark recommends use of teacher checklists as part of the overall process to document the identification of a gifted and talented student (1997).

A huge concern regarding predeveloped checklists, however, is the normed nature of the items and their potential bias. In other words, while the instrument was developed on one group of children, it may not work for the children that you work with. Different children develop differently and may have different language and cultural factors that must be considered in developing checklists.

Observation Charts. Observation charts are very popular in many early childhood programs. They are prepared blank forms for recording behavior within certain predetermined categories and within certain time frames. For an infant program, these categories might include liquid intake, solid intake, bowel movements, and behavioral notes, to name just a few (Martin, 1999). Each time these occur within the specified time frame, the teacher places a

▶ *Specific checklists can be used to determine a child's development in specific areas.*

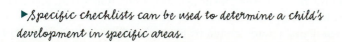

▶*Checklists provide a quick and easy way for a teacher to record certain behaviors and activities of children performing in natural, social and physical settings. (Will Faller)*

check in the space. This information provides a record of a pattern of behavior, and is an easy communication tool to use between a teacher and parent. Observation charts can be used for individual children and for groups of children. Clearly an observation chart only records the predetermined behaviors, so it is important to plan ahead carefully the behaviors you wish to record. It is also important not to initiate an activity or task simply to have it show up on the chart. The point of the chart is to record activities, not to use as a planning document of when activities should occur.

Rating Scales. Rating scales are tools in which each observation is rated according to a predetermined scale that records the degree to which the item being observed has occurred. The simplest form of the scale has one "yes" and one "no" column. Other scales include numerical ratings using the same numerical range for each item (especially popular when the results are to undergo statistical analysis), levels of behavior, and pictorial representations. Some scales provide clear criteria for determining each level of the scale. Use of rating scales requires well-trained observers who can make quick, accurate assessments of what they observe (unless it's a self-assessment scale). The results of many rating scales can be totaled to develop an overall score, profile, or picture.

The advantages of rating scales are that they are efficient, record information on a wide range of behaviors, often record behaviors other methods miss, and provide lots of information quickly. But use of rating scales require expert training, and they are open to bias because they require quick, inferential judgments. Several scales should be conducted at different times and in different contexts before a full picture is achieved.

Media Techniques

Various media techniques have been used for research on children's behavior and for documenting children's interactions and development. Media techniques provide a tangible record that can be stored, used to communicate with parents, and included in discussion with students about their development. Use of media techniques also provides a wonderful way to record children's growth over time in the program.

Photography. Photography can be used for a variety of assessment purposes, including making a record of children's physical development over time, significant events in children's lives, records of children's products and unique activities as part of their portfolios, and documenting social growth and development (Martin, 1999). Obviously, someone using photography must be a competent camera user. If the photos are to be used or stored in a computer, then digital photos should be taken. Finally, determine ahead of time the way the camera will be used, so it is a deliberate process—not just used randomly when something strikes your fancy.

The purpose of using a camera is to record children's growth and progress, not to take a world-class picture. Thus, a small, inexpensive, pocket-size 35-mm camera with built-in flash is ideal. Automatic shutter and exposure reduce the time it takes to set up a camera; a built-in zoom is an added bonus. Use a film that can be effective inside and outside (this often means that the flash will be needed inside). Use of instant cameras increases the cost and decreases quality—and with the availability and cost of one-hour processing, it really is not warranted. For use of a camera to be effective, children must become so used to it that they they ignore it. When I take pictures in a classroom, I first walk around with the camera with no intent of taking pictures; when I taught I always had a camera around my neck. Children soon totally ignored it.

To take good pictures, the photographer needs to be at the child's level—usually this means kneeling, crouching, or sitting. It helps to tell children you won't take their picture if they pose (except when you want this form of picture—maybe to go on their locker, portfolio record, or computer file). Creation of a chart that records each time children are photographed and what they are doing helps the teacher ascertain that all children are covered equally. The focus should be on naturalistic photos of children interacting with the environment and with each other, as well as on significant milestones (riding a trike for the first time, writing one's name, and so on).

Mounting photos on a predeveloped form enables the teacher to include needed information for each photo: name, date, time, activity, others in the picture, contextual information, and information about growth and progress (Martin, 1999). Photos can be stored in a variety of ways.

Video Recordings. Most people are very familiar with the use of video recorders—today they are used more than still cameras. All video recorders come with instructions, and the best way to learn to use one is simply to practice a lot. Newer camcorders automatically record the date and time of each recording; some can be preprogrammed with the child's name; and all adjust automatically to changing light conditions. Many have a speaker on the camera and mikes that can be placed close to the action. Video recordings can be used for a variety of observations. Some of these include play patterns; use of space; group interactions; fine and gross motor skills; products, creative activities, and activities in progress (for portfolios); behaviors, difficult behaviors and social interactions; formal class presentations of older students; and field trips (Martin, 1999).

All videos should be carefully labeled (child's name, activity, context, and comment) and stored next to the child's portfolio. A videotape recording log should accompany each tape.

Video recordings are also excellent for staff training and student teaching purposes. But additional permission from children's parents to use them in this manner is needed.

▶*Cameras and videos can be used to observe children outside the classroom.*

Audio Recordings. A portable and resilient tape recorder with mobile speaker can be an effective tool for collecting information on children. The teacher should become very familiar with the use of the tape recorder, and should develop a format for labeling and storing the recordings. A tape recorder that uses batteries and a cord enables the teacher to use the batteries when recording, and plug in the cord when rewinding and editing.

Many lab schools and some programs have built-in sound systems in the classrooms that allow student teachers and teachers to listen in on what children are saying. A recorder can easily be hooked up to these systems. A stationary mike can be used for children who are interacting in a small area; otherwise, a handheld mike will be needed to follow children around. Allow children to play with the recorder to familiarize themselves with its use in the classroom. Tape recordings can be used to record a large variety of activities, including circle time and group sharing; group singing and playing instruments; conversations, reading, and storytelling in the book corner; sociodramatic play; language difficulties; children reading out loud; bilingual children's conversations; emerging language development; problem solving, friendship tables, and other conflict resolution activities; field trips; school-age jokes, creative language and poems; and portfolio assessment meetings with students. From these and other recordings, a teacher can look for a number of things to analyze. These include (1) all sorts of language development—pronunciation, length of utterances, rhythm of speech, accent, speech patterns, grammar, communication difficulties, expression of ideas, use of rhyme, demonstrations of feeling in language, and imitation; (2) social relationships, social play roles, humor, talking to oneself, fantasy, realism, friendships, and peer interactions; and (3) repeating events, telling stories, imagination, logic, conversations with adults, and articulating moral views and attitudes.

Use the counter on the tape recorder carefully to document who is speaking and other important information. The audiotape should be labeled, dated, and accompanied by a numbered log, and it should be kept near the recorded child's portfolio. Recordings of individual children—or those focusing on one individual in a group—are easier to use and store than group recordings.

Combination Approaches

As I have suggested already, most good assessment approaches use a combination of methods to collect information and evaluate children and programs. Here I discuss a few specific approaches that combine a number of different instruments.

Case Studies

A case study is a profile of an individual, family, or group—classroom or other type—that is developed by collecting a variety of information using different sources and instruments. Its function is usually to address a specific concern, area, or function—often defined by time—such as to identify a child for a specific school program. This method is used a great deal by sociologists and social workers, and is becoming more popular in educational programs. Collecting data to develop an IEP or IFSP for a special-education student is a form of case study.

The second common use of case studies is to follow a child, family, or class of children over a period of time. For example, a case study following a welfare parent's return to work, and the children's enrollment in child care, school, and before- and after-school programs will provide information about whether the community's services for children work together, or there are gaps in services that need to be addressed. As an evaluation tool, case studies provide lots of details and tell us how and whether systems (family, school, child care) work well together.

The analysis of data gathered from a case study obviously depends on the purpose of the study. For the identification of a special education student, the analysis is designed to determine whether the child can benefit from intervention, and the nature of the program needed. An analysis of the relationship of publicly funded programs for children in one community will focus on barriers, overlaps, funding, transportation, and areas for improvement.

Portfolio Assessment

Portfolios are collections of information, including health records, test results, work samples, photos and other recordings, and parent input, on an individual child. The collection is kept over a period of time and periodically added to, enabling child-care professionals, teachers, and parents to follow the child's progress over time, create a plan to meet the child's needs, and evaluate the child's progress (Martin, 1999). The intent of the portfolio is to provide a developmental picture of the whole child. While some definitions of portfolios include only the child's products, the definition used here includes a variety of measures, observations, and products.

Items to Be Included in a Portfolio. Items to include in a child's portfolio cover a wide range of information. Some salient examples are elaborated here.

Health and medical information. Be careful about confidentiality.

Parent information. Interview parents on a variety of occasions to collect background information about the child—number and age of siblings, likes and dislikes, what the child enjoys doing at home, activities with the father and the mother and extended family members, and so on. Also find out parents' expectations of the program and the goals they have for their child.

Observations. Record examples of the child learning and interacting. A teacher might also record times a child is very successful at something or achieves a task, skill, or concept that has been a focus in the child's work. Anecdotal notes, videotapes, audiotapes, checklists, and photographs are used to record this information. Every area of development should be included in these observations—physical, social and emotional, cognitive, literacy, creativity, and self-concept.

Work samples. Children's own work is the most authentic way of documenting learning and development. Any products made by a child provide a great way to follow development—self-portraits, examples of artistic efforts, stages in learning to write, use of different tools, written and illustrated reports of field trips and books, and more. Be sure to collect products that represent growth in many areas. Keep real products, and photocopy or photograph objects that are too large or cumbersome to collect and store. Make sure to date all products as soon as they are made.

Developmentally Appropriate Practice

Summary sheets. Twice a year, the content of the portfolio should be summarized in terms of strengths and needs, based on the teacher's knowledge of growth and development. The child should not be compared to other children in the program.

Many early childhood programs are required to use one or more forms of standardized tests or screening tools, which should be added to the portfolio. Additional items should then be collected to complement and broaden the record.

A program's educational component should consider these factors in deciding what should be collected on each child (Martin, 1999):

- the purpose of each type of documentation;
- who will maintain the records;
- who can have access to the portfolio (confidentiality);
- how the data will be analyzed;
- the philosophy of the program and of its stakeholders—including parents;
- the time available to process and analyze information;
- staff attitudes and knowledge.

Managing Portfolios. Clearly portfolios can be bulky, unmanageable, and unwieldy. Here are some ideas for managing portfolios:

- Provide a place to keep children's work on an ongoing basis. Individual large folders, ring binders, large envelopes, shopping bags, and pizza and shirt boxes work well.
- Keep portfolios within children's easy reach. Children need to be able to view portfolios to review past work and add to the collection.
- Keep examples of growth and development in all areas. When products aren't created, use other methods to record progress—photos, checklists, and so on.
- Create a system. Determine ahead of time how you will use the observational system. You might pick a certain number of children to observe each week, or concentrate on observing events—circle time, lunch, field trips.
- Be prepared. Find ways to make sure you collect information on each child in each developmental area. Date and write comments on the back of a product as soon as it is made.
- Involve students. Talk to students about the portfolio process. Have them select products they would like to keep; encourage them to provide comments on pictures, photos, and other records. Review portfolio samples with children on a regular basis. Help children talk about their products and how they represent their development. Help them evaluate their own progress.
- Select products representative of a child's output, not just "the best" (Cohen, 1999).
- Use a CD to store portfolio information, if possible. New material can be copied on the CD each year, and it can follow the child throughout their school experience.

Child Observation Record

According to Schweinhart (1993), an early childhood assessment should be developmentally appropriate, reliable, valid, and user-friendly. Systematic observation of children's involvement in developmentally appropriate activities can be used to achieve these four criteria. Through careful development, norming of items and criteria, and field testing, such instruments can also be user-friendly. A method that uses this approach is the High/Scope Child Observation Record (COR), for children aged 2½ to 6 years. The COR assesses a child's behavior in six areas: initiative, creative representation, social relations, music and movement, language and literacy, and logic and math. For each of these categories, teachers observe a child over several months, then use their notes to rate the child's behavior on thirty items, on a five-point scale. For example, for the item "expressing choices," there are these five levels (Schweinhart, 1993, p. 33):

1. Child does not yet express choices to others.
2. Child indicates a desired activity or place of activity by saying a word, pointing, or some other action.
3. Child indicates desired activity, place of activity, materials, or playmates with a short sentence.
4. Child indicates with a short sentence how plans will be carried out ("I want to drive a truck on the road").
5. Child gives detailed description of intended actions ("I want to make a road out of blocks with Sara and drive the truck through it").

Teachers score the COR initially six to eight weeks into the program year, then one or two times throughout the remainder of the year. The instrument has also been used by outside observers (not teachers) to collect data for research purposes. The COR is philosophically consistent with the High/Scope curriculum (discussed in Chapter 4).

Work Sampling System

The Work Sampling System is a classroom assessment developed by Meisels (1992). The purpose of the instrument is to assess and document children's skills, knowledge, behavior, and accomplishments over a wide range of areas and over a period of time. The information is collected from children performing within the classroom in a range of tasks and situations (Meisels, 1993). The system has three components: developmental checklists, portfolios, and summary reports.

Developmental Checklists. There are six checklists, for children ages 3 to 8 (one for each year), covering each of these areas:

- personal and social development,
- language and literacy,
- mathematical thinking,
- scientific thinking,
- social studies,
- arts and music,
- physical development.

Each of these areas is subdivided into a number of skills, tasks, behaviors, and knowledge on which the student is rated. The checklists are standardized, and include guidelines to show teachers how to use the instruments consistently. Because these checklists record individual progress on basic curricular domains, they can be used to document children's progress over time, and to plan curricula and curricular activities.

Portfolio. In the work sampling system, two types of products are collected: core items and other items. *Core items* are items collected at the same time three times a year in the same area or domain for every child. Thus each child has the same amount of products collected at the same time. *Other items* are collected specifically for each child at different times, allowing teachers to view progress in a variety of domains and across time. Portfolios provide documentation of the entire range of a child's development—integrating instruction and assessment.

Summary Report. Teachers develop a summary report on each child three times a year, carefully summarizing the checklists and portfolio information, and using specific criteria to evaluate each domain. The summary report provides a profile of a child's progress for parents and administrators, and replaces the traditional report card. The report documents each child's progress in each domain in relation to expected norms—since the checklists are standardized—and documents whether the child needs assistance in specific areas. Based on the report, teachers can talk with parents about their child's progress, and administrators receive information about the success of their program.

The strength of the work sampling system is its reliance on interpreting children's accomplishments within the context of the classroom performance. It also reflects teacher activities in the classroom. To be effective, however, this approach requires teachers to be careful and objective observers of their children's performance. Further, the effective use of the work sampling system necessitates that parents and politicians become less enamored of the power and seduction of whole-group standardized tests, and that parents understand how to interpret the reports.

Issues in Testing

As I have discussed in other places in this book, at one point while I was a Head Start director, I became curious about the children in my program who were receiving services because they had special needs. Various assessments are used to determine who should receive these services and the kind of intervention each child needs. Common special needs are hearing and sight disabilities, delayed development, and being physically confined to a wheelchair; others include behavioral and emotional challenges, ADHD, and speech delays. Many of the children identified by Head Start with a disability move into special education programs in the local public schools.

To satisfy my curiosity, I examined a five-year period of records of my program. According to these records, 70 girls and 170 boys were identified as having special needs requiring intervention (Wardle, 1991). That's almost two and a half times as many boys as girls. This discrepancy is consistent with studies that indicate that five to nine times as many boys as girls are diagnosed as hyperactive in this country (Harris, 1986). These figures lead me to ask several questions:

1. Were the assessments we used to determine a child's disability accurate? Did more boys really have problems than girls, or did this discrepancy reflect a bias

against boys in our program (boys are more physical, louder, more difficult to discipline, and some teachers feel like they are not as much fun to be around)?

2. Are the instruments we used to place children in various disability categories based on accurate developmental scales of low-income normal boys and girls? There is a lot of research that suggests boys develop more slowly than girls in a variety of areas.

3. Were the assessments done in context and by people with whom the children were familiar, or were they conducted by strangers in an artificial setting?

Objectivity

On several occasions, my wife—a special-education teacher—was strongly encouraged by her principal before she evaluated a child that "You must find this child has some disability." Clearly this is a very subjective approach to testing (not to mention unethical!). No two people see the same child in the same way. But the intent of objectivity in assessment is to use an instrument that provides accurate information about a child, not to justify an opinion someone might already have. In other words, the objective use of any assessment enables the child to obtain a score that accurately reflects how the child does on the instrument, without the tester's bias, preexisting opinion, or judgment. Unfortunately, we all have biases—and if we are not careful, these biases affect the way we do assessments. Clean, white, middle-class, compliant, and respectful children tend to score higher on assessments than children who are poor, dirty, minority, boys, or less compliant (Wardle et al., 1989).

Reliability. An assessment tool is of little value if it is not reliable. **Reliability** means that the tool will give the same results each time it is used to measure the same knowledge or information. A metal ruler will always measure an inch as an inch, but a cloth tape may stretch when wet, and thus measure it differently. Thus the metal ruler is more reliable. A reliable test will not vary depending on the tester, the time of day, or other variables. One of the biggest problems with reliability is that the people who give the tests, do the observations, and interpret the information often let their own biases affect the results; or the test simply requires too much subjective interpretation by the tester. Another problem with reliability is that the testers are often poorly trained. Observation methods for research require **interobserver reliability**— all observers must agree on their observations, and they must score the observed behavior the same.

It is important to note, however, that just because an instrument is reliable does not mean it is necessarily of any value. A measuring tape is highly reliable in measuring the height of a child, but beyond height, it tells us nothing about the child.

Validity. Assessment instruments must be valid. This means they must measure what they claim to measure. A measuring tape is valid in determining a child's height. It is not valid in measuring a child's intelligence. A tool to screen kindergarten children is valid only if it truly predicts which children will succeed in kindergarten and accurately indicates those who need extra help to succeed. The tools used by my Head Start program that resulted in two and a half times more boys than girls being placed in special education probably were not very valid. Obviously, it is possible to have a highly valid instrument with no reliability, and a highly reliable instrument with no validity.

Naturalistic versus Controlled Assessments

As I mentioned at the beginning of this chapter, a great deal of research on children's behavior and development has been conducted in university laboratories. These are highly controlled environments, in which researchers carefully control or manipulate various factors to determine specific effects on specific behaviors (Irwin and Bushnell, 1980). The opposite of controlled laboratory research is **naturalistic research**—a process in which the child is observed doing what comes naturally, in a natural—familiar—environment (Irwin & Bushnell, 1980).

The question is, how controlled or naturalistic should child assessments be? Many standardized tests are highly controlled—children take the same test at the same time with the exact same instructions in an identical environment. Many believe that far more naturalistic approaches are needed, recording children's natural, daily performance interacting with peers and teachers in their familiar classroom and engaged in familiar classroom activities. Naturalistic methods also encourage children to demonstrate what they can do in context. A child in the block area with a friend will engage in different behavior from the same child when he is on the toilet or playing with another friend on the outside playground.

Clearly, naturalistic observations cannot be as precisely interpreted as controlled assessments, but many believe that results from naturalistic methods give us more valuable information about a child and are much more helpful in developing programs and activities to meet the needs of each child. Others believe there is a place for each kind of assessment and that careful selection of the assessment must be made depending on its purpose and interpretation.

Authentic Assessment. A concern regarding the limitations of standardized tests and assessments has led to an increased use of authentic assessments. An **authentic assessment** is "assessment of learning that focuses on performance of skills or knowledge in a manner that is within an appropriate context" (Martin, 1999, p. 350). *Authentic assessment* is a general term that covers observations, assessments, portfolios, and more. It is characterized by the following features (Martin, 1999):

- Children exhibit what they know and can do in a familiar context; focus is not on their deficiencies.
- It does not compare what the child can do to what other children can do or to external criteria.
- It focuses on the big picture (holistic, integrated knowledge), not isolated skills and knowledge.
- It includes areas such as creativity, initiative, attitude, perseverance, and social interaction.
- It is concerned with what the child typically does in the learning and social environment, not how the child responds to isolated questions and artificial problems.
- It includes what children produce as a part of the learning process—pictures, written labels, constructions of unit blocks, maps, written assignments, pictures.

▶ *Developmentally appropriate assessments allow us to evaluate children's progress of what they can do, within a familiar context.*

Developmentally Appropriate Assessment.

According to Schweinhart, early childhood assessments must be developmentally appropriate (1993). This means that assessments must cover not only language and mathematics but also initiative, social relations, creative representation, and music and movement. Further, the assessment should permit children to initiate their own activities as well as responding to a teacher's questions, and should allow children to perform within their normal context—in their classroom with their everyday teachers.

A great deal of testing of young children is, in fact, mistesting. It presents a series of demands that young children must answer immediately—even if they do not feel like it. Each question has a right answer. Although a DAP curriculum is child-centered, many tests are teacher-centered (though teachers have to rely on the test's questions and answers). By definition, such testing is foreign to a DAP program, and thus foreign to a child in such a program. These tests are more consistent with teacher-directed, back-to-basics philosophies such as E. D. Hirsch's core curriculum.

Many of these tests focus on numbers, letters, shapes, basic colors, and basic knowledge. Initiative, creativity, social relationships, art, and music and movement are not considered. Also, much testing is inappropriate to children's own cultural and daily experiences (National Center for Fair and Open Testing, 1991). White, middle-class testers have assumed that everyone shares the same experience and thus the same body of knowledge (Schweinhart, 1993). Recently, a colleague and I observed a 4-year-old child receiving a screening test. He was asked to identify a whistle from a picture. My colleague commented that unless he watched NFL football carefully or was a soccer referee, he would not know what a whistle looks like.

Confidentiality

All information collected on a child—test scores, portfolios, screening results, and more—are confidential. They are the property of the child and parent, and should be viewed only by professionals who need to see them to do their job. Further, parents need to sign a document allowing professionals access to their child's information; student teachers doing child observations and assessments need permission from the child's parent to do so. Parents have a right to see any information on their child at any time. (I discuss this issue regarding children with special needs in Chapter 6. Some states require personal information on special-education children to be kept under lock and key.)

Never should teachers discuss individual student information with people who do not need the information to do their job or for whom parents have not given written permission to see the data, including other parents, staff, and volunteers who can overhear a conversation. Also, staff must be careful not to post individual children's information, such as allergies and medication schedules, where everyone can see them.

Criticism of Standardized Tests

Standardized tests are group-administered assessments with specific instructions to assure consistent administration. They are normed so that results can be compared to those of other children of the same age across the country. These tests tend to focus on testing simple facts, low-level skills, superficial memorization, and isolated information. Content is generally abstract, favors verbally advanced children, and is biased against children who are not familiar with standard information (Meisels, 1993).

Standardized tests seem to test a child's ability to take a test far more than they assess the skills they are supposed to evaluate. Reading, language, math, and general knowledge are learned in context, yet these tests evaluate them out of context. They are also often given under circumstances that induce stress—especially for children not used to taking tests and for children who need a familiar person as the tester (Wodke et al., 1989).

Although the results of standardized tests provide information about a child's percentile ranking on a specific subtest, they do not tell us why the child can do certain things and cannot do others. They don't even tell us whether a child misunderstood the directions or doesn't know how to multiply by 5. According to most experts (Hills, 1993; Meisels, 1993; Schweinhart, 1993), there is little to justify the use of standardized tests for children in third grade and below.

A Deficit Model of Assessment. Because screening tools are used most often to identify children who need special services or who are "not ready" for kindergarten, assessment instruments have focused on finding what is wrong with a child. Assessment is often viewed as a deficit model (Hills, 1993). In Chapter 6, I discuss how we seem to be very comfortable identifying children who need special-education service but cringe at identifying young children who are gifted. The early identification of children with disabilities has led in large part to this idea of a deficit model. Although the intent of early identification is valid, the misuse of these assessments and the deficient nature of the process should cause educators to be very careful in their use of such tests.

Conclusion

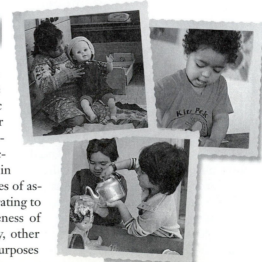

In early childhood programs, various assessments are used for a vast range of purposes. These purposes include screening to place children in specific programs and address particular needs, determining program effectiveness, driving curriculum and instruction, and assessing student progress in all domains. One of the chief purposes of assessment is accountability—demonstrating to parents and politicians the effectiveness of educational programs. Unfortunately, other uses of assessment can be at cross-purposes with programs, and don't always benefit children and their parents. Standardized tests are the favorite assessment tool of politicians and many administrators, but they are of little value in helping to provide the best possible educational programs for our children.

Questions and Projects

1. Obtain the kindergarten screening tool used by the district in which you live. Bring it to class and be prepared to discuss it.

2. Use one of the Harms and Clifford Early Childhood Environmental Rating scales on a program you have access to.

3. Conduct an observation of a child in a school program. Choose a checklist, rating scale, time or event sampling, or a running record.

4. Discuss in a short paper (3–5 pages) the pros and cons of using an IQ test as part of a child's portfolio assessment.

5. How would you communicate to parents your concerns that their child might have a learning disability and needs further assessment?

6. Develop a photo record of one child for one day in an early childhood program. Make sure you get written parent permission.

CHAPTER

15

Future Issues; Controversial Issues

*E*arly childhood programs, serving children from infancy through third grade, are experiencing a fantastic amount of change. This chapter focuses on some of the changes that are under way and helps students evaluate these changes. I believe that change is good, because it enables our early childhood institutions to do a better job of meeting the diverse and comprehensive needs of our children and families, and I believe teachers need to be comfortable with change, be agents of change, and be advocates for change. But change must be initiated and implemented based on what we know to be best for children and families; not out of fear, a desire for control and power, or simple political expedience. ■

Alternative Structures

One area of change impacting early childhood programs is in the structure of public schools. Because of growing dissatisfaction with public schools, alternative approaches are being tried, including charter schools, vouchers, and contracting out vital services. The use of uniforms—used by almost all public schools worldwide—is also being tried by some U.S. schools, and finally, in more and more cases, parents are educating their children at home.

Charter Schools

Historically, U.S. public schools have operated through the government unit known as the **local educational authority,** or local school district. The district is governed by an elected school board, is a legal entity created by the constitution of each state, and operates within some form of geographic boundary—county, city, town. Each local district is entrusted to determine the educational philosophy, curricula, policies, standards, and graduation requirements for each school in the district. While neighborhood schools reflect the characteristics of their own community, schools throughout the district have largely identical programs and policies.

As a result of the 1954 Supreme Court decision *Brown v. Board of Education of Topeka*, which outlawed segregation by race in public schools, busing was introduced into many urban school districts. Magnet schools were also created—to attract different populations to certain schools, thus "naturally" integrating those schools. Magnet schools are schools with a particular focus or emphasis—for example, technology, academics, Montessori curriculum, Outward Bound philosophy, bilingual education, British Infant Schools approach, or gifted programs. Magnet schools now exist to provide parent choice and to discourage families from choosing private alternatives (religious and nonreligious). Some families living in neighborhoods in which the local school has become a magnet are not happy, however, because they have lost their neighborhood school and often have to transport their children out of their neighborhood. Some schools have addressed this concern by providing magnet schools as distinct programs within existing neighborhood schools.

Recently, in several states such as Colorado and Arizona, the concept of choice within public schools has expanded to include **charter schools.** Each state must pass legislation to permit these schools, and each state creates its own rules regarding their development, operation, and funding. Thus charter schools differ from state to state. Concepts that characterize charter schools include the following:

- *A specific, narrow focus.* Examples are back-to-basics (core knowledge curriculum), Montessori, literacy, technology, small class size, the arts, or a combination of these.
- *Eligibility requirements.* Charter schools can select students based on objective criteria (entrance tests, having dropped out from other schools, and so on), but cannot discriminate based on race, gender, ethnic or national background, or special needs.
- *Parental involvement required.* Many of these schools have contracts with parents that require them to be directly involved with the school and their child's education.
- *Suspension of some rules that districts must follow.* Charter schools are not required to meet all of the rules the other schools in the district must follow—curriculum, some personnel policies, and others.
- *Small size.* Almost all charter schools are smaller than most of their regular school counterparts. Further, many of these schools also stress small class size.
- *Fewer services offered than those provided by traditional schools.* Because charter schools focus on a single philosophy, they often do not offer the gamut of services other schools might provide (extracurricular activities including sports and clubs, anti-drug curricula, anti-bullying programs, and so on).

Charter schools exist to provide parent choice. They may also be created by the state as a solution to failing public schools. The state has the final authority to determine the quality and effectiveness of every school in the state. It has a right—and a responsibility—to change or even close schools that are not performing. In Colorado the state legislature passed a law that would allow it to change schools that consistently fail the state's CSAP tests (see Chapter 14) into charter schools. Finally, some believe that charters came about in Colorado and Arizona as a way for state officials to defuse the public's clamor for voucher programs.

Many charter schools are at the elementary school level—and thus include the K–3 grades. Further, some of these schools have incorporated ideas from theories and best practices of early childhood education: small classes, parent volunteers and the requirement of parental involvement, focus on a single philosophy (say, Montessori), provision for children younger than 5, and extended-day programs. The latter programs are often provided in collaboration with other agencies, either private or public.

The concept of the charter school appears to be popular among parents and will continue to grow. There are many reasons for this growth:

- small schools have less bureaucratic red tape;
- there is more opportunity for parental involvement;
- it is possible to sidestep cumbersome rules;
- they focus on a target problem (dropouts, non–English-speaking students, and so on);
- they focus on a single philosophy or approach;
- it is possible to create both a school and a business climate based on the needs of specific clients, one school, and one community.

Private for-Profit Schools. The creation of charter schools has led to the involvement of private corporations in running public schools and the potential for other private organizations to become involved. The Edison Project and Mosaica are two national education corporations that run individual public charter schools. They are contracted by a district to run a school: hire the staff, provide staff training and development, use policies and procedures developed by the company, as well as curricular and instructional approaches that match the company's philosophy. For example, the Edison Project stresses small classes, a focus on literacy, and extensive use of technology. Mosaica has a generic curriculum that it tailors to the culture and needs of children in each specific school it runs.

Advocates of private enterprise view the involvement of these corporations in running public schools very favorably. There also is a group of public officials (educators, legislators, bureaucrats) who believe the "business model" will solve all of the problems and challenges facing our schools. People who believe that the education of our future citizens must transcend the **bottom line** mentality (comparing the "business" of education to the need for corporations to make a profit to satisfy their shareholders), however, view this trend with increasing alarm.

Private not-for-Profit Schools. To date, most charter schools are independent bodies created specifically to run single public schools. They are developed by a group of parents, teachers, or community members, or a combination of these groups. They have a board of directors made up of the founding members and additional parents and community members, and they develop policies and procedures, hire staff, and adopt a specific curriculum or series of curricula. Money to run these schools comes from the local school district and the state, with additional funds generated through grants, fundraising, and community and business support.

Charter schools can be created only in states that provide this choice. To create a charter school, interested parties must follow the laws of their state and apply to the local district in which the school will exist. Generally, to get approved, the new school must:

- demonstrate a need (the planners must show that they will provide a choice that is not currently available in the district, and for which there is demand);
- demonstrate a legal and fiscal ability to run a school;
- have the physical structure (building) and space needed in an area appropriately zoned;
- demonstrate parental and community support;
- include people who have a track record of running educational programs.

If the district rejects the charter application, the organization can appeal to the state's department of education, which has the final authority to decide. Regardless, the overall supervision of each charter school (making sure it follows relevant laws, meets the needs of the students and parents, and so on) is the responsibility of the school district in which the school resides.

Criticism of Charter Schools. Some people object to charter schools because they believe the relaxation of certain rules and policies allows these schools to limit enrollment of students with disabilities, as well as minority and low-income students. For example, schools that require parental participation discriminate against families who cannot participate; also, most charter schools do not provide transportation, which works against some families.

Vouchers

The idea of **educational vouchers** is not new. This approach was first suggested by Christopher Jencks, a Harvard University educator, in the 1960s and was tried in a limited fashion in Seattle and Minnesota. The concept is to give parents a voucher equal to the cost of educating their child in the public school system, which they can redeem at any school of their choice—public, private, or religious. Funding for public schools comes from three distinct sources: local property taxes, state funds, and federal funds— property taxes being the largest percentage, federal funds the smallest. Local funds are generated through taxes on all property (except not-for-profits such as churches and schools), state funds are allocated by the state each year, and federal funds are almost totally program-specific—Title I, Head Start, special education, and the like.

State Funds. To date, voucher programs in Florida, Wisconsin, and Ohio have provided vouchers only for the state component of the cost to provide education. In each case a parent is given this amount (or a percentage of the state's allotment) to use to help pay tuition in a private or religious school.

Vouchering All Funds. Theoretically it is possible that the local property-tax component could be vouchered. This would require a change in each state's laws. Further, federal money could be given to parents of eligible students, to be redeemed along with the other funds. The last time Title I was reauthorized by the federal government, a

▶*Vouchers would fund religious programs as well as other parent choices.*

proposal to voucher these funds was suggested; conceivably even Head Start funds could be vouchered.

One of the central arguments against vouchers is that the state contribution is not enough to cover most private school tuition, and that children with the greatest need (poverty, special education, and other issues) would be stuck in existing public schools, while middle-class children could use the money to supplement paying for expensive private schools. If all educational funds were vouchered, however, students with the greatest need would receive the greatest amount of money.

Separation of Church and State. The few voucher programs currently in place have allowed parents to choose religious schools as an option for their children. This has placed the entire voucher concept in jeopardy, because it would appear to violate the concept of the **separation of church and state.** The U.S. Constitution stipulates that the state cannot make laws either in favor of a particular religion or in opposition to one. In this case, *state* means tax money. Many argue that using tax money—through vouchers—to support religious schools does favor certain religions, and the courts have tended to agree. However, the most recent Supreme Court case, involving an Ohio voucher program, declared the use of tax money for vouchers constitutional despite the fact that almost all the parents enrolled their children in religious programs. The Supreme Court declared the fact that parents chose religious schools did not mean the state was supporting those schools. Clearly, voucher programs that prohibit the use of vouchers in openly religious schools would not pose the same constitutional issue. Paradoxically, many early childhood advocates strongly support the right of parental choice for children under age 6, yet also fully support the lack of choice that currently exists in most public-school approaches.

Contracting Services

A growing trend in public schools is to contract out specific services to public and private providers. The areas in which this is occurring most frequently are early childhood programs, special education, and before- and after-school programs. There are various reasons for this approach:

- reduced costs, because these companies pay lower salaries and benefits than the school district;
- increased efficiency, because of fewer bureaucratic rules and regulations;
- ability to provide services the district could otherwise not afford to provide—by charging tuition for specific services (such as a second half-day of kindergarten, before- and after-school programs, and so on);
- increasing the school's services without decreasing their core mission;

- ease and low cost of starting and discontinuing services, because the district simply signs a contract and does not have to deal with costly personnel issues.

As schools concentrate on the core areas of their mission, while at the same time addressing new areas such as anti-bullying programs and character education, this trend to contract out some of the school programs will probably increase in the future.

Home Schooling

"If I were you, I'd teach her at home," the kindergarten teacher told my wife when she visited the local public school to enroll Maia, our eldest child. "She will simply be too bored in this program." So for the next two years, my wife home-schooled Maia and our second child, Eirlys, while also caring for our baby, Kealan. Because my wife is a teacher, she was able to provide the early experiences they needed. We also joined a home-school group, which arranged group enrichment activities for the children on a regular basis.

Home schooling has increased rapidly over the past ten years and continues to expand. It has generated an entire industry of conferences, curricula, and advocacy groups. Many families who home-school work closely with their local district to receive services their children cannot receive at home—sports, special education, district-wide and state-wide contests, and the like.

By far the majority of the children who are home-schooled are of elementary-school age, because parents view this as the time a child's academic and moral foundations are being developed. Further, all subjects can be taught by one person at this age: unlike high-school classes, depth of content knowledge is not necessarily needed to teach elementary school children. Some parents who home-school have teacher preparation; some do not. Most, however, do have college degrees.

Most people home-school for religious reasons: they believe religion should be the central focus of their child's education. Other people choose to home-school because the local options available to them don't fit their child's needs and their family's values. Often this is a temporary solution, until the child is old enough to go to another school, the family moves, or other educational options become available. This is what happened with my family.

In the early 1970s and 1980s, many school districts and state departments of education were very hostile toward parents who home-schooled. They required approved curricula, and the teachers had to have specific qualifications (often stricter than those required for private-school teachers). Since that time, however, many of the authorities have relaxed and work cooperatively—if begrudgingly—with parents who home-school. Most state departments of education have a specific person assigned to act as liaison between parents who home-school and school districts that are not clear about—or willing to follow—their responsibilities to these children and their parents.

Uniforms

As a schoolboy attending English state schools, I had to wear a uniform, which included the school tie. Today I often joke to colleagues that one of the best outcomes of my English education is my ability to tie a necktie on the fly. Other countries—Brazil, South Africa, Australia, Japan—require students to wear a school uniform, as well as many religious and private schools in this country. Several school districts are also requiring uniforms, including Oakland and Riverside, both in California. Other districts, individual public schools, and magnet and charter schools are considering the use of school uniforms. Some of the arguments people make for school uniforms include the following:

- uniforms enable children from different economic backgrounds to appear equal;
- uniforms build school spirit, just as they do for sports teams, school clubs, police, and firefighters;
- uniforms reduce the distraction caused by children competing with one another over what they are wearing;
- uniforms reduce disciplinary problems and eliminate gang-related clothing;
- uniforms focus students' attention on learning.

Opponents of uniforms in public schools say that:

- uniforms are expensive for low-income families;
- uniforms deny personal expression through clothing;
- schools spend unnecessary time and effort on uniforms, with no demonstrable positive results;
- uniforms are opposed by many parents;
- many educators, politicians, and parents view uniforms as the purview of private and religious schools.

Uniforms for students will become more common as schools look for ways to reduce disciplinary problems and focus children's attention on learning. Uniforms will be particularly popular in charter, private, and religious schools, where they will be a condition of enrollment, along with parental involvement, discipline contracts, and homework requirements.

Funding Streams

A central challenge for providing high-quality early childhood programs is securing adequate funding. Traditional K–12 education is funded through the local district, with some kindergarten programs still being only half-day. Parents who want full-day kindergarten programs pay for the other half, and the extended service is often provided by private companies and paid for directly by parent tuition.

Programs for children under kindergarten age are paid for by a mishmash of funding sources—federal and state funds, grants, private tuition, religious and corporate subsidies. This variety of funding sources produces historically destructive turf issues, an uneven stream of services, and uneven program quality. Many of the programs are funded at such a low level that they cannot afford to hire full-time qualified teachers or provide other quality indicators.

Federal and State Funds

In Chapter 2 I described various state and federal early childhood programs that currently exist. To recap, federal programs include Title I (for low-income students), special education (IDEA), Head Start (including Early Head Start), and Even Start. The federal government also provides one-time grant money for contemporary educational trends: self-esteem, drug abuse prevention, literacy, anti-bullying programs, and the like. Federal funds are given in block grants for a variety of low-income child-care services called TANF (Temporary Assistance for Needy Families)—welfare, work training, transition, and so on. States fund a variety of early childhood programs. Georgia provides full-day programs in existing child-care facilities; Colorado funds part-day programs in local public schools. All state programs have specific eligibility criteria, which are not as strict as Head Start regulations. Federal and state support for programs serving infants to 8-year-olds will continue to grow; but this increase will be for existing programs and for programs viewed as educational, as opposed to quality child care.

Early Head Start. Ever since the inception of Head Start in 1965, the target age for this program has been the year before public school (usually ages 4–5). As more and more schools have instituted their own early childhood programs, more and more Head Starts are also serving 3-year-olds.

The original philosophy of Head Start was that one year of an intensive, comprehensive, high-quality early childhood program would inoculate children for future success in the public schools. Research on Head Start students since its inception, however, has consistently shown that this one year is simply not enough. As a result, Head Start has developed its Early Head Start initiative, for children from infancy to age 3. The program even works with expectant mothers. Some reasons for the creation of this new initiative are:

- The earlier the intervention in a child's life, the more successful it is.
- Recent brain research has further emphasized the importance of the early years, including the negative impact of poverty and stress.
- The number of single parents, teen parents, and grandparent homes has increased.
- There is an increased need for full-day, full-year child care for infants and toddlers.
- There is increased knowledge about best practices for the care of infants and toddlers.
- The U.S. public, and most professionals, increasingly accept high-quality, institutionalized infant and toddler care.

Employer-Supported Child Care

High-quality child care is considered by some companies to be an important benefit for their employees. Further, these companies realize that it is prohibitively expensive for parents to pay the full cost of their children's care. As a result, some employers—private and governmental—are willing to subsidize these services. Many of them contract with private companies to provide on-site care for their employees' children; others buy slots in existing community centers.

Companies that help support child-care programs insist on a certain level of involvement in running the programs, which often includes input into the curriculum, quality control, parent councils, and exposure of the company's name in the community. In employer-supported early childhood programs, teachers can receive better benefits than traditional child-care programs, and other quality aspects can be addressed—equipment, training, and the facility.

Public-School Early Childhood Programs

While some public schools administer Head Start and Title I early childhood programs, many also have early childhood programs that are funded out of their own budget. These are often programs for low-income children and are designed to establish behaviors and skills that the school believes will enable these children to succeed in their later school experience.

The curriculum and instructional methods of public early childhood programs tend to be a downward version of typical public-school elementary approach—direct instruction, large classes and classrooms, and expectations of quiet and sedentary behavior, with little play, choice, or social-skill development (Wardle, 1989). While this practice is partly due to the fact that school principals have no background in early childhood, it is also a reflection of policymakers who believe that early childhood programs for low-income, minority students should stress teacher-directed academic instruction (Hale, 1986; 1994).

Mixed Funding

In a brick building nestled next to public housing, a bar, and a few individual homes and facing a dramatic view of the Rocky Mountains, sits the Sheridan Early Childhood Center. This low brick building houses Head Start, the Sheridan School District's early childhood programs, and the district's K–3 school population; funding streams to support the programs include Head Start, the school district, Title I, the Colorado Preschool Project, and IDEA (special education).

Mixing a variety of funding sources is the trend of the future. Schools may also receive specific grant funds for before- and after-school programs, as well as tuition from families who can afford to pay for half-day kindergarten and before- and after-school programs. And enrichment programs, such as technology and anti-bullying efforts, will be funded with grants from businesses and the federal and state governments.

Add to this scenario wraparound child care for children under school age—child-care programs for children when they are not attending part-day, part-year early childhood education programs. Since some state, federal, and district early childhood programs are only part-day, wraparound programs are needed. Year-round early childhood programs—including K–3—also require programs to provide these options. These are sometimes offered in the same classroom as the other programs, or care for children is provided in other rooms in the same building, or transportation is provided to take the children to existing community child-care sites. Programs are funded through tuition fees, block-grant funds, specific federal and state grants, and a combination of two or more of these funding streams. Programs offered in existing school buildings are usually subsidized by the district, through the use of space, utilities, and janitorial services.

Curricula

There are several current trends in early childhood curricula that will continue into the foreseeable future. Many of these approaches were described in detail in Chapter 4. Because educational curricula have always been a reflection of society, as society changes, so do our curricula (Wiles & Bondi, 1998); further, every society continually changes

▶*How do we balance the need of young children to explore, discover, invent, experiment and investigate, with the increased focus on standards, outcomes, and assessments?*

its view of the role of education and the priorities of its schools (for example, after the Russians launched *Sputnik*, a national curricular initiative in math and science was launched in the United States, with targeted federal funds). Factors affecting current curricular trends in early childhood include the following:

- a back-to-basics view of education by much of the public and some politicians;
- a concern regarding deterioration in the behavior of students in school;
- school violence;
- increased state and federal involvement in local school affairs;
- increased use of technology in national and international business;
- concern on the part of the public regarding the effectiveness of U.S. public schools;
- increased concern for our world's environment;
- increased concern regarding the negative impact of TV, videos, and video-game violence;
- belief by many educators and politicians that early literacy is the foundation for all academic success;
- the globalization of commerce and business.

Core Knowledge Curriculum

E. D. Hirsch's Core Knowledge Curriculum and other back-to-basics approaches are gaining popularity in early childhood programs (especially K–3), particularly in private schools and public charter schools, as well as home school curricula. Hirsch's seminal work, *Cultural Literacy* (1987), is adored by politicians who believe that our schools are diluting the teaching of the basics, and who idealize our Eurocentric cultural heritage. Hirsch's ideas have been used to develop a series of books for parents, titled *What Every Kindergartener Needs to Know*, *What Every First Grader Needs to Know*, and so on, continuing on up to sixth grade. Middle-class parents of students who succeed in traditional school approaches like this approach because they believe it is a return to the basics they were taught, and a rejection of "soft" academic ideas such as self-esteem, multicultural education, global education, and special education.

Character Education

Character education programs have been instituted by early childhood programs and schools because of the increase in negative behaviors in school. Thomas Lickona and others have spearheaded a movement to include character education in schools. They argue that we need these programs because poor student behavior is negatively affecting teaching and learning; churches and some families are not teaching their children character; we already teach values in schools (bringing homework in on time, respecting the teacher, sharing, speaking in turn, and so on); and TV, videos, and computer games are destroying children's character development. Further, character education proponents argue that there are core values all Americans agree on, regardless of their cultural and religious affiliation.

The Heartwood Early Childhood Curriculum (1997) is a character education curriculum developed for programs serving children aged 3 to 5. The underlying purpose of this curriculum is to:

- model appropriate behavior to children;
- expect appropriate behavior of children;
- support appropriate behaviors in children;
- involve parents in a partnership in developing character in their children;
- provide words and ideas children can use to help them resolve conflicts and discuss appropriate behaviors;
- help children control their own behaviors.

The curriculum is centered on high-quality children's books that illustrate a core set of attributes (values), and it shows children and adults how to practice and use these attributes in classroom experiences. The attributes are telling the truth, being brave, respecting, being a friend, caring, and wishing. The curriculum also provides techniques and language teachers can use to reinforce these values.

Opposition to character education includes people who believe morals should be taught at home and by the family's religious institution; those who believe schools are already overburdened with too much to do; and those who believe that teaching morals is teaching religion. Others feel that the values these programs teach—such as telling the truth, respecting, being a friend, using words to solve problems—are not modeled by many role models in our society who lead our education efforts, such as politicians and school administrators and thus the program is hypocritical.

As our society wrestles with the poor social development of many of our children, character education will grow in popularity. But research indicates that while comprehensive, school and communitywide programs work, simply adding a character education program to a school does not. For a character education program to be effective, children must see the attributes modeled by their teachers, administrators, board members, coaches, security personnel, and politicians.

Standards-Driven Curricula

Goals 2000, discussed in Chapter 4, began a concerted move toward creating national educational standards. Many states continued the process, establishing a series of standards for each academic discipline, which set out exactly what a child should be able to know and do in each discipline at a given age or grade. Further, many states are developing assessments to determine how well students are meeting these standards (see Chapter 14).

Although standards are not strictly a curriculum, they act as one, because all local schools **align their curriculum to state standards.** This means that they make sure their curricular content not only teach the state standards but also teach them at the prescribed times. In reality, these state-approved standards *are* the curriculum, complete with outcomes and scope and sequence. Using state standards and assessments to create curricula is a radical shift away from the historical local control of curricula, and it is leading to a national curriculum that is often more content- than process-driven, as well as to high-stakes testing.

Standards-driven curricula directly affect K–3 public-school programs because the public-school curriculum is aligned with state standards. It also affects preschool programs—especially public preschool programs—because the standards are simply pushed down to younger children. Even programs like Head Start are pressured by local schools to align their educational outcomes to make sure children meet the local school entry requirements. The challenge for early childhood educators is that standards-based curricula are invariably not developmentally appropriate, and are driven by external factors rather than by the needs of individual children, families, and communities (Elkind, 1999; Wardle, 1989).

Outcome-Based Early Childhood Education

The new Head Start Performance Standards (Department of Health and Human Services [Head Start], 1999) include educational standards. Included in these standards are outcomes, such as recognizing letters and numbers and knowing letter–sound relationships. The authoritative document, *Not by Chance* (Kagan & Cohen, 2000), recommends that programs designed to care and educate America's young children "focus on goals and results for children" (Kagan & Cohen, 2000, p. 15). The authors believe this will lead to improved quality of programs, increased political and financial support for early childhood programs, and consistent, national accountability for early childhood care and education.

One of the realities of any outcome-based system is that it drives the curriculum. For example, if an outcome is that all 5-year-olds must be able to skip on both feet, alternately, for five minutes, then the curriculum will include activities that develop this specific skill to ensure that children master it to the level required by the outcome. Since program success and continued future funding are dependent on how well students perform on these specific outcome measures, they become the central components of the curriculum.

Outcome-based curricula are developed to assure that children can demonstrate specific learning outcomes after specific time periods (for instance, at the end of Head Start). Outcomes tend to be more focused on end results than standards in content, behavior, attitudes, and dispositions. Because more public money is being used for preschool programs across the country, and because most people who make policies for young children don't understand what constitutes appropriate development, outcome-based curricula will become ever more popular.

High-Stakes Testing

In the 1998 Head Start reauthorization act, Congress requires Head Start to assess each child's progress in specific language, math, and communication areas, such as "understands an increasing complex and varied vocabulary" and "knows at least ten letters of the alphabet" (Taylor, 2000). The results of state-required assessments reward good schools and give additional funds to struggling schools; they can also eventually result in struggling schools becoming charter schools or being taken over by the state. The net result of these federal and state mandates, besides moving us away from local control to state and national control, is high-stakes assessment—placing extreme importance on children's performance on narrowly defined, pressure-inducing tests and testing situations—a direct result of the call for accountability. It is clear, however, that this trend flies in the face of most early childhood philosophies and what we know about appropriate assessments for young children.

Foreign Languages

As businesses become more globalized, there is a need for Americans to know more languages than just English. U.S. business is expanding in a number of directions—Russia, Japan, China, eastern Europe, Africa, and South America. Clearly, to be competitive in these markets, U.S. corporations will need people fluent in the home languages of these countries.

U.S. schools have historically taught a second language beginning in middle school. These programs have often been fairly ineffective, however, because of poor non-native

Moyenne Section, École Maternelle (French Immersion Preschool)

It's a crisp, Colorado morning. There's a dusting of powder snow on the sidewalk, and the sky is cobalt blue. I'm outside a stately old public elementary school in a quiet residential area in south Denver. Built in the early 1900s, the school represents the typical public-school buildings of that time—massive walls, high ceilings, wide hallways, and high windows.

This is the home of the Denver International School—a twenty-five-year-old French–English immersion school. DIS is a private school substantially subsidized by the French department of education to serve children of French citizens in Denver. However, many non-French children attend the school.

Seven 4-year-olds are sitting around a large table in the middle of the room, working on Christmas cards and worksheets. Vicky, a young French Canadian woman from Quebec City, talks to the children in rapid, conversational French. Occasionally she switches to English, then back to French, but 90 percent of her conversation is in French. She provides feedback in French, gives instructions in French, and praises the children in French.

One child asks to go to the bathroom in English, but after modeling by the teacher, he repeats his request in French before leaving the classroom.

The room is a high-ceilinged old classroom, with high windows, old oak trim, and large black-boards at each end. Various learning centers radiate from the central table. French songs, *les règles de la classe* (classroom rules), numbers and letters in French, days of the week and months of the year in French are all up on the walls. There is a huge world map with the message "Christmas Tour of the World" (in French) and a map of *les continents* (both have Europe in the center, rather than the Americas, as U.S. maps do). There are French tapes, books, and computer programs.

There are seven white children—two girls and five boys—one child is absent. Two of the children have a French family background, and thus speak French; the rest do not.

The teacher comfortably switches between the children working at the table and others rehearsing for the evening's schoolwide Christmas program. All of the dialogue is in French. Children converse with each other in both French and English. Although the teacher speaks primarily in French, she does not admonish the children when they speak in English. When they ask her a question in English, she responds in French.

Vicky tells the children it's time for recess, so they hustle out into the hallway and retrieve their outdoor coats from their individual lockers. The whole class then leaves for the snow-covered playground, basking in the bright winter sun.

language teachers, unsuccessful approaches, and the age of the students. An increasing body of research pinpoints the window for best second-language acquisition as being between ages 3 and 10. Further, other research suggests that the full-immersion approach is by far the best way to teach a second language.

There is considerable professional opposition to the idea of starting to teach a foreign language in the early grades, as well as to full-immersion second-language programs, but it is clearly time for U.S. schools to catch up to the rest of the developed world in this area. Further, while the tendency is to focus only on Spanish as a second language, foreign-language needs will diversify as the educational community catches up with the business world and realizes that existing and potential marketplaces require us to teach a variety of languages.

Peace and Nonviolence Education

We live in an increasingly violent culture. In the past it was possible to protect young children, to some extent, from violence; now, however—with the access TV provides (often even in children's bedrooms), along with violent video and computer games, heavily marketed war toys, and violent movies being viewed by younger and younger children—children are being exposed to a great amount of violence at an early age. And because young children imitate their world, more violence is showing up in their play, creative work, and social interactions.

Educators view this trend with alarm. There are two main concerns: first, exposure and use of violence at a young age teach children not only that violence is okay but that violence is an appropriate way to solve conflicts, to deal with feelings of inadequacy, or simply to "illustrate power and control." And second, specific negative behaviors, such as school violence, adolescent crime, and domestic abuse are believed to be caused, at least in some measure, by this increased exposure to violence at a young age. Social learning theory, discussed in Chapter 9, explains how the media have such a powerful influence on our children.

As a result of this concern, several organizations have developed teacher training programs and curricular materials; two such organizations are Educators for Social Responsibility and the National Association of Mediation Educators. Character education efforts, peer counselors, and anti-bullying programs address other violence-related concerns. These organizations are developing and advocating approaches that include these core ideas:

- Work with parents to set limits on the amount of time children watch TV each day, and to control the content of the programs they watch. Encourage parents to watch TV with their children, and not to place TVs in children's rooms.
- Provide all sorts of healthy alternatives to TV and video watching: outdoor play and hikes, indoor creative activities, story reading, gardening, learning an instrument, sports, and more.
- Teach children to be critical TV viewers—especially of violence and commercials.
- Develop peer mediation programs, especially in schools and early childhood programs that include a variety of ages.
- Limit the use of TV and videos in early childhood programs, and carefully screen Internet sites and computer software (Haugland, 1992).

- Be very clear about what constitutes unacceptable behavior on the part of children in a program—racist, sexist, violent comments and violent behavior (regardless of the family's individual values regarding these issues).

Most early childhood teachers are committed to a peaceful world in which violence is not used to solve problems, and are aware of the power of teaching alternatives to violence to children at a young age. The challenge is to be able to do this in a society that glorifies violence through TV and video programs, films, war toys, professional sports, and other societal values that have a very strong impact on young children.

Ecology Education

The development of environmental awareness is a new curricular trend in early childhood programs. Through activities, children's books, thinking, and discussing, adults and children can slowly develop the concept that our planet is in our hands, and that it is up to us to take care of it. Very young children cannot conceive of global warming, recycled materials, and endangered species. But very young children can be aware of the freshness of the air on a spring day, the sight and sound of a fresh stream, the majesty of a great tree, and the mystery of mallard ducks pairing off at the same time each year to make a nest and have their young.

Ecological education is based on the concept that people are part of the ecological systems of the earth, and that the world and its resources are finite. It is based on a belief in the holistic interconnections of all living things. Another assumption is that teaching ecology to young children is an effective approach. Young children's inquisitiveness and openness allow them to learn about all living things. Their childlike view of the world embraces the ability to see the world from the perspective of, say, a caterpillar, panda, or baby frog. In their unique way, children see how flowers, insects, birds, animals, rain, sun, and people all function as part of the interwoven fabric of nature. They have a built-in reverence for all life, a desire to protect the fragile, and a simple understanding of all living things. Maybe because young children are themselves so fragile and dependent on others, they understand how each part of nature depends on other parts, and on protection by people. They also know how to role-play—take the perspective of—a spider creating a web, a duck making a nest, or a mole digging a hole, which helps them understand the need of animals and insects for a safe, protected environment.

A typical ecology curriculum for young children might have the following features:

- *Teaching knowledge about the natural world.* This includes basic knowledge, relationships (between rain and growth, wind and the shape of trees, and the like), all sorts of natural cycles (day and night, seasons, life cycle of frogs and butterflies), and the value of living things to the world.

▶ *Ecology education teaches children the importance of caring for the natural world.*

- *Exposing children to community examples of caring for the environment.* This usually involves field trips to observe city workers planting flowers, greenhouses, community vegetable gardens, using goats and sheep to eat weeds in city parks, and more.
- *Reading and providing books that cover various aspects of ecology.*
- *Creating classroom or center recycling and conservation projects.*
- *Instituting projects that involve nature.* These might involve planting a garden, collecting weather information, and so on.
- *Collaborating with the home on projects.* Examples include recycling, gardening, or reducing water and electrical use.
- *Teachers and other staff in a program modeling ways to care for our world.* Set an example by recycling, gardening, taking conservation measures, and so on.
- *Engaging in projects that explore local, national, and international conservation efforts.* This kind of project is fun for older children.

As the world's population increases and globalization leads to a "smaller world," competition for essential resources, such as electricity and fresh water, increases. And as Americans increasingly view themselves as global citizens, we will expect curricula to reflect ecological concerns.

Literacy

A current trend in early childhood curricular approaches is an emphasis on literacy. More and more educators and politicians believe that students who master literacy (reading and writing) early in their school experience will be successful; those who don't will struggle in their remaining school years (NAEYC, 2000). President Bush has promised to make Head Start a literacy program, the state of Colorado has made early literacy the cornerstone of its standards and increased spending on education, and curricula such as Success for All (developed by The Johns Hopkins University) and Six Trait Writing are examples of new literacy curricula.

The National Association for the Education of Young Children recently issued *Learning to Read and Write* (NAEYC, 2000), which contains a joint statement by the International Reading Association (IRA) and NAEYC. Other educational and governmental groups have joined the push for literacy. Some of this activity simply reflects a new trend, similar to what the country experienced after Russia launched *Sputnik*.

The new literacy focus, however, has not fully addressed teaching literacy to children from homes that provide no literacy stimulation, children with a variety of learning disabilities that directly limit their learning to read and write, children who are maturational slow learners, and the role of technology (instruction, methodology, and resources) in helping to teach literacy. While all early literacy approaches stress the need for home modeling, support, and involvement, few programs provide recommendations for teaching literacy to children from environments in which these elements don't exist.

And as I have already discussed, American educators, curriculum designers, and education policymakers are also very far behind our colleagues in other developed countries in understanding how to encourage early literacy and second-language acquisition at the same time. In fact, many American educators believe that both cannot be done simultaneously: that learning a second language automatically hinders literacy development in the first language.

Since educators and policymakers have declared that "all children should learn to read and write by the end of third grade" (NAEYC, 2000), literacy development will be a primary focus of all early childhood programs for the foreseeable future.

Diversity

As I have discussed at length throughout this book, our early childhood population is becoming more and more diverse. One result of this diversity is that traditional approaches to teaching and learning often do not work effectively with these children and their families. This is partly because much of our knowledge base is built on research on white, middle-class children; partly because most early childhood teachers are white, middle-class women; and partly because increased diversity naturally brings with it increased challenges that require new approaches.

Changing Demographics of Our Children

The 2000 census figures show a dramatic increase in the diversity of this country, especially in Hispanic and Asian populations. Furthermore, these increases are greatest among families with young children. Demographic changes will have a significant impact on early childhood programs across this country. In Chapter 6 I address the challenges of meeting the needs of all our students. Here I will focus on this challenge in the context of specific changing demographics.

Hispanic Children. The fastest-growing minority group in this country comes under the ethnic label of Hispanic. Hispanic Americans can be of any racial group; the three largest populations are from Mexico, Puerto Rico, and Cuba (Cruz-Janzen, 1997). Hispanics include people whose relatives lived here before it was part of the United States—in California, Colorado, New Mexico, Arizona, Texas—and people who have recently immigrated from Mexico and from Central and South America.

One of characteristics of this group is the tremendous within-group diversity—what I call diversity of diversity. Cuban American parents or parents recently from Colombia may have very different values and expectations for their children than parents recently from Mexico, or migrant parents. Other challenges Hispanics bring to our programs include

- *Speaking Spanish as a primary language.* Some parents wish to have their children continue to speak Spanish; others want their children to learn English as quickly as possible. And, of course, some of these children don't speak Spanish at all.

▶ *We all came from different backgrounds: families, communities, cultures, and religions. Early childhood programs have to work closely with each child's family and community.*

- *A strong religious orientation.* This often, but not always, means Catholic. Among other things, when publicly funded early childhood programs provide environments and curricula that reflect the culture of Hispanic families, they must understand laws regarding the separation of church and state. This religious orientation is an obvious advantage for Catholic schools.

Rocky Mountain Aztlan Head Start Program

The community center is across from a neighborhood swimming pool that boasts a large mural with Aztec themes. The community center is a modern building, housing a child-care program, several local community-college classrooms, the Denver Housing authority, and Aztlan Head Start Center. In the classroom are thirteen Hispanic Head Start children. Boys have neat crew cuts, girls have their straight and curly black hair flowing freely or held in a loose ponytail. The children are sitting on a carpet singing songs to the accompaniment of a children's record.

Songs alternate between Spanish and English. Children enthusiastically repeat phrases from "The Muffin Man," and then do big arm movements to a song about rainbows and "all kinds of people." They then select a variety of activities in different areas of the classroom.

Three middle-aged Hispanic women comfortably move among the children. Two are teachers, one a volunteer. The volunteer works with two children at a time making paper clothes for paper cutout dolls; one teacher is working with children making a huge butcher-paper poster of children's handprints in purple, red, and green. The other teacher helps two children with simple English computer programs, helps wash children's hands after they have done the handprint project, and responds to other issues. Two children are washing blocks, two are making art with stamps and ink prints, a little boy is building a house in the block area, and two girls are involved in an elaborate dramatic play with telephones, message pads, and women's clothes.

The classroom is bright, airy, and clean, with windows, child- and adult-size sinks, and doors to the bathroom. The floor is a rubberized surface with fixed and loose carpet. The classroom is very well equipped, with two computers, a variety of books in Spanish and English, toys, learning materials, and classroom equipment in good condition. Learning centers include the computer area, dramatic and pretend play area, listening area (tapes and earphones), block area, and reading area.

There's quite a hum in the room. Discussions between children are a comfortable mix of Spanish and English. The volunteer talks conversationally with the children as they work on the doll's clothes: "How was the weather when you came to school? Was it cold?" She switches between Spanish and English. The other two teachers speak primarily in English.

Books, environmental print, classroom rules, and instructional posters—colors, numbers, months and days, the classroom schedule (with photos of various activities)—are in English and Spanish, but not always both.

A child on the computer prints out his display, which already has his name printed on it. He then puts it in his locker. Another child uses a felt pen to add detail to her doll's clothes. A child washes his hands after making handprints, then decides to wash the sink. While an occasional conflict arises, for the most part the children are appropriately engaged. Teachers seem to anticipate potential friction and intercede calmly.

I quietly excuse myself as the children busily pursue their individual activities.

- *Family values that view male and female children differently.* Some Hispanic cultures still emphasize the role of the woman as the mother, nurturer, and homemaker, and of the man as provider and disciplinarian. This can lead to families having different educational expectations for boys and girls in our early childhood programs.

- *Rich culture of music, art, and dance.* These cultural groups have very rich cultural histories that include dance, stories, art, and music. Our challenge is to integrate these cultures into our curriculum and experiences for children, without creating a tourist curriculum (see Chapter 4).

- *Negative experience with schools.* Like other minorities, many Hispanic parents have had very negative experiences with public schools when they were students. Overcoming this negative history can be very difficult and can impact their relationship with their child's early childhood program.

Asian American Children. The second-fastest-growing group of people in this country is Americans with some Asian heritage. Again, these families include both people with a long history in this country and new immigrants. There are various issues to be aware of as we work with these families:

- *Diversity within the category. Asian Americans* is a misnomer, created by the U.S. Census Bureau. It is a misnomer because many people from countries that are part of Asia—eastern Russia, India, Pakistan, Iran, Turkey, Yemen, and more—are not considered part of this census category. National groups that make up this broad umbrella include communist and nationalist Chinese, Japanese, Korean, Vietnamese, Hmong, Filipino, Malay, and Indonesian, and many have historical hatreds toward other groups in the category resulting from bitter wars, conquests, and oppressions going back thousands of years. We must be cognizant of this diversity and of the arbitrary nature of the census category.

- *Cultural values of family and education.* Many parents of Asian American heritage place a very high value on education and family. They want to know what we are providing that will enable their children to be academically successful in school. We need to provide this information to them.

- *Respect for teachers.* In many Asian countries, teachers are considered highly respected professionals. Their advice is sought by parents; they are the experts. As a result, some parents struggle with the idea of parental involvement in the classroom, cooperative learning, and field trips. Also, some Asian parents expect issues such as behavior, discipline, and special education to be handled at home or by a community leader, but not at school.

- *Conflict between different generations regarding the Americanization of their children.* Part of the diversity within all groups is the difference between generations, especially if one generation is from the home country and the other was born in this country.

African American Children. Many of our early childhood programs serve a significant number of African American families. Issues these programs must consider, when working with these families, include:

- *Diversity of families.* As I discussed with Hispanic and Asian American families—and in line with my discussion of diversity within diversity in Chapter 6—African American children come from diverse homes; diverse religious, economic, and educational backgrounds; and diverse historical and geographic contexts.

- *Religious values.* Many black parents are very religious and expect their child's program to support their values. Special care must be taken in addressing issues that may challenge certain religious values, such as sexual orientation.

- *Value of education.* African American parents place high value on the education of their children and believe that learning the basics—math, reading, writing—is very important. This belief sometimes challenges a program's use of a developmentally appropriate philosophy.

- *A history of prejudice.* Because of slavery and a history of oppression and discrimination, African American parents are very concerned with equal rights. These parents are often actively engaged in civil rights efforts in their communities, and are deeply concerned regarding the quality and equity of their child's education.

- *Extended families.* While all American family structures are changing, many African American children have an extended network of people who help care for them, and programs need to find ways to work effectively with all of the child's caregivers, while maintaining legal issues of confidentiality and privacy.

Multiracial Children. The 2000 census was the first time in our modern history that people were allowed to select more than one racial or ethnic category to label their official identity. As a result, 6.8 million Americans checked more than one race (Bureau of the Census, 2001). The largest group of these are children, and most experts believe this figure is a very conservative one.

The increasing multiracial population has various implications for early childhood educators. Teachers must explore our own biases regarding mixed-race and mixed-ethnicity relationships and marriage. Pressure should be brought to bear on educational supply companies to create and market products for multiracial and multiethnic children and their families—books, puzzles, dolls, games, and more. We need to explore the best way to meet the educational needs of these children and their families. Because we have totally ignored multiracial and multiethnic children in our history and schools, we have no body of knowledge regarding their needs. Just as children with Hispanic and Asian American heritage are diverse, so are children with mixed backgrounds. A child of a black parent and a white parent has different needs from a child of Navajo Indian and black parents, Hispanic and Japanese, or Japanese and Korean parents, and teachers need to be responsive to these variations. Finally, we must develop ways to support a healthy multiracial identity in a country that stresses single race or ethnic group membership.

Research

We live in an ever more diverse society, yet much of our current body of knowledge—child psychology, learning theory, childrearing practices, best practices, and so on—is based on research that does not represent the diversity of race, ethnicity, national groups, gender, language, culture, and more (McCray, 1994). Since much of learning

► *Multiracial and multiethnic families will continue to increase, and their children add to the diversity of our programs.*

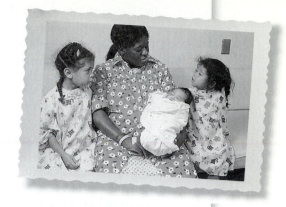

and child development is contextual—determined by environment, expectations, motivation, cultural context—it is incumbent on research to shift its paradigm to help us understand the impact of all these various forces on children's development and learning.

As I said earlier, most of our human-science knowledge is based on the dominant culture, and we consider information gathered from the dominant culture—through research, observation, and tradition—as the norm; all other groups and subgroups are compared to that standard (McCray, 1994). When behaviors, attitudes, and practices of people who belong to these groups correspond to dominant culture, they are considered okay; when they differ, they are considered abnormal or deviant. The terms *culturally disadvantaged* and *culturally deprived* derive from this concept. When I worked for a national child-care company, a parent complained to the Minnesota licensing authority because one of our caregivers had swaddled her 1-year-old infant. The parent felt this was inappropriate, and the licensing authority agreed. They told us that it was developmentally inappropriate to swaddle such an old baby. Yet when I worked with Mayan people in the Highlands of Guatemala, I saw 2-year-olds swaddled. The licensing authority was enforcing a value of the dominant culture.

We now recognize that every individual develops and functions within a cultural frame of reference shaped by unique forces. Each culture is valid and right, in and of itself; its values should not be compared to those of another culture—in this case, the dominant culture—and when this is done in research, it is called **bias.** Bias in research can occur in a variety of ways. For example, statistics used to create well-baby reports (height and weight norms doctors give parents when their infants visit for well-baby checks) were at one time based on a predominantly Irish American sample, because the university collecting the data used only children who lived close to the university, most of whom were Irish American. Irish Americans are, on the average, fairly large—resulting in biased data for, say, Asian and Hispanic children. When I took my eldest child, Maia, for a one-year checkup, she hardly even registered on the height and weight scales (my wife and my mother are both less than five feet tall). The nurse who checked her was quite worried; luckily, the doctor understood the bias in the norms.

One of the greatest scientific concerns is using research results gathered from one group of people—Asian, black, Native American, white, low income—and then **generalizing** the results to all people. Studies on parenting methods, learning approaches, teaching techniques, and the like could all fall victim to this kind of bias. Another problem found in research is a confusion of variables, which commonly occurs when a child's race and ethnicity are incorrectly assumed to be the same as their culture; yet many research studies and recommendations assume that race and ethnicity always equate to culture. Because we have only recently considered race, culture, and income as central parts of a child's experiences that affect their learning, we don't truly understand the relationships of these variables.

In Chapter 9, I discuss the theoretical and scientific body of knowledge on which we base our policies for children and families. This body of knowledge is based almost totally on the theories, research, writings, and practices of white European and North American professionals. Diversity experts believe it is simply wrong to take the general rules of development from this body of knowledge and apply them to all people (McCray, 1994). According to McCray (1994, p. 44), researchers need an ability to recognize problem areas that require a multicultural perspective; an awareness of how failure to embrace diversity contributes to research bias and perpetuates stereotypes; a critical review of existing knowledge; and **multicultural competency** within the research community.

A culturally competent researcher is someone who understands social diversity, social justice, and social identity, and uses this understanding when doing research on diverse populations or when generalizing results to these populations. *Social diversity* is the concept of an individual's membership in a reference group and how that membership affects the person's basic values. Further, social diversity is the recognition that all reference groups have values—none better than, or dominant over, another—a concept that recognizes that research from a one reference group may not apply to individuals from another reference group. *Social justice* is the idea that, historically, one cultural view (the dominant culture) has been foremost, and all others have been suppressed or oppressed. Thus diverse groups in America have been oppressed for years by the dominant group. A competent researcher understands this view. *Social identity* is the understanding that we all belong to one or more reference groups, and those memberships influence our values and the way we view others. A competent researcher understands how social identities—that of the researcher and those of the subjects—can create bias in methods, results, and interpretation of results.

Teachers

While the number of minorities continues to increase in America, most of our early childhood teachers are white women. Thus, more and more children are being taught by teachers of very different social, economic, racial, and ethnic backgrounds from their own. Not only does this pose the problem of teaching Other People's Children (Delpit, 1995) but it creates a gap between the teacher's background and that of the children's parents—an obvious challenge for programs, teachers, parents, and students.

A solution to this dilemma is to increase the number of minority teachers in our early childhood programs—which is, however, far easier said than done. The central problem is that all public-school K–12 teachers are required to be certified, and certification requires at a minimum a bachelor's degree. While many early childhood programs do not require a four-year degree, Head Start and state-funded programs are moving toward requiring a teaching certificate. Far fewer minorities are graduating from four–five-year colleges than white students; further, minorities with bachelor's degrees can generally demand far higher salaries from government jobs and the private sector than from teaching. It is, obviously, a vicious cycle.

Challenges to Developmentally Appropriate Practice

It does not take a genius to see that the information covered in Chapters 3 and 9 give a very powerful impression that our early childhood history is white, American (United States), and European. Froebel, Pestalozzi, Dewey, Rousseau, Erikson, and Skinner were

▶ *The diversity of immigrants to this country challenges our programs. What are the needs of these children from Belize?*

white men from Europe and the United States. Montessori, Mitchell, Pratt, and Johnson, white women from Europe and the United States. These theorists, researchers, and practitioners along with contemporary contributors such as Gardner, Bandura, and Bruner, are the architects of developmentally appropriate practice, the preferred philosophical basis of our field.

As we serve more families from every corner of the globe and from cultures and subcultures within our country, with diverse languages, customs, religions, and beliefs, many argue that we must expand our body of knowledge to reflect this diversity. Most nations outside Europe and the United States practice the family bed, many live in one- or two-room homes, and some have several families living in the same house. Schools in Asian countries differ markedly from those in France, Denmark, and Sweden; some childrearing practices in African American homes differ from those in Hispanic and white homes. While there is considerable agreement that we must include diverse cultural viewpoints in the care and education of children, this view poses certain dilemmas to our field. What should we do if the values of parents from one cultural group we serve conflict with the values of the dominant culture, such as equality, desegregation, best practices, and separation of church and state? What is the most effective way to prepare children from diverse cultural backgrounds to succeed in a world controlled by the dominant culture? And finally, what constitutes high-quality early childhood education and care—what are the standards we should use?

Teacher and Caregiver Preparation

As politicians have sought to reform American education, teacher preparation practices have been carefully scrutinized. In Chapter 7 I discussed at length the different methods used to prepare teachers and caregivers to work with young children. While a four-year degree (often with added teacher-preparation requirements and time) is still the preferred approach to preparing K–12 teachers, those who work with infants, toddlers, and preschoolers pursue a variety of routes to preparation, including four–five-year degrees, CDAs, and high-school diplomas.

What is the best way to prepare child-care professionals? Is there one best way—or a variety of approaches? Should preparation for an infant teacher be qualitatively different from preparation for a first- or second-grade teacher?

State Early Childhood Standards

There is a vast array of requirements for people who work with children under school age, from simply being over 18 years old and in good health to having a bachelor's degree in infant and early childhood development or elementary education (not to mention special education). Many of these requirements are developed by the state's department of health and human services, not the department of education.

One trend in the field, however, is to increase the qualification requirements for teachers working with young children. Head Start and many state-funded early childhood programs are requiring teachers to have early childhood degrees. Because many traditional four–five-year teacher-training colleges stress K–12 education and many students prefer to get teaching credentials that allow them to teach young children and elementary-school children, these degrees are often weighted toward elementary-school techniques, philosophies, methods, and curricular development.

The trend toward requiring bachelor's degrees for early childhood teachers will continue, especially in public-school early childhood programs and in programs funded directly by federal and state monies—because politicians believe the public equates high-quality education with a teaching certificate. But it will not become the requirement for caregivers in child-care programs—either for-profit and not-for-profit—though a variety of federal and state initiatives will continue to upgrade the child development skills and knowledge of child-care providers in centers and homes.

Practicums

A continual complaint of new teachers is that they have not been prepared for the reality of the classroom. They know the theory, history, philosophy, and content of teaching, but they are ill-prepared to handle the real life of a teacher. This complaint has increased as the diversity and challenges of the classroom have increased. Teachers today are expected to differentiate instruction to suit different learning styles; provide appropriate support to special-education students; teach to the state's standards; respond to cultural, racial, and linguistic diversity; and work effectively with parents.

Many states have responded to this criticism by requiring student teachers to spend far more hours in the school classroom and to enter the classroom earlier in their teacher education. The Stanley British Primary School in Denver, Colorado (discussed in detail in Chapter 4), has an agreement with the Metropolitan State College of Denver to provide classroom experience for its college students and to instruct them in the philosophy and practices of the British Infant School approach, an agreement that meets the requirements of the Colorado Department of Education's teacher-certification process.

Cultural Competence

I have already discussed the dilemma posed by the increasing number of minority children in our early childhood programs, which are still dominated by white, middle-class caregivers, teachers, and directors. One solution to the dilemma is to train more minority teachers, but the next-best solution is to train teachers in cultural competence. Teachers and caregivers are taught how to work effectively with minority students, families, and communities—making the school an accepting place for these students and families, and adjusting the curriculum and instruction to be meaningful to each child.

Cultural competence requires teachers from the dominant culture to understand some of the negative results of that culture; for example, an ability to see the negative impact of the western expansion of the United States on Native Americans and Hispanics, the negative impact of Christianity on tribal religions and customs, and the difficulty children from minority cultures have in changing their behaviors when they enter the (dominant culture) school. Cultural competence enables teachers to view the world from each child's point of view—even if this point of view differs radically from their own value orientation. Cultural competence is gained through training and direct experience with people from diverse cultures and communities.

Alternative Programs

While new teacher training programs are requiring more practicum experiences, and the CDA program is a national, field-based process, many child-care teachers are simply thrown into the classroom with little or no training at all. They learn by the seat of their pants. One alternative approach to these extremes that is being explored is that of a master-teacher apprenticeship. In this approach, experienced teachers are matched with students learning to be teachers. The master teacher is given a reduced teaching load in order to spend time and energy working with the student one on one. The student teacher learns the real-world methods of working with students, discipline issues, building politics, and family and community dynamics. This approach has been used successfully for years by the French educational system and is the foundation for training teachers in the Reggio Emilia model.

One goal of alternative approaches to teacher training is to develop teachers who are grounded in the real aspects of teaching and prepared for the increased responsibilities faced by teachers in today's programs. Another is to find a way to attract more minorities to the profession. The tension between requiring a four–five-year degree and the desperate need to provide qualified, competent minority teachers to our increasing number of minority students will continue and increase in the future.

Teacher Shortage

It is estimated that 2.2 million additional teachers will be needed in the next decade to accommodate increasing student populations, class-size reductions, and teacher attrition (CDF, 2001). To meet the challenge, more than 30 percent of newly hired teachers enter the field without full certification, 11 percent enter the classroom without a license, and 25 percent of public-school teachers are teaching outside their area of expertise (CDF, 2001). Further, schools with a high percentage of low-income and minority students have less-qualified staff. More than 20 percent of all new teachers leave the profession within three to four years.

The job of being a teacher continues to get more difficult—increased content standards and expectations, public scrutiny through test-score comparisons, greater curricular expectations (recently added anti-bullying programs being one example), more children coming from dysfunctional homes, and lack of parent support. In many cases, when our schools don't work—for whatever reason—teachers become the public's and politician's favorite whipping boy. Fewer and fewer people choose to place themselves in this position.

High-Quality Care and Early Childhood Education

As our society invests more money in early childhood care and education, there is an increased concern about quality. One of the results of this trend is the standards-based and outcome-based education discussed earlier in this chapter. Another is the use of various accreditation approaches. Central to the issue of quality, however, is the continued conflict between early childhood education and child care.

Early Childhood Education versus Child Care

For all practical purposes, there are two general programs for children under school age: early childhood education (learning) and child care (caring and supervision). The educational programs tend to be part-day (mother's day out, cooperative preschools, religious preschools, Head Start, local schools, gifted programs, special-education programs, Title I programs, state-funded programs), staffed by trained teachers, and funded by parents and public dollars. Child-care programs tend to be full-day (up to ten hours), provided by family child care, not-for-profit programs, for-profit centers, and employer child care, and often staffed by teachers with minimal qualifications.

Clearly these two approaches are radically different in quality, a difference that is largely due to program funding. As I have suggested, America seems willing to fund educational programs (direct learning programs) but reluctant to fund programs that are designed to care for children while their parents work or are in training. Until this philosophical difference is overcome, providing high-quality early childhood services will continue to be a major struggle.

What Is a High-Quality Early Childhood Program?

A central concern of everyone involved in the early childhood field is to make sure we are providing high-quality care to our future citizens. This is particularly important, since it is very clear that the early childhood experience sets the foundation for future school success. The questions then are: What constitutes high-quality early childhood programs and how can we recognize a high-quality program?

Teacher–Child Ratio. Considerable research points to the quality of teacher–child interactions as a crucial predictor of children's successful development. Children who received high-quality teacher interactions exhibited less stress, more verbal skills, higher intelligence, better social skills, and higher socio-emotional development than those who did not (Kontos & Wilcox-Herzog, 1997). High-quality interactions are described as those that are responsive to student needs—nurturing, intense, involved, and sensitive. While research indicates that the quality of these interactions, rather than their frequency, is the essential factor, research also shows that teachers are more sensitive and responsive in their interactions with children when there are fewer children per adult. Further, while teachers believe they are actively involved in interaction with all children, the research indicates that many children of these same teachers receive very little contact. The most needy, verbal, and pleasant children attract teacher attention, while other children are often ignored. To offset this problem, teacher–child ratios must be kept small, and teachers must be very aware of their interaction patterns. The fact that family child-care providers seem to be more engaged with children than teachers in center-based programs would seem to support this notion (Kontos & Wilcox-Herzog, 1997).

Classrooms that meet the recommended adult–child ratios have more responsive and sensitive interactions than classrooms that don't. Ratios and group sizes recommended by NAEYC (Greenberg, 2001) are:

	Ratio	Maximum group size
Infant–12 months	1:4	8
12–24 months	1:5	12
24–30 months	1:6	12
30–36 months	1:7	14
Preschool	1:10	20

Note, Brazelton and Stanley call for even smaller ratios, as discussed in Chapter 1.

Teacher Education. There is considerable research correlating teacher education and preparation to high-quality early childhood experiences. A consistent link has been established between increased training in early childhood education and responsive, sensitive teacher–child interactions (Hayes, Palmer, & Zaslow, 1990): the more education teachers have in child development and education, the more responsive and sensitive they are in their interactions with children. States that have increased licensing requirements and provided additional training for child-care providers have seen an increase in high-quality interactions. Further, research has shown a consistent relationship between quality teacher–child interaction and improved child development outcomes—cognitive, social, and emotional (Kontos & Wilcox-Herzog, 1997).

High-Quality Child Care and Future Success. "The quality of child care is primarily related to lower staff–child ratios, staff education, and administrators' prior experience. In addition, certain characteristics distinguish poor, mediocre, and good quality centers, the most important of which are teacher wages, education, and specialized training" (Cost, Quality, and Child Outcomes Study Team, 1995, p. 41). Research from a study of Early Head Start shows that 2-year-olds who attended the program performed better in language, cognitive development, and socio-emotional development compared to children who did not participate in the program. Furthermore, parents who were served by the program had more positive parenting skills, used physical punishment less frequently, and were more able to assist their child's development appropriately. Finally, programs that were fully implementing all Head Start performance standards (an indicator of quality) showed the strongest findings.

Another study determined that children who attended a high-quality preschool center were more likely to complete high school, less likely to be in trouble with the law, and less likely to repeat a grade. Boys who attended this program were 40 percent more likely to graduate from high school than boys who did not attend. The study determined that for every dollar invested in the program, the public saved $4.39 (in remedial education costs, crime, higher taxes, and so on; CDF, 2001). And the famous Perry Preschool research, discussed elsewhere in this book, reinforces the point. Finally, there is research documenting that children who attended high-quality school-age programs missed fewer days of school, outperformed their peers on statewide tests, and showed improvement in school behaviors and homework completion (CDF, 2001).

Accreditation

While standards and outcomes are politically attractive approaches to achieving quality in educational programs, another method to determine quality is **accreditation.** Several organizations have developed accreditation processes, including NSACA (for school-age programs), National Child Care Association (NCCA), and NAEYC. Programs such as Head Start and military child-care programs have long had their own internal quality control systems.

The idea of accreditation is to create indicators of quality, and then develop a system to evaluate programs according to these indicators. The principal difference between accreditation on the one hand and outcomes and standards on the other is that accreditation focuses on the process, such as adult–child interaction, whereas outcomes and standards focus on content, skills, and measurable objectives. Because the results of high-quality early childhood care often are not evident until many years after the care is provided, and because many of the things we should be doing with young children are difficult if not impossible to measure, accreditation is viewed by many as a better fit for quality control and accountability in early childhood programs, than outcomes and standards.

Standards of Accreditation. Any accreditation process is based on a standard of program quality. The NAEYC accreditation publication states that "the criteria listed in this book represent the current consensus of the early childhood profession regarding the definition of a high quality program for young children" (NAEYC, 1991A, p. ix). While many standards are universally accepted as indicators of high quality—such as the health and safety standards of active supervision, keeping immunization records, and sterilization of toys and clothing—others are open to debate, such as developmentally appropriate curricula and child–staff ratios. The philosophical underpinning of the NAEYC accreditation process is developmentally appropriate practice (Bredekamp & Copple, 1997). Research indicates that accreditation significantly increases program quality; accredited centers provide a high quality of service, and staff in these programs are more knowledgeable about early childhood and more professional (Bredekamp & Glowacki, 1995; Whitebook, Saki, & Howes, 1997).

NAEYC Accreditation Indicators. The NAEYC accreditation system was initiated in 1985 and has been revised several times since. The quality categories for the NAEYC accreditation process are:

- interactions among staff and children;
- curriculum;
- staff–parent interactions;
- staff qualifications and development;
- administration;
- staffing;
- physical environment;
- health and safety;

- nutrition and safety;
- evaluation.

Under each of these major categories are items designed to determine the level of the program's adherence to a standard. For example, under "interactions among staff and children," item A-1 is "Staff interact frequently with children. Staff express respect for and affection toward children by smiling, touching, holding, and speaking to children at their eye level throughout the day, particularly at arrival and departure, and when diapering or feeding very young children. Staff actively seek meaningful conversations with children" (NAEYC, 1991a, p. 15).

Some indicators are evaluated through observation, such as staff–child interactions; some are determined through the examination of paperwork, such as staffing ratios and staff qualifications; some are evaluated through parent questionnaires; and some are determined by staff interviews. Many use a combination of these methods.

NAEYC Procedure. The NAEYC accreditation process includes three primary steps: self-study, validation, and commission decision.

Self study. The program uses self-study materials to determine the strength of the program and areas in which improvement is needed. The program then makes the necessary changes and submits to the accreditation body a written program description.

Validation. A visit is arranged for an on-site evaluation of the program. The evaluator— or team of evaluators—compares the program's self-study assessment and record of improvement to the observation criteria. The results are then submitted to a commission.

Commission decision. Based on documents submitted by the program and the on-site evaluation, the commission decides whether the program should be accredited.

State Standards

States are funding more and more early childhood programs (see Chapter 2). Further, as state departments of education are implementing standards for their K–12 public-school programs, they are developing standards for their early childhood programs. They are motivated by concerns about accountability and a desire to justify the expenditure of public moneys on programs for young children. As states spend more money on early childhood programs and as educational standards become the hallmark of accountability, early childhood standards will increase. On the other hand, states seem fairly reluctant to develop quality standards for child-care programs—especially those that increase the costs. Some states do, however, support the adoption of the accreditation programs and pay higher reimbursement rates to programs that are accredited; other states provide a variety of scholarship funds to increase the knowledge base of child-care teachers and providers.

Class Size

Early childhood accreditation criteria include student–teacher ratios, as do most state licensing requirements. The ratios change by the child's age, with the smallest ratio being for infants. Small child–teacher ratios are considered one of the hallmarks of high-quality care for a variety of reasons, including teacher–child interactions. Curiously, these ratios are much smaller (fewer students for each teacher) than for public-school early childhood classrooms—including K–3 classrooms. If a small adult–child

Figure 15.1

Early Childhood Classroom Observation Form Used in NAEYC's Accreditation Process

B.   **Curriculum**   (Note: A page is not missing. The letters and numbers are not in consecutive order because only some of the Criteria are observed in each classroom.)

CRITERION	RATING			COMMENTS
	Not met	Partially met	Fully met	

B-3a.   **Modifications are made in the environment, staffing pattern, schedule, and activities to meet child's special needs.**   [1]   [2]   [3]

     ❑ Indoor and outdoor environments are accessible to special needs child including ramps, bathroom, and playground access as needed.

     ❑ Schedule is modified as needed, such as shorter day or alternative activities.

     ❑ Program is modified as needed, such as provision of special materials and equipment, use of supportive services, individualization of activity.

     ❑ Individual education plans are developed and implemented in a developmentally appropriate manner.

     ❑ Therapy is developed appropriately and incorporated within classroom activities as much as possible, rather than removing the child from the classroom.

B-4.   **The daily schedule provides a balance of activities in consideration of the child's total daily experience—what happens before, during, and after the program with attention to the following dimensions:**

B-4a.   **All age groups play outdoors daily, weather permitting.**   [1]   [2]   [3]

B-4b.   **The schedule provides for alternating periods of quiet and active play.**   [1]   [2]   [3]

B-4c.   **More than one option for group activity (individual, small group, or large group) is available most of the day. Infants and toddlers are not expected to function as a large group.**   [1]   [2]   [3]

B-4d.   **A balance of large muscle/small muscle activities is provided in the daily schedule.**   [1]   [2]   [3]

B-4e.   **A balance of child-initiated/staff-initiated activity is provided while limiting the amount of time spent in large group, staff-initiated activity.**   [1]   [2]   [3]

Source: National Academy of Early Childhood Programs, 1991 early childhood classroom observation. (Form to be used with *Accreditation criteria and procedures of the National Academy of Early Childhood Programs.*) Washington, DC: NAEYC. Reprinted with permission from the National Association for the Education of Young Children.

ratio is an important indicator of quality, why doesn't it exist in schools? Further, as our classrooms are filled with more and more diverse students, teachers must continually differentiate and individualize their instruction, which calls for smaller classes.

In 1985 the state of Tennessee initiated a huge research project on class size, called Project S.T.A.R. The initial four-year study compared student achievement of children in small classes (thirteen to seventeen students) to that of students in average-size classes (twenty-two to twenty-five students) in kindergarten to third-grade classrooms. The larger classes included a teacher and assistant. The math, science, and study-skills performance of 6,500 students in 330 classrooms in eighty schools was studied. All of the students in the small classes showed improvements over the other students in early learning and cognitive skills, with minority students' improvements double that of their white counterparts.

The second phase of this study, Lasting Benefits, showed that students from the smaller classes continued to perform better even after they returned to larger classes in fourth grade. Finally, the third phase of the study, Project Challenge, assigned all K–3 students in the seventeen economically poorest districts in Tennessee to small-size classrooms. The results in reading and math at the end of the year improved in these districts from below average for the state to above average (Mosteller, 1995).

Reducing class size poses two tremendous challenges. The first is philosophical: ever since educator Horace Mann returned from observing Prussian military schools, we have considered placing large numbers of students of the same age and ability in a single classroom as the standard public-school practice. It is simply accepted as the norm, like the school day and the annual calendar. Textbooks, curricula, and tests are geared to this idea, as is much of the training for K–12 teachers. The other problem is cost: clearly, more teachers must be hired, and teachers are the single most costly component of education. Further, many schools and early childhood programs would need additional classroom space to serve the same number of children. (Increasing the traditional school's scope to include children younger than kindergarten age already poses the same challenge for many schools.) In spite of these difficulties, reducing class size is a trend that will continue, especially for the early grades.

Use of Technology

The question to be addressed regarding schools and technology is not whether technology will become a more important part of education, but how. There are several challenges, including the lack of equipment in schools, poor teacher preparation, and the technology divide. Maybe of most interest to educators is just how technology can be integrated into all instruction, and not simply isolated as a separate subject or content area.

Equipment

There are two fundamental dilemmas regarding technology equipment for early childhood programs: the cost of the equipment, and the ever-changing state of the art. To some extent, grants from major computer companies are providing equipment for some schools. But—as is often the case—suburban schools are much more able to provide needed technology than rural and inner-city schools, resulting in inequitable access.

One of the dilemmas relating to access is that both early childhood experts and educators who advocate full integration of technology into all learning activities advocate that computers and other electronic equipment be placed in every classroom, with enough units that children can use them every time the task requires it (Haugland, 1992). The traditional approach of isolating computers in labs is not recommended. Clearly, integrating technology into all classrooms is more expensive than having a single computer lab, or even a technology cart that is wheeled into the classrooms.

With some of our poorest schools having problems providing adequate textbooks, it is not clear how schools will afford the needed equipment. As technology begins to replace textbooks, some of the money budgeted for textbooks can be shifted to technology expenses. It also appears that increased federal interest in local schools will translate into additional technology dollars.

Teacher Preparation

After lack of equipment and technology resources, lack of teacher expertise is the next most challenging problem in implementing technology in the classroom. There are two basic problems: lack of basic technology skills, and lack of knowledge about using technology for more than basic skills acquisition and skill and drill activities. These problems are partly the result of many of today's teachers not being technologically literate, since they did not grow up around computers. The next generation of teachers will enter college with all the basic skills and knowledge.

The second problem—knowledge of how best to integrate technology into the curriculum—is far more difficult to solve. Because technology is often marketed to parents and schools as a tool for developing basic skills, many of the available programs are either games or focus only on skill and drill. Further, new state standards and outcomes make computers ideal tools to help students prepare for the standardized tests, reinforcing its role for review and skill reinforcement.

Creative, innovative, open-ended use of technology to enrich, differentiate, and support the basic curriculum will not occur widely until early childhood programs place more value on creativity, innovation, problem solving, and individualizing the curriculum. Teachers and parents who understand this philosophy will have no problem integrating technology into the entire curriculum.

The Technology Divide

I have already discussed the imbalance between the technology resources of suburban schools and those of city and rural schools—called the **technology divide.** Exaggerating this problem is the reality that many low-income families do not have computers at home, and if they do, often do not have Internet access. Further, the parents in such families are usually not computer literate. All of this means that children from low-income homes are at a tremendous disadvantage compared to their middle-class counterparts. Because many children use computers to do research for schoolwork, type school papers, and present fancy, computer-generated reports, children without computers are at an additional disadvantage. Because of this inequality, a board member for the Oakland, California, school district proposed the elimination of homework. He felt it was not fair for some students to be able to present sophisticated, typed (with graphics), well-researched reports, while other students had to submit handwritten reports with no fancy graphics.

No one has come up with a workable solution to this dilemma. Certainly, as the cost of computers decreases, more families will be able to afford them. Some private schools—Edison schools, for example—buy a personal computer for each of their students, which they are allowed to take home.

Control of TV and the Internet

One of the most difficult issues facing families and early childhood programs is how to control inappropriate materials on the TV and Internet. Many believe that the increasing negative behavior of children in organized programs is partly due to the Internet and the media (Levin, 1998). Further, the media's focus on sex, greed, violence, exploitation, and materialism is in direct opposition to the philosophy of most early childhood programs. How can a program teach a child to "talk out his problems" when on TV, videos, and video games it's okay to shoot or hit someone you disagree with, and acceptable to use all the bad words you can think of? Clearly this desire to control the media runs head-on into our free-speech rights. Can libraries place blocking devices on their computers? What about schools? And, do these work?

The other dilemma, of course, is that parents often rely on TV and videos to baby-sit their children, and are not aware of the potential negative impact on their children's development. A central issue is that adults can to some extent separate the fantasy of TV from the reality of their lives, while young, impressionable children cannot.

The debate will rage on. Schools must find ways to capitalize on the tremendous educational value of the Internet without exposing students to hate speech, violence, pornography, and blatant commercialism. Parents must be educated about the negative effect of violence, sex, and commercials on TV.

One of the problems with TV watching is the increasing marketing to children by companies—soda, cereals, hamburgers, dolls, makeup, fashion, CDs, software, and on and on. It is disgusting that many schools across the country have exclusive contracts with Coke and Pepsi. What's particularly worrisome is that many of these products are very bad for children's health and negate any effort the program makes to teach children good food choices and eating habits.

Males in Early Childhood Programs

Currently there is an effort to increase the number of men in the early childhood field. This is because more and more families do not include a man in the home, and because more and more boys are at risk of school failure (more boys than girls are in special education, drop out of school, engage in substance abuse, and commit suicide). The emphasis on recruiting men for early childhood classrooms is especially strong in programs for minority children.

▶ *It is extremely difficult to attract men to the early childhood education field. (R. Benjamin-Wardle)*

Teachers

It is extremely difficult to attract men to the early childhood field, and even more difficult to retain them (Neugebauer, 1994; Cunningham, 1998–1999). The reasons are complex, but include a general mistrust by the public of men who choose to work with young children, the extremely low pay of early childhood professionals (obviously not acceptable for any teacher, regardless of gender), and the difficulty men experience trying to make inroads into a traditionally female occupation. As a male early childhood professional, I was almost always the only man in meetings, and I was the only male in the education department of a national early childhood company. People have assumed that I am gay on more than one occasion. Some years ago I applied to direct the Office of First Impressions, an early childhood initiative for my state. I entered the interview with state officials eager to demonstrate my knowledge and commitment to young children, families, and early childhood education. I left one hour later disgusted that more than three-quarters of the interview revolved around whether I was married, why a man would desire such a position, and my overall moral character. I discussed the issue of male teachers and caregivers in more detail in Chapter 7.

Father Involvement

Another way to get men more involved with young children is to support father involvement in our early childhood programs. Traditionally, the mother accepted the responsibility of taking young children to their program, and programs have developed effective ways of working with mothers. But now men are far more involved with the lives of their young children, and the number of single, male-headed households is increasing.

Early childhood programs are developing a variety of ways to be more responsive to fathers. Some of these include (Cunningham, 1998–1999):

- providing parent meetings and training just for fathers;
- providing bulletin boards with ideas of things fathers can do with their children;
- including fathers in newsletters, photos, marketing materials, and the like;
- providing staff training to address anti-male bias and teacher–father involvement;
- inviting men to be field trip volunteers and program resources;
- providing men's bathrooms in the center;
- including posters, children's books, and artwork that show positive father models.

Conclusion

Current and controversial issues affecting early child-hood programs include all the hot issues affecting K–12 schools, the age-old debate between early childhood education and child care, and the challenge of integrating technology into instruction. Two other powerful issues are the question of equity in education, and the role early childhood education should assume in increasing the overall quality of U.S. public schools, especially in academic areas. These—and other issues—will continue to dominate early the childhood field. And as more public money is used to support these programs (federal, state, and local), the debate will intensify.

Questions and Projects

1. Find a partner. Select one of the topics covered in this chapter. Develop a debate, with each one of you taking opposing sides of the issue. Present your debate to the class. Afterward, allow for questions and discussion.

2. Select one of the topics covered in this chapter. Conduct research in the library and on-line regarding the topic. Expand on the information presented here. Prepare a ten- to fifteen-minute presentation to the class on the topic. Give your opinion, and support your opinion.

3. In general, parents have a choice of programs for their preschool-age children. Further, college-age students have a choice of colleges (state, private, technical, religious and so on). Should all parents have a choice of schools for their K–12 children? Why? Why not?

4. After researching the topic—with politicians, experts, community leaders—develop a paper that suggests solutions to the technology divide.

5. Interview at least four parents of young children. Ask them if they believe children under kindergarten age should be served by the local school for free. Write a three- to five-page paper summarizing their responses. Include reasons for and against this idea.

GLOSSARY

absorbent mind A Montessori term to describe the preschool years when young children are highly receptive to learning lots of material through all their senses and in an integrated manner.

accommodation In Piaget's theory, accommodation is one of two ways children learn about the world, by being forced to change their internal view or schema of something, to make it more accurately correspond to the external reality of the object or concept. *Also:* An approach of absorbing new immigrants into the American way of life that requires new immigrants to reject much of their unique cultural heritage, including their language.

accreditation A process administered by a variety of child-care associations to improve the quality of child care and early education, both in centers and homes. Accrediting associations include NAEYC, NAFCC, and NSACA.

aligning curriculum to state standards The process of redesigning district curricula so that they teach the content, skills, and concepts of specific state standards, in the correct time frames.

Americans Technically, *Americans* includes all people who live on the North and South American continents, from Canada to Tierra de Fuego. In this book it is occasionally used synonymously with *U.S. residents.*

arousal-modulation theory of play A theory of play based on the work of Berlyne, which proposes that children play to maintain an optimal level of stimulation.

assessment Any effort to collect data and information on a student or a program with the intent of making some judgment regarding that student or program. The judgment might have to do with the success of a program, the needs of the student, or the improvement of a curriculum.

assimilation One of two ways Piaget believes children learn about the world. In assimilation, children change their view of the world to fit their own schema or internalized concept.

associative play The stage of social play in which children play together on a simple level—they might talk to each other, imitate each other, and share toys, but they are not fully cooperating (planning, directing, assigning roles, creating scripts).

atelierista An artist in Reggio Emilia schools who works with children to develop ways of presenting what they have learned. Works in the Atelier, where students work on artistic projects.

attachment A critical period, when, according to Bowlby and others, human infants must develop a bond with their mother or other significant adult.

attention The process of tuning in to aspects of the environment. The way we focus on information that we need to learn, which is accomplished by an interaction between the environment and our mind.

authentic assessment Assessment of a concept, skill or knowledge that is based on the child's demonstrated performance, within the appropriate context—home, classroom, community. A process that encourages the child to demonstrate what she knows and can do.

authoritative parenting One of three parenting styles; combines high levels of nurturing and control, with open and frequent communication.

autonomy Ability to perform independently: in the case of children, a child is able to do something without help.

autonomy vs. shame or doubt The second of Erikson's stages of psychosocial development, which occurs during ages 1–3, approximately. At this stage the child must learn to develop a healthy sense of independence.

basics The traditional subject matter of the curriculum: math, reading, writing, science, and so on.

behaviorism/behavioral theory A theory that describes the role of the environment on learning. Behaviorism is divided into two areas: operant conditioning and classical conditioning.

bias An approach that favors one side, position, or viewpoint over another. For example, a father who favors his son over his daughter is showing a male bias.

bicultural practice The ability to operate effectively within two distinctly different cultures—for example, a home culture and a school culture that is different from the home culture.

bilingual education Instruction in two languages—usually the child's home language and another language. In the United States it is used to describe a program that supports a child's home language while teaching English.

body of knowledge The information used to create philosophies, program goals, curricula, and best practices. In field of the early childhood education, it is theories, research, tradition, and ongoing practice.

bottom line For-profit companies must always consider the financial reality of making a profit; otherwise their shareholders get upset, and the company eventually folds. Quality, consistency, and even integrity are often sacrificed to this reality.

Brown v. Board of Education of Topeka The Supreme Court decision that declared that separate schools for black children and white children cannot be equal. The decision effectively outlawed separate school programs based on race, gender, language, and special needs.

call-and-response singing An approach to singing with children in which the leader (teacher, singer, recorded singer) sings a phrase and the children respond, alternating throughout the song.

canned curriculum A single curriculum taught for a specific period of time: character education, self-esteem, black history month, etc. The curriculum is usually highly prescribed by its creators.

CDA candidate A teacher or caregiver in an early childhood setting involved in the process that leads to a Child Development Associate credential.

center care A program that cares for children under school age in a community facility—either an independent center or one connected with a chain, Head Start program, school, or other agency.

cephalocaudal development The development of muscle control in infants that progresses from head to toe.

character education Aspects of the formal educational curriculum that address character development. U.S. schools have always taught character, but character education focuses on its development in children.

charter schools Unique schools created by specific state legislation. Although they are funded the same way as other public schools, they have fewer rules and more leeway to be creative and unique, and are centered on a specific approach—such as core knowledge of curriculum, second language, arts, technology.

Child Development Associate (CDA) A field-based, national certification program for child-care providers and teachers. Requires experience, knowledge, and on-the-job assessment.

classical conditioning Pavlov's theory of behaviorism in which two stimuli are presented at approximately the same time, and eventually the neutral stimuli (which initially caused no response) produces the response. In Pavlov's experiment, the sound of the bell caused the dog to salivate.

classifying Grouping objects together by one characteristic, such as size, color, function, or ability.

cognitive development The growth of mental and intellectual capacities. Occurs in a stepwise process.

cognitive play Piagetian levels of play, from functional play to games with rules.

competencies An outcome-based approach to developing knowledge and experience working with young children. Used by the CDA program to structure its curriculum and assessment.

concrete operations stage The period of cognitive development in which the child uses logical rules and operations to control thinking, even if they appear to contradict direct experience. The child at this stage has attained conservation.

conservation The ability to understand that volume, weight, mass, and number do not change when they physically appear to. Must be achieved before a child can move to the concrete operations stage.

constructive play The stage of cognitive play in which children use materials and toys to create something else: building a town with blocks, making a picture with paint, using sand to make tunnels, or building a boat on the workbench.

constructivism The process by which children use their active exploration of the environment, and materials in that environment, to create mental structures in their minds about the physical world and how things work.

constructivist theory A theory of cognitive development that postulates that we construct our own view of reality by taking in information from the environment and actively processing it.

continuum of change The gradation of change from one phenomenon to another: for example, the range of bounce heights between a very bouncy ball and one that hardly bounces at all.

cooperative play Children playing together and fully interacting with each other—planning, changing roles, and working together. A stage of cognitive play.

core knowledge curriculum The term used by E. D. Hirsch to describe his curriculum, which teaches cultural literacy—what every child in this country should know at specific time periods: basic skills and content.

cost–benefit analysis A research method that examines the relation between the cost of a social program and the cost savings generated as a result of the program's effectiveness. The Perry Preschool Project is a good example.

creative dramatics The improvisational communication of an emotion, an expression, a character, or a story.

criterion reference tests Assessment instruments that compare a subject's score to an outside criterion, such as a set qualification score to get into kindergarten or into a university.

critical feature A part of an object, idea, or person that is highly significant to describing and remembering it. We use critical features to remember objects or aspects of persons; we remember a Mercedes Benz by its three pronged emblem.

critical pedagogy An educational practice derived from the work of Paulo Freire, which stresses the role of students both to evaluate what they are taught and to use the information to change society.

cultural bias A slant in books, curricular materials, tests, policies, and so on that favors members of one cultural group—in this country, usually middle-class white Americans—over members of other groups.

curriculum The experiences, activities, and learning, planned and otherwise, that children experience under the direction of the program—in the center or school, on field trips, and in the community.

decontextualized language Language that does not include a variety of natural cues, such as voice inflection, facial expression, setting, or context. Books are an example of decontextualized language.

deductive A technique of thinking that applies general principles to specific facts or situations to come to a conclusion.

deficit model of assessment Screenings, assessments, and tests that focus on what a child does not know and cannot do—their deficits.

developmental delay The general term used by many early childhood programs and schools to classify a child with a disability that is covered by the federal IDEA law.

developmental goals and objectives Targets used by curriculum planners to support the developmental growth of children.

developmentally appropriate practice A philosophical guide developed by the National Association for the Education of Young Children, stressing developmental learning, individual differences, and social or cultural context.

developmental path The path children naturally take as they progress through each developmental stage; the natural direction of development.

didactic A teacher-directed approach to teaching, learning, curriculum, and educational philosophy. The teacher is in charge and is the expert.

differentiate A teaching and curricular approach that provides for a variety of learning styles, and a variety of abilities, approaches, and speeds of learning. Used to match diverse student learning needs.

disposition Developing a habit of mind that leads to the continuation of an activity or behavior, such as reading, creativity, enjoying math, or liking to write.

diversity of diversity The concept of variability and differences within traditional areas of diversity, such as racial groups, children with disabilities, and gender groups.

dominant culture The dominant and pervasive values of the U.S. mainstream. The laws, educational expectations, and religious values derived from a white Anglo-Saxon Protestant heritage.

ecological education A curricular approach that introduces children to their responsibility in caring for the world, and activities that help children understand the balance of all things on the globe.

educational goals and objectives Targets used by curriculum planners to support the educational attainment of children.

educational vouchers Vouchers representing a percentage of the total cost of educating a child. They are given to the child's parent, who can then choose any school for the child and use the voucher to help pay the tuition.

egocentric A characteristic of preschool children, who think and act with themselves at the center. This focus also influences children's sense of morality.

emergent curriculum The content and activities of the curriculum are developed from children's interactions with each other, staff, and parents, based on children's experiences and interests.

emotional intelligence A set of abilities that characterizes a child's emotional response to learning; it can be as powerful a predictor of future success as IQ.

emotional literacy A component of emotional intelligence, emotional literacy is the ability to master one's emotional domain and use that knowledge in future activities and learning.

enactive representation A way of remembering actions by physically repeating those actions; what some call muscle memory. Walking, dancing, swimming, and playing soccer are examples. Jerome Bruner believes young children are more enactive learners than older children and adults.

entrapment Any physical area between 3½ and 9 inches in size that can trap a falling child by the head, causing extreme injury and even death.

environmental checklists Documents designed to enable programs to assess all aspects of their physical environment. Several are available, including those that are part of the NAEYC accreditation process.

environmental print Examples of print in the environment: advertisements, traffic signs, building names, posters, directions, charts, and so on.

equality In early childhood programs, this term means that everyone has an equal opportunity to have access to a free education.

equity Children should receive the support, guidance, and instruction needed in early childhood programs to meet their full potential, whatever that potential is. Requires the program to go beyond equality.

ESL student English as a Second Language student. A name for children whose first language is not English.

ethics Every profession has a code of ethics, which stipulates the standards of the field, which are then used to guide decision making and professional behavior.

eurythmics Expressive whole-body movements in time to music: the central concept of the Dalcroze music education method.

event sampling An observation method that focuses on a preselected behavior or event.

expository text Written material that primarily gives information: about animals, how to fix a car, how to build a house, the population of a country.

extrinsic rewards Behavioral reinforcers that come from outside the person: food, money, praise, tokens, and the like.

family child care Care of children in someone's home. May be regulated or unregulated.

federal block grant money Money sent directly to states to provide child-care services for low-income families, often those involved in training, seeking a job, or in a low-paid job. Usually administered by counties.

field-based program An education preparation program that focuses on working with children in a specific educational setting.

formal operations stage The final stage in Piaget's cognitive theory. At this stage children can manipulate ideas, solve problems, and predict solutions—even ones that they have never directly experienced.

functional play Play that is based on the physical characteristics of materials and children: rolling a ball, jumping up and down, breaking sticks, throwing stones in a lake.

games with rules Play involving more than one child that requires all children to follow some externally imposed rules, and requires children to suppress their ego needs.

globalization The spread of ideas across the world; the spread of values, languages, trade, and media (including the Internet) across borders and political and philosophical barriers.

goals Broad, general subject areas that a program intends to cover: desired areas of learning, behavior, and development.

graduated challenge Materials and equipment that children can use in progressively more challenging and complex ways.

grantee agency The local agency that directly receives federal Head Start dollars and that is responsible for the legal and fiscal operation of the local Head Start program.

Great Society programs A series of federal antipoverty programs created during the administration of President Lyndon Johnson. Head Start is the best known and the one that has lasted the longest.

guidance Assisting children to develop internal controls to be able to function appropriately within social settings.

habituation Ceasing to respond to a stimulus that is repeatedly presented; the mind "shuts off" to what it considers irrelevant information. Commonly known as boredom.

hands-on Active learning that requires children to feel, manipulate, construct, and experiment with concrete materials.

heuristics An aid or cue for solving a problem or remembering a process, such as the saying "I before *e* except after *c*" or "The order of the information is the same as the alphabet."

hidden curriculum Aspects of the curriculum children learn that are not specified in a curriculum document. For example, social relationships, the value of athletics, whether parents are respected, and the like.

hierarchy of needs Maslow's theory of motivation: it states that basic needs must be met before higher-order motives apply.

high-stakes tests Standardized tests used to evaluate the performance of schools, teachers, students, and/or administrators. Since students' scores are used to determine the performance, this places extreme pressure on them.

home schooling Parents choosing to educate their children (K–12) at home. Each state has different rules and regulations regarding this practice.

iconic representation A way of remembering by means of pictures. Young children remember the signs of their favorite toy store, fast-food place, and TV character through icons. It's a very immediate, but not flexible, form of memory. Computers use icons a great deal.

idiom An expression that is not based on the individual meaning of the words: for example, "put your foot in your mouth." Idioms differ from language to language, culture to culture.

idiosyncratic Learning that is based on individual experiences, needs, learning styles, and preferences.

imprinting A behavior learned during a critical period: for example, ducklings following the first moving object they see within a short time period after being hatched.

inclusion Providing instruction to special-education students in the least-restrictive environment, which usually means they are with their same-age peers, even if not performing at the same level. Children under age 5 should stay at their local community center, if at all possible.

Individual Education Plan A written program for children with disabilities, aged 3 to 21 years, developed by school professionals and the parents, that outlines educational objectives, approaches, and materials to meet the student's unique needs.

Individual Family Service Plan A written program for children with developmental delays, from infancy to 2 years old, that outlines services they will receive.

inductive A technique of thinking that uses a set of specific facts to reach a general conclusion.

industry versus inferiority The fourth stage of Erikson's psychosocial stages, from about ages 6 to 12. Characterized by the child's mastery of tasks, skills, social rules, and peer and adult relationships.

information processing theory An approach to understanding learning that follows the child's entire learning process, from attending to the correct stimuli in the environment to recalling appropriate information from long-term memory and performing based on the knowledge learned.

in-home care Care provided by a nonrelative who comes into the home, such as a nanny.

initiative versus guilt The third stage of Erikson's psychosocial stages, from ages 3 to about 5½, which is characterized by the child's readiness to move out from under parental guidance.

institutional approach An approach that reflects the order and function of large institutions, such as hospitals and schools. Tends to be regimented, hard, and organized to meet group rather than individual needs.

integrated approach An educational approach that uses two or more of the traditional academic disciplines at one time. It encourages mixing skills, concepts, and ideas across disciplines—learning across the curriculum.

interactions Human connections and social contacts; in this book, they usually refer to child–adult relationships.

inter-observer reliability The extent to which the scores by each observer of the same event agree with each other; the closer they agree, the more reliable the results.

intrinsic motivation The internal drive children have to play, master tasks, explore the world, and do things that make them feel good.

intrinsic reward A reinforcer to a behavior that comes from within a person: self-praise, motivation, pleasure in mastery of a task, and so on.

invariant stages Stages in a development theory that must be followed in order, and cannot be repeated.

Israeli kibbutzim Communal settlements in Israel that include collective infant and early childhood programs.

kinesthetic Involves movement, bodily awareness, and the need to be active; one of Howard Gardner's eight intelligences

laboratory studies Research on animals and children conducted in highly controlled settings, usually research labs connected to universities.

language acquisition device The way the mind is hard-wired to learn language, according to Noam Chomsky. The environment simply activates this device.

learning centers Physical areas in a classroom designed for development and learning based on a particular theme or discipline. Includes furniture and appropriate materials and tools. Examples include art, math, science, and reading centers.

least-restrictive environment The legal mandate to serve children with disabilities in settings with same-age peers, whenever this does not have a negative impact on the learning of the children with disabilities.

life-span theory A theory of human development that covers a person's entire life.

local educational authority The local school district that is authorized by the state to run public schools. Each LEA has an elected school board and provides free K–12 education for children.

local match The 20 percent of the total budget that must be contributed to the local Head Start program to match the federal money. Usually this match is provided in space, services, and parent volunteer hours.

logical consequences   A guidance technique that is directly related to the undesired behavior. For example, the logical consequence of spilling paint is cleaning up the mess.

logical-mathematical learning   The basics of mathematical knowledge—understanding the relationship between size, shape, amount, order, sequence, etc., and numbers, measurement, etc.

long-term memory   The area of the brain where information is stored once it has been processed in our short-term memory.

looping   A teacher or team of teachers following the same group of children for at least two years.

marble rollways   A marble game that can be purchased or made with unit or other blocks. The player drops the marble into the top of the rollway, and then the marble runs back and forth until it reaches the bottom and exits onto the floor.

math manipulatives   Solid objects children use to explore various mathematical properties and concepts, such as volume, weight, adding, more than, and less than, and basic numbers. Traditionally available in the math learning center.

maturation   The genetically preprogrammed development of children as they grow older.

maturational theory   The idea that growth is preprogrammed, and that children develop naturally along this preprogrammed path. The environment has little effect on this development.

mental functions   Activities, structures, and processes of the mind.

metacognition   The way people use knowledge about their own learning and approach to memory to assist them in learning and memorizing.

metacommunication   Talking to yourself: providing instructions, motivation, and advice to yourself as you approach new tasks and challenges.

méthode clinique   A research method used by Piaget that asked children to explain how they resolved specific problems and dilemmas.

mission statement   A broad statement of a school or early childhood program that summarizes its educational philosophy.

modeling   Part of social learning theory: modeling teaches children through their observation of the behaviors of someone (real or symbolic) whom they respect, believe to be competent, and admire.

moral reasoning   The thinking children engage in as they determine moral responses and behaviors. "Why should I be good; why should I share; why should I be loyal?" According to Lickona and Kohlberg, the reasons for being good change as children mature.

morphemes   The smallest units of meaning.

multicultural competency   The ability to function equally well with people from a variety of diverse backgrounds, and in institutions that reflect a variety of communities.

multicultural education   The discipline that examines curricular and instructional approaches to teaching children from diverse groups within our educational programs.

multiple intelligences   Gardner developed an approach that categorizes learning into eight general areas, or intelligences. He proposes that individual children learn more effectively using one or more of these approaches, but that all children should be able to use each approach to some extent.

multiracial and multiethnic children   Children whose biological parentage makes it impossible to place them accurately within one of the U.S. Census's racial or ethnic categories.

nativism   A theory of language acquisition that states children are born preprogrammed to learn all essential elements of all languages. The environment provides the vehicle for this programming to unfold.

naturalistic research   Nonintrusive observation of children in their natural environments—home, community, classroom, playground—engaged in familiar activities with familiar children and adults.

Neonatal Behavior Assessment Scale   An instrument developed by Brazelton that determines the overall health and well-being of a newborn infant and may alert physicians to possible problems. Is more thorough and extensive than the Apgar Assessment Scale.

nonliterality   A characteristic of play that is not based on the real aspects of time, place, people, and things. A creation of the child's mind, rather than reality.

nonparticipant observer   Someone using an observation instrument who is not actively involved with the children being observed.

norm referenced   Assessment instruments that have been given to a large number of children of the same age across the country, and then averaged. Individual results are compared to these averages.

number   The abstract quantity or value associated with a number.

numeral   The label assigned to a numeral, such as "ten" or "27."

objectives   A narrowing of goals—more specific, observable, and often measurable.

objectivity   Assessments that are not influenced by personal opinion, bias, or judgment.

object permanence   The end of Piaget's sensorimotor stage, when infants understand that even though they can no longer see an object, it still exists.

one-drop rule   A uniquely American concept that holds that any person with any black heritage must be categorized as black. Also extends to others of mixed heritage (white and Hispanic, etc.).

one hundred languages of children   The many ways children in Reggio Emilia schools demonstrate their learning and development; a roving, worldwide exhibit of products made by children from Reggio Emilia schools.

one-to-one correspondence   An exact match between two groups of objects: one apple for every child; one knife for every plate.

operant conditioning   The use of positive and negative reinforcement, and punishment, to mold behaviors and teach new skills; the use of external control to modify a behavior.

ordering   Sequencing objects or sounds by one criterion: for example, from biggest to smallest, brightest to dullest, loudest to quietest, or favorite to least favorite.

outcomes   Very specific, measurable objectives for particular content areas at set time periods (say, the end of second grade, or the end of a specific subject curriculum).

parallel play   A stage of social play in which more than one child is playing at the same or similar activity, but they are not interacting with each other.

paraprofessionals   Staff members working with children in a public school, Head Start, or other educational program who have only a high-school diploma or GED, and who have no formal teacher education.

participant observer   Someone using an observation instrument who is also actively involved with the children.

patterning   A repeated sequence, by either sound (clapping, stamping, singing) or sight (colored beads in a certain sequence; the patterns on a peacock's feathers), or by activity (the daily classroom schedule).

pedagogista   An educational expert, or consultant, who works closely with teachers, parents, and city officials within Reggio Emilia schools.

peer mediators   Trained students who facilitate conflict resolution in school settings; mediators in a structured program to reduce and solve peer conflicts.

performance standards   The national Head Start regulations that local programs must adhere to, and that are reviewed every three years by a federal review team.

Perry Preschool Project   A comprehensive early childhood program operated by the High/Scope Education Foundation. Results from this program established a powerful cost benefit for Head Start–type programs. It is not a Head Start program.

personal identity   The part of a child's self-image that is based on the child's competence, mastery, and ability to control, order, and function effectively in the world.

philosophy   The belief system about students, learning, education, and the role of the school in society that determines the framework for the curriculum.

phonemes   The smallest units of sound, which collectively make up a specific language.

phonics   The relationship of letters and sounds in written words.

phonological awareness   Awareness of all the sound components in spoken and written language, including soft and hard letter sounds, rhymes, and syllables.

phonology   The sound system of a specific language.

physical/motor play   Gross and fine motor activities or the use of body parts in play—rolling, skipping, climbing, jumping, thumb wrestling, etc.

pink tower   The best known of Montessori's many specially designed toys and learning materials: a stacking unit that requires children to place each block in the correct place.

play training   Various approaches teachers can take in increasing the quality of play of children; ways to help children move to more complex forms of play.

pluralism   The approach of absorbing new immigrants and existing groups into the American mainstream without expecting them to reject their own cultural attributes—also called the salad-bowl approach.

policy council   One of the governance components of Head Start, made up of parents and community volunteers; it has specific functions, including approval of hiring and firing personnel in the program.

pragmatics   The use of language in practical settings, influenced by vocal inflection, volume, body language, and contextual cues.

preoperational stage   The second stage of Piaget's theory, in which children can represent experiences through abstract symbols—words, numbers, pictures—but not without the heavy influence of the physical world.

prescribed curriculum   The day-to-day decisions about what to teach and how to teach are predetermined in the written curriculum.

print-rich environment   A learning environment, such as a classroom, that provides lots of examples of different forms of print for children to use—posters, charts, advertisements, maps, directions, books, labels, and more.

private speech   Vygotsky's concept of young children talking to themselves out loud to structure or scaffold their learning. As children get older, they internalize this process, but still use it.

process skills The skills—such as observation, measurement, language, and so on—that are used and required in studying science.

progressive education An educational approach developed by Dewey and his colleagues that emphasizes a student's experiences and uses inquiry and problem-solving methods.

prosocial behaviors Behaviors that enable a child to function successfully and appropriately with other children and adults.

prototype A representative example, or typical member of a category, which is likely to incorporate features of the most typical, commonly observable characteristics of the concept.

proximo-distal development The development of muscle control in infants that progresses from the center of the body to the extremities of arms and legs.

psychosocial theory Erikson's theory of eight stages of development, which cover the entire span of human life and focus on social and emotional development.

punishment Strictly speaking, punishment is an operant conditioning method that reduces the likelihood of the targeted behavior being repeated. In common parlance, it is any unpleasant response to the undesired behavior of a child.

purposeful movement Movement undertaken with conscious thought and intent, which gives control and awareness to a child.

racial and ethnic constancy The idea that race and ethnicity are fixed, and do not change based on age, occupation, or other factors.

readiness In general, what it takes to prepare a child for something. Specifically, the term is used for school or kindergarten readiness: is the child ready for the rigors—academic and social—of school?

recapitulation theory A theoretical concept that maintains that the development of a discipline in an individual follows the same progression as the evolution of the same discipline through human history. Two examples are the development of play and the development of musical knowledge.

reciprocal agreements Agreements between states to allow state certification from one state to be valid in another.

reference-group orientation The groups children and people belong to: family, classroom, race, ethnicity, church, neighborhood, profession, gender, and peer groups.

refinement The process of muscle development from overall gross motor control—walking, sitting—to fine-motor control, such as using of fingers to hold a paint brush and pencil.

relative care Care provided by a relative in the child's home or the relative's home.

reliability The nature of an assessment instrument that enables it to provide the same results on the same subjects over repeated uses; consistency.

representation Reproducing a real, concrete experience to hold it in the mind, through pictures, actions, words, photographic memory, or sounds.

running record A continuous narrative of a child's behavior; a highly naturalistic observation.

sample A research term indicating the makeup of the group of children or people used in the research. The makeup of the sample—race, ethnicity, gender, income, and so on—determines how applicable the results are for future use.

scaffolding A metaphor to describe a process of assisting children in learning how to learn. Ideas, techniques, and methods provided by a teacher—or peer—that help children learn within the zone of proximal development, and which are eventually internalized by the child.

schema An idea, framework, or design that we create in our minds that is used to think about the world. According to Piaget, our schemata are constantly changing.

scope and sequence The way concepts and skills are placed within a curriculum so that children build on past knowledge and skills; often so highly prescribed as to ignore any individual differences.

self-correcting A toy or learning material that can be put together only in one way, thus requiring children to adjust, or self-correct, to complete the task; part of the Montessori method.

self-image The child's image of himself or herself, which is a combination of the way the world responds to the child and the way the child interprets the world. It's not all positive or all negative. In Cross's model, self-image is made up of personal identity and reference-group orientation.

semantics Variations in the meaning of language, as determined by cultural and geographic location and other factors.

sensitive period A time during a child's or adult's development when a particular influence is most likely to have an effect—a window of opportunity.

sensorimotor stage The first of Piaget's stages, characterized by learning about the environment through all the senses, reflexive response to stimuli, and a belief that "out of sight is out of mind."

separation of church and state The term used to describe the constitutional mandate that forbids the state (government) from either supporting any religion or persecuting any religion. Any organization that receives tax money, such as a public school, is considered the state.

simple unit; complex unit; super-complex unit A simple unit is a single manipulative component, a complex unit is two manipulative units, and a super-complex unit is three or more manipulative components. For example, a pile of sand is a simple unit, adding a shovel makes a complex unit, and adding a bucket of water makes a super-complex unit.

social competence A skill that allows students to learn in a variety of physical and social settings. An individual's ability to initiate and maintain relationships with peers. The basis of the Head Start philosophy.

social interactionist theory A theory of language acquisition that believes a child is born with a genetic predisposition to learn a language, but requires the parent (or caregiver) to continually provide appropriate verbal interactions.

social play Development of play from playing alone to playing cooperatively with other children.

sociocultural theory A theory of development that believes a children's cognitive development is strongly influenced by their social interactions and social context. Vygotsky's theory is known as a sociocultural theory.

sociodramatic play A combination of cooperative play and dramatic play, often called fantasy or make-believe play: more than one child involved in play that includes roles, scripts, and props.

solitary play Playing alone.

spiral curriculum A curriculum approach that uses the cycle of learning—a movement from the concrete and personal understanding to abstract and conventional knowledge—as a framework to determine curricula activities. This approach is followed for all new information, concepts, and skills, regardless of the age of sophistication of the child: thus its spiral nature.

stage theory A theory of development that holds that children develop through distinct, qualitatively different stages. Completion of each stage allows children to move to the next one.

stakeholders Individuals and organizations that have a direct, vested interest in an early childhood program and school: parents, financial supporters, teachers, the local community (or church), and others.

standards The level of accomplishment and mastery of specific content areas that children should demonstrate at points along the way, such as at the end of third grade. Standards are not the same as curriculum.

standing committee A committee that stays in place to address a variety of topics and tasks over time.

steady beat timing The ability to keep a steady beat independently, despite the distraction of environmental factors.

subjectivity Assessments that are highly influenced by personal opinion, judgment, and bias.

symbolic play Using materials and toys to represent something they are not: a doll becomes a baby, a block is a phone, a cardboard box is a house, and a child is the mother.

symbolic representation The use of symbols—numbers and words—to remember ideas, experiences, and facts. In Bruner's scheme, symbolic representation is the most complex representation; next is iconic representation including pictures and one-to-one icons; with enactive—muscle memory, being the most primitive.

syntax How the units of meaning are combined to create oral language: the grammar of the language.

tactile cues Information students gain through touch that helps them learn and helps students who have difficulty gaining information through sight, hearing, or other methods.

taxonomy of educational objectives Bloom's theory of the different ways we process cognitive information, from basic knowledge, to evaluation.

teachable moment Seizing the opportunity when a child is particularly open to being taught; the opposite of the idea that teaching should occur only at specified times and schedules.

teacher-directed learning An approach to learning used by traditional schools and the core knowledge curriculum, in which teachers are considered the experts, who direct and control the learning process.

technology divide The difference between low-income and middle-class families and schools regarding access to, and use of, technology in their educational programs.

theme A broad concept or curricular topic such as seasons, animals, transportation. Teachers use themes to develop experiences and activities in each content area.

theory The organization of data, ideas, and concepts to provide a more complete understanding of what this information means in a piecemeal fashion.

time sampling An observational method that is conducted at predetermined time intervals and focuses on predetermined activities or events.

Title I A large federal program targeted at low-income children who are not performing up to the state standards for their grade. Funding is distributed to schools with the most low-income students.

token economy A classroom management technique in which tokens—pieces of paper, play money, chips—are used to reinforce targeted behaviors, which are then redeemed for treats such as candy, supplies, time on the computer, lunch with the principal, and so on.

tourist curriculum An approach to diversity that focuses on celebrations, food, and music without investigating the true meaning of diversity—values, goals, expectations, and view of the world.

traditional lab school   A school—usually elementary—attached to a teacher's college or university to provide opportunities for prospective teachers to learn and practice being teachers, and to conduct school-related research.

transductive   Primitive kind of thinking that preschool children engage in. When objects or actions occur together, young children believe, simply because of their proximity, that they must be related, that one causes the other. To a young child, someone who wears a dress must be a woman.

transformational representation   The track or trail left by a scientific phenomenon. A good example is the erosion caused by the flow of water. By helping children see these records, they more easily learn the scientific concept.

transformation   The process of change. A scientific term to show the activity that occurs during change: the act of raining; the opening of the Evening Primrose at dusk.

transition   The change between activities, settings, and expectations. It includes moving from the bus to the program, from classroom to classroom, from classroom to bathroom, and more.

trust vs. mistrust   The first of Erikson's stages of psychosocial development, which occurs during infancy. During this period, infants must learn to trust that their basic needs will be met.

turf issues   Competition among different early childhood programs for funding, students, parent support, and jurisdiction.

twice-exceptional student   A student who has been diagnosed with one or more special needs and who also is gifted.

values clarification   A popular educational program of the 1960s and 1970s, that used Kohlberg's work to help children reason about moral dilemmas; it is now very much out of favor.

War on Poverty   President Lyndon Johnson's federal programs designed to remove poverty from U.S. society. These programs included Project Head Start, a federally funded program for young children.

webbing   The curriculum planning process of starting with an idea, word, or concept, and then extending the process in every direction that the child thinks of. Is also used as a prewriting device.

whole language   An approach to teaching reading and writing by constructing meaning through interactions with authentic written materials. It emphasizes reading and writing for meaning and in meaningful contexts.

whole-child approach   An approach to curriculum development based on a philosophy that a child's entire being—emotional, social, moral, physical, and cognitive—should be developed in the program.

working memory   The part of our memory in which incoming information is processed to place it into long-term memory; it has a very small capacity and is very short: thus we lose a lot of information.

wraparound child care   Child care that provides full-day child care for children who attend an early childhood education program for a few hours a day. The program might be run by the same organization that provides the early childhood program, or it might be provided by a different organization.

zone of proximal development   According to Vygotsky, this includes the range of what children can do on their own and what they can achieve with expert assistance from another child, teacher, parent, or volunteer.

REFERENCES

Aboud, F. E. (1987). The development of ethnic self-determination and attitudes. In J. S. Phinney & M. J. Rotheram, (Eds.), *Children's ethnic socialization: Pluralism and development* (pp. 29–55). Newbury Park, CA: Sage.

Aboud, F. E., & Christian, J. D. (1979). Development of ethnic identity. In L. Eckensberger, Y. Poortinga, & W. J. Lonner (Eds.), *Cross cultural contributions in psychology.* Lisse, Holland: Swets & Zeitlinger.

Adams, G., & Poersch, N. O. (1997). Who cares? State commitment to child care and education. *Young Children, 52*(4), 66–69.

Adams, M. (1990). *Beginning to read: Thinking and learning about print.* Cambridge, MA: MIT Press.

Allen, D. (1998). Trends in demand for center-based child care and early education. *Child Care Information Exchange, 123,* 8–11.

Allen, E. K., & Marotz, L. (1994). *Developmental Profiles: Pre-birth through eight.* Albany, NY: Delmar Publishers.

American Academy of Pediatrics. (1997). *Model child care health policies.* Elk Grove Village, IL: Author.

American Association for the Advancement of Science. (1999). *Dialogue on early childhood science, mathematics and technology education.* Washington, DC: Author.

Apple, M. (1986). *Teachers and tests.* New York: Routledge and Kegan Paul.

Arbett, J. (1989). Caregivers in day care centers: Does training matter? *Journal of Applied Developmental Psychology, 10,* 541–552.

Arnheim, R. (1969). *Visual thinking.* Berkeley, CA: University of California Press.

Association for Supervision and Curriculum Development. (1982). *Report for the Executive Committee of the Association for Supervision and Curriculum Development, Research and Working Group.* Alexandria. VA: Author

Atwell, N. (1987). *In the middle.* Portsmouth, NH: Heinemann.

Bachu, A. (2000). Fertility of American women: June, 1998. *Current Population Reports, P20–526.* Washington, DC: U.S. Bureau of the Census.

Ban, P. L., & Lewis, M. (1974). Mothers and fathers: Girls and boys: Attachment behavior in the one year old. *Lewis-Palmer Quarterly, 20,* 195–204.

Bandura, A. (1969). Behavioral modification through modeling practices. In L. Krasner and Ullman (Eds.), *Research in behavior modification.* New York: Holt, Rinehart and Winston.

Bandura, A. (1973). *Aggression: A social learning analysis.* Englewood Cliffs, NJ: Prentice Hall.

Bandura, A. (1989). Human agency in social cognition theory. *American Psychologists, 44,* 1175–1184.

Bandura, A., & McDonald, F. J. (1963). Influences of social reinforcement and the behavior of models in shaping children's moral judgment. *Journal of Abnormal and Social Psychology, 67,* 274–281.

Bandura, A., Ross, D., & Ross, S. A. (1961). Transmission of aggression through imitation of aggressive models. *Journal of Abnormal Social Psychology, 63,* 575–582.

Bandura, A., Ross, D., & Ross, S. A. (1963) Imitation of film-mediated aggressive models. *Journal of Abnormal and Social Psychology, 66,* 3–11.

Banks, J. A., & Banks, C. A. M. (Eds.). (1997). *Multicultural education: Issues and perspectives.* (3rd ed.). Boston, MA: Allyn and Bacon.

Barnes, H. (1991). Waldorf Education . . . an Introduction. Retrieved 1/21/01. From www.waldorfeducation.org/waldorf/hb_intro.htm

Bateson, G. (1955). A theory of play and fantasy. *Psychiatric Research Reports, 2,* 39–51.

Baumrind, D. (1967). Child care practices anteceding three patterns of preschool behavior. *Genetic Psychology Monographs, 75,* 43–88. Washington, DC: Heidref.

Behrmann, M. M., & Lahm, E. A. (1994). Computer application in early childhood special education. In J. L. Wright & D. D. Shade (Eds.), *Young children: Active learners in a technological age* (pp. 105–120). Washington, DC: NAEYC.

Bellis, M. (1999). Look before you loop. *Young Children, 54*(3) 70–73.

Berk, L. E., & Winsler, A. (1995). *Scaffolding children's learning: Vygotsky and early childhood education.* Washington, DC: NAEYC.

Berlyne, D. (1960). *Conflict, arousal and curiosity.* New York: McGraw-Hill.

Blendinger, J., & Jones, L. T. (1994). New Beginnings: Preparing future teachers to work with diverse families. *Action in Teacher Education 16*(3), 79–86.

Bloom, B. (Ed.). (1956). *Taxonomy of educational objectives. Handbook I: Cognitive domain.* New York: David McKay.

Bowlby, J. (1982). *Attachment and loss* (Vol. 1: Attachment) (2nd ed.). New York: Basic Books.

Bowles, D. D. (1993). Biracial identity: Children born to African American and white couples. *Clinical Social Work Journal, 21*(4), 417–428.

Boxhill, N. A. (1993). Making a place for Norma: Meeting the needs of homeless children. *Child Care Information Exchange, 95,* 35–37.

Brazelton, T. B., & Greenspan, S. I. (2000). *The irreducible needs of children: What every child must have to grow, learn and flourish.* Cambridge, MA: Perseus.

Bredekamp, S., & Copple, C. (Eds.). (1997). *Developmentally appropriate practice* (Rev. Ed.). Washington, DC: NAEYC.

Bredekamp, S., & Glowacki, S. (1995). *The first decade of NAEYC accreditation: Growth and impact on the field.* Paper presented at a conference sponsored by the McCormick Tribune Foundation and NAEYC, 18–20 September, Wheaton, IL.

Bredekamp, S., & Rosengrant, T. (Eds.). (1992). *Reaching potentials: Appropriate curriculum and assessment for young children,* volume 1. Washington, DC: NAEYC.

Bright Horizons Family Solutions. (1997). *The Horizons' Initiative: Helping hands for homeless children.* Dorchester, MA: Author.

Bronfenbrenner, U., & Morris, P. A. (1998). The ecology of developmental processes. *In handbook of child psychology* (Vol. 1; *Theoretical models of human development,* series ed. W. Damon, vol. ed. R. M. Learner (pp. 993–1082). New York: Wiley.

Bronson, M. B. (1995). *The right stuff for children birth to 8. Selecting play materials to support development.* Washington, DC: NAEYC.

Brown, S. L. (1994, December). Animals at play. *National Geographic, 186*(6), 2–35.

Bruner, J. (1972). The nature and uses of immaturity. *American Psychologist, 27,* 687–708.

Bruner, J. (1983). Play, thought and language. *Peabody Journal of Education, 60*(3), 60–69.

Bus, A., van Ijzendoorn, M., & Pellegrini, A. (1995). Joint reading makes for success in learning to read. A meta-analysis on intergenerational transmission of literacy. *Review of Educational Research, 65,* 1–21.

Canniff, D. L. (1990, November). Why the Waldorf movement is thriving in Eastern Europe. *Education Week, X*(13), 28.

Carlsson-Paige, N., & Levin, D. (1987). *The warplay dilemma: Balancing needs and values in early childhood classrooms.* New York: Teachers College Press.

Carlton, E. B. (2000). Learning through music: The support of brain research. *Child Care Information Exchange, 133,* 53–56.

Carpenter, C. J., Stein, A. H., & Baer, D. M. (1978). *The relation of children's activity to sex-type behavior.* Paper presented at the 12th Annual Convention of the Association for Advancement in Behavior Theories, Chicago.

Cartwright, S. (1998). Caregivers of quality— Essential attributes of teachers of young children. *Child Care Information Exchange, 120,* 18–20.

Center for the Child Care Workforce. (2000). *Current data on child care salaries and benefits in the United States.* Washington, DC: Author.

Chaillé, C., & Britain, L., (1997). *The young child as scientist.* New York: Longman.

Chang, H. (1993). *Affirming children's roots: Cultural and linguistic diversity in early care and education.* San Francisco: California Tomorrow.

Cherry, C. (1999). *Creative art for the developing child.* Revised by D. M. Nielsen. Torrance, CA: Fearon.

Child Care Information Exchange. (1999). Early childhood worldwide—more alike than different: An interview with David P. Weikart. *Child Care Information Exchange, 126,* 6–12.

Child Care Information Exchange. (1999). The Exchange top 40. *Child Care Information Exchange, 125,* 43.

Children's Defense Fund. (1996). *The state of American children.* Washington, DC: Author.

Children's Defense Fund. (1999). *Seeds of success: State prekindergarten initiatives 1998–1999.* Washington, DC: Author.

Children's Defense Fund. (2001). *The state of America's children.* Washington, DC: Author.

Children's Foundation. (1990). *Family day care licensing study.* Washington, DC: Author.

Children's World Learning Centers. (1979). *Parenting Series.* Golden, CO: Author.

Children's World Learning Centers. (1997). *Learning through the year.* Golden, CO: Author (Brochure).

Chomsky, C. (1972). Stages in language development and reading exposure. *Harvard Educational Review, 42*, 1–33.

Christie, J. F., Enz, B., & Vukelich, C. (2003). *Teaching language and literacy: Preschool through the elementary grades* (2nd ed.). Boston: Allyn and Bacon.

Christie, J. F., Roskos, K. A., Enz, B. J., Vukelich, C., & Neuman, S. B. (1995). *Reading for linking literacy and play.* Newark, DE: International Reading Association.

Christie, J. F., & Wardle, F. (1992). How much time is needed for play? *Young Children, 47*(3), 28–32.

Church, E. B. (2000). Music, movement and make believe. *Scholastic Early Childhood Today, 14*(8), 35–42.

Clark, B. (1997). *Growing up gifted* (5th ed.). Upper Saddle River, NJ: Merrill.

Clay, M. (1985). *The early detection of reading difficulties* (3rd ed.). Portsmouth, NH: Heinemann.

Cohen, L. (1999). The power of portfolios. *Scholastic Early Childhood Today, 13*(5), 22–29.

Colorado Department of Education. (2000). *Title I, Part A (Formerly Chapter 1)—Improving basic programs operated by local education agencies.* Denver, CO: Author.

Community Development Institute. (2001). Family Outcomes. *QIC News, 5*(1), 4.

Copeland, J., & Gleason, T. (1993). *Causes of speech disorders and language delays.* Unpublished manuscript. Speech and Language clinic, University of Arizona, Tucson, AZ.

Copley, J. V. (2000). *The young child and mathematics.* Washington, DC: NAEYC.

Corey, M. S., & Corey, G. (1998). *Becoming a helper.* Pacific Grove, CA: Brooks/Cole Publishing Co.

Cost, Quality, and Child Outcomes Study Team. (1995). *Cost, quality, and child outcomes in child care centers.* Denver, CO: Department of Economics, University of Colorado at Denver.

Crawford, J. (1987, April 1). Bilingual education: Language, learning and politics. *Education Week: A Special Report*, 43.

Cross, W. (1987). A two factor theory of black identity: Implications for the study of identity development in minority children. In J. S. Phinney & M. J. Rotheram (Eds.), *Children's ethnic socialization* (pp. 117–123). Newbury Park, CA: Sage Publications.

Crosser, S. (1994). Making the most of water play. *Young Children, 49*(5), 28–32.

Cruz-Janzen, M. I. (1997). Curriculum and the self-concept of biethnic and biracial persons. Dissertation. Denver, CO: University of Denver.

Cruz-Janzen, M. I. (1998, Fall). Culturally authentic bias. *Rethinking Schools*, 5.

Cunningham, B. (1998/1999). Men in child care. *Child Care Information Exchange.* Part 1, Sept. Oct, 1998, 20–22; Part 2, Jan/Feb., 1999, 66–69.

Curry, N. E., & Johnson, C. N. (1990). *Beyond self esteem: Developing a genuine sense of human value.* Washington, DC: NAEYC.

Curry-Rood, L. (1999, September/October). Creating readers. *Child Care Information Exchange. 129*, 48–52.

Daniel, G. R. (1992). Beyond black and white. In M. P. P. Root, *Racially mixed people in America* (pp. 333–341). Newbury Park, CA: Sage.

Dateline Child Care. (2000). State funding for preschool programs. *Child Care Information Exchange, 135*, 82–84.

Dattner, R. (1969). *Design for play.* Cambridge, MA: MIT Press.

Day Care Services Association. (n.d.). T.E.A.C.H. early childhood project. Chapel Hill, NC: Author.

Decker, C., & Decker, J. (1997). Planning and administering early childhood programs. (6th ed.). Columbus, OH: Merrill.

Delpit, L. (1995). *Other people's children: Cultural conflict in the classroom.* New York: The New Press.

Denver Waldorf School (n.d.). *Give your child the Waldorf advantage.* Denver, CO: Author.

Dewey, J. (1934). *Art as experience.* New York: Capricorn.

Dewey, J. (1938). *Education and experience.* New York: Macmillan.

Diegmueller, K. (1995, June 14). California plotting new tack in language arts. *Education Week, 19*(38), 1, 12, 17.

Doll, R. (1970). *Curriculum improvement* (2nd ed.). Boston, MA: Allyn and Bacon.

Dorrell, A. (1999). Equipping the computer learning center. *Early Childhood News, 11*(6) 18–22.

Duff, R. E., Brown, M. H., & Van Scoy, I. J. (1995). Reflection and self-evaluation: Keys to professional development. *Young Children, 50*(4), 81–88.

Dumas, J. E., & LaFreniere, P. J. (1993). Mother-child relationships as sources of support or stress: A comparison of competent, average, aggressive and anxious dyads. *Child Development, 64*, 1732–1754.

Dunbar, J. (2001). A Head Start garden: Nutrition education at its best. *Children and Families, 15*(3), 34–38.

Dunn, L., & Kontos, S. (1989, April). *Influence of family day care quality and child rearing attitudes on children's play in family day care.* Paper presented at the biennial meeting of the Society for Research in Child Development. Kansas City, MO.

Dunn, L., & Kontos, S. (1997). Research in review: What we have learned about developmentally appropriate practice. *Young Children, 52*(4), 4–13.

Dworetzky, J. P. (1995). *Human development: A life span approach* (2nd ed.). St. Paul, MN: West.

Edelsky, C. (1990). Whose agenda is this anyway? A response to McKenna, Robinson and Miller. *Educational Researcher, 19*(8), 7–11.

Elkind, D. (1999). Educating young children in math, science and technology. In *Dialogues on early childhood science, mathematics and technology education* (pp. 62–70). Washington, DC: American Association for the Advancement of Science.

Ellis, M. J. (1973). *Why people play*. Englewood Cliffs, NJ: Prentice Hall.

Ellis, M. J. (1993). *Why children play*. Englewood Cliffs, NJ: Prentice-Hall.

Endres, J., & Rockwell, R. (1994). *Food, nutrition, and the young child*. New York: Merrill.

Engel, B. (1995). *Considering children's art: Why and how to value their work*. Washington, DC: NAEYC

Epstein, J. L. (1984). *Single parents and the schools: The effects of marital status on parent and teacher evaluation* (Report 353). Baltimore, MD: Center for Social Organization of Schools, The Johns Hopkins University.

Epstein, J. L. (1985). Home and school connections in schools of the future: Implications of research on parent involvement. *Peabody Journal of Education, 62,* 18–41.

Erikson, E. (1963). *Childhood and society* (2nd ed.). New York: Norton.

Families and Work Institute.(1994). *The study of children in family child care and relative care: Highlights and findings*. New York: Author.

Featherstone, J. (1967). The primary school revolution in Britain. *The New Republic* (August 10, September 2, September 9), 2–16.

Feeney, S., & Chun, R. (1985). Effective teachers of young children. *Young children, 41*(1) 47–52.

Feeney, S., & Kipnis, K. (1992). *Code of ethical conduct and statement of commitment*. Washington, DC: NAEYC.

Feitelson, D., & Ross, G. (1973). The neglected factor—play. *Human Development, 16,* 202–223.

Fish, J. M. (1995, November/December). Mixed blood. *Psychology Today,* 55–61, 76, 80.

Fishbein, H., & Imai, S. (1993). Preschoolers select playmates on the basis of gender and race. *Journal of Applied Developmental Psychology, 14,* 303–316.

Foreman, G. E., & Kuschner, D. S. (1984). The child's construction of knowledge: Piaget for teaching children. Washington, DC: NAEYC.

Forman, G. E., & Hill, D. F. (1984). *Constructive play: Applying Piaget to preschool*. Reading, MA: Addison Wesley.

Fox, D. L., & Jordan, V. D. (1973). Racial preference and identification of Black, American Chinese, and white children. *Genetic Psychology Monographs, 88,* 229–286.

Freire, P. (1970). *Pedagogy of the oppressed*. New York: Seabury Press.

Frost, J. L., & Sweeney, T. B. (1996). *Cause and prevention of playground injuries and litigation: Case studies*. Wheaton, MD: Association for Childhood Education International.

Fuhr, J. E., & Barclay, K. H. (1998). The importance of appropriate nutrition education. *Young Children, 53*(1), 74–80.

Gallahue, D. (1993). Motor development and movement skill acquisition in early childhood education. In B. Spodek (Ed.), *Handbook of research on education of young children* (pp. 24–41). New York: Macmillan.

Gandini, L. (1993). Fundamentals of the Reggio Emilia approach to early childhood education. *Young Children, 49*(1), 4–8.

Gardner, H. (1980). *Artful scribbles: The significance of children's drawings*. New York: Basic Books.

Gardner, H. (1983). *Frames of mind: the theory of multiple intelligences*. New York: Basic Books.

Gardner, H. (1991). *The unschooled mind: How children think and how schools should teach*. New York: Basic Books.

Gardner, H., & Hatch, T. (1989). Multiple intelligences go to school: Educational implication of the theory of multiple intelligences. *Educational Research, 18*(8), 4–9.

Gay, G. (1997). Educational equality for students of color. In J. A. Banks. & C. A. M. Banks (Eds.), *Multicultural education: Issues and perspectives* (3rd ed.) (pp. 195–228). Boston, MA: Allyn and Bacon.

Gibbs, J. T. (1989). Biracial adolescents. In J. T. Gibbs, L. N. Huag, & Assoc. (Eds.), *Children of color: Psychological intervention with minority youth* (pp. 322–350). San Francisco: Jossey-Bass.

Gilligan, C. (1982). *In a different voice: Psychological theory and women's development,* Cambridge, MA: Harvard University Press.

Ginsburg, H. P. (1977). *Children's arithmetic*. New York: Van Nostrand.

Goelman, H., Shapiro, E., & Pence, A. R. (1999). Family environment and family day care. *Family Relations, 39,* 14–19.

Goleman, D. (1995). *Emotional intelligence. Why it can matter more than IQ*. New York: Bantam.

Gordh, B. (1996, Nov/Dec). Music to your ears. *Scholastic Early Childhood Today, 11*(3), A1–A9.

Graves, D. (1983). *Writing: Teachers and children at work*. Portsmouth, NH: Heinemann.

Greenberg, P. (1969). *The devil has slippery shoes: A biased biography of the Child Development Group of Mississippi (CDGM)—a story of maximum feasible poor parent participation*. Washington, DC: Youth Policy Institute.

Greenberg, P. (1987, July). Lucy Sprague Mitchell: A major missing link between early childhood education in the 1980s and progressive education in the 1890s–1930s. *Young Children, 42*(4), 70–84.

Greenberg, P. (2001). The irreducible needs of children: An interview with T. Berry Brazelton, M.D., and Stanley I. Greenspan, M.D. *Young Children, 56*(2), 6–14.

Greenman, J. (1985). Babies get out: Outdoor settings for infant and toddler play. *Beginnings: Going Outside, 2*(2) 7–10.

Greenman, J. (1988). *Caring spaces, learning places: Children's environments that work.* Redmond, WA: Exchange Press.

Greenman, J. (1993, May/June). It ain't easy being green. *Child Care Information Exchange. 97.*

Grief, E. (1976). Sex role playing in preschool children. In J. Bruner, A. Jolly, & K. Sylva (Eds.), *Play: Its role in development and evolution.* New York: Basic Books.

Grieshaber, S., & Cannella, G. S. (2001). *Embracing identities in early childhood education.* New York: Teachers College Press.

Hadley, R. G., & Mitchell, L. K. (1995). *Counseling research and program evaluation.* Pacific Grove, CA: Brooks/Cole Publishing.

Hakuta, K. (1986). *Mirror of language: The debate on bilingualism.* New York: Basic Books.

Hale, J. E. (1986). *Black children: Their roots, culture, and learning styles.* Baltimore, MD: Johns Hopkins University Press.

Hale, J. E. (1994). *Unbank the fire: Visions for the education of African America children.* Baltimore, MD: Johns Hopkins University Press.

Halpern, R. (1999). After-school programs for low income children: Promise and challenges. *The Future of Children, 9*(2), 81–95.

Harms, T., & Clifford, R. M. (1998). *Early childhood environment rating scale.* New York: Teachers College Press.

Harms, T., Cryer, D., & Clifford, R. M. (1989). *Family day care rating scale.* New York: Teachers College Press.

Harms, T., Jacobs, E. V., & White, D. (1995). *School-age care environment rating scale.* New York: Teachers College Press.

Harper, L., & Sanders, K. (1975). Preschool children's use of space: Sex differences in outdoor play. *Developmental Psychology, 11,* 119.

Harper, V. (1994). Multicultural perspectives in the classroom: Professional preparation for educational professionals. *Action in Education 16*(3), 66–78.

Harris, A. C. (1986). *Child development.* St. Paul, MN: West Publishing Co.

Hartup, W. (1991) *Having friends, making friends, and keeping friends: Relationships as educational contexts: An early report.* Minneapolis, MN: Center for Early Education and Development.

Haugland, S. W. (1992). The effects of computer software on preschool children's developmental gains. *Journal of Computing in Early Childhood Education, 3*(1), 15–30.

Haugland, S. W. (1997). Computers in early childhood classrooms. *Early Childhood News, 9*(4), 6–18.

Haugland, S. W. (1999). The newest software that meets the developmental needs of young children. *Early Childhood Education Journal, 26*(4) 245–254.

Haugland, S. W. (1999). What role should technology play in young children's learning? *Young Children, 54*(6), 26–31.

Hayes, C., Palmer, J., & Zaslow, M. (1990). *Who cares for America's children? Child care policy for the 1990s.* Washington, DC: National Academic Press.

Helm, J. H., & Katz, L. (2001). *Young investigators. The project approach in the young years.* Washington, DC: NAEYC.

Henderson, A. T. (1988). Parents are a school's best friends. *Phi Delta Kappan 70*(2), 148–153.

Hewes, D. W. (2000, May/June). Coops—Preschools with parents in charge. *Child Care Information Exchange, 133,* 75–78.

Hills, T. W. (1993). Assessment in context—teachers and children at work. *Young Children, 48*(5), 20–28.

Hirsch, E. D. (1987). *Cultural literacy. What every American needs to know.* Boston, MA: Houghton Mifflin.

Hirsch, E. D. (1996). *The schools we need.* New York: Doubleday.

Hirsch, E. S. (Ed.). (1996). *The block book* (3rd ed.). Washington, DC: NAEYC.

Hofferth, S. L. (1989). What is the demand for and supply of child care in the United States? *Young Children, 44*(5), 28–33.

Hofferth, S. L., & Phillips, D. A. (1991). Child care policy research. *Journal of Social Issues 47,* 1–13.

Hohmann, M., & Weikart, D. P. (1995). *Educating young children: Active learning practices for preschool and child care programs.* Ypsilanti, MI: High/Scope.

Honig, A. S. (2000). Singing with babies. *Scholastic Early Childhood Today, 14*(8), 20–21.

Honig, A. S., & Wittmer, D. A. (1996). Helping children become more prosocial: Ideas for classrooms, families, schools, & communities. *Young Children, 51*(2), 62–69.

Hoover-Demsey, K. B., & Sandler, H. M. (1997). Why do parents become involved in their children's education? *Review of Educational Research, 67,* 3–42.

Horn, W. (1998). *Father facts* (3rd ed.). Gaithersburg, MD. National Fatherhood Institute.

Huber, L. K. (1999). Woodworking with young children: You can do it! *Young Children, 54*(6), 32–34.

Hurwitz, S. C. (1998). War nurseries—Lessons in quality. *Young Children, 53*(5), 37–39.

Irwin, D. M., & Bushnell, M. M. (1980). *Observational strategies for child study.* New York: Holt, Rinehart and Winston.

Jaffe, K. (1999, Winter). Small children, sizeable needs. *Forum for Applied Research and Public Policy,* 84–87.

Johnson, H. (1996). The art of block building. In E. S. Hirsch (Ed.), *The block book* (pp. 9–26). Washington, DC: NAEYC.

Johnson, J. E., Christie, J. F., & Yawkey, T. D. (1999). *Play and early childhood development.* New York: Longman.

Johnson, J. L., Gallagher, R. J. Cook, M., & Wong, P. (1995). Critical skills for kindergartenrs: Perception from kindergarten teachers. *Journal of Early Intervention, 19*(4), 315–349.

Jones, E. (Ed.). (1993). *Growing teachers: Partnerships in staff development.* Washington, DC: NAEYC.

Jones, E. (1998, January/February). The elephants' child as caregiver. *Child Care Information Exchange, 119,* 48–52.

Kagan, S. L., & Cohen, N. E. (2000). *Not by chance: Creating an early care and education system for America's children.* New Haven, CT: Bush Center in Child Development and Social Policy at Yale University.

Kahn, D. (Ed.). (1995). *What is Montessori preschool?* Cleveland, OH: North American Montessori Teachers' Association.

Kalson, S. (1996, June 4). The world's best child care? The Reggio Emilia schools in Italy can help children find answers to their own questions. *Pittsburgh Post Gazette,* pp. 40–44.

Kamii, C. (1985). *Young children reinvent arithmetic.* New York: Teachers College Press.

Kamii, C. (1989). *Young children continue to reinvent arithmetic, 2nd grade.* New York: Teachers College Press.

Kamii, C., & DeVies, R. (1978). *Physical knowledge in preschool education: Implications of Piaget's theory.* Englewood Cliffs, NJ: Prentice Hall.

Karnes, M. (1979). Young handicapped children can be gifted and talented. *Journal for the Education of Gifted, 2*(3), 157–172.

Katz, L. (1972). Developmental stages of preschool teachers. *The Elementary School Journal, 73*(1), 50–59.

Katz, L. (1995). *Talks with teachers of young children: A collection.* Stamford, CT: Ablex.

Katz, L. G. (1998). The benefits of the mix. *Child Care Information Exchange, 124,* 46–49.

Katz, L. G., & McClellan, D. E. (1997). *Fostering children's social competence: The teacher's role.* Washington, DC: NAEYC.

Katz, P. A., Sohn, M., & Zalk, S. R. (1975). Perceptual concomitants of racial attitudes in urban grade school children. *Developmental Psychology, 11,* 135–144.

Kim, A. (2001, December 14). Weighty warning, *Rocky Mountain News,* p. 46A.

King, E. (1999). *Looking into the lives of children: A worldwide view.* Albert Park, Australia: James Nicholas Publishers, Ltd.

King, J. E. (1994). *Perceiving reality in a new way: Rethinking the Black/White duality of our time.* Paper presented at AERA annual meeting, New Orleans, LA.

King, N. R. (1979). The kindergarteners' perspective. *Elementary School Journal, 80,* 81–87.

Knowles, M. (1980). *The modern practice of adult education.* New York: Cambridge University Press.

Kohlberg, L. (1976). Moral stages and moralization: The cognitive-developmental approach. In T. Lickona (Ed.), *Moral development and behavior: Theory, research, and social* (pp. 34–55). New York: Wiley.

Kohlberg, L. (1981). *The philosophy of moral development.* New York: Harper and Row.

Kontos, S. (1992). *Family day care: Out of the shadows and into the light.* Washington, DC: NAEYC.

Kontos, S., & Dunn, L. (1989). Attitudes of caregivers, maternal experiences with day care, and children's development. *Journal of Applied Developmental Psychology 10,* 37–51.

Kontos, S., & Wilcox-Herzog, A. (1997). Teachers' interactions with young children: Why are they so important? *Young Children, 52*(2), 4–12.

Krajec, V. D., Bloom, P. J., & Clark, D. (2001). *Who's caring for the kids?* Wheeling, IL: Center for Early Childhood Leadership and the Illinois Network of Child Care Referral Agencies.

Krathwohl, D. R. (1994). Reflections on the taxonomy: Its past, present and future. In L. W. Anderson & L. A. Sosniak (Eds.), *Bloom's taxonomy: A forty-year perspective.* Ninety-third yearbook of the National Society for the Study of Education, part II, Chicago, IL: National Society for the Study of Education.

Kritchevsky, S., Prescott, E., & Walling, L. (1977). *Planning environments for young children: Physical space.* Washington, DC: NAEYC.

Kuhl, P. (1993). *Life language.* Seattle, WA: University of Washington.

Kupersmidt, J. (1983, April 21–24). *Predicting delinquency and academic problems from childhood peer status.* Paper presented at the biannual meeting of the Society for Research in Child Development, Detroit, Michigan.

Ladd, G. W. (1983). Social networks of popular, average rejected children in school settings. *Merrill-Pulmer Quarterly 29,* 283–308.

Lally, J. R. (1998). Brain research, infant learning, and child care curriculum. *Child Care Information Exchange, 121,* 47–48.

Lally, J. R., Mangione, P., & Honig, A. S. (1988). The Syracuse University Family Development Research Program: Long range impact of an early intervention with low income children and their families. In D. Powell (Ed.), *Parent education as early childhood intervention: Emerging directions in theory, research, and practice* (pp. 79–104). Norwood, NJ: Ablex.

LeBuffe, P. A., & Naglieri, J. A. (n.d.). *The Devereux early childhood assessment (DECA). A measure of within-child protective factors in preschool children.* Villanova, PA: Devereux Foundation.

Levin, D. E. (1998). *Remote control childhood? Combatting the hazards of media culture.* Washington, DC: National Association for the Education of Young Children.

Lewman, B. (1999). Read it again! How rereading-and rereading—stories heightens children's literacy. *Children and Families, 28*(1), 13–15.

Lickona, T. (1983). *Raising good children.* New York: Bantam.

Lind, K. K. (1999). Science in early childhood: Developing and acquiring fundamental concepts and skills. In *Dialogues on early childhood science, mathematics and technology education* (pp. 73–83). Washington, DC: American Association for the Advancement of Science.

Liss, M. B. (1981). Patterns of toy play: An analysis of sex differences. *Sex Roles, 7,* 1143–1150.

Malaguzzi, L. (1993). For an education based on relationships. *Young Children, 49*(1), 9–12.

Mark, M. L. (1996). *Contemporary music education* (3rd ed.). New York: Schirmer Books.

Martin. S. (1999). *Take a look. Observation and portfolio assessment in early childhood* (2nd ed.). Don Mills, Ontario: Addison Wesley.

Maslow, A. H. (1959). *New knowledge in human values.* New York: Harper and Row.

Maslow, A. H. (1973). Theory of human motivation. In R. J. Lowry (Ed.), *Dominance, self-esteem, self actualization: Germinal papers of A. H. Maslow.* Monterey, CA: Brooks/Cole.

Mayer, R. (1996). Learners as information processors: Legacies and limitations of education psychology's second metaphor. *Education Psychology, 31,* 151–161.

McCormick, M. (1988). *Mediation in schools: An evaluation of the Wakefield Pilot Peer mediation program in Tucson, Arizona.* Washington, DC: American Bar Association.

McCray, J. W. (1994). Multicultural diversity and ethical considerations in research design. *Journal of Home Economics. 86*(2), 41–46.

McRoy, R. G. (1981). *A comparative study of the self-concept of transracially and interracially adopted black children.* Dissertation Abstracts International 42 (03) Sec. A. 1318.

McWhirter, J. J., McWhirter, B. T., McWhirter, A. M., & McWhirter, E. H. (1998). *At-risk youth: A comprehensive response* (2nd ed). Pacific Grove: CA: Brooks/Cole.

Meisels, S. (1992). *The Work Sampling System™: An overview.* Ann Arbor: University of Michigan.

Miller, S. A. (1995). Parents' attributes for their children's behavior. *Child Development, 66,* 1557–1584.

Montessori School of Denver (n.d.). *Oh the things you'll learn.* Denver, CO: Author.

Moore, T. (2000). Music: the great connector. *Child Care Information Exchange, 133,* 50–52.

Mosteller, F. (1995). The Tennessee study of class size in early school grades. *The Future of Children, 5*(2), 113–127.

Muller, S. A. (1995). Parents' attributions for their children's behavior. *Child Development, 66,* 1557–1584.

Myers, C. (1992). *The British Primary School approach to learning.* Denver, CO: Stanley British Primary School.

National Association for the Education of Young Children. (1991). *Accreditation criteria and procedures.* Washington, DC: Author.

National Association for the Education of Young Children. (1991). *Early childhood classroom observation.* Washington, DC: Author.

National Asociation for the Education of Young Children. (1996a). *Guidelines for preparation of early childhood professionals.* Washington, DC: Author.

National Association for the Education of Young Children. (1996b). NAEYC Position Statement: Responding to Linguistic and Cultural Diversity—Recommendations for Effective Early Childhood Education. *Young Children, 51*(2), 4–12.

National Association for the Education of Young Children. (1998a). *Accreditation criteria and procedures.* Washington, DC: Author.

National Association for the Education of Young Children. (1998b). Continuum of children's development in early reading and writing. *Young Children, 53*(4), 40–45.

National Center for Fair and Open Testing. (1991). *Standardized tests and our children: A guide to testing reform.* Cambridge, MA: Author.

National Council for Accreditation of Teacher Education. (1994). *NCATE standards.* Washington, DC: Author.

National Council of Teachers of Mathematics. (2000). *Principles and standards for school mathematics.* Reston, VA: Author.

National Geographic Society. (1993). *National Geographic picture atlas of our world.* Washington, DC: Author.

National Institute on Out of School Time. (1998). *Fact sheet on school-age children's out of school time.* Wellesley College, MA: Center for Research on Women.

National Playground Safety Institute. (n.d.). *The dirty dozen.* Ashburn, VA: National Recreation and Parks Association.

National SAFE KIDS Campaign, 1301 Pennsylvania Ave, NW, Washington, DC, 20004.

Nelson, M. K. (1990). Mothering others' children: The experience of family day care providers. *Signs. Journal of Women in Culture and Society, 15,* 586–605.

Neugebauer, R. (1996). Employer child care continues to grow and consolidate. *Child Care Information Exchange. 109,* 7–11.

Neugebauer, R. (1998). Who's who in school-age care. *Child Care Information Exchange, 123*, 35–38.

Neugebauer, R. (1999). Kids on campus: Status report on child care. *Child Care Information Exchange, 122*, 20–22.

Neugebauer, R. (2000a). Booming economy fuels continued expansion of for-profit child care. *Child Care Information Exchange, 131*, 18–21.

Neugebauer, R. (2000b). Religious organizations taking proactive role in child care. *Child Care Information Exchange, 133*, 18–20.

Neugebauer, R. (2000). *Recruiting and retaining men in your center. In inside childcare trend 2000.* Redmond, WA: Exchange Press.

Neugebauer, R. (2000). Who provides child care in the USA? In R. Neugebauer (Ed.), *Inside child care trend report 2000* (pp. 39–41). Redmond, WA: Child Care Information Exchange.

Neuman, S. (1988). The displacement effect: Assessing the relationship between television viewing and reading performance. *Reading Research Quarterly, 23*, 414–440.

Neuman, S., Copple, C., & Bredekamp, S. (2000). *Learning to read and write: Developmentally appropriate practice for young children.* Washington, DC: NAEYC.

Noll, W. J. (2000). *Taking sides: Clashing views on controversial educational issues* (11th ed.) Guilford, CT: Dushkin/McGraw-Hill.

Northwest Regional Educational Laboratory. (1990). *Effective schooling practices: A research synthesis, 1990 update.* Portland, OR: Author.

Ogbu, J. U. (1987). Variability in minority school performance: A problem in search of an explanation. *Anthropology and Education Quarterly, 18*, 312–334.

Olds, A. (1982, Summer). Planning a developmentally optimal day care center. *Day Care and Early Education.*

Ormrod, J. (1999). *Human learning* (3rd ed.). Columbus, OH: Merrill.

Ovando, C. J. (1997). Language diversity and education. In J. Banks and C. A. M. Banks, (Eds.), *Multicultural education* (3rd ed.) (pp. 272–296). Boston: Allyn and Bacon.

Parke, B. N., & Ness, P. S. (1988). Curricular decisions-making for the education of young children. *Gifted Child Quarterly, 32*(1), 196–199.

Parker, J. G., & Asher, S. R. (1987). Peer relations and later personal adjustments: Are low-accepted children at risk? *Psychological Bulletin, 102*, 357–389.

Parten, M. B. (1932). Social participation among preschool children. *Journal of Abnormal and Social Psychology, 27*, 243–269.

Parten, M. B. (1933). Social play among preschool children. *Journal of Abnormal and Social Psychology, 28*, 136–147.

Peterson, J. (2001, November 18). As quoted in M. Whaley, Moving beyond drugs to fix attention woes. The *Denver Post*, pp. 29A–30A.

Phillips, C. (Ed.). (1991). *Essentials for child development associates working with young children.* Washington, DC: NAEYC.

Phillips, C. B. (1991). *Field advisor's guide for the CDA professional preparation program.* Washington, DC: Council for Early Childhood Professional Recognition.

Phillips, D., Mekos, D., Scarr, S., McCartney, K., & Abbott-Shim. (2001). Within and beyond the classroom door. Assessing quality in child care centers. *Early Childhood Research Quarterly, 15*(4), 475–496.

Phipps, P. (1999). Is your program brain compatible? *Child Care Information Exchange, 126*, 53–57.

Piaget, J. (1952). *The origins of intelligence in children.* New York: Wiley.

Piaget, J. (1954). *The construction of reality in the child.* New York: Basic.

Piaget, J., & Inhelder, B. (1958). *The growth of logical thinking from childhood to adolescence.* New York: Basic Books.

Podeschi, R., & Xiong, V. (1994). *The Hmong & American education: The 1990s.* Milwaukee, WI: Institute on Race and Ethnicity, University of Wisconsin.

Polya, G. (1957). *How to solve it: A new aspect of mathematical method* (2nd ed.). Garden City, NY: Doubleday.

Powell, D. R. (1998). Reweaving parents into the fabric of early childhood programs. *Young Children, 53*(5), 60–67.

Pratt, C. (Ed.). (1924). *Experimental practice in the city and county school.* New York: E. P. Dutton.

Pratt, C. (1948). *I learn from children.* New York: Cornerstone Library.

Pratt, C. (1973). The play school. In C. Winsor (Ed.), *Experimental schools revisited.* New York: Agathon.

Prescott, E. (1994, November/December). The physical environment—a powerful regulator of experience. *Child Care Information Exchange, 100*, 9–15.

Read, H. {1943} (1956). *Education through art* (3rd ed.). New York: Pantheon.

Rice, K. F., & Sanoff, M. K. (1998). Growing strong together: Helping mothers and their children affected by substance abuse. *Young Children, 53*(1), 28–33.

Ripple, C. (2000). *Economics of caring labor: Improving compensation in the early childhood workforce.* New York: A. L. Mailman Family Foundation and Foundation for Child Development.

Rivkin, M. S. (1995). *The great outdoors: Restoring children's right to play outside.* Washington, DC: NAEYC.

Root, M. P. P. (1996). *The multiracial experience.* Newbury Park, CA: Sage.

Rubin, K. H., Maioni T. L., & Hornung, M. (1976). Free play behavior in middle and lower-class preschoolers: Parten and Piaget revisited. *Child Development, 47,* 414–419.

Rudolph, K. D., Harmen, C., & Burge, D. (1995). Cognitive representations of self, family, and peers in school competence and sociometric status. *Child Development, 66*(5), 1385–1402.

Sample, W. (1993, March/April). The American Indian child. *Child Care Information Exchange, 90.*

Saylor, G. J., and Alexander, W. M. (1974). *Curriculum planning for schools.* New York: Holt, Rinehart and Winston.

Schickedanz, J. A. (1999). *Much more than the ABCs. The early stages of reading and writing.* Washington, DC: NAEYC.

Schiller, P. (1998). The thinking brain. *Child Care Information Exchange, 121,* 49–51.

Schulman, K., Blank, H., & Ewen, D. (1999). State prekindergarten initiatives: A varied picture of states' decisions affecting availability, quality and access. *Young Children, 54*(6), 38–41.

Schweinhart, L. J.(1993). Observing young children in action: The key to early childhood assessment. *Young Children, 48*(5), 29–33.

Schweinhart, L. J., & Weikart, D. P. (1997). *Lasting differences: The High/Scope preschool curriculum comparison study through age 23.* (Monograph of High/Scope education research foundation, 12). Ypsilanti, MI: High/Scope Press.

Schweinhart, L. J., & Weikart, D. P. (1998, March). *Why curriculum matters in early childhood. Educational Leadership,* 57–60.

Seitz, V., & Apfel, N. H. (1994). Parent-focused interventions: Diffusion effects on siblings. *Child Development, 65,* 666–676.

Semaj, L. (1980). The development of racial-classification abilities. *Journal of Negro Education, 50,* 41–47.

Shireman, J., & Johnson, P. (1980). *Adoption: Three alternatives (2nd Progress Report).* Chicago: Chicago Child Care Society.

Shore, R. (1997). *Rethinking the brain. New insights into early development.* New York: Families and Work Institute.

Silva, D. Y., & Johnson, J. E. (1999). Principals' preference for the N–3 certificate. *Pennsylvania Educational Leadership, 18*(2), 71–81.

Silverman, L. K. (1989). Invisible gifts, invisible handicaps. *Roeper Review, 12*(1), 37–42.

Singer, D., & Singer, J. (1990). *The house of make-believe: Children's play and development of imagination.* Cambridge, MA: Harvard University Press.

Smilansky, S. (1968). *The effects of sociodramatic play on disadvantaged preschool children.* New York: Wiley.

Smith, B. O., Stanley, W. O., & Shores, J. H. (1957). *Fundamentals of curriculum development.* New York: Harcourt Brace Jovanovich.

Smith, C. (2000). For the love of music—and children. *Child Care Information Exchange, 133,* 46–49.

Smith, K. (2000). Who's minding the kids? Child care arrangements: Fall, 1995. *Current population reports, P70–70.* Washington, DC: U.S. Bureau of the Census.

Synder, L. S., & Downey, D. M. (1991). The language-reading relationship in normal and reading-disabled children. *Journal of Speech & Hearing Research, 34,* 129–140.

Stanley British Primary School. (2000). *Stanley British Primary School; Kindergarten through 8th Grade.* Denver, CO: Author.

State of Colorado. (1991). *Colorado 2000: A plan for achieving the national educational goals in our communities.* Denver, CO: Author.

State of Colorado. (1994). *Rules for the administration of the Exceptional Children's Education Act.* Denver, CO: Author.

Steiner, R. (1926). *The essentials of education.* London: Anthroposophical Publishing Co.

Stephens, K. (1999). Supporting Resilience by connecting children with nature. *Child Care Information Exchange, 130,* 52–55.

Stiggins, R. J. (2001). *Student-involved classroom assessment* (3rd ed.). Upper Saddle River, NJ: Merrill/Prentice Hall.

Subotnik, R. F. (1997). Teaching gifted students in a multicultural society. In J. A. Banks & C. A. Banks (Eds.), Multicultural education (pp. 361–392). Boston: Allyn and Bacon.

Sulzby, E., Barnhart, J. E., & Hieshima, J. A. (1989). Forms of writing and rereading: A preliminary report. In J. Mason (Ed.), *Reading and writing connections.* Boston: Allyn and Bacon.

Sutton-Smith, B. (1979). Epilogue: Play as performance. In B. Sutton-Smith (Ed.), *Play and learning* (pp. 295–320). New York: Gardner Press.

Swartz, L. L. (1994). Calendar reading: A tradition that begs remodeling. *Teaching Children Mathematics, 1,* 104–109.

Sweet, A. (1993). *State of the arts: Transforming ideas for teaching and learning to read.* Washington, DC: Office of Research, U.S. Department of Education.

Swinger, M. (Ed.). (1999). *Sing through the day* (Rev. ed.). Farmington, PA: Plough Publishing House.

Swinger, M. (Ed.). (2000). *Sing through the seasons.* (Rev. ed.). Farmington, PA: Plough Publishing House.

Sylva, K., Roy, C., & Painter, M. (1980). *Childwatching at playgrounds & nursery school.* Ypsilanti, MI: High/Scope Press.

Szyba, C. M. (1999). Why do some teachers resist offering appropriate, open-ended art activities for young children? *Young Children, 54*(1), 16–20.

Taba, H. (1962). *Curriculum development: Theory and practice.* New York: Harcourt, Brace and Jovanovich.

Taylor, H. H. (2000). Curriculum in Head Start. *Head Start Bulletin, 67,* 1.

Thomas, R. R. (1991). *Beyond race and gender.* New York: American Management Association.

Trepanier-Street, M. L., Hong, S. M., & Baner, J. C. (2001). Using technology in Reggio-inspired long-term projects. *Early Childhood Education Journal, 28*(3), 181–188.

Turbiville, V. P., Umbarger, G. T., & Guthrie, A. C. (2000). Fathers' involvement in programs for young children. *Young Children, 55*(4), 74–79.

U.S. Bureau of the Census. (1990). *Who's minding the kids? Child care arrangements.* Washington, DC: Author.

U.S. Bureau of the Census. (1991). School enrollment. Social and economic characteristics of students. October 1989. *Current population reports.* Washington, DC: Author.

U.S. Consumer Product Safety Commission. *Public playground handbook for safety.* Washington, DC: Author.

U.S. Department of Education. (1997). *Father involvement in their children's schools* {on line}. Available: http://www.ed.gov/NCES/pubs98/fathers/intro/html#intro.

U.S. Department of Health and Human Services. (1990). *Multicultural principles for Head Start programs.* Washington, DC: Author.

U.S. Department of Health and Human Services. (1998). *The Head Start Act, amended.* Washington, DC: U.S. Government Printing Office.

U.S. Department of Health and Human Services, Administration on Children, Youth and Families. (2000). *Child Maltreatment 1998: Reports from States to the National Child Abuse and Neglect Data System.* Washington, DC: U.S. Government Printing Office.

U.S. Department of Health and Human Services, Administration for Children, Youth, and Families, Head Start Bureau. (1999). *Head Start fact sheet: Fiscal year 1998.* Washington, DC: Author.

U.S. Department of Health and Human Services, Administration for Children, Youth and Families, Administration for Children and Families, Head Start Bureau. (2001). *Fiscal year 2001 fact sheet.* Washington, DC: Author.

U.S. Department of Health and Human Services, Administration for Children, Youth and Families, Head Start Bureau. (2001, June). *The Head Start Path to Positive Child Outcomes.* Washington, DC: Author.

U.S. Department of Health and Human Services, Centers for Disease Control and Prevention.

(2001, July). *Death final data for 1998. National vital statistics reports 48, no. 11.* Washington, DC: Author.

U.S. General Accounting Office. (1997, May). *Welfare reform: Implications of increased work participation for child care.* Report #GAO/HEH-97-75. Washington, DC: Author.

Vandell, D. L., & Shumow, L. (1999). After school child care programs. *The Future of Children, 9*(2), 64–80.

Vygostky, L. (1962). *Thought and language.* Cambridge, MA: MIT Press.

Vygotsky, L. (1978). *Mind in society: The development of higher mental processes.* Cambridge, MA: Harvard University Press.

Waggoner, D. (1994). Language minority school age population now totals 9.9 million. *NABE News 18*(1), I, 24–26.

Walker, B., Hafenstein, N. L., & Crow-Enslow, L. (1999). Meeting the needs of gifted learners in early childhood programs. *Young Children, 54*(1), 32–37.

Wardle, F. (1975, March). Folk dance fun. Virginia reel, hora, tarantella—Folk dancing is an exciting way to explore other cultures. *Teacher,* 79–81.

Wardle, F. (1976, November). A first look at education of Guatemalan Indians in post-earthquake Guatemala. *New Schools Exchange Newsletter 136,* 12–15.

Wardle, F. (1977, October). Do they still kill cowboys? *Early years for teachers through age 8.* 32–33/78.

Wardle, F. (1978). *PACER model.* Urbana, IL: ERIC Clearinghouse Elementary and Early Childhood Education.

Wardle, F. (1987a, May/June). At the workbench. Woodworking for young children. *Scholastic Pre K Today,* 32–33.

Wardle, F. (1987, September). Getting back to the basics of children's play. *Child Care Information Exchange,* 27–30.

Wardle, F. (1989). *Case against public school early childhood programs.* Urbana, IL: ERIC Clearinghouse for Early Childhood Education, # ED310846.

Wardle, F. (1990). Bunny ears and cupcakes for all: Are parties developmentally appropriate? *Child Care Information Exchange, 74,* 32–42.

Wardle, F. (1991, May/June). Are we shortchanging boys? *Child Care Information Exchange,* 48–51.

Wardle, F. (1993, November). Criteria for selecting toys. *Beginnings: Child Care Information Exchange,* 43–44.

Wardle, F. (1995a). Alternatives . . . Bruderhof education: Outdoor school. *Young Children, 50*(3), 68–73.

Wardle, F. (1995, July). How young children build images of themselves. *Child Care Information Exchange, 47,* 44–47.

Wardle, F. (1996). Proposal: An anti-bias and eco-logical model for multicultural education. *Childhood Education, 72*(3), 152–156.

Wardle, F. (1998). Math and science ideas on the playground. From *Playground manual for the National Migrant Head Start program*. Denver, CO, Unpublished.

Wardle, F. (1999a). Adapting indoor environments for students with specific disabilities. In J. E. Johnson, J. E. Christie, & T. D. Yawkey, *Play and early childhood development* (2nd ed., pp. 173–175). New York: Longman.

Wardle, F. (1999). Educational toys. *Early Childhood News, 11*(1), 38.

Wardle, F. (1999c). In praise of developmentally appropriate practice. *Young Children, 54*(6), 4–12.

Wardle, F. (1999d). Some needs of gifted students. After Clark (1997), *Growing up gifted*. Upper Saddle River, NJ: Merrill.

Wardle, F. (1999e). *Tomorrow's children: Meeting the needs of multiracial and multiethnic children at home, in early childhood programs, and at school.* Denver, CO: Center for the Study of Biracial Children.

Wardle, F. (2000a). Field trips: Essential learning. How children learn. *Children and Families, 14*(3), 68–70.

Wardle, F. (2000b, fall). The order in mess. How children learn. *Children and families, 14*(4), 82–83.

Wardle, F. (2001). The value of teaching art. *Children and Families, 15*(1), 24.

Wardle, F. (2001, January/February). Giving your building a second chance. *Child Care Information Exchange, 137*, 82–87.

Wardle, F., & Moore-Kneas, K. (1995). (Eds.). Child-to-child sexual behavior in child care settings: Conference report. ERIC document #ED 381–258.

Weikart, P. (1998). Facing the challenge of motor development. *Child Care Information Exchange, 121*, 60–62.

Weikart, P. S. (1997). *Teaching folk dance: Successful steps*. Ypsilanti, MI High/Scope Press.

Weiss, H. B. (1999). Partnerships among families, early childhood educators, and communities to promote early childhood learning in science, mathematics, and technology. In *Dialogue in early childhood science, mathematics, and technology education*. Washington, DC: American Association for Advances of Science.

Wells, G. (1985). *Language development in the preschool years*. Cambridge, UK: Cambridge University Press.

Whaley, M. (2001, November 18). Moving beyond drugs to fix attention woes. *The Denver Post*, pp. 29A–30A.

Wheelock College Institute for Leadership and Career Initiatives. (2000). *Child care licensing re-quirements: Minimum preservice training, annual ongoing, and administrative training hours for directors in child care centers*. Boston, MA: Author.

Whitebook, M. (1989). *Who cares? Child care teachers and the quality of care in America*. Oakland, CA: Child Care Employee Project.

Whitebook, M. (1995). Salary improvements in Head Start: Lessons for the early care and education field. Washington, DC: Center for the Child Care Workforce.

Whitebook, M., Sakai, L., Gerber, E., & Howes, C. (2001). *Then and now: Changes in child care staffing, 1994–2000*. Washington, DC: Center for the Child Care Workforce.

Whitebook, M., Sakai, L., & Howes, C. (1997). NAEYC accreditation as a strategy for improving child care quality, executive summary. Washington, DC: National Center for Early Childhood Work Force.

Whitmore, J. (1981). Gifted children with handicapping conditions: A new frontier. *Exceptional Children, 48*(2), 106–111.

Wiles, J., & Bondi, J. (1998). *Curriculum development. A guide to practice* (5th ed.). Upper Saddle River, NJ: Merrill.

Will, J. A., Self, P. A., & Datan, N. (1976). Maternal behavior and perceived sex of infant. *American Journal of Orthopsychiatry, 46*, 135–139.

Willer, B., Hofferth, S. L., Kisker, E. E., Divine-Hawkins, P., Farqhar, E., & Glantz, F. B. (1991). *The demand and supply of child care in 1990*. Washington, DC: NAEYC.

Winsor, C. B. (1996). Blocks as a materials for learning through play. In E. S. Hirsch (Ed.), *The block book* (pp. 1–25). Washington, DC: NAEYC.

Wittmer, D. S., & Honig, A. S. (1994). Encouraging positive social development in young children. *Young Children, 49*(5), 4–12.

Wodke, K. H., Harper, F., Schommer. M., & Brunelli, P. (1989). How standardized is school testing? An exploratory observational study of standardized group testing in kindergarten. *Educational Evaluation and Policy Analysis, 11*, 223–235.

Wolery, M., & Wilbers, J. S. (Eds.). (1994). *Including children with special needs in early childhood programs*. Washington, DC: NAEYC.

Wright, J. C., Huston, A. C., Ross, R. P., Calvert, S. L., Rolandelli, D., Weeks, L. A., Raeisse, P., and Potts, R. (1984). Pace and continuity of television programs: Effects on children's attention and comprehension. *Developmental Psychology, 20*, 653–667.

Yettick, H. (2001). Giving HOPE to inner-city kids. Center identifies, challenges gifted and talented students who might fall through the cracks. *Rocky Mountain News*, Nov. 5, 22A–23A.

Zigler, E. F., & Finn-Stevenson, M. (1996, Fall). Funding child care and public education. *The Future of Children 6*(2), 104–121.

NAME INDEX

Note: Page numbers followed by f indicate figures.

SUBJECT INDEX

Note: Page numbers in boldface type indicate definitions of key terms.